Table of Contents

.ĸ must be

FEMINIST POLITICS AND HUMAN NATURE

Alison M. Jaggar

ROWMAN & LITTLEFIELD PUBLISHERS, INC.

To those who developed these ideas through their activity on behalf of women; the many generous and perceptive friends who have helped me to articulate them; my family who have always supported my work; Karuna, Sumita and their generation who will carry forward the ideas in this book.

Reprinted in 1988 by Rowman & Littlefield Publishers, Inc.

Published in the United States of America in 1983
by Rowman & Allanheld, Publishers
(A division of Littlefield, Adams & Company)
81 Adams Drive, Totowa, New Jersey 07512

Library of Congress Cataloging in Publication Data

Jaggar, Alison M.
  Feminist politics and human nature.

  (Philosophy and society)
  Includes bibliographical references and index.
  1. Feminism—Philosophy. 2. Feminism—Political
aspects. 3. Women and socialism. I. Title. II. Series
HQ1206.J33   1983   305.4'2   83-3402
ISBN 0-8476-7181-X
ISBN 0-8476-7254-9 (pbk.)

Acknowledgments

Every book is in some sense a social product, but this book is a social product in a sense that is especially obvious. Not only does it draw directly on the writings of many authors, but parts of it have been heard or read by many people, from all of whose comments I have benefited. I am particularly grateful to the members of the Society for Women in Philosophy, without whose support I might not have dared to devote so much of my energy to feminist philosophy. In addition, the following individuals generously gave me the benefit of their comments on at least part of the manuscript: Eunice Belgum, Teresa Boykin, Mary Elizabeth Branaman, Claudia Card, Frank Cunningham, Tim Diamond, Wendy Donner, Cedric Evans, Marilyn Frye, Judy Gerson, Nancy Gifford, Sandra Harding, Nancy Hartsock, David Jaggar, Sara Ketchum, Glorianne Leck, Rachel Martin, John McEvoy, Maryellen McGuigan, Zjemi Moulton, Harvey Mullane, Linda Nicholson, Joanna Parrent, Christine Pierce, David-Hillel Ruben, Nina Schiller, Carolyn Shafer, Vicky Spelman, Alan Soble, Karsten Struhl, Joyce Trebilcot, Bill Todd, Kerry Walters, Dick Wasserstrom, Bob Young, Iris Young and Jackie Zita. Sandra Bartky carefully read both of the first two drafts and part of the final revision. She contributed incisive philosophical criticisms and innumerable suggestions for stylistic improvements, as well as much practical wisdom and humor to help me find a way through the daily contradictions that confront us all. My family has been encouraging throughout, even though my work on this book has usurped much time I might otherwise have spent with them. Elaine Stapleton, with help from Cindy Curtis, typed the last draft of the manuscript with great speed and good humor, identifying and correcting a number of my mistakes. Finally, Jane Horine, with generous help from Rebecca Hanscom, worked with dedication and creativity to produce a systematic and comprehensive index.

My work has been supported financially by the Dorothy Bridgman Atkinson Endowed Fellowship, granted by the American Association of University Women, by a Fellowship from the National Endowment for the Humanities, by two Taft summer grants-in-aid of research and by a grant for typing from the University of Cincinnati Research Council. I gratefully acknowledge this assistance.

part one
Feminism and Political Philosophy

1
Feminism as Political Philosophy

In a sense, feminism has always existed. Certainly, as long as women have been subordinated, they have resisted that subordination. Sometimes the resistance has been collective and conscious; at other times it has been solitary and only half-conscious, as when women have sought escape from their socially prescribed roles through illness, drug and alcohol addiction, and even madness. Despite the continuity of women's resistance, however, only within the last two or three hundred years has a visible and widespread feminist movement emerged that has attempted to struggle in an organized way against women's special oppression.

The first unmistakably feminist voices were heard in England in the 17th century. In the next 200 years, more voices began to speak together and were heard also in France and the United States. Organized feminism emerged in a period of economic and political transformation: industrial capitalism was beginning to develop, and Britain, France and the United States were adopting political systems of representative democracy. These economic and political changes drastically altered women's situation and also the way in which women perceived their situation. Much of this alteration was a result of the transformation in the economic and political significance of the family.

In the early modern period, production was organized through the household and noble families still had substantial political influence, even though the feudal system had been replaced by the centralized nation-state. In virtue of their family membership, women were guaranteed a certain status both in production and in government, although this status was always lower than that of men. Noblewomen enjoyed considerable political power through the influence of their families, and married women who were not of noble rank had substantial economic power within their families because production was organized through the household. In the preindustrial era, most women were solidly integrated into the system of productive work necessary for a family's survival. In this era, childcare and what we now consider domestic work occupied only a small proportion of women's time. In addition to these tasks, most women made a substantial contribution to food production through keeping poultry and bees, making dairy products and cultivating vegetables; they were responsible for food processing and preservation; they spun cotton and wool and then sewed or knitted the results of their work into clothes; they made soap and candles, accumulated considerable empirical medical knowledge and produced efficacious herbal remedies. The importance of women's contribution to social survival was so evident that there seemed no reason to raise questions about it: women's place in the social order appeared as a natural necessity.

The impact of industrialization, together with the rise of the democratic state, undermined and finally transformed the traditional relationships that had defined preindustrial society. Among them, of course, it transformed the family and so disrupted women's traditional position. Women of the upper classes lost political power with the decline of aristocratic families and the rise of the democratic state. Similarly women of the lower classes had the basis of their economic power undermined as industrialization removed much of their traditional work out of the home and into the factory. Even though many women were employed in the factories, especially in the early ones, the industrialization of their traditional work meant that women's control diminished over such vital industries as food processing, textile manufacture and garment manufacture. Women's reduced contribution to the household increased their economic dependence on their husbands and diminished their power vis-à-vis their husbands.

At the same time as the decline in the economic and political significance of the family tended to undercut women's economic and political status, it held at least the promise of a new status for women, one not predicated on their family membership. For instance, the factory system and the opportunity for wage labor opened to women for the first time the prospect of economic independence outside the household and apart from husbands. Similarly, the new democratic ideals of equality and individual autonomy provided a basis for challenging traditional assumptions of women's natural subordination to men. The contradictory results of these economic and political developments meant that women's position in society no longer appeared as a natural necessity. Instead, women became what Marxists called "a question." That question concerned the proper place of women in the new industrial society and many answers were proposed. Organized feminism emerged as women's answer to this question.

In the two or three centuries of its existence, organized feminism has not spoken with a single voice. Just as feminism first arose in response to the changing conditions of 17th-century England, so changing circumstances since that time have altered the focus of feminist demands. For instance, suffrage, temperance and birth control have all been, at one time or another, the object of organized feminist campaigns. The most recent resurgence of feminism occurred in the late 1960s with the rise of what came to be known as the women's liberation movement. This movement surpassed all earlier waves of feminism in the breadth of its concerns and the depth of its critiques. It was also far less unified than previous feminist movements, offering a multitude of analyses of women's oppression and a profusion of visions of women's liberation. This book is part of the women's liberation movement. Through a critical examination of four major conceptions of feminism that this movement has appropriated or generated, I hope to strengthen the movement by contributing to the development of a theory and a practice that ultimately will liberate women.

"Feminism" and "Women's Liberation"

"Feminism" was originally a French word. It referred to what in the 19th-century United States was called "the woman movement": a diverse collection of groups all aimed, in one way or another, at "advancing" the position of women. When the word "feminism" was introduced into the United States in the early 20th century, however, it was used to refer only to one particular group of women's rights advocates, namely that group which asserted the uniqueness of women, the mystical experience of motherhood and women's special purity. Ehrenreich and English call this trend in the woman movement "sexual romanticism" and contrast it with the more dominant tendency of "sexual rationalism."[1] In opposition to the romantic "feminists," the sexual rationalists argued that the subordination of women was irrational not because women were purer than men, but because of the basic similarities between women and men. In contemporary usage, the 19th-century restriction on the meaning of "feminism" has again been lost. Now, "feminism" is commonly used to refer to all those who seek, no matter on what grounds, to end women's subordination. That is how I shall use the term in this book.

This inclusive definition of feminism is opposed to the usage of some speakers who employ "feminism" as what Linda Gordon calls "an imprimatur to bestow upon those we agree with."[2] Because feminist claims touch every aspect of our lives, the term *feminism* carries a potent emotional charge. For some, it is a pejorative term; for others, it is honorific. Consequently, some people deny the title "feminist" to those who would claim it, and some seek to bestow it on those who would reject it. Like Gordon, I think that this practice is not only sectarian but misleads us about history. Just as an inadequate theory of justice is still a conception of justice, so I would say that an inadequate feminist theory is still a conception of feminism. My goal is not the discovery of a Platonic ideal form of feminism and the exposure of rival theories as pretenders. Instead, I want to contribute to formulating a conception of feminism that is more adequate than previous conceptions in that it will help women to achieve the fullest possible liberation.

The "women's liberation" movement, as I have indicated already, is the major version of feminism in contemporary western society. The very name of the movement reflects the political context from which it emerged and provides a clue to some of the ways in which it differs from earlier forms of feminism. Earlier feminists used the language of "rights" and "equality," but in the late 1960s "oppression" and "liberation" became the key words for the political activists of the new left. In the proliferation of "liberation movements" (black liberation, gay liberation, third world liberation, etc.) it was inevitable that the new feminism should call itself "women's liberation." The change in language reflects a significant development in the political perspective of contemporary feminism.

The etymological origin of the word "oppression" lies in the Latin for "press down" or "press against." This root suggests that people who are oppressed suffer some kind of restriction on their freedom. Not all restrictions on people's freedom, however, are oppressive. People are not oppressed by simple natural phenomena, such as gravitational forces, blizzards or droughts.[3] Instead, oppression is the result of human agency, humanly imposed restrictions on people's freedom.[4]

Not all humanly imposed limitations on people's freedom are oppressive, however. Oppression must also be unjust. Suppose you are in the proverbial lifeboat with nine other people, that there is sufficient food only for six but that those in the lifeboat decide democratically to divide the food into ten equal parts. Here you would be prevented from eating your fill as the result of some human action but you could not complain that this restriction on your freedom was oppressive as long as you accepted that distribution as just. Thus, oppression is the imposition of unjust constraints on the freedom of individuals or groups.

Liberation is the correlate of oppression. It is release from oppressive constraints.

It is clear from these definitions that there are conceptual connections between oppression and liberation, on the one hand, and the traditional political ideals of freedom and justice, on the other. To speak of oppression and liberation, however, is not simply to introduce new words for old ideas. While the concepts of oppression and liberation are linked conceptually to the familiar philosophical concepts of freedom, justice and equality, they cannot be reduced without loss to those concepts. Talk of oppression and liberation introduces not just a new political terminology but a new perspective on political phenomena. It is a perspective that presupposes a dynamic rather than a static view of society and that is influenced by Marxist ideas of class struggle. Oppression is the *imposition* of constraints; it suggests that the problem is not the result of bad luck, ignorance or prejudice but is caused rather by one group actively subordinating another group to its own interest. Thus, to talk of oppression seems to commit feminists to a world view that includes at least two groups with conflicting interests: the oppressors and the oppressed. It is a world view, moreover, that strongly suggests that liberation is unlikely to be achieved by rational debate but instead must be the result of political struggle.

The emphasis on the process of struggle rather than on its ends relieves those who advocate liberation from the need to attempt a complete characterization of the end at which they aim. It weakens the temptation to plan utopias by the recognition that our conception of what it is to be liberated must be subject to constant revision. As human knowledge of nature, including human nature, develops, we gain more insight into possible human goods and learn how they may be achieved through the increasing control both of ourselves and our world. Through this process, the sphere of human agency is constantly increased. Drought is no longer an act of God but the result of failure to practice suitable water conservation measures; disease and malnutrition are no longer inevitabilities but the results of social policy. Consequently, constraints that once were viewed as natural necessities are transformed into instances of oppression; simultaneously, the possible domain of human liberation is constantly being extended. In principle, therefore, liberation is not some finally achievable situation; instead, it is the process of eliminating forms of oppression as long as these continue to arise.

Women's Liberation and Political Philosophy

New perspectives notwithstanding, there is a continuity between the traditional and the contemporary feminist projects. In seeking liberation, contemporary feminists necessarily take over the interest of their predecessors in freedom, justice, and equality. Their concern with the traditional concepts of political philosophy means that feminists cannot avoid the familiar philosophical controversies over the proper interpretation of these concepts. Apparently, interminable disagreement over what should count as freedom, justice and equality has led to the characterization of these concepts as "essentially contested,"[5] and much of political philosophy itself may be viewed as a continuing series of attempts to defend alternative conceptions of freedom, justice, and equality. In developing its own interpretation of these ideals, women's liberation engages in political philosophy.

Partly because of their traditional training and partly in an attempt to "legitimate" the philosophy of feminism, academic philosophers have tended to discuss feminist issues in terms of the older and more familiar concepts. By contrast, the grass-roots discussions of non-academic feminists have revolved around questions of oppression. This new language has raised new philosophical questions relating to the concepts of oppression and liberation. These are some of the questions. What is the precise nature of women's special oppression? Does the nature of their oppression vary for different groups of women? Can individual women escape oppression? If women are oppressed, who are their oppressors? Can one be an unknowing or unintentional oppressor? May oppressors themselves be oppressed? Can individual members of the oppressor group refrain from oppressing women so long as the group, as such, continues to exist? To each of these questions, contemporary feminists have provided a range of competing answers.

Feminist political philosophers thus use both traditional and nontraditional categories in attempting to describe and evaluate women's experience. In either case, they often raise issues that may seem foreign to political philosophy as it is currently conceived. For instance, they ask questions about conceptions of love, friendship or sexuality. They wonder what it would mean to democratize housework or childcare. They even challenge entrenched views about the naturalness of sexual intercourse and childbearing. Their demands or slogans are unfamiliar and may appear non-political. They demand "control of their bodies," "an end to sexual objectification," and "reproductive rights." They even assert that "the personal is political."

In focusing on these issues, feminist theorists are exploring the possibility of applying existing political categories to domains of human existence that hitherto have been considered to lie beyond the sphere of politics. Thus, feminist reflections on equality for women consider not only the questions of equal opportunity and preferential treatment for women in the market but whether equality requires paid maternity leave or even so-called test-tube babies. In raising such issues, contemporary feminists are giving a new focus to political philosophy. Rather than simply providing new answers to old problems, they seek to demonstrate that the problems themselves have been conceived too narrowly. In reconceptualizing old problems or in raising new ones, contemporary feminism is providing novel tests for the adequacy of existing political theories and, where traditional political theory seems inadequate, it is beginning to suggest alternative ways of conceptualizing social reality and political possibility. By seeking to extend the traditional domain of political philosophy, contemporary feminism challenges both existing political theories and our conception of political philosophy itself.

The Aims and Structure of This Book

Contemporary feminists share certain concerns that distinguish them both from non-feminists and from earlier feminists. But the very breadth of contemporary feminist concerns means that there is a "division of feminist labor," so that some feminists are preoccupied with some political struggles, some with others. Some feminists work in universities, some are active in left groups or in community organizing, some are black, some are lesbian. The variety of work and life experience of contemporary feminists results in a variety of perceptions of social reality and of women's oppression. This variety is a source of strength for the women's liberation movement. Earlier waves of feminism sometimes have been charged with reflecting primarily the experience of white middle- and upper-class women. While white middle-class women, at least, are still strongly represented in the contemporary women's movement, increasingly their perspective is challenged by perceptions that reflect the very different experiences of women of color, working-class women, etc. The rich and varied experience of contemporary feminists contributes fresh insights into women's oppression and provides the women's liberation movement with new and valuable perspectives.

It is not always obvious, however, how the new insights and perspectives should be translated into feminist theory. Standing in different social locations, some feminists experience certain aspects of women's oppression with particular sharpness while others are affected more immediately by other aspects. The differing perceptions of women's oppression are often used in developing systematic analyses of women's oppression which differ markedly from each other. For instance, some feminists have no hesitation in declaring unambiguously that women are oppressed by men. Others have adopted the less than self-evident position that, while they may *appear* to be oppressed by men, in reality women's specific oppression is a result of the capitalist system. Still other feminists, although they use the popular language of oppression, attempt to launder it by disconnecting its apparently radical presuppositions; they argue that *both* women and men are oppressed by the "sex-role system." It is clear that contemporary feminists hold a variety of theories concerning women's oppression and women's liberation.

My primary aim in this book is to evaluate these theories. In order to do this, I shall try to clarify the claims made by various feminists and to draw out the presuppositions and implications of feminist claims. I shall then attempt to organize the multifarious and often competing contemporary feminist claims by linking them to certain basic assumptions, in particular to four distinct conceptions of human nature. That is to say, I shall try to identify four alternative conceptions of women's liberation by exhibiting them as systematic political theories. I call these theories, respectively, liberal feminism, traditional Marxism, radical feminism and socialist feminism.

Although much of this book is expository and analytical, my goal is not simply to clarify feminist theorizing. In addition, I subject each theory to critical scrutiny and identify its strengths and weaknesses as a theory of women's liberation. This book is intended as a substantive contribution to feminist theory, insofar as it argues for the superiority of one conception of women's liberation over all the others. That one is socialist feminism.

As the discussion proceeds, it will become evident that it raises a number of meta-theoretical issues regarding the nature of political philosophy. These include the question of the proper domain of political philosophy, a domain which feminism, as I shall show, seeks to expand. Another meta-theoretical question concerns the conceptual connections between political philosophy, on the one hand, and theories of human nature, on the other. By linking feminist political claims to certain theories of human nature, I shall excavate the often-concealed structure of a political theory and encourage the resurrection of philosophical anthropology not only as a legitimate, but as a fundamental philosophical endeavor. In addition, I shall explore the relation between political philosophy and the human sciences. Finally, I shall discuss the question of theoretical adequacy in political philosophy.

The structure of the book will be as follows. Part I will discuss the logical status of a political theory, focusing particularly on the validity of the distinction usually drawn between philosophy and science. I shall argue that a theory of human nature is at the core of both political philosophy and the life sciences, that such a theory is inevitably both normative and empirical and that, consequently, it is wrong to view political philosophy and the life sciences as separate and autonomous disciplines.

In Part II, I shall identify the conception of human nature that lies at the heart of each of what I see as the four major contemporary theories of women's liberation. Part III will trace the connections between each theory of human nature, its correlated feminist critique of contemporary society and its recommendations for social change. It should be noted that Part III is not intended simply as a way of drawing out the logical consequences of the conceptions of human nature discussed in Part II. In spite of my occasional characterization of a certain theory of human nature as the "philosophical foundation" of a certain political theory, I think it is mistaken to present any political theory as a deductive system. Later I shall argue that, just as our beliefs about human nature affect the ways in which we conceptualize social reality, so the ways in which we understand and experience that reality affect our views about human nature. Consequently, a feminist theory is viewed better as a network of normative, conceptual, empirical and methodological claims than as a deductive system. Such a network is sometimes called a paradigm and is often associated with the work of Thomas Kuhn.[6] Occasionally I may refer to a feminist theory as a paradigm but my use of "paradigm" is rather different from Kuhn's insofar as I believe that paradigms or comprehensive ways of understanding reality are generated by specific historical conditions and reflect the material interests of particular social groups.

In the fourth and final part of the book, I take up the issue of theoretical adequacy in political philosophy. Since I argue that claims in the life sciences, political theories and epistemological claims are mutually dependent on each other, it follows that there can be no theory-neutral interpretations of the criteria for rational choice between competing political theories. I shall show that each of the feminist theories that I identify includes its own conception of theoretical adequacy and so justifies itself in its own terms. I break out of this circle by arguing that socialist feminism provides the most appropriate interpretation of what it is for a theory to be impartial, objective, comprehensive, verifiable and useful. I conclude by suggesting that, on this interpretation, socialist feminism is the most adequate of the feminist theories formulated to date.

Four Conceptions of Women's Liberation

Certain difficulties are endemic to any attempt to categorize social theory. The most obvious difficulty is that theory changes constantly, partly in response to changing social realities, partly in response to new theoretical perspectives. Women's situation is changing rapidly at the present time and feminist theory, in consequence, is constantly developing. Partly because feminist theory is a new intellectual discipline, moreover, feminist theorists are not working within an established paradigm and consequently often challenge their own fundamental assumptions. These rapid changes mean that the present analysis can be useful as a description only for a relatively short time, although I hope that its critical or prescriptive value may be longer lasting.

Another problem that confronts all attempts at classification is the problem of selecting the principles of organization. At any given moment, social reality can be perceived or conceptualized in a variety of different ways and existing feminist theory provides a variety of perceptions and conceptualizations of women's situation. Social theory, however, does not stand outside social reality; it is itself a part of that reality and, like the other parts, is capable itself of being variously analyzed. What kind of analysis one provides, what kinds of similarities and differences one emphasizes, depends on one's purposes in undertaking the analysis.

In my analysis of feminist theory, I am not interested in a taxonomic classification of as many subspecies as possible. Rather, I seek a sound methodology to provide the basis for a theory and a practice that will liberate women. Consequently, I seek to reduce rather than to proliferate theories. I am searching for the genera, the ways of conceptualizing women's situation that are fundamentally incompatible with each other. In order to do this, of course, I must decide which differences count as "fundamental," and I find it most useful to identify fundamental differences by reference to four distinctive conceptions of human nature. These conceptions, I shall show, are correlated with distinctive analyses of women's oppression and distinctive visions of women's liberation.

Like all systems of categorization, mine may be challenged in a number of ways. It collects within one category certain views that some might prefer to keep distinct; it separates views that some might think belong together; and it omits certain views entirely. In what immediately follows, I want to give a preliminary explanation of my system of categorization. The ultimate test of the adequacy of my system, of course, will be found in the body of the book, where I provide the detailed argument for the theoretical unity and for the plausibility of the paradigms that I identify.

Among the most obvious omissions from this book are religious and existential conceptions of women's liberation. Such conceptions have been significant historically; indeed, *The Second Sex,* published in 1949 by the existentialist Simone de Beauvoir, must be considered a forerunner of the contemporary women's liberation movement. I have omitted religious and existentialist conceptions primarily because I find them implausible. They are outside the mainstream of contemporary feminist theorizing, and they have little direct connection with socialist feminism, the version of feminist theory that I consider the most plausible.

Black feminism has not been omitted from the book, but it has not been treated as a separate theory because black feminists utilize a variety of theoretical approaches. Some discuss the situation of black women in terms of a liberal or a traditional Marxist framework; a few advocate their own version of separatism, black nationalism; a very few are radical feminists, though almost none seems to be a lesbian separatist; and some black feminists argue that the situation of black women can be fully understood only through a development of socialist feminist theory, a development that integrates conceptually the category of racial or ethnic identity with the categories of gender and class. Given the variety in the theoretical orientation of black feminism, I think it more useful to examine their contributions in the context of the four categories of feminism I identify than to present those contributions as reflective of a single black feminist perspective.

A relatively small body of written work is available by feminists of color other than black feminists, and what is available is mainly at the level of description. Of course, a fully adequate theory of women's liberation cannot ignore the experience of any group of women and, to the extent that socialist feminism fails to theorize the experience of women of color, it cannot be accepted as complete. So far, however, relatively few attempts exist by non-black feminists of color to develop a distinctive and comprehensive theory of women's liberation.

Another conspicuous omission from my list of feminist theories is anarchist feminism or anarcha-feminism. While a substantial number of contemporary feminists identify themselves as anarchists, their views do not receive a separate examination in this book. The reason for this decision is that, because anarchism is such a broad term, each of the four conceptions of women's liberation that I do consider contains views that may legitimately be described as anarchist. Anarchist elements can be found in the liberal (especially libertarian) suspicion of the state, in the classical Marxist hope that the state ultimately will "wither away," in the radical feminist attacks on patriarchal power in everyday life and in their self-help alternatives, and in the socialist feminist critiques of hierarchy and authoritarianism on the left. Because such a great diversity of views may be labeled anarchist, it seems impossible to identify a single conception of human nature and society that does not exclude substantial numbers of self-defined anarchists. Consequently, rather than identifying feminist anarchism as a distinct feminist theory, I shall simply note the elements of anarchism as they arise in the context of what I see as the four major contemporary paradigms of women's liberation.

A large number of contemporary feminists identify themselves as lesbian feminists. Once again, they have not been categorized separately, since lesbianfeminism has not yet developed a distinctive and comprehensive theory of women's liberation, although it may be in the process of doing so. In the meantime, some lesbianfeminist insights have been incorporated by socialist feminism and some even by liberal feminism. My most extended discussion of lesbianfeminism, however, occurs in the context of my examination of radical feminism. This is because lesbianfeminists typically recommend some form of separatism as a political strategy and separatist strategies follow most naturally from radical feminist analyses of women's oppression.

I say radical feminist "analyses" rather than "analysis" because there is no single radical feminist analysis of women's oppression. Neither, as we shall see, is there a single radical feminist conception of human nature. The political tradition that I call "radical feminism" had its roots in two different types of soil: in the basically liberal civil rights movement and in the Marxist-inspired new left. Because of this contradictory heritage, radical feminists found it difficult to locate their distinctive insights within a comprehensive theoretical framework and the radical feminist movement in fact generated a variety of analyses of women's oppression and a variety of visions of women's liberation. What unified all these analyses was a conviction that the oppression of women was fundamental: that is to say, it was causally and conceptually irreducible to the oppression of any other group. It is this conviction that I have taken as definitive of radical feminism and that also serves as my justification for identifying radical feminism as a distinctive feminist perspective. It may be that this justification will not serve for much longer. Within radical feminism, I note an increasing divergence between those who emphasize a fundamental and probably biologically based commonality in the experience of all women and those who place increasing emphasis on the way in which women are divided by race and by class. The latter group is moving closer to the position that I characterize as socialist feminism and in a few years the conceptual distinction between radical feminism and socialist feminism may have to be reexamined.

Socialist feminism is perhaps the most questionable of all the four paradigms that I have identified. On the one hand, it may not be clearly separable from some of the most recent expressions of radical feminism, since it does take domination by gender to be at least as fundamental as domination by class, in the Marxist sense of "class." On the other hand, socialist feminism may be viewed as a relatively minor revision of traditional Marxism and some might deny that its revisions of the central Marxist categories are sufficiently significant to warrant its being considered a separate paradigm. In my view, socialist feminism is still distinct from both radical feminism and traditional Marxism. On the one hand socialist feminism today is very different from the most popular versions of radical feminism which, as I shall argue later, either tend toward idealism or have failed to extricate themselves completely from the influence of biologism. On the other hand, I believe that the socialist feminist revisions of Marxism are fundamental, requiring a rethinking of every Marxist analysis, from domestic labor to imperialism. Later in the book, I shall provide the detailed argument necessary to support my claim that socialist feminism, although still in the process of development, is already a distinct and comprehensive, as well as an illuminating and useful, theory of women's liberation.

It is my belief that the four feminist paradigms that I present are the most widely accepted and plausible conceptions of women's liberation that presently exist. Furthermore, since there is a sense in which these theories developed chronologically, even though all are still current and continue to influence one another, it is easy to exhibit each as designed, at least in part, to answer problems inherent in the preceding theory. When each theory is examined in the context of its rivals, the understanding of each is deepened and a sense of the on-going and dialectical process of feminist theorizing emerges.

Given the rapid development and cross-fertilization characteristic of contemporary feminist theorizing, it is obvious that any attempt at categorization runs the risk of oversimplification at best and of distortion at worst. The feminist theories that I identify in terms of their basic assumptions about human nature are meant to be viewed as rational reconstructions or ideal types. This implies that perhaps no individual will accept every aspect of what I identify as a single theory. Those who accept the position in general terms may not have articulated the presuppositions on which I claim their position rests; or they may not wish to draw the conclusions that I think are implied by their view. Alternatively, challenged by other feminist theories, they may have tried to revise their own account, even at the expense of inconsistency with their own philosophical presuppositions. The reconstruction of feminist theories as ideal types minimizes the similarities between them and sharpens the differences. My ultimate aim is certainly not to deepen divisions among feminists; rather, it is to help resolve them. I think this can be done best, however, by an in-depth examination of our differences that clarifies exactly what is at stake. The way is then prepared for a resolution of those differences, a resolution that can provide a sound basis for future political work and for further theoretical development.

Notes

1. Barbara Ehrenreich and Deirdre English, *For Her Own Good* (Garden City, New York: Anchor Books, 1979), p. 20.
2. Linda Gordon, "The Struggle for Reproductive Freedom: Three Stages of Feminism," in Zillah R. Eisenstein, ed., *Capitalist Patriarchy and the Case for Socialist Feminism* (New York: Monthly Review Press, 1979), p. 107.
3. This view is opposed to that taken by Judith Farr Tormey in "Exploitation, Oppression and Self-Sacrifice," *Philosophical Forum* 5, nos. 1–2 (Fall–Winter 1973-74):216. Tormey believes that persons can be oppressed by such non-human phenomena as the weather.
4. The conceptual connection between oppression and human agency is presupposed, in fact, by the next feature of oppression that I mention, namely, that it is unjust. At least as justice is conceived in modern times, questions of justice are considered to arise only with regard to situations that result from human agency. For example, it is neither just nor unjust that some individuals are born with physical handicaps, so long as their handicaps cannot be traced to some prior unjust situation, such as the avoidable malnutrition of their mothers or exposure to avoidable environmental pollutants.
5. W. B. Gallie, "Essentially Contested Concepts," *Proceedings of the Aristotelian Society* 56(1955–56):168–98. Cf. also Alasdair MacIntyre "The Essential Contestability of Some Social Concepts," *Ethics* 84(1973):1–9.
6. Thomas S. Kuhn, *The Structure of Scientific Revolutions* (Chicago: University of Chicago Press, 1962). In subsequent chapters, I shall elaborate this view of a feminist theory as a paradigm.

2
Political Philosophy and Human Nature

Three Aspects of Political Philosophy

The goal of political philosophy is to articulate a vision of the good society. Political philosophy is essentially a normative enterprise that seeks to determine the ideals and principles that should inform social organization.

This is not to deny that much political philosophy, especially contemporary political philosophy, appears on the surface to be concerned less with arguing in favor of such ideals as equality, democracy or community than with attempting to define them. Every theory, after all, must clarify its own key concepts and, in the case of political philosophy, many of the central concepts are controversial not so much as abstract ideals but rather in their interpretation. Even in their debates over the "meaning" of "freedom" or "individuality," "justice" or "equality" however, political philosophers are not really trying to discover how those terms are ordinarily used. Instead, although they often express their conclusions as claims about meaning, political philosophers in fact argue for their own stipulated *interpretation* of the disputed concepts. And in arguing for their own interpretation, political philosophers take into account not only traditional usage and conceptual clarity; they also employ explicitly normative arguments about the superiority of a society that instantiates this rather than that conception of democracy, freedom or justice. Thus, even the conceptual arguments of political philosophers have a normative dimension.

The normative nature of political philosophy is uncontroversial. Indeed, it is customary to distinguish political philosophy from political science precisely by claiming that political science, which is said to investigate how political systems in fact work, is empirical, while political philosophy, which tells us how they ought to work, is normative. Political science is seen as descriptive, political philosophy as prescriptive. Although I do not wish to deny the normative nature of political philosophy, I shall challenge this customary way of distinguishing political philosophy from political science by arguing that both, as they are commonly defined, include both normative and empirical elements.

Interchangeably with "political philosophy," I shall also use the more ambiguous term "political theory," which is more generally recognized as including both claims in what is ordinarily called political science and also explicitly normative claims.[1]

Inseparable from a vision of the good society is a critique of the philosopher's own society. This critique may not be worked out in any detail but it is always at least implicit because a conception of justice is simultaneously a conception of injustice. Equality defines inequality; oppression defines liberation. How much emphasis a philosopher gives to the positive vision and how much to the negative critique depends on a number of things: on the philosopher's motives in writing, on her or his own situation (for some philosophers, an overt critique of their own society may be too dangerous to undertake) and also on the philosopher's conception of the nature and social function of political theory. Some philosophers may believe that their task is to provide a detailed blueprint for the future; others, like Marx, may have epistemological reasons for believing that the future society must be designed by its future inhabitants and that the immediate task is to struggle against specific forms of oppression. Thus Marx's philosophy, unlike Plato's, for instance, consists largely in a detailed critique of the capitalist future. Nevertheless, the vision of an alternative society, however indistinct, underlies every philosophical criticism of contemporary injustice or oppression, just as every philosophical theory of the good society contains an implicit condemnation of existing social evils.

A third aspect of political philosophy is a consideration of the means for traveling from here to there, a strategy for moving from the oppressive present to the liberated future. Many philosophers have failed to give explicit attention to the question of means. Some may have wished to avoid charges of subverting the status quo; others, however, have had an underlying epistemological rationale for ignoring the question of the means to social change. They have held an elevated conception of political philosophy as the articulation of universal ideals and have viewed the question of how to instantiate those ideals as being both logically secondary and non-universal. The Marxist tradition is one of the few that has given much weight to questions of means as well as of ends and this is because of the Marxist belief that theory is born from practice, that only in the process of struggling against oppression can people formulate new visions of liberation.

Whether or not one accepts this tenet of Marxist epistemology, there are other reasons for viewing questions of strategy as integral to political philosophy. One reason is that questions of means are not just questions of efficiency; they also involve normative issues about what means may be morally justifiable in achieving social change. Examples of such questions concern the justifiability as well as the effectiveness of propaganda, strikes, boycotts, restrictions on freedom of speech or movement, torture, sabotage, terrorism and war. Because questions of means have this normative aspect, they are related logically to questions of ends. So the basic principles of a political theory often seem to imply the propriety of some means to social change and to prohibit the use of other means. For instance, the liberal commitment to preserving individual rights seems to rule out censorship, let alone terrorism and assassination, as legitimate means to social change. On the other hand, a Marxist analysis of the state as an instrument of class domination undercuts the state's claims to political authority and justifies illegal and possibly violent forms of resistance to it on the part of the oppressed classes. For these reasons, as well as because political philosophy has an ultimately practical aim, I view a consideration of the appropriate strategies for social change as an integral part of political philosophy.

Political Philosophy and Scientific Knowledge

To acknowledge that political philosophy is concerned with means as well as with ends is to recognize that it must be practicable as well as practical; an adequate political theory must show how to translate its ideals into practice. To use a well-known if rather dated formula of analytic philosophy, "ought" implies "can." To know what can be, however, requires considerable information about what is. To know how certain political ideals can be instantiated, for instance, requires information about human motivation, in order to determine the circumstances in which people will cooperate; it requires information about the available technology, in order to determine the social possibility and social costs of satisfying certain human desires; and, in order to discover workable strategies, it requires information about the motors of social change. A political theory that is practicable as well as practical obviously depends heavily on scientific knowledge about the real world.

It is not only to discover the *means* of social change that political philosophers require scientific knowledge. In order to engage in a critique of contemporary society, a political philosopher must know what is going on in that society. Political ideals are designed to evaluate actual situations and actual situations must therefore be properly understood.

Finally, although it is obvious that the critical and the strategic aspects of political philosophy require a knowledge of the real world, it may be less obvious that to construct a positive vision of the good society also requires knowledge of the world. This is because abstract ideals need specific interpretations. For instance, the Marxist attack on the liberal conception of equality, a conception which defines that ideal primarily in terms of civil rights, draws on empirical data showing that individuals with more economic power in a society inevitably use that power to weaken or even eliminate the ability of those with less economic power to exercise their civil rights. It is partly on the basis of empirical considerations, therefore, that Marxists argue for an economic dimension to equality. To take an even more fundamental example, in order to make a general determination of what is socially desirable, it is necessary to be able to identify the basic human needs. For although "good" may not be definable in terms of human need, as one form of philosophical naturalism claims, yet there is a conceptual connection between them such that, if something fulfills a basic human need, this constitutes a prima facie, although not an indefeasible, reason for calling it good.[2]

An intimate relation exists, then, between political philosophy, on the one hand, and, on the other hand, such sciences as psychology, economics, political science, sociology, anthropology and even biology and the various technologies. Some political philosophers recognize this explicitly. For instance, Rawls requires that those who formulate the principles of justice in his ideal society should know "whatever general facts affect the choice of those principles" and gives examples that include "political affairs and the principles of economic theory; . . . the basis of social organization and the laws of human psychology."[3] A knowledge of many sciences is necessary to give substance to the philosophical ideal of human well-being and fulfillment, to add trenchancy to philosophical critiques of oppression and to avoid idle speculation by setting limits to social and political possibility.

Science, Politics and Human Nature

The dependence of political philosophy on information about the world, particularly the sort of information that the human or life sciences are designed to provide, raises for political philosophers not only the problem of acquainting themselves with the findings of those sciences but the deeper problem of determining which of those findings they should accept as valid. Scientific claims to provide the information for which Rawls calls, that is, "the principles of economic theory," "the basis of social organization and the laws of human psychology," are all highly controversial. For instance, there are no generally accepted laws of psychology, and no prospect that any will be discovered soon.

One aspect of the intractability of the human sciences is that disputes within them often lack clear criteria of resolution. This is not to say that there are no relatively straightforward empirical questions about, for instance, the voting patterns or divorce rates of certain groups. But the more persistent disputes within the human sciences concern not facts, but the *interpretation* of facts; that is, they concern which theoretical models will best explain or make sense of these facts. To take a current example, the new "discipline" of sociobiology has developed a theoretical framework that attempts to explain instances of apparently altruistic behavior in both animals and humans in terms of an evolutionary strategy through which genes seek to maximize their chances of reproductive success. This theoretical framework is in sharp contrast, of course, to older theories about altruism which may interpret it as a triumph of the moral will over the selfish instincts or as a flowering of the human potential for self-actualization through cooperation.

I think it is illuminating to see many of the disputes in the various human sciences as grounded ultimately in competing conceptions of what it is to be human. Psychology provides perhaps the most convincing examples of this claim with its variety of theoretical models of the human mind: the behavioristic model, according to which people are complicated stimulus-response mechanisms; the "humanistic" model, which sees people in basically existential terms as agents who are capable of making an individual choice about their own destiny; the Marxian model, which views humans as self-creating only through social action; the Freudian model; the model of humans as computers, and so on. Conflicts between schools of economists, too, seem to involve competing conceptions of human nature: classical economics rests on a conception of humans as beings whose individual interests are constantly likely to conflict, whereas Marxist economics posits a fundamental identity of interest between members of the same class and ultimately, indeed, between all members of the human species. Within sociology, the structural-functionalist school conceives of human individuals simply as the bearers of roles, while other approaches ascribe more or less autonomy to human agents. And alternative models of human motivation may also be found to underlie competing analyses in political science. Making this point, Charles Taylor writes:

> For a given framework [of explanation] is linked to a given conception of the schedule of human needs, wants, and purposes, such that, if the schedule turns out to have been mistaken in some significant way, the framework itself cannot be maintained. This is for the fairly obvious

reason that human needs, wants, and purposes have an important bearing on the way people act, and that therefore one has to have a notion of the schedule which is not too wildly inaccurate if one is to establish the framework for any science of human behaviour, that of politics not excepted. A conception of human needs thus enters into a given political theory and cannot be considered something extraneous which we later add to the framework.[4]

To attribute the divisions within the human sciences to the lack of a generally accepted conception of what it is to be human is not to diagnose the problem, but to re-state it.[5] Yet I think that this restatement has heuristic value because it leads us to focus attention on the whole notion of a theory of human nature. What questions should a theory of human nature be designed to answer, what are the methods by which it might discover those answers and what are the criteria for determining the adequacy of the answers offered?

No single issue, of course, can be identified as "the" problem of human nature. Rather, there is a cluster of interrelated questions, many of which have been perennial objects of study for philosophy. These questions include ontological issues, such as whether human beings can be thought of as existing prior to or independently of society; and metaphysical or methodological issues, such as whether human beings are irreducibly different from the rest of nature or whether their activities can be understood in principle by the concepts and methods of natural sciences. Other questions include the basis, scope and limits of human knowledge, and the nature of human fulfillment and self-realization. In modern times, a skeptical issue has been raised: is it possible to identify any universal characteristics of human nature which all human beings have in common and which distinguish them from animals, or are persons living at different places and times, in different social contexts, so diverse that the only characteristics they may safely be assumed to share are biological? An attempt to provide a comprehensive and systematic answer to these and other questions may be called a theory of human nature.

Given the range and extent of these problems, it is obvious that a complete theory of human nature stretches beyond the findings of any single discipline, be it anthropology, sociology or psychology. Rather, each of these disciplines provides a partial contribution to a comprehensive theory of human nature. But, as well as contributing to the development of such a theory, there is a clear sense in which research in each of these disciplines also *presupposes* a certain model of human nature. Let us take as an example the problem of understanding human motivation. Empirical data are certainly required to develop an explanatory model but a systematic account of motivation is not simply derivable from empirical data. On the contrary, what are to count as data is determined by the conceptual framework set up to guide the project of research. Empirical observations do not simply discover what motivates human beings; they must also presuppose certain very general features of human motivation. For example, if psychologists believe that human behavior is governed by innate biological drives or instincts, then psychological research obviously will focus on attempts to identify those drives and will tend to ignore environmental stimuli and rational agency. If psychology is dominated by a conception of human motivation according to which persons are complicated stimulus-response mechanisms, then psychological research will attempt to explain behavior through the discovery of the stimuli to which the organism is responding and will tend to ignore biology and rational agency. And if psychology takes people to be essentially rational agents, then research will tend to ignore human biology and environmental stimuli and will be directed instead toward discovering the individual's reasons for action—the exact direction of the research being determined, of course, by the researcher's own conception of rational behavior. This example brings out the now familiar interdependence between theory and observation and it also illustrates the way in which questions, answers and methods are not independent aspects of a conception of human nature—or of any other theory. What count as appropriate methods and appropriate answers are determined by what one takes the questions to be and, conversely, what one takes to be significant questions is in part a function of one's preexisting theoretical and methodological commitments.

Theories of human nature do not differ from theories of non-human nature in their interdependence of question, answer and method, but in another respect they are generally taken to differ from such theories: in their normative element. A few philosophers of science deny the alleged contrast by arguing that all knowledge is pervaded by normative moral and political assumptions. Whether or not this is true for the physical sciences, it is certainly true for the theories that constitute the human sciences. For instance, to determine an individual's reasons for action requires an inevitably normative decision about what counts as rational behavior. More generally, the core of any theory of human nature must be a conception of human abilities, needs, wants and purposes; but there is no value-free method for identifying these. Obviously, a theory of human nature requires us to separate out the "real" or basic or ineliminable needs and wants from among the innumerable things that people in fact say they need and want, and there seems to be a strong conceptual connection between the notion of a basic need or want and the notion of human flourishing and well-being. What constitutes flourishing and well-being, however, is clearly a question of value, both with respect to the individual and with respect to the social group. It has been a commonplace for some time that the notion of mental health has overtly normative and ideological ingredients and philosophers are now beginning to argue the same for the notion of physical health. Even the standard of physical survival cannot be used as a value-free criterion for determining human needs, for it raises normative questions about how long and in what conditions humans can and should survive.

This discussion of human well-being brings out one way in which values are embedded in the human sciences. In later chapters, I shall give other examples of how valuational, including political, considerations influence the ways in which we conceptualize human nature. I shall argue that this is true even of our assumptions about what constitutes genuine knowledge. For the moment, however, I hope I have shown that the human sciences are grounded on conceptions of human nature that are not straightforwardly empirical, both because they presuppose certain very general features of what it is to be human and because they rest on certain normative assumptions. The presuppositions of the human sciences, in fact, constitute varying answers to what the western tradition has taken to be the central problems of philosophy. These include questions regarding the relations between human and non-human nature, between mind and body, and between individuals and other individuals, questions regarding the possibility and source of genuine human knowledge and questions regarding human well-being and fulfilment. The original object of this section thus has been turned on its head. I began by looking for standards of well-established scientific knowledge about human beings that could be used by political philosophers in constructing a theory of the good society. But now it seems that the human sciences themselves rest on a philosophical foundation. In part, moreover, this foundation consists precisely in answers to the central questions of political philosophy.

If this argument is sound, political philosophy and the human sciences, certainly including political science, are ultimately inseparable. None of them is "autonomous." Philosophy, science and politics are not distinct endeavors. The human sciences do not constitute a reservoir of factual knowledge, uncontaminated by values, on which political philosophers can draw; nor, since political philosophy depends on the findings of the human sciences, can the former be viewed simply as a prologomenon to the latter. Instead, a certain methodological approach to the human sciences is correlated with a basic perspective in political philosophy in such a way that each reinforces the other.[6] The unifying element in each case is a certain very general conception of human nature.

Human Nature and the Nature of Women

In developing its vision of the good society, every political theory gives at least some indication of women's and men's relative positions in that society—even if its view is indicated as much as by what it fails to say as by what it actually says. Consequently, since every political theory is grounded on a certain conception of human nature, each political theory incorporates some assumptions about the nature of women and of men. In the case of most classical theories, claims about women's nature were explicit, although definitely not accorded a central place in the total system.[7] In contemporary times, systematic political philosophers, such as John Rawls and Robert Nozick, have rarely discussed women directly. Nevertheless, the very silence of contemporary philosophers on this topic is significant. Either it suggests that standard moral or political theories, such as natural rights theory, utilitarianism or even the theory of alienation, apply without modification to women, or it suggests that they do not apply to women at all. In other words, from contemporary philosophers' silence about women one might infer either that there are no differences between women and men that are relevant to political philosophy or that women are not part of the subject matter of political philosophy at all.

Feminists break this silence. Their critique of women's position in contemporary society demonstrates that every aspect of social life is governed by gender. In other words, it reminds us that all of social life is structured by rules that establish different types of behavior as appropriate to women and men.[8] Feminists subject these rules to critical scrutiny, arguing that, in many cases if not all, they are oppressive to women. To establish this critique, feminists are confronted inevitably by questions about women's nature, its potentialities and limitations. They are forced to reflect on the social and political significance of all the differences, including the biological differences, between the sexes. In other words, they are forced to develop a theory of human nature that includes an explicit account of the nature of women and men.

In Part II I shall trace the development of feminist theorizing about women and men's nature. I shall show how earlier feminists accepted, more or less uncritically, prevailing conceptions of human nature that took the male as paradigm, and concerned themselves primarily with demonstrating that women are as fully human as men. In making this argument, both liberal and Marxist feminists insisted on a sharp distinction between the biological attribute of sex and the cultural attribute of gender, and they argued that biological differences were, by and large, irrelevant to political theory. As contemporary feminism developed, however, it extended its critique to new areas of social life, including sexuality and childbearing. In those areas it was less plausible to assume the political irrelevance of biological differences between the sexes, and so some contemporary feminists have seen the need to reconsider the political and philosophical significance of biology. In some parts of the women's movement, this has led to a resurrection of biological determinism in the form of theories explaining gender as determined, at least in part, by sex. Other feminists have begun to look harder at the conceptual distinction between sex and gender, suggesting that the distinction itself may have what one feminist philosopher calls "a false clarity."[9] The result is a renewed series of attempts to conceptualize the nature of women and of men.

Although contemporary feminists focus mainly on women, their work has implications for political philosophy as a whole. One result of their work is that the adult white male can no longer be taken to represent all of humanity, nor the adult white male experience to encompass all that is important in human life. In examining four feminist theories of women's and men's nature, Part II of this book will show how contemporary feminism has come to challenge traditional androcentric paradigms of human nature and traditional androcentric definitions of political philosophy. If these feminist critiques are demonstrated to be valid, of course, they will necessitate a reconstruction not only of political philosophy, but of all the human sciences and perhaps of the physical sciences as well.

> Materialist feminism is therefore an intellectual approach whose coming is crucial both for social movements, for the feminist struggle, and for knowledge. This project would not be—could not be, even if desired— limited to a single population, to the sole oppression of women. It will not leave untouched any aspect of reality, any domain of knowledge, any aspect of the world. As the feminist movement aims at revolution in social reality, the theoretical feminist point of view (and each is indispensable to each other) must also aim at a revolution in knowledge.[10]

Notes

1. Not everyone, of course, regards "political philosophy" and "political theory" as interchangeable. For instance, the political science department in my own university lodged a territorial objection when I proposed to teach a course in feminist political theory. The political scientists claimed that "theory" was their turf; I was qualified to teach only philosophy.

2. Charles Taylor, "Neutrality in Political Science," in Alan Ryan, ed., *The Philosophy of Social Explanation* (New York, Oxford: Oxford University Press, 1972), p. 161.

3. John Rawls, *A Theory of Justice* (Cambridge: Harvard University Press, 1971), p. 137.

4. Taylor, "Neutrality," p. 155.

5. That conceptions of rationality are inevitably normative will be argued in the next chapter.

6. One of the clearest examples of this correlation may be found in the historical and conceptual connections between the nineteenth-century idea of progress and the idea of organic evolution. Darwin's theory of evolution was inspired by a reading of Malthus, and Darwin's theory, in turn, provided scientific respectability for the ideology of "Social Darwinism." The general conception shared by all these theorists was the promise of

progress at the cost of struggle. Underlying this conception was a view of human nature as "inert, sluggish and averse from labour, unless compelled by necessity." This quotation from Malthus and indeed the whole example is given by R.M. Young, "The Human Limits of Nature," in Jonathan Benthall, ed., *The Limits of Human Nature* (Frome and London: Allen Lane, 1973).

7. A fascinating collection of philosophers' views on women is Mary Briody Mahowald's *Philosophy of Woman: Classical to Current Concepts* (Indianapolis: Hackett Publishing Co., 1978).

8. A few societies are said to have more than two genders. For instance, Lila Leibowitz reports a four-gender system in traditional Navaho society (*Females, Males, Families* [North Scituate, Mass.: Duxbry Press, 1978], pp. 37–38). Contemporary feminism, however, focuses on modern industrial society, which has only two genders. Consequently, in this book I shall ordinarily assume the operation of a two-gender system, defining one standard of appropriate "masculine" behavior for males and a contrasting standard of appropriate "feminine" behavior for females.

9. Ann Palmeri, "Feminist Materialism: On the Possibilities and Power of the Nature/Culture Distinction," paper read to the mid-west division of the Society for Women in Philosophy, October 25, 1980.

10. Christine Delphy, "For a materialist feminism," *Proceedings of the Second Sex— Thirty Years Later: A Commemorative Conference on Feminist Theory,* September 27–29, 1979 (New York: New York Institute for the Humanities, 1979).

part two
Feminist Theories
of Human Nature

3
Liberal Feminism and Human Nature

Liberal philosophy emerged with the growth of capitalism. It raised demands for democracy and political liberties that often expressed deeply held moral convictions about the inherent equality of men; these demands also expressed the challenge of the rising merchant and later the industrial capitalist class against the restrictions on travel, finance and manufacture by which the feudal system hampered the growth of trade and industry. The confrontation between feudalism and capitalism reached its climax at different times in different countries; in England, it occurred in the mid-17th century with the Civil War. Naturally, women were affected as much as men by the social transformation that was taking place, and it was inevitable that the changing circumstances of their lives, coupled with the inherent persuasiveness of the new ideas, should lead women to wonder why the new egalitarianism was not extended to them. Simultaneously with the new bourgeois man's revolt against the monarch's claim to absolute authority by divine right, therefore, the new bourgeois woman began to rebel against traditional male claims to authority over her. Writing on marriage in the year 1700, Mary Astell asked:

> If absolute Sovereignty be not necessary in a State how comes it to be so in a Family? or if in a Family why not in a State? since no reason can be alleg'd for the one that will not hold more strongly for the other?

> If *all Men are born free,* how is it that all Women are born slaves? As they must be if the being subjected to the *inconstant, uncertain, unknown, arbitrary Will* of Men, be the perfect Condition of Slavery?[1]

Liberal feminism has always been a voice, though one that often has gone unheard, throughout the 300-year history of liberal political theory. Consistently over the centuries, feminists have demanded that the prevailing liberal ideals should also be applied to women. In the 18th century, they argued that women as well as men had natural rights; in the 19th century, they employed utilitarian arguments in favor of equal rights for women under the law; and in the 20th century, with the development of the liberal theory of the welfare state, liberal feminists demand that the state should actively pursue a variety of social reforms in order to ensure equal opportunities for women.

The long history of liberal philosophy makes it inevitable that it should contain a number of strands, not all of which are consistent with each other. Liberal theory is unified, however, by certain assumptions about human nature that constitute the philosophical foundation of the theory. Liberal feminism too is built on this foundation. Yet although liberal feminism has always begun from liberal principles, it has operated always on the progressive edge of liberal thought, pushing those ideals to their logical conclusion. In doing so, it has found itself forced to challenge not only the currently accepted interpretation of liberal principles but also liberalism's underlying assumptions about human nature. Thus liberal feminism contains contradictions that threaten ultimately to shatter its own philosophical foundation.[2]

Traditional Liberalism and Human Nature

Liberal political theory is grounded on the conception of human beings as essentially rational agents. Stated abstractly, this conception does not sound particularly innovative; after all, the notion of rationality had always been prominent in the western philosophical tradition, from Aristotle to the medieval philosophers. But liberal theorists have constructed their own, characteristic account of reason that uniquely distinguishes the liberal conception of human nature.

First, liberals assume that rationality is a "mental" capacity. The classical liberal theorists were metaphysical dualists; that is to say, they believed that the human mind and the human body represented two quite different kinds of beings, each irreducible to and connected only contingently with the other. Contemporary liberal theorists are not committed explicitly to metaphysical dualism, but their political theory rests on a kind of dualism that I call "normative dualism." Normative dualism is the belief that what is especially valuable about human beings is a particular "mental" capacity, the capacity for rationality. Liberals assume that the physical basis of this capacity is irrelevant to political theory. An early expression of this view may be seen in the discussion by John Locke, a 17th-century liberal philosopher, of the case of the abbot of St. Martin. Apparently the abbot, when he was born,

> had so little of the figure of a man that it bespake him rather a monster. It was for some time under deliberation whether he should be baptized or no. However, he was baptized and declared a man provisionally, till time should show what he would prove.[3]

Locke's point was that what made the abbot a "man" was not his physical shape but rather his capacity to reason, which could not be determined at birth. Like Locke, contemporary liberal theorists ascribe political rights on the basis of what they take to be the specifically human capacity for rationality and disregard what they conceive as "merely physical" capacities and incapacities.

A second feature of the liberal conception of rationality is that it is conceived as a property of individuals rather than of groups.[4] Like normative dualism, this view of rationality is connected with an underlying metaphysical assumption. The assumption in this case is that human individuals are ontologically prior to society; in other words, human individuals are the basic constituents out of which social groups are composed. Logically if not empirically, human individuals could exist outside a social context; their essential characteristics, their needs and interests, their capacities and desires, are given independently of their social context and are not created or even fundamentally altered by that context. This metaphysical assumption is sometimes called abstract individualism because it conceives of human individuals in abstraction from any social circumstances. It is easy to see how abstract individualism influences the liberal conception of rationality as an essential characteristic of human individuals. It does not force liberals to deny that the presence of a social group may be an empirical prerequisite for an individual's learning to exercise her or his capacity to reason, insofar as one's ability to reason is inferred primarily from one's ability to speak and speech develops only in groups.[5] But the metaphysical assumption of human beings as individual atoms which in principle are separable from social molecules does discourage liberals from conceiving of rationality as constituted by or defined by group norms, let alone as being a property of social structures. Instead, they identify as rational only individuals who are able to act in quite specific ways, ways that will be described shortly.

A third feature of the liberal conception of rationality is that it is assumed to be a capacity that is possessed in approximately equal measure at least by all men. Descartes, who was not a political liberal but whose radically dualistic metaphysics and individualistic epistemology were a formative influence on the foundations of liberal theory, puts it this way:

> Good sense is of all things in the world the most equally distributed, for everybody thinks himself so abundantly provided with it, that even those most difficult to please in other matters do not commonly desire more of it than they already possess.

The apparent irony of this formulation is mitigated by what follows it:

> It is unlikely that this is error on their part; it seems rather to be evidence in support of the view that the power of living a good life and of distinguishing the true from the false, which is properly speaking what is called Good Sense or Reason, is by nature equal in all men.[6]

Just what is the human capacity to reason? In answering this question, liberal theorists are not completely unanimous. Their views contain echoes of the classical conception of reason as the guide to morality and values, but these echoes are often dominated by the more instrumental conception of reason that began to develop with the rise of the new science in the 17th century. Consequently, it is possible to distinguish both a moral and a prudential aspect of the liberal conception of rationality. Some liberal theorists emphasize one of those aspects, some the other. Many have tried to hold both in balance. Rousseau and Kant, for instance, thought that the essence of reason was the ability to grasp the rational principles of morality. It was this capacity that distinguished humans from animals and gave them their special worth. For Hobbes and Bentham, on the other hand, rationality was seen simply in instrumental terms as the capacity to calculate the best means to an individual's ends. The ends themselves were taken as given, insusceptible to rational evaluation. Locke and such contemporary liberal theorists as John Rawls and Robert Nozick attempt to maintain a balance between the moral and the instrumental aspects of rationality, arguing that the establishment of the state, as they construe it, is rational both because it is morally acceptable and because it is in the self-interest of those who are subject to it. Rawls succeeds in maintaining a somewhat uneasy compromise between these aspects, but for Nozick, whose writing stresses heavily the prudential justification of the state, the instrumental aspect of rationality seems fundamental. Certainly it is the latter conception of rationality which dominates in orthodox economics and in game theory.

A related way of distinguishing between various liberal interpretations of rationality is through a distinction between the ends of human action and the means for achieving those ends. Some liberals believe that the ends of human action are susceptible to rational evaluation; others believe that reason is useful only in determining the most efficient means for achieving human ends. The ends/means distinction is related to the moral/prudential distinction because the rational evaluation of ends is typically made by liberals on moral grounds. In other words, those theorists who accept that reason has a moral dimension use whatever moral theory they happen to hold in order to criticize the rationality of immoral desires. Otherwise, however, liberals view each individual as the expert in identifying her or his own interest,[7] and they eschew any claim to criticize the rationality of an individual's desires except on formal grounds, such as consistency. For instance, so long as an individual has a number of desires, the liberal may criticize the rationality of that individual's desire to be a drug addict since addiction, for most people except the wealthy, means that the individual's other desires are unlikely to be fulfilled. But if an individual had no desires other than to be a drug addict, there would be no grounds, except for moral ones, on which the liberal could criticize the rationality of that desire. Thus for many liberal theorists the specific content of each individual's desires lies outside the scope of rationality. They see reason as instrumental, concerned with means rather than ends. As Russell put it, " 'reason' has a perfectly clear and precise meaning. It signifies the choice of the right means to an end that you wish to achieve. It has nothing whatsoever to do with the choice of ends."[8]

In spite of their acknowledgment of the possible variety of individual desire, liberal theorists have often attempted to identify desires that they take to be in fact universal. These attempts have not always produced the same results. Hobbes and Locke, for instance, give great weight to the desire for "reputation" or the esteem of others; Rawls, by contrast, places heavier emphasis on the desire for *self*-respect, which he views as the most important primary social good. In spite of such differences, liberals do tend toward a general agreement on the probable objects of most people's desire. This agreement results from two assumptions that underlie liberal thought. One of these is the metaphysical assumption of abstract individualism, mentioned earlier. According to this assumption, each human individual has desires, interests, etc. that in principle can be fulfilled quite separately from the desires and interests of other people. The second assumption is ostensibly about the world rather than about human nature. It is that the resources necessary to sustain human life are always limited; in other words, that humans always inhabit an environment of relative scarcity. Given these two assumptions, liberal political theorists tend to suppose that each human individual will be motivated by the desire to secure as large an individual share as possible of the available resources. Hobbes states explicitly that humans are motivated by the desire for gain, and Locke comes close to identifying rationality with the desire for unlimited accumulation.[9] It is noteworthy that he regards the propensity to unlimited accumulation as rational not just in the prudential sense but also in the moral sense of being in accord with the law of nature or reason. Rawls, too, assumes that it is rational for those who formulate his principles of justice, his parties to the "original position," to each want the largest possible share of what he calls the "primary social goods," which include "rights and liberties, opportunities and powers, income and wealth," even though Rawls also argues that rational individuals will balance the chance of receiving a large share of these goods against the risk of receiving a small one and in the end will act so as to minimize the risk of loss.

The assumption that people typically seek to maximize their individual self-interest is one way of expressing the assumption of universal egoism. This assumption reemerges constantly in liberal thinking, although it is rarely stated as an explicit motivational postulate. Only a few liberal philosophers, such as Hobbes and Bentham, claim that people always act in what they perceive to be their own self-interest.[10] Most of the other major liberal theorists, such as Locke, Kant, Mill, and Rawls, conceive people as able to act on a moral principle of impartiality, which requires them to refrain from placing their own selfish interests before the interests of others. Their assertion that people have this moral capacity means that the philosophers I have just mentioned cannot be viewed as claiming the thesis of universal egoism. Yet most of these philosophers certainly think that people tend naturally toward egoism, even though they are sometimes able to refrain from self-interested behavior. Mill, for instance, claims that the capacity to act on moral principle belongs only to "cultivated" adults. He thinks that the moral capacity is grounded on an innate propensity to what he calls "sympathetic selfishness," that is, the ability to take pleasure in the pleasure of some other people and to be saddened by their grief. People feel such sympathy only with a relatively few others, however, and do not feel it with all humanity. Consequently, Mill names his postulated innate capacity for sympathy *"l'egoîsme à deux, à trois* or *à quatre."*[11]

John Rawls is committed less obviously than the other major liberal theorists to an assumption of universal egoism. It is true that he bases his political theory on the assumption that those who formulate the principles, the parties to the "original position," are mutually disinterested; that is to say, they tend to "take no interest in one another's interest."[12] Nonetheless, Rawls denies explicitly that this assumption commits him to an egoistic theory of justice; instead, he claims that the assumptions of mutual disinterest, coupled with the requirement that none of the parties in the original position can know in advance her or his own place in the society being planned, results in the formulation of principles of justice that are identical with those that would result from an assumption of universal benevolence.[13] Rawls states that he uses the assumption of mutual disinterestedness only for the purposes of simplicity and clarity. In the final part of his book, Part III, he even takes pains to show how his theory of justice is compatible with a non-egoistic account of human nature. Nevertheless, one of the main criteria by which Rawls ultimately justifies his theory is its adequacy in maximinimizing each individual's share of what he calls the primary social goods, and this would not be an appropriate criterion of adequacy unless he assumed that actual individuals in ordinary life, as well as hypothetical individuals in the contract situation, actually did wish for the largest individual share. In general, even those liberal philosophers who believe in the human capacity for altruism or benevolence see human beings as confronted typically by a conflict between duty and inclination; in conditions of scarcity, one is forced often to choose between furthering one's own interests or furthering those of others, and one's natural inclination is invariably to favor what one perceives to be one's own interests.

From the preceding it is evident that liberal theory rests on the assumption that all persons, at all times and in all places, have a common essence or nature. Interpreted weakly, of course, this assumption is not peculiar to liberalism; indeed, it must be shared by any positive account of human nature. But the liberal account of human motivation and rationality indicates a belief that universal truths about human nature may be quite specific. No matter where or when they live, human beings are seen as tending naturally toward egoism or the maximization of their own individual utility, even though sometimes they may be constrained by moral considerations. Because of the assumption that human nature is essentially changeless, liberalism is sometimes described as being ahistorical; that is, it does not place any philosophical importance on such "accidental" differences between human individuals as the historical period in which they live, their rank or class position, their race or their sex. Human beings are defined in the abstract by their universal and "essential" capacity for reason.

Although liberal theorists view human nature as essentially changeless, they still acknowledge certain psychological differences between individuals and they accept that those differences may result from different social experiences. Liberals acknowledge differences in what individuals want, they recognize that different individuals care more or less about the interests of others, they see that some people are more receptive than others to moral arguments and they acknowledge that people vary in how far and by which emotions they are influenced. Many of these variations, liberals agree, are likely to result from differences in individual social experience. Thus, in contrast to Descartes' postulation of innate mental structures, Locke develops his empiricist conception of the mind as a *tabula rasa* which is inscribed by experience.

Liberals do not consider that their acknowledgment of individual differences is inconsistent with their basic assumption of a universal human nature, since they view rationality, the human essence, as a potential rather than as an empirically observable characteristic. This potentiality may be actualized to a greater or lesser degree; rational beings may behave irrationally in certain situations. Consequently, even though all humans may have an equal *capacity* for rationality, liberals do not conclude that actual individuals will be equally rational. So Locke was able without contradiction both to assert that reason is "the common rule and measure that God has given to mankind"[14] and to deny that those who lacked property (and, therefore, the opportunity to develop their powers of reason) were fully rational. He wrote that dispossessed laborers'

> opportunities of knowledge and inquiry are commonly as narrow as their fortune and their understandings are but little instructed, when all their whole time and pains is laid out to still the croaking of their own bellies, or the cries of their children. . . . So that a great part of mankind are, by the natural and unalterable state of things in this world, and the constitution of human affairs, unavoidably given over to invincible ignorance of those proofs on which others build.[15]

On these grounds, Locke justified the restriction of full civil rights to men of property. Similarly, John Stuart Mill, fearing the "tyranny" of the "masses," recommended that educated people should have more influence in government than the uneducated, even though he also looked forward to the day when all persons would have the opportunity to develop their capacity for reason.

The final point that should be emphasized with respect to the liberal conception of reason is that it is normative as well as descriptive. This means that individuals who fail to develop their capacity for reason are not just different from those who succeed; instead, they are regarded as *deficient* because they have failed to fulfill their uniquely human potential. We shall see later how liberal feminism takes over the normative as well as the descriptive element in the liberal conception of reason.

Liberal Political Theory

The liberal conception of human nature sets the terms of liberal political theory. It constitutes the ground of the basic moral and political values of liberalism, it poses the fundamental problems of liberal political philosophy and it prescribes the method that liberals use for resolving those problems.

The fundamental moral values of liberalism are predicated on the assumption that all individuals have an equal potentiality for reason. This assumption is the basis of liberalism's central moral belief, the intrinsic and ultimate value of the human individual. Because different liberal theorists construe reason differently, their belief in the value of the human individual is expressed in various terms. Those who emphasize the moral aspect of reason stress the value of individual autonomy; that is, they value reliance on individual judgment, uncoerced and unindoctrinated, rather than on established authority in determining matters of truth and morality. Those liberal theorists who emphasize the instrumental aspect of reason stress the value of individual self-fulfilment and the importance of each individual's being able to pursue her or his own self-interest as he or she defines it. Whether autonomy or self-fulfilment is the primary emphasis, liberalism's belief in the ultimate worth of the individual is expressed in political egalitarianism: if all individuals have intrinsic and ultimate value, then their dignity must be reflected in political institutions that do not subordinate any individual to the will or judgment of another. Compared with medieval political philosophy, which interpreted the social hierarchy as the god-given natural order, this basic egalitarianism in liberal theory was extremely radical.

The liberal conception of the good society naturally is one that instantiates the basic liberal values. The good society must protect the dignity of each individual and promote individual autonomy and self-fulfilment. Given these values, liberals have inferred that the good society should allow each individual the maximum freedom from interference by others. Unfortunately, however, liberals believe, interference from others and even attack from others is a permanent probability in the human condition. Liberals assume that the resources for human survival are limited and that each individual has an interest in securing as large a share as possible of those resources. From these assumptions, liberals conclude that every society contains the built-in likelihood of conflict between competing individuals.

Given all this, the fundamental problem for the liberal theorist is therefore to devise social institutions that will protect each individual's right to a fair share of the available resources while simultaneously allowing him or her the maximum opportunity for autonomy and self-fulfilment. Liberal answers to this dilemma are framed traditionally in terms of justifications and delimitations of the power of the state. For the state is the institution that liberals charge with protecting persons and property and, simultaneously, with guaranteeing the maximum freedom from interference to each individual.

In trying to determine the limits of legitimate state intervention in the life of an individual, liberal theory distinguishes between what it calls the public and the private realms. The ubiquitous terms *public* and *private* are used by different political theorists to mark a variety of contrasts. In the context of liberalism, those aspects of life that may legitimately be regulated by the state constitute the public realm; the private realm is those aspects of life where the state has no legitimate authority to intervene. Just where the line between the two realms should be drawn has always been controversial for liberals; but they have never questioned that the line exists, that there is some private area of human life which should be beyond the scope of legal government regulation.

The history of liberal political theory can be seen as the provision of a philosophical rationale for a gradual enlargement of the public realm, that is, for an extension of the responsibilities of the state. In charging the state with the preservation of individual freedom, early liberal theorists had a characteristic interpretation of what they meant by freedom. For them, it revolved around those issues that we have come to call "civil liberties": the right of all to own property, to be represented in government, to travel, to form associations, to worship according to their convictions, and to publish their opinions.[16] The state was legitimate only insofar as it guaranteed those rights. Twentieth-century liberalism retains these concerns but it has shifted the focus of its preoccupations. Seeing that one's ability to take advantage of these legal or formal rights is related closely to one's wealth or to its absence, contemporary liberals are concerned increasingly with questions of economic distribution. Where inequality of wealth is recognized as affecting other rights and opportunities, it comes to be seen as something requiring justification and possibly even rectification.

This development has meant radical changes in liberal views regarding the functions of the state. For early liberalism the primary task of the state was to secure external defense and internal order. The state's direct intervention in the economic realm was to be limited to upholding the sanctity of contracts. This "night watchman" theory of the state is still held by some contemporary liberals, notably by Robert Nozick. But the direct inheritors of this aspect of the classical liberal tradition are now commonly called conservatives, and those who are generally acknowledged as contemporary liberals would now assign to the state much further-reaching functions than did their classical predecessors. With the development of a modern economy, it has become obvious that all individuals are affected inevitably by others in far-reaching ways and, in particular, that those who possess great wealth have enormous control over the lives of those who lack it. Recognizing that it can no longer guarantee non-intervention in people's lives, liberals now expect the state itself to mitigate the worst effects of a market economy. In particular, the state is expected to guarantee a minimum standard of living and education, even for the poorest sections of its population. This is the theory of the welfare state, which has received its most systematic and influential expression in the work of John Rawls.

Historically, the liberal tradition in political theory has always been associated with the capitalist economic system. Liberal political theory emerged with the rise of capitalism, it expressed the needs of the developing capitalist class and the liberal values of autonomy and self-fulfilment have often been linked with the right to private property. Many liberal theorists, however, have tried to insist on a separation between political and economic theory and to deny or to minimize the implications that each has for the other. In spite of the historical association between liberalism and capitalism, several of the leading liberal philosophers of the 19th and 20th centuries, including John Stuart Mill and John Rawls, have been not unsympathetic to socialism.[17] Rawls, for instance, claims that his principles of justice are compatible in principle both with a society in which the major means of production are privately owned and with one in which they are publicly owned. As we shall see, however, the kind of socialism that is claimed to be compatible with liberal political theory is a very different kind from Marxist socialism. It is grounded on very different presuppositions about human nature and society and it contrasts with Marxism especially in its views about the nature and functions of the state. Unlike Marxism, liberalism views the state as a politically neutral instrument whose function is to guarantee to all individuals an equal opportunity for moral development and self-fulfilment. Changing historical circumstances, together with increased understanding about the ways in which an individual's opportunities for self-fulfilment are affected by that person's economic power or powerlessness, have resulted in a drastic modification of classical liberal views about the role of the state in economic life. But still the state is supposed to refrain from intervention in the "private" lives of individuals and from imposing moral values that would threaten individual autonomy. An emphasis on the preservation of civil liberties and of individual rights to freedom from intervention thus remains a central feature of contemporary liberalism.

These, in broadest outline, are the conclusions of liberal political theory. Liberals do not view these conclusions as limited in validity, appropriate to some societies but inappropriate to others. Instead, since human nature is eternally the same, liberals view the main tenets of their political theory as timeless and universal principles for the regulation of the good society. They believe that the principles have been discovered by reflection on the universal human condition and that our hope for social progress lies in persuading other individuals that these principles are both morally acceptable and in their own personal best interest.

Liberal Feminism and Women's Nature

The overriding goal of liberal feminism always has been the application of liberal principles to women as well as to men. Most obviously, this means that laws should not grant to women fewer rights than they allow to men. Liberal feminists have fought consistently against laws which do just this. In the 19th century, they fought for such basic liberties as women's right to own property and to vote. In the 20th century, liberal feminists have opposed laws that allow women special exemption from jury duty (an exemption that provides employers with an excuse for not paying their female employees if such women do choose to serve on a jury) and laws that give husbands more rights than their wives within marriage.[18] As well as opposing laws that establish different rights for women and for men, liberal feminists have also promoted legislation that actually prohibits various kinds of discrimination against women. Such legislation requires that women be equally eligible with men for credit, that they be considered equally in employment, that they should have equal access to professional and job-training programs, and that they should have the same basic educational opportunities. In addition, contemporary liberal feminists demand pregnancy benefits for female workers, maternity leaves and the establishment of childcare centers. This historical shift in the focus of liberal feminism, from the emphasis on opposing discriminatory laws to the more recent emphasis on using the law to oppose other forms of discrimination, has some interesting consequences for liberal political theory and for the theory of human nature on which it rests.

Early liberal feminists saw their task as relatively straightforward. Since traditional liberal theory ascribed rights to persons on the basis of their capacity to reason, early feminists had to argue for women's rights by showing that women were indeed capable of reason. This has been a major thrust of liberal feminist arguments since at least the eighteenth century.

The denial that women can be fully rational agents has a long history in philosophical writing. Aristotle believed that "the woman has [a deliberative faculty] but it is without authority."[19] Consequently, "the male is by nature superior and the female inferior; the one rules and the other is ruled."[20] Thinkers of the Middle Ages agreed with the Greeks that God made woman to be a helper in procreation for man because "woman's power of reasoning is less than a man's."[21] Modern philosophers, including many liberals, have held substantially the same view. Hume, Rousseau, Kant, and Hegel all doubted that women were fully rational.[22] Hegel, for instance, believed that women's deficiency in the "universal faculty" was such as to render women as different from men as plants were different from animals.[23] This was the philosophical tradition that had to be challenged by feminists who shared the characteristic liberal belief that individuals are entitled to political rights only in virtue of their capacity for reason.

The existence of this philosophical tradition, coupled with the growing acceptance of liberal political theory in the 18th and 19th centuries, determined the focus on women's rationality that we find in such thinkers as Mary Wollstonecraft in the 18th century and J.S. Mill in the 19th. In *A Vindication of the Rights of Women* (1792), Mary Wollstonecraft argued forcefully that women had the potential for full rationality and consequently were as capable as men of complete moral responsibility.[24] The fact that women did not always realize this potentiality was due to the fact that they were deprived of education and confined to the domestic sphere:

> Educated in worse than Egyptian bondage, it is unreasonable, as well as cruel, to upbraid them with faults that can scarcely be avoided, unless a degree of native vigour be supposed that falls to the lot of very few amongst mankind.[25]

In his *On the Subjection of Women,* Mill was concerned to emphasize the same point. If women's intellectual attainments were inferior to those of men, the most likely explanation was that women had been afforded less opportunity to develop their minds.

> They have always hitherto been kept, as far as regards spontaneous development, in so unnatural a state, that their nature cannot but have been greatly distorted and disguised; and no one can safely pronounce that if women's nature were left to choose its direction as freely as men's, and if no artificial bent were attempted to be given to it except that required by the conditions of human society, and given to both sexes alike, there would be any material difference, or perhaps any difference at all, in the character and capacities which would unfold themselves.[26]

Even in the 20th century, feminists have not been able to assume general acknowledgment that women's potentiality for rational and moral action equals that of men. Popular (as opposed to recent feminist) interpretations of Freud, for instance, have been used to rationalize the inevitability of the "fact" that, as Freud put it:

> Women have but little sense of justice, and this is no doubt connected with the preponderance of envy in their mental life . . . We also say of women that their social interests are weaker than those of men, and that their capacity for the sublimation of their instincts is less.[27]

In order to combat such views, much contemporary feminist research has been directed toward demonstrating that observed psychological differences between the sexes are not innate but rather are the result of what the researchers often call "sex-role conditioning." Betty Friedan writes about "the sex-directed educators,"[28] and others document the ways in which girls and boys are treated differently almost from the moment of birth.[29] Systematic investigation of the effects of social influences on cognitive and emotional development has shown how well-founded were the speculations by Wollstonecraft and Mill on the way in which women's upbringing discouraged them from developing their full capacity for reason.

What can be concluded from all this about the conception of human nature that is presupposed by liberal feminism? Is it identical with that of main-stream liberalism or does it diverge in some way? Does liberal feminism maintain that there is an essential identity between men's and women's natures, or that women's and men's natures are different? I shall conclude this section by outlining the "official" liberal feminist conception of human nature but in the next section I shall discuss how some features of liberal feminism undermine the "official" conception.

Liberal feminists, like everybody else, are forced to recognize the indisputable physical differences between women and men. We have seen already, however, that liberals view human beings as essentially rational agents and deny that the physical basis of the capacity to reason, if there is one, is part of the human essence. If individuals are rational in the required sense, their physical structure and appearance are unimportant. Just as height and weight are considered irrelevant to an individual's essential humanity, so too are the physical characteristics such as race and sex that historically have been more controversial. Liberal feminism is grounded squarely on an acceptance of this traditional view. It is presupposed by the feminist argument that an individual's sex is irrelevant to her rights and by the feminist concern to prove that women are capable of full rationality. So far, then, the liberal feminist position seems to be that male and female natures are identical; or, to put it more accurately, that there is no such thing as male and female nature: there is only human nature and that has no sex.

Even if the physical facts of women's sex do not preclude them from full humanity, the question of their mental capacities remains. For it is in virtue of these, of course, and specifically in virtue of the capacity for reason, that liberals assign to individuals full human rights. Liberal feminists, as we know, have campaigned consistently for educational opportunities for women, arguing that it is the lack of such opportunities which accounts for women's failure to develop fully their capacity for rationality. Yet these campaigns do not commit liberal feminists to the view that women's capacity for rationality is identical with that of men. Many liberal feminists may in fact believe that this is true, but their "official" claim is more modest. It is simply that, in the absence of equal educational opportunities for boys and girls, it is impossible to determine conclusively whether women and men have an equal capacity for reason—or, indeed, for anything else. Thus Mill writes:

> Standing on the ground of common sense and the constitution of the human mind, I deny that anyone knows, or can know, the nature of the two sexes, as long as they have only been seen in their present relation to one another. . . . What is now called the nature of women is an eminently artificial thing—the result of forced repression in some directions, unnatural stimulation in others. . . .
>
> Hence, in regard to that most difficult question, what are the natural differences between the two sexes—a subject on which it is impossible in the present state of society to obtain complete and correct knowledge . . . conjectures are all that can at present be made.[30]

Liberal feminism thus remains officially agnostic on whether there is indeed absolute equality in the rational potential of women as a group and of men as a group.

This limited agnosticism, however, does not infect the liberal feminist view on the question of whether women are fully human. Contemporary liberals, unlike some classical theorists, do not assign rights to human beings in proportion to how far they have actualized their capacity for reason. Once a certain minimum level of rationality has been reached, liberalism grants equal rights to all individuals. And liberal feminists state unambiguously that the capacity for reason in women as a group is developed to a level well above the minimum required for the assignment of full human rights. There may be questions about the rights of infants or idiots but not about those of women. Once again, therefore, liberal feminists seem to conclude that women and men may vary in their "accidental" properties, both physical and mental, but that they are identical in their essential nature.

What about the liberal feminist vision of the future? How do liberal feminists envision human nature in the good society? Because of their assumption that human nature is universal, liberal feminists are forced to answer that those humans who inhabit a just society in the future will be the same in their essential features as they are now. In their "accidental" features, however, future humans may differ considerably from present-day ones. In particular, the psychological differences between males and females are likely to be much less marked than they are today. Equalized opportunities for education will mean that most women and many men will actualize their potentiality for rationality more fully than they do at present, so the differences between women and men in the development of their reason, as well as other observed psychological differences between women and men, will diminish and possibly disappear. As long ago as 1792, Mary Wollstonecraft wrote:

> A wild wish has just flown from my heart to my head, and I will not stifle it, though it may excite a horse-laugh. I do earnestly wish to see the distinction of sex confounded in society, unless where love animates the behaviour.[31]

Wollstonecraft's vision still inspires many contemporary liberal feminists, although they would be more apt to describe themselves as wishing to confound the distinction of gender than as wishing to confound the distinction of sex. One common way of referring to the ideal of contemporary liberal feminism is to talk about the androgynous society. Members of the androgynous society would be physiologically male or female, but they would be unlikely to show the same extreme differences in "masculine" or "feminine" psychology as those characteristics are currently defined. That is to say, there would not be the current extreme contrast between logical, independent, aggressive, courageous, insensitive and emotionally inexpressive men and intuitive, dependent, compassionate, nurturant, and emotional women. Boys and girls would receive the same educational opportunities and no attempt would be made to impose those character traits that are considered traditionally to be masculine or feminine. Instead, every individual would be free to develop, in any combination, any psychological qualities and virtues. People would be free to pursue their own interests and develop their own talents regardless of sex. Gendered psychological differences would lessen and possibly disappear.

Liberal feminists have used a variety of arguments to recommend this ideal. On utilitarian grounds, they argue that the increased options for personal development would reduce the discontent of frustrated individuals. For society as a whole, they claim that there would be a larger pool of human resources to draw on and, to the extent that competition would increase, they promise that everyone would benefit from "the stimulating effect of greater competition on the exertions of the competitors."[32] The latter claim, of course, is an attempt to make feminist use of Adam Smith's "Invisible Hand" argument.[33] Finally, moving out of a utilitarian framework, liberal feminists argue that androgyny constitutes the most consistent application of the liberal principle of individual freedom, the only ideal that allows every individual to develop her or his full "human potential." Ultimately, indeed, androgyny is a humanistic rather than simply a feminist ideal, since it "liberates" men as well as women from the strait-jacket imposed by "sex-role conditioning" for the "sex-role system." In using this variety of arguments, liberal feminists follow the strategy of such social contract theorists as Locke and Rawls, who try to provide both prudential and moral arguments for the legitimacy of the state. By claiming that gender constitutes an arbitrary and oppressive constraint on the freedom both of women and men, liberal feminists argue simultaneously that gender is unjust and that its abolition is in the general human interest. If this argument can be substantiated, liberal feminists will have strengthened that optimistic strand of liberal theory which holds that, in the good society, moral rightness and individual self-interest invariably coincide.

Problems for the Liberal Theory of Human Nature

Liberal feminism, as I have characterized it so far, is a logical extension of traditional liberalism. It accepts the traditional liberal conception of human nature and the characteristic liberal values of individual dignity, equality, autonomy and self-fulfillment. Along with these, it accepts the liberal ideal of creating a society which maximizes individual autonomy and in which all individuals have an equal opportunity to pursue their own interests as they perceive them. In applying this ideal to women, however, underlying difficulties emerge. Liberal feminists may not confront those difficulties directly but, implicitly or explicitly, their demands raise questions about the viability of some of the major tenets of liberal theory and even about the consistency of the liberal theory of human nature. In Chapter 7, I shall examine the way in which liberal feminist practice poses a challenge to liberal political theory. In the remainder of this chapter I look critically at the liberal conception of human nature and its associated conception of political philosophy and philosophical method. Not all of the problems that I consider here are catalyzed by liberal feminism, but some of them are.

1. NORMATIVE DUALISM

Liberal political theory developed within the framework of philosophical assumptions that constitute the Cartesian problematic. The assumptions made by Descartes, especially that the mind is in principle separable from the body and that knowledge is a product of individual minds, have given rise to a number of intractable metaphysical and epistemological problems. Since the 17th century, the western tradition has taken these problems to constitute the core problems of philosophy. They include problems about the relation between mind and body, about our knowledge of the existence of other minds and about our knowledge of the so-called external world. Within the Cartesian problematic, these questions are unanswerable. As Richard Rorty says:

> In every generation, brilliant and feckless philosophical naifs (Herbert Spencer, Thomas Huxley, Aldous Huxley, Piaget, B.F. Skinner, Noam Chomsky) turn from their own specialities to expose the barrenness of academic philosophy and to explain how some or all of the old philosophical problems will yield to insights gained outside of philosophy—only to have the philosophy professors wearily explain that nothing has changed at all.[34]

Contemporary liberalism is not committed to an explicitly dualistic metaphysics. Nevertheless, it does presuppose what I have called normative dualism, namely, the view that what is especially valuable about human beings is their "mental" capacity for rationality. It is interesting to note that normative dualism generates problems for liberal political theory that are quite analogous to the epistemological problems generated by metaphysical dualism. In other words, normative dualism encourages political scepticism and political solipsism.

What I mean by political solipsism is the liberal assumption that human individuals are essentially solitary, with needs and interests that are separate from if not in opposition to those of other individuals. This assumption is the starting point of liberal theory. It generates what liberals take to be the fundamental questions of political philosophy: what are the circumstances in which essentially solitary individuals might agree to come together in civil society, what would justify them in doing so and how might conflict be prevented when they do? Liberals typically have answered these questions with various versions of social contract theory. These specify the interests individuals have in civil association and limit the legitimate powers of association to fulfilling those interests. Central to the interests postulated is always the assumed interest in the protection of life, civil liberties and property.

Much of the credibility of social contract theory derives, of course, from the plausibility of the questions that it is designed to answer. But these questions are plausible only if one begins with the assumption of political solipsism, the assumption that human individuals are essentially self-sufficient entities. Individual self-sufficiency, however, is an unrealistic assumption even if one conceives of all human beings as healthy adults, which most social contract theorists have done. As soon as one takes into account the facts of human biology, especially reproductive biology, it becomes obvious that the assumption of individual self-sufficiency is impossible. Human infants resemble the young of many species in being born helpless, but they differ from all other species in requiring a uniquely long period of dependence on adult care. This care could not be provided by a single adult; in order to raise enough children to continue the species, humans must live in social groups where individuals share resources with the young and the temporarily disabled. Human interdependence is thus necessitated by human biology, and the assumption of individual self-sufficiency is plausible only if one ignores human biology.[35] Normative dualism, however, encourages liberal theorists to ignore human biology, and we can now see how it generates a political solipsism that fundamentally shapes liberal theory. If liberals were to stop viewing human individuals as essentially rational agents and were to take theoretical account of the facts of human biology, especially, although not only, the facts of reproductive biology, the liberal problematic would be transformed. Instead of community and cooperation being taken as phenomena whose existence and even possibility is puzzling, and sometimes even regarded as impossible, the existence of egoism, competitiveness and conflict, phenomena which liberalism takes as endemic to the human condition, would themselves become puzzling and problematic.

Liberal political theory expresses a kind of scepticism as well as a kind of solipsism. This is scepticism about the justifiability of establishing political institutions designed to promote any specific conception of human well-being and fulfilment. This scepticism has two sources. One is the liberal value of individual autonomy, which requires that each individual have the maximum freedom to make her or his individual determination of what is true and what is good. The other source is the instrumental interpretation of rationality which holds that an individual can make a rational choice between a variety of means to a given end, but that one cannot give a rational justification for any particular rank ordering of ends. On this interpretation of rationality it is because each individual is the ultimate authority on her or his own needs and desires that political society must allow maximum freedom for individuals to define their own needs. For both these reasons, liberals claim that political institutions must be as neutral as possible about the ends of human life. Ronald Dworkin, a contemporary liberal theorist, expresses what I call liberal scepticism in this way:

> political decisions must be, so far as is possible, independent of any particular conception of the good life, or of what gives value to life. Since the citizens of a society differ in their conceptions, the government does not treat them as equals if it prefers one conception to another.[36]

Mary Gibson, in a discussion of Rawls's political philosophy, makes explicit some of the implicit problems in the scepticism promoted by the liberal conception of rationality.[37] She constructs hypothetical examples of a voluntary M-S (master-slave) and a voluntary S-M (sadist-masochist) society and points out that the liberal conception of rationality has no grounds for condemning either of these societies, no matter how "inegalitarian, exploitative or otherwise morally repugnant." In opposition to liberal scepticism, Gibson argues that it is impossible to develop any useful account of rationality that is value-neutral. Instead, she argues that a politically useful conception of human rationality must refer to such normative notions as personhood, human good and harm to persons (p. 209) and inevitably, therefore, must incorporate value judgments. If Gibson's argument is correct, liberal scepticism, the insistence on what Rawls calls the thinnest possible theory of the good, itself begins to seem irrational.

For it demands a perpetual scepticism with regard to the fundamental questions of political philosophy, namely, what are real human needs and what are the objective criteria of their fulfillment.

In my view, the scepticism of liberal political theory results, at least in part, from its normative dualism. By ignoring the fact that humans are a biological species, liberals deprive themselves of one important route for identifying human needs. This is not to say that purely biological criteria exist for the identification of human needs. People want and need far more than physical survival. Moreover, as I stated in Chapter Two, even the notion of physical survival itself is problematic, for it raises all kinds of questions about how long and under what conditions humans can and should survive. But I do think that our common biological constitution provides part of the groundwork for determining objective criteria of human need. No adequate philosophical theory of human need can ignore the facts of human biology: our common need for air, water, food, warmth, etc. Far from being irrelevant to political philosophy, these facts must form its starting point.

In this section so far, I have discussed one aspect of the liberal theory of human nature, namely its normative dualism. I have argued that an adequate political theory must abandon the assumption of normative dualism because this assumption leads to political solipsism and political scepticism. Political scepticism constitutes a withdrawal from the most fundamental problems of political philosophy, while political solipsism poses for political philosophy certain characteristic questions that I shall argue later are misdirected. I shall return to these issues later in this chapter and, from different perspectives, in future chapters. Later in this chapter, I shall also argue that normative dualism generates a conception of equality that is biased against women. In the meantime, I next turn to a different but related aspect of the liberal theory of human nature.

2. ABSTRACT INDIVIDUALISM

The word "individualism" can be used in many different ways, some of which have complex interrelations.[38] I shall here discuss abstract individualism, the assumption that the essential human characteristics are properties of individuals and are given independently of any particular social context.

Liberal feminism provides at least an implicit challenge to abstract individualism. The basis of this challenge is feminist investigations into the causes of the psychological differences between the sexes. As we saw earlier, liberal feminists have been concerned to prove that women are as capable as men of being fully rational agents. This concern has inspired much recent feminist research, which has demonstrated conclusively that most if not all of the cognitive and emotional differences between the sexes can be attributed to the different experiences of males and females, especially in their early years.[39] As the research continues, it demonstrates increasingly how heavily individuals' desires and interests depend on the social context in which they are reared and from which they learn their values. Obviously this research, if sound, presents a serious empirical challenge to abstract individualism, which takes human nature as a presocial given.

Naomi Scheman has developed a conceptual rather than an empirical argument against abstract individualism. She points out that abstract individualism rests on an assumption that mental states attach primarily to individuals.

Without this assumption, it would be impossible to conceive of individuals as feeling emotions, expressing wants, and defining interests outside any system of social organization. In opposition to what she calls the individualistic conception of the objects of psychology, Scheman argues, following Wittgenstein and others, that complex psychological objects such as beliefs or emotions cannot be assimilated to objects of introspection or to nonintrospectible bodily states. Scheman writes:

> The problem with this assimilation is that it ignores the nature of the complexity of our identification of our own (let alone others') complex psychological objects. What we take to be our emotions, our belief, our desire is a bundle of introspectible states and behavior, unless we are simply assuming that some one thing underlies them all. What it is that we know, what it is that is so definitely and particularly there in us, is not the thing itself (our *feeling* of anger is not the anger itself, surely not all of it) but, we usually think, some sign of it. We can, I think, maintain that our twinges, pangs, and so on are particular events no matter what our social situation, but it does not follow that the same is true for more complex psychological objects, such as emotions, beliefs, motives, and capacities. What we need to know in order to identify *them* is how to group together introspectible states and behavior and how to interpret it all. The question is one of meaning, not just at the level of what to call it, but at the level of there being an "it" at all. And questions of meaning and interpretation cannot be answered in abstraction from a social setting.[40]

Scheman concludes that humans have "emotions, beliefs, abilities and so on only in so far as they are embedded in a social web of interpretation that serves to give meaning to the bare data of inner experience and behavior" (page 12). For this reason, Scheman claims that the liberal conception of human individuals as existing outside a social context is logically as well as empirically impossible. It is a conceptual as well as an empirical truth that human interests are acquired only in a social context.[41]

This argument cuts more deeply against abstract individualism than the liberal feminists' identifications of what they call "sex-role conditioning" or "sex-role socialization." Using the language of roles seems to suggest that behind the role exists an independent human individual whose real nature is concealed when she or he is forced to play a certain role. If Scheman's argument is correct, however, the notion of a presocial human being with any determinate kind of nature is conceptually incoherent.

The challenge to the notion of the abstract individual has profound consequences for liberal political theory and metatheory. For instance, it undercuts the liberal conception of freedom as non-interference; we can now see that, without what liberals construe as "interference," there would be no human individual at all. As I shall argue shortly, it also undercuts the traditional liberal conception of equality. Most seriously, perhaps, an abandonment of abstract individualism invalidates the liberal justification of the state, which presupposes that individuals have certain fixed interests, and it displays the unhelpfulness of the liberal assumption that the good society is one that fulfils the interests of its members. If we reject abstract individualism and suppose instead that human desires and interests are socially constituted, then we can expect that the members of any society are likely to learn to want just those things that the society provides. To attempt to justify forms of social organization by reference to the existing desires of individual members of society can thus be seen, as Scheman remarks, to be a pointlessly circular procedure.

Later I shall argue that abstract individualism generates inadequate conceptions of freedom and of equality and so is politically unacceptable. I shall end this part of my discussion of abstract individualism however by commenting on its implications for the liberal conception of philosophical method. If abstract individualism is untenable, then we cannot discover the human essence by the a prioristic method of abstracting all those human characteristics that are not universal. If this is true, the principles of good social organization cannot be timeless or universal; instead, such principles must be addressed to the problems of specific groups in specific situations. With the rejection of abstract individualism, then, political philosophy becomes an unending process, and one that must rely on a much closer examination of actual social conditions than liberals traditionally have thought it necessary to undertake. In other words, a rejection of abstract individualism is a rejection of the whole a prioristic liberal approach to both human nature and political theory.

3. LIBERAL RATIONALITY

The liberal conception of rationality is not independent of the epistemological and methodological assumptions that I have just been discussing. I think it is worthwhile to give it separate consideration, however. Although the liberal theory of rationality cannot provide the basis for an adequate political theory, a discussion of its shortcomings can help to define the questions that an adequate theory of political rationality must answer.

One important feature of the liberal conception of rationality is the concept of autonomy. Respect for autonomy is basic to the liberal conceptions of freedom and equality and provides one of liberalism's main arguments for limiting the power of the state. Central to the concept of autonomy is the idea of self-definition, a reliance on the authority of individual judgment. If individual desires and interests are socially constituted, however, the ultimate authority of individual judgment comes into question. Perhaps people may be mistaken about truth, morality or even their own interests; perhaps they may be systematically self-deceived about these matters or misled by their society. This possibility is recognized implicitly by liberal feminists when they talk about "sex-role conditioning," or when they claim that so-called "happy housewives" in fact are deeply dissatisfied, notwithstanding their protestations of contentment. In this way, liberal feminists give implicit recognition to the possibilities of self-deception and the social perversion of human need. These possibilities may not be ultimately incompatible with individual autonomy, but they do imply that individual preferences cannot be taken at face value. The liberal respect for autonomy must take account of the ways in which human beliefs, desires and interests are socially constituted. The Marxist tradition has addressed the issue in terms of such concepts as "ideology," "hegemony," and "false consciousness," but these approaches leave the status of individual judgment extremely uncertain. Various attempts have been made within the liberal tradition to distinguish conceptually between (stated) wants and (genuine) needs, but these attempts are not easily reconciled with the instrumentalist strand within the liberal conception of rationality. The liberal concept of autonomy thus remains problematic.

The instrumentalist strand within the liberal conception of rationality equates rational behavior with the efficient maximization of individual utility. To be rational in this sense it is necessary, although not sufficient, for an individual to be egoistic. As we saw earlier, liberal theorists assume that all individuals tend toward egoism, even though they may be capable of a greater or lesser degree of limited altruism. While this model may provide a plausible approximation to the behavior of contemporary males, it is obvious immediately that it is much less appropriate to the behavior of women, who often find their own fulfillment in serving others. As one feminist psychologist has put it, the assumption of innate human selfishness and competitiveness "overlooks the fact that millions of people (most of them women) have spent millions of hours for hundreds of years giving their utmost to millions of others."[42]

If liberal feminists reject the view that psychological differences between the sexes are innate, two alternative ways remain in which they can account for this fact. On the one hand, they can accept the egoistic model of rationality by arguing that women's socialization up to now has forced them to develop in a direction contrary to the natural human tendency toward egoism.[43] Alternatively, they can reject the egoistic paradigm of rationality. This latter course is increasingly being taken by feminists, including liberal feminists. It is now quite common to hear feminists deny that they wish to become, psychologically, like men. Instead, they stress the desirability of such "feminine" characteristics as the capacity for nurturing others and deny that such behavior is irrational. Even though some liberal feminists may be repelled by the egoistic conception of rationality, however, it is doubtful that its rejection is consistent with their overall philosophical outlook.[44]

One way of defending the egoistic conception of rationality might be through an argument that this conception has heuristic value by providing the foundation for a fruitful social science.[45] This argument cannot be discussed fully here, but it seems doubtful, to say the least. For instance, in an interesting critique of the foundations of classical economics, Amartya K. Sen points out that in revealed preference theory, according to which individuals always maximize their own utility by definition (unless their behavior is inconsistent), it is impossible to account for choices in which her own interest is merely one of an agent's considerations.[46] He argues that an economic theory based on the assumption of universal egoism is unable to account for the allocation of "public goods" such as libraries or parks, or even for what occurs in such a central economic field such as work motivation. To resolve these problems, Sen proposes that the traditional conception of "economic man" be replaced by a model of human behavior that recognizes the rationality of individuals' commitment to groups as well as dedication to their own self-interest.

Just as the egoistic conception of rationality is inadequate for economics, it is inappropriate for political theory. A number of philosophers have argued that the degree of individual want satisfaction cannot be the criterion for measuring the good society. R.P. Wolff has attempted to summarize many of these arguments by claiming that a political philosophy founded on the value of individual want satisfaction can never admit what he calls the values of community.[47] The egoistic model of human nature is unable to acknowledge the values intrinsic to participating in an affective, a productive or a rational community because these values involve, by definition, a concern for individuals other than oneself. Wolff suggests that the values of community constitute legitimate parts of a conception of the public good that cannot be reduced to the sum of individuals' private goods. A theoretical model that does not allow us even to formulate the question whether or not these values should be part of our conception of the public good must be considered seriously inadequate.

The liberal paradigm is male-biased in several respects. Some of these will emerge in Chapters 7 and 11. In this section, I shall suggest just a few of the ways in which the liberal conception of human nature is male-biased.

One obvious example of male bias is liberal normative dualism, the excessive value placed on the "mind" at the expense of the body. Of course, both men and women have both minds and bodies but, throughout the western philosophical tradition, women have been seen consistently as being connected with (or entangled in) their bodies in a more intimate way than men are with theirs. Women's bodies have been thought to commit them to the biological reproduction of the species; they have been seen as closer to "nature." Men, on the other hand, have been thought to express their creativity through the creation of "culture." The traditional view, in short, is that women are more closely associated with nature and men with culture; women with the body and men with the mind.[48]

The association of women with body and men with mind has been reinforced if not generated by a sexual division of labor in which (some) men have dominated the "intellectual" fields of politics, science, culture and religion, while women have been assigned the primary responsibility for many day-to-day tasks necessary for physical survival, tasks which include food preparation, psychological nurturance and the care of infants and young children. In later chapters, I shall outline the materialist theory of knowledge that seeks to provide an explanation of the connection between systems of ideas and the life circumstances of those who produce them. Even without such a theory, however, it is easy to see how certain features of the liberal theory of human nature are far more likely to have been produced by men than by women. For instance, it is easy to see how men, at least men of a certain class, would be likely to place supreme value on "mental" activity and to ignore the fact that such activity would be impossible without the daily physical labor necessary for survival, especially the physical labor of women. It is even harder to imagine women developing a political theory that presupposed political solipsism, ignoring human interdependence and especially the long dependence of human young. Nor would women be likely to formulate a conception of rationality that stressed individual autonomy and contained such a strong element of egoism as the liberal conception.[49]

Just as it is unlikely that women's experience would have led them to frame the liberal conception of human nature, so it is unlikely that women would ever have developed the conception of equality that is associated with abstract individualism. According to this conception of equality, every rational individual is entitled to equal rights regardless of age (so long as the "age of reason" has been attained), and regardless of race, sex or economic class. When it was first formulated, this conception of equality was extremely progressive, and indeed it is progressive in many contexts even today. It also has serious drawbacks. The most obvious is that real human beings are not abstract individuals but people of a determinate race, sex or age, who have lived different histories, who participate in different systems of social relations, and who have different capacities and different needs. Some, though probably not most, of the differences in capacity and need are linked to biological differences. To take an obvious example, the needs of the physically handicapped differ from the needs of those who are not so handicapped. We may say, if we like, that both groups have the same need for transportation, but this obscures the special arrangements that have to be made for the disabled. Similarly, it is true that certain features of women's biology may mean that occasionally their needs are different from those of men. Most evidently, women's reproductive functions may mean that women have needs for pregnancy leave, maternity services and arrangements for easy access to their nursing babies. On a commonsense level, of course, everyone knows that women (and other groups) have varying needs. But the liberal insistence on "formal" equality, which comes from viewing people as abstract individuals, makes it easy not only to ignore these varying needs but even to claim that satisfying the needs of a certain group would amount to "reverse discrimination" or giving special privileges to women. A good example of this is the 1976 U.S. Supreme Court decision in the case of *Gilbert* v. *General Electric Company*.[50] In this case, female employees of General Electric charged that the exclusion of pregnancy-related disabilities from their employer's disability plan constituted sex discrimination. The U.S. Supreme Court ruled that this was not so, in part because it argued that the exclusion of pregnancy was not in itself a gender-based discrimination but instead merely removed one physical condition from coverage. The justices counted as quite irrelevant the biological fact that this was a physical condition to which only women were subject!

That this liberal argument is even possible results from the related assumptions of abstract individualism and normative dualism. The absurdity of the argument provides an additional demonstration of the implausibility of these assumptions and brings out their hidden male bias. The *Gilbert* case makes plain that the "accidental" biological fact of sex does have political relevance and, in so doing, it challenges the liberal feminist ideal of the "sex-blind" androgynous society. Increasingly, indeed, liberal feminist demands themselves require a recognition of the political relevance of at least some aspects of sex and of gender. In Chapter 7, I shall investigate how far contemporary feminist demands are compatible with the political structure of traditional liberalism and how far that structure, generated by what we have seen to be an androcentric conception of human nature, is itself male-biased.

Conclusion

Feminism owes a great deal to liberalism. Indeed, it owes so much that some Marxists characterize feminism as an essentially bourgeois phenomenon. In my view, that characterization is entirely mistaken, but it is certainly true that the earliest feminists were inspired by liberal ideals of human dignity, autonomy, equality and individual self-fulfillment. Given that women are still defined conventionally in terms of their relations to men and to children, given that women are still seen as less rational than men and given the fact that the Equal Rights Amendment to the U.S. Constitution has been defeated, I believe that these ideals must remain in some way part of feminism, even though in later chapters I shall also argue that the liberal ideals should be revised or reconceptualized.

In spite of liberalism's contribution to feminism, I believe that the liberal conception of human nature and of political philosophy cannot constitute the philosophical foundation for an adequate theory of women's liberation. In this chapter, I have pointed out a number of problems with the liberal theory of human nature. My criticisms have been organized around the overlapping topics of normative dualism, abstract individualism, and rationality. I have also begun to argue that the liberal paradigm is male-biased. One of the fundamental problems that I have identified in liberal theory is its incapacity to provide a substantive conception of the good life and a way of identifying genuine human needs. These questions certainly are not simple; as we shall see, they confront every political theory, including every theory of women's liberation, and it is far from clear that any theory has an entirely satisfactory answer to them. What is clear, however, is that an adequate answer can never be found so long as one retains the assumptions of abstract individualism and the view of rationality as morally and politically neutral.

Notes

1. Quoted in Juliet Mitchell, "Women and Equality," *Partisan Review* 42(1975):381. Mitchell's article is reprinted in *The Rights and Wrongs of Women,* edited by Juliet Mitchell and Ann Oakley (Harmondsworth: Penguin, 1976), pp. 379–99.
2. Since I wrote this, Z. Eisenstein has published *The Radical Future of Liberal Feminism* (New York: Longmans, 1981), which makes a similar claim though on rather different grounds.
3. John Locke, *An Essay Concerning Human Understanding,* 2 vols, edited by Alexander Campbell Fraser (New York: Dover Publications, 1959), Book 3, chap. 6, para. 26.
4. I did not formulate this point until I heard Naomi Scheman read her paper "Individualism and the Objects of Psychology" to a meeting of the mid-west division of the Society for Women in Philosophy, held in Detroit on 25 October 1980. The paper is to be published in *Discovering Reality: Feminist Perspectives on Epistemology, Metaphysics, Methodology and the Philosophy of Science,* edited by S. Harding and M. Provence Hintikka (Dordrecht: Reidel, 1983). I shall explain later Scheman's criticism of this liberal assumption.
5. The use of speech is one of Descartes' main criteria for the existence of reason and for distinguishing humans from animals. Hobbes, too, believes that reason is intimately connected with speech; indeed, from the fact that humans are not born with speech, he concludes that they are not born with reason.
6. R. Descartes, *Discourse on the Method of Rightly Conducting the Reason and Seeking for Truth in the Sciences,* Part 1, in *The Philosophical Works of Descartes,* Vol. 1, translated by E. S. Haldane and G.R.T. Ross (Dover Publications, 1931), p. 81.
7. Each mature individual "is the person most interested in his own well-being: the interest which any other person, except in cases of strong personal attachment, can have in it, is trifling, compared with that which he himself has; the interest which society has in him individually (except as to his conduct to others) is fractional, and altogether indirect; while with respect to his own feelings and circumstances, the most ordinary man or woman has means of knowledge immeasurably surpassing those that can be possessed by anyone else." J.S. Mill, *On Liberty,* in Max Lerner, ed., *Essential Works of John Stuart Mill* (New York: Bantam Books, 1961), p. 323.
8. Bertrand Russell, *Human Society in Ethics and Politics* (New York: Simon & Schuster, 1955), p. vi.
9. C.B. Macpherson, *The Political Theory of Possessive Individualism* (Oxford: Oxford University Press, 1964), pp. 234–36.
10. Hobbes had such an important influence on Locke and other early liberal philosophers that I am counting him here as a liberal theorist, even though his political theory and his underlying theory of human nature differ in a number of significant respects from the main tradition of liberal theory.

11. J.S. Mill, "Nature," in Max Lerner, ed., *Essential Works of John Stuart Mill,* p. 392.

12. John Rawls, *A Theory of Justice* (Cambridge: Harvard University Press, 1971), p. 127.

13. Ibid., pp. 148–49. My discussion of egoism, both here and later in the chapter, owes much to the persistent and painstaking criticism of Alan Soble.

14. John Locke, *The Second Treatise of Government* (Indianapolis: Bobbs-Merrill, 1952), p. 8.

15. John Locke, *An Essay Concerning Human Understanding,* B. IV, Chap. XX, Section 2.

16. Sandra Bartky has pointed out to me that some liberal theorists attempt to derive specific civil liberties from human nature itself. For example, Locke tries to justify a "right to property" in terms of humans' natural efforts to secure for themselves the necessities of life. In one place, Locke construes the human right to property as analogous to the bird's right to its nest, and he treats the natural rights to life and liberty in a similar way.

17. J.S. Mill, "Chapters on Socialism" in *The Collected Works of John Stuart Mill,* edited by John M. Robson and Jack Stillinger (Toronto and Buffalo: University of Toronto Press, 1967), pp. 703–53. John Rawls, *A Theory of Justice,* pp. 270–74.

18. A survey of the laws that discriminate against women in the United States is given by Leo Kanowitz, *Women and the Law: The Unfinished Revolution* (Albuquerque: University of New Mexico Press, 1969). Cf. also Karen DeCrow, *Sexist Justice* (New York: Vintage Books, 1974) and K.M. Davidson, R.B. Ginsburg and Herma Hill Kay, *Sex Based Discrimination* (St. Paul, Minn.: West Publishing Co., 1974). As late as December 1980, the National Organization of Women was in court opposing a Louisiana law which recognized the husband as "head and master" and which allowed him to mortgage and sell his wife's property even if it was hers before she entered the marriage.

19. Aristotle, *Politics,* 1 13. 1260 al3.

20. Ibid., 15. 1254 b13–14.

21. Thomas Aquinas, *Summa Theologiae,* 1, q. 92, art. 1; cf. q. 98, art. 2; q. 96, art. 3. Cited by Maryellen MacGuigan, "Is Woman a Question?" *International Philosophical Quarterly,* December 1973, p. 487.

22. For substantiation, see Maryellen MacGuigan, "Is Woman a Question?" See also Christine Garside, "Can A Woman be Good in the Same Way as a Man?" *Dialogue* 10, no. 3 (September 1971):534–44, and Steven Burns, "The Humean Female," *Dialogue* 15, no. 3 (September 1976:415–24. Cf. also the comments on Burns's paper by Louise Marcil Lacoste in the same issue of *Dialogue.*

23. G.W.F. Hegel, *Philosophy of Right* (London: Oxford University Press, 1967), p. 263.

24. See Carolyn W. Korsmeyer, "Reason and Morals in the Early Feminist Movement: Mary Wollstonecraft," *The Philosophical Forum* 5 nos. 1–2 (Fall–Winter 1973-74).

25. Quoted in ibid., p. 104.

26. John Stuart Mill, "On the Subjection of Women," in Alice S. Rossi, ed., *John Stuart Mill and Harriet Taylor Mill: Essays on Sex Equality* (Chicago: University of Chicago Press, 1970), p. 190.

27. Sigmund Freud, "Femininity," *New Introductory Lectures on Psychoanalysis* (New York: W.W. Norton & Co., 1933), p. 184.

28. Betty Friedan, *The Feminine Mystique* (New York: W.W. Norton & Co., 1963).

29. So much feminist research has focused on this issue that it is impossible to cite here even the main sources. However, one fascinating study of "social conditioning and its effects on the stereotyped role of women during infancy" (in Italy) is Elena Bianini Belotti's *Little Girl* (London: Writers and Readers Publishing Co-operative, 1975). Feminist research on social influences on males and females has utilized many theoretical approaches, from behaviorism to various versions of psychoanalysis. I shall argue later in this chapter that the terminology of "sex-role conditioning" reflects a distinctively liberal perspective on human nature.

30. *John Stuart Mill and Harriet Taylor Mill: Essays on Sex Equality,* pp. 148-50.

31. Quoted by Juliet Mitchell in "Women and Equality," reprinted in *The Rights and Wrongs of Women*, p. 392.

32. *John Stuart Mill and Harriet Taylor Mill: Essays on Sex Equality*, p. 184.

33. In his classic *Wealth of Nations* (1776), Adam Smith argued that the "Invisible Hand" of providence, through the mechanism of a market economy, coordinated the selfish strivings of each so that they worked to the ultimate benefit of all.

34. Richard Rorty, "Keeping Philosophy Pure," *Yale Review* 65 (1976):351. Alan Soble drew Rorty's article to my attention.

35. Nancy Hartsock made this point to me in a letter. A similar point is made by Sara Ann Ketchum, "Female Culture, Womanculture and Conceptual Change: Toward a Philosophy of Women's Studies," *Social Theory and Practice* 6, no. 2 (Summer 1980):159.

36. Ronald Dworkin, "Liberalism," in Stuart Hampshire, ed., *Public and Private Morality* (Cambridge: Cambridge University Press, 1978), p. 127. Naomi Scheman pointed out to me this clear statement of a basic liberal assumption.

37. Mary Gibson, "Rationality," *Philosophy and Public Affairs* 6, no. 3:193–225. Ted Benton argues similarly that the concept of "interests" has an inevitably normative component. "Realism, power and objective interests" in Keith Graham, ed., *Contemporary Political Philosophy: Radical Studies* (Cambridge: Cambridge University Press, 1982) pp. 7-33.

38. A very useful analysis of the different senses of "individualism" has been made by Steven Lukes in his *Individualism*, New York: Harper and Row, 1973.

39. Carol Gilligan has established that males and females also differ in their moral reasoning. Such differences have often been noted, for example by Freud, as quoted earlier in the chapter, and usually they have been interpreted as evidence of women's moral inferiority. Gilligan argues instead that both women's and men's moral reasoning contains important insights and that an adequate moral theory must integrate both types of reasoning. Gilligan does not estabish the genesis of the different perspectives on morality held ᵢ women and men, but she gives the impression that these perspectives derive from ' distinctively different life experiences of each sex. Carol Gilligan, "In a Different Voiᴄ Women's Conceptions of Self and of Morality" and "Woman's Place in Man's Life Cycle," *Harvard Educational Review* 47, no. 4 (November 1977) and 49, no. 4 (November 1979). See also Carol Gilligan, *In a Different Voice: Psychological Theory and Women's Development* (Cambridge: Harvard University Press, 1982).

40. Scheman, cited in note 3 above, pp. 7 and 8 of the typescript.

41. This is not to deny that human interests also have a biological component. The relationship between social and biological influenes on human nature will be discussed more fully in the next three chapters.

42. Jean Baker Miller, *Toward a New Psychology of Women* (Boston: Beacon Press, 1976), quoted in A.A.U.W. *Journal*, November 1976, p. 4.

43. I owe this point to Sandra Bartky.

44. Sandra Harding has pointed out to me that feminists who are not liberals may challenge the whole egoism/altruism dichotomy as a male construct; many are beginning to do precisely this.

45. This is suggested by Milton Friedman in "The Methodology of Positive Economics," reprinted in May Brodbeck, *Readings in the Philosophy of the Social Sciences* (New York: Macmillan Co., 1968).

46. Amartya K. Sen, "Rational Fools: A Critique of the Behavioural Foundations of Economic Theory," *Philosophy and Public Affairs* 6, no. 4:317-44.

47. R.P. Wolff, *The Poverty of Liberalism* (Boston: Beacon Press, 1968). chap. 5: "Community."

48. See Sherry B. Ortner, "Is Female to Male as Nature is to Culture?" in Michelle Zimbalist Rosaldo and Louise Lamphere, eds., *Women, Culture and Society* (Stanford; Stanford University Press, 1974).

49. Carol Gilligan's work (n. 36) suggests that prevailing moral theory has focused too exclusively on men's lives and so has come to overvalue autonomy and achievement at the expense of such women's values as attachment and intimacy.

50. This decision was later reversed by Congress, and the Disability Amendment took effect in October 1978.

4

Traditional Marxism and Human Nature

Marxist theory was formulated in the mid-19th century, at a time when the worst results of the Industrial Revolution were becoming manifest and when most of the liberal democratic or "bourgeois" revolutions had already occurred or were just occurring in Europe. Contrary to liberal theory, which is associated historically with capitalism and indeed often provides a rationale for it, Marxism offers a devastating critique of the capitalist system. Marxism charges, moreover, that the liberal theory employed to justify the bourgeois revolutions is mere egalitarian rhetoric, serving only to disguise the deep inequalities that inevitably characterize all societies divided by class. For Marxists, the notion of class is the key to understanding all social phenomena, including the phenomenon of women's oppression. The good society is the classless society.

Marxist theory has its own special account of women's oppression, what constitutes it, what causes it, and how it can be ended. Underlying its account, of course, is a special conception of women's nature, which I examine in this chapter.

A major problem in undertaking this task is to determine just what counts as Marxism. Marx and his friend and collaborator, Engels, produced a huge corpus of writings, from early exploratory essays in the 1840s, through their classic summary of their main ideas in *The Communist Manifesto* of 1848 (the "year of revolutions"), to Marx's vast but unfinished technical treatise *Capital,* and to Engels' attempts to develop and popularize his and Marx's ideas after Marx's death in 1883. Because the two wrote over a period of half a century, there is inevitable change and perhaps inconsistency in their ideas. In addition to this difficulty, many authors since their deaths have attempted to interpret, revise, and extend Marxist theory, and in the process have strongly disagreed not only over what Marx meant by what he actually said, but over what he would have said if he had lived into the 20th century. I believe there is no certain way to resolve the continuing controversy over how to characterize Marxist theory. Marx himself was often ambiguous, and to a number of issues, including the status of women, he devoted little attention; Engels, who did undertake a systematic analysis of women's oppression after Marx's death, has often been criticized for distorting Marx's ideas; and contemporary Marxist theorists cannot be guaranteed to have extended Marx's ideas correctly.[1] On the other hand, since Marxist theory is supposed to be a developing science, it is unfair to take the century-old writings of Marx and Engels as the final word on anything, let alone on women's liberation, especially in the light of the enormous social changes that have affected women's situation in the last hundred years. Intensifying these difficulties is the fact that "Marxism," like "feminism," is a politically charged term that carries intensely honorific or pejorative connotations for different groups. Consequently, strong interests other than pure scholarship are involved for those who claim to be the inheritors of Marx, as well as for those who try to dissociate themselves from his ideas.

The course that I shall attempt to steer through these difficulties will not satisfy all those who view themselves as Marxists; indeed, it may satisfy none of them. I propose to identify an interpretation of Marxism, and particularly of Marxist feminism, that, whether or not it is ultimately true to Marx's most mature intentions, has been the most widely accepted interpretation of Marxist feminism for a hundred years, at least until the emergence of the contemporary women's liberation movement led to a sudden flurry of attempts to reinterpret Marx on women. It is the interpretation of Marxism that was dominant in the new left of the 1960s and the interpretation against which radical feminism rebelled. Many Marxists still hold to this interpretation, and it does, indeed, receive considerable support from the writings of Marx and Engels, whom I shall quote regularly. Some readers may complain that Engels cannot be considered an entirely reliable expositor of Marx's ideas, but we know that Marx himself respected and was deeply influenced by Engels. In any case Engels, not Marx, undertook a systematic analysis of women's oppression, and Engels' *The Origin of the Family, Private Property and the State* has been accepted as the classic statement on women by generations of Marxists.[2] I shall argue later that the interpretation that I identify as "traditional Marxism" is not a consistent application of the central insights of the Marxist method. In other, slightly paradoxical, words, I shall argue that "traditional" Marxism is not "orthodox" Marxism and that the view that is popularly labeled "socialist feminism" in fact applies the central principles of Marxism more consistently than did Marx himself.[3]

Marxism and Human Nature

Marxist theory was designed as a deliberate refutation of liberalism. It rejects not only liberal political theory but even the liberal conception of rationality and philosophical method. Almost as an afterthought, it proposes an alternative to the liberal feminist conception of the constitution, cause and remedy of women's oppression. Its whole approach is grounded on a conception of human nature which, in many respects, is directly oppposed to the liberal conception.

Most of Marx's explicit discussions of human nature occur in his earlier and unpublished writings, which have been rediscovered only in comparatively recent years. In Marx's later and published work, the stress is upon the scientific status of his social analysis; here, discussions of the philosophical foundations of this analysis are infrequent, and Marx even ridicules his earlier use of such terminology as "human essence." Considerable controversy has arisen over the continuity between Marx's earlier and his later work. Some scholars claim that the later Marx made a sharp break with his earlier self, while others argue that the differences between Marx's earlier and his later work are better seen as differences of stress and emphasis rather than as substantive differences of content; a recent suggestion is that Marx chose to emphasize a "scientific" approach in his published work but found it necessary for his own clarification to establish the philosophical foundations of that analysis in writings that he chose not to publish.[4] In my view, the last suggestion is quite plausible, and I believe that a characteristic conception of human nature underlies all Marx's work. In my attempt to identify this conception I shall try to side-step the controversy as far as possible by drawing chiefly, though not entirely, on Marx's later work.[5]

One of the most fundamental contrasts between the liberal and the Marxist conceptions of human nature is the Marxist denial of metaphysical dualism. For Marxists, the human essence is not a capacity for rationality that may be embodied in a variety of forms. On the contrary, Marxists view human beings as one biological species among others. For them, it is a necessary rather than an accidental fact that humans have a certain kind of biological constitution. Moreover, it is a fact with profound consequences for human social life and thus for political theory.

The physical structure of the human body requires that, to survive, humans must draw on the resources of the non-human world. They need food, drink, shelter, clothing, etc., and they obtain these from non-human nature. Because human beings have many biologically based needs, humans can be conceived only in relation to a world in which these needs may be satisfied. Partly for this reason, Marxists deny that it is possible to make a sharp conceptual distinction between human and non-human nature. The two are "internally related," aspects of a larger whole.

Nothing said so far indicates any differences between the human and other biological species. Animals, too, must draw on the non-human world for physical survival. In the *German Ideology,* Marx writes:

> Men can be distinguished from animals by consciousness, by religion or by anything else you like. They themselves begin to distinguish themselves from animals as soon as they begin to *produce* their means of subsistence, a step which is conditioned by their physical organization.[6]

In other words, human beings differ from animals in that they do not simply utilize what the world provides in order to fulfill their needs; they also transform the world. People do not simply graze or find ready-made shelter; they also grow food and prepare it, and they construct their own shelters.

Some animals, too, produce their means of subsistence by building dams, nests, webs, and so on. Marx considers this question in the *Economic and Philosophic Manuscripts of 1844* and also later in *Capital* where he writes:

> A spider conducts operations that resemble those of a weaver, and a bee puts to shame many an architect in the construction of her cells. But what distinguishes the worst architect from the best of bees is this, that the architect raises his structure in imagination before he erects it in reality. At the end of every labour-process, we get a result that already existed in the imagination of the labourer at its commencement. He not only effects a change of form in the material on which he works, but he also realises a purpose of his own that gives the law to his modus operandi, and to which he must subordinate his will.[7]

Although there is a superficial similarity between the way in which humans and animals utilize the world's resources, Marx considers that there is a fundamental difference. Contrary to the activity of animals, human activity is conscious and purposeful. Marx calls it "praxis."

The word *praxis* can be traced to the time of Homer. It is a noun derived from the Greek verb meaning "to do" or "to act," so that its earliest meaning was that of conscious action or achievement, as opposed to the making of an object. Later praxis became more closely associated with economic activity and was used to mean a transaction, business, or even the exaction of money or recovery of debt.[8] As Marx uses it, praxis consists in conscious physical labor directed toward transforming the material world so it will satisfy human needs. For Marx, it is praxis rather than pure rational thought which is the essential human activity. An examination of the Marxist notion of praxis provides a key to understanding the Marxist conception of human nature.

A central feature of praxis is that it is essentially a social activity. This does not mean that individuals do not sometimes plan their own labor, or work alone. But no individual could lead a life that was entirely solitary. It is doubtful, indeed, that a solitary human individual could survive physically; as I remarked in Chapter 3, the human biological constitution seems to require human interdependence for simple survival.[9] In any case, even if an isolated individual were able to survive alone, through some uniquely fortuitous circumstances, that individual would lack language and any of the accumulated experience of the human species. Her or his efforts to survive would resemble the instinctive efforts of animals. Human praxis, by contrast, is cooperative in that it invariably involves some division of labor and draws on the knowledge, skills, and experience of earlier workers. Consequently, the worker's conception of what needs to be done, how it should be done and when it has been done successfully are all determined in outline by previous social experience and by the social context within which the individual is working. For these reasons, praxis is a fundamentally social phenomenon.

Praxis is directed toward satisfying human needs, needs based on human biology.

> Men must be in a position to live in order to "make history." But life involves before everything else eating and drinking, a habitation, clothing and many other things. The first historical act is thus the production of the means to satisfy these needs, the production of material life itself.[10]

But praxis does not end there.

> The second point is that the satisfaction of the first need (the action of satisfying and the instrument of satisfactions which have been acquired) leads to new needs; and this producing of new needs is the first historical act.[11]

"The first historical act," therefore, has a double aspect. It provides the means of satisfying existing needs and simultaneously creates new needs. In this way, praxis changes not only the non-human world but also the human producers themselves. As new needs emerge, people develop new means of satisfying those needs; the new products, in turn, give rise to still further needs, until the original human nature is completely transformed. Engels' essay on "The Part Played by Labour in the Transition from Ape to Man" (1876) is a development of this idea that human beings create their own nature through productive activity.

The notion that human beings create themselves opens up infinite possibilities for human control of their own destiny. It may seem paradoxical that these vistas are displayed to us by a theory that lays such emphasis on the biological basis of human nature. Ordinarily, a philosophical emphasis on human biology is used for the purpose of announcing biologically imposed limits to social possibility. But the way in which Marxism conceptualizes the relation between human biology and human society does not even allow for the usual form of questions as to the extent of the biological determination of human nature. Just as, on the Marxist view, human nature is not conceptually distinct from non-human nature, so Marxists do not see a line between the biological and the social components of human nature. Instead, Marxist theory views human biology and human society as related "dialectically." In other words, biology and society are not, in the end, conceptually separable from each other; rather they are related in such a way that each partially constitutes the other. Human biology is seen as having permitted the development of certain types of social organization at the same time as those particular forms of social organization permitted and encouraged a certain direction in biological evolution. For instance, tool use is seen as a cause as well as an effect of bipedal locomotion. A limited bipedalism freed the hands to pick up sticks and stones; the use of these objects gave their users an evolutionary advantage that led both to more bipedalism and to more developed tool use. So Engels writes: "the hand is not only the organ of labour, *it is also the product of that labour*."[12] Of course, the mutual interaction between human biology and human society still continues as humans continue through praxis to modify and develop human nature. For instance, science is still expanding our conceptions of what is biologically possible, from sporting achievements to test-tube babies and flights to the moon. The expansion of biological possibility, resulting from social developments, in turn expands the possibilities of social organization. I shall argue later that this dialectical conception of the relation between human biology and human society has special significance for feminism.

The notion of praxis is not only the key to Marx's general conception of human nature. In addition, Marx claims that the specific form of praxis undertaken in a given society determines the fundamental features of that society and of the nature of its inhabitants. The "peculiar, distinctive character" of every society is constituted ultimately by its "mode of production," that is, by the way in which the members of that society organize their productive activity.[13] Marx's best known and most succinct statement of this view is the following passage from his Preface to *The Critique of Political Economy:*

> In the social production of their life, men enter into definite relations that are indispensable and independent of their will, relations of production which correspond to a definite stage in development of their material productive forces. The sum total of these relations of production constitutes the economic structure of society, the real foundation, on which rises a legal and political superstructure and to which correspond definite forms of social consciousness. The mode of production of material life conditions the social, political and intellectual life process in general. It is not the consciousness of men that determines their being, but, on the contrary, their social being that determines their consciousness.[14]

One interesting feature of this passage is that it expresses a sharp contrast with the liberal view of rationality. Not only do Marxists claim that praxis rather than pure rational thought is the characteristic human activity, but they see rational thought itself as inseparable from praxis. This is true both because thought is typically expressed in productive activity and also because, for Marxists, the very parameters of rational thought are determined in some ultimate sense by the dominant mode of production. For Marxists, therefore, rationality is not some universal or transcultural standard of thought. Instead, rationality is expressed in action, and what counts as rational action is defined within a given society.

This active and historical conception of rationality is a part of the general historical approach that Marxists take to understanding human nature. Far from seeing human nature as changeless, Marxists believe that people's capacities, needs and interests are determined ultimately by the mode of production that characterizes the society they inhabit. Thus, human nature itself is a historical product. In the Marxist view, the liberal notion of the abstract individual is conceptually incoherent. Because people realize their human potentialities only in a specific historical context, it is impossible even to conceive of a human individual outside any such context. As Marx put it, perhaps rather less than perspicuously: "*Man* is not an abstract being, squatting outside the world. Man is the *world of men,* the State and Society . . . the human essence is no abstraction inherent in each single individual. In its reality it is the ensemble of social relations."[15]

If human nature is necessarily historical, as Marx argues, it cannot be investigated by the method of abstracting from particular circumstances. For human nature is precisely the particular circumstances which pertain in any given society; if we abstract those circumstances, we abstract precisely what is human. Instead, human nature must be investigated empirically within specific historical contexts and in particular with regard to the prevailing mode of organizing productive activity. This, in outline, is what is meant by the "historical materialist" method of investigation.

In pursuing a historical materialist investigation of human nature, it is particularly important to take account of the division of society into classes. For "the history of all hitherto existing society is the history of class struggles."[16] With the institution of private property, Marx saw societies as having been split into opposing groups, members of which shared a common relation to the means of production and, consequently, shared similar economic conditions, interests and cultural affinities. Under capitalism, the primary focus of Marx's interest, the two main classes are the proletariat, or working class, and the bourgeoisie, or capitalist class. Because members of the same class participate in similar kinds of productive activity and experience similar social conditions, they are influenced to develop certain physical characteristics and certain aspects of their personality and are blocked from developing others. For example, the material conditions of class society result in members of the capitalist class being, on average, taller, healthier and having a longer life expectancy than members of the working class. Similarly, their social circumstances will encourage members of the capitalist class to be greedy, insensitive and hypocritical, while the circumstances of the working class block them from developing their capacities for poetry or for intellectual work. Thus, Marx sees class society as creating broad social types of human beings. The nature of individuals is determined not only by the mode of production that prevails in the society they inhabit, but also by their place within the class system of that society. Individuals are likely to develop a character structure that is shared by other members of their class; that is, individuals of the same class are likely to have in common a relatively permanent set of habitual attitudes that determine the general way in which they think and react to the world.[17]

The specific character structures that typify a certain form of class society are reinforced both by the dominant ideology and, on a deeper level, by the very structure of daily life. The dominant ideology of a society is the framework of beliefs and values that is generally employed to explain and justify social experience. This ideology is expressed not only in systematic theories, but also through the legal system, through the prevailing religion, and through various forms of artistic and cultural expression. Marxists believe that in every class society there is a dialectical relation between the dominant ideology and the mode of production, such that each influences the other. As we saw earlier, however, they believe that the mode of production ultimately determines the ideology, in the sense that it sets limits to the sort of ideas that will be accepted within a given society.

In class society, the ruling class ultimately dominates the production and distribution of scientific, religious and artistic ideas. For this reason, it can exert fairly direct control over the concepts and values that are generated and disseminated. More indirectly and subtly, however, the mode of production also determines the prevailing ideology through its structuring of daily life. For instance, in the conditions of capitalist society, most people experience work as the repression rather than the expansion of their creative abilities. Consequently, they become "lazy," turning their interests from production to consumption. Competing with each other for scarce goods, they experience themselves and others as acquisitive and predatory. In class societies, the prevailing mode of production thus generates specific forms of "false consciousness," perceptions of human nature and reality distorted in ways that tend to make the status quo seem inevitable or "natural," and which thus serve the interests of the ruling class. Since the 19th century, a number of Marxist theorists have tried to develop the notion of false consciousness so as to explain, among other things, the absence of working-class revolutions in the advanced capitalist nations of the world.

In his earlier writings, notably the *Economic and Philosophic Manuscripts of 1844,* Marx uses the concept of alienation to characterize the particular manifestation of human nature that typifies capitalist society. For the "humanistic" interpreters of Marx, who emphasize his earlier work, the concept of alienation forms the basis of the Marxist critique of the capitalist system. (In Part III of this book, I shall discuss the concept of alienation in some detail and show how socialist feminist authors have tried to reinterpret it.) In spite of its promise as a critical tool, "alienation" is a somewhat problematic concept for Marxists because it may be taken to presuppose a human essence from which people under capitalism are alienated, and the concept of a human essence seems quite at odds with the conception of human nature as a product of history. Whether for this reason or another, the word "alienation" slips only rarely into Marx's later work, and many scholars believe that the later Marx dropped the notion. Even in Marx's later descriptions of human beings under capitalism, however, he retains many of the elements of his earlier concept of alienation. Consider the famous passage in Volume 1 of *Capital,* in which Marx describes the plight of the worker under capitalism:

> within the capitalist system all methods for raising the social productiveness of labour are brought about at the cost of the individual labourer, all means for the development of production transform themselves into

means of domination over, and exploitation of, the producers; they mutilate the labourer into a fragment of a man, degrade him to the level of an appendage of a machine, destroy every remnant of charm in his work and turn it into a hated toil; they estrange from him the intellectual potentialities of the labour-process in the same proportion as science is incorporated in it as an independent power; they distort the conditions under which he works, subject him during the labour-process to a despotism the more hateful for its meanness; they transform his life-time into working time and drag his wife and child beneath the wheels of the Juggernaut of capital.[18]

In this passage, Marx gives an unforgettable sketch of how the capitalist system enslaves workers apparently to machines and, in consequence of the capitalist division of labor, "converts the labourer into a crippled monstrosity, by forcing his detail dexterity at the expense of a world of productive capabilities and instincts."[19] In other words, capitalism overdevelops a few potentialities in workers, principally those for a certain kind of manual dexterity, but denies the possibility for the development of many others, particularly intellectual potentialities. Consequently, "labour always appears as repulsive, always as *external forced labor;* and not labour, by contrast, as 'freedom and happiness.' "[20] These observations show the similarity between Marx's later views of human nature under capitalism and his earlier conception of it as alienated. In particular, they make plain Marx's belief that capitalism seriously impedes human self-realization and the full flowering of human potentiality, however these notoriously vague phrases are interpreted. Moreover, the capitalist organization of production obscures the ways in which the members of a society are interdependent; it sets individuals in competition with each other so that they learn to view one another as potential enemies and are unable to perceive their mutual dependence and the interests they have in common. They conceive of themselves as isolated individuals, alienated from each other, rather than as beings who are necessarily social.

Human alienation can be overcome only by the abolition of capitalism and its replacement by socialism, under which private individuals would no longer own and control the means of production. Instead, the means of production would be "socialized"; that is, they would belong to society as a whole. Marxists believe that the establishment of socialism, like any other transformation in the mode of production, would engender new developments in human nature. There is no way to predict these developments with certainty, but some speculations can be made. It seems likely, for instance, that the competitive behavior engendered by capitalism would gradually be replaced by cooperation and, as the underlying commonalities in human interests emerged, the narrow egoism of capitalism would no longer appear to be rational. Production would be designed to satisfy human needs rather than to accumulate capital. Human needs themselves, moreover, would be redefined. As workers regained control over their productive activity, they would cease to believe that their chief interests lay in the consumption of commodities. If work were no longer defined by the needs of capital and no longer undertaken only for profit or for pay, human beings would acknowledge their need not only to consume but also to undertake free and socially meaningful activity. Labor would become

attractive work, the individual's self-realization, which in no way means that it becomes mere fun, mere amusement. . . . Really free working, e.g., composing, is at the same time precisely the most damned seriousness, the most intense exertion. The work of material production can achieve this character only (1) when its social character is posited, (2) when it is of a scientific and at the same time general character, not merely human exertion as a specifically harnessed natural force, but exertion as a subject, which appears in the production process not in a merely natural spontaneous form, but as an activity regulating all the forces of nature.[21]

In addition, the end of capitalism would transform not only production, but also consumption. No longer bombarded by advertising, people would begin to rethink what would count as good food and attractive clothing and even what would constitute sport, entertainment, leisure and fun.

In general, Marxists believe that the abolition of classes would end the truncated and distorted forms of human development that class society inevitably produces. In socialist society, some people would not be condemned to work eternally at machines, damaging their bodies through industrial diseases and their minds through boredom and repetition, and there would be no capitalist class characterized by its own special form of dehumanization. Instead, the socialization of the means of production would result inevitably in the reorganization of the labor process and particularly in attempts to reintegrate mental with manual labor. Within a developed socialism, therefore, people would be able to utilize more fully both their "mental" and their "physical" capacities in the course of their work. Although no one can say yet just how these human potentialities would be actualized, it is certain that there would emerge under socialism a more universal type of human nature, no longer bifurcated by class society.

[W]hen the limited bourgeois form is stripped away, what is wealth other than the universality of individual needs, capacities, pleasures, productive forces etc., created through universal exchange? The full development of human mastery over the forces of nature, those of so-called nature as well as of humanity's own nature? The absolute working out of his creative potentialities, with no presupposition other than the previous historical development which makes this totality of development, i.e., the development of all human powers as such the end in itself, not as measured on a *predetermined* yardstick? Where he does not reproduce himself in one specificity, but produces his totality?[22]

Human nature would be created consciously by human beings. Rather than the accumulation of capital, indeed, the goal of social organization would be the full development of human nature.

Marxist Political Theory

Marx's concept of alienation provides the moral if not the "scientific" foundation for his critique of capitalism. His general conception of human nature provides the metaphysical foundation for a political theory very different from that of liberalism. Not only does it provide different answers; it even asks different questions.

Its rejection of dualist presuppositions enables Marxist theory to avoid entirely many of the central metaphysical and epistemological problems that have dogged metaphysical dualism. For instance, the problem of how it is possible for interaction to occur between an ontologically distinct mind and body disappears. Similarly, the recognition of the necessarily social construction of language and thought abolishes the classical problems of epistemological scepticism and solipsism. Once we recognize that language and thought can develop only through praxis, or collective action to satisfy our needs through the transformation of nature, we can no longer doubt the existence of other people or of our "external" world. As for the problem of identifying human beings, they are identified in the first place by their biological constitutions and in the second place by their capacity for praxis.

The Marxist emphasis on the biological aspect of human nature is expressed in Marxism's rejection not only of metaphysical dualism but also of normative dualism, the view that what is special and valuable about human beings is their capacity for rational thought. The rejection of both kinds of dualism has direct consequences for Marxist political theory. For one thing, the Marxist acknowledgment that human capacities, needs and interests have a biological base, although they are certainly not biologically determined, opens up a possible way of escaping from liberal political scepticism about the possibility of identifying real human needs and interests. Unfortunately, it must be admitted that no Marxist theorist, to my knowledge, has succeeded yet in giving an account that is entirely satisfactory.

The Marxist insistence that humans are a biological species also makes plain the mutual dependence necessary for human physical survival, an interdependence connected intimately with our biological constitution. Liberal political solipsism, the assumption that human individuals are essentially solitary, is revealed as contrary to the facts of our socially conditioned biology and this revelation undercuts the whole problematic of liberal political theory. Rather than community and cooperation being seen as puzzles, the existence of serious conflict instead requires explanation.

Marxists find this explanation not in "the human condition," but rather in the division of society into classes. Under capitalism, the basic conflict is not between competing individuals, but between the working class and the capitalist class. Competition between individuals is not inevitable but results rather from the imperatives of the capitalist mode of production, which force capitalists to compete for markets and workers to compete for jobs. This state of affairs produces the egoistic motivation that liberals take to be endemic to human nature. The historical materialist conception of human nature denies any such universal motivation, and argues instead that the contemporary prevalence of egoistic behavior must be understood as the inevitable response to a capitalist society which rewards only the relentless pursuit of individual self-interest. A major transformation of the mode of production would result in major changes in human motivation.

The problem for Marxist political theory, then, is not to explain how social conflict may be contained within acceptable bounds, but rather to explain how the underlying causes of conflict may be eliminated. The answer that Marxism provides is the elimination of class society. Marxists believe that the capitalist mode of production must be replaced by a socialist mode of production. In other words, the means of producing the necessities of life must be taken out of the control of the capitalist class and placed in the hands of society as a whole. At least in the short term, "society as a whole" is to be represented by a workers' state, which is to make the main decisions about the production of the necessities of life: what is to be produced, under what conditions, and how it is to be distributed. The "Invisible Hand" of the market is to be replaced by many visible, and self-consciously cooperative, human hands.

The central task that liberal political theory sets itself is the definition of the legitimate power of the state: To this end, it distinguishes between the "public" realm, where the state may intervene legitimately, and the "private" realm, where the state has no legitimate authority. Although Marxist theorists often make a distinction between "public" and "private" realms, their use of these terms is quite different from that of the liberal theorists. Marxist theorists believe that there are two reasons why it is impossible to provide a general characterization of those situations in which the state has legitimate authority. One reason is that the Marxist conception of human nature as a continuous social creation precludes the view that there is any aspect of an individual's life which, in principle, is of concern only to that individual. The other reason is that, in spite of the prevailing capitalist belief that Marxism requires the state to control every aspect of social life, Marxists in fact do not accept the ultimate legitimacy of any state power.

In liberal political theory, the state is viewed as an impartial mediator between competing individuals. Apart from external defense, its main functions are to guarantee a (varying) degree of noninterference from others and to equalize opportunities. Marxist political theory differs from liberalism not simply in assigning the state a dominant role in economic affairs. More fundamentally, it perceives the state as a means by which the dominant class strengthens and legitimates its dominance over the subordinate classes, both by passing laws that favor its own interest and by punishing any attempts by members of the subordinate classes to challenge the status quo. Marxists do not claim that even the socialist state would be neutral between classes. But because it would represent the workers who are the overwhelming majority of the population, Marxists believe that the socialist state would be more genuinely democratic than the capitalist state, which represents primarily the interests of the relatively minuscule capitalist class. This increase in democracy would mean that the socialist state would need to be far less repressive than the capitalist state, which must enforce the interests of a ruling minority. Under socialism, the state's administrative functions would gradually come to overshadow its police functions, and the latter would ultimately "wither away." Communism would have arrived.

In a genuinely socialist society, by definition, it would be impossible for a tiny minority of individuals to control the lives of the vast majority of others through its ownership of the means of production. Instead, all would share a common relation to the means of production, the simultaneous relation of owners and workers. Because of this common relation, there would be no great inequalities of wealth between individuals; no one would be deprived of access to food, heat, education, or health care; nor would some individuals have an overwhelming advantage over others in utilizing their political rights to do such things as travel, publish their opinions or be candidates for political office. For this reason, Marxists claim that a more genuine freedom would exist in a planned socialist society than in the so-called free market of capitalism. They argue that freedom must include not only "formal" or legal entitlement, the guarantee of non-intervention, but also the provision of the material conditions in which individuals would have the real possibility of exercising their legal rights. It should be noted that even this expansion of the liberal conception does not fully capture the Marxist view of freedom, which will be discussed in more detail in Chapter 8.

The relation between socialism and democracy or between individual wealth and individual political freedom is one example of the connections that Marxists see between politics and economics. Unlike liberal political theory, Marxism views politics and economics as inseparable. For Marxism, the economy is not an autonomous realm, regulated by "natural" laws of supply and demand. Instead, every economic system is a social creation whose structure and vicissitudes reflect political choices and which, in turn, opens some political possibilities and limits others. For Marxism, then, the domain of political theory is defined much more broadly than it is for liberalism. Rather than focusing on government, its legitimacy and its limits, Marxist political theory centers on what it calls "political economy."

Even from this brief outline of Marxist political theory, one can see the absence of some of the insoluble dilemmas that confront the liberal. For instance, the Marxist political philosopher is not forced to walk the tightrope between the ideal of freedom as nonintervention and the postulated necessity for coercive means to preserve this freedom; the Marxist political philosopher is not enmeshed in the contradiction between the ideal of equal opportunity· to achieve unequal rewards and the impossibility of achieving this ideal in a society where "rewards" are conspicuously unequal; nor is the Marxist political philosopher confronted by the demand to treat people equally, as abstract individuals, at the same time as the voices of women and minorities make it increasingly clear that they are not abstract individuals and that their different needs require equal consideration. Another issue for contemporary liberalism has been the nature/ nurture controversy. This concerns the relative importance of genetic versus environmental factors in determining human behavior and has been central to a number of political disputes within the liberal framework. (How much social inequality is the result of the environment and how far should the state intervene to modify environments?) Within the Marxist conceptual framework, this question does not arise; it expresses a false dilemma since it rests on the mistaken assumption that human biology and human society are in principle separable from each other.

The Marxist view of human nature changes not only the domain and problematic of liberal political philosophy; it also changes our conception of political philosophy itself. I have quoted already the well-known if rather extreme statement of historical materialism in which Marx claims that "It is not the consciousness of men that determines their being but, on the contrary, their social being that determines their consciousness."[23] From this materialist perspective, our political theories, our conceptions of human nature, and our visions of what forms of social organization are desirable seem to be inevitably ideological; they are products of a particular historical situation and must be reconceptualized as that situation changes. We can achieve little of substance by reflecting on some notion of human nature in abstraction from society and attempting to derive specific but a priori and universal truths about how society should be organized. We must acknowledge that we can go only one step at a time in our attempts to elaborate a full conception of human liberation. According to historical materialism, of course, the prevailing mode of production limits not only our philosophical vision; it also sets limits to the kinds of social organization and human possibility that may be realized in actuality. A political theory that focuses on abstract principles while ignoring the existing material conditions is utopian and unrealistic. Finally, even where the material preconditions for progressive social change do exist, Marxists do not believe that such change will result from philosophical persuasion. Social revolution results when "the material productive forces of society come in conflict with the existing relations of production"[24]; philosophical debate is merely the ideological expression of a conflict already under way. All history is the history of class struggle. Consequently, changes in human nature and in forms of social organization can be achieved only through a revolutionary transformation of the mode of production. "The philosophers have only interpreted the world in various ways; the point, however, is to change it."[25]

Marxism and Women's Nature

The Marxist approach to the questions of women's nature and women's oppression is governed, naturally, by its allegiance to the method of historical materialism. This method presupposes the outline of a certain conception of women's nature: insofar as women are human beings, women's nature must be formed by the dialectical interrelation between women's praxis, their biological constitution and their physical and social environments. Other than this conceptual framework, however, the historical materialist method implies that we can have no a priori knowledge of women's nature. One can know a priori that women's nature, like men's, inevitably has changed and continues to change as the result of historical developments; but in the absence of empirical investigation, one cannot know anything specific about the extent and direction of those changes, let alone the answers to the crucial feminist questions concerning the ways in which women have differed or continue to differ systematically from men in their capacities, needs and interests. To answer these sorts of questions, it is necessary to investigate actual women in their actual historical situation. In particular, since human nature develops and is expressed through praxis, we must look at women's productive activity. Thus, in order to understand women in a given society, we must examine the kinds of labor they perform, the ways in which this labor is organized, and the social relations that women form with each other and with men as a result of their labor and its mode of organization.

Because Marxists are concerned primarily with the critique and overthrow of capitalist society, their interest in women focuses particularly in women's situation under capitalism, in which productive activity is organized around the division between the working class and the capitalist class. To understand women's nature under capitalism, therefore, it is necessary to investigate it through the lens provided by the notion of class. Because they see capitalist society as being split by a division that cuts across sex lines, Marxists do not assume that the nature of women in the capitalist class will be identical with the nature of working-class women.

In practice, how have traditional Marxists applied the general Marxist method of investigating women's nature, and what conclusions have they drawn from it? Marx himself did not undertake a thorough investigation of women's situation under capitalism. Instead, that task was left to Frederick Engels. In *The Origin of the Family, Private Property and the State,* Engels discusses briefly the sexual division of labor under capitalism but, surprisingly, he allocates far more space to a consideration of women's situation in precapitalist societies. To undermine conventional claims that women's subordination under capitalism is "natural," in the sense that it is an inevitable result of biological differences between women and men, Engels argues that women's subordination is a form of *oppression,* resulting from the institution of class society and maintained into the present because it serves the interests of capital.

It is often assumed that Engels' theory must be taken as a package, that his account of women's oppression under capitalism is inseparable from his account of women's situation in precapitalist societies. In my view, this assumption is doubtful; I think the issue of the origin of women's subordination may be separated from the issue of how that subordination is maintained today. Thus, I question the widespread belief that, in determining how far the capitalist system itself should be blamed for perpetuating women's subordination, we first have to discover whether women's original subordination resulted from or antedated class society. On the other hand, information about women's status in various types of societies may suggest ways of explaining the apparent intensification of women's subordination under capitalism and may indicate the material conditions for women's liberation. Regardless of its logical relevance, in any case, Engels' account of the origins of women's subordination has been of tremendous historical importance. Most Marxist and much feminist theory has taken this account as its starting point, and those theorists who have not done so have felt obliged to explain why not. Engels' account, moreover, taken together with Marx's scattered remarks on the topic, reveals a number of important Marxist assumptions about women's nature. For these reasons, I shall sketch briefly the classical Marxist account of the origins as well as the maintenance of women's subordination.

Marx and Engels assume that every society has been characterized by a sexual division of labor "which was originally nothing but the division of labor in the sexual act."[26] Even in the most primitive societies, however, the division of labor between women and men went beyond that required for conceiving children. From earliest times, Engels claims, there was a "natural" division of labor, with men specializing in producing the means of subsistence while women worked in the household. "According to the division of labor within the family at that time it was the man's part to obtain the food and the instruments of labour necessary for the purpose."[27]

Despite this early sexual division of labor, Engels does not believe that the earliest women were in any way subordinate to men. Instead, each sex was dominant in its own sphere and, since the work of both was vital to survival, women's status in the community was at least equal to that of men. Engels even suggests that in very early times women may have been dominant:

> The communistic household, in which most or all of the women belong to one and the same gens, while the men come from various gentes, is the material foundation of that supremacy of the women which was general in primitive times.[28]

Women's supposed supremacy was finally destroyed by developments in the sphere of what Engels calls production. With the invention of agriculture and the domestication of animals, the forces of production greatly expanded and a surplus was created. It now became profitable to own slaves and so the first form of class society came into being. Because these developments occurred in the male sphere of production, Engles argues, they gave men social dominance over women. Moreover, having acquired wealth, men now wanted to be able to control its disposal and in particular to be able to bequeath it to their own biological offspring.

> Thus on the one hand, in proportion as wealth increased it made the man's position in the family more important than the woman's and on the other hand created an impulse to exploit this strengthened position

in order to overthrow in favor of his children, the traditional order of inheritance. This, however, was impossible so long as descent was reckoned according to mother right. Mother right, therefore, had to be overthrown, and overthrown it was.[29]

In other words, men changed the old kinship system in such a way that it became patrilineal rather than matrilineal. For Engels, "the overthrow of mother right was the world historic defeat of the female sex."[30]

With this defeat, the egalitarian "pairing" marriages that had characterized the preceding form of society were replaced by what Engels calls "monogamy." It is important to note that Engels' use of the term "monogamy" is quite different from its contemporary use, in which it signifies primarily the restriction of sexual activity to a single partner. For Engels, by contrast, monogamy is primarily an economic rather than a social or a sexual institution. It is also, by definition, male supremacist.

It was not in any way the fruit of individual sex love, with which it had nothing whatever to do; marriages remained as before marriages of convenience. It was the first form of the family to be based not on natural but on economic conditions, on the victory of private property over primitive, natural communal property. The Greeks themselves put the matter quite frankly: the sole exclusive aims of monogamous marriage were to make the man supreme in the family and to propagate, as the future heirs to his wealth, children indisputably his own. . . .

Thus when monogamous marriage first makes its appearance in history, it is not as the reconciliation of man and woman, still less as the highest form of such reconciliation. Quite the contrary, monogamous marriage comes on the scene as the subjugation of the one sex by the other; it announces a struggle between the sexes unknown throughout the whole previous period. . . . The first class antagonism that appears in history coincides with the development of the antagonism between men and women in monogamous marriage, the first class oppression coincides with that of the female sex by the male."[31]

Engels believes that this ancient struggle continues into modern times because monogamy remains the primary institution that keeps women subjugated. By making women economically dependent on their husbands, monogamy forces them into subordination and deprives them of full participation in society at large. Only the abolition of monogamous marriage will liberate women. Monogamous marriage as Engels defines it, however, is tied inextricably to class society and, in contemporary times, to capitalism. It appears with the emergence of class society; it is defined in terms of male ownership of private property; and contemporary Marxists have developed a number of arguments to demonstrate that it remains one of the main institutional supports of capitalism, the contemporary form of class society. Marxists conclude that, in order to liberate women from monogamy, it is necessary to end capitalism.

Thus far, Engels has spoken in a very general way simply of "women." But under capitalism, at any rate, he believes that his analysis applies primarily to bourgeois women. For working-class women, matters are quite different.

[N]ow that large scale industry has taken the wife out of the home onto the labor market and into the factory, and made her often the breadwinner of the family, no basis for any kind of male supremacy is left in the proletarian household, except, perhaps, for something of the brutality toward women that has spread since the introduction of monogamy. The proletarian family is therefore no longer monogamous in the strict sense, even where there is passionate love and firmest loyalty on both sides and maybe all the blessings of religious and civil authority. . . . The wife has in fact regained the right to dissolve the marriage, and if two people cannot get on with one another, they prefer to separate. In short, proletarian marriage is monogamous in the etymological sense of the word, but not at all in its historical sense.[32]

In other words, Engels believed that, paradoxical as it may sound, there is a sense in which women of the capitalist class are more oppressed than working-class women. For the entry of working-class women into the labor market has made them independent of working-class men in a way that bourgeois women are not independent of capitalist men. Rather than being oppressed by working-class men, therefore, working-class women share with them a common class interest in overthrowing capitalism.

Bourgeois women share this interest too, but because of their gender rather than their class. Engels's analysis purports to show that, on the deepest level of social analysis, it is the capitalist system that oppresses women as a group and the working class as a whole. That men as a group oppress women as a group is false, for working-class men have no more real power than women. Their privileges are ultimately illusory, an ideological appearance concealing the social reality and allowing the capitalist class to divide and rule.

Bourgeois women are more likely than working-class women to be deceived by this appearance. After all, the men with whom they are in closest contact, capitalist men, really do enjoy substantial privileges in virtue of their sex as well as their class. On the traditional Marxist analysis, however, working-class women are more likely than bourgeois women both to feel and to be equal with the men of their class, especially if they work outside the home. The circumstances of their lives encourage them to recognize their basic identity of interest with the men of their class; hence feminist ideas have less appeal for them. It is more difficult for housewives within the working class to develop a sense of class consciousness, because of their relative isolation within the home. For this reason, Marxists believe that housebound women tend to be more "backward" or conservative than their husbands or than women with paid jobs. Even they, however, are unlikely to become feminists, because the work available to them outside the home is far less attractive and well paid than that available to women of the upper classes. In the Marxist view, therefore, bourgeois women are much more likely to be feminists than working-class women. The Marxist interpretation of this phenomenon is that the class position of working-class women gives them a clearer perception of social reality and enables them to see that most versions of feminism are versions of ruling-class ideology. Traditional Marxists argue that most prevailing feminist ideas are ideological because they postulate that women of all classes share a common interest in abolishing male privilege; by obscuring class divisions, they serve the interests of the ruling class. As we shall see, Marxists certainly believe that, with a few significant exceptions, women should be equal with men but they think that liberal and radical feminism are forms of false consciousness, generated by the experience of women who do not belong to the working class. Traditional Marxists argue that, rather than focusing their attack on the apparent privileges of all men, women should instead ally with working-class men in struggling for their common, long-term interest in the defeat of capitalism. Feminists must be brought to see that women and the working class are natural allies because the liberation of both requires the end of capitalism.

What view of women's nature is imbedded within this Marxist account of women's situation? What does this account have to tell us about women's capacities, needs and interests? In particular, what does it have to say about the genesis of the observable differences between women and men in capitalist society? What is the nature of those differences, what is their origin and what is the likelihood of eliminating them? Is Marxism like liberalism in seeing human nature as basically sexless and is it committed to the vision of a genderless or androgynous future? In my view, there is some ambiguity and even inconsistency in the Marxist answers to these questions. In the remainder of this section, I shall establish that this ambiguity exists. In the next section, I shall uncover its conceptual roots.

The dominant tendency in Marxist reflections on women's nature resembles in some ways the rationalist approach that characterizes liberal feminism. This may seem an odd claim to make about a theory whose fundamental orientation is away from rationalism or idealism and toward an emphasis on the material basis of human life. Certainly it is true that Marxism, unlike liberalism, sees human nature as being biologically sexed, as being necessarily male or female. Since the propagation of the species is a "circumstance which, from the very outset, enters into historical development"[33] and since human beings are a biological species that reproduces sexually, being sexed must be a necessary part of what it is to be human. In spite of their belief that the biological differences between women and men is ontologically basic, however, Marx's and Engels' anxiety to deny the "naturalness" of women's subordination often leads them to minimize the social and political significance of that difference. They emphasize continually that women's subordination results not from biology, but from the social phenomenon of class, that women in pre-class society were not a subordinate gender, nor are women among the contemporary working class. When they talk about the future, moreover, they foresee an undermining of the sexual division of labor that has been the material basis of women's subordination. Thus, in a much-quoted phrase Engels wrote that: "the first condition for the liberation of the wife is to bring the whole female sex back into public industry."[34] The major thrust, indeed, of Marxist theorizing seems to have been toward the abolition of gender distinctions in the market and thus toward what liberal feminists have called an androgynous future. This side of Marxist theory may be summed up in the following well-known quotation from *Capital,* Volume 1:

> However terrible and disgusting the dissolution, under the capitalistic system, of the old family ties may appear, nevertheless modern industry, by assigning as it does an important part in the process of production outside the domestic sphere to women, to young persons, and to children of both sexes, creates a new economic foundation for a higher form of the family and of the relationship between the sexes. . . . Moreover, it is obvious that the fact of the collective working group being composed of individuals of both sexes and all ages, must necessarily under suitable conditions, become a source of human development.[35]

This radical call to abolish sexual distinctions in the market (and, apparently, distinctions based on age as well) represents the dominant tendency in traditional Marxist theorizing about women. But another side to Marxist theory does emphasize the significance of the biological differences between women and men. On this view, expressed mainly in "asides" rather than in explicit argument, the biological differences between the sexes have not only determined a sexual division of labor in the past, but mean that the future can never be totally androgynous.

Marx and Engels believe that there has always been a sexual division of labor and that this, at least until the advent of capitalism, has taken a remarkably constant form. Apart from "the division of labour in the sexual act," they believe that women have always been concerned primarily with the household and men with obtaining "the food and instruments necessary for the purpose." In many passages Marx and Engels refer to this division of labor as "natural" or "spontaneous." For instance, in *The German Ideology* they write about the origins of the division of labor as being "originally nothing but the division of labour in the sexual act, then that division of labour which develops spontaneously or 'naturally' by virtue of natural predisposition (e.g., physical strength, needs, accidents, etc.)."[36] On the following page, they refer again to "the natural division of labour in the family." These remarks are not just youthful slips. In his mature work, *Capital,* Marx several times repeats the suggestion that there is a sexual division of labor in the family that is natural. For instance, he writes about the "spontaneously developed" system of organizing labor in "the patriarchal industries of a peasant family, that produces corn, cattle, yarn, linen, and clothing for home use." This family

> possesses a spontaneously developed system of division of labour. The distribution of the work within the family, and the regulation of the labour-time of the several members, depends as well upon the differences of age and sex as upon natural conditions varying with the seasons.[37]

Later in the first volume of *Capital,* Marx repeats the point. "Within a family . . . there springs up naturally a division of labour, caused by differences of sex and age, a division that is consequently based on a purely physiological foundation."[38]

Marx and Engels clearly believe that the division of labor within the family is natural because it is biologically determined, "based on a purely physiological foundation." Yet they never explain just what the division is, why it occurs nor whether it can be overcome in future forms of the family. In his *Critique of the Gotha Programme,* moreover, Marx even seems to reconsider his call to abolish the sexual division of labor in the market. He writes:

> The standardization of the working day must include the restriction of female labour insofar as it relates to the duration, intermissions, etc., of the working day; otherwise it could only mean the exclusion of women from branches of industry that are especially unhealthy for the female body or objectionable morally for the female sex.[39]

This passage carries the alarming suggestions that women's capacity to enter public industry is limited *both* by biological *and* by moral factors. The latter suggestion is repeated in Marx's apparent endorsement of the view of the British factory inspectors that one of the most deplorable effects of the factory system was the *moral* degradation it imposed on women and girls. It caused them to be dirty, to drink, to swear and to wear men's clothes—none of which Marx considered to be especially injurious for men.[40]

One more aspect of gender needs to be considered, the "division of labor" that is supposed to occur in sexual activity. In the passage quoted already from

The German Ideology, Marx and Engels write that the social division of labor originates in "the division of labor in the sexual act." If we take this remark seriously, it implies that, no matter how much society may seek to abolish the division of labor, such divisions are always likely to reemerge so long as "the division of labor in the sexual act" remains. Whether or not it is true that divisions of labor, such as the class division and the division of mental from manual labor, will always be regenerated by "the division of labor in the sexual act," it does seem at least plausible that a division of labor in sexual activity will always encourage a regeneration of the more extensive sexual division of labor that constitutes the basis of the institution of gender. This is because, in capitalist society though perhaps not in all others, sexual orientation is one of the defining features of gender identity. If an individual's primary sexual and emotional interest is in members of her or his own sex, then her or his gender identity is conventionally called into question. Thus, gay men are considered conventionally to lack masculinity, to be less than men, and lesbians to lack femininity, to be less than women. If gender is to be eliminated entirely, then, it seems that it may be necessary to abolish normative heterosexuality, the notion that heterosexual relations are more "natural" and legitimate than homosexual relations. In other words, "the division of labor in the sexual act" will have to be abolished. Neither Marx nor Engels, however, considers seriously and explicitly the radical implications of their own suggestion in *The German Ideology.* In an admittedly early work, Marx writes that "the relation of man to woman is *the most natural* relation of human being to human being,"[41] and Engels always assumes that normal sexual relations are heterosexual. For instance, he condemns the Athenian men who "fell into the abominable practice of sodomy and degraded alike their gods and themselves with the myth of Ganymede,"[42] and his discussion of the "mutual sexual love" that will be possible for us all only under socialism is conducted exclusively in heterosexual terms.

From this examination of Marx's and Engels' writings, I conclude that there is considerable ambiguity and even inconsistency in their view of women's nature. They waver between the radical ideal of full female participation in every area of life and the assumption that, while women's biology may allow for considerable participation, the complete achievement of this goal is impossible. The compromise view seems to be that, under socialism, women's nature would be much more like men's nature than it is under capitalism, especially among the capitalist class, but would not be identical with it. Certain unspecified biological differences between women and men would mean that there could never be a complete abolition of the sexual division of labor, either in the family, in the workplace, or in bed. Consequently, while gender differences under socialism would be considerably muted, complete psychological androgyny would be impossible.

Problems for the Marxist Conception of Human Nature

The Marxist conception of human nature escapes many of the fundamental problems that undermine the liberal conception. Its historical materialist approach promises to provide a fruitful method for understanding and, ultimately, for taking conscious control of human nature. But feminists complain that the classical Marxist theorists did not apply that method consistently to the questions of women's nature and women's oppression. The traditional Marxist analysis fails to acknowledge the extent and depth of women's oppression, and so it does not provide a satisfactory vision of liberation for women nor a workable strategy for achieving liberation. Part III of this book explores in detail the shortcomings in the traditional Marxist analysis of women's situation. In this final section of Chapter 4, I shall look at the underlying conceptual reasons for these shortcomings. I shall argue that one of the most important of these reasons is a conception of human reproduction that is insufficiently historical. Because of this, traditional Marxists see women's lives as being determined by their biology to a greater degree than men's. The implication, implicit though never explicit, is that women are not historical agents in as full a sense as are men.

The distinguishing feature of the Marxist analysis is the causal link that it seeks to establish between women's oppression and class society. Marxists deny that women's oppression is universal or biologically determined. Instead, they claim that women's oppression resulted from the institution of class society, that its form is determined by the current form of class society and that it can be abolished only by the abolition of class society. Under capitalism, Marxists claim, women are oppressed primarily because their oppression benefits capital. At first sight, this analysis is implausible. Women's oppression is far more evidently in the interest of men than of capital. In order to make their case, Marxist theorists have developed a number of arguments. I shall mention the most representative.

From a Marxist perspective, the material basis of women's oppression must be found in the sexual division of labor. Under capitalism, this division is defined characteristically by two spheres: the "public" sphere of the market and the "private" sphere of the family. The former is defined as the sphere of men; the latter as the sphere of women. To our generation, this slightly Victorian-sounding opposition needs some qualification. The massive entry of women workers into the paid labor force since World War II means that the market is no longer (if indeed it ever was) a totally male sphere in the sense that women are excluded from it. But it is still a masculine preserve in the sense that it is controlled by men (despite a few token women executives, politicians and higher civil servants) and also in that women workers are segregated into the lowest-paying jobs: currently in the United States the average woman worker earns only 59¢ for every dollar earned by the average male worker, and comparable wage differentials exist in other industrialized countries. As for the "private" sphere, this is still a feminine preserve in the sense that women, with virtually no exceptions, are responsible for housework and childcare. Thus, despite "help" from husbands, the average working woman spends 80 hours a week on her paid employment and on housework combined, compared to 50 hours for the average man. (That women do most of the housework does not mean, of course, that the home is their preserve in the sense that they have ultimate control there. But this is a question that will be considered in the second part of the book.)

There seems to be little doubt that this division of labor is in the interest of men. Contemporary Marxist theorists claim that it can also be shown to benefit capital. One of the most influential arguments has been formulated by Eli Zaretsky, who emphasizes that the sharp split between the "economy" and "the family" was an innovation contemporary with the rise of capitalism. While women certainly were subordinated in precapitalist societies, Zaretsky claims that, as capitalism matured, women's subordination was transformed and intensified by their exclusion from commodity production.[43] Other Marxist theorists have sought to explain why capital created and maintains its characteristic split between home and market. They argue that capital has taken over those areas of production that can be made profitable easily, but that it has chosen to neglect other forms of labor where profits are harder to come by. If women perform without pay such necessary social tasks as childrearing, care of the aged and the sick, cooking, etc., capital is relieved of the need to pay for the reproduction of the labor power on which it ultimately depends. Thus, Mariarosa Dalla Costa and Selma James theorize that the work women do in the home "frees" the male worker to work longer hours for capital and so increases the rate of surplus value.[44] Another Marxist theorist, Paddy Quick, argues that male dominance is ultimately the result of the desire of the ruling class to control the reproduction of labor power.[45] Post-Freudian Marxists, such as Wilhelm Reich,[46] the Frankfurt school, and Juliet Mitchell,[47] explain male dominance as an ideological or cultural phenomenon that helps to discipline the working class by imposing the kind of "authoritarian" character structure needed by the capitalist production process. Finally, it is often pointed out that the ideological definition of women's place as in the home offers a convenient rationalization for paying women less in the market. This not only provides capital with a pool of low-paid labor, but exerts a downward pressure on all wages and so increases the rate of exploitation of the working class as a whole.

These arguments all explain the contemporary sexual division of labor as being functional to capital. They have been challenged by feminists on a number of grounds, one of them economic. Some feminists have questioned the claim that the family system is indeed the cheapest way for capital to reproduce its needed labor power. They remind us that Marx and Engels themselves predicted that, rather than being left in the home, women would be drawn increasingly into commodity production. Whether or not this claim turns out ultimately to be correct, it is certainly plausible to suppose that capital might profit more from the direct exploitation of women than from allowing them to occupy so much of their time in reduplicative, "unproductive," or unprofitable housework.[48]

Second, many feminists have pointed out that, while the split between home and market is typical primarily of capitalist society, nevertheless some basic features of the sexual division of labor under capitalism were also to be found in pre-capitalist and even in pre-class societies. By definition, these features of noncapitalist societies cannot be explained as being functional to capital and so feminists have argued that their existence under capitalism requires an explanation more universal than the Marxist functionalist explanations that we have been considering.

The most obvious defect in Marxist functionalism, however, is that it never really explains why it is women who do "women's work." In other words, even if unwaged household labor is profitable to capital, there is no explanation of why it is *women* who perform this labor. Similarly, even though it is clearly profitable to capital that there should be a pool of low-paid marginal workers, there is no explanation why it is women who constitute that pool. Heidi Hartmann explains the problem this way. Marxism is a theory of class society and in particular of capitalism. It explains how capitalist society develops in a relentless drive for capital accumulation. In this process, capitalism creates a certain type of social structure in which the majority of people are poor or near poverty and it creates an ideology characterized by the values of individualism, competitiveness, domination and a certain kind of consumption. These are all necessary by-products of the process of capital accumulation:

Marx's theory of the development of capitalism is a theory of the development of "empty places." Marx predicted, for example, the growth of the proletariat and the demise of the petit bourgeoisie. More precisely and in more detail, Braverman among others has explained the creation of the "places" clerical worker and service worker in advanced capitalist societies. Just as capital creates these places indifferent to the individuals who fill them, the categories of Marxist analysis, class, reserve army of labor, wage-laborer, do not explain why particular people fill particular places. They give no clues about why *women* are subordinate to *men* inside and outside the family and why it is not the other way round. Marxist categories, like capital itself, are sex-blind.[49]

To explain why certain spaces are filled by women and others by men, Marxists appeal to "historical" reasons. In fact, however, as I shall argue next, these historical reasons are obscure; no Marxist theory provides a satisfactory historical account of the sexual division of labor. Engels's account is the most influential, but it contains all kinds of problems: factual mistakes, logical gaps, and unsupported assumptions.

First, contemporary anthropological data question the sexual division of labor that Engels claims to have characterized even the earliest societies. As we saw earlier, Engels believed that women in primitive societies were concerned primarily with household tasks. In the light of more recent data, this picture turns out to be seriously inaccurate. It is indeed true that in primitive as well as developed societies women seem always to be allocated the childcare and the routine cooking—the household tasks, in other words; but in primitive hunting and gathering societies of the type that Engels considers, women as well as men seem to be concerned with food collection. Men do indeed tend to hunt the larger animals while women concentrate on the collection of vegetable foods but women's labor is, if anything, often a more reliable source of food. There is even considerable anthropological evidence to support the claim that women rather than men developed horticulture and hence that it was within the sphere of women rather than men that the initial development of a productive surplus occurred. If this is so, then we need an explanation of why women did not come to dominate men rather than vice versa. Certainly the possibility of accumulating wealth provides women with a motive equal to men's for seizing the means of production.

In any case, even if Engels were correct in his characterization of the sexual division of labor in primitive society, his account would leave unanswered the vitally important question of why this occurred at all. Were there biological reasons for it and, if so, could those reasons still operate today? Since women's oppression, according to Engels, stemmed ultimately from the original sexual division of labor, his account is incomplete as long as this division remains unexplained.

Further problems concern the early sexual division of labor postulated by Engels. For one thing, this division sounds remarkably similar to that obtaining in contemporary society, obtaining, at any rate, ideologically though changing somewhat in practice. Yet when it occurs in contemporary society, such a division of labor is seen as the foundation of male supremacy because it makes women and their children economically dependent on men. In order to make his account consistent, Engels needs to explain why the economic dependence that he postulates for early women nevertheless allowed them to become the social equals of men, let alone their social superiors. Furthermore, if the wealth were owned by the gens and the gens were matriarchal, why was it that men became the owners of cattle and slaves in the changeover to class society? If the women were matriarchs, why didn't they retain possession of the new means of production? And why did the men, who were originally indifferent to biological paternity, suddenly develop such an intense concern for their own biological offspring?

All these questions tend to undermine Engels's claim that the women in pre-class societies were the social equals and even the social superiors of men. Among anthropologists this issue is extremely controversial and raises fascinating methodological questions.[50] The current evidence is inconclusive. So far as it goes, however, it seems to indicate that women were not systematically exploited and degraded in pre-class societies, but that such systematic subjugation occurred with the introduction of class society; to this extent, Engels's account is vindicated. But evidence also exists that even in pre-class societies (and even with the importance of their contribution to food production) women were not entirely the social equals of men. It is interesting that Engels himself even provides some of this evidence. For instance, in his discussion of pairing marriage which, he claims, occurred during a period when women were still equal or even superior to men, Engels remarks that the capture and purchase of women began at this time.[51] He attributes this development to a shortage of women, although he never explains why women should become scarce with the advent of pairing marriage. Whatever the reasons for this shortage, it should be obvious immediately that persons who are being captured and purchased are not the equals of those who are doing the capturing and purchasing. If women were the superiors of men, as Engels suggests, it should have been they who were capturing and purchasing men. If they were even the equals of men, they should have been selecting, accepting or rejecting husbands according to preference, rather than being themselves captured or sold. That Engels does not see that this method of betrothal is incongruous with female supremacy and even with women's equality is a glaring example of how certain aspects of women's subordination may seem so natural that they are invisible, even to those who are committed to women's emancipation. (The contemporary feminist process of consciousness-raising consists largely in making visible previously unnoticed aspects of women's oppression.)

What Marxist theory lacks is a convincing account, in historical materialist terms, of the reasons for the sexual division of labor. Why are women responsible for some types of work and men for others? Without such an account, women's subordination is unexplained and we have no indication of how, if at all, the situation may be changed.

Although this is a real problem, at first sight it does not seem to constitute a fundamental flaw in Marxist theory. It seems to be rather a gap in the theory, a gap which can surely be plugged through an application of the historical materialist method. Engels himself outlines this method in his famous introduction to the *Origin of the Family, Private Property and the State*:

> According to the materialistic conception, the determining factor in history is, in the final instance, the production and reproduction of immediate life. This, again, is of a twofold character; on the one side, the production of the means of existence, of food, clothing and shelter and the tools necessary for that production; on the other side, the production of human beings themselves, the propagation of the species. The social organization under which the people of a particular historical epoch and a particular

country live is determined by both kinds of production: by the stage of development of labor on the one hand and of the family on the other.[52]

Engels' own work is an attempt to trace the development of the family and, consequently, of women's work in relation to what he calls, revealingly, the development of "labor." Even though Engels' own account may be unsatisfactory, there seems to be no problem in principle with seeking to repair it.

In fact, however, the job of repair is less simple than it seems, at least so long as one's repair kit is limited to the conceptual tools of traditional Marxism. The traditional Marxist categories were not designed to capture the essential features of the sexual division of labor, and it is doubtful whether they are capable of doing the job. Within the public economy, for instance, there is in fact a sharp separation between jobs that are considered appropriate for men and those that are considered suitable for women; men and women rarely work side by side at the same job. The gender-blind categories of Marxist theory, however, obscure rather than reveal this fact. Even more seriously, the central Marxist categories hardly apply at all to the household, which is the traditional area of women's work. Marxist theory focuses primarily on production, and it defines household work, especially the household work of capitalism, as being outside production. Instead, household work is defined as reproduction, that is, the reproduction of human labor power. Reproduction itself is broken down into two parts: the daily regeneration of the labor power of existing workers, through rest and food; and the production of new workers through childbearing and childrearing. Thus, reproduction consists in both consumption and pro-creation. Women are responsible traditionally for much of the former, though of course men must eat the food that women prepare, and women are held traditionally to be responsible for almost all of the latter.

Marxism provides a clear acknowledgment of the social necessity of this woman's work. It recognizes explicitly the obvious fact that no society could continue without both consumption and procreation. In contrast with its close examination of production, however, Marxism does not provide much theoretical analysis of either of these other two aspects of social life, relying instead on an intuitive understanding of them. I shall argue that this failure to look closely at reproduction, especially at procreation, deprives Marxism of the conceptual resources necessary to understanding women's oppression. Indeed, it actually obscures that oppression and so contributes to maintaining it.

When we think of consumption, we think ordinarily of using certain objects: drinking tea, eating beans, wearing shoes, watching television, playing with toys, sleeping in beds, inhabiting flats or apartments. All the objects that we use are in part the products of human labor. According to Marxist theory, production and consumption are both aspects of an economic whole in which each aspect partially determines the other: developments in production stimulate new consumer needs, which in turn stimulate further developments in production. Although there is reciprocal interaction between production and consumption, however, production ultimately determines consumption. People in all societies have needed food, sleep, shelter and play, but the stage and mode of development of the productive forces determine ultimately what counts as an adequate meal, bed, house or entertainment. From a feminist point of view, this is unproblematic. What is more problematic is the way that the line is drawn between production and consumption. A modern meal, for instance, is the result of an enormously long and complex labor process that includes growing, picking, transporting, packaging, shopping and cooking. In Marxist theory, however, the last two processes count as consumption rather than production, at least if they are done in a household rather than in a restaurant. This point is independent of the question whether or not women's household work is productive in the technical Marxist sense of producing surplus value or profit. Domestic cooking or home decorating is not construed even as the production of use values; instead, they are conceived as consumption. This conceptual distinction serves to define even the nonprocreative part of women's household work not only as being outside the market, but as being outside production altogether. Yet it is not obvious that the distinction has any other rationale.

The question of procreation is more complex. Stated in general terms, procreation is the production of new adult humans. It includes conception, gestation, birth, physical childcare and the socialization of children. It is a process that requires much human labor, in part because human infants are born ignorant and virtually helpless. Like every human labor process, procreation is socially organized in a certain way. Each society has its own rules about who may conceive children and under what conditions, about how pregnant women should conduct themselves, about the proper process of birth, about proper standards of physical childcare and especially about what counts as proper socialization. Marxists do not see these alternatives as having emerged by chance. On the contrary, they believe that these various social practices are determined ultimately by the prevailing mode of production. Engels's work on the family is an attempt to demonstrate how, throughout history, changes in the mode of production have resulted in changes in the norms that dictate who may have sexual relations and conceive children with whom.

Whatever the historical changes in procreation, however, Marxists seem to assume that certain basic features remain constant. In particular, they assume that there is a constant division of labor by sex. Men impregnate women, who then bear children and perform infant care and early socialization; men step in again later to take charge of certain aspects of the education of older children, especially boys. This division of labor by sex in procreation is unquestioned in Marxist theory. It receives little direct attention but, wherever it is mentioned, we have seen that it is referred to as being "natural." This seems to mean that it is biologically determined. Yet Marxism provides no theoretical analysis of procreation and gives no explanation of just which features of women's biology make them uniquely suited to perform which aspects of procreative labor. Marxism takes it as self-evident that human biology requires women to conceive and bear children and to be responsible at least for infant care. Unlike what Marxists call production, therefore, human procreation is seen as a process relatively fixed by human biology. Biology sets fairly rigid limits to how far procreation is susceptible to historical change. We can see this assumption operating in *The German Ideology,* where Marx and Engels talk in general terms about the basic requirements of human life. When they talk about production, they say that the act of satisfying the biologically based human needs for food, shelter, clothing, etc., leads immediately to the production of new needs, and so the process of the historical construction of human nature is set in motion. When they talk about procreation, however, "the third circumstance which, from the very outset, enters into historical development,"[53] they allow only for limited changes in the social organization of conception, that is, for changes in the social rules governing which men and women are eligible to marry each other. Human nature is transformed through what Marxists call productive rather than procreative labor.

If human procreation is a process that is biologically determined to such a large extent, it is not a very interesting topic for political analysis. It will make little sense to talk about the "means" or the "forces" of procreation, except by a stretched analogy with production. Certainly there will be no possibility of distinguishing different "modes" of procreation and no political reason to distinguish conceptually between different aspects of it. Procreation will be closer to an animal process than to fully human praxis. While it may undergo peripheral changes, as a result of changes in the mode of production, procreation cannot be totally transformed. Consequently, those who are engaged in procreative labor will be, to a large extent, outside history. Even where their procreative labor is subject to historical development, it will ultimately be as a function of production, and so they will be the objects rather than the subjects of historical change. They will not be able to control their own destiny through a collective transformation of the mode of procreation. These points are not made explicitly by Marxist theory, which deals with procreation primarily by ignoring it, but they are consequences of the traditional Marxist approach to procreation. They imply that women, who are the primary procreative laborers, are biologically determined to a greater extent than men. Consequently, the hidden implication of Marxist theory is that women are less fully human than men.

As we shall see in future chapters, contemporary feminists are challenging this conception of procreation. Their challenge takes many forms. Some feminists distinguish conceptually between different aspects of procreation, separating the prenatal from the postnatal processes and arguing that, while men cannot bear children, there is no reason why they cannot rear them. Other feminists claim that recent technological advances have made it possible for the first time to overcome even the sexual division of prenatal labor. They point to such developments as artificial insemination, extra-uterine fertilization and even extra-uterine gestation. Other feminists still raise questions about the assumption that changes in procreation depend ultimately on changes in production and suggest that, conversely, the mode of procreation may partially determine production. For instance, these feminists point out that the organization of capitalist production and the length of the working day under capitalism are predicated on the assumption that someone else is taking care of children in some other place. They suggest, further, that the kind of technology available for procreation is determined by assumptions about who "has" children (there is no "pill" available for men) and about how the children are going to be reared. The general concern of all these feminists is to conceptualize procreation as a historical process constituted by the ever-changing dialectical relationship between human reproductive biology and the forms of social organization. Only by conceptualizing procreation in this way, they believe, will it become possible to discover, for instance, how far the organization of procreation in earlier societies was biologically inevitable, given the low level of development of the forces of production. And only by answering this question, they believe, will it be possible to discover whether or not early women were oppressed. Similarly, feminists believe that only by conceptualizing procreation as a historical process will it be possible to discover how far the contemporary division of labor in procreation is biologically inevitable and how far it is an indication of women's oppression. Finally, feminists believe that only this conceptual approach will reveal the real possibilities of transforming and democratizing the process of procreation.

Marxist theory was not designed primarily to provide an account of women's nature and women's oppression. What Marxism has to say about women is peripheral to the central claims of the theory, so that Marxist reflections on women's situation could be dropped entirely without changing the system in any substantial way. Instead, Marxism was designed to explain how a minority of individuals is able to control the lives of the majority because of their control over the productive resources of a society. In order to explain this, Marxists have recourse to their theory of class, a theory which has been enormously successful indeed in providing a unified explanation of many historical phenomena and much of the direction of historical change. In analyzing contemporary society, we have seen that traditional Marxism focuses on human beings in relation to commodity production and in this relation, of course, people appear only as members of classes such as the bourgeoisie or the petit bourgeoisie. They are seen as having neither sex nor gender. Thus, women in the market are viewed simply as workers rather than as women workers.

While women in the market are invisible to Marxist political economy, women in the home are virtually ignored. Verbal acknowledgment is given to the necessity of procreative labor, but this long and complex process receives no theoretical attention. Marxist political economy assumes that, as Sartre puts it, an individual is born at the time of applying for "his" first paid job. Women's procreative labor is not part of commodity production; that is, it is not part of the mode of production that defines capitalist society. Consequently, women who work at home do not have an independent place within a Marxist analysis of capitalism; they take their class position from that of their husbands and fathers. (Often, indeed, women's class position is assumed to be identical with that of their husbands or fathers, even when they do work in commodity production.) The result is an essentially gender-blind picture of social reality.

Social reality, of course, is not at all gender-blind, and on a personal level all political theorists are aware of this. Even on a theoretical level, Marx and Engels not only acknowledge the necessity of procreative labor but make a tremendous contribution in pointing out that women's subordination is not "natural"; that women are indeed oppressed. But the remarkable success of their theory of class has led Marxists to assume that this concept of class is the master key to unlocking the secret of all domination. They assume that the most significant feature of contemporary society is its division into classes; that all history is the history of class struggle. They assume that, as Engels states, class has replaced kinship as the major organizing principle of society.[54] Consequently, they believe that class is what counts in the life of an individual: gender conflict is only apparent; class conflict is real. Thus, while traditional Marxists recognize that there is indeed a "woman question," they interpret this question as asking how women fit into the capitalist system of commodity production.

The traditional Marxist way of formulating the "woman question" assumes that women are oppressed primarily as a result of their exclusion from public production. In contemporary times, this exclusion is disappearing; yet it is far from clear that women's oppression is diminishing. Feminists argue that many manifestations of women's oppression are not captured in the categories of Marxist political economy. Women share common experiences of oppression which, though they may be mediated by class, race and ethnicity, nevertheless cut across class lines. All women are liable to rape, to physical abuse from men in the home, and to sexual objectification and sexual harassment; all women are primarily responsible for housework, while all women who have children are held primarily responsible for the care of those children; and virtually all women who work in the market work in sex-segregated jobs. In all classes, women have less money, power, and leisure time than men.

Marxism's failure to provide an adequate historical account of the sexual division of labor is more than just an omission from the theory. It is an omission that works systematically to obscure women's oppression. Within the conceptual framework of traditional Marxism, some questions cannot be raised. For instance, there seems to be no specifically Marxist way of raising. the question why it is men who routinely beat and rape women, rather than vice versa. Again, given the Marxist conception of class, it makes no sense to ask whether women might occupy a special class position: women in the market share the class of their male co-workers and women outside the market are, in their own right, outside the class system altogether. Finally, given the Marxist conception of procreation as a process that is relatively fixed by biology, it makes no sense to subject this process to political analysis. It makes no sense to raise political questions about what is done in this process and how it is done, about who does the work and who makes the decisions, or about how the organization of procreation might be improved or made more democratic. From the point of view of Marxist political economy, men have no special privileges and there are no special needs and interests that are shared by women and which are in opposition to the interests of men. The only exception is women's exclusion from so-called public production, and that is only arguably in the interest of men and is, in any case, rapidly disappearing.

By obscuring women's oppression, Marxist theory provides a rationale for its perpetuation. The biologistic conception of procreation legitimates women's continuing responsibility for procreative labor. This responsibility, in turn, hinders women's full participation in nonprocreative labor and legitimates sex-segregation in that sphere. At the same time, the biologistic conception of procreation leads to the devaluation of procreative labor: women's work may be socially necessary, but it is not fully historical and hence not fully human work. Similarly, the biologistic assumption of heterosexuality, together with the view that men's sex drive is biologically determined to be stronger than that of women, legitimates sexual harassment and rape.[55] Taken together, these biologistic assumptions about procreation legitimate Marxism's focus on the "masculine sphere" of commodity production as the main stage of history and its emphasis on class as the fundamental social division. They obscure the special oppression of women and so legitimate the view that any conflict of interest between the sexes is apparent rather than real. Women's struggle against their oppression itself is delegitimated.

The apparent gender-blindness of Marxist categories is in reality a gender-bias. As we shall see in the next chapter, gender is a constitutive structure of contemporary human society. By concealing this, Marxist theory mystifies social reality and legitimates the continued oppression of women. Insofar as it does this, it is another ideology of male domination.

Just as the traditional Marxist categories of social analysis are apparently gender-blind, so too is the traditional Marxist account of human nature on which they are based. One writer states that Marxism presents us with a conception of human nature that is essentially of "abstract, genderless individuals."[56] The gender-blindness of the traditional Marxist account of human nature, however, like the gender-blindness of Marxist social categories, is apparent rather than real. In fact it is not a conception of humans as genderless but rather a conception of humans as male—and, one might add, as permanently adult. According to the Marxist conception of human nature, human beings create themselves and their world by laboring to transform nature to satisfy their needs. Although this account is apparently gender neutral, Marxists in fact have interpreted "labor" to mean primarily the production and exchange of objects—the kind of work that they associate with men. As I have argued, they exclude much women's work, and especially procreative work, from the category of labor and construe it more as biological processes. So women are excluded from history and even from full humanity. The traditional Marxist account of human nature is in fact androcentric and constitutes the conceptual basis for a political theory that is profoundly gender-biased.

Is it possible to provide a feminist revision of Marxism, one that would view human nature as fully historical even in its procreative aspect? If so, would such a revision challenge the core of Marxist theory? The answers to these questions obviously depend both on the kind of feminist revision one wishes to advocate and on what one takes to be the core of Marxist theory. In Chapter 6, I shall answer both questions in the affirmative, after Chapter 5's discussion of radical feminism.

Notes

1. One example of the controversy surrounding the identification of Marxist theory is Frederic L. Bender's *The Betrayal of Marx* (New York: Harper & Row, 1975). In this book, Bender distinguishes "original Marxian thought" from its alleged distortions by theorists who include Engels, Plekhanov, Lenin, and Stalin.

2. Frederick Engels, *The Origin of the Family, Private Property and the State* (New York: International Publishers, 1972). Since I shall cite this book frequently, I shall often refer to it simply as *"Origin."*

3. My conception of "orthodox" Marxism is essentially that of Georg Lukács in his influential essay "What is Orthodox Marxism?" (in G. Lukács, *History and Class Consciousness: Studies in Marxist Dialectics* [Cambridge, Massachusetts: M.I.T. Press, 1971]). Lukács argues that the core of orthodox Marxism is the historical materialist method, not any particular results of the application of that method.

4. The suggestion that Marx's philosophical conception of human nature was developed in his unpublished rather than his published writings was made by Bertell Ollman at the 4th Annual Conference on the Current State of Marxist Theory, Louisville, Kentucky, November 1979. In his book *Alienation,* Ollman had earlier insisted that there is a basic continuity in Marx's earlier and his later work. This is disputed by Louis Althusser and other scholars.

5. Karsten Struhl suggested this strategy for avoiding the controversy surrounding the work of the early Marx. My present exposition of Marx's theory of human nature has benefited greatly from the paper "Marx's Theory of Human Nature" read by Karsten Struhl to the Radical Caucus at the American Philosophical Association's Western Division meeting in April 1978. The paper is still unpublished.

6. Karl Marx and Frederick Engels, *The German Ideology,* edited with an introduction by C.J. Arthur (New York: International Publishers, 1970), p. 42. Marx always uses the masculine gender, "man," "he," etc., in contexts where he purports to be referring to all human beings. Later I shall argue that Marx is in fact thinking primarily of male human beings and that this focus leads him to ignore some fundamentally important features of human nature.

7. Karl Marx, *Capital: A Critique of Political Economy,* vol. 1 (New York: International Publishers, 1967), p. 178.

8. Thanks to Rebecca Hanscom for this information about the history of "praxis."

9. Throughout history, there have been persistent reports of feral children, abandoned as infants, who have somehow survived. Often they are said to have been raised by animals, such as wolves. In his *Wolf Children and the Problem of Human Nature* (New

York: Monthly Review Press, 1972), Lucien Malson investigates some of these cases and the failure of the children to develop "normally" even when rescued. Malson concludes that "without education, there is scarcely the possibility of man, let alone the promise" (p. 80).

10. Marx and Engels, *The German Ideology*, p. 48.

11. Ibid., p. 49.

12. Frederick Engels, "The Part Played by Labor in the Transition from Ape to Man," in Karl Marx and Frederick Engels, *Selected Works* (New York: International Publishers, 1968), p. 359.

13. Karl Marx, "Wage Labor and Capital," in Marx and Engels, *Selected Works*, p. 81.

14. Karl Marx, "Preface to *the Critique of Political Economy*," in Marx and Engels, *Selected Works*, p. 29.

15. Karl Marx, *Theses on Feurbach*, no. 6 in Marx and Engels, *Selected Works*, p. 29.

16. "The Communist Manifesto" in Marx and Engels, *Selected Works*, p. 35. In fact this claim is hyperbolic. As Marx and Engels well knew, there are pre-class societies.

17. The concept of "character structure" derives originally from the psychoanalytic tradition and was then found useful for certain concerns of social psychology. Freud used the idea of "character" to designate a relatively permanent set of habitual attitudes that develop primarily in infancy, and which determine the general way in which a person thinks and reacts to the world. The concept "character structure" as such was first given a more elaborate treatment by Wilhelm Reich, who thought of it as a total configuration of general modes of expression and reaction, including defense mechanisms, personality traits, behavior patterns, somatic orientations, and the like. Karsten Struhl, "Human Nature," p. 49.

18. *Capital*, vol. 1, p. 645.

19. Ibid., p. 360.

20. Karl Marx, *Grundrisse: Foundations of the Critique of Political Economy*, translated with a foreword by Martin Nicolas (New York: Vintage Books, 1973), p. 611.

21. Ibid., pp. 611–12.

22. Ibid., p. 488.

23. Karl Marx, "Preface to *The Critique of Political Economy*," in Marx and Engels, *Selected Works*, p. 182. Cf. also the statement that "life is not determined by consciousness but consciousness by life," Marx and Engels, *The German Ideology*, p. 67.

24. Ibid., p. 183.

25. *Theses on Feurbach*, vol. 11 in Marx and Engels, *Selected Works*, p. 30.

26. Marx and Engels, *The German Ideology*, p. 51.

27. Engels, *Origin*, p. 119.

28. Ibid., p. 113.

29. Ibid., p. 119.

30. Ibid., p. 120.

31. Ibid., pp. 128–29.

32. Ibid., p. 135.

33. Marx and Engels, *The German Ideology*, p. 49.

34. *Origin*, pp. 137-38.

35. Marx, *Capital*, pp. 489-90.

36. *The German Ideology*, p. 51.

37. *Capital*, pp. 77-78.

38. Ibid., p. 351.

39. Karl Marx, *Critique of the Gotha Programme*, in Marx and Engels, *Selected Works*, p. 334.

40. Compare *Capital*, pp. 257(n), 399, 464, 498-99. I owe these references to Sandra Bartky.

41. Karl Marx, *The Economic and Philosophic Manuscripts of 1844*, edited with an introduction by Dirk J. Struik (New York: International Publishers, 1964), p. 134.

42. *Origin*, p. 128.

43. Eli Zaretsky, "Capitalism, the Family and Personal Life," *Socialist Revolution:* Part 1, nos. 13/14, pp. 69–125; Part 2, no. 15, pp. 19–70. Reprinted by Canadian Dimension and by Harper, 1976.

44. Selma James & Mariarosa Dalla Costa, *The Power of Women and the Subversion of Community* (Bristol: Falling Wall Press, 1973).

45. Paddy Quick, "The Class Nature of Women's Oppression," *The Review of Radical Political Economics* 9, no. 3:42-53.

46. Wilhelm Reich, *Sex-Pol: Essays, 1929-34,* edited by Lee Baxandall (New York: Vintage Books, 1972).

47. Juliet Mitchell, *Psychoanalysis and Feminism* (New York: Vintage Books, 1975).

48. Irene Bruegel, "What Keeps the Family Going?" *International Socialism* 2, no. 1: 2-15.

49. Heidi I. Hartmann, "The Unhappy Marriage of Marxism and Feminism: Towards a More Progressive Union," in Lydia Sargent, ed., *Women and Revolution* (Boston: South End Press, 1981), pp. 10-11.

50. One problem is that much of the evidence in favour of the claim that women have been subordinated universally has been collected and interpreted by men; by men, moreover, who are immersed in the assumptions of western and male-dominated culture. Male observers have tended to focus almost exclusively on the activities of men in the cultures that they have observed. This has been partly due to the fact that, as men, they have been excluded from all-women activities; it has been partly due to the fact that male informants, at least in a colonial situation, have been easier to talk to because they have been the ones to learn a European language; and it has been partly due to the fact that, as men, male anthropologists have been more interested in male activities and, being from a male-dominated culture themselves, have assigned more importance to such activities. The most sophisticated existing defense of the view that the supposed universality of male dominance in fact results from western anthropologists' unconscious assumptions of male dominance is given by Eleanor Leacock in her *Myths of Male Dominance* (New York: Monthly Review Press, 1981).

Anthropologists who have entered a society with male supremacist assumptions have ordinarily found what they expected to find. For instance, they have interpreted the isolation of women's menstrual huts to mean that women were unclean, whereas the isolation of men's huts has been taken to mean that men's activities were sacred. They have failed to note that the male authority they observed was likely to have been enhanced by the impact of colonialism, which often made conscious efforts to strengthen men's power over women. One study even demonstrates that, with respect to the status of aboriginal women, male and female anthropologists have drawn conclusions that totally contradict each other. Male anthropologists have viewed such women as "domestic cows," or as "mere drudges, passing a life of monotony and being shamefully ill-treated by their husbands"; whereas female anthropologists show us "men and women living together in equal partnership, the rights and dignity of the members of both sexes being guaranteed." The authors of this study suggest that the explanation of this extreme divergence in conclusions is that female anthropologists, as women in a sexist society, have developed a kind of "double-consciousness" that helps them in their work by enabling them to combine the "anthropologist's categories" with those of the native. (Ruby Rohrlich-Leavitt, Barbara Sykes, and Elizabeth Weatherford, "Aboriginal Women: Male and Female Anthropological Perspectives," in Rayna R. Reiter, ed., *Toward an Anthropology of Women* [New York: Monthly Review Press, 1975], pp. 110-26. This anthology is a fascinating collection of challenges to conventional and male-biased anthropological assumptions.)

Certainly it is true that western assumptions of male dominance can blind anthropologists to the real authority that women may exercise in primitive societies. On the other hand, the same assumptions can also lead them to assume an authority that is lacking. A good example is the way in which investigations of the position of women have focused usually on descent systems. Finding that a society was matrilineal or matrilocal, anthropologists have often concluded that it was therefore matriarchal. This is what Engels seems to have done when he asserted that the communal household was the basis of female supremacy and when he called the overthrow of mother right (matriliny) "the world historical defeat of the female sex." Nevertheless, although women do seem to have a somewhat higher status in matrilineal and matrilocal societies than they do in patrilineal and patrilocal ones, this certainly does not warrant the inference that women in such societies are the social superiors of men or even their social equals.

51. *Origin*, p. 112.
52. Ibid., pp. 71-72.
53. Marx and Engels, *The German Ideology*, p. 49.
54. *Origin*, p. 72.
55. This assumption is made in numerous places in the Marxist corpus. One of them is where Engels assumes that women had to overcome men's resistance in order to secure the restrictions of sexual relations to a single partner. *Origin*, p. 117.
56. Gayle Rubin, "The Traffic in Women: Notes on the 'Political Economy' of Sex," in Reiter, ed., *Anthropology of Women*, p. 171.

5
Radical Feminism and Human Nature

The liberal and the traditional Marxist conceptions of feminism are rooted in philosophical traditions that are, respectively, 300 and 100 years old. Radical feminism, by contrast, is a contemporary phenomenon generated by the women's liberation movement of the late 1960s. This is not to say that certain ingredients of radical feminist thought were not prefigured by earlier thinkers. It is invariably possible to find precursors of even the most apparently novel and radical ideas in the literature and philosophy of an earlier time: some of Marx's central ideas, for instance, were foreshadowed for centuries before his birth and may even be traced to Plato. While utilizing some earlier feminist insights, radical feminism is developing a perspective on women's situation that in many ways is startlingly original, for it presents a fundamental challenge both to the liberal and to the Marxist ways of conceptualizing human nature and social reality.

Radical feminism is unmistakably a 20th-century phenomenon. Its emphasis on the importance of feelings and so-called person relationships is characteristic of the 20th century, and this emphasis was reflected in the ideals and documents of the new left, which was where women first began articulating the ideas of radical feminism. In addition, although reasonably effective means of contraception had been known for centuries, most women could not be freed from incessant childbearing and childrearing until infant mortality rates dropped and substitutes for human milk became widely available. Consequently, although the drudgery of women's traditional work had long been acknowledged, not until the 20th century did the possibility of minimizing and perhaps even abolishing the burden of women's traditional responsibility for childbearing and childrearing come to be recognized.

Radical feminism, however, did not burst full-blown into the consciousness of 20th-century women. It was sparked by the special experiences of a relatively small group of predominantly white, middle-class, college-educated, American women in the late 1960s. Some of them had been active in the recently formed National Organization for Women, which they perceived as being too conservative in its demands; others had been involved in various new left organizations, in civil rights organizing or in the movement opposing American involvement in Vietnam. The latter were shocked and outraged by their experience of sexual domination in organizations supposedly devoted to peace, justice and the end of oppressive institutions. As these women discussed their experiences and the systematic and widespread nature of their oppression became apparent to all, they came to feel that their primary political task must be to explore, to explain and to combat the oppression of women. Their self-designation as radical feminists originally signified their commitment to uncovering and eradicating the systematic or root causes of women's oppression. Later this label also came to indicate the radical feminist belief that the oppression of women was at the root of all other systems of oppression.

Since its birth in the late 1960s, radical feminism has changed a great deal. Most of the younger radical feminists no longer have previous political experience in left organizations, their thinking is less influenced by Marxist categories and they no longer address themselves to a left audience. Radical feminists regularly produce writings of striking power and originality but radical feminists are not identified by adherence to an explicit and systematic political theory. Instead, they are part of a grass-roots movement, a flourishing women's culture concerned with providing feminist alternatives in literature, music, spirituality, health services, sexuality, even in employment and technology. This culture is strongest in the United States but also exists in other industrialized nations. Because of the nature of their political practice, some of those whom I identify as radical feminists might now prefer to call themselves cultural feminists or lesbianfeminists.

The most important insights of radical feminism probably spring from women's own experience of oppression, but the grass-roots radical feminist movement is also influenced by many other traditions, from astrology to zen. Naturally, it is not easy to make all these ideas consistent with each other and radical feminism has generated a variety of theories about women's oppression. This variety is an indication of the originality and vitality of the movement. Out of the political and intellectual ferment of radical feminism, many important insights have emerged. Although these insights are not yet embedded in a single unified theory of women's liberation, they are grounded in a common political practice and on certain widely, though not universally, shared assumptions about human nature and social reality.

The early radical feminists of the 1960s came from a common class background and had similar political experiences. Today, those who are attracted to radical feminism still tend to be primarily white and college-educated. The similar class background and educational experience of radical feminists not only generated new insights about the situation of women in contemporary society; they also made it difficult for many radical feminists to perceive certain other aspects of women's experience, particularly the experiences of working-class women and women of color. In addition, as we shall see, early radical feminist theory was influenced and limited by the categories of prevailing academic thought. Some radical feminists are now moving beyond the early attempts at theory; they are making efforts to avoid the false universalization of women's experience and to develop categories of analysis that are materialist, rather than idealist, and dynamic, rather than static. This increasing theoretical sophistication results partly from the influence of a small group of French radical feminist writers. Radical feminism is thus changing rapidly, and my characterization of its theory may soon be outdated. Yet while it may be even more transitory than other political theories, radical feminist theory is still worth examining both because of its strengths and because of its weaknesses. On the one hand, radical feminism has revealed a radically new perspective on social reality which should fundamentally and permanently transform traditional political theory. On the other hand, radical feminism often is still unable to free itself from conventional, especially biologistic, ways of thinking. To develop a fully adequate theory of women's liberation, it is necessary to understand both the contribution of radical feminism and the conceptual mistakes that some radical feminists have made.

One of the first sustained and systematic works by a contemporary radical feminist was Shulamith Firestone's *The Dialectic of Sex.*[1] The opening words of this book are "Sex class is so deep as to be invisible," and they express the most profound insight of radical feminism. This is that distinctions of gender, based on sex, structure virtually every aspect of our lives and indeed are so all-pervasive that ordinarily they go quite unrecognized.[2] Instead of appearing as an alterable feature of our social organization, gender constitutes the unquestioned framework in terms of which we perceive and interpret the world. Gender constitutes the spectacles whose influence on our vision goes unnoticed until they are removed.

Radical feminism seeks to remove the spectacles. It makes visible distinctions between the sexes not only in the obvious areas of law and employment, but also in our personal relationships in the home, in bed, and even in our internalized perceptions of ourselves. Radical feminism shows how, in contemporary society, distinctions of gender structure the whole of life: men and women dress differently, eat differently, engage in different activities at work, at home and in their leisure time, and have different kinds of social relationships, including sexual relationships. Feminists for more than 200 years have recognized a sense in which women are made rather than born, but radical feminists have driven this insight deeper than before and used it as their main tool in constructing a comprehensive critique of women's oppression.

Radical feminism argues that gender is not only the way in which women are differentiated socially from men; they see it also as the way in which women are subordinated to men. The genders are not "different but equal." Instead, gender is an elaborate system of male domination. The theoretical task of radical feminism is to understand that system; its political task is to end it.

Radical Feminist Conceptions of Human Nature

The theoretical variety within radical feminism results in part from the fact that radical feminists have not yet succeeded in establishing a new feminist paradigm of human nature. Although they do share some common assumptions, different theorists have grounded their work on different views of human nature. Rather than explaining "the" radical feminist conception of human nature, therefore, this section will outline four different conceptions. In my view, these conceptions reflect a growing political radicalism and a deepening theoretical sophistication on the part of radical feminism.

1. SEX ROLES AND ANDROGYNY

In the late 1960s, feminists were paradoxically exhilarated by their rediscovery of women's oppression. Women's lives were transformed by the radical feminist shift in perspective that redefined women's problems not as symptoms of individual failure but as symptoms of oppression by a system of male dominance. Almost daily, fresh insights confirmed the superiority of the new perspective. Not only apparently "external" problems, such as sexual harassment and job discrimination, but even apparently "internal" problems, such as indecisiveness or inability to reach orgasm, were diagnosed as results of male gender privilege. Because the problem now seemed so clear, early radical feminists assumed that the solution was equally clear. If the problem was gender, then gender must be eliminated: the goal of feminism must be androgyny.

The early radical feminists did not always use the word "androgyny." Kate Millett coined the word "unisex" and that term gained wide currency, although it was taken up more by the mass media to describe the new fashions in clothing and hairstyles than by feminists to describe their new ideal of human nature. Sometimes radical feminists used terminology that may seem inappropriately biological, as when they talked about the "sex-role" or the "male-female" system. Whatever terminology they used, however, radical feminists agreed that the solution was to eliminate social distinctions between the sexes. One radical feminist put it this way: "There shall be no characteristic, behavior or roles ascribed to any human being on the basis of sex."[3] Similarly, "The Feminists," an influential, New York–based, radical feminist group, defined themselves as "A Political Organization to Annihilate Sex Roles" and stated:

> The sex roles themselves must be destroyed. If any part of these role definitions is left, the disease of oppression remains and will reassert itself again in new, or the same old, variations throughout society.
>
> We need a new premise for society: that the most basic right of an individual is to create the terms of its own definition.[4]

Like all political theorists, these early radical feminist authors made certain assumptions about human nature. As women emerging from a society saturated by liberal ideology, it was inevitable that the early radical feminists should absorb some basic liberal assumptions about human nature. One of their assumptions, implicit in the language of sex-roles, was a strong belief in the possibility and desirability of individual freedom of choice. Sex-role language suggests the abstract individualist belief that human beings exist as actors logically, if not temporally, prior to their entry onto the social stage. When they enter this stage, individuals assume a role that seems appropriate for the time being but that may be discarded at some future date. On this conception of human nature, human beings are not necessarily constituted by society but instead are capable, in principle, of withdrawing from society to redefine their own identity. Thus, an individual is able to throw off the identity imposed by society and can consciously choose her or his own future destiny.

This conception of human nature is essentially that of liberalism, and it is no accident that liberal feminists continue to talk about sex-roles. Radical feminists, however, soon dropped this terminology and its associated perspective on reality. One reason was simply the recalcitrance to change that they encountered in women as well as in men, and in feminist as well as in non-feminist women. Feminist analyses notwithstanding, women did not find it easy to discard the attitudes of a lifetime: to feel positive about their unadorned bodies, to abandon exclusive heterosexuality, to listen to women with the same respect as men, or to enjoy work that involved machinery, mathematics or heavy physical labor. Because of such difficulties, it soon seemed inapt to describe semipermanent character structures in terms of "roles," with the implication that these could be assumed or discarded at will.

Another reason for the abandonment of "sex-role" terminology was a general shift away from psychologically based accounts. In 1969, the New York Radical Feminists had claimed that:

the purpose of the male power group is to fulfill a need. That need is psychological, and derives from the supremacist assumptions of male identity—namely, that the male identity must be sustained through its ability to have power over the female ego. Man establishes his "manhood" in direct proportion to his ability to have his ego override woman's, and derives his strength and self-esteem through this process.[5]

Whether or not this is true, it is obviously incomplete as an explanation of women's subordination. It does not explain why "manhood" has been defined in terms of dominance nor why "womanhood" has been defined as passivity and subservience. Neither does it explain why men should have won the postulated psychological struggle between the sexes: are men *psychologically* stronger than women? In general, even if one were to grant that individuals could modify or abandon their roles at will, to describe women's oppression exclusively in terms of sex-roles would be to ignore questions about why the sex-role system developed and why it is maintained. The need to answer these questions has encouraged radical feminists to seek a less "idealist" and more "materialist" account of women's oppression. In other words, radical feminism has ceased to posit the ideal of a social role as a sort of superhuman pigeon hole into which real people are slotted, and instead has begun to try to identify the "material interests" that are promoted by the systematic domination of women. The remaining three radical feminist views of human nature are all variants of "feminist materialism."

Among the early radical feminists, a commitment to abolishing sex-roles was taken to imply a commitment to androgyny. Androgynous people would remain biologically male or female but, socially and psychologically, they would no longer be masculine or feminine.

Thus if "masculine" violence is undesirable, it is so for both sexes; "feminine" dumb-cow passivity likewise. If "masculine" intelligence or efficiency is valuable, it is so for both sexes equally, and the same must be true for "feminine" tenderness or consideration.[6]

Since the early days, however, androgyny has fallen out of general favor as a radical feminist ideal. Where it has survived, it has been given an interpretation quite different from the usual social/psychological one, as I shall explain later. One problem is that, although the term was designed to express a transcendence of traditional conceptions of masculinity and femininity, in fact it is said to perpetuate those stereotypes by assuming them. "In an 'androgynous' . . . society, it would be senseless to speak of 'androgyny' . . . since people would have no idea of the sex-stereotyped characteristics and/or roles referred to by the components of the term."[7] At best, therefore, "androgyny" should be seen only as a "traditional" or "self-liquidating" word.[8]

We may object that there is no harm in a knowledge of history, that to refer to sex stereotypes is not necessarily to endorse them. But radical feminists find deeper problems with the ideal of androgyny. Mary Daly has argued that the notion of androgyny suggests "two distorted halves of a human being stuck together—something like John Wayne and Brigitte Bardot scotch-taped together—as if two distorted 'halves' could make a whole."[9] Daly's point is that it is a mistake to conceive of women and men in contemporary society as having been encouraged to develop just "one side" of their personalities, so that men need only to supplement their rationality with emotional expressiveness, and women need only to supplement their gentleness with assertiveness. Within contemporary society, vices as well as virtues are associated with femininity and masculinity. Women are often passive, vain and subservient, while men are often belligerent, reckless, and domineering. To endorse an ideal that implies a conjunction of masculinity and femininity, as these are conceived ordinarily, is as absurd, according to Janice Raymond, as putting "master and slave language or imagery together to define a free person."[10] We need a new ideal of human nature, one not based on a "pseudo-organicism."[11] For some radical feminists, as we shall see later, this new ideal cannot be derived from any mixture of masculinity and femininity as we know them. Instead, it must be a development of the special powers inherent in women.

Even if androgyny were an adequate moral ideal, many radical feminists argue that it would be totally inappropriate as a political objective. Androgyny may be a broad humanistic ideal for both sexes, but it contains no recognition of the fact that, in order to approach that ideal, women and men must start from very different places. Both masculinity and femininity may be distortions of the human personality, but they are distortions of very different kinds. Most notably, being masculine carries benefits that being feminine does not. For radical feminists, it is just not true that masculine and feminine persons can work harmoniously together to reach androgyny. Instead, radical feminists argue that men derive concrete benefits from their oppression of women, and they conclude that feminists must struggle against rather than with men in order to achieve liberation. A general commitment to human liberation, which is implicit in the notion of androgyny, is unobjectionable morally but is always far too broad to be the focus of any political struggle. Feminist activists have to challenge specific forms of women's oppression; to take androgyny as an ideal could serve in practice only to distract them from their focus on these forms. As Adrienne Rich puts it, androgyny "fails in the naming of difference." Radical feminists argue that, because men oppress women, feminists must struggle against men and so must acknowledge the need for separatism and a polarization of the sexes. The ideal of androgyny obscures the necessity of struggle and is simply a form of "cheap grace."[12]

2. WOMEN'S BIOLOGY AS THE PROBLEM

The earlier radical feminists were impressed by their discovery that some form of male privilege existed in every known society. From this, they inferred that women's subordination was universal, that there had never been a time when women were the equals of men. Dissatisfied with psychological explanations of this phenomenon and searching for a "materialist" account, it was inevitable that radical feminists should look to biology to provide an explanation. For the most obviously relevant circumstances shared by male-dominant societies that were so different in other respects seemed to be the biological distinction between women and men.

Anti-feminists have always appealed to biology in their efforts to justify women's subordination. Assuming that human biology is fixed, anti-feminists have concluded that women's subordination is inevitable. Indeed, since they have seen that subordination as designed by "nature" rather than by men, anti-feminists have argued that it does not even constitute a form of oppression. Given the popularity of biological arguments among anti-feminists, at first it may be surprising to discover that radical feminists also appeal to biology. As we shall see, however, radical feminists believe that they can find ways of avoiding the conclusions of the anti-feminists. All the following arguments purport to explain women's subordination in biological terms and all have been characterized, by their authors or by others, as being radical feminist arguments, although not all turn out to be so upon closer examination.

One theory of women's subordination that was promulgated during the 1960s took for its starting point the "scientific discovery," then recently popularized by W. H. Masters and V. E. Johnson, of women's capacity for multiple orgasm.[13] This discovery so impressed the physician Mary Jane Sherfey that she speculated that women's oppression by men was necessary in order to suppress women's *"biologically determined,* inordinately high, cyclic sexual drive."[14] According to Sherfey,

> the *forceful* suppression of women's inordinate sexual demands was a prerequisite to the dawn of every modern civilization and almost every living culture. Primitive woman's sexual drive was too strong, too susceptible to the fluctuating extremes of an impelling, agressive erotism to withstand the disciplined requirements of a settled family life—where many living children were necessary to a family's well-being and where paternity had become as important as maternity in maintaining family and property cohesion. For about half the time, women's erotic needs would be insatiably pursued; paternity could never be certain; and with lactation erotism, constant infant care would be out of the question.[15]

Sherfey worries about the recent "decided lifting of the ancient social injunctions against the free expression of female sexuality." She continues:

> It is hard to predict what will happen should this trend continue—except one thing is certain: if women's sexual drive has not abated, and they prove incapable of controlling it, thereby jeopardizing family life and child care, a return to the rigid, enforced suppression will be inevitable and mandatory. Otherwise the biological family will disappear and what other patterns of infant care and adult relationships could adequately substitute cannot now be imagined.[16]

Sherfey's theory bears an unmistakable resemblance to ancient justifications of women's subordination, which also rested on the view of women as sexually insatiable. Her theory is, however, quite original in the context of modern thinking, which has tended to assume the contrary and Victorian view that women are, in general, less interested than men in sexual activity. To the extent that Sherfey argues for the possible necessity of women's continuing subordination, she can hardly be counted as a feminist, let alone a radical feminist. Nevertheless, her article was published without comment in *Sisterhood Is Powerful,* the pioneering and best-selling radical feminist anthology.

Susan Brownmiller provides a different, but also biologically based, account of women's subordination. She writes:

> From the humblest beginnings of the social order based on a primitive system of retaliatory force—the *lex talionis:* an eye for an eye—woman was unequal before the law. By anatomical fiat—the inescapable con-

struction of their genital organs—the human male was a natural predator and the human female served as his natural prey.[17]

On Brownmiller's account, women's original subordination is rooted in the fact that human anatomy allows men the possibility of raping women, while women cannot retaliate in kind.

> This single factor may have been sufficient to have caused the creation of a male ideology of rape. When men discovered that they could rape, they proceeded to do it . . .
> This accomplished, rape became not only a male prerogative, but man's basic weapon of force against woman, the principal agent of his will and her fear. His forcible entry into her body, despite her physical protestations and struggle, became the vehicle of his victorious conquest over her being, the ultimate test of his superior strength, the triumph of his manhood.
> Man's discovery that his genitalia could serve as a weapon to generate fear must rank as one of the most important discoveries of prehistoric times, along with the use of fire and the first crude stone axe. From prehistoric times to the present, I believe, rape has played a critical function. It is nothing more or less than a conscious process of intimidation by which *all men* keep *all women* in a state of fear.[18]

Since human genital construction has remained relatively unchanged since prehistoric times, Brownmiller's account seems to imply that women will continue to be subordinated through the continuing threat of rape. Brownmiller avoids this conclusion by advocating that women be fully integrated into the state apparatus for legislating against rape and for enforcing that legislation. Thus she relies on the power of a sexually integrated state to protect women from sexual assault. She assumes that, without such protection, weaker individuals will always be at the mercy of stronger ones who seek constantly, by all possible means, to achieve power over others. As soon as they are made explicit, it is obvious that Brownmiller's Hobbesian assumptions about human motivation and her views about the functions of the state are essentially those of the liberal. Although she is often taken to be a radical feminist and her work contains many radical insights, Brownmiller must be characterized in the end as a liberal feminist.

The most distinctive and original of these biologically based theories has been constructed by Shulamith Firestone.[19] As is suggested by the title of her book, *The Dialectic of Sex,* Firestone is influenced by Marxism, and she consciously attempts to provide an account of women's subordination that is both historical and materialist. Firestone believes that Marx's and Engels' interpretation of the historical materialist method was too narrow, since it focused primarily on the way in which the production of food, shelter, clothing, etc., was organized and paid little attention to procreation. For Firestone, however, the relations of procreation, rather than production, constitute the base of society; what is ordinarily called the economy is better viewed as part of the superstructure. She claims that "beneath economics, reality is psycho-sexual" (p.5) and concludes that the primary class division is that between women and men. Working from these assumptions, Firestone produces a revision of the famous definition that Engels gives of historical materialism in his *Socialism: Utopian or Scientific.* The following is Firestone's revised definition:

> Historical materialism is that view of the course of history which seeks the ultimate cause and the great moving power of all historic events in

the dialectic of sex: the division of society into two distinct biological classes for procreative reproduction, and the struggles of these classes with one another; in the changes in the modes of marriage, reproduction and childcare created by these struggles; in the connected development of other physically-differentiated classes (castes); and in the first division of labor based on sex which developed into the (economic-cultural) class system.

"All past history (note that we can now eliminate "with the exception of primitive stages") was the history of class struggle. These warring classes of society are always the product of the modes of organization of the biological family unit for reproduction of the species, as well as of the strictly economic modes of production and exchange of goods and services. The sexual-reproductive organization of society always furnishes the real basis, starting from which we can alone work out the ultimate explanation of the whole superstructure of economic, juridical and political institutions as well as of the religious, philosophical and other ideas of a given historical period" [pp. 12–13].

Thus Firestone sees herself as developing "a materialist view of history based on sex itself" (p. 5). She claims to

enlarge historical materialism to *include* the strictly Marxian, in the same way that the physics of relativity did not invalidate Newtonian physics so much as it drew a circle around it, limiting its application—but only through comparison—to a smaller sphere [p. 5].

Using her revised conception of historical materialism, Firestone concludes that the sexual division of labor has a biological base. She argues that human reproductive biology has dictated a form of social organization that she calls "the biological family." She believes that the basic reproductive unit of male/female/infant has persisted in every society and throughout every transformation of what Marxists call the mode of production. The persistence of this unit is the result of two universal features of the human biological constitution: that women are physically weaker than men as a result of their reproductive physiology, and that infants are physically helpless relative to adults. These biological relationships necessitate certain social relationships, if women and infants are to survive. Women must depend on men for physical survival and infants must depend on adults; since human milk, or a close substitute, is one of an infant's primary needs, infants depend primarily on adult women. Firestone concludes:

That a basic mother/child interdependency has existed in some form in every society, past or present, and thus has shaped the psychology of every mature female and every infant.

That the natural reproductive difference between the sexes led directly to the first division of labor at the origins of class, as well as furnishing the paradigm of caste (discrimination based on biological characteristics) [pp. 8–9].

Although Firestone locates the basis of women's subordination in the facts of human reproductive biology, she believes that biological imperatives are overlaid by social institutions, particularly sexual and child-rearing practices, that reinforce male dominance. Firestone describes, in essentially Freudian terms, the development in girls and boys respectively of "feminine" and "masculine" personalities. It is this development that equips men to win the psychological battle of the sexes identified by the New York Radical Feminists. In spite of her underlying reliance on a biological explanation, Firestone's reinterpretation of Freudian theory "de-biologizes" Freud by claiming that the development of the feminine and masculine personalities is not a direct and inevitable response to observed physiological differences between the sexes, but rather a reaction to differences in the perceived *social power* of women and men. Thus, penis envy is not the envy of a physical organ, but rather the envy of the social power of the male. In a further attack on biological determinism, Firestone challenges conventional assumptions about the biological inevitability of childhood, arguing instead that it is a social invention. She also provides exciting and insightful analyses of the ways in which male dominance is expressed and strengthened through the contemporary ideology of love and romance. She even interprets racism as grounded ultimately in male dominance.

Despite the influence of social institutions, however, Firestone believes that their power derives ultimately from what she thinks of as their material base in the human biological constitution. The patriarchal family, which generates the typically masculine and feminine character structures, is determined itself by the biologically given weakness and dependence of women and children. Ultimately, for both Freud and Firestone, anatomy determines destiny. Where Firestone differs from Freud is in her refusal to accept the destiny of male dominance and her consequent determination to change anatomy—or, at least, to change human reproductive biology.

Firestone believes that developments in technology have now made it possible, for the first time in history, to transform the biological basis of women's subordination. She has in mind, on the one hand, reliable contraceptive technology and, on the other, extra-uterine gestation, or what is popularly called test-tube babies. She argues that these technological developments now make it possible to eliminate the basic and hitherto biologically determined sexual division of labor. Finally, there can be "*The freeing of women from the tyranny of their reproductive biology by every means available, and the diffusion of the childbearing and childrearing role to the society as a whole, men as well as women*" (p. 206; italics in original).

As Firestone describes her proposal, it goes beyond a challenge to gender or to the sexual division of labor. She views it as an attack on "the sex *distinction* itself" (p. 11; italics in original). In one sense, it is obviously false that she is attacking the sex distinction: she is not proposing physical androgyny or hermaphrodism. Her goal is rather that there should be a transformation of procreation such that "genital distinctions between the sexes would no longer matter culturally" (p. 11). As Firestone understands this transformation of procreation, however, it would be quite unlike any transformations that have occurred or might occur within the sphere of production. Nor would it involve merely the replacement of one set of cultural practices by another. Instead, it would be the imposition of a set of consciously designed and deliberately chosen cultural practices onto a sphere of human life where the practices until now had been determined by human biology. Thus, Firestone sees it as a victory over "the Kingdom of Nature" (p. 9). "(T)he 'natural' is not necessarily a 'human' value. Humanity has begun to outgrow nature: we can no longer justify the maintenance of a discriminatory sex class system on grounds of its origins in Nature" (p. 10).

In the last section of this chapter, in the context of examining the various radical feminist conceptions of human nature, I shall look more closely at Firestone's assumptions about the line between nature and culture. For the moment, it is enough to note the significance of Firestone's work in attempting to provide a systematic and feminist account of women's subordination that deals comprehensively with such apparently diverse issues as human reproductive biology, childhood and racism. Later theorists must now consider the links between these issues.

In spite of the power and originality of Firestone's theory, it was never taken up by grass-roots radical feminism. The reason for this was not its inaccessibility as a theoretical work; Mary Daly's *Gyn/Ecology* is much less readable but has been extraordinarily popular with the grass-roots radical feminist movement. My guess is that there are several related reasons for the unpopularity of Firestone's work. One may be her belief that advanced technology is a prerequisite for women's liberation. Women in general are not trained in technology, and they know that it is controlled by men. Radical feminists observe that technology, especially reproductive technology, has been used in the past against women and to reinforce male dominance; they do not see how women could take control of advanced technology, at least in the short term, and use it for their own ends. Even apart from the fact that technology is male-controlled, it is viewed with suspicion by a significant counter-culture in all the advanced industrial nations. The catastrophic effects of contemporary technology are receiving increasing publicity: nuclear fall-out, toxic wastes, hazardous industrial materials, contaminated food, air and water pollution, even threats to human health from sophisticated medical technology. The general reaction against technology has stimulated a "back to nature" movement, which has influenced many radical feminists. For this reason, too, they are unlikely to be attracted by Firestone's liberation strategy, which she describes so unabashedly as "artificial" (p. 11) and a victory over "nature." The final problem with Firestone's theory, from the perspective of many radical feminists, lies perhaps in the fact that she does not hold men responsible for the system of male dominance. Instead, it is female biology that is at fault, and men appear in her theory as being ultimately women's protectors. Consequently, Firestone does not stress the need for a political struggle against male power; and her vision of the good society, as the full integration of women, men, and children into all areas of life, is clearly a version of the androgynous ideal. These politics do not fit comfortably with the increasingly militant and separatist tendencies of the grass-roots radical feminist movement.

3. WOMEN'S BIOLOGY AS THE SOLUTION

Since the early 1970s, radical feminists have become increasingly reluctant to locate the cause of women's subordination in anything about women themselves. For radical feminism, accounts which see the problem as stemming from either women's psychology or women's biology simply blame the victim, and are further expressions of the misogyny that pervades contemporary society. In consequence, many recent radical feminist writings have tended to see the fault as some flaw in male biology.

The belief that male biology is somehow to blame for women's subordination has been strengthened by research during the 1970s, research prompted in part by feminist agitation. This research has revealed that physical force plays a far larger part in controlling women than previously had been acknowledged. In Ohio, for instance, the report of the State Attorney General suggests that at least 50 percent of marriages involve some physical abuse of the wife, and other statistics show that half the women in the United States suffer beating at least once—and usually more than once. Rape is another form of physical assault, and it is estimated that a rape occurs every two minutes in the United States. If present trends continue, one out of every three women in the United States will be sexually assaulted in her life time. These figures are staggering, but their significance lies not only in their effects on the lives of those women unlucky enough to be the direct victims, but also in their more subtle effects on the lives of those who are lucky enough to avoid beatings or rape. Whether or not she is actually assaulted, the knowledge that assault is a permanent possibility influences the life of every woman. Women are afraid to hitchhike, to take walks in the moonlight, to travel at night by bus or on a subway, to frequent certain areas of the city or campus. This fear restricts women's areas of residence, their social and political activities and, of course, their study and work possibilities. If they live with a potentially abusive man, and at least half of all men are potentially abusive, much of women's attention goes to avoid "provoking" assault. Women live so constantly with the fear of physical violence that they may not notice it until it is removed, often at women-only feminist events. The recognition that women live continually under the threat of physical violence from men has led many radical feminists to the conviction that men are dangerously different from women and that this difference is grounded in male biology.

One example of this conviction is a mimeographed document circulated in 1973.[20] The radical feminist authors of this document speculate that men dominate women because men are innately more aggressive than women, due to the effects on the brain of the male hormone, testosterone. It is interesting to note that this is exactly the same explanation of male supremacy as that given by the anti-feminist writer Steven Goldberg, whose book, *The Inevitability of Patriarchy,* enjoyed a brief notoriety in the mid-70s.[21] The radical feminists avoid Goldberg's conclusion by suggesting that women should form their own societies from which men are excluded. This suggestion is elaborated in *The Wanderground,* a utopian novel that has become very popular among radical feminists.[22]

For some radical feminists, the main problem with male biology is simply that it is not female. At its most obvious, this has meant that men lack the special life-giving power that women possess in virtue of their biological capacity to become mothers. Except for a very few privileged women, however, being a mother has always involved caring for a child as well as giving birth to it; motherhood is associated conventionally not just with female reproductive biology, but with certain psychological qualities such as nurturance, warmth, emotional expressiveness, endurance and practical commonsense. Most feminists have been at pains to argue that this association results simply from the social fact that mothers have always provided childcare. For some radical feminists, however, there is a biological as well as a social connection between women's manifestation of these psychological qualities and their biological ability to become mothers. In the early 1970s Jane Alpert, a member of the Weather Underground, wrote the following to *Ms.* Magazine:

It seems to me that the power of the new feminist culture, the powers which were attributed to the ancient matriarchies (considered either as historical or as mythic archetypes), and the inner power with which many women are beginning to feel in touch and which is the soul of feminist art, may all arise from the same source. That source is none other than female biology: the *capacity* to bear and nurture children. It is conceivable that the intrinsic *biological* connection between mother and embryo or mother and infant gives rise to those *psychological* qualities which have always been linked with women, both in ancient lore and in modern behavioral science. Motherhood must be understood here as a potential which is imprinted in the genes of every woman; as such it makes no difference to this analysis of femaleness whether a woman ever has borne, or ever will bear, a child.[23]

The contemporary radical feminist movement is characterized by a general celebration of womanhood, a striking contrast to the devaluation of women that pervades the larger society. This celebration takes many forms. Women's achievements are honored; women's culture is enjoyed; women's spirituality is developed; lesbianism is the preferred expression of sexuality. In addition, women's bodies are celebrated, particularly those aspects that have been devalued in male-dominated society. In conscious opposition to the stereotyped models of female beauty that are acknowledged under "the patriarchy," radical feminism glorifies the physical variety of women's bodies and gives special respect to those parts and processes that the male dominant culture has considered to be unclean. Rather than being "the curse" of God, for instance, menstruation is viewed as the blessing of the Goddess.

Contemporary radical feminist writings abound with references to "the power inherent in female biology"[24] and "the creative power that is associated with female biology."[25] Mary Daly, for instance, appears to endorse the "native talent and superiority of women."[26] None of these authors attempts to provide a systematic account of just what are women's special powers, other than their capacity to give birth, nor of the relation of these powers to female biology. Moreover, the authors' style of writing is invariably poetic and allusive rather than literal and exact. But there is a repeated suggestion that women's special powers lie in women's special closeness to non-human nature. The radical feminist author Susan Griffin, for instance, has written a very popular book that draws parallels between men's attitudes toward women and their attitudes toward non-human nature. Of course, as we shall see later, such parallels are capable of a number of interpretations, but Griffin herself suggests that women and non-human nature are inseparable from each other.

We know ourselves to be made from this earth. We know this earth is made from our bodies. For we see ourselves. And we are nature. We are nature seeing nature. We are nature with a concept of nature. Nature weeping. Nature speaking of nature to nature.[27]

Women's special closeness with nature is believed to give women special ways of knowing and conceiving the world.[28] Radical feminists reject what they see as the excessive masculine reliance on reason, and instead emphasize feeling, emotion and nonverbal communication. In the following passage, Susan Griffin shows how men have defined reason so as to exclude and oppress women. The italics are all in the original.

Reason
They said that in order to discover truth, they must find ways to separate feeling from thought *Because we were less* That measurements and criteria

must be established free from emotional bias *Because they said our brains were smaller* That these measurements can be computed *Because we were built closer to the ground* according to universal laws *Because according to their tests we think more slowly, because according to their criteria our bodies are more like the bodies of animals, because according to their calculations we can lift less weight, work longer hours, suffer more pain, because they have measured these differences and thus these calculations, they said,* constitute objectivity *because we are more emotional than they are* and based they said only on what *because our behavior is observed to be like the behavior of children* is observably true *because we lack the capacity to be reasonable* and emotions they said must be distrusted *because we are filled with rage* that where emotions color thought *because we cry out* thought is no longer objective *because we are shaking* and therefore no longer describes what is real *shaking in our rage, because we are shaking in our rage and we are no longer reasonable.*[29]

Radical feminists believe that women's ways of understanding the world contrast with "patriarchal" ways of knowing. According to radical feminism, patriarchal thinking imposes polarities on reality, conceptually separating aspects of reality that in fact are inseparable. Patriarchy opposes mind to matter, self to other, reason to emotion and enquirer to object of enquiry. It posits dualisms within which one side of the dualism is superior to the other side and in this way imposes a hierarchy on nature. By contrast with the dualisms of patriarchy, this version of radical feminism claims to be nondualistic. Women are said to recognize that they are part of nature rather than separate from it; consequently, they trust in their direct and intuitive mode of knowing, which perceives the wholeness and oneness of the universe, the way in which "everything is connected with everything else."[30] Many radical feminists believe that this reality is obscured by the artificial hierarchies imposed by patriarchal culture. Women must peel off the patriarchal distortions and uncover the reality beneath.

This tendency in radical feminist writing has an interesting relationship with conventional "patriarchal" views. The long western philosophical tradition equates women and "the feminine" with nature, men and "the masculine" with culture. That tradition has been explicitly misogynistic. Women have been seen as closer to animals, both because they lacked reason and because the functioning of their bodies has been thought to commit them to the repetitive biological reproduction of the species. Men's bodies, by contrast, have been thought to allow them to transcend this biological repetition through the creation of "culture." De Beauvoir expresses the contrast in this way:

On the biological level a species is maintained only by creating itself anew; but this creation results only in repeating the same Life in more individuals. But man assures the repetition of Life while transcending Life through Existence (i.e., goal-oriented, meaningful action); by this transcendence he creates values that deprive pure repetition of all value. In the animal, the freedom and variety of male activities are vain because no project is involved. Except for his service to the species, what he does is immaterial. Whereas in serving the species, the human male also remodels the face of the earth, he creates new instruments, he invests, he shapes the future.[31]

The usual feminist response to this glorification of male culture has been to claim that women's subordination is a cultural or a social, rather than a biological, phenomenon and to deny that women's bodies inevitably involve women more closely than men with nature. The contemporary radical feminists whom we are considering, however, have taken the unusual step of accepting the claim that women are indeed closer to nature than men, but then have claimed that this is a source of special strength, knowledge and power. Culture does not transcend nature; instead, it disguises and mutilates it. Women's task is to

> find our way back to reality by destroying the false perceptions of it inflicted upon us by the language and the myths of Babel. We must learn to dis-spell the language of phallocracy, which keeps us under the spell of brokenness. This spell splits our perceptions of our Selves and of the cosmos, overtly and subliminally. Journeying into our Background will mean recognizing that both the "spirit" and the "matter" presented to us in the father's foreground are reifications, condensations. They are not really "opposites," for they have much in common: both are dead, inert. This is unmasked when we begin to see through patriarchal language.[32]

Given that these radical feminists make an explicit commitment to overcoming "patriarchal dualisms," one might suppose that their ideal of human nature would be the ideal of androgyny, of transcending the patriarchal opposition between masculinity and femininity. In fact, however, this is not so. On the one hand, many radical feminists deny that the patriarchal polarities of mind-body, masculine-feminine, and even male-female are ontologically basic. On the other hand, some of the same radical feminists believe that the long history of patriarchal oppression has established these polarities deeply in our experience. Androgyny implies a mixture of masculine and feminine qualities but, for many radical feminists, the most valuable qualities are those that are special to women.

> Feminist culture is based on what is best and strongest in women, and as we begin to define ourselves as women, the qualities coming to the fore are the same ones a mother projects in the best kind of nurturing relationship to a child: empathy, intuitiveness, adaptability, awareness of growth as a process rather than as goal-ended, inventiveness, protective feeling toward others, and a capacity to respond emotionally as well as rationally.[33]

The human ideal, therefore, is that of a woman—but not of a woman under patriarchy, where women are diminished and mutilated, even though they are never reduced to the moral or spiritual level of men. Thus the human ideal is that of a woman who has been able to develop her full human powers, the powers that have been suppressed, though not eliminated, by the patriarchy. We cannot know in advance how far these powers extend. In *The Wanderground,* Sally Gearhart fantasizes that eventually women may develop the extraordinary mental powers of "mindstretch" and "lonth." A popular button sums up the ideal: "The Future is Female."

It is undoubtedly a healthy and revolutionary impulse that generates this radical feminist celebration of women. Radical feminists challenge the woman-hating values of patriarchy by turning them on their head. They glorify women precisely for the same reasons that men have scorned and sometimes feared them; in so doing they give special value to women's reproductive functions and to the psychological characteristics that have distinguished women and men. By grasping the nettle so firmly, radical feminists intend not only to crush the sting, but even to produce some celebratory wine.

This bold confrontation with the patriarchy, however, takes place on the patriarchy's own ground. Here the landscape is dominated by sex differences, differences that appear as biologically given. Traditionally, feminists have engaged in a kind of archaeology on this ground. In attempts to show that its features are not prehuman, they have dug to uncover the socially constructed foundations of the hills and valleys. They have sought to demonstrate that the vegetation, including the nettles, has not sprung up spontaneously, but instead has been planted by human hand—and sometimes in quite unsuitable soil. By accepting sex differences as biologically given, many radical feminists in the United States have turned away from the traditional task of feminism. As we shall see, however, a few radical feminists, especially in France, have pushed ahead with the traditional project.

4. "ONE IS NOT BORN A WOMAN"

The distinctive contribution of radical feminism has been to make visible the invisible, to bring into focus the thoroughgoing but previously unacknowledged gender-structuring of human society and human nature. Practices that previously had gone unexamined, often on the assumption that their form was determined by human biological imperatives, were suddenly subjected to political analysis. They included the institutions of childrearing, marriage, housework, prostitution, rape and even heterosexuality. Contemporary French radical feminists, and a very few American ones, are carrying this analysis even further. They are challenging the "naturalness" of childbearing, of the female body, and even of the sex difference itself.

The French radical feminists whose theoretical writings have become most widely known in the United States are a group of intellectuals who have been deeply influenced by Althusserian Marxism, Lacanian psychoanalysis, and Derridian de-constructionist philosophy.[34] Although they call their approach "feminist materialist," like a number of radical feminists in the United States, the European intellectual influence makes their work very different from the work of most of their American sisters. In spite of the unavoidable influence of certain male intellectuals, the French radical feminists seek to distinguish themselves from what they see as male thinking. They are trying to elaborate a theory of *écriture féminine* (feminine writing) and also to exemplify that writing. The group includes Christine Delphy, Hélène Cixous and Luce Irigaray, but in the United States its best-known member is Monique Wittig.[35] In 1979, some of the group attended The Second Sex conference in New York City where Wittig presented a short paper, "one is not born a woman."[36] This paper provides an unusually concise outline of a certain feminist materialist approach to human nature, and I shall draw on it heavily in what follows.

Many American radical feminists, as we have seen, take the fact that women give birth to children as being central to women's subordination. Childbirth has been conceived as "natural" and "biological," both by those who seek to tune in to nature and by those who seek to overcome it. Wittig rejects this view. She argues instead that giving birth is a historical process of "forced production." To see birth as a biological given allows

> forgetting that in our societies births are planned (demography), forgetting that we ourselves are programmed to produce children, while this is the only social activity "short of war" that presents such a great danger of death [pp. 70–71].

Wittig denies that even women's bodies are biologically given.

In our case, ideology goes far since our bodies as well as our minds are the product of this manipulation. We have been compelled in our bodies and in our minds to correspond, feature by feature, with the *idea* of nature that has been established for us. Distorted to such an extent that our deformed body is what they call "natural", is what is supposed to exist as such before oppression. Distorted to such an extent that at the end oppression seems to be a consequence of this "nature" in ourselves (a nature which is only an *idea*) [p. 70].

It is misleading to describe this situation as the patriarchal mutilation of women's bodies by men. For Wittig, it is more accurate to say that patriarchy has actually created women and men. She denies that women constitute a "natural group"; instead, she calls the category of woman an "artificial (social) fact" (p. 70).

[Women] appear as though they existed prior to reasoning, belonging to a natural order. But what we believe to be a physical and direct perception is only a sophisticated and mythic construction, an "imaginary formation" which reinterprets physical features through the network of relationships in which they are perceived. (They are seen *black,* therefore they *are* black, they are seen *women,* therefore they *are* women. But before being *seen* that way, they first had to be *made* that way.) [p. 71]

Andrea Dworkin is one of the few American radical feminists who makes a similar point. She is particularly concerned with the way in which we have conceptualized human beings as necessarily either male or female, as falling into one or the other of "two discrete biological sexes."[37] On Dworkin's view, this ontology falsifies the reality that human individuals exhibit a wide variety of cross-sexed characteristics. She gives a number of arguments to support her conclusions that *"We are, clearly, a multisexed species which has its sexuality spread along a vast fluid continuum where the elements called male and female are not discrete"* (p. 183; italics in original). What stops us recognizing this continuum is the fact that our gendered society is structured around the belief that "there are two polar distinct sexes" (p. 175), a belief that it is obviously in most men's interest to perpetuate. Dworkin believes that "we will discover cross-sexed phenomena in proportion to our ability to see them" (p. 181).

Dworkin recognizes not only that our biological theory is a social construct whose categories reflect the interests of the socially dominant group, namely men. Like Wittig, she believes that human biological reality itself is socially constructed, at least in part. She suggests that a process of cultural selection has operated "to ensure that deviant somatypes and cross-sexed characteristics are systematically bred out of the population" (p. 182). Unfortunately, American radical feminists so far have shown little interest in exploring these suggestions.

At the beginning of this chapter, I commented that the talk of early American radical feminists about the "male-female system" might seem inappropriately biological. From the perspective of this version of materialist feminism, however, such talk is not at all inappropriate, because even "male" and "female" are not interpreted as categories that are simply "given" by human biology. On the contrary, for this version of radical feminism it is not just masculinity and femininity, but the very categories of " 'man' and 'woman' that are fictions, caricatures, cultural constructs."[38] As Monique Wittig puts it, "women are a class, which is to say that the category 'woman', as well as 'man', is a political and economic category, not an eternal one" (p. 72).

If this view is correct, it makes no sense for feminists to fight for an ultimate matriarchy or a separatist society, for these ideals would leave unchallenged the patriarchal categories of sex. Dworkin advocates the traditional feminist ideal of androgyny, but her interpretation goes far beyond its usual psychological meaning to a reconceptualization and possibly a physical transformation of human biology. Wittig has much the same goal. It is, literally, to use Firestone's words, "the elimination of the sex distinction itself." Wittig writes, "Our fight aims to suppress men as a class, not through a genocidal, but a political struggle. Once the class 'men' disappears, women as a class will disappear as well, for there are no slaves without masters" (p. 72).

It is in this sense that the goal of these radical feminists is "a sexless society" (p. 72). And it is in this spirit that Wittig and Zeig's *Lesbian Peoples: Material for a Dictionary* omits an entry for "man" and gives the following definition for "woman":

> Obsolete since the beginning of the Glorious Age. Considered by many companion lovers as the most infamous designation. This word was once applied to beings fallen in an absolute state of servitude. Its meaning was "one who belongs to another".[39]

Radical feminism is still in its early stages. Much theoretical work remains to be done in order for it to develop its own feminist conception of human nature. From the various starts that have been made, however, we can already discern the outlines of a feminist challenge to the prevailing androcentric conceptions of human nature. Radical feminism views humans not only as embodied in a specific form, but as having bodies that are created from the bodies of others. It attempts to take theoretical account of the familiar but philosophically neglected facts that all humans begin life as infants, that all are sexed, and that all are sexual beings. This transformed conception of human nature provides the conceptual foundation for a transformed conception of political philosophy.

Sexual Politics:
The Political Theory of Radical Feminism

Radical feminism is far more than an attempt to make existing political theory consistent or to plug its gaps. Instead, it constitutes an entirely new way of perceiving and even identifying political phenomena. We have already seen how Marxism, rather than providing new answers to old questions, redefines the central problems of political philosophy and, in doing so, provides a wider conception of the domain of politics. In an analogous way, radical feminism reconstitutes the problematic of political theory and enlarges still further our conception of the political domain.

Radical feminism is the first approach to politics to take the subordination of women as its central concern. In practically every known society, half the population has been dominated by the other half; yet this fact has been virtually ignored, except in asides, by every traditional political theory. Radical feminism seeks first to delineate the structure of this domination and then to discover how it can be destroyed.

"The personal is political" was a 1960s slogan that encapsulated a basic insight of radical feminism. Although the slogan was adopted by various groups of feminists who gave it a variety of interpretations, radical feminists used it to sum up their recognition that men systematically dominate women in every area of life. On this view, there is no distinction between the "political" and the "personal" realms: every area of life is the sphere of "sexual politics." All relations between women and men are institutionalized relationships of power and so constitute appropriate subjects for political analysis. Much radical feminist theory consists in just such analyses. It reveals how male power is exercised and reinforced through such "personal" institutions as childrearing, housework, love, marriage and all kinds of sexual practices, from rape through prostitution to sexual intercourse itself. The assumption that these institutions and practices are "natural" or of purely individual concern is shown to be an ideological curtain that conceals the reality of women's systematic oppression.

According to radical feminists, this oppression is universal. In spite of the wide cross-cultural variety in ways of organizing sexuality, marriage and child-rearing, radical feminists find underlying commonalities in women's experience. One of the earliest radical feminist theorists, Ti-Grace Atkinson, wrote, "the oppression of women has not changed significantly over time or place,"[40] and others agreed with her.

> The differences of national culture . . . are the superficialities that cover up the fundamental similarity of all national cultures the world over. This fundamental similarity is the split between male culture and female culture. . . .
> Women in practically all parts of the world, whether they are working outside the home or not, have responsibility for the cooking, cleaning and child "raising" chores of the society. This means that most women spend their time with children. This in itself is a cultural split as men go out and mix mainly with other males in the male world outside the home.[41]

In the "sado-rituals" of five very different societies, Mary Daly finds the common meaning of "the re-enactment of goddess murder."[42] She claims that there is a strong sense in which the women who suffer Indian *suttee,* Chinese foot-binding, African genital mutilation, European witchburning and American gynecology are all victims of a common oppression. Similarly, Kathleen Barry's exposé of the worldwide traffic in women, as well as her characterization of pimping as the oldest profession, suggests strongly that women's sexuality has always been controlled by men.[43]

The apparent universality of women's subordination has encouraged radical feminists to conclude that it is the primary or fundamental form of domination. This claim is open to a number of possible interpretations: that women were, historically, the first group to be systematically dominated; that women's subordination causally maintains other forms of domination; that women's subordination is the form of domination that should be tackled first (perhaps because it is causally primary; perhaps because women are in the most acute emergency situation); that the domination of women provides a conceptual model for understanding all other forms of oppression (Firestone's claim). Most radical feminists accept that women's subordination is fundamental in all these senses, although some radical feminists reject one or more of these claims. The answers to the questions posed by these different interpretations are independent of each other to varying degrees. For instance, whether knowledge of the origins of women's subordination has any relevance for contemporary political theory depends on whether women's contemporary subordination is maintained by the same factors that brought it about in the first place. Because so many radical feminists do believe that "the oppression of women has not changed significantly over time or place," they view women's original and contemporary subordination as manifestations of the same phenomenon. Consequently, they often see no reason to distinguish between historical and causal interpretations of the claim that women's oppression is primary or fundamental. The conflation of these two questions can be seen in the following passage:

> All political classes grew out of the male-female role system, were modeled on it, and are rationalized by it and its premises. Once a new class system is established on the basis of this initial one, the new class is then used to reinforce the male-female system. . .
>
> The pathology of oppression can only be fully comprehended in its primary development: the male-female division. Because the male-female system is primary, the freedom of every oppressed individual depends upon the freeing of every individual from every aspect of the male-female system.[44]

Whether or not they believe that women's subordination is primary in the historical sense, radical feminists generally agree that it is primary in the causal sense of constituting the root of many other social problems. For instance, not only class society and racism, but war, violence and the destruction of the environment have all been explained as symptoms of male dominance. These accounts, in turn, are used to justify the radical feminist view that women's liberation is primary in the political sense, because other struggles for social improvement are doomed to failure as long as women remain subordinated.

The belief that there are underlying commonalities in all women's experience of domination supports the radical feminists' claim that women are a class, a class whose membership is defined by sex.[45] The claim that women constituted a class aroused much controversy in the early days of the women's liberation movement, particularly between radical feminist and Marxist theorists. Marxist objections were based on the fear that "To oppose women as a class against men as a class can only result in a diversion of the real [sic] class struggle."[46] The radical feminist movement is now separated so far from the Marxist left that these debates no longer occur. In general, radical feminists no longer feel the need to legitimate their analyses by using quasi-Marxist terminology and American radical feminists, at least, have not attempted recently to provide a theoretical explanation of how women constitute a class. Nevertheless, the radical feminist insistence that women share a common oppression reinforces the assumption that women indeed are a class, and the claim continues to be made, though often in an intuitive and nontheoretical way. It continues in use because it implies not only that male dominance is not "natural," but that it is more than a set of prejudices or an ideology. Instead, the description of women as a class implies that men receive concrete material benefits from their domination and exploitation of women.

Within the sex class system postulated by radical feminism, the ruling class is known as "the patriarchy." (Mary Daly also calls it "the planetary Men's Association.")[47] Literally, "patriarchy" means "rule by the fathers" and, prior to the emergence of radical feminism, the term was used mostly by anthropologists, for whom it has a much narrower meaning. Within anthropology, patriarchal societies are "Old Testament-type pastoral nomads," where the basic social unit consists of the family centering around "one old man whose absolute power over wives, children, herds, and dependents was an aspect of the institution of fatherhood, as defined in the social group in which he lived."[48] Radical feminists, however, use the term much more broadly to refer to all systems of male dominance. For them, "Patriarchy appears to be 'everywhere.' Even outer space and the future have been colonized."[49]

Radical feminists share certain basic assumptions about the political structure of existing reality. Because of their varying conceptions of human nature, they maintain less agreement about the shape of the future and about what should replace the patriarchy. Some radical feminists advocate a gender-free or even a sexless society, while others advocate a matriarchy. Yet even these terms are not unequivocal. For Firestone, the sexless society will require test-tube babies and will be a "communist anarchy," characterized by a sexuality that is "polymorphously perverse"; Wittig, on the other hand, states that the sexless society will not exclude lesbianism because lesbians are not women (p. 74). (For Wittig, of course, "woman" is a social construct that feminists must reject.) Similarly, for some radical feminists, a matriarchy means a society in which women rule or which is even all female; for others, it means simply the reversal of "patriarchal priorities" and the substitution of "matriarchal" for "patriarchal" values.

> In both capitalist and socialist states, the production of things that produce wealth and military power dominates and determines the quality of life in the society. The way in which the next generation is conceived, born, and reared—that is, the mode of reproduction—is dictated by the interests of production.[50]

Matriarchy, by contrast, is "*a society in which production serves the interests of reproduction; that is, the production of goods is regulated to support the nurturance of life.*"[51] "*By 'matriarchy' we mean a society in which all relationships are modeled on the nurturant relationship between a mother and her child.*"[52]

The variety in their conceptions of the good society makes it difficult for radical feminists to agree on a single strategy for women's liberation. It is hard to decide on a route when one is uncertain about one's destination. An additional difficulty is that, although radical feminists share certain basic assumptions about the political structure of social reality, there are some respects in which they differ considerably. Nevertheless, just as a certain characteristic view of how women's liberation should be accomplished is incorporated within the political theories of liberalism and Marxism, so the political theory of radical feminism generates, at least in outline, its own conception of feminist political struggle and how it should be undertaken.

One distinctive feature of the radical feminist strategy for social change is that women's liberation can be accomplished only by separate and autonomous women's organizations. If women are a class, then they must organize as a class to fight their oppression. Since men constitute the class which benefits from women's subordination, only women can be trusted not to betray women's interests. Monique Wittig's *Les Guérillères* is an extremely popular work of fiction in which women become warriors and ride into battle against the armies of men. "They say that they sing with such utter fury that the movement that carries them forward is irresistible. They say that oppression engenders hate. They are heard on all sides crying hate hate."[53] An interesting feature of Wittig's description is that the women begin by exploring and celebrating their genitals, but that later

The women say that they perceive their bodies in their entirety. They say that they do not favor any of its parts on the grounds that it was formerly a forbidden object. They say that they do not want to become prisoners of their own ideology. They say that they did not garner and develop the symbols that were necessary to them at an earlier period to demonstrate their strength. For example they do not compare the vulvas to the sun moon stars. They do not say that the vulvas are like black suns in the shining night.[54]

This softening of the focus on female biology is in line with Wittig's long-term goal of a sexless society but it has not yet been taken up by American radical feminism.

Within the real world, the radical feminist struggle against the patriarchy is usually considerably less dramatic than the pitched battles of Wittig's fictional warriors. How radical feminists actually do challenge the patriarchy depends in part on how they conceptualize it. Some radical feminists view the patriarchy as a transhistorical and all-embracing culture. In the writings of Mary Daly, for instance, patriarchy appears as a seamless web within which all women are trapped. This conception of patriarchy encourages the adoption of a "cultural feminist" strategy for social change. On the one hand, if patriarchy is indeed everywhere, as Daly asserts, then every departure from traditional femininity may seem equally to constitute a challenge to the patriarchy. Becoming a female plumber, organizing a union of secretaries, learning self-defense or coming out as a lesbian may all be equally effective as feminist strategies. On the other hand, the fact that patriarchy is everywhere may seem so overwhelming that the short- and medium-term possibilities of social change may come to be viewed as hopeless. In either case, the totalistic and nonanalytical conception of patriarchy encourages radical feminists to withdraw from what has been viewed traditionally as political action and to turn instead to the creation of an alternative and separate women's culture. In *Gyn/Ecology,* for instance, Mary Daly describes how women are "spooked" by the male control of language and history. She recommends that women "Spook/Speak back" by renaming reality, responding to the "Call of the Wild." Such resistance to male culture is a process of "Exorcism, Escape and Enspiriting." Women's resistance is made possible by "Sparking: The Fire of Female Friendship" and by "Spinning: Cosmic Tapestries," creating a new culture with new symbols, new rituals, even a new language. In general, radical feminists tend to put their main energy not into organizing direct confrontations with "the patriarchy," but rather into developing alternative social arrangements, such as exploring herbal medicine, building women's businesses, creating women's music and rediscovering witch-craft. In chapter 9, I shall examine more carefully this strategy for social change.

Some radical feminist theorists view the patriarchy in a more analytical way. They have made a variety of attempts to uncover the roots of women's subordination or, what is the same thing, to uncover the material basis of patriarchy. They have questioned whether this basis was biological or social and, according to their answers, they have gone on to consider either how the biological imperatives operated or what were the key institutions maintaining women's subordination. For many radical feminists, women are kept in subordination by direct physical coercion, coercion which is sometimes seen as resulting from innate male aggression. In western society, this coercion is institutionalized through rape and battery; in other societies, by other means. For Firestone, as we have seen, childbearing and childrearing, love and romance, are the institutional expressions of another kind of biological imperative. Those radical feminists who are not biological determinists point to a number of different social institutions as basic to women's subordination. For Christine Delphy, "the appropriation and exploitation of their labour within marriage constitutes the oppression common to all women."[55] She agrees with Sheila Cronan that marriage is female slavery.[56] Kathleen Barry sees female *sexual* slavery as fundamental: "for women colonized both the economic and political are based in the sexual."[57] Charlotte Bunch believes that compulsory heterosexuality is basic to women's oppression and writes that "Lesbianism threatens male supremacy at its core."[58] Artemis March looks to "religious and medical institutions and sources as the primary agencies solidifying, enforcing and reproducing male control and misogyny."[59] Catharine MacKinnon writes: "feminism fundamentally identifies sexuality as the primary social sphere of male power"; "sexuality is the linchpin of gender inequality."[60]

Underlying this variety of views about the structure of patriarchy, there does seem to be a certain unity. No matter how they characterize it, many radical feminists seem to agree that the basis of women's subordination is connected somehow with what Marxists call the sphere of reproduction: i.e., it has something to do with sexuality, childbearing and childrearing. Thus radical feminists have not only brought these areas of life within the domain of politics; many of them also seem to believe that these areas of life are fundamental insofar as they determine the organization of what is thought of ordinarily as economic production and other forms of culture. Thus March complains that

> This economic reductionism of gender issues—such as pornography, prostitution . . . , rape, Lesbianism—is one of the most pernicious forms of androcentric thinking that we as feminists have to deal with, and . . . it starkly reveals the heavy investment of Marxism in male supremacy, and its inadequacy to deal with the infrastructural core of society, named the organization of sexuality and gender.[61]

This view has obvious implications for feminist strategy. Rather than organizing around conventional political or economic issues, it implies that feminists should concentrate their main efforts on transforming sexual and procreative practices, since these constitute the material base of women's subordination. On this view, "sexual politics" means not only that the relations between the sexes are political; it means also that any permanent and far-reaching change in that political situation requires a transformation of human sexual arrangements.

Problems with the Radical Feminist Conception of Human Nature

It is tempting to say that the main problem with the radical feminist conception of human nature is that it doesn't yet exist, that radical feminists have not yet agreed on a unified methodological approach to the question of human nature. But although there are differences between the various groups of radical feminists, there are also some areas of fundamental agreement. Those areas of agreement, in my view, constitute both the most important contribution that radical feminism has made to the human nature issue and, simultaneously, the source of the biggest problems in radical feminism as it has been developed so far.

The radical feminist conception of human nature is similar to the Marxist conception insofar as it explicitly rejects metaphysical dualism. Like Marxism, radical feminism insists that human beings are necessarily embodied. This insistence not only frees radical feminism from the persistent metaphysical problems that dog all forms of dualism; as I shall argue in Part III, the emphasis on the indispensability of the body also has far-reaching significance for political theory. The radical feminist conception of the human body, moreover, is less abstract than the traditional Marxist conception. Most notably, it pays specific attention to human reproductive biology. Radical feminists acknowledge explicitly that humans have a sex, that their sex is defined by differences in reproductive physiology, that women bear children, that infant survival depends on human milk or a close substitute and that human young require a long period of adult care. Of course, liberal and Marxist theorists know these facts too, but they give them little theoretical attention. Questions of sex, gender and procreation are virtually ignored by liberal and Marxist political theory: where the sexual division of labor *is* examined, it is primarily in connection with so-called economic production, not in connection with sexuality, childbearing, or childrearing. The radical feminist conception of human nature, by contrast, makes possible systematic reflection on the political significance of human reproductive biology. It provides the conceptual foundation for bringing sexual, childbearing and childrearing practices into the domain of politics.

In its emphasis on the social and political significance of differences between the sexes, the radical feminist conception of human nature is less abstract and more specific than the apparently gender-neutral conceptions of liberalism and of Marxism. Nevertheless, in other ways, radical feminism, at least in the United States, is more abstract and less specific than traditional interpretations of Marxism. This abstractness is a result of the fact that American radical feminists are often unaware of the need to use a historical as well as a materialist method in understanding human nature and society. In the following sections, I shall show how the failure to use a sufficiently historical approach has flawed American radical feminist conceptions of human biology, human psychology, and social reality.

1. BIOLOGICAL DETERMINISM

It is a familiar idea that there is some relationship between human biology and the forms of human social organization. Conservatives have used the idea frequently to argue for the inevitability of the status quo. Marxists too, although they have neglected procreation, have given theoretical expression to the evident truth that human biology is relevant to human history. The Marxist view differs from the conservative one, however, in that it views human biology itself as having a history. For Marxists, human biology is not a prehistorical given; the hand is the product of labor as well as the organ of labor. In contemporary western culture, this latter point often goes unrecognized. Human biology is acknowledged to be the product of evolution, but of a "natural" rather than a "historical" process of evolution. It is seen as the conclusion to a series of fortunate mutations in our prehuman ancestors, rather than as something shaped by human social organization, as a presocial given rather than as a continuing process which is, in principle, susceptible to conscious social control.

Developing in a contemporary western context, it was almost inevitable that radical feminism should absorb some of these "naturalistic" assumptions about human biology. It is ironic, indeed, that radical feminist insistence on the political significance of reproductive biology should challenge traditional conceptions of the "natural" basis of human life, at the same time as many radical feminists themselves continue to treat reproductive biology as a given and the procreative process as natural. This is least true of the French radical feminists, who are more deeply influenced by the historical approach that is characteristic of Marxism, but it is also quite evident in the work of many American radical feminists. It can be seen, for instance, in the way that Firestone draws the line between nature and culture. She describes a certain kind of social unit as "the biological family"; she views the relations that define this unit as "natural"; she describes the changes that she advocates as "artificial" reproduction; and she looks forward eagerly to the victory of "culture" over "nature." Authors such as Griffin, Daly, and the matriarchal theorists reverse Firestone's values insofar as they are more hostile to what they conceive as culture, which has always been patriarchal, and more sympathetic to nature. But they seem to share her assumption that women's lives are ruled to a greater degree than men's by natural rather than social forces. Thus they assume that, at least to some extent, the social relationship between women and men is biologically determined.

Of course there are many kinds of biological determinism. What they have in common is the claim that the genetic constitution of human beings uniquely determines quite specific features of human social life. Usually, these features are distinctly unattractive; they have included racial inequality, slavery, warfare, laziness, drug addiction, competition, rape, poverty, violence, corruption, political hierarchy and, of course, male dominance. Such biological determinist claims are obviously of interest to political philosophers since they can be used either to attack or to justify a particular form of social organization, to diagnose the causes of human discontent or to set the limits of social change. Overwhelmingly, although not necessarily, such theories tend to encourage a sort of fatalism: either they claim that we must adapt society to take account of whatever basic, unchangeable human propensities they assert, or else they claim that a society closely resembling the presently existing one is inevitable. For this reason, it is unusual for advocates of social change, such as feminists, to accept any kind of biological determinism.

There are many ways of challenging biological determinism and, particularly, the ancient view that the relations between the sexes are determined by human biology. A favorite approach of feminists has been simply the method of empirical counterexample. If a culture can be discovered where the sexual division of labor is quite different from the division that is alleged to be determined biologically, then the claim of biological determinism must be false. The work of Margaret Mead has often been used by feminists in this way. Sometimes it takes a feminist anthropologist to discover the counterexamples: biological determinist claims about human nature rest on universal generalizations that often in fact are unjustified, because investigators commonly attribute to other societies certain features of their own society. Without a feminist consciousness, investigators may simply fail to see that rape and warfare are not universal, or that primitive women and their children do not depend for survival on the food supplied by men.[62]

Even where universal generalizations do seem to hold, biological determinism does not follow. All kinds of logical and methodological flaws in the argument may be discovered. For instance, Goldberg's "proof" of the inevitability of patriarchy rests on a postulated "X-factor" or innate male characteristic that he calls "aggression." Goldberg, however, is able to adduce no independent evidence for the existence of innate male aggression; that it exists is pure speculation. Consequently, Goldberg's explanation of male dominance is vacuous because it assumes what it needs to demonstrate, namely that women are inherently less aggressive than men.[63] Many other studies of aggression are worthless because the definition of aggression is too vague or even defines aggression in terms of typical masculine behavior. Thus the definition may exclude such "feminine" phenomena as verbal aggression, "passive aggression," or "the silent treatment."[64]

Arguments from animal behavior to biologically determined male dominance are equally inadequate. It is not necessary to counter the male leader of the wolf pack with the female praying mantis or spider who eats her male alive.[65] For one thing, it is becoming notorious that observations of animal behavior are infected by the assumptions, often unconscious, of the observer. Thus ethologists from hierarchical, competitive, and male-dominant societies invariably interpret animal behavior in terms of hierarchy, competition and male dominance, although often such categories are quite inappropriate. For instance, the sexual behavior of female primates is described typically in terms of submission, even though this terminology may be quite misleading since it is often the female who initiates sex.[66] Even where similarities between animal and human behavior do exist, we cannot infer a common genetic cause. Many similarities, even of physical structure, are not "homologous" traits, sharing a common descent and a common genetic constitution, but rather are separately evolved "analogous" traits, examples of evolutionary convergence.[67] Most claims of homology in behavioral traits, especially in human behavior, are purely conjectural. Finally, the most important flaw of all in arguments resting on a certain "sexual division of labor" among animals is that they ignore the fact that animal "labor" is quite unlike human labor because it is much more largely instinctive, much less flexible, much less dependent on post-natal learning, and is not subject to the same sort of self-conscious reappraisal.

No matter how successful feminists may be in identifying flaws in specific biological determinist arguments, a persistent worry always remains. For, no matter how decisive feminist refutations of specific arguments may be, they always leave open the possibility that a valid form of biological determinism may be invented. Feminists, like other political radicals, ordinarily take themselves to have an interest in developing an argument against biological determinism in general. Such an argument would tell against all the ways in which political conservatives have sought to provide a naturalistic justification for an endless catalogue of prejudices and social evils.

One approach often contrasted with biological determinism is the so-called "environmentalist" approach, which attempts to explain human behavior completely in terms of environmental influences. This approach presupposes that the human mind is more or less a blank slate which is inscribed by the individual's experiences in society. Various kinds of environmentalist theories attempt to identify the mechanisms through which this inscription occurs. Much controversy exists over the empirical adequacy of the various environmentalist theories as explanations of individual behavior, but even if an environmentalist theory were to succeed in its own terms, there would be much else that it would fail to explain. For instance, it would provide no insight into why certain messages rather than others are inscribed on the individual's "slate"; why society is organized in certain ways; or why, indeed, society exists at all. Moreover, environmentalism suggests that all alternative ways of organizing future society are equally possible.

In order to answer these sorts of questions, human biology cannot be ignored. Obviously, the human biological constitution does mean that we require food, air, sleep, etc.; these requirements, together with our approximate size, strength, speed and so on, have always been important influences on how we have organized our social life. If biological determinism meant no more than this, it would be indisputable and quite innocuous. In fact, however, biological determinists make much more specific claims about the inevitability of certain features of human social organization. Rather than examining each of these individually, I shall identify certain general considerations that tell against all of them.

One such consideration is that our form of social organization is determined not by our biology alone, but rather by a complex interplay between our biological constitution, the physical environment we inhabit and our current type of technological and social development. Thus, although it may be true that, in a moderately harsh environment and with little technology, social survival depends on infant care by women, it does not follow that infants must be cared for by women where bottle feeding is available or where other kinds of productive work do not require heavy physical labor or long absences from home. We may say, if we wish, that the human biological constitution requires a certain form of social organization *within certain material circumstances.* But we cannot universalize from this to what is required in other circumstances. And we should note that this way of putting it focuses on human biology in a way that is quite arbitrary. It would be equally true to say that the material circumstances determine a certain form of social organization, given certain features of the human biological constitution.

Biological determinism claims that the human biological constitution sets limits to what is socially possible. In fact, however, the human biological constitution is not just a pre-social given, remaining constant throughout the changes in human social life. It is a result as well as a cause of our system of social organization. It is too simple, for instance, to say that sex differences determine certain forms of social organization; we must also note that certain forms of social organization produce differences between the sexes. Feminists have recognized for a long time that many of the psychological differences between the sexes are socially produced, but few have realized that this is also true of many biological sex differences. Biological sex differences are in part socially produced both on the level of the individual and the level of the species.

On the level of the individual, it is easy to see how a sexist society has different effects on the biological constitution of males and females. An obvious example is women's feet which, while no longer mutilated by foot-binding, are often still deformed by what used to be called winkle-picker shoes. In general, women have been prevented from developing their capacities for physical speed and strength, and the effects of this prohibition can be seen simply by looking at women's bodies, particularly their upper bodies. The rate at which women's athletic records are being broken and the speed with which women's bodies have changed even over the past decade indicates that in the past social norms have limited the way in which women fulfil their genetic potential so that we have no idea of the extent of that potential.

Even the genetic potential that women and men inherit, however, is influenced by the social history of our species. The hand is not the only organ that is a result as well as a cause of our system of social organization. Even our reproductive biology, the most basic sex difference of all, is in part a social product. In the course of human evolution, as our ancestors became bipedal tool-users through the historical process described in Chapter 4, bipedalism reduced the size of the bony birth canal in women. Simultaneously, tool use selected for larger brain size and consequently for larger bony skulls in infants. This "obstetrical dilemma" of large-headed infants and small birth canals was solved by the infants' being born at an earlier state of development. But this in itself was possible only insofar as adults, being already bipedal, were able to carry the infants who were too small to cling on by themselves. And it was also possible only because human social organization was so far developed that other adults would cooperate with the mother sufficiently to support a long period of infant dependence.

Just as the process of human reproduction was a social as well as a biological development, so the fairly exaggerated sexual dimorphism that we see in contemporary industrial society also seems to be at least partly a result of social factors.[68] In some ethnic groups, there is little sexual differentiation between men and women. Women are as tall as men, have equally broad shoulders and narrow hips, and have breasts so small that it is often difficult to tell an individual's sex even when seen from the front. The relatively smaller size of females in other ethnic groups is often due directly to the fact that their nutrition is inferior because of their lower social status. Differential feeding may also have resulted in selection for shorter females, since taller women would have found it harder to survive on minimal food.[69] Similarly, the cultural preference for shorter and more slender women in modern industrial society may have resulted in more of these women being able to reproduce than their larger sisters. Andrea Dworkin, as we have seen, has suggested that even the sex distinction itself may be in part a social product, because "intersex" individuals were less likely to be preferred as marriage partners. These are some of the ways in which society produces genetically inherited sex differences, as well as sex differences, society.

What is true of our gross physical structure is also true of our internal biology, such as our neurophysiology and our hormonal balances. These affect our social life, but our social life also affects them. It is indeed true that a higher level of the hormone testosterone is correlated with aggressive behavior, both in animals and in humans, but biological determinists confuse this correlation with one-way causation. A male monkey's testosterone levels diminish as he drops in the dominance hierarchy, but the latter is not a simple result of the former. Similarly, human menstruation is not a simple result of changing balance of sex hormones; the balance of sex hormones itself is affected by a wide range of social factors, such as exercise, body fat, work, anxiety or roommates.[70]

In citing these examples, I am not trying to counter a simplistic biological determinism by an equally simplistic "environmentalism" nor to claim that the human biological constitution is entirely a social product. Instead I want to show that the historical and dialectical conception of human nature that we owe to Marx and Engels can illuminate our understanding of human sex differences—even though Marx and Engels themselves, inconsistently with their own fundamental methodological commitments, took human sex differences as biologically given. A historical and dialectical conception of human biology sees human nature and the forms of human social organization as determined not by our biology alone, but rather by a complex interplay between our forms of social organization, including our type of technological development, between our biological constitution and the physical environment that we inhabit. It is impossible to isolate or quantify the relative influence of any one of these factors, because each is continually being affected by as well as affecting the others. In other words, the factors are not only related to each other but are dialectically related. For instance, the physical environment does not just set limits to human social organization; organized human activity also affects the environment—by draining, damming, clearing, terracing, leveling, fertilizing or polluting. The humanly caused changes in the environment in turn affect human social life, which in turn affects the environment in a new way, and so on. Similarly, although the creatures from which humans evolved were certainly sexed, their characteristic sex differences were modified by specific forms of human social life, and these forms in turn were affected by and continue to affect the continually evolving differences between the sexes.

As we have seen, there are all sorts of interrelated ways in which society produces sex differences as well as sex differences society. The conclusion of this sort of reasoning, however, is not simply that human biology and the forms of social life are more "cultural" and less "natural," more "social" and less "biological," than biological determinists have supposed. The conclusion is rather that, where human nature is concerned, there is no line between nature and culture. Dorothy Dinnerstein puts it this way:

> Humans are by nature unnatural. We do not yet walk "naturally" on our hind legs, for example: such ills as fallen arches, lower back pain, and hernias testify that the body has not adapted itself completely to the upright posture. Yet this unnatural posture, forced on the unwilling body by the project of tool-using, is precisely what has made possible the development of important aspects of our "nature": the hand and the brain, and the complex system of skills, language, and social arrangements which were both effects and causes of hand and brain. Man-made and physiological structures have thus come to interpenetrate so thoroughly that to call a human project contrary to human biology is naive: we are what we have made ourselves, and we must continue to make ourselves as long as we exist at all.[71]

When this is understood, biological determinism becomes not so much false as incoherent. We cannot say abstractly that biology determines society, because we cannot identify a clear, non-social sense of "biology" nor a clear, non-biological sense of "society." The thesis of universal biological determinism cannot be stated coherently.

This is not to say that we cannot focus sometimes on human biology and sometimes on human society, just as we can talk about human and non-human nature even though we recognize a dialectical relationship between them. It does mean, however, that we cannot talk about human biology, any more than about any other aspect of human beings, in isolation from a social context. In ordinary life, the social context is taken for granted, but it must be identified explicitly when we attempt to make theoretical generalizations about men and women, their needs, abilities and limitations. For human needs, abilities and limitations exist only in a certain social context. Human nature is both historical and biological, and the two aspects are inseparable.

This conception of human nature has far-reaching implications for political theory. Most important, it refutes the biological determinist claim that the human biological constitution sets universal limits to what is socially possible. In a given historical situation, this claim may approximate the truth; for instance, human beings cannot often work 24 hours in a day. But what biological determinism overlooks is the plasticity of human nature, which ensures that the limits of human nature are so elastic that they can never be identified with finality. Of course there is a biological basis for human needs, abilities and limitations. Human social organizations must allow for the satisfaction of these needs by human abilities and in spite of human limitations. But human needs are flexible and they are modified according to the means available for their satisfaction. And human abilities can be expanded, for example by technology, to overcome human limitations. For this reason, it makes sense to talk about human needs, abilities, and limitations only within a particular historical context. For it is that context which determines the specific form taken by our needs, abilities and limitations.

If it has far-reaching implications for political theory in general, the dialectical conception of the relation between human nature and human society has special significance for feminism. One interesting consequence of this conception is that it challenges the conceptual distinction between sex and gender that earlier feminists painstakingly established.[72] As it is conceived ordinarily, sex is thought of as a set of fixed biological characteristics, whereas gender is construed as a set of variable social norms about the proper behavior of sexed individuals. If, however, we acknowledge human biology, including sexual biology, as created partly by society, and if we acknowledge human society as responding to human biology, we lose the clarity of the distinctions between sex and gender. We see that sex does not uniquely determine gender but that it is not irrelevant to it either; moreover, we see that sex itself is partly created by gender. Once we see how sex and gender are dialectically and inseparably interrelated, the original clarity of the distinction between sex and gender comes to seem "a false clarity."[73] It becomes important for feminists to question not only gender but also sex.

Given this dialectical conception of sex and gender, we can see that there is no simple answer to the question of whether women's subordination has a biological cause. Instead, we can see that the question itself is misleading, suggesting a linear model of causality which is quite inapplicable to this context. Radical feminists are right to acknowledge that female biology is clearly relevant to the sexual division of labor in which women's subordination is rooted, but they are wrong to infer from this that women's biology causes women's subordination. Such an inference is mistaken because it ignores the ways in which women's biology is determined, in part, precisely by that subordination.

A further implication of this dialectical conception of the relation between sex and society is that no social activity or form of social organization is any more natural than any other. Male dominance is no more or less natural than female dominance. It is no more or less natural for mothers than for fathers to rear children. Heterosexual intercourse is no more or less natural than any other forms of sexual activity. Giving birth in a field is no more or less natural than giving birth in a hospital or even than providing an ovum for a test-tube baby. Some of these practices have a longer history and more ideological support than others, but none of them is determined by human biology or beyond the reach of conscious social control. Since both sexes are equally human, no sense can be given to the suggestion that women are closer to nature than are men. Going to war is neither more nor less natural than composing music or doing philosophy.

If nothing is natural in human social life, then we can give a conceptual as well as a political explanation of why the domain of traditional political theory is far too narrow. Traditional political theory has always made a distinction between the public and the private spheres of human existence and, while there has been disagreement over the precise extent of the public sphere, political theorists have unanimously agreed that the areas of sexuality, childbearing and childrearing should be defined as the private sphere because these activities have been conceived as natural or biologically determined. If this assumption of naturalness is false, however, then the distinction drawn between the public and the private realms is seen to be philosophically arbitrary, without sufficient reason. When so much of the work in the "private" realm is invariably done by women, moreover, it is not just irrational but sexist to assume that women are biologically determined to continue performing this work. An adequate political theory must evaluate traditional sexual, childbearing and childrearing practices and consider more liberatory alternatives.

In the preceding discussion of biological determinism I have tried to establish a conceptual basis from which the strengths and weaknesses of the radical feminist conception of human nature may be established. From this basis, we can see that one of the main strengths of radical feminism is its insistence, in opposition to liberalism and Marxism, that sex does make a difference, that feminists cannot afford to ignore the biological differences between women and men. Radical feminism contributes the insight that, for women, the problem is not gender alone; the problem is also sex. The main weakness of much radical feminist thinking about biology, however, is the way in which it often poses the problem of sex. It asks what it is about human biology that enables men to dominate women, but it asks this question without reference to any historical context, implying that human biology is unchanging, a fixed, pre-social given. Hence, radical feminism has a constant tendency to fall into biological determinism.

2. RADICAL FEMINIST PSYCHOLOGY

The first radical feminists were working in a context where women's oppression was invisible in political theory and denied in political practice. Given this context, their primary political and theoretical task was to demonstrate the systematic and pervasive nature of women's oppression. In order to emphasize that women were subordinated in all known previous societies and that they continue to be subordinated in all classes and ethnic groups of contemporary industrial society, radical feminists have tended to speak in very general terms about the relations between women and men. As I have suggested already, the focus on women as women has been extremely enlightening and has constituted perhaps the main contribution of radical feminism. Sometimes, however, the focus on sex and gender has been so intense that other aspects of human nature and social reality have become blurred. In the last section, I suggested that the tendency to generalise about women not only has encouraged radical feminists to consider the significance of biological sex differences but has also predisposed them to look favourably on biological determinist claims. In this section, I shall argue that the tendency to generalise about women has generated important insights about women's minds, but that it has also encouraged the emergence of a simplified and politically unacceptable psychology.

Because radical feminism has developed no unified theory of human nature, it has no systematic psychology. Nevertheless, the theoretical writings of radical feminism reveal certain common if not universal assumptions about the minds of women and men. Perhaps the most significant of these is that, under patriarchy, women's minds as well as women's bodies are under constant attack. The problem is not just that women are "socialized" into the approved "feminine" characteristics of passivity, compliance, emotionality, etc., although radical feminists would not disagree with these findings of liberal feminist psychology. The deeper problem, according to radical feminism, is that women's perceptions of reality are systematically distorted or denied. This happens not simply on an individual level; the patriarchal picture of human nature and society is integral to patriarchal culture and science. Even language itself becomes a weapon by which "the Fathers" diminish the range of women's thought:

> This applies to male-controlled language in all matters pertaining to gynocentric identity: the words simply do not exist. In such a situation it is difficult even to imagine the right questions about our situation. Women struggling for words feel haunted by false feelings of personal inadequacy, by anger, frustration, and kind of sadness/bereavement. For it is, after all, our "mother tongue" that has been turned against us by the tongue-twisters.[74]

Submerged in patriarchal culture, women are robbed of their mental as well as their physical powers and become confused and depressed. "In universities, and in all of the professions, the omnipresent poisonous gases gradually stifle women's minds and spirits."[75] The few women who do challenge the patriarchal picture are categorized as lesbians, as abnormal and eventually as mad.

The radical feminist critiques of the dominant culture have been extraordinarily illuminating. They have demonstrated the male bias of the prevailing conceptual framework within which human experience is described and interpreted. They have shown how history, anthropology, medicine, psychology and many other disciplines have perpetuated the patriarchal picture and reinforced patriarchal power. In spite of these contributions, however, I think there are problems with the way in which American radical feminists have attempted to reconceptualize reality in general and psychology in particular.

Some of these problems concern the radical feminist characterization of male and female psychology. Radical feminists are correct to note that prevailing conceptions of rationality and mental health are male-biased and that, from a feminist perspective, men are neither particularly rational nor particularly mentally healthy. In an effort to invert patriarchal perceptions, however, some of the most prominent radical feminists portray men as monsters. They see them as necrophiliacs, incorrigible rapists and torturers, irrational woman-haters.[76] While this portrayal brings out certain destructive aspects of masculinity that are often ignored and need to be revealed, I think that it is inadequate both descriptively and theoretically. Descriptively, it ignores not just the relatively unimportant and always questionable individual exceptions to masculine behavioral norms; it also ignores the way in which those norms themselves vary cross-culturally and, in contemporary society, by race and by class. Theoretically, radical feminism provides no explanations of why men have developed these bizarre characteristics and so leaves the impression, sometimes reinforced by explicit suggestion, that these characteristics are simply innate.[77] As I shall argue in Chapter 9, this impression generates a political practice that is full of difficulties.

The radical feminist picture of female psychology is somewhat more complicated. On the one hand, in their eagerness to subvert patriarchal values, radical feminists emphasize the valuable aspects of the qualities that are associated traditionally with women, qualities such as nurturance, sensitivity and emotional expressiveness, and they show how these qualities contribute to a special female strength. On the other hand, in an effort to emphasize that patriarchal oppression pervades even the inner life, radical feminists portray women not only as trapped by "external" constraints, but as mystified by male lies and trickery of male texts. Thus, women's minds as well as women's bodies are seen as the victims of patriarchal power.

Theoretically, the radical feminist account of women's psychology is no more satisfactory than its account of male psychology. That is to say, it provides no better explanation of why women develop what are claimed to be their distinctive psychological characteristics. Descriptively, however, the radical feminist portrayal of women is somewhat more adequate than its portrayal of men. It emphasizes both the existence of what Marxists call "false consciousness" and also the neglected value of many psychological characteristics that are considered feminine in contemporary society. Just as in its description of male psychology, however, the radical feminist characterization of women ignores class and racial differences in the ways that women perceive and respond to the world. Moreover, its portrayal of women as helpless victims is ultimately a "patriarchal" representation. In explaining the perpetuation of male dominance, all feminists are naturally concerned to avoid blaming the victim and one way of doing this is to emphasize the relative power of men over women. To *over*emphasise this power, however, not only distorts reality, but also depreciates the power that women have succeeded in winning and minimizes the chances of further resistance. By portraying women as helpless victims, it seems to me that some radical feminists have overemphasized men's control over women's minds and in this way may have unwittingly reinforced the power of those whom they wish to subvert.

I want to conclude this section by reflecting on how some radical feminists have conceptualized the relation between reason and emotion. In my view, the way in which certain American radical feminists have conceptualized this distinction reflects the ahistorical approach that is manifested in other aspects of radical feminist psychology, in the radical feminist conception of human biology and, as we shall see in the next section, in the social categories of radical feminism.

Some radical feminist theorists, such as Susan Griffin, reject reason because they identify it with the instrumental, quantitative technocratic and supposedly value-free conception of reason that began to become dominant with the scientific revolution of the 17th century. If this is reason, radical feminists want no part of it, and many rush in reaction to identify women with feeling, emotion, nature and wildness. For reasons explained in Chapter 3, I believe that radical feminists are correct to reject a reason conceived as purely instrumental, but I also believe that it is a mistake to abandon reason altogether. On the one hand, this move mystifies the emotions, identifying them with "pure feelings," instead of recognizing that, as we saw in Chapter 3, every emotion also presupposes certain social norms. For instance, we cannot understand what it is to feel awe, anger, admiration, envy, disappointment, hope or fear unless we can imagine the sorts of situations in which those emotions typically occur. On the other hand, the rejection of reason by some radical feminists assumes that reason must always be technocratic and patriarchal. It forces feminists into an antiintellectual and antiscientific position and encourages a romantic fusion with wordless nature and with animals.[78] It is ironic to note that, by accepting these historically bound definitions of reason and of emotion, which are both conceptually and politically inadequate, radical feminism in fact takes over one of the most fundamental of the patriarchal dualisms that it wishes to reject. A more fruitful approach for radical feminism would be to reject the dominant conceptions of reason, of emotion and of the relation between them and instead to develop new conceptions that would be more coherent, comprehensive and appropriate to feminist values. In Chapter 9, we shall see that some radical feminists are beginning to move in this direction.

3. UNIVERSALISM AND SOCIAL CATEGORIZATION

The strengths and weaknesses in the radical feminist conception of human nature are reflected in corresponding strengths and weaknesses in its political theory. For instance, the radical feminist focus on human reproductive biology allows feminists to enlarge enormously the domain of politics and to make visible forms of oppression that hitherto have been concealed. Paradoxically, however, the ahistorical way in which radical feminism conceptualizes human biology has the contradictory effect of tending to push sexuality, childbearing and childrearing back into the realm of "nature," to separate them from "culture," which is defined as a male creation. I have argued already that such a dichotomization of nature and culture is confused conceptually. I would add that it is disastrous politically because it perpetuates the patriarchal version of history and present reality. Not only does it give men undeserved credit for the achievements of human culture; by construing women's traditional work as natural, it discourages reflection on alternative ways of organizing that work and makes it inconceivable that we might ever overcome the sexual division of labor on which the traditional conception of "women's work" is based.

The ahistorical way in which radical feminism conceptualizes human biology also encourages it to develop an equally ahistorical conception of "the patriarchy." As I mentioned earlier, the term *patriarchy* has been used traditionally in anthropology to refer to a specific system of pastoral and nomadic social organization. The radical feminists who have taken over this term, however, use it much more broadly to refer to a universal system of male domination. Redefinition of terms is always possible, and some feminist theorists do use the term *patriarchy* in an unobjectionable way.[79] Within the context of radical feminist theory, however, *patriarchy* often seems intended both to retain some of its original specific meaning and also to have universal application. To use *patriarchy* in this way implies that patriarchy or male dominance is a transhistorical social structure, and this suggestion is seriously misleading. Here is a more appropriate way of conceptualizing male dominance.

> Male dominance, though apparently universal, does not in actual behavioral terms assume a universal content or a universal shape. On the contrary, women typically have power and influence in political and economic life, display autonomy from men in their pursuits and rarely find themselves confronted or constrained by what might seem the brute fact of male strength. For in every case in which we see women confined, by powerful men or by the responsibilities of child care and the home, one can cite others which display female capacities to fight back, to speak out in public, perform physically demanding tasks, and even to subordinate the needs of infant children (in their homes or on their backs) to their desires for travel, labor, politics, love, or trade. For every cultural belief in female weakness, irrationality, or polluting menstrual blood, one can discover others which suggest the tenuousness of male claims and celebrate women

for their productive roles, their sexuality or purity, their fertility or perhaps maternal strength. Male dominance, in short, does not inhere in any isolated and measurable set of omnipresent facts. Rather, it seems to be an aspect of the organization of collective life, a patterning of expectations and beliefs which gives rise to imbalance in the ways people interpret, evaluate, and respond to particular forms of male and female action. We see it not in physical constraints on things that men or women can or cannot do but, rather, in the ways they think about their lives, the kinds of opportunities they enjoy, and in their ways of making claims.[80]

The author of this passage, M. Z. Rosaldo, is not claiming that the universality of male dominance is brought into question by the fact that women as well as men often have considerable power, either individually or as a group. She also writes:

Some women, certainly, are strong. But at the same time that women happily and successfully pursue their ends, and manage quite significantly to constrain men in the process, it seems to me quite clear that women's goals themselves are shaped by social systems which deny them ready access to the social privilege, authority, and esteem enjoyed by a majority of men.[81]

Rosaldo's point, then, is not that men do not dominate women universally, but rather that they do so through a variety of social structures which vary tremendously both across and even within cultures. Her point needs to be taken seriously by radical feminists because it tells against too rapid generalizations about women and women's situation.

As Rosaldo remarks, generalizations about women's subordination invariably lead to a search for its "origins," a search which is bound to be unsuccessful because women's subordination is not a single phenomenon.

To look for origins is, in the end, to think that what we are today is something other than the product of our history and our present social world, and, more particularly, that our gender systems are primordial, transhistorical, and essentially unchanging in their roots. Quests for origins sustain (since they are predicated upon) a discourse cast in universal terms; and universalism permits us all too quickly to assume—for everyone but ourselves perhaps—the *sociological* significance of what individual people *do,* or even, worse, of what, in biological terms, they *are.*[82]

In other words, if we attempt to abstract "patriarchy" from the specific social practices through which men dominate women, we lose the history and only an ahistorical biology seems to remain.[83] Thus an ahistorical conception of patriarchy or male dominance and an ahistorical conception of human nature reinforce each other and together encourage biological determinism. The appearance of universality is in fact part of the ideology by which contemporary male dominance sustains itself.

Another problematic aspect of radical feminist's social categorization is its conception of women and men as opposing classes. This conception has the advantage of emphasizing that women's subordination is not natural and that men derive benefits from it. Yet it can also lead easily to an oversimplification of the experience both of women and of men. Mary Daly's talk of "the planetary Men's Association" draws attention to the fact that all men have a shared interest in the subordination of women, but it obscures the fact that men are also staggeringly unequal with each other in the amount of control that they are able to exert over their own lives and over the lives of women. Most men, in fact, are victims of a small, white ruling class that maintains its domination through the interrelated structures of racism, imperialism, and class society. Similarly, the view that women as such constitute a class draws attention to certain commonalities in women's experience of oppression, but it also obscures wide differences in the oppressive experiences of different women and even the fact that some women dominate others. Mary Daly, for instance, has been accused of "erasing" the special oppression suffered by poor women, colonized women, and women of color by assimilating their suffering to that of white, middle-class women.[84] In the same way, the radical feminist emphasis on the universality of women's oppression encourages it to neglect the fact that certain differences in the position of women in different societies are quite significant from a feminist perspective. As Barbara Ehrenreich remarks:

> There is something timeless and universal about women's oppression [but] it takes different forms in different settings, and . . . the *differences* are of vital importance. There is a difference between a society in which sexism is expressed in female infanticide and a society in which sexism takes the form of unequal representation on the Central Committee. And the difference is worth dying for.[85]

Not all radical feminists fall into the trap of falsely universalizing women's experience. Even in the early 1970s, two members of The Furies collective published an anthology on *Class and Feminism* in which radical feminist authors grappled with the problems engendered by class differences among feminists.[86] The most searching criticisms of Mary Daly's "erasures" were authored by lesbian radical feminists, and a sensitive study of the relationship between "feminism, racism and gynephobia" has been written by the radical feminist Adrienne Rich.[87] American radical feminists are giving increasing priority to overcoming their tendency to oversimplify the complexity of women's experience of domination. They are paying increasing attention to the varying experience of Jewish women, women of color, physically challenged women, etc. In order to move beyond description, however, and to provide an adequate theory of women's liberation, radical feminism will have to revise its ahistorical conceptualizations of class, of patriarchy, and of women and men themselves. To attempt such a conceptual revision, while retaining the main radical feminist insights, is the distinctive theoretical project of socialist feminism.

Notes

1. Shulamith Firestone, *The Dialectic of Sex: The Case for Feminist Revolution* (New York: William Morrow, 1970).

2. Here, as earlier in the book, I am assuming the commonly made distinction between sex—the biological property of being male or female—and gender—the social attribute of being masculine or feminine. At the end of the chapter, I shall discuss the validity of this assumption. For the time being, I shall also assume that there are only two sexes and two genders. Some individuals are said to be "intersex," and a few societies are said to have more than two genders, but I shall ignore these complications for the time being. In our society, only two sexes and two genders are recognized, and contemporary radical feminism focuses naturally on our society.

3. Bonnie Kreps, "Radical Feminism: I," in *Radical Feminism,* edited by Anne Koedt, Ellen Levine, and Anita Rapone (New York: Quadrangle Books, 1973), p. 239.

4. "The Feminists: A Political Organization to Annihilate Sex Roles," in Koedt, Levine, and Rapone, *Radical Feminism,* p. 370.

5. "Politics of the Ego: A Manifesto for New York Radical Feminists," in Koedt, Levine, and Rapone, *Radical Feminism,* p. 380.

6. Kate Millett, "Sexual Politics: A Manifesto for Revolution," in Koedt, Levine, and Rapone, *Radical Feminism,* pp. 366-67.

7. Mary Daly, "the qualitative leap beyond patriarchal religion," *Quest* 1, no. 4 (Spring 1975):31.

8. Ibid.

9. Ibid., p. 30.

10. Janice Raymond, "the illusion of androgyny," *Quest* 11, no. 1 (Summer, 1975):61.

11. Ibid., p. 58.

12. Ibid., p. 65.

13. W. H. Masters and V. E. Johnson, *Human Sexual Response* (Boston: Little, Brown, 1966).

14. Mary Jane Sherfey, "A Theory on Female Sexuality," in *Sisterhood Is Powerful,* edited by Robin Morgan (New York: Vintage Books, 1970), p. 225 (italics in original).

15. Ibid., p. 224.

16. Ibid., pp. 225-26.

17. Susan Brownmiller, *Against Our Will: Men, Women and Rape* (New York: Bantam, 1976), p. 6.

18. Ibid., pp. 4-5.

19. Firestone, *The Dialectic of Sex.* The following quotations from Firestone give page references to this book.

20. Alice, Gordon, Debbie and Mary, "Lesbian Separatism: An Amazon Analysis," 1973 (mimeographed).

21. Steven Goldberg, *The Inevitability of Patriarchy* (New York: William Morrow, 1973).

22. Sally Miller Gearhart, *The Wanderground: Stories of the Hill Women* (Watertown, Mass: Persephone Press, 1979). This theme is quite common in feminist fiction. Perhaps the earliest example is *Herland: A Lost Feminist Utopian Novel* by Charlotte Perkins Gilman, written for serial publication in 1915 and finally issued as a book in New York by Bantam in 1979.

23. Jane Alpert, "MotherRight: A New Feminist Theory," *Ms.* August 1973, p. 92.

24. Adrienne Rich, *Of Woman Born* (New York: W.W. Norton, 1976), p. 40.

25. Janice Raymond, *The Transsexual Empire* (Boston: Beacon Press, 1979), p. 107. Cf. also pp. xvi, 28. I owe these references to Mary Vetterling-Braggin in correspondence.

26. Mary Daly, *Gyn/Ecology: The Metaethics of Radical Feminism* (Boston: Beacon Press, 1978), p. 194 and many other places.

27. Susan Griffin, *Woman and Nature: The Roaring Inside Her* (New York: Harper Colophon, 1980), p. 226.

28. The following brief characterization of radical feminist views of knowledge owes much to Gerri Perreault's "Futuristic World Views: Modern Physics and Feminism. Implications for Teaching/Learning in Higher Education," a paper presented at the Second Annual Conference of The World Future Society—Education Section, October 18, 1979. The paper was also read at the National Women's Studies Association Second National Conference, Indiana University, Bloomington, May 16–20, 1980. I also benefited from reading Joyce Trebilcot's "Conceiving Women: Notes on the Logic of Feminism," *Sinister Wisdom* 11 (Fall 1979):43-50.

29. Griffin, *Woman and Nature,* pp. 117-18.

30. Daly, *Gyn/Ecology,* p. 11.

31. Simone de Beauvoir, *The Second Sex,* translated and edited by H. M. Parshley (New York: Bantam Books, 1961), pp. 58-59.

32. Daly, *Gyn/Ecology,* p. 4.

33. Jane Alpert, "MotherRight", p. 92.

34. This preliminary characterization of French radical feminism is derived largely from Suzanne Relyea's handout for "None of the Above: Gender Theory and Heterosexual

Hegemony," paper read to the American Philosophical Association, Dec. 28, 1980. A much fuller introduction to the work of contemporary French feminists and an understanding of some of the significant differences as well as the similarities between them may be derived from *New French Feminisms: An Anthology,* edited and with introductions by Elaine Marks and Isabelle de Courtirron (Amherst: University of Massachusetts Press, 1980).

35. Monique Wittig's books include *Les Guérillères* (New York: Avon, 1971); *The Lesbian Body* (New York: Avon, 1973); *Oppoponax* (Houston: Daughters, Inc., 1976).

36. In the proceedings of the Second Sex conference, New York (New York Institute for the Humanities, 1979). My page references are to this publication. The paper was published later in *Questions Féministes.*

37. Andrea Dworkin, *Woman Hating* (New York: E.P. Dutton, 1974), p. 175. The following quotations from Dworkin give page references to this book.

38. Ibid., p. 174.

39. Monique Wittig and Sande Zeig, *Lesbian Peoples: Material for a Dictionary* (New York: Avon, 1979).

40. Ti-Grace Atkinson, "Radical Feminism and Love" (1970), p. 2 (mimeographed)

41. Barbara Burris, "The Fourth World Manifesto," in Koedt, Levine, and Rapone, *Radical Feminism,* pp. 337 and 338.

42. Daly, *Gyn/Ecology.*

43. Kathleen Barry, *Female Sexual Slavery* (Englewood Cliffs, N.J.: Prentice-Hall, 1979).

44. "The Feminists: A Political Organization to Annihilate Sex Roles," in Koedt, Levine, and Rapone, *Radical Feminism,* p. 370.

45. This claim is made by most radical feminists, from the Redstockings collective up through Firestone to Monique Wittig.

46. Evelyn Reed, "Women: Caste, Class or Oppressed Sex?" in *Problems of Women's Liberation* (New York: Pathfinder, 1970), pp. 64-76. Reprinted in Alison M. Jaggar and Paula R. Struhl, eds., *Feminist Frameworks: Alternative Theoretical Accounts of the Relations between Women and Men* (New York: McGraw-Hill, 1978), p. 128.

47. Daly, *Gyn/Ecology,* p. 326.

48. Gayle Rubin, "The Traffic in Women," in *Towards an Anthropology of Women* (New York: Monthly Review Press, 1975), p. 168. Reprinted in Jaggar and Struhl, *Feminist Frameworks,* p. 157.

49. Daly, *Gyn/Ecology,* p. 326.

50. Barbara Love and Elizabeth Shanklin, "The Answer Is Matriarchy," in *Our Right to Love,* edited by Ginny Vida (Englewood Cliffs, N.J.: Prentice-Hall, 1978), p. 186.

51. Ibid. Italics in original.

52. Ibid., p. 185. Italics in original.

53. Wittig, *Les Guérillères,* p. 116.

54. Ibid., pp. 57-58.

55. Christine Delphy, *The Main Enemy: A Materialist Analysis of Women's Oppression,* translated by Lucy ap Roberts (London: Women's Research and Resources Centre Publications, 1977), p. 16.

56. Sheila Cronan, "Marriage," in Koedt, Levine, and Rapone, *Radical Feminism,* pp. 213-21.

57. Barry, *Female Sexual Slavery,* p. 237.

58. Charlotte Bunch, "Lesbians in Revolt," in *Lesbianism and the Women's Movement* (Oakland, Calif: Diana Press, 1975), pp. 29-37. Reprinted in Jaggar and Struhl, *Feminist Frameworks,* p. 136.

59. Artemis March, "A Paradigm for Feminist Theory," paper delivered at the Second Sex conference, NYC, September 1979, p. 2 of typescript.

60. Catharine A. MacKinnon, "Feminism, Marxism, Method, and the State: An Agenda for Theory," *Signs: A Journal of Women in Culture and Society* 7, no. 3 (Spring, 1982):529, 533.

61. March, "Paradigm," p. 2.

62. For further discussion of this phenomenon, see Chapter 4, n. 50.

63. I owe this point to Marilyn Myerson Ferrandino, "Patriarchy and Biological Necessity: A Feminist and Anarchist Critique," Ph.D. dissertation, S.U.N.Y. Buffalo, 1977.

64. Mary Ellen McGuigan made this point at a SWIP meeting in 1979.

65. This is one strategy recommended by Pat Mainardi, "The Politics of Housework," in Morgan, ed., *Sisterhood Is Powerful*, pp. 447-54.

66. This and a number of other examples are given by Elizabeth Fisher, *Woman's Creation: Sexual Evolution and the Shaping of Society* (New York: McGraw-Hill, 1980). Cf. also Donna Haraway, "Animal Sociology and a Natural Economy of the Body Politic," Parts I and II, *Signs: Journal of Women in Culture and Society* 4, no. 1 (Autumn 1978):21-60. Two other critical feminist discussions of this theme are Leila Leibowitz, " 'Universals' and Male Dominance Among Primates: A Critical Examination," and Ruth Bleier, "Social and Political Bias in Science: An Examination of Animal Studies and Their Generalizations to Human Behavior and Evolution," both in Ruth Hubbard and Marian Lowe, eds., *Genes and Gender: II* (Staten Island, N.Y.: Gordian Press, 1979), pp. 35-69.

67. Stephen Jay Gould, *Ever Since Darwin: Reflections in Natural History* (New York: W.W. Norton, 1977), pp. 240-41.

68. Ann Oakley, *Sex, Gender and Society* (London: Temple Smith, 1972), chapter 1, "The Biology of Sex."

69. Fisher, *Women's Creation*, p. 279.

70. These examples came from Marilyn Lowe, "The Biology of Exploitation and the Exploitation of Biology," a paper read to the National Women's Studies Association Second National Conference, Indiana University, Bloomington, May 16-20, 1980. In saying that human menstruation is affected by roommates, Lowe is referring to the empirically well-documented fact that the menstrual cycles of women who live together tend to co-ordinate with each other.

71. Dorothy Dinnerstein, *The Mermaid and the Minotaur: Sexual Arrangements and Human Malaise* (New York: Colophon, 1977), pp. 21-22. Dinnerstein herself, of course, can be identified as a radical feminist insofar as she recognizes the extent of contemporary misogyny, insofar as she roots this in childrearing practices, and insofar as she engages in universal generalizations about the relations between women and men. I have hesitated to characterise her as a radical feminist, in part because she does not identify herself that way, and because the radical feminists have not yet claimed her as one of their own. The other reason I have hesitated to classify Dinnerstein as a radical feminist is that her political theory is so different from the political theory of radical feminism. In particular, Dinnerstein never discusses the need for an organized political struggle by women against men.

72. My discussion here is inspired by Ann Palmeri's "Feminist-Materialism: On the Possibility and the Power of the Nature/Culture Distinction," a paper read to the mid-western division of SWIP in Detroit, October 1980.

73. Ibid., p. 1 of typescript.

74. Daly, *Gyn/Ecology*, p. 330.

75. Ibid., p. 8.

76. Mary Daly writes, "Woman hating is at the core of necrophilia," *Gyn/Ecology*, p. 62. Andrea Dworkin writes, "Men love death. In everything they make, they hollow out a central place for death, let its rancid smell contaminate every dimension of whatever still survives. Men especially love murder. In art they celebrate it, and in life they commit it" ("Why So-Called Radical Men Love and Need Pornography," in Laura Lederer, ed., *Take Back the Night: Women on Pornography* [New York: William Morrow, 1980], p. 148).

77. Shulamith Firestone is the only major radical feminist author to attempt a theoretical explanation of male psychology. Her work is one of the earliest examples of attempts by feminists to reclaim Freud. Today, however, her work receives little attention from radical feminists.

78. Mary Daly sometimes even seems to recommend that we abandon language. She writes: "Some attempt to imitate/learn from the language of 'dumb' animals, whose nonverbal communication seems superior to androcratic speech. Thus, in the midst of

the cackling (of the Hags) there can be detected meowing, purring, roaring, barking, snorting, twittering, growling, howling. The noise of these solemn assemblies functions to distract the would-be invaders, baffling them. In fact, however, the tactic of distracting is not even a major intent of the singing Spinners. Our sounds are sounds of spontaneous exuberance, which the demon wardens vainly try to translate, referring to their textbooks of Demonology and Female Psychology" (*Gyn/Ecology,* p. 414).

79. Heidi Hartmann, for instance, denies explicitly that patriarchy is a "universal, unchanging phenomenon" and states that "patriarchy, the set of interrelations among men that allow men to dominate women, has changed in form and intensity over time" (H. Hartman, "The Unhappy Marriage of Marxism and Feminism: Towards a More Progressive Union," in Lydia Sargent, ed., *Women and Revolution* [Boston: South End Press, 1981], p. 18).

80. M. Z. Rosaldo, "The Use and Abuse of Anthropology: Reflections on Feminism and Cross-Cultural Understanding," *Signs: Journal of Women in Culture and Society* 5, no. 3 (1980):394.

81. Ibid., p. 395.

82. Ibid., pp. 392-93.

83. This point was made by Juliet Mitchell in *Women's Estate* (New York: Pantheon, 1971), pp. 83-84. It has been reiterated more recently by Joan Smith in "Women and the Family: History and Biology," a paper read to National Women's Studies Association Second National Conference, Indiana University, Bloomington, May 16-20, 1980.

84. Elly Bulkin, "Racism and Writing: Some Implications for White Lesbian Critics," *Sinister Wisdom* 13 (Spring 1980):3-22. Also André Lorde, "An Open Letter to Mary Daly," in Cherríe Moraga and Gloria Auzaldúa, ed., *This Bridge Called My Back: Writings by Radical Women of Color* (Watertown, Mass.: Persephone, 1981), pp. 94-97.

85. Barbara Ehrenreich, "What Is Socialist Feminism?", revision of speech given at the National Socialist/Feminist Conference in July 1975, published in *WIN* Magazine 7, 3 June 1976, and reprinted as a pamphlet by Nationwide Women's Program, AFSC, 1501 Cherry St., Philadelphia, Pa. 19102.

86. Charlotte Bunch and Nancy Myron, eds., *Class and Feminism: A Collection of Essays from THE FURIES* (Baltimore, Md.: Diana Press, 1974).

87. Adrienne Rich, "Disloyal to Civilization: Feminism, Racism and Gynephobia," *Chrysalis: A Magazine for Woman's Culture* 7:9-27. Radical feminists are speaking out increasingly against racism. One outstanding example is *Conditions:*. *Five, the Black Women's Issue,* edited by Lorraine Bethel and Barbara Smith, 1979. Bulkin's article on "Racism and Writing" ends with "A short reading list on women/people of color and racism." The radical feminist press Persephone has published not only *This Bridge Called My Back,* but *Nice Jewish Girls: A Lesbian Anthology,* edited by Evelyn Torton Beck (Watertown, Mass.: Persephone Press, 1982). (There is considerable current debate over whether anti-semitism is a form of racism.) Cf. also Gloria T. Hull, Patricia Dell Scott, and Barbara Smith, eds., *But Some of Us Are Brave* (Old Westbury, N.Y.: The Feminist Press, 1982). This contains excellent bibliographies. The number of feminist publications on the varied experiences of women from different class and ethnic backgrounds is increasing rapidly at present, but of course not all of these publications come from a perspective that is radical feminist.

6

Socialist Feminism and Human Nature

> It is probably true quite generally that in the history of human thinking the most fruitful developments frequently take place at those points where two different lines of thought meet. These lines may have their roots in quite different parts of human culture, in different religious traditions: hence if they actually meet, that is, if they are at least so much related to each other that a real interaction can take place, then one may hope that new and interesting developments may follow.
>
> Werner Weisenberg, quoted by Fritjof Capra,
> *The Tao of Physics* (New York: Bantam, 1977).

Like radical feminism, socialist feminism is a daughter of the contemporary women's liberation movement. It is a slightly younger daughter, born in the 1970s and, like most younger daughters, impressed by its elder sister, while wanting at the same time to avoid her mistakes. The central project of socialist feminism is the development of a political theory and practice that will synthesize the best insights of radical feminism and of the Marxist tradition and that simultaneously will escape the problems associated with each. So far, socialist feminism has made only limited progress toward this goal: "It is a commitment to the *development* of an analysis and political practice, rather than to one which already exists."[1] In spite of the programmatic nature of its achievement so far, I believe that socialist feminism constitutes a distinctive approach to political life, one that offers the most convincing promise of constructing an adequate theory and practice for women's liberation.

Any attempt to define socialist feminism faces the same problems as attempts to define liberal feminism, radical feminism or Marxism. Feminist theorists and activists do not always wear labels and, even if they do, they are not always agreed on who should wear which label. Moreover, there are differences even between those wearing the same label and, in addition, dialogue between feminists of different tendencies has led to modifications in all their views. Most Marxists, for instance, now take the oppression of women much more seriously than they did prior to the emergence of the women's liberation movement, while radical feminists are paying increasing attention to class, ethnic and national differences between women. As a result, the line between socialist feminism and other feminist theories is increasingly blurred, at least on the surface. For all these reasons, it is inevitable that my account of socialist feminism, like my account of the other feminist theories, will be stipulative as well as reportive. As in defining the other theories, I shall identify socialist feminism primarily by reference to its distinctive, underlying conception of human nature.

The easiest way to provide a preliminary outline of socialist feminism is in terms of its similarities and contrasts with the other feminist theories, especially with Marxism and radical feminism to which it is most closely linked. In a very general sense, all feminists address the same problem: what constitutes the oppression of women and how can that oppression be ended? Both liberal feminists and traditional Marxists believe that this question can be answered in terms of the categories and principles that were formulated originally to deal with other problems. For them, the oppression of women is just one among a number of essentially similar types of problems. Socialist feminism shares with radical feminism the belief that older established political theories are incapable, in principle, of giving an adequate account of women's oppression and that, in order to do so, it is necessary to develop new political and economic categories.

Like radical feminists, socialist feminists believe that these new categories must reconceptualize not only the so-called public sphere, but also the hitherto private sphere of human life. They must give us a way of understanding sexuality, childbearing, childrearing and personal maintenance in political and economic terms. Unlike many American radical feminists, however, socialist feminists attempt to conceptualize these activities in a deliberately historical, rather than a universal and sometimes biologistic, way. A defining feature of socialist feminism is that it attempts to interpret the historical materialist method of traditional Marxism so that it applies to the issues made visible by radical feminists. To revise Juliet Mitchell's comment, it uses a feminist version of the Marxist method to provide feminist answers to feminist questions.[2]

Ever since its inception in the mid-1960s, the women's liberation movement has been split by a chronic dispute over the relation between feminism and Marxism. This dispute has taken a number of forms, but one of the most common ways of interpreting it has been in terms of political priorities. The political analysis of traditional Marxism has led to the position that the struggle for feminism should be subordinated to the class struggle, whereas a radical feminist analysis has implied that the struggle for women's liberation should take priority over the struggle for all other forms of liberation. Socialist feminism rejects this dilemma. Not only does it refuse to compromise socialism for the sake of feminism or feminism for the sake of socialism; it argues that either of these compromises ultimately would be self-defeating. On the socialist feminist analysis, capitalism, male dominance, racism and imperialism are intertwined so inextricably that they are inseparable; consequently the abolition of any of these systems of domination requires the end of all of them. Socialist feminists claim that a full understanding of the capitalist system requires a recognition of the way in which it is structured by male dominance and, conversely, that a full understanding of contemporary male dominance requires a recognition of the way it is organized by the capitalist division of labor. Socialist feminists believe that an adequate account of "capitalist patriarchy" requires the use of the historical materialist method developed originally by Marx and Engels. They argue, however, that the conceptual tools of Marxism are blunt and biased until they are ground into precision on the sharp edge of feminist consciousness.

One question that arises from this preliminary characterization is whether socialist feminism is or is not a variety of Marxism. Obviously, the answer to this question depends both on one's understanding of socialist feminism and on one's interpretation of Marxism. Political motivations are also involved. Some Marxists do not want the honorific title of Marxism to be granted to what they see as heresy;[3] others want to appropriate for Marxism at least those aspects of socialist feminism that they perceive as correct. Similarly, some socialist feminists want to define themselves as Marxists in opposition to other types of socialists; others see no reason to give Marx credit for a theory and a practice that reveals a social reality ignored and obscured by traditional Marxism. My own view is that socialist feminism is unmistakably Marxist, at least insofar as it utilizes the method of historical materialism. As I promised in Chapter 4, I shall argue that socialist feminism is in fact the most consistent application of Marxist method and therefore the most "orthodox" form of Marxism. Indeed, as I shall argue in Chapter 11, the general validity of the socialist feminist approach is suggested by Marxist epistemology itself.

The Socialist Feminist Conception of Human Nature

Socialist feminism is commited to the basic Marxist conception of human nature as created historically through the dialectical interrelation between human biology, human society and the physical environment. This interrelation is mediated by human labor or praxis. The specific form of praxis dominant within a given society creates the distinctive physical and psychological human types characteristic of that society.

Traditional political theory has given theoretical recognition only to a very limited number of human types. It is true that liberals acknowledge individual human variation; indeed, this acknowledgment is a necessary part of their arguments for a firm limitation on the extent of state power. As we have seen, Locke and Mill explain the reasons for at least some of this variation in terms of the social opportunities available to different classes, and liberal feminists explain psychological differences between the sexes in terms of sex-role socialization. Ultimately, however, liberals view the differences between people as relatively superficial, and they assume that underlying these superficial differences is a certain fixed human nature which is modified but not fundamentally created by social circumstances. Marxists, by contrast, view human nature as necessarily constituted in society: they believe that specific historical conditions create distinctive human types. Within contemporary capitalism, they give theoretical recognition to two such types, the capitalist and the proletariat. As we have seen earlier, however, the traditional Marxist conception of human nature is flawed by its failure to recognize explicitly that all human beings in contemporary society belong not only to a specific class; they also have a specific sex and they are at a specific stage in the life cycle from infancy to death. In addition, although this point was not emphasized earlier because it is not a specifically feminist point, all humans in modern industrial society have specific racial, ethnic and national backgrounds. Contemporary society thus consists of groups of individuals, defined simultaneously by age, sex, class, nationality and by racial and ethnic origin, and these groups differ markedly from each other, both physically and psychologically. Liberal political theory has tended to ignore or minimize all these differences. Marxist political theory has tended to recognize only differences of class. The political theory of radical feminism has tended to recognize only differences of age and sex, to understand these in universal terms, and often to view them as determined biologically. By contrast, socialist feminism recognizes all these differences as constituent parts of contemporary human nature and seeks a way of understanding them that is not only materialist but also historical. In particular, it has insisted on the need for a more adequate theoretical understanding of the differences between women and men. Given that its methodological commitment is basically Marxist, it seeks this understanding through an examination of what it calls the sexual division of labor.[4] In other words, it focuses on the different types of praxis undertaken by women and men in order to develop a fully historical materialist account of the social construction of sex and gender.

The differences between women and men are both physical and psychological. Socialist feminists have begun to look at both these aspects of human nature. Some theorists, for instance, have studied variations in menstruation and menopause and have discovered that often these variations are socially determined.[5] Marian Lowe has begun to investigate the ways in which society influences women's sporting achievements, as well as their menstrual patterns.[6] Iris Young has explored some of the socially determined ways in which men and women move differently from each other and experience space, objects, and even their own bodies differently.[7] She has observed that women in sexist society are "physically handicapped." Interesting work has also been done on women's body language.[8] In undertaking these sorts of investigations, socialist feminists focus on the dialectical relationship between sex and society as it emerges through activity organized by gender norms. The methodological approach of socialist feminists makes it obvious that they have abandoned an ahistorical conception of human biology. Instead, they view human biology as being, in part, socially constructed. Biology is "gendered" as well as sexed.

In spite of their interest in the physical differences between women and men, contemporary feminists have been far more concerned with psychological differences, and socialist feminist theory has reflected that priority. Its main focus has been on the social construction not of masculine and feminine physical types, but rather of masculine and feminine character types. Among the many socialist feminist theorists who have worked on this project are Juliet Mitchell, Jane Flax, Gayle Rubin, Nancy Chodorow and, perhaps, Dorothy Dinnerstein.[9] All these theorists have been impressed by how early in life masculine and feminine character structures are established and by the relative rigidity of these structures, once established. To explain the mechanism by which psychological masculinity and femininity are imposed on infants and young children, all utilize some version of psychoanalysis. This is because they view psychoanalytic theory as providing the most plausible and systematic account of how the individual psyche is structured by gender. But unlike Freud, the father of psychoanalysis, socialist feminist theorists do not view psychological masculinity and femininity as the child's inevitable response to a fixed and universal biological endowment. Instead, they view the acquisition of gendered character types as the result of specific social practices, particularly procreative practices, that are not determined by biology and that in principle, therefore, are alterable. They want to debiologize Freud and to reinterpret him in historical materialist terms. As Gayle Rubin puts it: "Psychoanalysis provides a description of the mechanisms by which the sexes are divided and deformed, of how bisexual, androgynous infants are transformed into boys and girls. Psychoanalysis is a feminist theory manqué."[10]

Its utilization of psychoanalytic theory should not be viewed as a defining characteristic of socialist feminism. Not only do all kinds of feminist and non-feminist theorists utilize certain insights of psychoanalysis, but ultimately socialist feminists themselves may reject all versions of Freudian theory—perhaps in favor of a more elegant theory, perhaps in the belief that Freud's fundamental assumptions about human nature are incompatible with historical materialism. Neither is socialist feminism distinguished by its recognition of the social determination of our "inner" lives. Awareness of this determination has been growing throughout the 20th century, in part as a result of the general popularization of Freudian theory, in part as a result of the need felt by the left to explain such political phenomena as the occurrence of fascism rather than socialist revolution in Western Europe. In the 1930s, for instance, Wilhelm Reich and the members of the Frankfurt School explored the ways in which the sexually repressive German family created the so-called authoritarian character structure, which easily accepted Nazism.[11] These explorations on the left have begun to enrich the 19th-century Marxist view of "man" which, as Sartre put it, treated "him" as having been born at the time of applying for "his" first job.[12]

The distinctive aspect of the socialist feminist approach to human psychology is the way in which it synthesizes insights drawn from a variety of sources. Socialist feminism claims all of the following: that our "inner" lives, as well as our bodies and behavior, are structured by gender; that this gender-structuring is not innate but is socially imposed; that the specific characteristics that are imposed are related systematically to the historically prevailing system of organizing social production; that the gender-structuring of our "inner" lives occurs when we are very young and is reinforced throughout our lives in a variety of different spheres; and that these relatively rigid masculine and feminine character structures are a very important element in maintaining male dominance. Given this conception of human psychology, one of the major theoretical tasks that socialist feminism sets itself is to provide a historical materialist account of the relationship between our "inner" lives and our social praxis. It seeks to connect masculine and feminine psychology with the sexual division of labor.

Because it views human beings as constantly recreating themselves through historically specific forms of praxis, socialist feminism's conception of human nature is inseparable from its social theory. Consequently, the following elaboration of the socialist feminist account of the way in which women and men are socially constructed includes not only claims about human psychology and physiology but also claims about social institutions and ways of organizing social life.

It is generally accepted, by non-feminists and feminists alike, that the most obvious manifestation of the sexual division of labor, in contemporary society if not in all societies, is marked by the division between the so-called public and private spheres of human life. The line between these two spheres has varied historically: in the political theory of ancient Greece, for instance, "the economy" fell within the private sphere, whereas in contemporary political theory, both liberal and Marxist, "the economy" is considered—in different ways—to be part of the public realm. Wherever the distinction has existed, the private realm has always included sexuality and procreation, has always been viewed as more "natural" and therefore less "human" than the public realm, and has always been viewed as the realm of women.[13] Although women have always done many kinds of work, they have been defined primarily by their sexual and procreative labor; throughout history, women have been defined as "sex objects" and as mothers.

Partly because of this definition of women's work and partly because of their conviction that an individual's gender identity is established very early in life, much socialist feminist theory has focused on the area of sexuality and procreation. Yet the theory has been committed to conceptualizing this area in terms that are historical, rather than biological, and specific, rather than universal. Socialist feminism has accepted the radical feminist insight that sexual activity, childbearing, and childrearing are social practices that embody power relations and are therefore appropriate subjects for political analysis. Because of its rejection of biological determinism, however, socialist feminism denies the radical feminist assumption that these practices are fundamentally invariant. On the contrary, socialist feminists have stressed historical variation both in the practices and in the categories by which they are understood. Zillah Eisenstein writes:

> None of the processes in which a woman engages can be understood separate from the relations of the society which she embodies and which are reflected in the ideology of society. For instance, the act of giving birth to a child is only termed an act of motherhood if it reflects the relations of marriage and the family. Otherwise the very same act can be termed adultery and the child is "illegitimate" or a "bastard." The term "mother" may have a significantly different meaning when different relations are involved—as in "unwed mother." It depends on what relations are embodied in the act.[14]

In the same spirit, Ann Foreman writes that "fatherhood is a social invention . . . located in a series of functions rather than in biology."[15] Rayna Rapp writes that even "being a child is a highly variable social relation."[16] Using the same historical approach, Ann Ferguson has argued that the emergence of lesbianism, as a distinct sexual identity, is a recent rather than a universal phenomenon insofar as it presupposes an urban society with the possibility of economic independence for women.[17] More generally, "It was only with the development of capitalist societies that 'sexuality' and 'the economy' became separable from other spheres of society and could be counter-posed to one another as realities of different sorts."[18]

Other authors have claimed that there is no transhistorical definition of marriage in terms of which the marital institutions of different cultures can be compared usefully.[19] Even within a single society, divisions of class mean that the working-class family unit is defined very differently from the upper-class family unit, and that it performs very different social functions.[20] One author denies that the family is a "bounded universe" and suggests that "we should extend to the study of 'family' [a] thoroughgoing agnosticism."[21] In general, socialist feminist theory has viewed human nature as constructed in part through the historically specific ways in which people have organized their sexual, childbearing and childrearing activities. The organization of these activities both affects and is affected by class and ethnic differences, but it is seen as particularly important in creating the masculine and feminine physiques and character structures that are considered appropriate in a given society.

The beginnings of this conception of human nature are already evident, to some extent, in the work of Marx and Engels. Engels' famous definition of the materialist conception of history in his introduction to *The Origin of the Family, Private Property and the State* states clearly:

> The social organization under which the people of a particular historical epoch and a particular country live is determined by both kinds of production: by the state of development of labor on the one hand and of the family on the other.[22]

Moreover, Marx and Engels warn explicitly against conceptualizing procreation in an ahistorical way. In *The German Ideology,* they mock an ahistorical approach to "the concept of the family,"[23] and Engels' own work in *Origin* is designed precisely to demonstrate historical change in the social rules governing the eligibility of an individual's sexual partners. As we have seen in Chapter 4, however, Marx and Engels view changes in the social organization of procreation as ultimately determined themselves by changes in the so-called mode of production, at least in postprimitive societies. Consequently, they see procreation as being now only of secondary importance in shaping human nature and society. One reason for this view may be that Marx and Engels still retain certain assumptions about the "natural," presumably biological, determination of much procreative activity. Thus, they do not give a symmetrical treatment to the human needs for food, shelter, and clothing, on the one hand, and to sexual, childbearing and childrearing needs, on the other. They view the former as changing historically, giving rise to new possibilities of social organization, but they regard human procreative needs as more "natural" and less open to historical transformation. Socialist feminists, by contrast, emphasize the social determination of sexual, childbearing and childrearing needs. They understand that these needs have developed historically in dialectical relation with changing procreative practices. Consequently, they are prepared to subject sexual and procreative practices to sustained political analysis and to reflect systematically on how changes in these practices could transform human nature.

Although socialist feminist theory stresses the importance of the so-called private sphere of procreation in constructing the historically appropriate types of masculinity and femininity, it does not ignore the so-called public sphere. It recognizes that women have always worked outside procreation, providing goods and services not only for their families but for the larger society as well. Socialist feminism claims that the conception of women as primarily sexual beings and/or as mothers is an ideological mystification that obscures the facts, for instance, that more than half the world's farmers are women,[24] and that, in the United States, women now make up almost half the paid labor force. Indeed, the Department of Labor projects that women will constitute 51.4 percent of the U.S. paid labor force by 1990.[25]

For socialist feminism, women, just as much as men, are beings whose labor transforms the non-human world. Socialist feminists view the slogan "A women's place is everywhere" as more than a call for change: for them, it is already a partial description of existing reality.

Only a partial description, however. Although socialist feminism recognizes the extent of women's productive work, it recognizes also that this work has rarely, if ever, been the same as men's. Even in contemporary market society, socialist feminism recognizes that the paid labor force is almost completely segregated by sex; at every level, there are "women's specialities." Within the contemporary labor force, moreover, women's work is invariably less prestigious, lower paid, and defined as being less skilled than men's, even when it involves such socially valuable and complex skills as dealing with children or sick people.

Socialist feminism sees, therefore, that the sexual division of labor is not just a division *between* procreation and "production": it is also a division *within* procreation and *within* "production." Consequently, socialist feminism does not view contemporary masculinity and femininity as constructed entirely through the social organization of procreation; these constructs are elaborated and reinforced in nonprocreative labor as well.

Just as socialist feminists stress the historical variation in women's work as sexual servants, as wives, and as mothers, so too they stress the historical variation in women's nonprocreative work. Changes in the mode of "production" as well as in the mode of procreation have affected prevailing conceptions of femininity. For instance,

> Only in a capitalist society does it make sense to look down on women as emotional or irrational. As epithets, they would not have made sense in the renaissance. Only in a capitalist society does it make sense to look down on women as "dependent." "Dependent" as an epithet would not make sense in feudal societies.[26]

Even within modes of production, the variation in the non-procreative work that women have been expected to perform has been especially influential in creating cross-class differences in conceptions of masculinity and femininity. In the 19th-century United States, for instance, black women were required to be physically strong and privileged white women to be physically weak, and the same distinction held between working-class and upper-class women in England.

We can now summarize the socialist feminist view of human nature in general and of women's nature in particular. Unlike liberalism and some aspects of traditional Marxism, socialist feminism does not view humans as "abstract, genderless" (and ageless and colorless) individuals,[27] with women essentially indistinguishable from men. Neither does it view women as irreducibly different from men, the same yesterday, today and forever. Instead, it views women as constituted essentially by the social relations they inhabit. "(T)he social relations of society define the particular activity a woman engages in at a given moment. Outside these relations, 'woman' becomes an abstraction."[28]

Gayle Rubin paraphrases Marx thus:

> What is a domesticated woman? A female of the species. The one explanation is as good as the other. A woman is a woman. She only becomes a domestic, a wife, a chattel, a playboy bunny, a prostitute, or a human dictaphone in certain relations. Torn from these relationships, she is no more the helpmate of a man than gold in itself is money.[29]

To change these relationships is to change women's and so human nature.

Since history is never static, continuing changes in human nature are inevitable. As Marx himself remarked, "All history is nothing but a continuous transformation of human nature."[30] Socialist feminists want women to participate fully in taking conscious social control of these changes. They deny that there is anything especially natural about women's relationships with each other, with children or with men. Instead, they seek to reconstitute those relationships in such a way as to liberate the full power of women's (and human) creative potential.

No contemporary feminist would deny this goal, stated in the abstract. Just as at one time everyone was against sin, so now everyone is in favor of liberating human potential. Just as people used to disagree over how to identify sin, however, so now there is disagreement over what are human potentialities, which ones should be developed and how this development should be undertaken. Every conception of human nature implies an answer to these questions, and socialist feminism has its own distinctive answer. Unlike liberalism, the socialist feminist ideal of human fulfilment is not individual autonomy; for reasons that were suggested in Chapter 3 and that will be explained more fully later, socialist feminism views the ideal of autonomy as characteristically masculine as well as characteristically capitalist. The socialist feminist conception of human fulfilment is closer to the Marxist ideal of the full development of human potentialities through free productive labor, but socialist feminism construes productive labor more broadly than does traditional Marxism. Consequently, the socialist feminist ideal of human well-being and fulfilment includes the full development of human potentialities for free sexual expression, for freely bearing children and for freely rearing them.

To many Marxists, the theory of alienation expresses Marx's conception of human nature in capitalist society. As the theory is traditionally interpreted, alienation characterizes primarily workers' relation to wage labor; however, Marx saw that the way workers experience wage labor also affects the way they experience the rest of their lives. Because their wage labor is coerced, their activity outside wage labor seems free by contrast.

> We arrive at the result that man (the worker) feels himself to be freely active only in his animal functions—eating, drinking and procreating, or at most also in his dwelling and in personal adornment—while in his human functions he is reduced to an animal. The animal becomes human and the human becomes animal.[31]

To socialist feminists, this conception of alienation is clearly male-biased. Men may feel free when eating, drinking, and procreating, but women do not. As the popular saying has it, "A woman's work is never done." An Englishman's home may be his castle, but it is his wife's prison. Women are compelled to do housework, to bear and raise children and to define themselves sexually in terms of men's wishes. The pressures on women to do this work are almost overwhelming:

> When I say that women are subject to a form of compulsive labor, I mean that they may only resist with great difficulty, and that the majority succumb. The same may be said of non-owners when it comes to wage work. In both cases, it is not compulsive in the sense that one is driven to it with whips and chains (though that happens, too!), but in the sense that no real alternative is generally available to women, and that everything in society conspires to ensure that women do this work. While a non-owner may attempt small independent production, or simply refuse to work and live off begging or state welfare, that is not proof of his freedom. The same is true of women. While a woman may with great difficulty resist doing reproductive work, that is no proof that she is "free" not to do it.[32]

One way in which socialist feminists are attempting to conceptualize contemporary women's lack of freedom is by extending the traditional Marxist theory of alienation. A more detailed account of these attempts will be given in Chapter 10, but a few authors may be mentioned here. Iris Young's reflections on "the struggle for our bodies," cited earlier in this chapter, suggest that women suffer a special form of alienation from their bodies. Similarly, Sandra Bartky claims that women are alienated in cultural production, as mothers and sexual beings. She believes that feminine narcissism is the paradigm of a specifically feminine form of sexual alienation.[33] Ann Foreman argues that femininity as such is an alienated condition: "While alienation reduces the man to an instrument of labour within industry, it reduces the woman to an instrument for his sexual pleasure within the family."[34] One may define the goal of socialist feminism as being to overcome all forms of alienation but especially those that are specific to women.

If it is difficult to envision what nonalienated industry would be like, it seems almost impossible to foresee the form of nonalienated sexuality or parenthood. Because of the ideological dogma that these are determined biologically, it is even harder to envision alternatives to prevailing sexual and procreative practices than it is to the capitalist mode of production. Alternative ways of organizing procreation tend to be viewed as science fiction; indeed, they are considered more often in fiction than in political theory. As we shall see in Chapter 10, a number of socialist feminists are experimenting with alternatives in procreation, but the extent and validity of those experiments is limited, of course, by their context in a society that is emphatically neither socialist nor feminist.

The one solid basis of agreement among socialist feminists is that to overcome women's alienation, the sexual division of labor must be eliminated in every area of life. Just as sexual segregation in nonprocreative work must be eliminated, so men must participate fully in childrearing and, so far as possible, in childbearing.[35] Normative heterosexuality must be replaced by a situation in which the sex of one's lovers is a matter of social indifference, so that the dualist categories of heterosexual, homosexual and bisexual may be abandoned. Some authors describe the ideal as androgyny,[36] but even this term is implicitly dualistic. If it is retained for the present, we must remember that the ultimate transformation of human nature at which socialist feminists aim goes beyond the liberal conception of psychological androgyny to a possible transformation of "physical" human capacities, some of which, until now, have been seen as biologically limited to one sex. This transformation might even include the capacities for insemination, for lactation and for gestation so that, for instance, one woman could inseminate another, so that men and nonparturitive women could lactate and so that fertilized ova could be transplanted into women's or even into men's bodies. These developments may seem farfetched, but in fact they are already on the technological horizon;[37] however, what is needed much more immediately than technological development is a substantial reduction in the social domination of women by men. Only such a reduction can ensure that these or alternative technological possibilities are used to increase women's control over their bodies and thus over their lives, rather than being used as an additional means for women's subjugation. Gayle Rubin writes: "We are not only oppressed *as* women, we are oppressed by having to *be* women or men as the case may be."[38] The goal of socialist feminism is to abolish the social relations that constitute humans not only as workers and capitalists but also as women and men. Whereas one version of radical feminism takes the human ideal to be a woman, the ideal of socialist feminism is that women (and men) will disappear as socially constituted categories.

The Political Theory of Socialist Feminism:
Toward a Political Economy of Sex and Gender

Political theories share the common objectives of diagnosing the causes of human malaise and of writing prescriptions for its cure. They are rivals to each other in the sense that they provide conflicting visions of the good society and alternative critiques of existing societies. As we have seen already, however, political philosophers not only differ in their diagnosis of and prescription for human malaise; often they also disagree on some of the symptoms of the disease. It is not just that they give different answers to the same questions; they also ask the questions differently.

Feminist political theories follow the same pattern. The overriding objective of each theory is to understand women's oppression in contemporary society in order to discover how to end that oppression. Each feminist theory that we have considered, however, perceives women's oppression in a different way. It provides an alternative to the other theories not only in its prescription for ending women's oppression, but in its diagnosis of what that oppression is.

There is no way to formulate the problems of political philosophy that is politically or theoretically neutral. The manner in which one formulates the problem is in large part a function of one's own political priorities and of the methodological commitments implicit in one's conception of human nature. Socialist feminists have their own political priorities and their own conception of human nature. Consequently, their political theory is distinct from the other theories that we have considered not only because of the answers it gives but because of the questions it asks.

Traditional Marxism stresses commonalities between women and men of the same class, as Marxism defines classes, and it stresses differences between women of different classes. Evelyn Reed poses the following rhetorical question:

> Tens of thousands of women went to Washington antiwar demonstrations in November, 1969, and again in May, 1970. Did they have more in common with the militant men marching beside them on that life-and-death issue—or with Mrs. Nixon, her daughters, and the wife of the attorney general, Mrs. Mitchell, who peered uneasily out of her window and saw the specter of another Russian Revolution in those protesting masses?[39]

For Reed, class differences are far more fundamental than differences of sex or gender. Consequently, on the traditional Marxist view that she expressses, a feminist political theory is adequate insofar as it explains why the most fundamental interests of working-class women and men are shared, rather than in conflict.

Radical feminism, on the other hand, stresses the commonalities in the experience of all women, from the president's wife to the antiwar demonstrator. For radical feminism, women's shared interest in overthrowing male domination is far more fundamental than the divisions between women of different classes, as "class" is ordinarily understood. For radical feminism, therefore, a feminist theory is adequate just as far as it accounts for those commonalities. Because it views the common features of women's experience as consisting primarily in women's universal definition as mothers and as sexual servants and because it sees the subordination of women to men as the most fundamental division in all societies, it concludes that the domain of procreation and sexuality constitutes the material base of society as a whole. For it is in this domain, radical feminists believe, that women's subordination is rooted. On the radical feminist view, therefore, the Marxist class analysis applies to a relatively superficial level of social reality.

Socialist feminists have their own view of the problem of women's oppression. As they see it, a contemporary individual's life experience is shaped by her sex and gender assignment from birth to death. Equally, however, they believe that an individual's experiences are shaped by her class, race, and nationality. The problem for socialist feminism, then, is to develop a theoretical account of these different types of oppression and the relation between them with a view to ending them all. Unlike the two theories just mentioned, socialist feminism is not committed in advance to any view on the question of which type of oppression is more fundamental.

In answering the questions that it sets itself, socialist feminism draws on the historical materialist method of Marxism. It seeks the underlying reasons for women's subordination in human praxis, in the way that people in each society organize to produce and distribute the basic necessities of life. Socialist feminists, like traditional Marxists, believe that politics cannot be separated from economics. Consequently, their project is to construct a political economy of women's subordination. Although the socialist feminist method is fundamentally Marxist, the way in which it utilizes this method results in a transformation of some central Marxist categories.

1. THE CONCEPTUAL FRAMEWORK

For traditional Marxism, class struggle is the key to understanding the form of social phenomena and the direction of historical change. According to Marxism, as soon as humans learned how to produce and store a surplus of goods beyond their own immediate needs, they began a struggle to control the productive resources of society in order to appropriate that surplus for themselves. The group which achieved control of the means of production became the ruling class and it used this control to dominate the other classes, to control the conditions of their labor, and to appropriate its product. As one mode of production succeeds another, classes are reconstituted, but the basic motor of history remains the struggle to control society's productive resources.

Socialist feminists do not disagree with that view, stated in the abstract. But they do disagree with how Marxists traditionally have interpreted it. On the traditional interpretation, "labor" refers primarily to the work involved in producing the means of satisfying human "material needs," understood primarily as food, shelter, clothing, etc.[40] Marx and Engels state explicitly that there are two aspects to "the production of life, both of one's own in labor and of fresh life in procreation."[41] In most of their writings, however, "production" is understood as meaning the production of food shelter, clothing, etc., and "classes" are defined by their relationship to the "means of production," in this sense. The "economy" of a society is taken to be the way it organizes "production," and its "political economy" is the complex system of interrelationships between its specific forms of political power and of "economic" organization. The prevailing "economic system" or "mode of production" is thought to determine ultimately what happens in the "noneconomic" realm and thus constitutes the "material base" or "economic foundation" of society.

Of special interest to feminists is the fact that childbearing and childrearing practices are taken to be part of the noneconomic or "superstructural" realm.

Socialist feminists propose a much wider interpretation of all these categories. I shall first give a brief and necessarily abstract statement of their position and then provide some of the socialist feminist arguments in favor of their view.

Socialist feminists begin from the fact, acknowledged at least in part by Marx and Engels, that human material needs include not only food, shelter, clothing, etc. Equally fundamental to the survival of the species are the social and often individual human needs for bearing and rearing children, for sexual satisfaction and, on one view, for emotional nurturance. Every society has to produce the means to satisfy these needs. Insofar as their satisfaction requires human labor, the system designed to satisfy them is a system of production—even though it does not always produce tangible objects.

All human adults, both male and female, are capable of virtually all types of labor. Both sexes can contribute to producing the means of satisfying human needs for food and shelter, for sexual satisfaction, and for emotional nurturance. Men as well as women are capable of caring for and socializing children, and there is even some evidence that men can lactate.[42] At previous and existing levels of technological development, however, there is one difference between the productive capacity of women and men: the biologically grounded difference that only men have been able to impregnate women, and only women have been able to give birth to children. Because of this difference in the male and female contribution to procreation, women's capacity for reproduction historically has been far more limited than men's. A woman has been able to produce a maximum of only 20 or so children in her lifetime, whereas a man has been able to father literally hundreds of children. For this reason, women's reproductive capacity has been an especially important productive resource in all previous societies.

On the socialist feminist view, there is considerable historical variation in the systems through which people have attempted to fulfill the need for children. The same is true of the ways in which people have organized to satisfy their needs for sexual and emotional satisfaction. Just as human needs for food, shelter and clothing assume specific form through the means available to satisfy them, so too the needs for children, for sexual satisfaction and for emotional nurturance undergo a continuous historical process of transformation. For instance, in spite of the valuable because limited reproductive capacity of women, a desire for male rather than female children has sometimes caused women to be killed for failing to produce sons.

Not only are the means to satisfy the needs for children and for sexual and emotional satisfaction produced through human labor; humans can also distribute and exchange the means of fulfilling these needs. Historically, two of the main institutions for effecting such transactions have been marriage and prostitution. Because these sorts of transactions are possible, the system of producing and distributing the means to satisfy needs for children, for sexual satisfaction and for emotional nurturance is in fact an economic system, or part of one—even though money is not always the currency of exchange.[43] In making this point, socialist feminists are building on the insight of radical feminists. Radical feminists have identified sexuality and procreation as areas of human activity that are susceptible to political analysis. Socialist feminists claim that these practices fall within the domain of political economy.

Within this part of the economic system, to which different socialist feminist theorists give different names, it has often happened that some people have controlled the labor of others. The controlling group has forced the subordinate groups to do sexual, procreative and emotional labor for them; it has defined what work was done and how it was performed; it has benefited disproportionately from the labor of the subordinate groups; and it has used the work done by the subordinate groups to bring those groups even further under its control. In this sort of situation, the dominant and subordinate groups are in what is essentially a class relation to each other, although socialist feminists often refrain from using the terminology of class, since "class" already has a well-defined and narrower meaning within Marxist theory.

Socialist feminists believe that the ruling group in the production of children and of sexual and emotional satisfaction has always been predominantly, though not exclusively, composed of men and that the laboring group in the production of these goods has always been composed predominantly and almost exclusively of women. Certainly they believe that this is true in contemporary society where they see a systematic difference in power between women and men, a difference defined in large part by men's control over the sexual, procreative, and emotional labor of women. This control may not be used to extract surplus value or profit from women's labor, but it is still a form of exploitation in the Marxist sense. On the Marxist view, exploitation is forced, unpaid, surplus labor, the product of which is not controlled by the producers. Exploitation is a defining feature of all class societies and, in pre-class societies, is usually clearly visible. Only under capitalism has exploitation been concealed by assuming the form of surplus value.[44] Therefore, so long as men as a group control and derive primary benefit from the labor of women as a group, socialist feminists view men as a group or class that exploits women as a group or class.

Socialist feminists do not believe that the sexual and procreative aspects of production are determined ultimately by what is defined ordinarily as "the economy"; in other words, sexuality and procreation are not part of the superstructure. Neither, however, do socialist feminists believe that they alone constitute the material base of society as a whole. Instead, sexuality and procreation are a part of the economic foundation of society, partially determining "the economy," in the narrow sense, and partially determined by it.

The socialist feminist claim, then, is that the productive resources of society include the human capacity to perform a wide variety of types of labor. One of the most important of these productive resources historically has been women's capacity to bear children. On the socialist feminist view, therefore, the perennial struggle to control society's productive resources has always included a struggle to control the reproductive capacity of women. This struggle has occurred not only between men of different economic classes but also between women and men. To the extent that women and men have stood in different relations to the productive resources of society, this struggle may be viewed as a class struggle. One cannot achieve an adequate understanding of social phenomena and the direction of historical change without reference to this continuing struggle. It is a struggle in which women and men have always been on different sides as groups, although not necessarily as individuals, and it is a struggle in which men invariably have dominated women, although women have sometimes made limited gains in controlling their reproductive capacity or other productive resources.

This conceptual framework defines the primary problems of socialist feminist political theory and also the method for approaching those problems. Socialist feminist theorists must use the conceptual tool of the sexual division of labor to explore the relations between women's subordination, specific economic systems (in the narrow conventional sense of "economic"), and specific ways of organizing childbearing and childrearing, sexuality and emotional life.

2. THE ECONOMIC FOUNDATION OF SOCIETY

Why have socialist feminists developed this distinctive approach to political theory? They have two sorts of arguments. Their "negative" arguments point out inadequacies in alternative theories; their "positive" arguments point to new theories which utilize this approach and which, in their view, provide a more adequate understanding of women's subordination and hence more insight into how to end it.

The "negative" arguments of socialist feminism have been sketched in previous chapters. Their critique of the conceptual framework of traditional Marxist theory can be summed up by saying that, according to socialist feminism, traditional Marxism represents the world view of men. Like radical feminists, socialist feminists believe that traditional Marxist categories ignore women's labor outside the market, overlook the gender-defined character of women's work within the market, and so obscure the systematic domination of women by men. Whatever the economic system, conventionally defined, radical and socialist feminists perceive that the conditions of women's lives are determined not only by the ruling class, conventionally defined, but also by men. And they see that men of all classes benefit directly though in different ways from women's labor. In contemporary society, for instance, the sexual desires of men of all classes are taken as primary in the definition of women as sexual objects and in the overt or tacit acceptance of such institutions as rape, prostitution and the sexual double-standard. Men of all classes enjoy women's domestic services and the extra leisure that these services give them. In earlier societies, men appropriated the labor of the children whom women reared. Even now, men still appropriate children by giving them their name. Male capitalists determine the conditions of women's wage labor; but male workers receive monetary and other advantages from the fact that women's wage labor is invariably less prestigious, often more stressful, and always lower paid than men's. Male dominance pervades every area of life under capitalism, yet it is little more than a footnote to Marxist political economy.

Although the domination of women is not central to Marxist political economy, it does not follow that it cannot be explained in terms of Marxist categories. Traditional Marxists claim that all social phenomena occurring within a given society should be understood as determined ultimately by the "economic base" of that society. In understanding simple or "primitive" societies, where the main organizing principle was kinship, Engels seemed to accept that procreative relations should be included within the economic base of society. Nevertheless, he explains that:

> Within this structure of society based on kinship groups the productivity of labor increasingly develops, and with it private property and exchange, differences of wealth, the possibility of utilizing the labor power of others, and hence the basis of class antagonisms: new social elements, which in the course of generations strive to adapt the old social order to the new conditions, until at last their incompatibility brings about a complete upheaval. In the collision of the newly developed social classes, the old society founded on kinship groups is broken up. In its place appears a new society, with its control centered in the state, the subordinate units

of which are no longer kinship associations, but local associations; a society in which the system of the family is completely dominated by the system of property, and in which there now freely develop those class antagonisms and class struggles that have hitherto formed the content of all written history.[45]

Engels' explanation is in accord with the view that he and Marx expressed thirty years earlier in *The German Ideology:* "The family, which to begin with is the only social relationship, becomes later, when increased needs create new social relations and the increased population new needs, a subordinate one."[46] In more complex societies, therefore, Marx and Engels see the relations between men and women and between adults and children as being determined ultimately by the prevailing system of production, defined so as to exclude sexuality and procreation.

This claim is denied by radical and socialist feminists. Gayle Rubin writes:

> No analysis of the reproduction of labor power under capitalism can explain foot-binding, chastity belts, or any of the incredible array of Byzantine, fetishized indignities, let alone the more ordinary ones, which have been inflicted upon women in various times and places.[47]

Of course, one would hardly expect an analysis of the reproduction of labor power under capitalism to explain social phenomena in pre-capitalist societies, but neither does any such concept explain male dominance in the contemporary world. Traditional Marxism conceals rather than illuminates the facts that:

> While women represent half the global population and one-third of the [paid] labor force, they receive only one-tenth of the world income and own less than 1 percent of the world property. They are also responsible for two-thirds of all working hours.[48]

In order to account for male dominance, radical and socialist feminists believe either that Marxism must construct some new explanations of how this dominance is determined by the prevailing mode of production or it must revise its conception of what constitutes the mode of production and thus of what constitutes the economic base of society. Radical and socialist feminists alike are sceptical of the fruitfulness of the former path. Instead, each has chosen to develop a new conception of the material base of society that will give a more adequate explanation of the pervasiveness and persistence of male dominance. To do this, both radical and socialist feminists look to the sphere of sexuality and procreation. Each group, however, conceptualizes this in quite different ways.

Radical feminists tend to view procreation as a cross-cultural universal, biologically determined or not. For many of them, women's subordination is rooted in the fact that women in all societies are childbearers, childrearers and sexual servants to men. Radical feminists express this by saying that men control women's bodies, forcing them to bear children and to be sexually available. On this view, as we have seen, the central or basic institutions of male dominance are those that organize sexuality, childbearing and childrearing, including such institutions as normative heterosexuality and marriage. The fundamental task of feminism then becomes the smashing of these institutions and the key slogan for women becomes the demand for control over their bodies. Because radical feminists view male dominance as the most significant feature of contemporary society, and because they view the organization of procreation as the material basis of male dominance, they conclude that the material base of society as a whole, that which ultimately determines every other social phenomenon, is the organization of sexuality, childbearing and childrearing. All existing societies are patriarchal and the power of the patriarchy is rooted in male control of procreation. What Marxists call "economic systems" or "modes of production" are simply manifestations of a more basic and universal "mode of reproduction," to use Firestone's terminology.

Socialist feminists agree that the domination of women cannot be explained without reference to procreation. But they do not agree that it can be explained entirely by this reference. For one thing, as we have seen, socialist feminists deny that male dominance has a universal form or can be identified with any set of cross-cultural institutions. Instead, it is manifested in different ways in different societies. In addition, socialist feminists believe that, in viewing women primarily as mothers and as sexual servants, radical feminists accept too much of the male-dominant ideology that discounts women's labor in nonprocreative and nonsexual areas. A full understanding of women's oppression must examine the sexual division of labor outside as well as within procreation and between procreation and "production." Moreover, it must examine the "endless variety" as well as the "monotonous similarity" in women's experience,[49] both the experiences of women in other societies and especially the experience of women of different classes, races and nationalities in contemporary industrial society. Even within contemporary society, there is "endless variety" not only in women's nonprocreative experiences but also in women's sexual experience and in their experience as mothers. Depending on their class or race, some women have been forced to "mother" the children of other women; some women are prostitutes; some women are virtually a-sexual wives. "Class and race determine access to contraception and abortion on the one hand, and sterilization on the other."[50] In short, just as traditional Marxism does not account for the commonalities in the experience of women, on the socialist feminist view, radical feminism does not account for the differences in women's experience.

Socialist feminists have made a number of attempts to provide a more adequate explanation of women's subordination. All these attempts refer to types of productive activity not ordinarily considered economic, and seek to show how they can be understood in economic terms. Lynda Lange, for instance, grounds women's subordination in the fact that women, unlike men, are compelled to engage in reproductive labor, which she conceptualizes primarily as the bearing and rearing of children. This labor varies within different classes and within different racial or ethnic groups, but it is always assigned to women. Lange points out that one of the main sanctions forcing women to perform reproductive labor is the limitation on their access to wage labor, although this coercion is mystified by the ideology of marriage and motherhood. Realistically, however, "Marriage to a wage-worker remains for most women the best bargain for a livelihood that they can make. Hence it appears as a 'free' choice."[51]

Gayle Rubin develops a more elaborate, though not incompatible, account of women's subordination. She grounds that subordination in a particular form of the "sex-gender system," that is, "the set of arrangements by which a society transforms biological sexuality into products of human activity and in which these transformed sexual needs are satisfied."[52] Rubin views kinship as a widely prevailing empirical form of sex-gender system, one based on the subordination of women. Within kinship systems, women are exchanged as wives, thus enforcing exogamy and creating and consolidating extrafamilial ties. In order for this system to work, a norm of heterosexuality must be imposed on both sexes and a passive feminine nature must be created in girls. Rubin sees Freudian theory as a description of the process by which a passive feminine psychology is imposed on females. Freud describes correctly boys' and girls' different emotional reactions to their own anatomy but, as Rubin points out, he fails to see that these different reactions are generated by a social context in which heterosexuality is the norm and in which, because of male dominance, women's biology is devalued. By utilizing the concept of a sex-gender system, Rubin, like Lange, seeks to explain women's subordination by reference not to "the economy" but rather to the prevailing system of organizing sexuality and procreation.

Nancy Chodorow is another theorist who believes that women's contemporary subordination is grounded in the prevailing organization of procreation, but she focuses on mothering rather than sexuality.[53] Chodorow begins from the fact that women are typically the primary caretakers of their children and that, consequently, an individual's most intense early relationship is invariably with her or his mother. Both girls and boys initially react to their mothers with love and later, in order to separate themselves, with hostility. In a sexist society, however, boys can become masculine only by separating themselves completely from their mothers. They do this by developing a contempt for women, by denying their own emotional needs and by generally creating a rigid and punitive superego. Girls, on the other hand, achieve femininity by being like their mothers. Consequently, they retain their capacity for empathy with others and develop superegos that are open to persuasion and vulnerable to the judgments of others. In the end, boys grow up to be men who are achievement-oriented and well adapted to work outside the home, while girls grow up to be women whose psyches are well adapted to emotional work both inside and outside the home. According to Chodorow, the results of the sexual division of labor in parenting go beyond the fact that mothers produce daughters who become mothers (in the social sense) themselves and men who don't. Because the male-dominated social and family structure recreates itself in the psychic structure of individuals, male dominance in general is reinforced, especially through the unequal prestige enjoyed by the domestic and nondomestic spheres. Chodorow adds that the prevailing system of procreation creates small privatized family units, a tendency which contributes to the mobility and interchangeability of families and to the belief that the polity has no responsibility for young children. In this way, Chodorow's theory tries to establish that the prevailing system of procreation has a significant determining influence on the organization of nondomestic production.

Although Chodorow's work is currently very popular, critics have pointed out that, from a socialist feminist perspective, it is not without problems. One difficulty is that Chodorow tends to view the organization of childrearing and the consequent development of psychological masculinity and femininity in the universalistic and ahistorical way that is characteristic of much, though not all, psychoanalytic theory. Moreover, Chodorow focuses on how the prevailing organization of procreation affects children and ignores its effect on parents, especially on mothers. Finally, she does not provide a materialist explanation for the sexual division of labor in procreation, which is the starting point of her theory; consequently, even if Chodorow is correct in her account of how the sexual division of labor in parenting reproduces itself, generating characteristically masculine and feminine attitudes towards children, this account is incomplete as a theory of women's subordination.

Ann Ferguson and Nancy Folbre attempt to conceptualize the relation between "economics," procreation, and male dominance in a way that avoids these flaws. They develop the concept of "sex-affective production," which includes "the bearing and rearing of children—and the provision of affection, nurturance and sexual satisfaction." Ferguson and Folbre claim that every society must have such a system and they argue that, although men do perform some of this work in contemporary society, women currently do the bulk of the labor involved. As a result, women in contemporary society have:

> a longer working day with less material and emotional rewards than men, less control over family decisions, and less sexual freedom combined with less sexual satisfaction. Specialization in sex-affective production is also associated with restrictions on options, choices and remuneration available to women in work outside of family—restrictions often directly attributed to their presumed or actual mothering role.[54]

Ferguson and Folbre conceptualize women's work outside the market more broadly than Lange, but their general conclusions are similar to hers: the contemporary organization of sex-affective production not only allows men to benefit directly from women's labor in this area but also allows the increased exploitation of women in wage labor.

Although it has always been true that men have exploited women's sex-affective labor, Ferguson and Folbre insist that the system of sex-affective production is not unchanging. For instance, they argue that under capitalism women's participation in work outside the home has increased and the amount of time women devote to sex-affective production has diminished substantially. At different periods in history, there are different possibilities for women to throw off male control in the area of sex-affective production.

The concept of sex-affective production is far from being universally accepted by socialist feminists. Ferguson and Folbre's work is a good example, however, of the continuing socialist feminist efforts to conceptualize what I have called the sphere of procreation. These efforts are all characterized by a view of sexual and procreative activities as labor, as political and economic, and as existing in dialectical interrelation with what is ordinarily called "production." Socialist feminists insist only that procreation and "production" are mutually determining but that one is not a more "ultimate" determinant than the other; both are part of the economic foundation of society. The fact that women in "developing" countries engage primarily in subsistence agriculture for their families while men engage in wage labor, either in industry or in cash crop agriculture for export, is surely in part a result of the sexual division of labor in procreation which assigns to women the major childcare and domestic responsibilities.[55] Similarly, in the industrialized nations, the characteristic sexual division of labor in the market, which assigns women disproportionately to the nurturing and service occupations (nurse, waitress, school teacher, secretary, social worker, entertainer, prostitute) is justified ideologically as an extension into the so-called public realm of women's work in the home. On the other hand, procreative practices are deeply affected by the prevailing system of market production. One example is the switch from breast-feeding to bottle-feeding babies as corporations discover the possibility of profiting both from the employment of mothers and from the manufacture of infant formula. Another example is Bowles's and Gintis's demonstration of differences in the types of skills that schools and colleges teach to working- and upper-class youth, respectively.[56]

Within Marxist theory, there has been much controversy over the concepts of "base" and "superstructure." The concepts are traced to Marx's *Preface to "The Critique of Political Economy"* where he writes:

In the social production of their life, men enter into definite relations that are indispensable and independent of their will, relations of production which correspond to a definite stage of development of their material productive forces. The sum total of these relations of production constitutes the economic structure of society, the real foundation, on which rises a legal and political superstructure and to which correspond definite forms of social consciousness. The mode of production of material life conditions the social, political and intellectual life processes in general. It is not the consciousness of men that determines their being, but, on the contrary, their social being that determines their consciousness. . . . With the change of the economic foundation the entire immense superstructure is more or less rapidly transformed. In considering such transformations a distinction should always be made between the material transformation of the economic conditions of production, which can be determined with the precision of natural science, and the legal, political, religious, aesthetic or philosophic—in short, ideological forms in which men become conscious of this conflict and fight it out. Just as our opinion of an individual is not based on what he thinks of himself, so can we not judge of such a period of transformation by its own consciousness; on the contrary, this consciousness must be explained rather from the contradictions of material life, from the existing conflict between the social productive forces and the relations of production.[57]

For many years after Marx's death, the preceding extract was usually interpreted to mean that the "superstructure" was rigidly determined by the "base" in the sense that it was little more than a reflection of the base, and that human beings were little more than pawns of historical forces. This "economic determinist" understanding of base and superstructure is now receding, although traces still remain. Instead of interpreting "determine" to mean "uniquely specify," most contemporary Marxists are now willing to acknowledge that the superstructure may have considerable "autonomy" and to interpret the assertion of a dialectical relation between base and superstructure to mean that the mode of production "ultimately" determines the superstructure only in the weaker sense of finally setting the limits to what cultural forms are possible. Socialist feminists do not want to deny this view so much as to reinterpret it. They claim that the economic foundation of society includes a characteristic system of organizing procreation which, in historical times, has been defined in part by a characteristic sexual division of labor. This system of procreation is among the most pervasive influences on the culture of a society, understood in the sense of its "legal, political, religious, aesthetic and philosophic . . . forms" and is important in setting limits to what forms can ultimately exist in that society. Much feminist theory consists precisely in tracing connections between the sexual division of labor in procreation, the sexual division of labor in the market and the ideological sexism embodied in law, politics, religion, aesthetics and philosophy.

The socialist feminist claim that the organization of procreation (or reproduction or sex-affective production) constitutes part of the economic foundation of society is not a simple empirical claim, although empirical facts are certainly relevant to it. For one thing, acceptance of the claim presupposes a willingness to conceptualize procreative and sexual practices as forms of human labor, historically changing rather than biologically determined. Second, acceptance of the socialist feminist claim depends on a political evaluation of the significance of women's subordination and what one is prepared to accept as an adequate account of it. If one views women's contemporary subordination simply as one "question" within capitalism, one can dispose of it merely by the standard Marxist functionalist explanations. If one believes, however, that the subordination of women is a structural feature of contemporary society and contemporary human nature, regulating every aspect of life in a fundamental way, then one will find Marxist functionalism inadequate. If one is impressed chiefly by the fact of male domination and takes that as the primary question to be answered, a Marxist class analysis will be viewed as describing a more superficial level of social reality. In other words, one may choose to stress similarities or differences between the experience of women and men in the same class, and one may choose to stress similarities or differences between the experience of women in different classes.

Suzanne Langer writes: "The 'technique' or treatment of a problem begins with its first expression as a question. The way a question is asked limits and disposes the ways in which any answer to it—right or wrong—is given."[58] Langer's point is that any theoretical explanation will reflect one's formulation of the problem. As we saw earlier, however, no formulation of a problem can be politically or theoretically neutral: what one seeks to explain is determined, in large part, by one's own political priorities and preexisting methodological commitments. Socialist feminism formulates the question of women's oppression in a distinctive way, and this formulation is related, in turn, to its distinctive methodology for answering it. Moreover, the socialist feminist way of asking and approaching the question of course sets limits to what counts as an adequate answer. In Chapter 11, I shall discuss further the interdependent relationship between theories and criteria of theoretical adequacy.

3. THE PUBLIC/PRIVATE DISTINCTION

The socialist feminist conception of procreation as part of the economic foundation of society has carried forward the radical feminist challenge to the traditional distinction between public and private life. This distinction has characterized all previous political theory, although it plays a different role in different theoretical contexts and is construed differently, for instance, by liberal and by Marxist theorists. In the previous chapter, we saw how the insight implicit in the radical feminist slogan "The personal is political" had opened up a new way of understanding such areas of life as sexuality and procreation. Socialist feminists have developed this radical feminist insight into an explicit critique of existing political and economic theory, especially the theories of the liberal and Marxist traditions.

Within the liberal tradition, we have seen the conceptual distinction between economic theory, on the one hand, and political philosophy, on the other. Economic theory is supposed to describe how the economy in fact works; political philosophy is supposed to prescribe how the political system ought to work. The distinction between the public and the private spheres of human life occurs both in liberal political philosophy and liberal economic theory. However, because both types of theory are understood as having a different logical status and as being designed to answer different sets of questions, the public/private distinction functions differently in liberal economics and in liberal political theory.

Liberal economics presupposes a distinction between the public, "economic" world of the market and the private, "non-economic" sphere of the home. This distinction reflects the development of industrialization and commodity production which moved many traditional forms of production out of the home and into the factory. In contrast to earlier societies, therefore, the home ceased to be viewed as a center of economic production and came to be seen rather as a refuge from economic production, "a haven from the heartless world", a "utopian retreat from the city."[59] As we know, the public world of commerce and industry was defined as the world of men; the home was defined as "women's place."

Socialist feminists point out that the public/private distinction postulated here is covertly normative and that, in the 19th century, it functioned in several ways to rationalize the exploitation of women:

> The conception of two social spheres existing side by side simply masked this more complex social reality. It did not describe the society in which it arose so much as reflect it ideologically. Wittingly or unwittingly, it served to legitimate certain of the bourgeois patriarchal practices of that society. At worst, by separating women out of production and making them "the Sex", it drew a veil of Motherhood over the forms of women's oppression that bourgeois society intensified: the economic super-exploitation of working women; gross abuse of the sexual advantage this gave middle-class men; subordination of bourgeois women to the property and personal interests of men of their class; and the subjection of women to the demand for ever-increasing population to meet the needs of war and production.[60]

Within liberal political theory, the public/private distinction is explicitly rather than covertly normative. It was formulated to answer the characteristic liberal question of the legitimate extent of government authority. In this context, the public realm is understood to comprise those aspects of life that are properly subject to government regulation; the private realm is those aspects which should be exempt from such regulation. Just how to define the limits of each realm has been a chronic problem for all liberal philosophers but, in spite of many differences between them, there has been general agreement that the family is the center of private life. It has been generally supposed that the relations between family members ordinarily should be exempt from state intervention. This is not to say that family members can do anything they like to one another. But parents are regarded as having extensive rights over their children, especially to control their children's education, and the physical abuse and even rape of wives by their husbands is in fact normally tolerated by the law. Liberals also argue frequently that individuals' sexual lives are their own affair and should be free from state regulation. In spite of the difference in the meaning of "public" and "private" within liberal political theory and liberal economic theory, there is clearly a connection between the two uses. For instance, the view of the home as a haven from the heartless world is used sometimes to justify exempting the home from government regulation: if the home is the sphere in which people exercise natural human affections, these will be degraded if subjected to the impersonal scrutiny of the law.[61]

Socialist feminists claim that, by drawing the public-private distinction in this way, liberal theorists deny needed protection to women (and also to children). Because the sexual division of labor forces women into childcare and sexual service for men, and because women are segregated from men in the paid labor force, women's main contacts with men are often at home or in bed. In these situations, women are frequently subject to rape, incest and physical abuse. By defining sexual and family relations as private, however, liberal theorists provide grounds for arguing that these assaults are no business of the law and so for allowing them to continue. As we shall see in Chapter 7, liberal feminists have recognized this problem in traditional liberal theory and have begun to argue for a narrower distinction of the private sphere. Socialist feminists argue for abolishing the public/private distinction entirely.

> Areas that have been traditionally kept private certainly are not those that should be kept that way; to do so is only to serve further the ideology of male dominance that underlies our most basic thinking about political and legal matters.[62]

The Marxist tradition differs from the liberal tradition in its conception of the intimate connection between economics and politics. Rather than distinguishing between economic theory and political philosophy, therefore, Marxism focuses on the study of political economy: the mutual constitution of economic and power relations between classes defined by their relation to the means of production. Marxist political economy is simultaneously a description and a critique of the capitalist system. Consequently, unlike liberalism, it has no reluctance to acknowledge that its use of the public/private distinction is simultaneously descriptive and normative. Traditional Marxists believe that the public/private distinction is particularly important for understanding women's oppression; Engels, for example, claims frequently that women are oppressed not because they do household work (presumably he has in mind childrearing, cooking, cleaning, etc.) but because, with the collapse of primitive communistic households, "Household management lost its public character. It no longer concerned society. It became a private service; the wife became the head servant, excluded from all participation in social production."[63] Engels's point seems to be that women are oppressed not because they do work that is essentially degrading, but because of the social relations that define this work in contemporary society.

Unfortunately, Engels never defines precisely the difference in social relationships that constitutes public and private work. He does not explain, for instance, why a man should not be described as engaged in "private service" for his feudal lord or even for an individual capitalist. It seems probable that Engels has in mind the conditions of 19th-century capitalism and that he means that female household workers typically work alone or in much smaller groups than male industrial workers. Household work is not characterized by an extreme division of labor; in fact, women in the household often perform a variety of tasks that are separated in the market: nurse, cook, cleaner, dishwasher, laundress, chauffeur, etc. Industrial work, by contrast, is "socialized" through an extremely detailed division of labor.[64] Consequently, industrial workers work in large groups, while women in the household are often isolated from other adults and reduplicate the work of other women in similar situations. It seems to be because of their relative isolation that Engels perceives housewives as excluded from society. He even suggests that women outside the market are not doing real work. As we saw earlier, he says that they are "estranged from all real work" and "excluded from all participation in social production." On the same page, Engels writes that, in primitive communistic society, "the task . . . of managing the household was as much a public, a socially necessary industry as the procuring of food by men." Here, Engels almost seems to suggest that household work today is no longer socially necessary, although he acknowledges elsewhere the obvious facts that procreation, cooking, cleaning, etc. will be necessary in every society. Whatever Engels thinks is the defining feature of "private" production, it is clear that he regards it as having less importance than "public" production. The traditional Marxist view, which has been outlined already, is that the sets of relations which define specific forms of the family are determined ultimately by the dominant "mode of production" in the narrow economic sense. Consequently, women in the household are seen as excluded from the main action of history, passively absorbing the impact of "economic" changes in "social production."

It is interesting to notice that, although the terms "public" and "private" have quite different meanings within the context of liberal and Marxist theory, both liberals and Marxists assign sexual and family relations to the realm of the private. Unlike liberals, Marxists do not define the private realm as entirely outside the realm of politics, but they do think that it is less central, politically, than the "economic" realm. Socialist feminists charge that, by accepting even a modified version of the public/private distinction, traditional Marxists are accepting a basic feature of capitalist ideology. They add that this distinction is also part of an ideology of male dominance because it minimizes the importance of women's work outside the market. In the socialist feminist view, the distinction between the so-called public and private spheres obscures their interpenetration and essential unity. In so doing, it obscures the fact that the subordination of women is part of the economic foundation of society. The point is not simply that an individual's position in one sphere affects her or his position in the other: that men's superior access to "production" enables them to dominate women sexually and to exploit their procreative labor, while women's responsibility for procreation limits their access to wage labor. It is true that these things happen, but it is not clear that the best way of explaining them is to view them as results of people's participating in two separate spheres or systems of production. The more fundamental point, for socialist feminists, is that it is misleading to think of there being two distinct spheres at all. Rosalind Petchesky expresses the socialist feminist view in this way:

> "Production" and "reproduction", work and the family, far from being separate territories like the moon and the sun or the kitchen and the shop, are really intimately related modes that reverberate upon one another and frequently occur in the same social, physical, and even psychic spaces . . . Not only do reproduction and kinship, or the family, have their own, historically determined, products, material techniques, modes or organization and power relationships, but reproduction and kinship are themselves integrally related to the social relations of production and the state; they reshape these relations all the time.[65]

Joan Kelly makes the same point:

> We can no longer focus upon productive relations of class, suppressing those of consumption (sexuality/family) as Marx did, or focus on sex and familial arrangements (Freud, and Juliet Mitchell in *Psychoanalysis and Feminism*) without those of class, any more than we can place one sex in the category of sexuality/family and the other in that of society. To do so violates our social experience and the new consciousness that is emerging out of it. A more complex pattern of sociosexual arrangements is called for—and is appearing in feminist social thought. Feminist thought

regards the sexual/familial organization of society as integral to any conception of social structure or social change. And conversely, it sees the relation of the sexes as formed by both socioeconomic and sexual-familial structures *in their systematic interconnectedness.*[66]

All feminists are concerned to end male dominance, and all feminist political theory is designed to show how this can be done. A distinctive feature of each contemporary feminist theory is its analysis of the basis of male dominance in contemporary society. For liberalism, male dominance is rooted in irrational prejudice; it must be overcome by rational argument. For traditional Marxism, male dominance is an ideology by which capital divides and rules; it must be overcome by a "cultural revolution" based on a socialist transformation of the "economy." For radical feminism, male dominance is grounded on men's universal control over women's bodies, meaning their sexual and procreative capacities; it must be overcome by women's achieving sexual and procreative self-determination. The political theory of socialist feminism differs from all these views by conceiving of contemporary male dominance as part of the economic foundation of society, understanding "economic" to include child-bearing and sexual activity. On the socialist feminist view, therefore, the abolition of male dominance requires a transformation of the economic foundation of society as a whole. It is necessary to transform not just education, nor simply work, nor sexuality, nor parenting. We must transform everything.

> The current political goals of the women's movement also indicate how the earlier, split vision of bourgeois patriarchal society is fading. These goals are neither to participate as equals in a man's world, nor to restore to woman's realm and values their dignity and worth. Conceptions such as these are superseded in the present will to extirpate gender and sex hierarchy altogether, and with them all forms of domination. To aim at this, as almost all parties (at least within the women's movement in the United States) now seem to do, is to make a program out of the essential feminist perception, that the personal is political. It is a program that penetrates both to the core of self and to the heart, or heartless center, of the male domain, for it will require a restructuring of all social institutions to change our subjective experience in this way. To restructure how we come to know self and others in our birthing, growing up, loving and working, feminist politics must reach the institutions that fatefully bear upon sexuality, family, and community. Schools and all socializing agencies will have to be rid of sex and sexual bias. Work and welfare will have to be placed in the humane context of the basic right to all to live, work, and love in dignity. And there will have to be genuine participation by all in shaping the modes and purposes of our labor and distributing its returns. A feminist politics that aims at abolishing all forms of hierarchy so as to restructure personal relations as well as relations among peers has to reach and transform the social organization of work, property and power.[67]

Radical feminism enlarged the domain of politics. Socialist feminism enlarges the domain of political economy. In doing so, it sets new tasks for political and economic theory. One of these tasks is what Gayle Rubin calls "a political economy of sex." Using "politics" and "economics" in their conventional sense, Rubin writes:

A full-bodied analysis of women in a single society, or throughout history, must take *everything* into account: the evolution of commodity forms in women, systems of land tenure, political arrangements, subsistence technology, etc. Equally important, economic and political analyses are incomplete if they do not consider women, marriage, and sexuality. Traditional concerns of anthropology and social science—such as the evolution of social stratification and the origin of the state—must be reworked to include the implications of matrilateral cross-cousin marriage, surplus extracted in the form of daughters, the conversion of female labor into male wealth, the conversion of female lives into marriage alliances, the contribution of marriage to political power, and the transformations which all of these varied aspects of society have undergone in the course of time. . . .

Eventually, someone will have to write a new version of *The Origin of the Family, Private Property and the State,* recognizing the mutual interdependence of sexuality, economics, and politics without underestimating the full significance of each in human society.[68]

Political theory is prescriptive as well as explanatory. To enlarge its domain is not simply to show the need for more extensive analyses; it is also to show the need for more comprehensive ideals. Radical and socialist feminists have shown that the old ideals of freedom, equality, and democracy are insufficient. Women are not free as long as their sexuality is male-defined and as long as they cannot make their own decisions to bear or not to bear children. Women are not equal with men as long as they are forced to do a disproportionate amount of childcare, maintenance work and nurturing. An ideal of democracy is inadequate if it focuses solely on participation in selecting a government or even on workers' control over the production of the means to satisfy human needs for food, shelter, and clothing. Socialist feminism declares the need for new conceptions of freedom and equality and for a new conception of democracy that will include democracy in procreation or what Clark and Lange call "reproductive democracy."[69] Democracy in procreation will come to pass only when every member of society is able to participate fully in decisions over how many children are born, who bears them, who cares for them, and how they are reared.

Problems for Socialist Feminism

In my view, the socialist feminist conception of human nature, with its corelated conception of political economy, constitutes the most promising approach to an adequate understanding of the nature and basis of women's subordination. It provides a conceptual framework in terms of which we can understand how biological sex has been interpreted and transformed through human labor. Personal experience, as well as theoretical analysis, convinces us of the overwhelming importance of sex and gender in our lives. Yet, although these structure human nature and society in a fundamental way, they are taken as given by most political theories. Mother Jones, for instance, is alleged to have said "God almighty made the women and the Rockefeller gang of thieves made the ladies." But God almighty did not make the women and neither did Mother Nature. A traditional class analysis explains the transformation of some women and men into ladies and gentlemen. But only socialist feminism makes a serious attempt to explain how human beings continuously transform themselves into men and women.

Promising as it is, socialist feminism at the moment is far from fulfilling its promise. It conceptualizes women's subordination in a more historical and nuanced way than either traditional Marxism or than radical feminism, and its conception of human nature provides it with a more powerful method for understanding the issue. So far, however, its theory of women's liberation remains incomplete. In what follows, I shall identify three areas that are conceptually problematic within the existing socialist feminist analyses of human nature and social reality.

1. INTERNALIZED OPPRESSION AND FEMINIST RESISTANCE

Feminist theorists, by definition, advocate social change. In order to achieve such change, they recommend specific strategies. If these strategies are to be successful, they must be predicated on an understanding of the obstacles to change. Feminist theorists have identified many such obstacles, from discriminatory legislation, to the corporate interest in underpaying women, to the male interest in controlling women's bodies. In addition to "external" obstacles to feminist changes, however, there also appear to be "internal" obstacles, obstacles in women's own minds. Women often seem to accept male values and perceptions, even when it is obvious, from a feminist perspective, that these values and perceptions distort reality and are directly opposed to women's own interests. In other words, women seem to "internalize" the oppressive "external" reality. One of the most important questions confronting all feminist theorists is why women, who are, after all, a majority in most populations, so often seem to submit to or even collude with their own subordination. At its simplest, the question is: why are not all women feminists?

Answers to these questions are located at one intersection between political theory and political anthropology. They draw on claims both about social structure and about human nature. Each feminist theory that we have examined so far provides its own characteristic account of women's resistance to domination in contemporary society and its own explanation of why that resistance has been limited in its success. Liberal feminists, as we have seen, believe that non-feminist women are victims of their socialization or sex-role conditioning; consequently, liberal feminists rest great hopes in educational reform. Traditional Marxists see the problem differently. Since they believe that most prevailing versions of feminism are contaminated by ruling-class ideology, the question for Marxists is not "Why are most women not feminists?" but rather "Why do most women, feminist and non-feminist alike, fail to perceive their long-term interest in socialist revolution?" Traditional Marxists find the answer in the related notions of ideology and false consciousness. They believe that the ruling class's control of the production of knowledge, coupled with the very structure of daily life, combine to convince most women that true happiness lies in the acquisition and consumption of more and more commodities. Within radical feminism, two main lines of reasoning are offered to explain women's submission to domination. One line stresses the lack of objective options for women, portraying them as almost totally trapped by the patriarchy, often victims of sheer physical violence, and as submitting to men in order to survive. The other line of reasoning sees women as deluded, tricked and bewildered by patriarchal culture, patriarchal science and even the language of the patriarchy.

As we have seen, there are problems with all these explanations. Liberal feminism's concept of sex-role conditioning presupposes an unacceptable conception of human nature which postulates an asocial substratum. The Marxist concepts of false consciousness and ideological obfuscation are promising in principle, but in practice acknowledge only capitalist ideology, ignoring the ideology of male dominance to which Marxism itself in some ways unwittingly contributes. Radical feminism offers incisive critiques both of the patriarchal illusions of choice and of the patriarchal bias of prevailing culture; however, its picture of reality seems oversimplified insofar as it portrays women as almost helpless victims. For instance, at a time when weapons can far outweigh any differences in physical strength, the radical feminist account fails to explain adequately why women often allow themselves to become the victims of male violence.

Socialist feminism claims the need for an alternative to all these views. Although so far it has been only partially successful in providing such an alternative, its historical materialist method, together with its feminist political priorities, generate important criteria for evaluating the adequacy of proposed theoretical explanations of "internalized oppression," including the adequacy of those offered by socialist feminists. According to these criteria, an adequate political psychology must be materialist or non-idealist; that is to say, specific motives and character traits must be grounded in specific forms of praxis or in the mode of production. It must be sensitive to feminist concerns so that it takes a comprehensive view of the sexual division of labor and interprets "production" in the inclusive, feminist sense. It must be historical, which is to say that it should take account of historical variations in gendered psychological traits. Finally, it should be nondeterministic, recognizing the ways in which certain historical circumstances allow specific groups of women to transcend at least partially the perceptions and theoretical constructs of male dominance and in which this feminist "raised consciousness" can inspire and guide women in a struggle for social change.

The political economy of socialist feminism has shown how men in general and capitalist men in particular have specific material interest in the domination of women and how they construct a variety of institutional arrangements to perpetuate this domination. In addition, socialist feminists offer several psychological accounts which purport to explain why women themselves often seem to collude with their own subordination and neglect apparent opportunities for individual or collective resistance. Most of the current socialist feminist accounts depend on a psychoanalytic theory of character formation, arguing, for instance, that the mother-rearing of children, in a sexist and heterosexist social context, results in psychologically passive girls with "soft ego boundaries," who are dependent on others for affection and approval, and aggressive boys with "rigid ego-boundaries," who separate themselves sharply from others. These distinctively masculine and feminine character structures are thought to provide strong psychological reinforcement for the sexual division of labor that generated them.

Given its materialist presuppositions, socialist feminism recognizes that a psychological theory alone could never constitute a complete explanation of male domination. In developing psychological accounts of male aggression and apparent female submission, socialist feminist theorists are not assigning ultimate blame to the victims, nor are they claiming that the roots of male dominance lie in distinctive features of male and female psychology; they are claiming merely that certain forms of praxis generate psychological predispositions to perpetuate those forms of praxis. The socialist feminist use of psychoanalytic theory for this purpose, however, is somewhat problematic. For one thing, there is the well-known anti-feminist bias of Freud, exemplified in his extremely negative portrayals of women as dependent, irrational, emotional, passive, narcissistic, masochistic and motivated by penis envy and his inability to see such female strengths as flexibility, openness, sensitivity, practicality, and nurturance. A deeper problem is Freud's underlying theory of human nature, which seems fundamentally incompatible with a historical materialist view.[70] Freud portrays human nature as unchanging, ahistorical and anti-social. Civilization, for him, is a process of repressing the instincts. Freud's view, in fact, is basically that of Hobbes: humans are naturally selfish and regulated by the pleasure principle. Such a theory of human nature inevitably generates a political philosophy that is deeply pessimistic about the possibilities of freedom and community.

Those socialist feminist theorists who draw on psychoanalytic theory believe that it is possible to revise Freud in such a way as to overcome his anti-female bias, his universalism and his determinism. They view his insights about infant sexuality, the unconscious and the bisexuality of infants at birth as indispensable ingredients in any explanation of how gendered character structures are socially imposed and remain so relatively rigid. They believe that Freud's political pessimism can be avoided by refusing to ground their revised psychological account in an inevitable, infantile response to a universal sexual anatomy. Instead, they claim that infants respond to a sexual anatomy whose meaning has been assigned by a male-dominant and heterosexist culture and to a sexual division of labor that has been universal in human history but is, in principle, susceptible to alteration. Even in the absence of thoroughgoing social change, socialist feminists, like Freud, see the character structures established in infancy as relatively rigid but not as impervious to conscious modification by the individual. Consequently, socialist feminists claim that their use of psychoanalytic theory is nondeterministic as well as being historical and non-idealistic, and that it provides a theoretical justification for the radical feminist insight that the personal is deeply involved.

The problem of developing a historicized and feminized version of psychoanalysis is similar in several respects to the problem of developing a feminist political economy, which I shall discuss later in this chapter. Both projects, for instance, require the construction of a new terminology.[71] Nevertheless, socialist feminism does not stand or fall according to its success in reconstructing psychoanalytic theory. It may turn to other conceptual frameworks for explaining women's apparent acquiescence to male domination, perhaps by developing a feminist version of the notion of false consciousness,[72] or by expanding Gramsci's concept of hegemony.[73] The latter is designed to explain how a dominant class maintains control by projecting its own particular way of seeing social reality so successfully that its view is accepted as commonsense and as part of the natural order by those who in fact are subordinated to it. Whatever theoretical framework it finally adopts, socialist feminism has made a genuine contribution to political theory by articulating the need for a political psychology which is historical, materialist and nondeterministic and which is motivated by feminist politics.

2. PRODUCING HUMAN BEINGS

In many ways, it seems appropriate to view procreation as a form of production. We have seen already that the view that procreation consists primarily of a series of biological functions is in fact an ideological obfuscation of the historical nature of procreative work. In fact, procreation is no more determined by human biology than other forms of human labor, which, of course, are also affected by human physiological structure such as our lack of prehensile feet or tails. Every society has its own norms about the proper methods and social context for conceiving children, its own views about the proper treatment of pregnant women and its own conception of the proper way to give birth.

> We find, for example, that the behavioral display of uterine contractions during labor differs from culture to culture to such an extent that in the most extreme case it would be impossible to interpret a woman's behavior during labor if one didn't know the culture's rules for appropriate displays during birth.[74]

Standards of acceptable childrearing are determined equally by the social context. What young people are taught and how they are taught depend on the type of adults desired. What should young people learn to accept as food or as appropriate toilet habits? What should they accept as legitimate authority? What skills and interests should they acquire? These are all determined by prevailing social values including, in contemporary society, values about the proper place of the children of working-class parents, of ethnic minority parents, and of course, about the proper place of women.

Lynda Lange is a feminist theorist who has taken the lead in emphasizing that procreation is a form of labor. She denies, however, that it is a form of production:

> If children are products, it makes sense to ask who should own and control them, a question which seems to me not only morally unsavoury, but also impossible to make sense of within historical materialism. If women in the role of child-care workers are really exploited productive workers, from whom should they withdraw their service in a strike, in order to improve their condition?[75]

Lange believes that these questions are unanswerable and so she categorizes procreative labor as a form of consumption. It is hard to reconcile this with her stated desire to give procreation "equal billing" with production when, on the Marxist view, as we saw in Chapter 4, production and consumption form a dialectical unity in which production ultimately determines consumption.

In my view, the questions raised by Lange are not unanswerable. The answer to her second question, from whom childcare workers' labor would be withdrawn in the event of a strike, is the more obvious. In principle, I think it is no different from the answer to the same question raised about any service workers, such as hospital workers or teachers. If female childcare workers were indeed to strike, they would simply stop changing diapers, cooking food, etc. Their services, like the services of hospital workers or teachers, would be withdrawn directly from those for whom they care: children, patients or pupils. Indirectly, their services would be withdrawn from those who exploit or who oversee the exploitation of their labor: hospital administrators, school boards and, in a domestic context, husbands.

The main reason why Lange's question sounds odd is that we know a strike by female procreative workers in the home (housewives!) is extremely unlikely. For one thing, as many Marxist and feminist theorists have pointed out, it is difficult for isolated housewives to develop a sense of political solidarity with others in a similar situation. In addition, the pervasive and suffocating ideology of the family links "love and marriage," sentimentalizes mother love as the highest, because the most self-sacrificing, form of love and makes parents, especially mothers, feel individually responsible for the welfare of their offspring. This ideology is so strong that even those who are most exploited by the prevailing system of organizing procreation, the wives and mothers (increasingly, these are separable relations), often fail to perceive their exploitation clearly and instead suffer guilt over their feelings of discontent. Finally, housewives have the certain knowledge that innocent people, in this case their own children, would suffer if they withdrew their labor. Of course, hospital workers, teachers and transit workers also know that their strike would affect innocent people. But they are less emotionally tied than mothers to those people who would be hurt, they feel no individual responsibility for them, and they do not believe that the withdrawal of their services would be as shattering for patients, pupils and travelers as the withdrawal of mothers' care would be for most children. For all these reasons, a strike by housewives is extremely unlikely, but it is not in principle impossible—just as a strike by serfs was very unlikely but not, in principle, impossible. In fact, housewives have often undertaken individual protest strikes, becoming depressed, developing headaches in bed and, in the extreme case, escaping into madness.

Lange's other problem with regarding procreation as production is that it forces us to view children as products and so makes it possible to ask who should own and control them. Just as Lange's question about striking sounded odd because it is hard to rid oneself of the prevailing ideology of the family, so I think this question sounds reasonable because it is hard to rid oneself of the prevailing ideology of the market. In a market society, everything has an owner and, in contemporary society, young people are still viewed as something like the property of their parents. Parents are seen as having a right to control their children's behavior, including sexual behavior, and their education. In the contemporary United States, efforts by parents to ban certain books in the classroom are increasing, and bills are regularly introduced into Congress that would require doctors to inform parents if their children have venereal disease or seek an abortion. In *The Communist Manifesto,* Marx and Engels mock

> the bourgeois [who] sees in his wife a mere instrument of production. He hears that the instruments of production are to be exploited in common, and, naturally, can come to no other conclusion than that the lot of being common to all will likewise fall to the women.
> He has not even a suspicion that the real point aimed at is to do away with the status of women as mere instruments of production.[76]

Analogously, to conceptualize a democratized, presumably socialized system of procreation as part of a system of production is not necessarily to imagine transferring the "ownership" of young people to the community as a whole. We fear this only if we already view young people as property. A democratized system of procreation in fact is a precondition for doing away with the status of young people as mere products to be owned.

On the Marxian view of human nature, adult humans, in producing the goods they need for their survival, also produce themselves. That adult humans are social products, however, does not necessarily raise questions about who owns and controls them. Similarly, to view procreation as a form of production is not necessarily to raise morally objectionable questions about who owns and controls young people. These questions arise only if one views young people as passive objects of the rearing process. This view of young people is implicit in a number of contemporary theories of human nature, such as Skinnerian behaviorism or any kind of liberal environmentalism, but it is quite incompatible with a feminist or a Marxist approach that stresses the agency of human subjects. Within the framework of socialist feminism, it is not appropriate to view the socialization of children as the imposition of human civilization onto "little animals." A more appropriate model of childrearing might utilize the educational theory of Paulo Freire, who views education as a dialogic relation between teacher and student.[77] If "toilet training" their children seems to many mothers like housetraining their dogs, it is only because this educational process is being undertaken in a social context where children, like pets, are viewed as the property and responsibility of their parents (or owners) and where excretory functions are viewed with disgust and embarrassment as dirty and animal. Young people can indeed be "trained" to conform, but to be fully "humanized," as Freire puts it—that is, to become conscious of themselves in historical perspective and to participate actively in the creation of their culture— they must participate actively with adults in the learning process.

While Lange's objections to viewing procreation as a form of production are not unanswerable, the answers point to a weakness in contemporary socialist theory. Because most of the theorists have been concerned primarily with women's liberation, they have looked at procreation primarily from women's perspective, emphasizing how the prevailing system of organizing procreation is alienating and exploitative for women. Their concern with procreation from the child's perspective has been limited mainly to a critique of the ways in which classist, racist and sexist values are embedded in the educational system. What socialist feminists so far have failed to do, however, is to examine critically the relations of dominance and subordination that distinguish adults from children. Shulamith Firestone is almost alone in her radical critique of the whole institution of childhood and in her demands for its.abolition.[78]

Socialist feminists need to think systematically about the institution of childhood, about the limitations it imposes on young people and about the "privileges" it offers in compensation for those limitations. They may well find that those privileges are as illusory as the false respect accorded to women in sexist society. Socialist feminism needs to look critically at the relation between adults and young people and consider how far that relation is oppressive, alienating or exploitative for young people as well as for women (and men). It needs to consider how far the helplessness of children, like that of women, is socially imposed. Just as oppression creates females who are "feminine" (whining, irresponsible and competitive with other women), so it may be that oppression creates young people who are "childish" (whining, irresponsible and competitive with their siblings).

In developing new conceptions of freedom, equality and democracy, socialist feminism should not fail to question why young people are excluded from these in almost every society. If democracy in procreation requires that every member of society should participate fully in decisions over how many children are born, who rears them and how they are reared, socialist feminists should not forget that young people too are members of society. There is a tendency to treat young people as *future* members of society and to consider their education only in terms of its effects on them when they become adults. But young people exist now, and decisions about procreation affect them more immediately than anyone else. Those decisions affect them now and not just when they "grow up." An important task of socialist feminism is to determine how young people can participate fully in those and other fundamental decisions about the organization of social life.

3. NAMING THE SYSTEM

The socialist feminist conception of human nature is inseparable from the socialist feminist conception of political economy. The problems faced by the latter are similar to those of the former. The political and methodological commitments of socialist feminism have redefined from a feminist and a historical materialist perspective the task of political theory and the criteria for evaluating theoretical adequacy. The task, however, remains to be completed. Socialist feminism has indicated a new domain for political economy; it has identified the questions that a feminist political theory must ask, and it has shown the sorts of answers that are acceptable. However, socialist feminism has not yet provided the answers, in part, because of continuing uncertainty about how the redefined domain of political economy should be conceptualized.

The general method of socialist feminism commits it to an account of the subordination of women that refers in some way to the sexual division of labor. As a political economic theory, this account might mention the content of the work that women do, that is, the kind of goods that women produce. The main emphasis of the account, however, must be on setting that work in its social context, explaining the social relationships that hold between women performing different kinds of work and between others in the society, especially men. For instance, the citizen housewife who sews at home for her family inhabits quite a different set of social and economic relations from the un-documented immigrant woman who sews at home on a piecework system for a garment manufacturer, and men exploit her labor in quite a different way. The sexual division of labor in different societies has varied so widely that it is notoriously difficult to construct general economic categories for understanding women's work cross-culturally, but one might suppose that it would be easier to develop categories explaining the sexual division of labor within a given society. Even in the case of contemporary industrial society, however, it is far from obvious how to provide a general and illuminating characterization of women's work that goes beyond the tautology that it is done by women.

All contemporary feminists have been impressed by the amount of work done by women that falls outside the sphere of the market. This is recognized by women themselves in such popular sayings as "A woman's work is never done," but it is unrecognized by traditional political economy. National economic statistics ignore both women's unpaid labor in the home and, especially in developing countries, their work in subsistence agriculture.[79] Socialist feminists believe that women's subordination consists not only in their limited access to the market, but also in the exploitation of their labor through non-market economic relationships. In contemporary industrial society, most non-market labor is performed at home. Consequently, socialist feminists, seeking to explain the subordination of women in contemporary industrial society, have sought to provide a theoretical account of women's work in the home. Different theorists have stressed different aspects of this work and have named it differently. Clark and Lange have defined women's work at home to consist primarily in the bearing and rearing of children, and they follow traditional Marxist usage in calling this work the system of reproduction.[80] Ulrike Prokop defines women's domestic labor to include not only cooking, cleaning, and childrearing but also a type of "immaterial production": the production of interpersonal relationships.[81] Folbre and Ferguson identify a system of "sex-affective production" that includes the bearing and rearing of children and the provision of nurturance and sexual satisfaction.[82] And Gayle Rubin focuses particularly on the set of arrangements for organizing human sexuality that she calls a "sex/gender system."[83]

In traditional Marxist theory, the area of life that these theorists are struggling to conceptualize is called "reproduction." Some socialist feminists, such as Clark and Lange, retain traditional Marxist terminology but others, as we have seen, substitute a new vocabulary. They have several reasons for doing so. One is that traditional Marxists use "reproduction" to cover a wide variety of social practices. In its broadest meaning, "reproduction" is that aspect of production devoted to replacing the means of production, such as the production of seed-corn or replacements for existing machinery. "Reproduction" is also used in a more restricted sense to refer to those institutions that maintain and reproduce the social relations of production. As Marxists construe them, these are capitalist social relations. In this usage, "reproduction" is taken to include entertainment, education, advertising, in short, the whole realm of culture and ideology—what Marxists call the superstructure. Finally, "reproduction" is sometimes used to refer to what I have been calling "procreation," those activities involved in bearing and rearing children. When it is used in this last sense, however, procreative reproduction is always identified as being part of reproduction in one of the first two senses. That is to say, procreation is viewed either as one aspect of production or as one aspect of the ideological superstructure.

There is a certain rationale for labeling procreation as "reproduction" in the first sense, since it does indeed reproduce that most important means of production, labor power. Moreover, if procreation is viewed as reproduction in this sense then it must be part of the economic foundation of society: since seed-corn or machine parts are produced through the same physical process and even at the same time as corn and machines for exchange on the market, the "relations of reproduction" are seen to be identical with the "relations of production." The distinction between them is purely conceptual. If, however, procreation is construed as "reproduction" in the second sense, then it does not appear as part of the economic foundation of society. Instead, there is a suggestion that the functions of the family are largely ideological and that the form of the family in capitalist society is determined ultimately by the relations of commodity production. Socialist feminists recognize that these multiple uses of "reproduction" in the Marxist tradition can only lead to confusion. Moreover, Rubin points out that to characterize procreation as reproduction, "links 'the economy' to production and the sexual system to 'reproduction.' It reduces the richness of either system, since 'productions' and 'reproductions' take place in both."[84] She believes that the sex/gender system "has its own relations of production, distribution and exchange."[85] Finally, Sandra Harding complains that to describe procreation as reproduction "incorrectly suggests that humans are merely duplicated, generation after generation, in immutable forms. In fact, humans truly create themselves in new forms continually and the new forms are both social and biological."[86]

The characterization of women's procreative work as "reproduction" may thus be viewed as ideological, insofar as it misleadingly and invidiously suggests that women's work is less fundamental and less creative than men's: the suggestion is that men create the system of production; women merely maintain it. It is to avoid all these problems that socialist feminist theorists have suggested their various new terminologies and that I have spoken throughout either of "sexuality", "childbearing" and "childrearing" or of "procreation."

Regardless of their differences in emphasis and terminology, socialist feminist theorists have succeeded in identifying types of labor that political economy traditionally has ignored. They have also succeeded in expressing genuine insights about the exploitation of women's labor outside the market. But they have been less successful in analyzing this labor through a conceptual framework that goes beneath the level of description. In describing women's non-market labor, socialist feminist theorists naturally identify it first in terms of its content: rearing children, fulfilling emotional needs, etc. Their theoretical terminology, however, often follows their first descriptions. They identify the system of production in question by reference to the types of needs it is designed to satisfy: needs for sex, affection, children, etc. By using a terminology that refers to the content rather than to the relations of women's work, these theorists suggest that women's labor can be identified primarily by the type of goods that it produces. Their terminology carries a suggestion that women's work is concerned chiefly with nurturance or with what one might call the production of people rather than of things.

By using this sort of theoretical terminology, socialist feminists suggest that there are two systems of production, geared to produce two different types of goods. In a trivial sense, of course, this is true. In this sense, indeed, one could say that there are indefinitely many systems of production, depending on how narrowly one wishes to define the goods in question. One can speak of the system for producing food, for producing health care, for producing garden implements or for producing hairpins. The question is why one should wish to make these distinctions or to multiply systems in this way. Some socialist feminists make these distinctions in order to identify work that is specifically female. But of course women as well as men produce "things," and men as well as women are involved in producing "people": not simply in begetting them, but in socializing them through the media and education and caring for them through medicine.

In general, the distinction between "production" and "reproduction" or between "production" and procreation, seems artificial. It seems to be a relic of the public/private distinction that socialist feminists have criticized in other contexts. To postulate two systems of production, defined in terms of their "contents" or objects of production, disguises the essential inseparability of procreation and production in the conventional sense. Lynda Lange writes:

> Reproduction, in the sense in which we are using the term (to include the socialization of children) both largely determines the productive needs of society and provides an essential means to their being met, namely, labour. The productive needs of society are determined by reproduction, not merely because there are new mouths to be fed (or not fed, as the case may be), but also because the cultural level of their socialization determines to a very large extent how much and what type of production will be required to satisfy their needs. It is apparent at the very least that production and reproduction function as limits one upon the other.[87]

The inseparability of "production" and procreation is illustrated in all kinds of ways. For instance, a high birthrate may be thought to be a cause of poverty by producing too many mouths to feed. But poverty is equally a cause of high birthrates: "for every mouth to feed, there are two hands to work"[88] and, where infant mortality is high, people produce many children to ensure that a few will survive. Conceptually, one may distinguish developments in "the means of production" from developments in "the means of procreation." But the food grown to feed the next generation of adults is separable only conceptually from the food grown to feed the present generation, and the medical advances that reduce adult mortality. One might ask whether feminist theory gains anything from making a conceptual distinction between procreation and "production." Since the distinction is not in fact adequate to distinguish women's work from men's work—for both sexes engage in "production" and both engage in procreation, though in different ways—it is simpler and less liable to mislead if contemporary society is viewed as a single system of production, a system that produces both people and things, often in the same process, and which, of course, has its moments of reproduction and of consumption. The question then remains, of course, how to characterize this system so that the subordination of women is both described and explained, both seen and understood.

The conceptual framework of traditional Marxism was designed to deal with an analogous problem: how to explain the domination of a majority of the population by a ruling minority. Rather than focusing on the content of the work done, Marxism focuses on the relations between individuals and especially between groups of individuals, defined as classes. When Marxism characterizes the contemporary economic system as the capitalist system, it describes it in terms of economic relations. To talk about the system of commodity production is to refrain deliberately from mentioning the specific kinds of goods that are produced and to emphasize their common economic relationship: insofar as they are commodities, they are all produced for sale on the market. Women's subordination is a relation that holds between women and men and, in order to understand that relation, feminist theory needs a conceptual framework that is constructed out of relations. As Engels saw clearly, women are not oppressed by what they do so much as by the social context in which they do it. So he tried to explain women's subordination by showing that women in contemporary society had a special relation to production. In his view, this was the relation of exclusion.

Socialist feminists have criticized Engels' answer because they perceive that women are not excluded from production. They have pointed correctly to the vast quantity of productive work done by women, outside as well as inside the market. As we have seen, however, some socialist feminists have conceptualized this as a system of production additional to the capitalist system of commodity production. So far, I have criticized their suggestion on the grounds that there is no feminist point in distinguishing two systems of production by reference to the types of goods they produce. It is also possible, however, to interpret socialist feminists as suggesting that the system additional to the capitalist system can be identified not in terms of its products, but rather in terms of the relations by which it is constructed: gendered relations of male dominance rather than genderless relations of capitalism. This suggestion is made explicitly by Christine Delphy when she postulates a "family" system of production that defines the work of married women not in terms of its content, but in terms of the workers' relation to their husbands.[89] No matter whether they work on the family farm, in the family business or do housework, Delphy argues that the proceeds of women's labor are appropriated by their husbands and that they receive only maintenance in return.

Just as one can distinguish between different types of products, so one can distinguish market relations from non-market relations. The question is, does this distinction help to illuminate women's subordination? In part, it does seem to do so; certainly it identifies a type of exploitation that is ignored by traditional political economy. To emphasize women's domination outside the market, however, is often to neglect women's domination within the market. While men's labor force participation has been dropping slightly in this century, women's has been increasing by leaps and bounds. But the gender domination of women does not disappear when they enter the market. It is maintained in all kinds of ways, the most obvious being that full-time female workers in the United States earn, on average, only 59¢ for every dollar paid to full-time male workers. Thus many socialist feminist attempts to repair Engels' account of women's subordination in fact retain one of Engels' basic assumptions: that the distinction between capitalist and noncapitalist production is vital for understanding women's contemporary subordination. This may have been true in the 19th century, but the distinction does not seem to cast much light on women's subordination in contemporary society. Women's move into the market, far from eliminating gender domination, is more like a move "from private to public patriarchy."[90]

Socialist feminists, as their self-chosen name implies, are the inheritors of two political traditions. They are trying to synthesize the insights of radical feminism with those of traditional Marxism, and this is not easy to do. The dichotomous roots of the movement are reflected in dualistic categories that recur continually within socialist feminist theory. As we have seen, socialist feminism tends to postulate two systems of production, characterized by different sorts of relations and designed to fill different human needs. One system is the capitalist system where, in the process of producing the means to satisfy human needs for food and shelter, cars and televisions, genderless capitalists exploit genderless workers. The other is the patriarchal domestic system where, in the process of producing the means to satisfy human needs for sexuality, emotional gratification and children, men exploit women. As some socialist feminists recognize, however, these dualisms conceal as much as they reveal about women's subordination. The three sets of distinctions implicit above, distinctions between market and family relations, between the production of things and the production of people, and between class domination and gender domination, simply do not coincide. Instead, they all cut across each other. Women participate in market as well as in domestic production and suffer gender domination in both places. Their experience in both places also depends on their economic class in the conventional sense. Moreover, it is false that home and market produce different kinds of products. While not many physical goods are currently produced at home, an increasing amount of procreative, sexual, and emotional work is organized through the market. Leaving aside the actual sale of babies (though this does exist) and the still-rare practice of paying women to bear children for those who are unable to do so, much of the socialization of children now occurs through the market in the form of daycare, private schools and the media.[91] Similarly, the emotional life at least of the privileged class is entrusted increasingly to paid therapists, and their sexual needs are augmented increasingly through the market. Quite apart from the booming sales of pornography and "sexual aids" and the growing business of sex clinics, Iris Young has pointed out that women in the labor market are used to create and then to gratify certain kinds of sexual needs. She writes:

In contemporary society not only images of "sexy" women foster capitalist accumulation, but real live women are employed for their "sexual" labor— for being sexy on their jobs, suggesting sexiness to customers, and in many jobs whose main function is being sexy in one way or another.[92]

From the perspective of women, therefore, it seems to make sense to view contemporary society as a single system structured by male dominance. Neither the categories of production/procreation nor the categories of market/family seem adequate for understanding women's subordination. It is not that the distinctions can't be made nor that they may not be useful for some purposes. But they seem to hamper as much as to help the feminist project, suggesting that women are oppressed as women within a single sphere, and obscuring the pervasiveness of male domination throughout contemporary society.

Radical feminists see this. They view contemporary society as a single system they call patriarchy. To socialist feminists, however, the radical feminist concept of patriarchy is inadequate both as description and as explanation. The ahistorical radical feminist conception of patriarchy does not describe women's situation adequately, insofar as it obscures differences between the experience of women in different societies, and between the experience of women in the same society who have different class, race, or ethnic backgrounds. And the universalism of the radical feminist description of women's situation makes that situation inexplicable except in terms of some transhistorical and possibly biologically determined male drive for power. The socialist feminist conception of human nature renders unacceptable any such "explanation" of male dominance. Because of their commitment to a historical materialist method, as well as their own observations of variety in the sexual division of labor, socialist feminists view the struggle between women and men as changing historically with changes in modes of production. For them, an adequate theory of women's subordination "must account for male dominance as structured into a set of specific, though variable, social and economic relations, with specific material effects on the relations of men and women."[93]

Traditional Marxism, too, views contemporary society as a single system. It calls this system capitalism, and it sees the system as motivated by the continual drive for capital accumulation. Socialist feminism has advanced beyond traditional Marxism in seeing that this view is too simple. Socialist feminism sees that recorded history is characterized by a conflict of interest between women and men. Its historians, anthropologists and sociologists have produced many examples of how women have struggled for control over the certain productive resources of society, especially their own bodies. What socialist feminism lacks, however, is a comprehensive theoretical framework for interpreting its scattered insights into the reasons why men have sought to control women's labor, the means they have used to do so and the ways in which women have resisted men's control. The political economy of traditional Marxism provides a general characterization of modes of production in a specified sense and shows in general terms why one mode of production succeeded another. Socialist feminism needs an analogous way of identifying different "epochs" or types of male dominance by reference to transformations in the sexual division of labor, of relating these transformations to developments in the forces of production, including procreation, and of showing how such transformations are correlated with specific changes in the nature, basis and extent of men's power over women.

An important criterion for the adequacy of such a feminist political economy would be its ability to provide a consistent account of the relation between gender domination and conventional class domination. Traditional Marxism deals with this problem by saying that conventional class relations are causally more fundamental than relations of male dominance and describe a deeper level of social reality; by contrast, radical feminism reverses the order and says that gender relations are causally fundamental and that they describe a deeper level of social reality. Socialist feminism rejects both views and so is left with the problem. A major attraction of the various "two-spheres" models is that they seem to avoid this problem; they represent social reality as two systems of social relations existing side by side. But if one postulates a single social system, structured by two sets of economic relations, then one still has to explain the relation between them. Some socialist feminists claim that capitalist and "patriarchal" relations reinforce each other;[94] some claim that capitalist and "patriarchal" relations undermine each other.[95] In either case, one is left with the picture of a social system that has two different motors which may or not be driving that system in the same direction. Obviously, this picture is another version of dualism. Things become even more confused if, as a few theorists have done, one uses a similar theoretical strategy to account for the added complications of race or age. A multisystemic model rapidly emerges which has limited explanatory power and no theoretical elegance at all.

It may be that social reality is best understood in such dualistic or multi-systemic terms, but a few socialist feminists deny this. They believe that the problem of the relation between various forms of domination must be solved by the development of new categories of class. "We have to break down the abstract category of the 'working class' and place its division into men and women—and also black and white—at the center of our understanding."[96] In other words, we must develop gendered and racially specific economic categories, where the notions of gender and race are built into the new concepts of class. Only by developing more precise categories can we comprehend the ways in which developments in capitalist patriarchy tend to intensify some existing forms of gender or racial domination, to decompose others, and to recompose gender and race domination in new forms. Iris Young is one of the most articulate critics to date of all versions of what she calls "dual systems theory," and she calls for a feminist political economy that would interpret the complex social reality of domination by conventional class, by sex and by race within a unified conceptual framework. Young writes:

> Our nascent historical research coupled with our feminist intuitions tells us that the labor of women occupies a central place in any system of production, that gender division is a basic axis of social structuration in all hitherto existing social formations, and that gender hierarchy serves as a pivotal element in most systems of social domination. If traditional Marxism has no theoretical place for such hypotheses, then it is not merely an inadequate theory of women's oppression, it is an inadequate theory of social relations, relations of production, and domination. *We need not merely a synthesis of feminism with traditional Marxism, but a thoroughly feminist historical materialism, which regards the social relations of a particular historical social formation as one system in which gender differentiation is a core attribute.*[97]

Young is prepared to offer no examples of what such a "single system" political economy would look like. Others have suggested, however, that Ehrenreich's and English's account of the transition from what they call "patriarchy" to what they call "masculinism" might constitute a fragment of such a theory. For Ehrenreich and English, "patriarchy" describes a specific pre-capitalist social order organized around household production; "masculinism" is an industrial capitalist system. Interrante and Lasser believe that, in addition to identifying patriarchy as an historically specific social system, this categorical distinction might

> help overcome the dichotomous analysis of the family and the economy which continues to plague both left and feminist work. It suggests a method for analyzing, in a unified and interconnected way, both the political economy of sex and the sexual economy of work. With this method, the subordination of women would no longer be viewed as a parallel system or as an adjunct to class relations. Instead, it would become *central* to any Marxist understanding of capitalist expansion. For example, as we read the book, the transition from patriarchal to masculinist society involves neither the "removal" of certain kinds of work from the home, nor what Douglas calls the "disestablishment" of women's work, but the very creation of work as "work"—that is, the transformation of role-defined useful work into value-producing wage labor. Finally, masculinism would highlight the complex importance of gender in distinguishing public and private spheres of activity and in identifying individuals and groups in relation to those spheres. Maculinism could move beyond sex to a more complex division of labor based simultaneously on sex, class, and race. Thus, the "sexual double standard" of ladies/girls would no longer be viewed merely as another example of male hypocrisy. It could be seen as an aspect of social organization which reproduced class divisions—by regulating the kinds of kin and non-kin contacts which supported household operation, and by exporting the demographic burdens of sexual behavior from the upper to the lower classes.[98]

Interrante and Lasser bemoan the fact that Ehrenreich and English in fact fail to use these conceptual tools to develop "a materialist analysis of women's oppression." Nevertheless, whether or not it proves ultimately tenable, the patriarchy/masculinism distinction does provide a hint of the sort of categories that might be constructed by a feminist political economy, one that would fully "dissolve the hyphen" in "socialist-feminism."[99]

Like other aspects of its theory, the political economy of socialist feminism is incomplete. So far it consists more in a critique of prevailing conceptual models of women's contemporary situation than in the presentation of a systematic alternative framework. Even the critique has positive value, however, because, in making it, socialist feminism articulates criteria for the theoretical adequacy of proposed alternative models and so indicates directions and methods for future work by feminist political economists.

4. THEORY AND PRACTICE

It is obvious that socialist feminism faces large theoretical problems. It is still far from constructing a consistent, comprehensive and unified account of women's subordination. Nevertheless, already it has considerable fragments of theory, a sound method and, equally important, is developing a distinctive political practice. Political theory is not only a guide to political practice; it also develops as a result of practical political experience. We can expect that socialist feminist activism as well as socialist feminist scholarship will provide new insights for the theory.

As we saw in Chapter 2, political philosophy is devoted ultimately to practical ends. Consequently, the adequacy of a political theory is tested ultimately by the types of political activity that it encourages and their success in overcoming forms of domination. In the next part of this book, I shall examine the political practice of socialist feminists and of their sister feminists, a practice grounded on their respective presuppositions about human nature. This examination will prove a further basis for evaluating the political philosophy of various feminist tendencies.

Notes

1. Margaret Page, "Socialist Feminism—a political alternative?", *m/f* 2 (1978):41.

2. Juliet Mitchell, a pioneering author whose work broke the ground for socialist feminism but whose basic orientation is ultimately Marxist, writes, "We should ask the feminist questions, but try to come up with Marxist answers." *Women's Estate* (New York: Pantheon Books, 1971), p. 99.

3. Pun intended. There is in fact an exciting journal named *Heresies: A Feminist Publication on Art & Politics.*

4. A clear statement of this methodological approach is given by Iris Young, "Socialist Feminism and the Limits of Dual Systems Theory," *Socialist Review* 50–51, pp. 169-88. Cf. also Iris Young "Beyond the Unhappy Marriage: A Critique of the Dual Systems Theory," in Lydia Sargent, ed., *Women and Revolution* (Boston: South End Press, 1981), pp. 43-69. Young in fact uses the term "gender division of labor", but I prefer to follow Nancy Hartsock in using the more familiar "sexual division of labor." Hartsock justifies her use of the latter term in part because of her belief that the division of labor between women and men is not yet entirely a social affair (women and not men still bear children), in part because she wishes to keep a firm hold of "the bodily aspect of existence." Nancy Hartsock, "The Feminist Standpoint: Developing the Ground for a Specifically Feminist Historical Materialism," in Sandra Harding and Merrill Hintikka, eds., *Discovering Reality: Feminist Perspectives on Epistemology, Metaphysics, Methodology and the Philosophy of Science* (Dordrecht: Reidel Publishing Co.), 1983 (forthcoming).

5. Janice Delaney, Mary Jane Lupton, and Emily Toth, *The Curse: A Cultural History of Menstruation* (New York: E.P. Dutton, 1976).

6. Marian Lowe, "The Biology of Exploitation and the Exploitation of Biology," paper read to the National Women's Studies Association Second National Conference, Indiana University, Bloomington, May 16-20, 1980.

7. Iris Marion Young, "Is There a Woman's World?—Some Reflections on the Struggle for our Bodies," proceedings of *The Second Sex—Thirty Years Later: A Commemorative Conference on Feminist Theory* (New York: The New York Institute for the Humanities, 1979). See also Young's "Throwing Like a Girl: A Phenomenology of Feminine Body Comportment, Motitility and Sexuality," *Human Studies 3* (1980):137-56.

8. For example, see Nancy M. Henley, *Body Politics: Sex, Power and Non-Verbal Communication* (Englewood Cliffs, N.J.: Prentice-Hall, 1977).

9. Juliet Mitchell, *Psychoanalysis and Feminism* (New York: Vintage Books, 1975); Gayle Rubin, "The Traffic in Women: Notes on the 'Political Economy' of Sex," in Rayna R. Reiter, ed., *Toward an Anthropology of Women* (New York: Monthly Review Press, 1975), pp. 157-210; Nancy Chodorow, *Mothering: Psychoanalysis and the Sociology of Gender* (Berkeley and Los Angeles: University of California Press, 1978); Dorothy Dinnerstein, *The Mermaid and the Minotaur: Sexual Arrangements and Human Malaise* (New York: Harper & Row, 1977). Dinnerstein's work is idiosyncratic and consequently

difficult to categorize. Many of her assumptions, however, are identical with the assumptions of the other theorists mentioned here.

10. Rubin, "Traffic," p. 185.

11. Wilhelm Reich, *Sex-Pol: Essays, 1929–34* (New York: Vintage, 1972); also *The Sexual Revolution* (New York: Farrar, Straus & Giroux, 1979); also *The Mass Psychology of Fascism,* trans. Vincent R. Carfagho (New York: Pocket Books, 1978). Perhaps the best known result of the work by members of the Frankfurt School on this topic is Theodor W. Adorno, Else Frenkel-Brunswik, Daniel J. Levinson, and R. Nevitt Sanford, *The Authoritarian Personality* (New York: Harper & Row, 1950; repr. New York: W.W. Norton Library, 1969).

12. J.P. Sartre, *Critique de la raison dialectique* (Paris: Gallimard, 1960), p. 47.

13. The significance of this distinction for feminist theory will be discussed later in this chapter and also elsewhere in the book. Other theorists who have examined the distinction include Jean Bethke Elshtain, "Moral Woman and Immoral Man: A Consideration of the Public-Private Split and its Political Ramifications," *Politics and Society,* 1974; Jean Bethke Elshtain, *Public Man, Private Woman: Women in Social and Political Thought* (Princeton: Princeton University Press, 1981); and Linda Nicholson, *Feminism as Political Philosophy* (in progress). Cf. also M.Z. Rosaldo, "The Use and Abuse of Anthropology: Reflections on Feminism and Cross-Cultural Understanding," *Signs: Journal of Women in Culture & Society* 5, no. 3 (1980): esp. pp. 396-401.

14. Zillah Eisenstein, "Some Notes on the Relations of Capitalist Patriarchy," in Zillah Eisenstein, ed., *Capitalist Patriarchy and the Case for Socialist Feminism* (New York: Monthly Review Press, 1979), p. 47.

15. Ann Foreman, *Femininity as Alienation: Women and the Family in Marxism and Psychoanalysis* (London: Pluto Press, 1977), pp. 20 and 21.

16. Rayna Rapp, "Examining Family History," *Feminist Studies* 5, no 1 (Spring 1979):177.

17. Ann Ferguson, "Patriarchy, Sexual Identity and the Sexual Revolution," paper read at University of Cincinnati's Seventeenth Annual Philosophy Colloquium on "Philosophical Issues in Feminist Theory," November 13–16, 1980. This paper was later published in *Signs: Journal of Women in Culture and Society* 7, no. 1 (1981) :158-72.

18. Robert A. Padgug, "Sexual Matters: On Conceptualising Sexuality in History," *Radical History Review* 20 (Spring/Summer 1979):16.

19. Kathleen Gough, "The Nayars and the Definition of Marriage," in P.B. Hammond, ed., *Cultural and Social Anthropology* (London, New York: Collier-Macmillan, 1964).

20. Rayna Rapp, "Family & Class in Contemporary America: Notes Toward an Understanding of Ideology," *Science and Society* 52, no. 3 (Fall 1978).

21. Ellen Ross, "Rethinking 'the Family' ," *Radical History Review* 20 (Spring/Summer 1979):83.

22. Frederick Engels, *The Origin of the Family, Private Property and the State* (New York: International Publishers, 1972), pp. 71-72.

23. Karl Marx and Frederick Engels, *The German Ideology* (New York: International Publishers, 1970), p. 49.

24. *Isis Bulletin 11,* Geneva, Switzerland.

25. U.S. Bureau of the Census, *A Statistical Portrait of Women in the U.S.* (Washington, D.C.: Department of Commerce, Bureau of the Census, 1977); Current Population Reports, Special Studies Series, P-23, no. 58, pp. 28, 30, 31.

26. Heidi I. Hartman, "The Unhappy Marriage of Marxism and Feminism: Towards a More Progressive Union," in Lydia Sargent, ed., *Women and Revolution* (Boston: Southend Press, 1981), pp. 28-29.

27. Rubin, "Traffic," p. 171.

28. Eisenstein, "Capitalist Patriarchy," p. 47.

29. Rubin, "Traffic," p. 158.

30. Karl Marx, *The Poverty of Philosophy* (New York: International Publishers, 1963), p. 147.

31. Karl Marx, *Early Writings,* translated and edited by T.B. Bottomore (New York: McGraw-Hill, 1963), p. 125.

32. Lynda Lange, "Reproduction in Democratic Theory," in W. Shea and J. King-Farlow, eds., *Contemporary Issues in Political Philosophy,* vol. 2 (New York: Science History Publications, 1976), pp. 140-41.

33. Sandra L. Bartky, "Narcissism, Femininity and Alienation," *Social Theory and Practice* 8, no. 2 (Summer 1982):127-43.

34. Ann Foreman, *Femininity as Alienation,* p. 151.

35. Some feminists are beginning to speculate on whether advanced technology will ultimately make it possible for men to be equally involved with women in bearing children. Two authors who consider this question are Shulamith Firestone, *The Dialectic of Sex: The Case for Feminist Revolution* (New York: W.W. Morrow, 1970), and Marge Piercy, *Woman on the Edge of Time* (New York: Fawcett Books, 1977).

36. Ann Ferguson, "Androgyny as an Ideal for Human Development," in Mary Vetterling-Braggin, Frederick A. Elliston, and Jane English, eds., *Feminism and Philosophy* (Totowa, N.J.: Littlefield, Adams, 1977).

37. Barbara Katz Rothman, "How Science is Redefining Parenthood," *Ms,* August 1982, pp. 154-58.

38. Rubin, "Traffic," p. 204.

39. Evelyn Reed, "Women: Caste, Class or Oppressed Sex?" in Alison M. Jaggar and Paula Rothenberg Struhl, eds., *Feminist Frameworks: Alternative Theoretical Accounts of the Relations between Women and Men* (New York: McGraw-Hill, 1978), p. 127.

40. Engels, for example, explicitly contrasts procreative activity with "labor" in *Origin,* pp. 71-72. Marx and Engels do the same in *The German Ideology.*

41. Marx and Engels, *The German Ideology,* p. 50.

42. I am grateful to Judith Archer for bringing to my attention a number of references to male lactation. Not all of them can be cited here, but they include: Robert B. Greenblatt, M.D., "Inappropriate Lactation in Men and Women," *Medical Aspects of Human Sexuality,* June 1972, pp. 25-33; John Knott, "Abnormal Lactation: in the Virgin; in the Old Woman; in the Male; in the Newborn of Either Sex ('witches' milk')," *American Medicine,* n.s. 2, no. 6 (June 1907):373-78; R.C. Creasy, "Lactation from the Mammary Gland in the Male," *Journal of American Medical Association,* Chicago, 1912; P.L. Ponte and L. Pacilli, "L'allataments fuon della grairdanze nella stone e rella realta" [Suckling without pregnancy in fiction and reality], *Minerva Medica* 58, 29 August 1967.

43. The word "economics" derives from the Greek *oikonomia* meaning "management of a household or state." With the advent of industrialization, much work moved out of the home and "the economy" came to be contrasted with the household or the family. In its older and broader sense, however *economy* means any system of producing, distributing, and consuming goods. It may even be used of non-human systems, as in a recent book published by Harvard University Press on *Bumblebee Economics.*

44. Nancy Holmstrom, "Exploitation," *Canadian Journal of Philosophy* 7, no. 2 (June 1977):353-69.

45. Engels in *Origin,* p. 72.

46. Marx and Engels, *The German Ideology,* p. 49.

47. Rubin, "Traffic," p. 163.

48. U.N. Secretary General Kurt Waldheim, *Report to the U.N. Committee on the Status of Women,* reported in *Ms,* April 1981, p. 18.

49. Rubin, "Traffic," p. 160.

50. Joan Kelly, "The Doubled Vision of Feminist Theory: A Postscript to the 'Women and Power' Conference", *Feminist Studies* 5, no. 1 (Spring 1979):222. E.g., "Fully 20 percent of married black women in the United States have been sterilized, often during childbirth without their informed consent. In Puerto Rico, it is reported that 35 percent of women of child-bearing age have been sterilized. Ironically, white middle-class women in the United States often have difficulty in obtaining sterilization." Lisa Leghorn and Mary Roodkowsky, *Who Really Starves? Women and World Hunger* (New York: Friendship Press, 1977), p. 33.

51. Lange, "Reproduction," p. 141.

52. Rubin, "Traffic," p. 159.

53. Chodorow, *Mothering.*

54. Ann Ferguson and Nancy Folbre, "The Unhappy Marriage of Patriarchy and Capitalism," in Sargent, *Women and Revolution*, p. 319. For an earlier discussion of sex-affective production, see Ann Ferguson, "Women as a New Revolutionary Class," in Pat Walker, ed., *Between Labor and Capital* (Boston: South End Press, 1979).

55. Leghorn and Roodkowsky, *Who Really Starves?*

56. Samuel Bowles and Herbert Gintis, *Schooling in Capitalist America* (New York: Basic Books, 1977).

57. Karl Marx, "Preface to *A Contribution to the Critique of Political Economy*" in Marx and Engels, *Selected Works* (New York: International Publishers, 1968), pp. 182-83.

58. Suzanne K. Langer, *Philosophy in a New Key* (London: Oxford University Press, 1942), p. 3.

59. The former quotation is the title of a book by Christopher Lasch, *Haven in a Heartless World: The Family Besieged* (New York: Basic Books, 1977). The latter quotation is part of the title of an article by Kirk Jeffrey, "The Family as Utopian Retreat from the City: The Nineteenth-Century Contribution," in Sallie Teselle, ed., *The family, communes and utopian societies* (New York: Harper Torchbook, 1972).

60. Joan Kelly, "Doubled Vision," pp. 222-23.

61. An argument something like this is used by Richard Wasserstrom in "Privacy: Some Arguments and Assumptions," in Richard Bronaugh, ed., *Philosophical Law* (Westport, Conn: Greenwood Press, 1978). Cf. also David A.J. Richards, *Sex, Drugs, Death, and the Law: An Essay on Human Rights and Overcriminalization* (Totowa, N.J.: Rowman and Littlefield, 1982), chap. 2.

62. Lorenne Clark, "Privacy, Property, Freedom and the Family," in R. Bronaugh, ed., *Philosophical Law*, p. 183.

63. Engels, *Origin*, p. 137.

64. This is well described in Harry Braverman, *Labor and Monopoly Capital: The Degradation of Work in the Twentieth Century* (New York: Monthly Review Press, 1974).

65. Rosalind Petchesky, "Dissolving the Hyphen: A Report on Marxist-Feminist Groups 1-5," in Zillah R. Eisenstein, *Capitalist Patriarchy*, pp. 376-77.

66. Joan Kelly, "Doubled Vision," p. 223.

67. Ibid., pp. 223-24.

68. Rubin, "Traffic," pp. 209-10.

69. Lorenne M.G. Clark and Lynda Lange, *The Sexism of Social and Political Theory: Women and Reproduction from Plato to Nietzsche* (Toronto, Buffalo, London: University of Toronto Press, 1979).

70. For an excellent discussion of this problem, see Richard Lichtman's series of three articles on "Marx and Freud" in *Socialist Revolution:* vol. 6, no. 4 (Oct.–Dec. 1976); vol. 7, no. 3 (May–June 1977); and vol. 7, no. 6 (Nov.–Dec. 1977). In the 20th century, there has been considerable debate over whether Freudian theory can be incorporated into a "Marxist" psychology and many attempts at a Marx/Freud synthesis. They began with Wilhelm Reich in the 1930s and continued with the work of the Frankfurt School. In the 1960s, the popularity of Herbert Marcuse, an erstwhile member of the Frankfurt School, led to a revival of such efforts by the New Left in the United States and in Britain. A recent and influential attempt at a Marx/Freud synthesis has been made by Michael Schneider, *Neurosis and Civilization: A Marxist Freudian Synthesis* (New York: Seabury Press, 1975).

71. Joseph Interrante, "The Sexual Politics of Speech," *Radical History Review* 22 (Winter 1979–80):157.

72. One socialist feminist currently working on this project is Sandra Bartky. Bartky links women's false consciousness and male supremacist ideology to a socialist-feminist concept of alienation. Sandra L. Bartky, "On Psychological Oppression," in Sharon Bishop and Marjorie Weinzweig, eds., *Philosophy and Women* (Belmont, Calif.: Wadsworth, 1979), pp. 33-41; also "Narcissism, Femininity and Alienation," *Social Theory and Practice* 8, no. 2 (Summer 1982):127-43. Bartky's work will be discussed in Chapter 10.

73. Goeffrey Nowell-Smith and Quinton Hoare, eds., *Selections from the Prison Notebooks of Antonio Gramsci* (London: Lawrence & Wishart, 1971).

74. Brigitte Jordan, *Birth in Four Cultures: A Crosscultural Investigation of Childbirth in Yucatan, Holland, Sweden, and the United States* (Montreal: Eden Press, 1980), p. ii.

75. Lynda Lange, "Towards a Theory of Reproductive Labour," paper prepared for presentation at the workshop on Marxist-Feminism, Canadian Philosophical Association Congress, June 4–7, 1979, p. 13 of typescript.

76. Karl Marx and Frederick Engels, *The Manifesto of the Communist Party*, in Marx and Engels, *Selected Works*, p. 50.

77. Paulo Freire, *The Pedagogy of the Oppressed* (New York: Seabury Press, 1973).

78. Shulamith Firestone, *Dialectic of Sex*. See especially chapter 4, "Down with Childhood."

79. With no children in the house, the value of the work done by unpaid houseworkers is now calculated at $8,400.00 per year. With children present, the amount is much higher. *The Dollar Value of Housework* (Cornell Distribution Center)—*Ms.*, 7 Research Park, Ithaca, N.Y. 14850.

80. Clark and Lange, *Social and Political Theory*.

81. Ulrike Prokop, *Weiblicher Lebenszusammenhang* [The Context of Women's Daily Life], Frankfurt am Main, 1976. Guntram Weber translated pp. 64-82 and 213-15 of this book and published them under the title of "Production and the Context of Women's Daily Life" in *New German Critique* 13 (Winter 1978). Sandra Bartky drew this article to my attention.

82. Ferguson and Folbre, "Unhappy Marriage."

83. Rubin, "Traffic."

84. Ibid., p. 167.

85. Ibid., p. 177.

86. Sandra Harding, "What Causes Gender-Privilege and Class-Privilege?", unpublished, p. 4 of typescript. This paper was an early draft of Harding's "What is the Real Material Base of Patriarchy and Capital?" in Sargent, ed., *Women and Revolution*, pp. 135-63. In the later version, however, Harding dropped the passage that I have quoted.

87. Lynda Lange, "Why are Women Oppressed?", paper read at a workshop on feminist philosophy, Canadian Philosophical Association, May 1976, pp. 5–6 of typescript.

88. "Study on the Interrelationship Between the Status of Women and Family Planning", United Nations World Population Conference, E/CN.6/575. Cited by Leghorn and Roodkowsky, *Who Really Starves?* p. 30.

89. Christine Delphy, *The Main Enemy: A Materialist Analysis of Women's Oppression*, translated by Lucy ap Roberts (London: Women's Research and Resources Centre Publications, 1977).

90. This phrase is attributed to Carol Brown by Linda Nicholson in "Rationality and Gender," a paper read at the University of Cincinnati's Seventeenth Annual Philosophy Colloquium on Philosophical Issues in Feminist Theory, November 13–16, 1980.

91. Joan Kelly, "Double Vision," p. 221.

92. Iris Young, "Socialist Feminism and the Limits of Dual Systems Theory," (see note 4), pp. 179-80.

93. Ibid., p. 177. Tim Diamond, in private correspondence, was one of the first people to articulate for me this need in socialist feminist theory.

94. Heidi I. Hartman, "The Unhappy Marriage," has a section entitled "The Partnership of Patriarchy and Capital." Zillah R. Eisenstein talks about "the mutually reinforcing dialectical relationship between capitalist class structure and hierarchical sexual structuring," "Capitalist Patriarchy," p. 5.

95. Ferguson and Folbre, "Unhappy Marriage." Also Alison Edwards, "Women and Modern Capitalism", *Urgent Tasks* 6 (Fall 1979). Of course, this was the view of Marx and Engels.

96. Anne Phillips, "Revolutionary Socialism," *Big Flame Magazine* 6 (Winter 1980–81):22.

97. Iris Young, "Socialist Feminism and the Limits of Dual Systems Theory," pp. 180-81 (italics in original).

98. Joseph Interrante and Carol Lasser, "Victims of the Very Songs They Sing: A Critique of Recent Work on Patriarchal Culture and the Social Construction of Gender," *Radical History Review* 20 (Spring/Summer 1979):34.

99. Rosalind Petchesky, "Dissolving the Hyphen."

part three
Feminist Politics

As it is understood within the western tradition, "politics" is an extremely broad concept that can refer to many aspects of the management or government of a city or a state. According to Webster's dictionary, "politics" may be used to refer to the science or art of government, to participation in governmental affairs, to methods or tactics for affecting governmental policies, or to opinions or principles regarding how society should be governed. In male-dominated society, feminists are rarely involved directly in governing society; typically, they work outside established institutions in attempts to change how society is governed. The following exploration of feminist politics will examine the values that inspire different groups of feminists and which they would like to see instantiated in political society, the correlated feminist critiques of existing political institutions and practices and the strategies by which different groups of feminists try to bring about political change and realize their vision of the good society.

As we have seen already, much feminist criticism concerns the contemporary organization of childbearing, childrearing, sexuality and personal maintenance. Within the western tradition, these areas of life have been defined as outside the sphere of politics. Traditionally, political life has been contrasted with so-called private life and political economy has been contrasted with domestic or household economy. Given the sexual division of labor in contemporary society, which still defines the home as women's proper place, the traditional conception of politics thus excludes much of women's world. By including the household within their critique, some feminists challenge the traditional conception of politics as male-biased and androcentric. They claim a new definition of politics that includes the management or government of every aspect of social life.

A few feminists even challenge the customary identification of management with government. They distinguish between management, as a system of social organization, on the one hand, and government, as a system of coercion, on the other hand. If politics is defined as the management of a state, and if a state is defined as a set of permanent institutions through which a unified code of behavior is established and enforced within a certain territory, then politics by definition is concerned with coercive authority. Some feminists believe that the good society should have no coercive government, but should be managed through noncoercive forms of organization. The implication of this view is that, while all of contemporary life may be political insofar as it is structured by coercive relationships, eventually politics, with government, should be abolished altogether.

Feminist politics are grounded on feminist values. Not all feminists share the same values, however. There is some overlap between the values held by various groups of feminists but differences emerge in a number of ways. The most obvious way is in disagreements over how to analyze or explain various aspects of women's contemporary oppression. Even where feminists may agree that a certain feature of contemporary society is oppressive to women, they may have different reasons for their belief. For instance, both liberal feminists and traditional Marxists oppose women's being assigned the primary responsibility for housework. But while the liberal sees this assignment as unjust, denying women equal opportunity for self-fulfilment, the Marxist sees it as a way in which the working class is divided, creating antagonisms between women and men and hindering the development of class solidarity. When feminists provide different analyses of what is wrong with a certain feature of women's situation, inevitably they diverge in their recommendations about how that situation should be changed. In the present example, liberal feminists propose that housework should be "professionalized" through the market, whereas Marxists propose that it should be socialized through the state. The former recommendations would result in a society where individual competition was intensified and where relations between people were even more mediated by money; the latter would result in a society where the performance of necessary social tasks was seen as the ultimate responsibility of society as a whole, rather than of certain individuals. Obviously, which of these societies one would prefer depends on one's overriding values.

Value differences emerge in a less obvious way at the level of description as well as at the level of explanation. This is not too hard to see when feminists differ over what counts as equality; it is harder to see when feminists disagree over what counts as sexual harassment, as prostitution or as rape. Disagreements over these sorts of issues may be based in part on disagreement over "the facts," perhaps over who typically makes sexual advances to whom and in what sorts of contexts. More fundamentally, however, disagreements about how to describe or characterize women's situation may be grounded in disagreement over such philosophical and evaluative questions as the proper interpretation of freedom or of coercion. In Chapter 2, I argued that all interpretations of reality reflected certain values: the conceptual system through which reality is understood inevitably picks out certain regularities in social life or in non-human nature and ignores others. In Part III of this book, I shall identify some of the values reflected in the various feminist accounts of women's contemporary situation. In Part IV, I shall discuss criteria for choosing between these accounts.

The values that identify each group of feminists are connected conceptually with their characteristic view of human nature. This is not to say that a certain conception of human nature logically implies a certain set of values that, in turn, entails a particular approach to politics. Although the organization of this book may suggest that there is a deductive relationship between a certain conception of human nature and a certain cluster of political views, this is not so. The conceptual connections between an individual's social or political values, her beliefs about contemporary society and her beliefs about human nature are far more complex. It is probably nearer the truth to say that these various beliefs and values form an interconnected web or network, within which changes in any one part are likely to necessitate changes elsewhere if the whole is to remain coherent and consistent. In what follows, I shall try to show the continuity between the values that inform a certain conception of human nature and the values that inform each distinctive feminist approach to political life.

7
The Politics of Liberal Feminism

The liberal conception of human nature is radically individualistic in several ways. One of these is a view of human beings as individuals who share a common essence that may vary in its manifestations but which remains basically unaffected by variations in the social context. The essence of human nature is the uniquely human capacity for reason, a concept that, as we saw earlier, is itself understood by liberals in a way that is distinctively individualistic. The liberal conception of reason is influenced by the traditional western association between reason and goodness, and that influence emerges in the view held by some liberals that rationality consists in the human ability to recognize the validity of the moral law. The more dominant strand in the liberal interpretation of reason, however, is the instrumental conception associated with the rise of 17th-century science; on this conception, rationality consists primarily in individuals' ability to be consistent in pursuit of their own ends.

The liberal conception of human nature is informed by certain characteristic values, and these values also inspire the liberal conception of the good society. The most fundamental liberal value is a belief in the intrinsic dignity and worth of every human individual, a worth grounded in each individual's capacity for reason. Liberals express this value in their political theory through the demand for equality. As we have seen in Chapter 3, however, the way in which equality has been understood has changed substantially during the 300-year development of liberal thought. In this chapter, I shall show how liberal feminists have pushed the concept of equality so far that its instantiation threatens other liberal values and its interpretation threatens the basic structure of liberal political theory and even the liberal conception of human nature.

Since liberals view rationality as the essential human characteristic, they infer that the good society must allow the maximum opportunity for the development and exercise of individuals' capacity to reason. Moreover, since each human being has at least the potential capacity to reason, this opportunity must be available to all. The value that liberals place on individual rationality is expressed in their political theory through the demand for liberty. The notion of liberty is liberalism's distinctive contribution to political theory and the political value that gave the tradition its name. It means freedom from interference either by other individuals or by the state. Liberty is thought to guarantee individual autonomy, the right of each individual to establish her or his own interpretation of truth and of morality, uncoerced by established authority. Liberty is also thought to guarantee individuals the right to pursue their own interests or self-fulfilment, as they define their interests and understand their fulfilment.

The importance that liberals ascribe to liberty is manifested in their determination to set firm limits on the authority of the state. In liberal theory, those limits are marked by the conceptual distinction between the public realm, which is susceptible to state regulation, and the private realm, which is exempt from such regulation. Not only must the state refrain from intervening in certain areas of individual life; it must also protect those areas from interference by others. Some of the protected areas are identified by specific civil liberties; they include freedom of expression, particularly political or religious expression, freedom of worship and freedom of assembly. In addition, the contemporary liberal state even allows a limited right of civil disobedience; that is, it respects the right of individuals to "follow their conscience" when their moral beliefs conflict with the demands of the state. In recognition of this right, the liberal state has sometimes tolerated individual refusal to pay taxes or to serve in the armed forces. The liberal insistence on an inviolable private sphere of human life is sometimes characterized as "the right to privacy." It is the political expression of liberal respect for individual rationality in both its moral and its instrumental interpretations.

Because of their respect for individual judgment, liberal philosophers seek to develop a political theory that is independent of any substantive claims about the nature of the good life or of human happiness or fulfilment. Individuals are entitled to set their own ends and, so long as they do not violate the rights of others, there are in principle no limits to what they may want to do or believe they ought to do. In principle, therefore, liberals are committed to the belief that individuals are fulfilled whenever they are doing what they have decided freely to do, however unpleasant, degrading or wrong this may appear to someone else. Liberals seem to have no grounds for speculating how people might choose to occupy themselves in the good society and so try to make their theory neutral between various conceptions of the good life.

In practice, however, liberals are not scrupulously agnostic about what constitutes human fulfilment. Paradoxically, one limitation on their agnosticism springs from that agnosticism itself: because of their agnosticism, they have no critical standpoint from which to resist conventionally accepted criteria of achievement or success. Consequently, liberals tend in practice if not in principle to accept conventional accounts of happiness or self-fulfilment. If most people compete for certain socially defined goods and positions, and if individuals are the best judges of their own interest, liberals are forced to conclude that in fact happiness consists in the acquisition of those goods and the achievement of those positions, at least for the majority of people who compete for them. As Mill notoriously and fallaciously observed, "the sole evidence it is possible to produce that anything is desirable is that people do actually desire it."[1] Like many other liberal philosophers, Mill identifies the good for an individual with what that individual wants. The liberal concludes that the happiest individuals, in general although not universally, are those who achieve what most people want: wealth and social prestige. Those who fail in the competition are likely to be less happy and fulfilled. Naturally, this conclusion reinforces the liberal belief in the importance of equal opportunities for all.

In addition to this tendency to accept conventional views of happiness, there is another way in which liberals often depart in practice from their "official" scepticism regarding human fulfilment. This second departure is generated by the liberal respect for reason and by the characteristic liberal conception of what reason is. Because they view the exercise of reason as the distinctively human capacity, liberals tend to place the highest value on those activities which they perceive as requiring the most use of reason. Prior to the 19th century, this meant that liberals disdained most kinds of physical production and viewed the good life as the opportunity to devote oneself to intellectual reflection. This anti-work attitude was modified in the 19th century, perhaps partly as a result of the Industrial Revolution and the systematic application of science to increasing production. It now became possible for individuals to be seen as fulfilled through work, so long as this work was primarily mental rather than manual. Manual work was still thought to be degrading, especially if it was performed under the direction of another. It is easy to see the connection between this attitude to work and liberal normative dualism (see Chapter 3), according to which the body is the unfortunately necessary but mortal and fallible container of the mind.

Justice is the final value that informs liberal political theory. The question of justice, for liberals, is the question of the proper distribution to individuals of what John Rawls calls "the benefits and burdens of social co-operation."[2] These benefits and burdens are taken to include both political rights and obligations, such as the right to freedom of expression or the obligation to obey the law, and economic rights and obligations, such as the right to a minimum standard of living and the obligation to pay taxes. In both the political and the economic realm, contemporary liberals see it as the responsibility of the state to impose just burdens and to allocate just benefits. Within the liberal tradition are several "theories of justice"; that is, there are a number of conflicting views about how costs and benefits, duties and rights, should be apportioned between individuals. In disputes about which theory is correct, liberals have taken the ideal of equality as a starting point and then sought to justify departures from equality. The historical tendency of the liberal tradition has been for the state to play an increasing role in helping individuals to exercise their rights, for instance through the provision of legal aid, and also for the state to be increasingly active in the redistribution of income, through progressive taxation and various welfare programs. Thus there has been a historical trend away from purely formal or legal interpretations of equality and toward more substantive or economic interpretations. This tendency is often referred to as "socialistic." In fact, however, the concern with justice remains a typically liberal preoccupation, insofar as it rests on a conception of society as composed of essentially separate individuals, each competing with the others for his or her "fair share."

The Liberal Feminist Analysis
of Women's Oppression

Liberal feminists believe that the treatment of women in contemporary society violates, in one way or another, all of liberalism's political values, the values of equality, liberty, and justice. Their most frequent complaint is that women in contemporary society suffer discrimination on the basis of sex. By this, they mean that certain restrictions are placed on women *as a group,* without regard to their individual wishes, interests, abilities or merits.

Liberal feminists believe that sex discrimination is unjust because it deprives women of equal rights to pursue their own self-interest. Women as a group are not allowed the same freedoms or opportunities granted to men as a group. In a discriminatory situation, an individual woman does not receive the same consideration as an individual man. Whereas man is judged on his actual interests and abilities, a woman's interests and abilities are assumed to be limited in certain ways because of her sex. In other words, a man is judged on his merits as an individual; a woman is judged on her assumed merits as a female. Liberal feminists believe that justice requires equal opportunities and equal consideration for every individual regardless of sex. This view is obviously connected with the liberal conception of human beings as essentially rational agents. On this conception, sex is a purely "accidental" or non-essential feature of human nature. The sex of an individual should be considered only when it is relevant to the individual's ability to perform a specific task or to take advantage of a certain opportunity.

Within contemporary society, liberals believe that women suffer a variety of forms of discrimination. The most obvious form is legislation that provides different responsibilities, obligations, and opportunities for women and for men. Both Britain and the United States, for example, have so-called "protective" labor legislation that applies to women only and may establish maximum hours of work, minimum wages, mandatory rest periods, or may restrict certain types of nighttime work. Liberal feminists complain that these laws are used to exclude women from better-paying jobs and to deny them promotion. In some states, women receive special exemptions from jury service and consequently may not have their salaries paid if they do choose to serve. There is further asymmetry in the legal rights assigned to married women and men. For example, the husband often has more extensive rights than the wife to dispose of communal property such as real estate, cars and furniture; a wife sometimes is still restricted from making contracts and engaging in business on her own; a married woman's domicile is normally expected to follow her husband's, and so on.

In spite of these sorts of legal discrimination, liberal feminists believe that most discrimination against women is not mandated by the legal system but is rather informal or based on custom. An extremely significant form of customary discrimination consists in reluctance to appoint qualified women to certain jobs, particularly prestigious, well-paying or supervisory positions, and in reluctance to allow women to gain necessary qualifications for those positions, perhaps by refusing them entrance into professional schools or other job-training programs. Such discrimination begins in the nursery, where male and female infants are perceived and handled differently, and continues in the educational system, where boys are encouraged to train for prestigious or well-paying "masculine" occupations while girls are channeled into preparing for the lower-paying but more "feminine" service occupations. Women also suffer discrimination in obtaining credit to buy a house or to start a business and they may have more difficulty than men in renting accommodation. Liberals view all these sorts of discrimination as unjust because they deprive women of equal opportunities for pursuing their own self-interest, as they define that interest.

Informal discrimination is manifested not only in assumptions that women are not suited to certain sorts of work; it can also be expressed through assumptions that women are particularly well-suited for other sorts of work. Within contemporary society, there are strong expectations, often shared even by women themselves, that women should take primary responsibility for the work involved in raising children and in running a home. Women are also expected to provide sexual satisfaction for their husbands or their male partners. Within the paid labor force, they are expected to perform similar sorts of work, providing sexual titillation if not satisfaction to men and other sorts of nurturing services to men, women and children.

If this sexual division of labor were freely chosen, liberal feminists would have no grounds for challenging it. In fact, however, they assume that it is not freely chosen, that women congregate in these occupations because discrimination denies them access to the prestigious, powerful, and well-paying positions that are held predominantly by men. Behind this assumption, one can see the characteristic liberal values about what constitutes desirable or fulfilling work. The work that women typically perform is not well-paying and has little conventional prestige and liberal feminists show little inclination to challenge the conventional valuation of that work. Liberal feminists view childcare and housework as forms of unskilled labor, servicing the despised body and requiring little exercise of the respected mind. They regard clerical and service workers as typically obeying instructions, with few opportunities to make autonomous decisions. And liberal feminists perceive the provision of sexual titillation or gratification for men as requiring more in the way of physical than of mental qualifications. As we have seen already, the view of rationality that underlies these perceptions is far from unproblematic; however, it is a necessary premise for the liberal feminist conclusion that contemporary women are assigned work that is menial and degrading because it does not allow the exercise of the human capacity for reason, either in its moral or in its prudential dimension. The teaching profession may seem to be an exception to this conclusion, insofar as it is defined conventionally as a female occupation yet obviously requires the exercise of intellectual capacities. In this case, however, women predominate particularly in the early stages, where education is inseparable from physical care. As young people grow older, male teachers gradually increase until, by the college years, men predominate. The most prestigious educational work, and that which seems to require the greatest development of the capacity to reason, has been reserved traditionally for men.

Women's relegation to certain kinds of work degrades them not only while they are performing that work. According to liberal feminism, the conditions of women's work also diminish their liberty and autonomy in the rest of their lives. Women are paid so little that they figure disproportionately among the poor and most contemporary liberals recognize that poverty makes it difficult or impossible for individuals to exercise their formal or legal rights. For instance, poor people cannot exercise their right to travel when they cannot afford the fares; their right of free expression is diminished by their lack of control over the media; and their right to stand for public office is worth little when they cannot afford to finance an electoral campaign. Instead of saying that poorer individuals have less liberty or fewer rights than wealthier ones, Rawls prefers to say that "the worth of liberty" is less for poor people.[3] However one expresses the point, liberal feminists complain that poverty makes most women unequal to most men.

The situation is worst for those women who do unpaid childcare, sexual and maintenance work in the home: economic dependence on their husbands makes it difficult or practically impossible for housewives to exercise their autonomy. More than a hundred years ago, John Stuart Mill wrote: "The *power* of earning is essential to the dignity of a woman, if she has not independent property."[4] A century later, Betty Friedan concurred:

> For women to have full identity and freedom, they must have economic independence. . . .
> Equality and human dignity are not possible for women if they are not able to earn. . . . Only economic independence can free a woman to marry for love, not for status or financial support, or to leave a loveless, intolerable, humiliating marriage, or to eat, dress, rest, and move if she plans not to marry.[5]

In addition, the assignment of most domestic work to women diminishes even further their opportunities for prestigious and well-paying jobs and so constitutes a difficult trap to escape.

As liberal feminists perceive contemporary society, women lack equal opportunities for the more fulfilling types of work and are consigned instead to work that is degrading, menial and diminishes their liberty and autonomy. On the liberal feminist view, this is not only unjust; for two centuries, liberal feminists have claimed that it is also an inefficient use of society's human resources. Mary Wollstonecraft argued that a more equal treatment of women would allow them to be more useful to society and J. S. Mill complained that the denial of equal opportunities to women deprived society of valuable contributions that women might otherwise make:

> Is there so great a superfluity of men fit for high duties, that society can afford to reject the service of any competent person? Are we so certain of always finding a man made to our hands for any duty or function of social importance which falls vacant, that we lose nothing by putting a ban upon one-half of mankind, and refusing before hand to make their faculties available, however distinguished they may be? . . . To ordain that any kind of persons shall not be physicians, or shall not be advocates, or shall not be members of parliament, is to injure not them only, but all who employ physicians or advocates, or elect members of parliament, and who are deprived of the stimulating effect of greater competition on the exertions of the competitors, as well as restricted to a narrower range of individual choice.[6]

On Mill's argument, the abolition of sex discrimination is not only required by justice but will also maximize each individual's contribution to society as a whole. This claim, of course, is a version of Adam Smith's classic belief that, when each individual is free to pursue his own self-interest, the "invisible hand" of Providence, working through a market economy, will co-ordinate these selfish strivings to the net benefit of all. Justice is in our economic as well as our moral interest.

Women's lack of equality in public life is the major focus of liberal feminism. But liberal feminists also perceive women as oppressed in other ways. In particular, like all feminists, they believe that contemporary standards of sexuality are oppressive to women. Naturally, they formulate their critique of contemporary sexual norms in terms of their characteristic values of equality, liberty and justice.

Women have always had less sexual liberty than men, and even today liberal feminists see strong social and sometimes legal impediments to women's freedom of sexual expression. Among these restraints are social and sometimes legal impediments to sex education, contraception, abortion: and lesbianism, and the familiar sexual double-standard that requires women to be passive rather than active in sexual encounters and that condemns women who want a variety of sexual partners while admiring men who seek the same. The contemporary perception of women as sexual objects imposes social penalties on women who do not express their sexuality in a way pleasing to men. Women are expected to present themselves as subtly or blatantly titillating to men and to achieve sexual gratification through intercourse, even though this sexual practice is far more conducive to male than to female orgasm. The perception of women as sexual objects restricts more than their sexuality: it also encourages sexual harassment, makes it difficult for women to be taken seriously in non-sexual contexts, and provides a covert legitimization of rape. In these ways, it limits women's freedom to travel safely alone and denies them equal opportunities in public life.

Some of the restraints mentioned above, such as restrictions on sex education, contraception, and homosexual activity, may seem to affect men as much as women and thus fail to constitute examples of sex discrimination. In fact, however, liberal feminists see that inadequate sex education and contraception harm women much more than men since it is women who become pregnant and who are supposed to take responsibility for any children who may be born. Even normative heterosexuality in some ways is more oppressive to women than to men. Because it is difficult for unmarried women to maintain themselves above the poverty level, greater economic pressure to marry is felt by lesbians than by gay men. In social terms, the status of bachelor is not considered deserving of pity or ridicule as is the status of spinster or "old maid"—hence the tendency for some unmarried heterosexual women to refer to themselves as "bachelor girls"!

It is characteristic of liberal feminism to express its critique of contemporary sexual norms only in terms of such "political" concepts as liberty and equality. Within the liberal framework, these concepts are construed as values that properly regulate the public realm; they are not seen as "moral" values which are thought of as regulating the private realm. Liberal feminists deliberately avoid characterizing contemporary sexual mores in such overtly moral terms as *promiscuous, perverse, alienated, puritanical, repressed,* or *mechanical.* There are two reasons for this restraint on the part of liberal feminists. One reason is their commitment to the characteristically liberal scepticism about the possibility of providing a general but substantive account of human fulfilment. Consequently, like all liberals, they try to utilize what Rawls calls the thinnest possible theory of the good; that is, they try to make their political theory as neutral as possible between various conceptions of the good life. The other reason for the limits on the liberal feminist critique of sexual norms is connected with liberalism's basic conception of human nature. As we have seen already, the liberal tradition presupposes a conception of human nature that is normatively, if not metaphysically, dualistic. This normative dualism is expressed in the view that the characteristic human activity is the exercise of one's reason. Since persons, on the liberal view, logically may be male, female, multisexed or sexless, there is nothing intrinsically human or valuable about sexual activity. Nor is there any reason to suppose that there is any one intrinsic or exclusive purpose in sexual activity Although obviously they are aware that sexual activity is necessary for procreation, liberal feminists see no reason to limit sexual activity to procreation. Sexual activity can be used to conceive children, to obtain pleasure or to make money; to communicate or to avoid communication; to express aggression, friendship or love. Liberal theory provides no basis for claiming that any of these uses is more "natural" or objectively desirable than any other; correlatively, it provides no basis for claiming that any of these uses is in itself is wrong, unnatural or perverse. The normative dualism of liberal theory provides no conceptual foothold for a normative philosophical theory of sexuality. Particular sexual practices and sexual activity in general are valuable only insofar as individuals define them as good or wish to engage in them.

Within the liberal framework, sexual activity is paradigmatically a private matter unless it infringes on the rights of other individuals. Consequently, state intervention in the sexual lives of its citizens violates their rights to privacy unless the sexual activity in question violates other individuals' rights. On this basis, liberal feminists argue that restraints on sex education, on contraception or on abortion violate the individual's right to privacy.[7] Restrictions on masturbation, homosexuality or any other sexual practice are equally unjustified, according to the liberal feminists, so long as no unwilling partners are involved. Of course, liberal feminists always oppose rape, even within marriage, since this is an obvious case of sexual coercion and the violation of individual rights. Typically, they also object to sexual activities involving children, on the grounds that children are not yet able to give an informed and rational consent to sexual participation.

The liberal commitment to liberty and the inviolability of private life places liberal feminists among most other feminists in their opposition to restraints on contraception, abortion, homosexuality, etc. The same commitment, however, separates liberal feminists from most other feminists on the issue of pornography. The contemporary women's liberation movement has always been critical of pornography. In the 1960s and early 1970s, feminists complained that glamorized, sexualized and infantilized images of women perpetuated the view that women were the sexual playthings of men. In the 1970s and early 1980s, the focus has shifted to images of violence against women. Feminists complain that these make the rape, torture and even murder of women appear to be legitimate and even erotic. Pornography presents a special problem for liberal feminists because of liberalism's historic commitment to freedom of expression and the right to privacy. Liberal feminists may be "personally" or "privately" revolted or titillated by pornography, but they have no "political" grounds for opposing it unless it can be shown to have a direct causal connection with the violation of women's rights.

Whereas pornography is a fairly recent issue for feminists, prostitution has always been a major target of feminist attack. Since liberal feminists perceive prostitution to be an occupation involving little opportunity for the autonomous exercise of rationality, they do not consider it a model of human fulfilment. On the other hand, liberals do not conceive one's body to be an essential part of oneself, so there seems to be no reason why one's sexual services may not just as well be sold as one's other abilities. Indeed, the propriety of selling one's intellectual capacities might be more problematic, on liberal grounds, than the sale of one's sexual services. So long as prostitution is freely chosen, therefore, liberal feminists do not see grounds for imposing on prostitution restrictions any more severe than those which regulate other occupations. Liberal feminists do point out, however, that women can be seen as having made a free choice to enter prostitution only when they have been given the opportunity to develop their rational faculties, when they are not perceived and taught to perceive themselves primarily as sexual objects and when they have equal opportunities to enter other kinds of employment.

In sum, liberal feminists believe that the treatment of women in contemporary society violates their rights to liberty, to equality, and to justice—as well as constituting an irrational and inefficient use of society's human resources. In order to solve these problems, liberal feminists propose several characteristic strategies.

The Liberal Feminist Proposals for Social Change

Liberal feminists often state that their goal is to incorporate women fully into the mainstream of contemporary society. By "mainstream" they mean the so-called public life of industry, commerce, education and political office. Liberal feminists have no overt objection to women's choosing a so-called private life of family and friends, but they believe this life to be regulated primarily by affection and emotion, rather than by rationality, and so to offer little opportunity for the exercise of women's specifically human capacities. Consequently, liberal feminists assume that women's conspicuous underrepresentation in public life is less a result of choices made freely by women than it is a result of women's lack of equal opportunities to enter and rise in public affairs. Liberal feminists want to eliminate sex-based discrimination in all areas of life and to guarantee women equal opportunities with men to define and pursue their own interests. They argue for a meritocracy within which jobs and offices would be awarded entirely on the basis of relevant qualifications. Because they believe that the effects of present discrimination permit no firm conclusions about the "natural" potentials of women and men, liberal feminists are unable to predict exactly what would be the results of allowing women equal opportunities with men. Less cautious or consistent liberal feminists, however, assume that increased freedom of choice would issue in a sexually integrated or androgynous society where individuals' occupations, sexual choices, etc., were largely unrelated to their sex.

In order to achieve a more just society, liberal feminism's first strategy is reasoned argument. Viewing human beings as essentially rational, liberal feminists take every opportunity to educate the public about the irrationality and injustice of discrimination against women. Liberal feminists write books, seek access to the media and sit on committees to investigate the status of women and to determine how that status may be improved. Liberal feminists may also engage in public demonstrations. Unlike riots, however, the purpose of these demonstrations is not to intimidate nor to coerce; instead, it is to draw public attention to the injustices that women suffer in an attempt to challenge popular prejudices and to change popular attitudes.

For liberal feminism, the most basic injustice suffered by women in contemporary society is, of course, the existence of sex-biased laws. Liberal feminists seek the repeal of all laws that ascribe different rights, responsibilities and opportunities to women and to men. They even oppose so-called protective legislation for women, believing that the same standards of health and safety should apply to everyone. They believe that women as well as men should be subject to military service if it is compulsory and the more consistent liberal feminists also argue that women should be trained for combat as well as non-combat duties.

During the 1970s, a steady trend toward increasing the formal or legal equality of women has occurred in most of the industrialized countries. In the United States, a major focus of liberal feminist activity has been the proposed Equal Rights Amendment to the Constitution which reads: "Equality of rights under the law shall not be denied or abridged by the United States or by any State on account of sex." It was approved by the United States Congress in 1972, and liberal feminists then spent ten years struggling for its ratification by the needed 38 states until their efforts were finally defeated in 1982. If the ERA had been ratified, any sex-specific law would have become unconstitutional. Hence, employment legislation could no longer have applied only to women, marriage laws would have had to apply equally to men and women, and women would have become eligible for conscription into the armed forces. Government at all levels would have been prohibited from discriminating against women in public employment and in job-training programs. Most important, males and females in public education would have had to receive the same treatment. The ERA would have prohibited sex-segregated public schools and universities, special programs for boys or girls, and discrimination in admissions policies.

Liberal feminists demand sex-blindness in the application as well as the formulation of the laws. They believe that this can be guaranteed only when legislators, the judicial branch, and law enforcement officers are no longer predominantly male. Consequently, liberal feminists argue that the sexual integration of legislatures, law courts and police forces is necessary not only to ensure equality of opportunity for female politicians, lawyers and police officers; it is also a precondition for the impartial administration of the laws. For this reason, liberal feminists in the United States have joined in attempts to elect more women to public office, regardless of their candidates' politics on issues that are not defined as "women's issues."

Prior to the contemporary women's liberation movement, formal equality seemed to be an adequate goal for liberal feminism. It was thought that, in the absence of legal constraints, women would quickly achieve substantive equality with men; lingering prejudice would be dispelled by rational arguments appealing both to justice and to efficiency. Contemporary liberal feminists, however, have discovered that informal or customary discrimination against women, though not legally mandated, is nevertheless extremely pervasive and extremely powerful. When it became apparent that such discrimination was recalcitrant to rational argument, liberal feminism's next move was to attempt to use the law to abolish discrimination against women. In consequence, liberal feminists have sought laws which not only require equal pay for equal work, but which forbid discrimination in educating, hiring, promoting, housing or granting credit to women. Many of these laws now exist in the United States, where liberal feminism has recently achieved the legal recognition of sexual harassment as a form of discrimination. In one respect, this feminist resort to legal recourse is quite compatible with traditional liberalism, which views the state as the impartial protector of the rights of all its citizens. Yet in another respect feminist reliance on the law is contrary to the spirit of traditional liberalism, which views any growth in state power as a threat to individual liberty. Later in this chapter I shall discuss this apparent conflict between the traditional liberal values of liberty and of equality.

One interesting result of liberal feminist efforts to abolish discrimination against women is that these feminists have been led to abandon their original requirement of "sex-blindness": the requirement that laws should be written in sex-neutral language and applied without regard to sex. For instance, liberal feminists have recognized that employee pregnancy and maternity leaves are a necessary part of women's equality of opportunity, and liberal feminists have also pressed for the establishment of so-called affirmative action programs, which require employers to provide evidence of good faith efforts to hire women and members of ethnic minority groups. In arguing for the justice of these sex-specific practices, liberal feminists find themslves going far beyond traditional liberal conceptions of equality and the role of the state. They now argue that, to achieve genuine equality of opportunity, the state should take positive steps to compensate for what they perceive as biologically and socially caused handicaps. Women, in their view, are often the victims of both.

Like other contemporary liberals, liberal feminists increasingly believe that there are certain material preconditions for genuine equality of rights. Not only must there be no discrimination in detěrmining who is eligible to take advantage of various opportunities; individuals must also be able to make use of this eligibility. Poverty is the nːost obvious and common factor which prevents individuals from exercising their rights. For instance, poverty may preclude obtaining adequate childcare to free women for study or work; poverty may prevent an abortion, even when abortion is legally permitted; and poverty may even make it impossible for a woman to leave her abusive husband. Contemporary liberal feminists believe that if the state is really to enforce equality of rights, it must make it economically possible for women to exercise those rights. Consequently, they argue that the state should fund abortions for the poor, fund public childcare facilities,[8] and fund temporary refuges for the victims of domestic abuse. Some liberal feminists have also argued that the state should fund special job-training programs for women. Obviously, all these proposals move far beyond the original liberal feminist commitment to a formal, sex-blind equality for women.

It is obvious that, in pursuit of equality for women, liberal feminists are prepared to make extensive use of the state; yet in certain areas they believe that state intervention is unjustified. Their commitment to freedom of speech and freedom of information, for instance, forces liberal feminists to oppose restrictions on pornography as well as on sex education unless either of these can be shown to contribute directly to the violation of others' rights. (For this reason, liberal feminists are particularly interested in studies investigating the subsequent behavior of those who use pornography.) Similarly, because of their commitment to the right of privacy, liberal feminists advocate the abolition of laws (other than health and safety regulations) that restrict contraception, abortion, or any sexual behavior between "consenting adults in the privacy of their homes."[9] On the same grounds, they advocate legislation that would outlaw discrimination against homosexuals or unmarried mothers. Liberal feminists also believe that liberty or privacy requires the abolition of laws prohibiting prostitution although, in recognition of the possibilities of coercing women, they simultaneously advocate severe penalties for the use of coercion in procuring prostitutes.[10]

The fact that liberal feminists have found it necessary to pursue women's equality through such an extensive use of the law is an admission that rational argument is insufficient, or at least too slow, to eradicate discrimination against women. Of course, the same inefficacy of rational argument also presents a problem for getting feminist legislation passed and enforced. Having found that legislators as well as law enorcement officials are not particularly open to moral argument, liberal feminists have resorted to traditional lobbying techniques and other liberal democratic means of influencing legislation. Occasionally, liberal feminists might believe so strongly in the justice of their cause that they would resort to civil disobedience. The purpose of such disobedience, however, would be to challenge only the justice of selected laws or practices. Liberal feminists could not consistently challenge the legitimacy of a government elected in open elections by universal suffrage.

Contemporary liberal feminists are convinced of the importance of public law in changing private attitudes, but not all their activity is directed at legal reform. Liberal feminists are also much concerned with self-improvement— and with helping other women to improve themselves. "Improvement" · is generally understood to mean increasing one's skills for survival or advancement within contemporary society. Thus, liberal feminists have set up special classes or programs for women in areas such as assertiveness training, auto mechanics, self-defense, preparing a resumé, being interviewed, dealing with the health care system, financial management, buying and selling a house, writing a marriage contract, or coping with a divorce. Although some of these programs are offered at no charge, women are increasingly expected to pay for such courses. In consequence, their organizers have the double gratification of earning money themselves and of feeling that they are promoting the feminist cause—a satisfying coincidence of private and public interest. A related U.S. phenomenon is the emergence of women's networks: sets of social ties between professional women developed with the explicit aim of enabling women to help each other in their careers. A recent advertisement for a network claimed that women professionals should compete with men rather than with each other.[11]

Not all liberal feminist ventures are economically self-supporting. In addition to organizing various kinds of classes, liberal feminists have participated in establishing free services for women in distress. These services often include counseling for women in crisis, such as survivors of rape, domestic abuse or incest, and temporary refuges for battered women. From the liberal feminists' point of view, however, these services should be provided by the state. Consequently, once the services—together with the need for them—are established, liberal feminists seek public funding to maintain them. The start-up staff of such agencies are often volunteers, but wherever possible liberal feminists seek to move toward a paid staff. This is in part because their liberal assumptions about human motivation suggest that paid workers are more likely to be committed to their work; in part it is because of their belief that the tradition of female volunteerism rests on the assumptions of women's economic dependence and self-sacrifice, and they believe that feminists must challenge that tradition.

The liberal feminist vision of how women's service agencies should function reflects the liberal feminist attitude toward society in general. Liberal feminists, as we have seen, support the right of each individual to pursue self-fulfilment as he or she defines it, but they believe that this fulfilment is most likely to be found in the competitive world of public life. When opportunities for women are truly equal, liberal feminists predict, women will be no more eager than men to engage in unpaid work, whether in the home or as a public service volunteer. The obvious question is how that work will be accomplished, and liberal feminists have a ready answer: it will be "professionalized"; i.e., people will be paid to perform hitherto unpaid work. Thus, women will no longer be expected to care at home for elderly, sick or handicapped members of their families. Instead, institutional care will be made available or a caretaker will be hired. Clothes will be washed by laundries, food will be prepared by restaurants, children will be reared in childcare centers, and homes will be cleaned by paid cleaners. Liberal feminists such as Caroline Bird predict that women with salaries will be able and willing to pay for such services:

> More women could afford the housekeeping services that now exist for the very rich alone. More charge-and-deliver grocers would be needed to serve the growing number of housewives who would not mind paying more to save the time they now spend shopping in self-service supermarkets. Cleaning services could contract to keep a house in shape by sending in teams of machine-equipped professionals to tidy for an hour or so every day; maintenance services employing salaried mechanics could keep all household gear operating for a flat annual fee; yard services like those run by teams of Japanese gardeners in Los Angeles could contract to keep lawns mowed and garden beds weeded. Food take-out services and caterers proliferating around the country would increase to serve the growing number of women who like to entertain but don't have time to cook.[12]

Bird argues that such professionalization would have a number of advantages:

> These new services would be cheaper in real economic terms because specialists working at what they enjoy are more efficient than amateurs doing chores they may detest. But the big gain would be a better use of talent. If the born cooks, cleaners, and children's nurses were paid well enough so that they could make careers out of their talents, domestic services would attract women who now enjoy household arts but hesitate to practice them professionally because they don't want to be treated as "servants." . . .

> For hundreds of years now, many tasks have been passing from what the economists call "customary" work, done without pay, to wage work. Canning, clothes-making, and the care of the sick now are jobs, not unpaid chores. The hired hand has replaced the farmer's son, the paid baby-sitter has replaced neighborly child-watching, and young people learn to drive, skate, ski, and swim from paid instructors, rather than older relatives. The shift has always increased efficiency and improved the status of the task.[13]

In these speculations, Bird assumes that the new services would be paid for by women consumers through the market. Where consumers cannot afford certain necessary services, however, contemporary liberal feminists would certainly assume that these services should be provided by the state as part of its responsibility to guarantee a minimum standard of living for its citizens.

Problems with Liberal Feminist Politics

Primarily through the efforts of liberal feminists, the legal status of women in most of the industrialized nations has improved considerably in the last fifteen years. In the United States, many kinds of sex discrimination have been outlawed, new forms of discrimination, such as sexual harassment or denial of maternity leave, have been legally recognized, affirmative action programs are often required by law, the legal right to abortion has been established, although it remains under attack and in some areas the right to express one's sexual preference is legally protected. A few states even outlaw rape within marriage. At least a few women exist in almost every occupational category, and Britain has elected its first woman Prime Minister. While these primarily legislative changes have made possible a transformation in the lives of some women, it is not clear how far they have benefited the average woman who continues to earn little more than half the average male wage. Although women are continuing to enter the paid labor force in large numbers, most women remain in sex-segregated and low-paying occupations; they continue to be primarily responsible for housework and childcare and so are often forced to work "two jobs". Economic access to abortion is restricted in the United States, reported rape is on the increase and the incidence of domestic battery seems to be rising.

The continuing inequality of women does not in itself indicate the failure of liberal feminist politics. Liberal feminists certainly do not regard their program as complete and are focusing increasingly on the economic reforms they see as necessary to allow women to take advantage of their existing legal gains. At the end of this chapter, I shall discuss the question whether genuine equality for women can be achieved through reliance on state instituted reforms. First, however, I want to consider a number of other questions which concern both the internal consistency of liberal feminism and the normative desirability of the liberal feminist vision.

1. SOMATOPHOBIA AND HUMAN FULFILMENT

The word "somatophobia" was coined by E. V. Spelman.[14] It refers to the hostility toward the body that is displayed throughout the western philosophical tradition and which liberalism expresses by identifying the human essence with the "mental" capacity for reason. Liberal feminism retains a number of so-matophobic assumptions and these raise problems for liberal feminist theory and vitiate the liberal feminist vision of the good society.

One aspect of liberal somatophobia is its theoretical disregard for the significance of the body. In Chapter 3 I argued that this disregard for the body encouraged a misleading formulation of the main problems of political theory, as well as making the already difficult question of identifying genuine human needs especially difficult for liberals. The latter difficulty was illustrated earlier in this chapter when I suggested that their disregard for the body deprived liberals of any basis for developing a normative theory of sexuality. In Chapter 3, I also argued that the liberal disregard for the body generated an unduly abstract or formal conception of equality which could be used to justify the refusal to remedy inequalities related to specifically female conditions, such as pregnancy. Of course, this abstract conception of equality can be used against women only because women are already subordinated. In a male-dominated society, political theory is inevitably androcentric and so takes the male as the norm and construes female divergences from the male paradigm as anomalies or handicaps. Somatophobia, therefore, is one, although not the only, source of the inadequacy that feminists find in the liberal conception of equality.

Another aspect of somatophia, as we have seen, is disdain for physical work, and this aspect has always been criticized by Marxists on the grounds that it disvalues the work that is most basically and directly necessary for human survival. On a deeper level, Marxists point out that the distinction between so-called mental and manual labor is socially created, like all distinctions, and that it serves particular social and political interests. Marxists argue that all human labor has both intellectual and physical aspects: on the one hand, human labor is distinguished from animal activity precisely by the fact that it is designed deliberately to fulfil certain conscious purposes; on the other hand, those purposes can be fulfilled only through physical activity, for even the most abstract thought requires physical expression. In all class societies, some kind of division between mental and manual labor has been established, and that division has always served the interest of the ruling class. Under capitalism, the division between so-called mental and manual labor has been vastly extended and is continually being pushed even further to fragment forms of labor whose mental and manual aspects were previously integrated. For instance, factory production separated conception from execution, dividing the "mental" work of designers and managers from the "manual" work of machine operators; in the modern office, the thoughts of one person are transcribed by other people. Harry Braverman provides a detailed explanation of how the separation of mental from manual labor has been intensified and systematized in the 20th century.[15]

Every complex system of production requires a certain division of labor. Marxists do not oppose divisions of labor as such, but they are critical of the way that the capitalist system organizes production by separating mental from manual labor. Through this division, the working class is deprived of knowledge that belonged originally to them and it becomes possible for that knowledge to be used to exploit them. New productive technology is then designed with a view to controlling the work force and extracting the maximum productivity or surplus value from the workers, rather than with a view to making the process of production easier, safer, and more fulfilling.[16] Thus, the separation of mental from manual labor deprives workers of the possibility of controlling the process as well as the product of their labor and condemns them to unfulfilling activity that is also often stressful, dangerous, and exhausting. In contrast with manual workers, mental workers have real privileges. The status of their work is higher, they are usually better paid and the actual process of their work often seems easier, safer and more fulfilling. Because they have literally lost touch with physical reality and the life experience of most people, however, the ideas produced by exclusively mental workers tend increasingly toward abstract conceptions that distort the nature both of physical reality and of human social life. This rather enigmatic claim will be amplified in Chapter 11.

Both radical and socialist feminists sympathize with the spirit of this Marxist critique and agree that the mental/manual distinction has been used to control and exploit workers. What they add to this critique is the claim that the mental/manual distinction has also been used by men as a way of controlling and exploiting women. We have seen already that the western philosophical tradition has associated women with the body and men with the mind. Western society has excluded women from the so-called "life of the mind" and has defined women's traditional work of caring for the body and especially of producing the next generation as non-rational, even animal, and unworthy of scientific study.[17] With the rise of capitalism, however, what counted as science was extended to include the development of productive technology and, in the 19th and 20th centuries, established science was further extended into the domain of women's traditional work. Science was now applied to healing, childrearing, food preparation, emotional counseling and even to giving birth. The resulting "sciences," however, were developed by men, and women were largely excluded from them. Thus, men appropriated the "mental" labor of developing theories about nutrition, medicine, child development, psychotherapy and obstetrics, while women were assigned the "manual" labor of following the male experts' instructions. In this way, the mental/manual distinction was used by some men as a way of gaining control over women's traditional work and reorganizing it in their own interests.[18]

So-called medical science provides many examples of this phenomenon. In the United States, health care is controlled directly by the male medical profession and manipulated indirectly by the male-controlled companies that manufacture medical technology and pharmaceuticals. In consequence, the kind of health care that is considered appropriate in the United States, as well as the organization of its delivery, reflects the interests not only of capitalism but also of male dominance. These interests are promoted by the distinction between mental and manual labor, which is central in justifying both the content and the form of the health care system. In this system, women appear primarily as low-status medical workers, such as nurses, nurses' aides and technicians, or else as patients. Women's low status as medical workers and their correspondingly low pay are rationalized by a separation of mental from manual labor which deprives women of "scientific" knowledge and does not value the considerable practical knowledge that they often develop from close and sensitive contact with patients. Even as patients, women are considered primarily as physical bodies to be medicated by the physician who knows best what is good for them. Many of the medical procedures currently imposed on women are technologically complex and highly profitable but of doubtful safety or even necessity. Since the 1960s, for instance, "the pill" has become the most popular form of birth control; hysterectomy has become one of the most frequently performed surgeries and the number of births occurring through Caesarian-section has more than tripled since 1970. Even with vaginal childbirth, women are invariably forced to labor in a supine, "stranded beetle" position, a position that is difficult and uncomfortable for them but convenient for the physician and for the increasingly complex technological systems that have become routine even in normal births. The use of complicated obstetric technology makes it impossible for women to control the process through which they give birth, sometimes results in injury to infants and increases the likelihood of post-partum depression in their mothers.[19] Yet the use of such complex medical technology is justified by the veneration of science, a category which, as currently interpreted, itself presupposes a separation of mental from manual labor. From this technology, high profits are made and, through it, the men who are considered to be knowledgeable experts gain increasing control over the lives of so-called ignorant women.

These Marxist and feminist reflections on the mental/manual distinction suggest that there are shortcomings in the liberal feminist vision of human fulfilment. Liberal feminists assume that most individuals are likely to discover fulfilment through the exercise of their rational capacities in the public world and consequently these feminists emphasize the importance of equality of opportunity in that world. They do not challenge the contemporary structuring of work by the mental/manual distinction.[20] Instead, they accept conventional definitions and valuations of existing job categories and seek opportunities for women to enter intellectual, "professional" or supervisory occupations. Liberal feminist assumptions rest on a devaluation of women's traditional work and indeed of the labor of most working people. According to these assumptions, producing a book on childrearing earns more respect than producing a happy baby and research on nutrition is seen as a more valuable and fulfilling endeavour than preparing a meal. Karen DeCrow, one-time president of the National Organization for Women, the largest liberal feminist organization in the United

States, puts it this way: "Love and Marriage" is "The Canary's Cage"; "The Outer World Is Where the Fun Is."[21] Non-feminist women are often repelled by these liberal feminist values. Often they find considerable fulfillment in their traditional work, in spite of its oppressive aspects, and they know its importance. They sense, at least intuitively, the deprivation and alienation of a life lived primarily "in the head" and lacking the satisfactions inherent in the development and exercise of bodily strength and skill. Although they would not view themselves as socialists or as radicals, they would probably have some sympathy with the Marxist view that liberal feminism's conception of fulfilment embodies bourgeois values or with the radical and socialist feminist view that this conception embodies the values of male dominance. Of course, the tacit acceptance of conventional or dominant values is an inevitable result of the scepticism about human good that lies at the heart of liberal theory.

Liberal feminism fails to challenge one of the fundamental assumptions of male dominance and capitalism, the assumption that it makes sense to divide mental from manual labor. In fact, all human labor requires the exercise of some so-called intellectual and some so-called physical capacities, even though the work process of course can be organized into tasks that require minimal use of one or the other. What should be questioned, however, is why the work process should be organized around this particular principle of dividing labor. The usual answer to this question relies on some notion of efficiency: oversimply, it is claimed to be "more efficient" for some people to plan the work process and others to execute it. It is also sometimes claimed that people "are happier" performing those tasks, mental or manual, that they are best equipped to perform, the assumption being that people differ innately in their mental and physical capacities.

These conventional answers overlook several aspects of the labor process. First, there is empirical reason to question whether so-called mental workers who are removed from the physical process of production in fact do design the most efficient work processes. Similarly, manual workers who have no control over their work process have little motivation to work responsibly and efficiently. On a deeper level, one can question a concept of efficiency that is defined entirely by producing the maximum quantity of goods at the minimum cost while ignoring such considerations as worker safety and satisfaction. Everyone has both a mind and a body, although use of this language acknowledges a dualism which in fact should be challenged, and everyone should surely derive satisfaction from the productive utilization of both. To organize the labor process in such a way that people are able to develop only their mental or only their physical capacities, and probably only a small part of each of these, is to institute an organization of work that systematically deprives all workers of the possibility of fulfilment.

The distinction between mental and manual work rationalizes not just a division of labor; it rationalizes a division of labor that is hierarchical, a hierarchy justified by the claim that those at the top are those who know best. In a very limited sense, this is true: those at the top do tend to be those who have had the most formal education. Yet the correlation between formal education, on the one hand, and income and status, on the other, cannot be interpreted to mean that those who are at the top have superior mental capacities; because of their class, race and gender, they have only been allowed to acquire more schooling.[22] In fact, the distinction between mental and manual labor diverts attention from distinctions that may be more illuminating in explaining the contemporary structuring of the work process. These are distinctions between the relative degrees of control that different groups or classes of people have over the product and the process of their labor.

The distinction between mental and manual labor is inherently antidemocratic and serves to rationalize and perpetuate, even if unwittingly, oppression and domination. As long as work appears to be organized around a division between mental and manual labor, most people will be relegated to some form of manual work and so will be subject to the apparently superior knowledge of the so-called experts. Even in its own terms, therefore, liberal feminism is incapable of guaranteeing a fulfilling life for all. If one accepts that fulfilment consists primarily in the exercise of the individual human mind, rather than in developing both so-called mental and so-called physical capacities in cooperation with other people, then fulfilment becomes a condition to which relatively few may aspire.

2. JUSTICE AND PREFERENTIAL TREATMENT

One of the most controversial proposals of liberal feminism in the United States has been its advocacy of programs of "affirmative action." "Affirmative action" referred originally to the policy adopted by the U.S. government on the basis of President Johnson's Executive Order 11246. The order required that all colleges, universities and other institutions which did business with the federal government or which received federal grants should not only refrain from direct racial, sexual, or religious discrimination, but should also "take affirmative action to ensure that applicants are employed, and that employees are treated during their employment, without regard to their race, color, religion, sex, or national origin." "Affirmative action" is now used more generally to refer to any institutional policy designed to open up fields dominated by white males to any individuals previously excluded from those fields. Affirmative action includes the advertising of available positions in places where women of all races and male members of racial or ethnic minorities are likely to see them and public reassurances that non-racist and non-sexist criteria will be used in evaluating candidates. In addition, it is sometimes taken to require that specific numbers of minorities or women should be hired within a specific time in order to raise their numbers to a certain proportion of the staff in areas where they are strikingly underrepresented relative to their numbers in the pool of applicants. While the use of rigid quotas is not required or even permitted under U.S. law, there is much fear that informal quotas will be put into effect. Consequently, affirmative action has become extremely controversial in the United States. Its opponents claim that it violates the merit criterion by allowing less qualified candidates to succeed over the better qualified ones; consequently they label it "reverse discrimination"; less tendentiously, affirmative action is also sometimes called "preferential treatment."

Most colleges and universities in the United States receive some form of federal government money and consequently are subject to affirmative action regulations. The requirement to enforce these regulations has occurred in a period when educational institutions face economic difficulties, partly due to declining enrollments after the post-World War II baby boom left college, partly due to economic recession. During the 1970s, a drastic reduction in the academic positions available coincided with increased pressure to hire white women and members of ethnic minorities. As the competition for academic positions has become more severe, debates over the justice of affirmative action have filled the pages of academic, and particularly philosophy, journals.[23]

Within these debates, there has sometimes been uncertainty over exactly what constitutes preferential treatment. Some writers have interpreted "preference" in a relatively weak sense, believing that it obliges an employer to select a white woman (or a minority group member) only when her (or his) qualifications are as good as those of the best male (white) candidate. Other writers interpret "preference" more strongly, believing that it requires an employer to select a woman (or a male minority group member) for a position she (or he) is minimally qualified to fill, even though her (or his) qualifications may not be as good as those of the best male (white) candidate. U.S. law requires preference only in the first and weaker sense; yet strong arguments support the view that, within the liberal framework, justice requires preference in the second and stronger sense. I shall outline these arguments as they apply to women, although most of them also apply to males who belong to minority groups.

One argument in favor of giving strong preference to female job applicants is that this is necessary in order to counteract the bias, both conscious and unconscious, against women. It has been well established that the same piece of writing is rated lower when signed by a woman than when it is signed by a man, and that job recommendations are both written and read with sexist prejudice. Until this sort of bias can be eliminated, liberal feminists claim that it must be balanced by the preferential treatment of women. A second argument points out that the circumstances of women's lives have often deprived them of the opportunity to become as well qualified as men. Apart from the damaging effects of sex-role conditioning on women's self-confidence and motivation, women have often been the victims of discrimination by being refused admission to the training programs that would enable them to acquire the most prestigious qualifications. In addition, conventional family expectations concerning child care, housework and the priority of a husband's career may have limited women's mobility and the time to acquire the best possible job qualifications. The proponents both of this argument and of the previous one claim that women's paper credentials may not reflect accurately their real qualifications and that preferential treatment of women may be necessary to select the candidate who has the most real ability or merit.

The argument for preferential treatment that has received perhaps the most publicity has been the so-called "reparations" argument. This argument has been used more by blacks, but some feminists have also claimed that to hire a woman who is less qualified on paper may be a way of compensating her for past injustice suffered by her and perhaps by all women. Finally, there are those who argue that being a woman is in itself a qualification (although not, of course, a sufficient one) for certain highly paid and prestigious jobs and offices: the presence of a woman in those positions is necessary to encourage the aspirations of young women who otherwise might fail to strive for comparable posts. This "role-model" argument, like the first two arguments that I mentioned, views the so-called preferential treatment of women as being necessary simply to ensure genuine equality of opportunity for women.

Inevitably, these liberal feminist claims have inspired a number of objections. The most obvious one states simply that preferential treatment is an example of the same unfair discrimination that feminists oppose when it is applied to women. The objectors charge further that feminists are inconsistent when they claim that sex is an irrelevant criterion for excluding women from certain positions but then advocate its use for including them. Liberal feminists reply that they advocate preferential treatment only as an interim measure to offset the effects of past discrimination; as soon as these results are eliminated, preferential treatment will be abandoned.

Another common objection to the preferential treatment of women is that, since women are less qualified than some male candidates, they will "lower standards" and reduce efficiency, thereby harming society in general and discrediting women in particular. In reply, liberal feminists may argue that justice is a higher social ideal than efficiency, and that compensatory justice requires preferential treatment. Such a reply, however, is inconsistent with the meritocratic view of justice that is the basis both for the liberal feminist attack on sex discrimination and for most of the liberal feminist arguments in favor of preferential treatment. A more consistent reply for liberal feminism is to deny that the preferential treatment of women produces inefficiency in any but the shortest run. To buttress their denial, liberal feminists draw on arguments purporting to show that paper credentials often fail to reflect women's real ability. They may even argue that qualified women candidates, having overcome discrimination to acquire their qualifications, are likely to be superior to most male candidates who have not undergone such a rigorous process of selection.

One topic that has received considerable attention in the philosophical literature concerns the question of who, if anybody, deserves compensation. Some writers argue that women as a group should not receive preference, since women as a group have not suffered unjust discrimination; only those individual women who can show a clear case of unjust discrimination should receive compensation, and that compensation must be proportional to the injury they have received. Liberal feminists respond to this attack in two ways. On the one hand, they may simply deny that compensation is a reason for preferential treatment, choosing instead to justify it on other grounds. Alternatively, liberal feminists may argue that *all* women who have grown up in male-dominated society have suffered discrimination, but that this has not usually consisted in the blatant denial of a job or an office for which they were the best qualified. Rather, they may argue, the discrimination has been deeper, more subtle and more insidious. Through sex-role conditioning, discrimination has affected not only women's opportunities, but their very motivation and ability to take advantage of their opportunities. Since all women have suffered this sort of discrimination, liberal feminists might argue, all women deserve preferential treatment in compensation.[24]

The main opposition to the preferential treatment of women (and of male minority group members) probably arises from the belief that it is unfair to their white male competitors. Even if women have suffered discrimination in the past, this discrimination was perpetrated by older men who have now achieved positions of power and authority. It is objected that young men did not benefit from this discrimination and that it is unjust to penalize them for it. The liberal feminist response to this argument is to point out that the preferential treatment of women is not designed as a means of retribution and often is not even claimed to be a means of reparation. Consequently, the point that young white men did not perpetrate the original discrimination is irrelevant. Liberal feminists remind their objectors that the main reason for preferential treatment is to guarantee that women will have *opportunities* equal to those of white men, since women are struggling against the effects both of past and present prejudice. If preferential treatment were to operate as planned, it is true that a larger proportion of women than at present would achieve high-paying and prestigious jobs and offices, and that some men who would otherwise have received those positions would be excluded. But, liberal feminists argue, this result is not unjust to the men involved, and men perceive it as unfair only because they expect to benefit from male privilege in the same way their fathers did. If women are to receive fair equality of opportunity, men must lower their traditional expectations of monopolizing the best-paid and most prestigious jobs and offices. Liberal feminists point out that in fact it will be many years before men have to compete with women on a genuinely equal basis. Since subtle forms of discrimination discourage so many women from even entering into competition with men, even those men who suffer currently from the effects of preferential treatment are still sheltered from the full competition of women.

For liberal feminism, the just society is a fair meritocracy. The liberal feminist strategy for achieving that society is to use rational argument coupled with legal coercion to secure equality of opportunity. When opportunities are already unequal, liberal feminists advocate preferential treatment in order to establish what has been called a "counterfactual meritocracy";[25] that is, a society in which jobs and offices are awarded to those people who have the minimum qualifications for them and who would have had the best qualifications if they had not been victims of previous unjust discrimination. The preferential treatment of women is a way of attempting to institute a counterfactual meritocracy; it is a temporary expedient designed as a step on the way to a fair meritocracy. Within the meritocratic framework of liberal political theory, I believe that the preferential treatment of women is required by justice. Yet I also think that serious questions can be raised about the whole meritocratic framework that structures the liberal feminist vision of the good society.

3. EQUALITY OF OPPORTUNITY AND MERITOCRACY

Equality is a fundamental liberal value, and it provides a major inspiration for liberal feminism. Contemporary feminist interpretations of this concept, however, pose a number of problems for liberal theory. It is not clear that contemporary interpretations of equality are compatible either with liberty or indeed with the liberal theory of human nature. In addition, the vision of a society structured according to the liberal feminist conception of equality is open to serious criticism.

Equality is notoriously an ideal that is open to many different interpretations. Contemporary liberal feminists believe that its traditional interpretation as "formal" or legal equality is too weak because they see that it fails to exclude the possibility of many kinds of discrimination against women. They also reject the "strong" interpretation of approximate economic equality since they believe that its instantiation would require massive economic redistribution by the state. Liberals believe that such massive state intervention would infringe on individuals' rights to liberty, especially their liberty to accumulate property; their assumptions about human motivation also entail that such economic redistribution by the state would remove people's incentive to work, thus leading to general impoverishment. The interpretation of equality advocated by contemporary liberal feminists is therefore equality of opportunity, an interpretation designed to respect individuals' rights to liberty while providing maximum incentive to compete.

Although the notion of equal opportunity is an attempt to provide a more precise interpretation of equality, it contains its own ambiguities. To have an opportunity to do or to have something, one must be *able* to do or to have it; there must be nothing preventing one from doing or having it. The thing in question, moreover, must be to some extent a good thing. As one writer remarks, "It is bitter sarcasm to say someone had the opportunity to lose his life pointlessly in the Battle of the Somme."[26] To claim that someone has an opportunity, then, one must have some conception of what is the good thing that the person is able to do or to have and of what would constitute a restriction on that person's ability to do or to have it. As we have seen, liberal feminism has a rather problematic conception of the good things people should be able to pursue. It runs into more problems in identifying the restrictions that diminish and finally eliminate many people's opportunities to pursue those good things.

When liberal feminists talk about opportunities, we have seen that they are concerned ordinarily with opportunities for achievement in a competitive society. They mean opportunities for securing the prestige, power and (usually) wealth that are the rewards of success in industry, commerce, scholarship, the arts, entertainment, politics or sport. Liberal feminists believe women are subject to special restrictions so that their opportunities to succeed in these fields are not equal to those of men. Liberal feminism has continually lengthened the list of women's special restrictions. Liberal feminists have moved rapidly from identifying legal restrictions and irrational prejudice to identifying unequal education, unfair social expectations, childbearing and poverty as limitations on women's opportunities.

In identifying barriers to women's achievement, liberal feminists have become increasingly aware of "internal" as well as "external" barriers. They have seen how the total environment of male supremacy shapes women's perceptions of themselves; molds women's interests, needs and wants; and limits women's ambition, determination and perseverance. Liberal feminists conclude that equality of opportunity requires equality in children's early education and environment. This conclusion accords both with psychological theory and with commonsense, but it is incompatible with one aspect of the "abstract individualist" conception of human nature that is central in liberal theory. This aspect is the assumption I have called liberal scepticism and that Alan Soble calls "the autonomy of empirical desires."[27] On this assumption, there are no rational criteria for identifying what is good for human individuals other than what those individuals say is good for them. Consequently, individuals' expressed desires are taken as identical with their "real" needs, wants and interests. Each individual is viewed as the authority on what is good for him or her, and so expressed desires are accepted as unquestionable data, given prior to political theory.

By presupposing that what women in fact want or need is not always identical with what they say they want or need, liberal feminist practice challenges the autonomy of empirical desires. This challenge does not necessarily imply that individuals are not the authorities, in some ultimate sense, on what is good for them, but it does imply that knowledge of their true interests is not automatic for "normal" individuals; rather, such knowledge is an achievement with complex social preconditions. Individuals' expressed desires may be different from their "real" desires or from what they would have chosen if they had had more knowledge. Once desires are no longer accepted as immediately self-validating, moreover, it becomes necessary to develop criteria for distinguishing genuine choices from those that are coerced or manipulated, real desires from expressed desires. A basic shortcoming of liberal theory is its inability to provide such criteria. The liberal tradition conceives of freedom simply as the absence of external obstacles to individual action and assumes that individuals are autonomous agents so long as they are not blatantly dysfunctional. To provide criteria for genuine choice that are sufficiently sensitive to the ways in which people's beliefs and feelings are determined by their social context, liberalism would have to abandon one of its central doctrines, namely, its pretensions to moral neutrality, and make precisely the kinds of value judgments about human fulfilment that it is committed to avoiding. In this way, the liberal feminist pursuit of equal opportunity raises deep problems for the very theory of human nature that it took as its starting point. Indeed, the political practice of liberal feminism points to the need for an alternative theory of human nature, one which recognizes the social constitution of human needs, interests and qualities of character and which provides a conception of human rationality that goes beyond liberal instrumentalism.

There is another way in which the liberal feminist search for equality of opportunity in practice may contradict the liberal theory of human nature. As we have seen, liberal feminists are committed to the view that members of both sexes have equal moral worth because both sexes have at least a minimal capacity to reason; however, liberal feminists are not committed to the view that members of both sexes have, on average, equal reasoning or other capacities. Consequently, they claim not to know whether or not equality of opportunity would result in the sexes becoming completely integrated in all areas. In order to discover whether opportunities have been equalized in any particular area, however, the criterion that liberal feminists use in fact is the resulting distribution of the sexes: a predominance of men in any area is taken as evidence that opportunities in fact have not been equalized. Thus, while liberal feminist theory professes agnosticism over the results of equalizing opportunities between women and men, liberal feminist practice assumes that those results can be predicted. Liberal feminism can avoid this contradiction only by finding an alternative standard for measuring whether opportunities have been made equal, but it is not easy to formulate an appropriate alternative criterion.

In its pursuit of equal opportunities, liberal feminism challenges not only the liberal conception of human nature; it also challenges the liberal value of individual liberty. We have seen already that, in their attempts to eliminate restrictions on women's equality of opportunity, contemporary liberal feminists place heavy reliance on the action of the state. Several writers have pointed out, however, that, if liberal feminists were to follow their own logic through to the end, the notion of equal opportunity could be used to justify state control of every aspect of life. For example, both Onora O'Neill and D. A. Lloyd Thomas argue that genuine equality of opportunity would require that children be removed from their parents' care and control to be reared in state nurseries. Only in this way, they argue, would it be possible to guarantee to each child the equal "distribution of health care, diet, socialization, consideration and respect, as well as of schooling, which would ensure the same distribution of competences."[28] If these arguments are correct, then equality of opportunity is incompatible with individual liberty, a value which is at least as basic as equality within the liberal tradition.

Some may object that this kind of intensive state intervention in childrearing and education would be unnecessary after the first generation in the liberal utopia, when hereditary privileges and disadvantages would have been abolished. Not so. The meritocracy advocated by liberal feminism does not allocate social goods equally; instead, it distributes the goods to those who most deserve them, however desert is defined. In such a system, those who rise to the top of the social pyramid will accumulate all sorts of advantages from which their children can benefit, even if the inheritance of property is forbidden. When this happens, the opportunities of the second generation are no longer equal. Meritocracy, in fact, is an inherently unstable social arrangement which constantly tends to dissolve itself. It presupposes equality of opportunity, but its effect is constantly to make opportunities unequal. Meritocracy can be maintained only by constant state intervention.

Even with this intervention, it is not obvious that strict equality of opportunity could be achieved. Even if children were reared in state nurseries, differences would occur in the ways in which the attendants treated the children and in the ways the children treated each other. Since it has been established that individuals' interests, motivation and abilities depend to a considerable extent on the social relations they are able to establish with others, even state nurseries could not guarantee complete equality of opportunity. Thomas argues that, when the goal of equal opportunity is carried to its logical conclusion, "the doctrine must end up by not permitting persons to be dependent for their self-development on others at all; in other words, the doctrine is incompatible with the existence of any society at all."[29] This is a *reductio ad absurdum* of the whole concept.

Even if complete equality of opportunity is impossible in principle, a liberal feminist might reply that the ideal still serves a valuable heuristic function. Even though it must be balanced by considerations of individual liberty and social cost, the ideal of equal opportunity continues to point toward the removal of unjust barriers to individual ambition. Yet some critics of liberal feminism question the desirability of equal opportunity and the meritocratic society even as a moral ideal. Gertrude Ezorsky, for example, argues that the moral underpinning for the meritocratic ideal lies in the intuitive notion that, when opportunities have been equalized, the best qualified individual will have tried harder to achieve her or his qualifications than any other individual and will therefore *deserve* the job or the office in question. Suppose, however, that one candidate is better qualified than the rest due to some biologically inherited talent. Ezorsky argues that this individual had no responsibility for the fact that she or he turned out to be the best qualified and therefore does *not* deserve the job or the office in question. She concludes that, since competitive opportunities are inevitably unequal and therefore unjust, feminists should abandon the idea of a meritocracy, counterfactual or otherwise. She suggests instead, that

> we might consider minimizing such unfairness by eliminating the merit competition for jobs, where the good effects of the competition are of no great consequence, and of separating other benefits, like status and salary, from the outcome of such unavoidably unfair competition.[30]

Sandra Harding is another feminist who explicitly attacks the Siamese twin ideals of meritocracy and equal opportunity. Harding argues that these ideals are incompatible with what she calls the democratic ideal. The democratic ideal, in Harding's view, includes the principles that each member of the community has an equal right to construct her own purposes and sense of self and to participate equally in debating all issues affecting the quality of life. Harding argues that these principles cannot be instantiated in a meritocracy. Within a meritocracy, those who occupy positions of power and influence will determine what counts as a meritorious performance. Because they have achieved their own favored position by accepting prevailing standards of merit, they will not tolerate criticism of those standards. Thus a meritocracy will tend inevitably toward conservatism and will tend to stifle democratic consideration of ways for improving the quality of life for all members of the community. By rewarding only certain characteristics, moreover, a meritocracy denies respect to people who lack those characteristics and so denies them an effective right to construct their own purposes and sense of self. In general, meritocracy legitimates a system of unequal rewards which results inevitably in unequal access to political power. In this way, it perpetuates the values of the status quo and limits the possibility of challenge to those values by denying political power to those who do not share them. Harding concludes that:

> Taken as an issue about how the society might best fill its jobs, the equality of opportunity principle probably functions pretty well within "normal" institutional growth, where standards of merit are more or less universally shared and uncontroversial (if there ever was such "normal" institutional growth); but it is a reactionary device at times when the social relations structured by our institutions need deep changes.[31]

There is now a voluminous and growing literature on the topics of equal opportunity and meritocracy, but the issues it raises are too complex for further discussion here. I shall conclude my own brief discussion of equal opportunity by mentioning one final criticism of the meritocratic ideal. This criticism is made by Marxists, but it is shared by many non-Marxists both on the left and on the right. It concerns the quality of human relationships which would result from the instantiation of the liberal feminist ideal, when all work is "professionalized";[32] that is, organized through the competitive market system. In the *Communist Manifesto,* Marx and Engels claim that:

> The bourgeoisie, wherever it has got the upper hand, has put an end to all feudal, patriarchal, idyllic relations. It has pitilessly torn asunder the motley feudal ties that bound man to his 'natural superiors', and has left remaining no other nexus between man and man than naked self-interest, than callous "cash payment". It has drowned the most heavenly ecstasies of religious fervour, of chivalrous enthusiasm, of philistine sentimentalism, in the icy water of egotistical calculation. It has resolved personal worth into exchange value, and in place of the numberless indefeasible chartered freedoms, has set up that single, unconscionable freedom—Free Trade.[33]

Of course, Marx and Engels do not wish to idealize the quality of human relationships under feudalism where religious fervor, chivalrous enthusiasm and philistine sentimentalism invariably cloaked brutality and exploitation. Yet they do want to point out the alienation and dehumanization resulting from the capitalist transformation of almost all human relationships into undisguised economic contracts. In this situation, the basic assumptions of liberal theory come to seem indisputable as individuals become the overt maximizers of their own self-interest, as rationality is reduced to egoism and as the ties of human community are attenuated to ties of convenience. Under capitalism, alternatives to the liberal vision can easily be dismissed as unrealistic or utopian. Repugnance at this social vision is the moral and emotional source of much feminist and Marxist opposition to liberal feminism. It is surely also the source of much contemporary "conservative" opposition to feminism in general, since liberal feminism is often thought to be the only feminism there is.

4. PRIVACY

The concern for privacy is a defining feature of the liberal tradition. A central question for liberal political theory has always been how to define the right to privacy and so set the limits of legitimate state authority. In previous chapters, we have seen how non-liberal feminists have challenged the validity of the liberal conception of the private sphere. Socialist feminists, in particular, have developed a searching critique of the public/private distinction as it appears both in liberal and in Marxist theory. Contemporary liberal feminists offer no such direct challenge to the right to privacy. Indeed, they appeal to that right in order to justify the abolition of restrictions on abortion and on women's sexuality. Within liberal feminist practice, however, there is an implicit challenge to the traditional liberal conception of privacy.

As we saw earlier, the liberal tradition as a whole has been characterized by a continuing tendency toward a diminution of the private sphere. In particular, liberals have justified increasing state intervention in what they define as the economic realm. Liberal feminists have encouraged this tendency by demanding state action to ensure equality of opportunity. Within the liberal tradition, however, the most serious challenge to the notion of private life comes from the liberal feminist interpretation of the slogan that "the personal is political."

Although liberal feminism has focused primarily on discrimination in what it calls public life, it has not ignored the family. Liberal feminists believe it unjust that women are expected to assume primary responsibility for childcare and housework. They are particularly outraged by the fact that differential responsibilities are sometimes written into the marriage law, so that any woman who marries automatically commits herself to being at least a part-time housekeeper. It is predictable that liberal feminists should recommend that the laws be changed so as to provide identical rights and responsibilities for each partner. Some liberal feminists, however, believe that a single form of marriage contract, even if it is written in sex-neutral language, unduly restricts individual choice and constitutes undue state restriction on how individuals may choose to live; therefore they have advocated individualized marriage contracts, which would allow for individual choice about the rights and responsibilities of marriage partners.[34] From one point of view, this would make marriage more of a "private" matter, since it would increase individual freedom of choice. From another point of view, however, it would make marriage much less private. As marriage contracts became more detailed, explicit and enforceable under the law, they would become indistinguishable from business contracts and it would become generally accepted that the details of family life should be regulated by the state.

Liberal theorists of the 17th and 18th centuries often assumed that the authority of husbands over wives was a natural authority or even that the family, including the wife, was a single individual.[35] Once women were acknowledged to be rational human beings, these views were obviously inconsistent with equal rights for individuals, and 19th-century feminism fought for women's legal right to retain and control their own property as well as their maiden names on marriage. Contemporary liberal feminists are now subjecting marriage to further political criticism. Some argue that any woman who now chooses the role of homemaker is entering a situation that is unjust since it provides no legal recognition of the economic value of her domestic services. Just as some liberals have argued historically that individuals should not be able to sell themselves into slavery, so some liberal feminists now claim that women should not be able to enter a traditional marriage contract which resembles servitude for women, since even an agreement by the husband to pay the wife for her services is not legally binding.[36] Some liberal feminists demand, therefore, that the law should recognize the economic value of a housewife's services. This could be done by declaring that the economic contribution of the homemaker should have value equal to that of the spouse who works outside the home, thus providing the wife with a claim on the wages or assets of her husband during a marriage in which he is the sole wage earner. Alternatively, the husband could pay his wife a wage for the domestic work she performs. In any case, liberal feminists argue that housewives should be eligible for full social security benefits. In arguing for such legal changes, one liberal feminist claims that marriage should be "a true partnership, legally and financially, as well as personally."[37] Apart from their proposals regarding the relationship between husband and wife, the liberal feminists' demand that the state should take on the responsibility of providing daycare as well as formal schooling for children may also be seen as a demand to extend the public vis-à-vis the private sphere.

In a decision relating to individuals' rights to view pornography, Warren Burger, chief justice of the U.S. Supreme Court, provided the following definition of the right to privacy guaranteed by the Fourteenth Amendment: "This privacy right encompasses and protects the personal intimacies of the home, the family, marriage, motherhood, procreation, and child rearing."[38] Nevertheless, many liberal feminist proposals represent a clear departure from this traditional liberal conception of the family as the center of private life. By evaluating marriage in terms of such political concepts as equality and justice, liberal feminism strips away the ideological mystification of "love and marriage" and makes explicit that marriage is primarily an economic rather than an affective relationship. We have seen already that several aspects of liberal feminist practice are incompatible with some of the basic assumptions of liberal theory, both its political values and its conception of human nature. The liberal feminist critique of the contemporary family does not imply that liberal feminists want to abandon entirely the traditional liberal conception of privacy. Liberal feminism does allow some areas of privacy to remain, most notably the areas of sexuality.[39] If liberal feminist arguments are accepted, however, the sphere for the private exercise of individual autonomy is much reduced and privacy becomes a less prominent value. As the liberal feminist emphasis on justice comes increasingly to overshadow its respect for so-called private life, one may begin to wonder whether the basic values of liberalism are ultimately consistent with each other.

5. THE STATE

In discussing the problems associated with liberal feminist politics, I have focused so far on the internal consistency of liberal feminism and on the normative desirability of the liberal feminist vision. I have not focused at all on the absence in liberal feminism of any direct challenge to the capitalist system. One reason for this absence is the liberal insistence on separating supposedly normative political philosophy from supposedly empirical economic theory. Liberal feminists take their task to be the extension to women of the liberal political values of liberty, equality, autonomy, self-fulfilment and justice, which they believe can be achieved through limited legal reforms. They do not view the oppression of women as a structural feature of the capitalist economic system, so that women's liberation requires the overthrow of that system. In opposition to this liberal feminist belief, Marxist critics have argued that the operation of the capitalist system itself makes impossible the genuine establishment of liberal political values and allows only their empty forms. Feminist critics have added that capitalism fosters values of individual competition which are incompatible with the feminist values of interdependence and nurturance. These criticisms of capitalism are made in various places throughout this book and will not be gathered together here. Instead, I shall conclude my discussion of liberal feminist politics by considering the liberal feminist reliance on the state to enforce liberty, equality and justice for all so that women may have the opportunity for autonomy and self-fulfilment.

Within liberal political theory, the state is the only permanent, legitimate and socially inclusive form of human association. Of course, liberals recognize that people form other sorts of associations: families, business, churches, clubs, etc., but they see these as differing from the state in ways that are politically significant. Contemporary liberals do not necessarily agree with the traditional liberal belief that the family is a "natural" association; in fact, as we have seen, liberal feminists tend to deny this. However, liberals do see families as relatively small groups, founded only partially on the consent of their members, temporary in duration, and regulated by ties of affection and sentiment rather than rational self-interest. Businesses, churches, clubs, etc., are voluntary associations but they too are temporary in duration and are designed to promote specific interests of limited groups. By contrast, liberals view the state as the only association that is non-exclusive, that is founded on the consent of its members and that is concerned with protecting the basic rights of all. For this reason, liberals see the state as the only association that is justified in using physical coercion, although even that coercion must be used in accordance with carefully specified procedures and for certain very limited purposes.

Given these assumptions, liberal feminists take it for granted that the state is the proper and indeed the only legitimate authority for enforcing justice in general and women's rights in particular. They see the state as the neutral arbiter of conflicting social interests, whose task is to protect individual rights and so to defend against the tyranny of any individual or group. Liberal feminists accept that established democratic procedures, such as universal suffrage, free elections, freedom of assembly and freedom of the press, are sufficient to guarantee that no minority will seize control of the state and use its coercive apparatus of law, police and armed forces to further its own special interests.

Marxists reject the liberal conception of the state. In class society, they believe, the state is primarily an instrument of the ruling class—under capitalism, of the capitalist class. On the Marxist view, the economic power wielded by the capitalist class allows it to manipulate state power in all kinds of ways: to influence legislation through direct and indirect bribery, to influence judicial decisions and, perhaps most important, to control the information purveyed by the mass media. In the mass media issues are defined and information is presented in a way that is favorable to the interests of the capitalist class. The general public is so misled that it fails to see where its true interest lies and so it votes for legislators and political programs that do not represent its own interests. In this way, Marxists believe, the appearance of democracy conceals a reality of subtle manipulation and coercion.

Although this sketch represents the main outlines of the Marxist view of the state, it is something of an oversimplification. For instance, it ignores the fact that the interests of the capitalist class are not entirely unified so that there may be conflicts between various sectors of that class, conflicts that the state has to mediate. My sketch also ignores the Marxist recognition that the working class can exert some control over the state. In favorable circumstances, the working class is able to win some legislation that promotes its own interests; consequently, the state is not an unambiguous instrument of class domination. Nevertheless, Marxists believe that, under capitalism, the state generally reflects the power of capitalist class and operates to reinforce that power and to give it the appearance of legitimacy. Given this view of the state, Marxists have no reason to believe that it can be trusted to protect individual rights. On their view, for instance, the inequalities of the capitalist reward system make any genuine equality of opportunity impossible. Just as the appearance of democracy disguises the reality of coercion, so they believe that the appearance of equal opportunity can only disguise the reality of privilege. Marxists conclude that liberal feminist attempts to achieve equality through legislation are worse than useless because they lend legitimacy to the authority of the state. For Marxists, by contrast, the capitalist state represents the interests of only a minority of the population and so has no legitimacy at all. The state can be trusted to promote women's equality only after the working class has seized state power.

It is easy to construct a feminist critique of the state that is parallel to the Marxist critique. Such a critique would point out that men's economic power gives them control of the state and allows them to use it to perpetuate the subordination of women. The election of a few token women does not alleviate this situation so long as men retain economic power. On this view, the state is an instrument of the patriarchy which cannot be trusted to enforce women's rights, and women owe no allegiance to it. Some feminists have already suggested such a critique in their denial that women can be bound by laws made by dead men.

Zillah Eisenstein argues that the practice of contemporary liberal feminists will force them eventually to develop a feminist theory of the state. This theory must recognize that the state is not a neutral arbiter between conflicting social groups, but rather "the condensation of a balance of forces," a balance in which one of the strongest forces is that of male dominance.[40] Eisenstein argues that this recognition will come about as feminists realize the full implications of their demands, for instance, the demands made at the government-funded Women's Conference held in Houston, Texas, in 1978. These demands included: the elimination of violence against women, support for women's businesses, a solution to child abuse, federally funded nonsexist childcare, a policy of full employment, the protection of homemakers, an end to the sexist portrayal of women in the media, reproductive freedom, a remedy for the double discrimination suffered by minority women, a revision of criminal codes dealing with rape, elimination of discrimination on the basis of sexual preference, the establishment of nonsexist education, and an examination of all welfare reform proposals for their specific impact on women.[41] While none of these demands directly challenges the liberal state, Eisenstein believes that they do presuppose what she calls a sex-class analysis of women's oppression. Eisenstein argues that this class analysis is fundamentally incompatible with the individualist presuppositions of liberal theory. As liberal feminists continue to struggle for state-instituted reforms, they will discover that "the motive of the state, via liberal feminism, is to keep women in their place as secondary wage earners and as mothers."[42] Eisenstein concludes:

> If feminists understand this, then they can begin to understand, as a women's movement, that their feminism cannot be met by the liberal

state, which has no commitment to women's liberation . . . if feminists are to be a part of the struggles with the state on questions of the ERA, abortion rights, welfare payments, and the like, they need to develop a strategy that fully utilizes the subversive content of feminism. As women continue to become more conscious of themselves as an oppressed sexual class, they will be able to develop a political strategy which recognizes this. This is in essence the real difference between liberalism and liberal feminism: feminism is potentially subversive to liberalism and the capitalist patriarchal state.[43]

The French-Canadian feminist Nicole Laurin-Frenette is less optimistic about the probable outcome of liberal feminism's reliance on the state to bring about women's liberation. Eisenstein sees the liberal feminist emphasis on legal reform as being at least potentially revolutionary because she believes that liberal feminists will come to realize that what she calls the "capitalist patriarchal state" is unable to guarantee genuine equality for women; consequently, liberal feminists will come to a more radical understanding of the functions of the state and to a radical critique of the system that sustains it. Laurin-Frenette, by contrast, fears that the liberal feminist reliance on the state will strengthen the state, an institution whose interests are ultimately opposed to those of the majority of women. She fears that reliance on the state will co-opt rather than radicalize the women's movement. She writes:

Thus women have obtained, mainly from the State, recognition of certain rights and the improvement of various conditions. In most cases, these victories of women are also victories of the State; they have, to a certain extent, increased its ability to control women and their movement. Some of the institutions set up by the State in the last few years look very much like permanent mechanisms for the control of women and their organizations, as, for example, the various councils, offices, commissions whose mandate is to study women, to listen to their protests, to formulate solutions to their problems and even, in some cases, to fund feminist projects. These bodies proliferate in societies where the feminist movement has the greatest impact; they also have their counterparts at the regional and international levels. Women are associated with them, especially on a professional footing; certain feminist organizations are represented in them, and sometimes even eminent figures in the movement. In spite of all this, relations between women and the State are not harmonious; nor have they ever been. For the State has not solved, and is not in the process of solving, the contradictions which foster women's revolt and resistance. It has, however, provided an audience for feminism and a channel for its dynamism, while blunting the movement's subversive potential: its power of liberation.[44]

Laurin-Frenette's arguments in this passage tell only against the liberal state, which reinforces and legitimizes the systems of capitalism and male dominance. She does not claim here that state power is inherently oppressive, even in a society that is no longer characterized by exploitation. But Laurin-Frenette is writing in a Canadian anarchist journal, her translator spells "state" with a capital S, and the section in which this quoted passage appears is headed "Feminism and Anarchism"; thus there is reason to believe that Laurin-Frenette shares the anarchist condemnation of all state power. On the anarchist view, the coercive power that is a defining feature of the state is never legitimate.

Anarchists reject theoretical devices, such as consent theory, which are designed to justify the limited use of state power. For anarchism, means are inseparable from ends and the good society cannot be ruled by a power which rests ultimately on force.

As we shall see in Chapter 9, there is a strand of radical feminism whose ideas are very close to those of communist anarchism. Like communist anarchists, many radical feminists believe that the good society must instantiate the values of interdependence, mutual aid and non-coercion, although their language differs somewhat from the language of the traditional anarchists. Moreover, the feminist slogan that the process is the product encapsulates exactly the anarchist view that means are inseparable from ends. The anarchist tendency within radical feminism generates a critique of liberal feminism that is deeper than the critique made by Marxists: it would criticize not just liberal feminism's failure to challenge the liberal state but liberal feminism's failure to challenge all state power.

How far this criticism is justified cannot be explored further in this chapter. Whereas most of my earlier criticisms of liberal feminist politics were "internal" ones, identifying inconsistencies between liberal feminist practice and certain central tenets of liberal theory, the anarchist critique of liberal feminism presupposes an entirely different theory of human nature and correspondingly different political values. Unlike liberal feminism, it asserts the possibility of a community where human relations are not based on individual self-interest kept in check ultimately by the threat of force. Whether or not this vision is utopian will be explored in later chapters.

Notes

1. J. S. Mill, "Utilitarianism," in Jeremy Bentham/J.S. Mill, *The Utilitarians* (New York: Anchor Books, 1973), p. 438.
2. J. Rawls, *A Theory of Justice* (Cambridge: Harvard University Press, 1971), p. 4.
3. Ibid., pp. 204ff.
4. John Stuart Mill, "The Subjection of Women," in J.S. Mill and Harriet Taylor Mill, *Essays on Sex Equality,* ed. by Alice Rossi (Chicago: University of Chicago Press, 1970), p. 179.
5. Betty Friedan, *The Feminine Mystique* (New York: Dell, 1974), pp. 370–71.
6. Mill, "The Subjection of Women", pp. 183–84.
7. The largest (100,000 member) liberal organization dedicated primarily to opposing current attempts to outlaw abortion in the US is NARAL (The National Abortion Rights Action League). As NARAL defines the abortion controversy, "The real issue is not abortion. The issue is the right of individuals and families to live free of government intrusion." The American Civil Liberties Union, following the 1973 Supreme Court decision in the case of *Roe* v. *Wade,* also defends abortion in terms of a woman's right to privacy.
8. The NOW (National Organization for Women) Bill of Rights, adopted at NOW's first national conference, Washington, D.C., 1967, calls for "Child Day Care Centers" as its fifth demand: "We demand: That child-care facilities be established by law on the same basis as parks, libraries, and public schools, adequate to the needs of children from the pre-school years through adolescence, as a community resource to be used by citizens from all income levels."
9. This phrase occurs in the 1963 British *Wolfenden Report: Report of the Committee on Homosexual Offences & Prostitution,* Authorized American ed. (New York: Stein & Day, 1963), and has since become a liberal catch phrase.
10. The report on the NOW Task Force on prostitution supports "full prosecution of any acts of coercion to any person, public agency or group to influence women to

become prostitutes" (NOW Resolution 141, passed at the sixth national conference of the National Organization for Women in Washington, D.C., in February, 1973).

11. A currently popular book is Mary Scott Welch's *Networking: The Great New Way for Women to Get Ahead* (New York: Warner Books, 1981). Cf. also Carol Kleiman, *Women's Networks: The Complete Guide to Getting a Better Job, Advancing Your Career, and Feeling Great as a Woman Through Networking* (New York: Lippincott and Crowell, 1980).

12. Caroline Bird with Sara Welles Briller, *Born Female: The High Cost of Keeping Women Down* (New York: Pocket Books, 1969), pp. 186–87.

13. Ibid., p. 187.

14. Elizabeth V. Spelman, "Woman as Body: Ancient and Contemporary Views," *Feminist Studies* 8, no. 1 (Spring 1982):109–31. Spelman has explored the philosophical foundations and the political implications of "somatophobia" in a number of papers.

15. Harry Braverman, *Labor and Monopoly Capital: The Degradation of Work in the Twentieth Century* (New York: Monthly Review Press, 1974).

16. This is argued by Braverman, ibid. Cf. also Mike Cooley, *Architect or Bee? The Human/Technology Relationship* (London: Langley Technical Services, 1980); Bernard Gendron, *Technology and the Human Condition* (New York: St. Martin's Press, 1977); and Les Levidow and Bob Young, eds., *Science, Technology and the Labour Process: Marxist Studies, Volume 1* (London: CSE Books; Atlantic Highlands, N.J.: Humanities Press, 1981).

17. E. V. Spelman gives an excellent account of the misogyny implicit in the western identification of women with the body in "Woman as Body."

18. A fascinating account of this development is given by Barbara Ehrenreich and Deirdre English in *For Her Own Good: 150 Years of the Experts' Advice to Women* (New York: Anchor Books, 1979).

19. Shelley Day, "Is Obstetric Technology Depressing?", *Radical Science Journal* 12 (1982):17–45.

20. It is true that some liberal feminists are among those currently involved in campaigns demanding equal pay for work of comparable worth. This demand obviously implies a challenge to conventional valuations of various occupational categories (clerical work is the occupational category most frequently declared to require "upgrading"), and it also implies a challenge to the determination of wage scales by the market. Rather than allowing wages to be determined by market forces, it requires that they be determined by the "worth" of the labor performed. The problem with this demand is that it provides little indication how the worth of a job should be measured. Should it be measured by the length of training or degree of skill required for its performance, by the amount of stress or danger it involves or by the social indispensability of its product? Questions can be raised about the interpretation and appropriateness of all these criteria. In practice, feminists who argue for the upgrading of clerical work tend to talk about the skill and responsibility that their work involves. If these criteria were to be accepted as the only standards of a job's worth, and if they were to continue being measured by the length of formal training required by the workers, then the current stratification of occupations by the mental/manual distinction would be reinforced. If both the market and schooling criteria for wage determination were challenged seriously, however, the whole structure of the capitalist economy would be called into question.

21. These catchy phrases are chapter headings from her book, *The Young Woman's Guide to Liberation* (Indianapolis: Bobbs-Merrill, 1971).

22. Samuel Bowles and Herbert Gintis, *Schooling in Capitalist America: Educational Reform and the Contradictions of Economic Life* (New York: Basic Books, 1976), chap. 4; "Education, Inequality and the Meritocracy."

23. The debate has been too extensive to document here. A good bibliography up to 1976 can be found in Barry R. Gross, ed., *Reverse Discrimination* (Buffalo, N.Y.: Prometheus Books, 1977). Another useful collection of papers on this topic is M. Cohen, T. Nagel, and T. Scanlon, eds., *Equality and Preferential Treatment* (Princeton, N.J.: Princeton University Press, 1976).

24. On this topic, see Alan H. Goldman, "Limits to the Justification of Reverse Discrimination," *Social Theory and Practice* 3, no. 3 (Spring 1975):289–306. Cf. also Alison Jaggar, "Relaxing the Limits on Preferential Treatment," *Social Theory and Practice* 4, no. 2 (Spring 1977):227–35, and Goldman's "Reply to Jaggar," pp. 235–37 in the same issue.

25. Hardy Jones, "Fairness, Meritocracy and Reverse Discrimination," *Social Theory and Practice* 4, no. 2 (Spring 1977):211–26.

26. D. A. Lloyd Thomas, "Competitive Equality of Opportunity," *Mind* 86, no. 343 (July 1977):388.

27. Alan Soble, "Paternalism, Liberal Theory and Suicide," *Canadian Journal of Philosophy* 12, no. 2 (June 1982):335–52.

28. Onora O'Neill, "How Do We Know When Opportunities Are Equal?" in Jane English, ed., *Sex Equality* (Englewood Cliffs, N.J.: Prentice Hall, 1977), p. 150. D. A. Lloyd Thomas, "Competitive Equality of Opportunity." p. 400.

29. Lloyd Thomas, "Competitive Equality of Opportunity,"

30. G. Ezorsky, "Reply to Professor Jones," delivered as a comment on Hardy Jones's paper ("Fairness, Meritocracy, and Reverse Discrimination") when he read it to the Western Division of the American Philosophical Association in New Orleans, April 1976. Page 5 of Ezorsky's typescript.

31. Sandra G. Harding, "Is the Equality of Opportunity Principle Democratic?" *The Philosophical Forum* 10, nos. 2–4 (Winter–Summer 1978–79):219.

32. The concept of "professionalism" is often used by liberals to suggest that certain kinds of work have a special dignity because they require high educational qualifications and because professionals are perceived to be autonomous insofar as they set their own standards for the quality of the service they offer and for the "professional ethics" of their occupation. In fact, "professionalization" has usually functioned as a way in which certain occupational groups have sought to insulate themselves from market competition and from public accountability. (For more on this, see my "Philosophy as a Profession," *Metaphilosophy* 6, no. 1 [January 1975]. Reprinted in *Teaching Philosophy Today: Criticism and Response,* edited by Terrell Ward Bynum and Sidney Reisberg [Bowling Green, Ohio: Bowling Green State University, 1977.) Use of the term "professional work" often serves the ideological purpose of disguising the exploitative class structure of certain (often predominantly female) occupations such as teaching and nursing, blunting potential class consciousness by imposing ideals of service and responsibility.

33. Karl Marx and Frederick Engels, *Manifesto of the Communist Party,* in Marx and Engels, *Selected Works* (New York: International Publishers, 1968), pp. 37–38.

34. The National Organization for Women, for instance, proposes legislation to validate marriage contracts other than the present unwritten one. *Do it NOW* 9, no. 3 (1976).

35. Early liberal views on marriage are discussed briefly by Sara Ann Ketchum, "Liberalism and Marriage Law," in Mary Vetterling-Braggin, Frederick A. Elliston, and Jane English, ed, *Feminism and Philosophy* (Totowa, N.J.: Littlefield, Adams & Co., 1977), pp. 264–76. In this connection, Ketchum cites Hobbes, Locke and Rousseau. Cf. also Mary Lyndon Shanley, "Marriage Contract and Social Contract in Seventeenth Century English Political Thought," *Western Political Quarterly* 32 (1979):79–91.

36. "Marriage Contracts for Support and Services," *NYU Law Review* (Dec., 1974): 1166.

37. Ann Crittenden Scott, "The Value of Housework," *Ms.* 1, no. 1 (July 1972), reprinted in Alison M. Jaggar and Paula R. Struhl, *Feminist Frameworks: Alternative Theoretical Accounts of the Relations between Women and Men* (New York: McGraw-Hill, 1978), p. 241.

38. Chief Justice Warren Burger, "Majority Opinion in *Paris Adult Theatre I* v. *Slaton,*" U.S. Supreme Court, 413 U.S. 49 (1973).

39. This reinforces the assumption of many young liberals that morality is coextensive with sexual morality, although they no longer believe that the basic moral injunction is "Don't!"

40. Zillah Eisenstein, *The Radical Future of Liberal Feminism* (New York: Longmans, 1981), p. 226. The direct quotation, used by Eisenstein, is from Nikos Poulantzas, *Classes in Contemporary Capitalism* (London: Verso Editions, 1971), p. 161.

41. This summary of the demands generated by the Houston conference comes from ibid., p. 232. Eisenstein's source is *An Official Report to the President, the Congress, and the People of the United States, March, 1978, The Spirit of Houston* (Washington, D.C.: National Commission on the Observance of International Women's Year, 1978), p. 15.

42. Eisenstein, ibid., p. 248.

43. Ibid.

44. Nicole Laurin-Frenette, "On the Women's Movement, Anarchism, and the State," *Our Generation* 115, no. 2:37.

8
The Politics of Traditional Marxism

The Political Values of Traditional Marxism

A distinguishing feature of the Marxist conception of political theory is that such theory should not focus on the elaboration of ideals to be instantiated in some absolutely good society of the future. According to historical materialism, ideals are not only developed by people in specific material circumstances; they are shaped by people's experience of those circumstances. The ideals that inspire political struggles are directed toward the elimination of specific institutions of domination, institutions that become the focus of political attack only when the material preconditions for abolishing them already exist. There is no reason to suppose that these ideals will be valid for all time nor that they are adequate for the regulation of every society. On the Marxist view, there is no ultimately good society, only a continual struggle to overcome specific obstacles to human fulfillment as these become apparent. Given this view of political theory, it is futile for political philosophers to pretend that they can finally and authoritatively articulate social ideals and principles of universal validity. The most they can do is to provide a systematic formulation and defense of the most progressive ideals that emerge in their time.

This view is both plausible and problematic. As I observed in Chapter 2, any critique of existing society presupposes some vision of a better alternative, no matter how blurred that vision might be. The diagnosis of human alienation presupposes a conception of human fulfillment that has a certain substantive content. If the conception were totally abstract, one would have no way of determining which ideals were more progressive. Although Marx deliberately limits his explicit predictions about "the good society," he characterizes it as communist, and his critique of capitalism inevitably rests on a certain vision of what communism would be like. As his own method would predict, this vision is shaped by Marx's own experience as a Jewish male intellectual in 19th-century Europe. In this chapter, I want to look critically at the politics which spring from that vision and in particular, to consider how far that vision is adequate as an ideal for contemporary feminists.

According to Marx, as we have seen, "All history is nothing but the continuous transformation of human nature."[1] The psychological and even the biological constitution of human beings changes constantly with changes in the mode of production. The one constant in human life is the necessity for praxis, for conscious physical labor that transforms the material world in the course of satisfying human needs and which, in transforming the non-human world, transforms human nature itself.

> The work-process . . . is human action with a view to the production of use-values, appropriation of natural substances to human requirements; it is the necessary condition for effecting exchange of matter between man and Nature; it is the everlasting Nature-imposed condition of human existence, and therefore is independent of every social phase of that existence, or rather, is common to every such phase.[2]

If the human essence consists in anything, therefore, it consists in praxis. Human beings express their humanness through their productive activity or work. Given this conception of human nature, it is obvious that work, as productive activity, must be a central value within the Marxist tradition.

Work is also, of course, a value for capitalism, especially for early capitalism. The rise of capitalism in Europe after the 16th century was accompanied and assisted by the emergence of the so-called Protestant work ethic.[3] The pre-capitalist separation of spiritual and economic life was superseded by a conception of material labor as itself sacred. The sanctity of such labor, however, did not mean that the actual process of work was perceived as valuable. Instead, the work process was viewed as an unpleasant necessity (perhaps imposed by God as a penalty for eating the forbidden fruit in Eden) whose value lay in its results. Under contemporary capitalism, the work process is still not regarded as valuable in itself—except, perhaps, for the few relatively autonomous "mental" workers. Instead, work is seen as the unfortunately necessary condition of survival. People are thought to work only because they want the results that work brings: goods, money and, occasionally, prestige.

The Marxist tradition, by contrast, values work not only for its results. Within the Marxist tradition, the actual process of work is seen as valuable, too. Not only does work enable human beings to change the non-human world in accordance with their needs; it is also the primary means by which human beings develop their own capabilities. Thus it is the basis of human self-development:

> Labor is, in the first place, a process in which both man and Nature participate, and in which man of his own accord starts, regulates, and controls the material re-actions between himself and Nature. He opposes himself to Nature as one of her own forces, setting in motion arms and legs, head and hands, the natural forces of his body, in order to appropriate Nature's productions in a form adapted to his own wants. By thus acting on the external world and changing it, he at the same time changes his own nature. He develops his slumbering powers and compels them to act in obedience to his sway.[4]

The human development that occurs through work is not just mental or intellectual development. Because the physical transformation of nature is required to fulfill human needs, work inevitably has a physical aspect and so requires the development of physical strength, skill and dexterity. The development of human physical capabilities is no less important than the development of mental ones. Humans are necessarily embodied and human praxis thus consists in both physical and mental exertion. Ultimately, indeed, the distinction between mental and physical abilities cannot be maintained; the physical and mental aspects of a skill, for instance, are quite inseparable.

For Marx, work is valuable because it is the condition of the full and free development of human potentiality:

> What is wealth other than . . . the absolute working out of [human] creative potentialities, with no presupposition other than the previous historical development, which makes this totality of development, i.e. the development of all human powers as such the end in itself?[5]

Two sorts of conditions, however, limit the free development of human potential through work. The first is that, within specific material conditions, survival requires a certain kind and amount of work, the kind and amount depending on the prevailing level of development of the forces of production and the correlated level of development of human needs. Marx calls this inescapable work "the realm of physical necessity."

> Just as the savage must wrestle with Nature to satisfy his wants, to maintain and reproduce life, so must the civilised man, and he must do so in all social formations and under all possible modes of production. With his development this realm of physical necessity expands as a result of his wants; but, at the same time, the forces in this field can only consist in socialised man, the associated producers, rationally regulating their interchange with Nature, bringing it under their common control, instead of being ruled by it as by the blind forces of Nature; and achieving this with the least expenditure of energy and under conditions most favourable to, and worthy of, their human nature. But it nonetheless still remains a realm of necessity.[6]

Marx believes that the fullest development of human potential can occur only when human beings have transcended the realm of physical necessity.

> In fact, the realm of freedom actually begins only where labour which is determined by necessity and mundane considerations ceases; thus in the very nature of things it lies beyond the sphere of actual material production. . . . Beyond [the realm of necessity] begins that development of human energy which is an end in itself, the true realm of freedom, which, however, can blossom forth only with this realm of necessity as its basis. The shortening of the working-day is its basic prerequisite.[7]

The full and free development of human potentialities is limited not only by the necessity of survival but also by class domination. A defining feature of class society is exploitation; the members of the dominant class exploit the members of the subordinate class(es) by forcing them to do more work than is required to satisfy the workers' own needs. The dominant class seizes the surplus produced and uses that surplus for its own benefit. Thus, even where the productive forces are developed sufficiently to be the basis of an extensive "realm of freedom," the existence of exploitation prevents that realm from emerging. Under capitalism, the contemporary form of class society, work is organized entirely for the goal of capitalist accumulation. It leaves the worker

> physically exhausted and mentally debased. . . . His work is not voluntary
> but imposed, *forced labour.* . . . Its alien character is shown clearly by
> the fact that as soon as there is no physical or other compulsion it is
> avoided like the plague.[8]

Clearly, the realm of freedom can become accessible to the majority of the population only if class society and the forced labor that defines it are abolished. The free and full development of human potential requires that individuals can freely and consciously choose their own work and their own means of self-development and self-realization. Marx believes that this is possible only under communism.

Not all work, then, is equally valuable for Marxists; indeed, under some conditions work can be positively harmful. The most valuable kind of work is freely undertaken. Humans characteristically achieve self-fulfillment through free productive activity. That such work is freely undertaken, of course, does not imply that it is not strenuous and demanding. In fact, it must be strenuous and demanding in order to develop human potentialities. Freedom, for Marx, is in no way "mere fun, mere amusement. . . . Really free working, e.g., composing, is at the same time precisely the most damned seriousness, the most intense exertion."[9] This exertion, of course, stretches both "physical" and "mental" capacities.

It is interesting to contrast Marx's assumptions about the human propensity to work with those of Malthus, many of whose views about human nature have become part of the liberal tradition. Malthus says:

> The savage would slumber for ever under his tree unless he were roused
> from his torpor by the cravings of hunger or the pinchings of cold, and
> the exertions that he makes to avoid these evils, by procuring food, and
> building himself a covering, are the exercises which form and keep in
> motion his faculties, which otherwise would sink into listless inactivity.[10]

Malthus obviously shares with Marx the belief that work develops human capacities, but he claims that political economy must be guided by a conception of "man as he really is, inert, sluggish, and averse from labour, unless compelled by necessity."[11] Malthus's beliefs about human motivation make him see what Marx would call the realm of necessity as the basic precondition for human self-development: "Necessity has with great truth been called the mother of invention."[12] Malthus's views are in complete contrast with Marx's belief that full human self-development requires the transcendence of the realm of necessity.

Although freedom is a value both for liberals and for Marxists, their contrasting views of human nature generate a striking contrast between the ways in which freedom is understood in each tradition. For the liberal, freedom belongs to (or is withheld from) humans as individuals. It has both an "internal" and an "external" aspect. Its internal aspect consists in autonomy, the mental capacity of the individual to make his or her own moral decisions. This is what is called "free will." The external aspect of freedom is liberty, the freedom from interference by others, typically physical interference. This is political freedom. On the liberal view, individuals are free when their "civil rights" are respected by other individuals and by the government, when they are left alone to carry out their autonomously made decisions. For the liberal, freedom is not expressed in any particular kind of activity or work; indeed, it may be expressed by one's choosing autonomously to do nothing at all. Contemporary liberals, as we have seen, have modified the classical liberal understanding of freedom, because they recognize that coercion may be economic as well as physical, and so demand economic aid from the government to safeguard individual rights. Yet contemporary liberals still retain the central conception of freedom as non-interference, as the absence of constraints on individual choice. If liberals were to talk about a "realm of freedom," they would identify it with the private sphere, with those aspects of life that are not regulated by the state. Thus, within the liberal tradition, freedom is defined in terms of the liberty, autonomy and privacy of the individual citizen.

The Marxist conception of freedom differs from the liberal conception in almost every respect. For one thing, as we have seen, Marx understands freedom in terms of conscious productive activity. This activity is simultaneously "mental" and "physical": Marx rejects completely the possibility of a purely "mental" freedom, such as that contained in the liberal conception 'of autonomy. In addition, Marx believes that the productive activity that characterizes freedom is typically demanding and strenuous; a free individual would not choose to be idle. The most fundamental contrast between the liberal and the Marxist conception of freedom, however, lies in the fact that freedom, for the Marxist, is a social achievement. One could not have freedom in the absence of society, nor while others lacked it. Thus, Marxism utterly rejects the liberal view of freedom as a property of single individuals.

Individual freedom, for the Marxist, has two social preconditions. The first precondition is the extensive development of the forces of production, which will reduce the realm of necessity:

> It is only possible to achieve real liberation in the real world and by employing real means, . . . slavery cannot be abolished without the steam-engine and the mule and spinning-jenny, serfdom cannot be abolished without improved agriculture, . . . in general, people cannot be liberated as long as they are unable to obtain food and drink, housing and clothing in adequate quality and quantity. "Liberation" is an historical and not a mental act, and it is brought about by historical conditions, the development of industry, commerce, agriculture, the conditions of inter-course.[13]

The second precondition of free productive activity is, of course, the abolition of the forced labor that characterizes class society. Actually, this condition is inseparable from the first, since the way in which the forces of production are developed is shaped by political considerations of ruling-class interest. A genuinely liberatory technology which did not enslave the worker to the machine would be possible only in a classless society where the goal of production would be the satisfaction of human need and not the accumulation of a surplus for the ruling class.

For Marxists, the liberal conception of freedom as guaranteed by civil rights is totally inadequate. Not only can the majority of the population never rely on government to defend those rights since, in a class society, government is an instrument of class rule; even more fundamentally, the emphasis on civil rights completely ignores the lack of freedom inherent in "wage slavery." Within capitalist society, most individuals are forced by economic necessity to become "wage slaves" whose productive activity, as we shall see in the next section, is alienated rather than free. Even the few individuals who are able to escape this necessity do not have the opportunity for genuinely free productive activity under capitalism. They may have hobbies or even be self-employed, but these activities permit only the limited development of their creative powers. This is because work is always a social project, as we saw in Chapter 4, conceived in relation to historically specific needs and performed according to historically defined standards. Artistic and craft work constitute perhaps the closest contemporary equivalent to the Marxist conception of free productive activity, but even this kind of production is very different under capitalism from what it would be under communism. As people's lives change, so will their ideas about good art and desirable crafts. New techniques will be developed under communism, and the organization of artistic and skilled craft activity may be entirely transformed. Indeed, the contemporary distinctions between arts, crafts and mass production may entirely disappear, along with the conception of the artist as a uniquely gifted individual. Within class society, one cannot even imagine the kind of productive activity that would result in the full development of one's human potentialities. It is in this sense that individual freedom, for Marx, is a social achievement. It cannot be attained by a few individuals in advance of general social development.

It is now obvious why Marxists reject the liberal attempt to safeguard individual freedom by guaranteeing an extensive private realm beyond the reach of state regulation. Even in class society, Marxists see the economic system rather than the state as the fundamental enemy of freedom. To the extent that a state apparatus survived in a classless society, it would no longer be an instrument of class domination and certainly would not limit the free productive activity of its citizens. For the Marxist, in fact, it is the public rather than the private sphere which is, at least potentially, the realm of human freedom. Of course, this view is not a straightforward reversal of the liberal position, since Marxists make the distinction between public and private in a different way from liberals. It is unclear exactly how Marx and Engels understood the public/private distinction: although they used the distinction, they gave it no exact definition or sustained discussion.[14] They appear, however, to have considered public life to be the realm of politics in the classical sense, the arena within which people engage in collective action to shape the course of history. In this arena, people are not bound to each other by ties of personal affection, but by the reciprocal consciousness of each other as members of a common community. As we have seen already, Marx and Engels included economics, ordinarily understood, within the public realm of politics. On their view, it is this realm that provides the opportunity for people to work together in pursuit of common interests, to transform the world and themselves through their productive activity, to take conscious control over "the forces of nature," including "humanity's own nature."[15] For this reason, it is the public realm that is the realm of freedom.

The fact that the public realm is the realm of freedom does not mean, of course, that people's choices within that realm are infinite: "Men make their own history but they do not make it just as they please; they do not make it under circumstances chosen by themselves, but under circumstances directly encountered, given and transmitted from the past."[16] How much freedom exists in the public realm at any given time depends on the prevailing material conditions that determine the possibilities of human development. Under capitalism, the public realm is extremely repressive and offers little possibility of free productive activity. Nevertheless, Marxists believe that the level of development of the forces of production under capitalism, the "socialization" of the work process through the division of labor, the polarization of classes and the development of class consciousness are all necessary preconditions for the kind of revolutionary social change that will permit a new flowering of human potential. Engels writes:

> The possibility of securing for every member of society, by means of socialised production, an existence not only fully sufficient materially, and becoming day by day more full, but an existence guaranteeing to all the free development and exercise of their physical and mental faculties— this possibility is now for the first time here, but *it is here.*[17]

In the meantime, people achieve the maximum freedom possible under capitalism by pushing against the limitations on human development that capitalism imposes. This struggle necessarily takes the form of conscious political and economic action in the public sphere. For this reason, and contrary both to appearances and to bourgeois ideology,[18] the public realm remains the realm of human freedom even under capitalism. The private realm, by contrast, is the realm of emotion, biology, and narrow family interest. Although Marx and Engels include economics, ordinarily defined, within the realm of politics, they believe that, under capitalism, household labor, child-bearing, child-rearing and sexuality fall outside that realm. Given their conception of the public and the private realms, it is easy to see why privacy is not a value within the Marxist tradition. Instead of being seen as the ground of freedom, privacy is viewed as opposed to true individual freedom.

The inherent worth of free productive activity is the basic value informing Marxist political theory. Liberalism, too, values freedom and work, but its conception of these is totally different from that of Marxism. Two other central values of liberalism, the values of justice and equality, seem hardly to have a place within the Marxist framework. The Marxist critique of capitalism, for instance, stresses its specific harmful effects on human beings, rather than its injustice. Similarly, Marxists often seem more critical of the hypocrisy involved in capitalist boasts of equal rights than they do of the actual inequalities created by capitalism.

Marx avoids explicit appeals to justice because he views it as a moralistic notion that has emerged from societies whose members are preoccupied by private accumulation. He thinks of justice as an ideological term which legitimates certain ways of distributing social goods by suggesting that a particular pattern of distribution is in accord with some universal or transhistorical ideal. The existence of such ideals is incompatible, of course, with Marx's historical materialism; as we saw in Chapter 4, the materialist approach interprets moral ideals or standards as integral parts of the particular socio-economic systems from which they emerge, rather than as transcendent standards against which such systems can be measured. Different societies have held different conceptions of justice, but no conception transcends all of them.[19] To criticize bourgeois society as unjust, therefore, is to invite abstract speculation, confusion and disagreement. It is far more effective to point to specific problems inherent in the capitalist system: its instability, its wasteful use of productive resources, the damage it does to workers and their families. For this reason, Marx writes to Engels that, when he read a certain criticism of the first volume of *Capital,* "I . . . cried with laughter . . . , bona fide tears of mirth . . . And so now even political economy is to be dissolved in drivel about conceptions of justice."[20]

This long-accepted interpretation of Marx's views on justice has been challenged recently in fresh philosophical debate over the question whether socialists need a theory of justice, whether Marx himself had at least a rudimentary theory of justice (perhaps that summed up in the well-known slogan from his *Critique of the Gotha Programme:* "From each according to his ability, to each according to his needs!"), and whether it is possible to develop a theory of justice that does not rest on liberal presuppositions.[21] On the one hand justice, at least as it is interpreted within the liberal tradition, seems to rest on a liberal conception of humans as individuals whose primary concern is for their separate and competing interests, particularly their interest in the accumulation of wealth; on the other hand, individuals in post-capitalist society will certainly retain a conception of themselves as having interests that are not identical with those of others and will have a concern for those interests. During the socialist period of transition between capitalism and communism, it will be necessary to develop principles that are perceived as fair for the distribution of social goods and social positions. Debate over these principles may well be formulated in terms of justice. Gradually, however, the preoccupation with distribution may be replaced by a concern for the more fundamental question of what Iris Young calls "the justice of the social processes and institutional relations that bring these positions and goods into being."[22] The resulting "theory of justice" would not give new answers to old questions, but would reformulate the questions. The current debate over "socialist justice" is too complex to be continued here. At any rate it is clear that Marx is relatively uninterested in the questions of just distribution that preoccupy liberal theorists and that, unless the concept of justice were radically reinterpreted, he would not agree with Rawls that "Justice is the first virtue of social institutions, as truth is of systems of thought."[23] The ideal of justice is not the guiding principle of Marxist politics.

It is often thought that equality is an important value for Marxism. Those who oppose Marxism often accuse it of "trying to make everybody the same" or of "bringing everybody down to the same level." Apart from its obviously propagandistic value, this accusation may arise because Marxists often mock liberal interpretations of equality. Whether equality is understood as equal political rights or as equality of opportunity, Marxists believe that it is a sham under capitalism because capitalism is a system that perpetuates, by definition, not only inequality of wealth but also inequality of power. The solution to this situation, however, does not consist in an equal distribution of material goods to each individual. Although anti-communists fear this solution, in fact Marx attacks it explicitly in one of his early works. Rather than transcending the values of capitalism, Marx thinks that the proposal of equal distribution springs directly out of them. In this proposal,

> The domination of material property looms so large that it aims to destroy everything which is incapable of being possessed by everyone as private property. It wishes to eliminate talent, etc. by *force*. Immediate physical possession seems to it the unique goal of life and existence. The role of *worker* is not abolished, but is extended to all men. The relation of private property remains the relation of the community to the world of things . . .
> This communism, which negates the *personality* of man in every sphere, is only the logical expression of private property, which is this negation. Universal *envy* setting itself up as a power is only a camouflaged form of cupidity which re-establishes itself and satisfies itself in a different way. The thoughts of every individual private property are *at least* directed against any *wealthier* private property, in the form of envy and the desire to reduce everything to a common level; so that this envy and levelling in fact constitute the essence of competition.[24]

By contrast, communism as it is understood by Marx consists in genuine collective ownership of the means of production and in corresponding collective decisions about what is produced and how it is produced.

> *Communism* is the *positive* abolition of *private property,* of *human self-alienation,* and thus the real *appropriation* of *human* nature through and for man. It is, therefore, the return of man himself as a *social,* i.e. really human, being, a complete and conscious return which assimilates all the wealth of previous development.[25]

Under communism, people would be equal in the sense that the fundamental structure of society would not allow some individuals to control the conditions of others' lives, and in that all would participate in making important social decisions. In this situation, however, individual talent would not be suppressed; rather, communism would be the precondition for the full flowering of human individuality. From this discussion, it is obvious that the Marxist conception of equality, like the Marxist conceptions of freedom and of justice, is entirely different from the liberal conception. Whereas liberals view equality as a relation between individuals, Engels writes: "the real content of the proletarian demand for equality is the demand for the *abolition of classes.* Any demand for equality which goes beyond that of necessity passes into absurdity."[26]

The Traditional Marxist Analysis of Women's Oppression

For Marxists, the defining feature of contemporary western society is that it is capitalist. Marxists believe that within capitalist society women are subject to a special form of oppression which affects primarily those women who are excluded from wage labor. The absence of discussion about the special position of women within wage labor suggests that traditional Marxists assume that women wage laborers suffer the same sort of oppression that is experienced by the rest of the working class. In other words, women wage laborers are exploited; presumably they are also, as Marx says in his early work, alienated as wage laborers. Within capitalist society, therefore, Marxists believe that women are subject to two distinct, though related, kinds of oppression. In this section, I shall outline the Marxist conception of women's two forms of oppression under capitalism and the relation between them. I shall begin with women's oppression in the paid labor force.

The distinguishing feature of capitalist society is the sharp division between the capitalist class, which owns the means of production, and the working class or the proletariat, which the capitalists pay to operate those means of production. The relation that holds between the capitalist and the working classes is a relation of exploitation. As we saw in earlier chapters, exploitation is forced, unpaid, surplus labour, the product of which is not controlled by the producers. Exploitation has existed in all class societies, but capitalism is the first form in which the existence of exploitation is hidden rather than obvious. This is because, under capitalism, the working class is not generally forced to work by physical or legal sanctions (although this may happen during a strike). Instead, the employer and the employee seem to "contract as free agents, and the agreement they come to is but the form in which they give legal expression to their common will."[27] Beneath the appearance of freedom, however, lies the reality that, because the capitalist class owns the means of production, the working class must work for the capitalists or starve. Its ownership of the means of production gives the capitalist class ultimate control over production, allowing it to determine what goods are produced and the process by which they are produced. Its criteria for making these decisions, the appropriately-called "bottom line," is profitability and the further accumulation of capital. Ironically, the more the working class produces, the more the capitalist class is enriched. The result of the working class's own productive activity is a constant increase in the power of its class enemy.

Like all modes of production, capitalism is distinguished by certain characteristic relations that prevail between human beings and the non-human world, between different societies, between classes within the society and between human individuals. Under capitalism, remnants of earlier modes of production remain, and so not all these relations are typically capitalist; however, capitalist relations predominate. In his earlier writings, Marx described capitalist relations as "alienated." In his later writings, the name "alienation" is rarely used, but there is no reason to suppose that Marx altered his perception of the structure and quality of those relations. The central feature of alienated relationships is that things or people that in fact are interdependent or dialectically related to each other come to seem alien, separate from or opposed to each other. In one of his early works, now called *The Economic and Philosophical Manuscripts of 1844,* Marx explains the alienated character of certain key relationships within which wage workers are enmeshed. Wage workers are alienated from their product because what they produce is taken from them by the capitalists and used to enslave them further: "The life which he has given to the object sets itself against him as an alien and hostile force."[28] In addition, wage workers are alienated from their actual work activity because they are forced to undertake that activity in conditions over which they have little control.

> the work is *external* to the worker, . . . it is not part of his nature; . . . consequently, he does not fulfil himself in his work but denies himself, has a feeling of misery rather than well-being, does not develop freely his mental and physical energies but is physically exhausted and mentally debased.[29]

The structure of work under capitalism also alienates wage workers from what Marx calls their "species-life." In other words, capitalism prevents workers from engaging in the free productive activity that is the mark of their humanity, the activity of transforming nature not just in order to fulfil direct physical needs, as animals do, but for the sake of the full development of human potentialities. Wage workers do not work for enjoyment; they work in order to survive. One aspect of this feature of alienation is that workers are alienated from non-human nature, viewing it as an external object that must be subjugated for the sake of physical survival rather than as the ground of human freedom and "the inorganic body of man."[30] "For labour, *life activity, productive life,* now appear to man only as *means* for the satisfaction of a need, the need to maintain his physical existence. . . . Life itself appears only as a means of life."[31]

Marx emphasizes one final aspect of alienation, the fact that under conditions of wage labor, workers are alienated from other human beings. The structure of the capitalist mode of production makes other people seem to workers to be simply competitors for scarce resources, either competitors for their jobs or employers who are attempting to exhaust their life energies. There are other aspects of alienation under capitalism; for instance, capitalists are alienated from their "species being" too and relations between societies may also be alienated. However, Marx focusses particularly on the aspects of alienation that I have just described.

When women enter the paid labor force, Marxists seem to view them as alienated in exactly the same way as male wage laborers. At any rate, they say nothing to indicate the contrary. I have already begun to argue that the traditional Marxist conception of alienation is sex-biased, but on the surface alienation does not seem to be a sex-specific condition. Marxists do believe, however, that women suffer from a sex-specific form of oppression that is additional to the alienation of the wage laborer. In contemporary society Marxists believe that this form of oppression is rooted in the specific sexual division of labor that characterizes capitalism; this division excludes many women from the wage labor force and assigns them to work in the home.

Under capitalism, women's work in the home is very peculiar. What is peculiar about it is not the content of the work: from a certain perspective, there is nothing strange about the fact that under capitalism, women bear and rear children, prepare and occasionally produce food and clothing, and provide sexual services for their husbands. In most societies throughout human history women have performed these tasks, although naturally they have done them in different ways in different historical circumstances. What is peculiar about women's domestic work under capitalism, however, is that it involves women in relations that are not characteristically capitalist relations. When women grow vegetables or sew for their families, they are not producing commodities for the market. Nor are women producing commodities when they bear and raise children: although labor power is a commodity under capitalism, it is not mothers or even fathers who sell their children's labor power—not, at least, where child labor is abolished. Nor can women be said to be employed by their husbands, much less by their children. Wives and mothers under capitalism are not paid for the services they perform in the home; indeed, contracts for husbands to pay their wives for domestic services have been found invalid by the courts.[32] If housewives do not like the conditions of their work, they are hardly free to move to another household; instead, they are tied by an elaborate legal contract which can only be broken on special grounds. Marriage is, in fact, a relation that is remarkably similar to the feudal relation of vassalage: it provides a means for exchanging support and protection from the husband in return for services and devotion from the wife.[33]

Some Marxists have debated the question whether domestic work under capitalism is productive or unproductive, but a number of writers have pointed out that, in the required technical sense, domestic work is neither.[34] To understand this seemingly odd conclusion, it is necessary to realize that Marx and Engels use the term "productive" in different senses in different contexts. Sometimes they use "productive" in a broad transhistorical sense to refer to any kind of labor directed toward the satisfaction of human need. Within the context of the capitalist mode of production, however, Marx and Engels also use "productive" in a narrower sense to refer to labor that produces surplus value or profit. In a capitalist society, the labor of women who work outside the market may be productive in the broader sense because it produces use value for consumption in the home. It is not productive in the narrower capitalist sense, however, because housewives are not paid a wage to produce commodities for sale on the market and so no profit is derived from their labor. The contemporary organization of domestic work is a remnant of an earlier mode of production and of these Marx writes:

> Within capitalist production there are always certain parts of the productive
> process that are carried out in a way typical of *earlier modes of production,*
> in which the relations of *capital and wage* labour did not yet exist, and
> where in consequence the capitalist concept of *productive* and unproductive
> labour are quite inapplicable.[35]

Since housewives are not engaged in capitalist production, their relations with
other members of their families, with other housewives, with nature and with
themselves are not the relations that are characteristic of capitalism. Since
alienation characterizes the special quality and structure of relations under
capitalism, housewives cannot be described as alienated.

That housewives are not alienated under capitalism does not imply that
they are not oppressed. Paradoxically, for Marxists, the housewife's freedom
from one kind of oppression is the condition for her subjection to the other:
it is precisely the housewife's freedom from the alienation of wage labor that
subjects her to the oppression of her husband. Women's oppression by their
husbands is not to be understood in terms of the quality of the relationship
established by individual married couples. Some of these relationships may be
extremely tyrannical; others may be distinguished by affection and respect. The
oppression of housewives is to be understood rather in structural terms: it is
a function of the economic dependence of the wife on the husband. The
economic structure of the marriage relation means that housewives depend on
their husbands for survival and, consequently, are materially subordinate to
them. Any respect shown by the husband comes from his individual good will;
it is not grounded in material equality between the marriage partners. Reform
of the marriage law, so that it prescribes equal rights and responsibilities for
each partner, in itself will do nothing to alleviate this material inequality. Engels
writes:

> In the great majority of cases today, at least in the possessing classes,
> the husband is obliged to earn a living and support his family, and that
> in itself gives him a position of supremacy without any need for special
> legal titles and privileges. Within the family, he is the bourgeois and the
> wife represents the proletariat.[36]

This last sentence of Engels should not be taken too literally. In the sentence
immediately previous to the passage quoted here, he has characterized the
housewife's position as domestic slavery. In *The Communist Manifesto,* Marx
and Engels compare the wife to a "means of production."[37] Engels is less
concerned to provide a precise characterization of the husband/wife relation
than he is to show that it is a relation of dominance and subordination—a
domination based on the economic rather than on the physical or legal power
of the husband.

Engels points out that the dominance of the husband, grounded in his
economically privileged position, is expressed in many ways, both inside and
outside marriage. One of the major ways this dominance is expressed is in the
constraints it imposes on women's sexuality. Because women need a husband
for the economic support of themselves and their children, they are afraid to
engage in sexual activity outside marriage in case they become pregnant. "The
anxiety about the 'consequences' . . . today is the most essential social—moral
as well as economic—factor that prevents a girl from giving herself completely
to the man she loves."[38] Indeed, the need to find husbands who can support
them forces many women to marry for economic security rather than for love.

Occasionally men, too, marry for economic security, but their access to other means of support makes them less likely to marry for money. Thus Engels writes:

> In both cases this marriage of convenience turns often enough into the crassest prostitution—sometimes of both partners, but far more commonly of the woman, who only differs from the ordinary courtesan in that she does not let out her body on piecework as a wage worker, but sells it once and for all into slavery.[39]

Once married, the dominance of the husband is expressed in a continuing sexual double standard. "What for the woman is a crime entailing grave legal and social consequences is considered honorable in a man or, at the worse, a slight moral blemish which he cheerfully bears."[40] Female adultery certainly occurs, but it is far more risky and subject to far greater social sanctions than adultery by men. "Economic considerations . . . make women put up with the habitual infidelity of their husbands—concern for their own means of existence and still more for their children's future."[41]

Finally, in addition to the constraints it imposes on women's sexuality, Engels hints that the economic dominance of the husband may be the basis of what is now called "wife battery" or "wife abuse." Engels does not name this directly, but he mentions, as if it were a matter of common knowledge, "the brutality towards women that has spread since the introduction of monogamy."[42]

The analysis given by Engels now seems dated in some ways. The ideology of romantic love has now become so pervasive that most women in contemporary capitalism probably believe that they marry for love rather than for economic support. Once the marriage begins to sour, however, many women are quite clear that it is the need for economic support for themselves and their children that keeps them from leaving. Most feminists would still agree with Engels that, underlying the ideology of romantic love and in spite of women's entry into wage labor, women's low pay means that most marriages still approximate the almost feudal model in which services are exchanged for support. And contemporary feminists would certainly agree with Engels that this type of marriage is a relation that systematically subordinates women to men, they would agree that this subordination is expressed in the ways that Engels describes, and they would agree that women's subordination results from the sexual division of labor that assigns husbands the role of economic provider. In addition, liberal feminists would claim that housewives are oppressed because they are assigned work that is menial, that does not exercise their rationality and that consigns them to tending mere bodily needs. It is at this point that Marxist critics of women's domestic labor part company with liberal feminists. On the Marxist view of human nature, persons are necessarily embodied in human form and so the work involved in satisfying human bodily needs is not considered to be menial. Instead, it is a form of praxis, the activity through which human beings create their world and themselves. It is true that Lenin characterized housework as "barbarously unproductive, petty, nerve-racking, stultifying and crushing drudgery."[43] To be consistent with Marxist theory, however, Lenin should not mean that there is anything intrinsically degrading about childbearing and childrearing, cooking, etc. Instead, he must be understood as criticizing the way in which these tasks are organized under capitalism.

On the traditional Marxist view, the organization of work under capitalism subjects housewives to a form of oppression that is even deeper than the direct oppression that they may suffer from their husbands. No matter how gentle and respectful their husbands may happen to be, housewives are oppressed by their exclusion from public life. In pre-class societies, women also did childcare, cooking, etc., but the organization of their work was not "privatized"; that is to say, their work did not consist in services performed for a single individual. Instead, women's work was done cooperatively by all the women and its products, including children, were shared by the whole group. We have seen already, in Chapters 4 and 6, that Engels does not believe that household work was oppressive when it was organized in this way. In those circumstances, he believes, household work had a "public character." With monogamy, however, he claims that "Household management . . . no longer concerned society. It became a private service; the wife became the head servant, excluded from all participation in social production."[44]

In this situation, women suffer not only the direct humiliations of servitude; they also suffer because they are excluded from participation in the public realm. Engels writes:

> Among peoples where the women have to work far harder than we think suitable, there is often much more real respect for women than among our Europeans. The lady of civilization, surrounded by false homage and estranged from all real work, has an infinitely lower social position than the hard-working woman of barbarism, who was regarded among her people as a real lady (lady, *frowa, Frau*—mistress) and who was also a lady in character.[45]

The relative isolation of such European "ladies" allows them no opportunity to participate in and to develop a conception of themselves as members of a community that is any wider than that of the capitalist family. Wage labor may be more repetitive and constraining than "leisure" or even than housework, but it offers wage workers the possibility of collective action to reshape their own destiny by overthrowing the capitalist mode of production. Under capitalism, Marxists believe, housework offers no such opportunity. The home is not even potentially the realm of freedom.

Since the Marxist view is that women's special form of oppression is grounded in their exclusion from the public realm, the Marxist analysis of women's oppression does not apply primarily to women wage workers. In Engels' time, women wage workers belonged mostly to the (male-defined) working class, and we have noted already Engels' view that the subordination of women is not inherent in the structure of the relation between working class women and men. On Engels' view,

> Now that large-scale industry has taken the wife out of the home onto the labor market and into the factory, and made her often the breadwinner of the family, no basis for any kind of male supremacy is left in the proletarian household, except, perhaps, for something of the brutality toward women that has spread since the introduction of monogamy.[46]

Women wage earners may be alienated, but they have achieved the material basis of equality with men. They have entered the public realm and are now in a position to recognize themselves as members of a wider community, as full social beings, and to participate self-consciously in transforming their physical and social world.

Writing in the 19th century, Marx and Engels believed that the special oppression of women was being undermined by women's entry into wage labor.

A hundred years later, it is clear that women's oppression continues to structure every aspect of social life. (Whether or how far the situation of women has improved over the intervening century is, of course, a problematic philosophical question; to answer it may require separate consideration of the position of women from different class, racial or ethnic backgrounds and it certainly requires careful specification of the criteria for "liberation.") One explanation for the persistence of male dominance may be that a proportional decrease in the numbers of women in the paid labor force occurred in the first part of the 20th century. Since the middle of the century, however, women have been rapidly reentering the paid labor force and now, as we have seen, they represent almost half of that labor force in the United States. In spite of this increase in the proportion of women wage workers, there seems to be no weakening in the sexual objectification of women, a fact which is obvious from the continuation of prostitution, from the emerging evidence of the sexual harassment of working women and from the most cursory acquaintance with the mass media. The segregation of women into low-paying, "feminine," service occupations is increasing, and women are still frequent victims of rape and domestic battery. These continuing aspects of women's oppression present a problem for traditional Marxist theory. The incorporation of women into the wage labor force does not seem to have undermined the sex-specific form of their oppression. Nor do alienation and the sex-specific form of women's oppression seem to be inversely related to each other, as traditional Marxism assumed. Women wage workers do not seem to be oppressed in the same way as male wage workers. On the contrary, the sex-specific form of women's oppression persists and is reinforced in the so-called public as well as in the private sphere, in the market as well as in the home.

Traditional Marxists cannot deny the persistence of these aspects of women's oppression in contemporary society and, needless to say, they do not endorse them. The question is, can Marxism provide an adequate theoretical account of these continuing aspects of women's sex-specific oppression? In other words, does Marxist theory provide illumination concerning the oppressive character of these social practices and does it explain their perpetuation?

The Marxist treatment of prostitution at first sight may seem to promise some illumination. Although male prostitutes do exist, prostitution has often been taken as the paradigm form of women's oppression, and Marx's treatment of prostitution could provide the model for a theoretical understanding of women's sex-specific oppression. Moreover, Marx and Engels state explicitly that prostitution is a form of alienation, and this claim promises to link the Marxist treatment of women's sex-specific oppression with Marxism's main theoretical system, incorporating domination both by class and by gender in the same explanatory framework. In an early work, indeed, Marx claims that prostitution is indistinguishable from wage labor:

> Prostitution is only a *specific* expression of the *universal* prostitution of the worker, and since prostitution is a relationship which includes both the one who is prostituted and the one who prostitutes (and the latter is much more base), so the capitalist, etc. comes within this category.[47]

Rather than being immediately illuminating, however, Marx's assimilation of prostitution to wage labor is puzzling because prostitution is not ordinarily structured in a way that is typical of wage labor under capitalism. The pimp may exploit the prostitute, but his power over her does not come from his ownership of certain means of production to which she has no access. Other than the physical body of the woman, prostitution requires no elaborate means of production which can be owned by another, and the work is not "socialized" through an elaborate division of labor. Alienation is supposed to characterize relationships that are typically capitalist, but prostitution seems closer to slavery. Either Marx is speaking metaphorically and moralistically in the passage quoted, seeking to discredit wage labor by its similarity to prostitution; or else he believes that the structure of the economic relationships within which prostitution occurs is irrelevant to the qualitative experience of the prostitute. Obviously Marx sees the prostitute as forced to work by economic necessity, and perhaps he is to be interpreted as saying that it is economically forced labor that is the basis of alienation.

In my view, the former interpretation is correct. This interpretation is suggested by the fact that the passage quoted occurs in one of Marx's early works, when he was more prone to making explicit moral judgments and before he had developed the systematic economic theory that provided, he thought, purely scientific reasons for the rejection of capitalism. The view that Marx is speaking metaphorically in this passage is also reinforced by the fact that he and Engels frequently describe bourgeois marriage as a form of prostitution.[48] Yet it seems quite contrary to the main theoretical drift of Marxism to view the housewife as literally alienated from her husband. In addition to describing the relation between the housewife and her husband as a form of prostitution, we have seen earlier that Marx and Engels also liken it to the relation between the slave owner and the slave, between the bourgeoisie and the proletariat and between the capitalist and his machines.[49] My conclusion from these varied and inconsistent characterizations of bourgeois marriage is that Marx and Engels were not concerned to provide a careful analysis of the husband/wife relation. Their main purpose was to undermine the bourgeois ideology of love and marriage as a voluntary partnership between free and equal individuals and to show that bourgeois marriage is in reality a relation of economic domination. Marx seems to have had a similar purpose in his few remarks about prostitution.

Traditional Marxism in fact devotes little sustained attention to the theoretical analysis of marriage or prostitution, and it spends even less time discussing rape, physical violence against women, sexual harassment, the sexual objectification of women and the sexual segregation of the paid labor force. Marxism offers no theoretical framework for understanding the oppressive nature of these relationships. In explaining why they are oppressive, we are forced to resort to the sort of conventional moral judgments that presuppose a liberal rather than a Marxist framework, judgments such as those condemning coercion, treating other people as means to one's own ends, inflicting suffering, etc. It may be, however, that Marxism spends little time in providing a theoretical analysis of these phenomena because it considers that the oppressiveness of these practices is less concealed than the oppression inherent in wage labor. Perhaps Marxists see the main task for a theory of women's sex-specific oppression as being not to explain *why* these practices are oppressive, when *that* they are so is obvious; perhaps they view the main task as being rather to show how such practices can be ended. In order to do this, a Marxist theory must show us why these practices persist and what, if anything, is their material basis. As I said earlier, this is a difficult question for Marxism. If male and female workers were really approaching a situation of material equality, one would expect a weakening of the perception that women are primarily sexual objects and a decline in female prostitution, in sexual harassment, in rape and in physical violence by men against women. If Marxism is to be accepted as an adequate theoretical and practical basis for women's liberation, it is vital that Marxism explain why these practices are not in decline. For the practices mentioned are not isolated phenomena nor tangential to women's lives; they reveal the sex-specific oppression of women and shape the daily life of every woman in contemporary society.

In answering this question, traditional Marxism contends that, once women are fully integrated into wage labor, there is *no* material basis for the sex-specific oppression of women. If such oppression persists, it must be generated by an outdated ideology, appropriate to an earlier set of material conditions. Many contemporary Marxists, unlike their "economistic" predecessors, recognize that ideology can be extremely influential—a "material force," as it is sometimes put. Some Marxists, such as Juliet Mitchell, even locate the source of women's sex-specific oppression in the human unconscious, an unconscious whose contents were established during an earlier stage in human history.[50] But this suggestion does not affect the basic Marxist position, that, once women have entered the wage labor force, there is no material basis for women's oppression. Sexual objectification, rape, wife-beating and the sexual segregation of the paid workforce do not reflect a gendered split in the fundamental economic structure of society and, in order to be abolished, they do not require a fundamental restructuring of the economic relations between the sexes.

If the ideology of male dominance is not embedded in some basic economic conflict of interest between the sexes, why does it continue to flourish under capitalism, even as more women enter the paid labor force? The basic reason, according to traditional Marxism, is that the continued subordination of women is in the interests of capital. For example, sexist ideology provides a rationale for paying women less than men, thus exerting a downward pressure on all wages and permitting the increased exploitation of the working class as a whole. Many feminists, by no means all Marxists, have pointed out that the use of women as sexual objects in advertising and entertainment is extremely profitable; pornography, as a booming industry, is even more clearly in the capitalist interest. Moreover, the sexual objectification of women distracts working-class men from their own oppression as workers, while rape and battery provide working-(and other) class men with an outlet for their own frustrations. So women become scapegoats for the capitalist class. Because this class controls science, education and the media, it will continue to perpetuate sexist ideology so long as it remains in its interest to do so. Thus prostitution, sexual objectification, sexual harassment, the sexual segregation of the paid labor force, rape and other forms of violence against women will continue so long as capitalism remains. They are all explained as functional to the capitalist system.

The same functionalist approach is applied by traditional Marxists to all other aspects of women's contemporary oppression. For instance, the strong resistance to women's right to abortion is explained as capital's way of forcing women to reproduce the labor power and the population of consumers that capitalism needs for its continued expansion. Similarly, the opposition to lesbianism and male homosexuality is seen as a way in which capital buttresses the belief that the nuclear family is "natural" and even biologically determined.[51] Many contemporary Marxists have pointed out that capital has an interest in maintaining the nuclear family at all class levels. In the upper classes, the family acts as a conduit for the accumulation of capital through inheritance, while in the working class it fulfills other vital economic functions for capital. For example, it provides a way in which socially necessary work such as childrearing and care of the sick and old is performed cheaply by unpaid women workers. Further, it maintains an artificially high level of demand for durable consumer goods, since each small household is forced to buy its own refrigerator, stove, washing machine, lawn mower, etc., even though many of these items may stand idle for most of the time. In addition, the nuclear family is thought to provide a "reserve army of labor" by acting as a sponge which absorbs women during periods of unemployment and which squeezes them out for seasonal work or whenever labor is scarce. Contemporary Marxists also claim that the nuclear family performs functions of social control, because its economic insecurity fosters submission to the discipline of the workplace, encourages competition between workers, and provides a way in which future workers are disciplined. Indeed, the nuclear family is viewed as making so vital a contribution to the capitalist production process that, as we have seen, many contemporary Marxists have been engaged in an elaborate debate over whether women's domestic labor should be viewed as "productive," in the technical Marxist sense of creating surplus value.

Examples of Marxist functionalist explanations of various aspects of women's sex-specific oppression could be multiplied, but the general point is clear. Appearances to the contrary, the sex-specific oppression of women is perpetrated not by men but by capitalism. Working-class men, at least, are only the ignorant tools of capital. The real material interests of working-class men, though not, of course, of capitalist men, are identical with those of women.

The Traditional Marxist Proposals for Social Change

The traditional Marxist analysis of women's oppression generates, at least in outline, a fairly clear conception of the social changes that are required to liberate women. On the traditional Marxist view, the sex-specific oppression of women under capitalism consists fundamentally in their exclusion from the public realm of social production. Therefore, in a much quoted sentence, Engels writes, "The first condition for the liberation of the wife is to bring the whole female sex back into public industry."[52] For women to enter public industry is both an end in itself and a means to further change. As participants in public industry (wage labor, under capitalism), women will no longer be on the sidelines of history. Instead they will be in a position to shape history, to realize their potentialities for social action to transform the existing world. As wage workers, women in public industry will suffer a new form of alienation. But they will struggle together with men to overcome that alienation by overthrowing the wage system and by establishing a socialist society, the necessary precondition of communism.

Socialism will provide the material basis for overcoming all alienation. A socialist revolution will consist in the means of production being taken over by the working class, which will also take control of the state apparatus. Until it finally "withers away," the socialist state will play a major role in reorganizing production, making decisions about what goods and services are produced, the process by which they are produced and how those goods and services are distributed. Since the state will represent the working class, those decisions, for the first time, will be genuinely democratic and they will be made on the basis of social need rather than profit. With the abolition of the capitalist mode of production, alienation will disappear: the capitalist class will no longer control the workers' productive activity, and the workers' products will no longer be used against them. When workers regain control of production, they will no longer have to be forced to work. Instead, their attitudes toward work will change: they will realize that self-fulfillment comes through work, and work activity rather than leisure activity will move to the center of their lives. Ultimately, indeed, the distinction between work and leisure may disappear. Meanwhile, workers will recognize the social nature of all productive activity and will develop cooperative rather than alienated and competitive relationships with their co-workers, relationships based on their acknowledged interdependence.

On the traditional Marxist view, socialism will be the basis for overcoming not only alienation but also the specific forms of oppression suffered by a variety of groups under capitalism. For instance, socialism will make it possible to end the oppression specific to ethnic minorities, to young people, to old people and to women, for there will no longer be a capitalist class with an interest in perpetuating these forms of oppression. Under socialism, work will be reorganized in such a way that everyone will be able to develop his or her potentiality for free and cooperative productive activity. This belief is expressed in the following passage from *Capital,* previously quoted in Chapter 4:

> However terrible and disgusting the dissolution, under the capitalist system, of the old family ties may appear, nevertheless, modern industry, by assigning as it does an important part in the process of production, outside the domestic sphere, to women, to young persons, and to children of both sexes, creates a new economic foundation for a higher form of the family and of the relations between the sexes. . . . Moreover, it is obvious that the fact of the collective working group being composed of individuals of both sexes and all ages must necessarily, under suitable conditions, become a source of humane development.[53]

The participation of all in public production, that is, in work outside the domestic sphere, will eliminate the material basis for the oppression of any group by another.

Of course, it will be difficult for women to participate fully in public production if they are also responsible for domestic work. Marx recognized this when he wrote: "Compulsory work for the capitalist usurped the place, not only of the children's play, but also of free labour at home within moderate limits for the support of the family."[54] The context of this sentence makes clear that Marx is talking about women's domestic work—though a woman might not have described this work as "free." Engels, too, saw that, if a woman

> carries out her duties in the private service of her family, she remains excluded from public production and unable to earn; and if she wants to take part in public production and earn independently, she cannot carry family duties.[55]

So far as I know, Marx never suggested a solution to this problem, but Engels did. Engels' solution was to socialize the work that, under capitalism, is done in the home, particularly the work of childrearing. Under socialism, he wrote, "Private housekeeping is transformed into a social industry. The care and education of the children becomes a public affair; society looks after all children alike, whether they are legitimate or not."[56] As Engels envisioned it, this solution is quite different from the childcare centers, restaurants and cleaning services suggested by liberal feminism. On the liberal feminist proposal, most people would pay for these services; services would be free only to the very poor. Most services, then, would be business enterprises, aimed primarily at making a profit. Consequently, their quality would vary considerably depending on people's ability to pay for them. Under socialism, however, such services would be designed not for profit but in order to meet people's needs. They would be of a uniformly high quality, regardless of their client's ability to pay.

The availability of these services would eliminate the economic basis of the family. As Engels puts it, "With the transfer of the means of production into common ownership, the single family ceases to be the economic unit of society."[57] By this, Engels does not mean that the single family would cease to be the productive unit of society. So far as the production of goods and services go, the advent of industrialization has meant that this kind of production typically has moved outside the home already. But the family has remained the unit for the production of children and the unit which takes responsibility for the immediate satisfaction of human needs for food, shelter, nurturance and so on. If those responsibilities were undertaken by society as a whole, relations within the family would be transformed. In particular, mothers, children and those family members too old or too ill to work would no longer be dependent for their survival on the wage earner(s), typically the husband and father. Thus the basis for male dominance within the family would disappear—and so, at least theoretically, would the basis for the oppression of children and old people.

While all family members would be affected by these changes, women would stand most obviously to gain. They would no longer be forced to marry for the sake of economic security, or stay in an unsatisfactory marriage. They would have no reason to tolerate a sexual double-standard or physical abuse. By removing the economic motivation to marry, then, socialism would provide the material foundation for a genuinely free and equal relationship between marriage partners. As Engels puts it:

> Full freedom of marriage can therefore only be generally established when the abolition of capitalist production and of the property relations created by it has removed all the accompanying economic considerations which still exert such a powerful influence on the choice of a marriage partner. For then there is no other motive left except mutual inclination.[58]

If the economic basis of the family disappeared, what would hold it together under socialism? Much of Engels' discussion has consisted in demonstrating how the structure of the family, and particularly norms about permissible sexual partners, has changed historically with changes in the mode of production. Since the establishment of socialism constitutes such a radical break with the capitalist way of life, one might speculate that it would become the basis for entirely new forms of social and sexual groupings. In fact, however, such speculations are entirely absent from traditional Marxist theory. Engels, for instance, claims that in a situation of "full freedom of marriage" people would continue to live in heterosexual couples. "And as sexual love is by its nature exclusive—although at present this exclusiveness is fully realized only in the woman—the marriage based on sexual love is by its nature individual marriage."[59]

Engels' claim is challenged neither by contemporary Marxist theorists nor by the family policies that have been established in those societies that are viewed ordinarily as having undergone socialist revolutions. Within the Marxist tradition, it is assumed that the heterosexual couple will constitute the normal social unit within which occurs deep affection, sexual expression and the production of the next generation. The family will be destroyed as an economic unit, in the Marxist sense, but it will remain a sexual, affective and procreative unit. Indeed, Engels believes, as we have seen, that the absence of economic considerations will strengthen the sexual and affective ties between heterosexual couples.

Although a socialist revolution is not directed primarily toward the transformation of sexual norms, traditional Marxist theorists would claim that it provides the material basis for such a transformation. Traditional Marxist theorists have written relatively little about how the establishment of socialism would affect the situation of women, but their existing theory implies that women would be among the primary beneficiaries of this transformation, just as they would be the primary beneficiaries of changes in family relations. We have seen already that women's entry into public production would mean that they would no longer be forced to sell themselves in marriage. Moreover, as women came to define themselves primarily in terms of their work outside the home, the ideological definition of women as sexual objects would become decreasingly congruent with social reality. Men would learn to value women's non-sexual qualities and women would be in a position to refuse to tolerate sexual objectification and sexual harassment. Women who were strengthened by physical labor would be less vulnerable to rape, but rape attempts would in any case diminish as men learned to perceive women in other than sexual ways. Rape attempts might also diminish because, under socialism, sexual activity would be less of a forbidden fruit: although coerced forms of sexuality would tend to disappear, there would probably be an increase in forms of sexual activity that were freely chosen, especially by women. For instance, Engels writes that the provision of public child care would "remove all the anxiety about the 'consequences' which today is the most essential social . . . factor that prevents a girl from giving herself completely to the man she loves."[60]

Obviously, the possibility of economic independence, the lack of economic pressure to marry and the disappearance of sexual objectification would benefit lesbian women at least as much as heterosexual women. Traditional Marxist theorists have seldom discussed the prospect of sexual freedom for lesbians (and gay men) as a benefit that would result from socialism. Many of these theorists, in fact, are homophobic, as is Engels when he talks about "the abominable practice of sodomy"[61] and as are contemporary Marxist groups which describe homosexuality as "bourgeois decadence." Engels' whole discussion of sexuality reflects his assumption that "normal" sexual expression is heterosexual as well as the bourgeois prejudice that women would naturally value chastity more than men.[62] These prejudices, however, may not be integral to Marxist theory (though they are rooted in it more deeply than appears at first sight), and Engels seems more consistent when he acknowledges ignorance about the organization of sexuality under socialism:

> What we can now conjecture about the way in which sexual relations will be ordered after the impending overthrow of capitalist production is mainly of a negative character, limited for the most part to what will disappear. But what will there be new? That will be answered when a new generation has grown up: a generation of men who never in their lives have known what it is to buy a woman's surrender with money or any other social instrument of power; a generation of women who have never known what it is to give themselves to a man from any other considerations than real love or to refuse to give themselves to their lover from fear of the economic consequences. When these people are in the

world, they will care precious little what anybody today thinks they ought to do; they will make their own practice and their corresponding public opinion about the practice of each individual—and that will be the end of it.[63]

On an enlightened (non-homophobic) Marxist view, therefore, lesbians stand to gain at least as much as heterosexual women from the establishment of socialism.

Some earlier Marxists theorists apparently assumed that the elimination of women's sex-specific oppression would follow automatically from the establishment of socialism. Contemporary Marxists do not make this assumption. They recognize that "after the revolution" people will still retain many ways of thinking and feeling that were appropriate to capitalist society. These will include ideas of competition, racism, disdain for manual labor and, of course, male supremacy. Once socialism has been established, there will still be a need for continued political struggle in the form of intense debates and actions, particularly around the situation of women. This struggle, however, will be "ideological" struggle. The liberation of women will not require any further transformation of the economic foundation of society: this is what Marxists mean when they claim that socialism provides the material base for women's liberation.

Although socialism is necessary to women, on the traditional Marxist view, women are also necessary to socialism. The (male) working class can never prevail as long as women press their husbands to submit to capitalist conditions of work for the sake of economic support or, even worse, as long as women undercut male workers' bargaining power by working for even lower pay. For traditional Marxists, then, it is necessary to "organize" women. This means both unionizing women wage workers and also attracting women into the revolutionary party which, on the traditional Marxist view, must lead the socialist revolution. To attract women into revolutionary parties and groups, Marxist activists of the 1970s and 1980s have placed a new emphasis on so-called "women's issues." Earlier socialist and communist groups had often been narrowly "economistic" in their demands, focusing their struggles around such issues as rates of pay, the length of workday and working conditions. The rise of the contemporary women's liberation movement, however, has made it almost impossible to ignore the fact that large numbers of women are less interested in these traditional class issues than they are in such "social" issues as sex discrimination, sexual objectification and harassment and violence against women. Marxist groups in capitalist countries have therefore begun to support some of these struggles.[64] Their purpose in providing such support, however, is not primarily to achieve reforms for women. Given their analysis of the material basis of women's oppression, they do not believe that either aspect of women's oppression can be eliminated under capitalism. It is their view that any reforms instituted by the capitalist state will be little more than tokenism, aimed at mystifying the sex-specific oppression of women even further by concealing it under the rhetoric of "freedom of choice," "equality of opportunity" and "reward according to merit." Nevertheless, contemporary Marxists believe that their involvement in women's struggles will provide them with an opportunity to introduce socialist ideas, convince women that socialism is necessary for their liberation and make the "contacts" necessary for recruiting women into the revolutionary party.

Problems in Traditional Marxist Politics

The politics of traditional Marxism illuminate a number of the problems that are endemic to liberal feminism. For instance, Marxism can help liberal feminists understand why their strategies of rational persuasion and legal reform are so ineffective in achieving genuine equality for women. Marxism's analysis of the political economy of capitalism shows how the capitalist class benefits from the superexploitation of women and why that class will abandon women's superexploitation only if an alternative group, such as recent immigrants, can be found to take women's place as the reserve army of labor. Similarly, Marxist analysis explains the reluctance of capitalism to provide quality childcare for children. If capital has enough interest in exploiting women's labor, it may indeed provide such care; but the care offered will never be enough, and it will always be inferior to private care, which the rich can afford to buy. Consequently, mothers will still be reluctant to leave their children and will still have "two jobs." The Marxist contribution to feminist politics goes beyond a negative critique of liberal feminism. Not only does Marxism show how the liberal feminist goal of equal opportunity can never be achieved under capitalism, but it offers an alternative to that goal. The recognition that economic independence for women is a precondition for women's liberation is not a specifically Marxist insight, but what Marxism offers is a reply to the woman who does not want to be "liberated" if "liberation" means only to be waged. Marxism offers a vision of work outside the home which goes beyond the alienated labor characteristic of capitalism. Its challenge to wage labor and to the distinction between mental and manual labor suggests how work can be reorganized to provide the possibility of fulfillment to all women, not just to a few women with a certain class privilege.

Recognizing the limits of the liberal feminist vision, many women turned to Marxism for a less class-biased and more "scientific" conception of women's liberation. In the 1960s, however, Marxism itself came under attack from the women's liberation movement. In the remainder of this chapter, I shall outline the criticisms of Marxist politics that contemporary feminists have made and I shall link those criticisms with the basic theoretical and political perspective of Marxism. In the next two chapters, I shall examine the alternative politics that contemporary feminists are developing.

The following discussion of traditional Marxist politics will focus primarily on Marxist-Leninist organizations in advanced capitalist countries, organizations which seem far from seizing state power. Insofar as the adequacy of traditional Marxist politics is tested ultimately in practice, it may seem unfair to focus so exclusively on the practice of relatively small organizations whose work is necessarily affected by the capitalist context in which it occurs. A better test of the adequacy of traditional Marxist politics would surely be found by examining the position of women in societies that claim already to have undergone a revolutionary transformation guided by the principles of Marxism-Leninism. In my view, the position of women in some of these societies has improved substantially but male dominance still persists, often in quite blatant forms, and the central structures of the society continue to reproduce it.[65] Although the fate of women in existing socialist societies is undoubtedly relevant to determining the adequacy of traditional Marxist politics, such an examination is beyond the scope of this book. Here I will focus on the current feminist debate only within the advanced capitalist nations. However, I do think that a close examination of the status of women in so-called socialist societies will bear out the fears that we shall see expressed by feminist critics of traditional Marxist organizations operating under capitalism.

The most common complaint made by feminists since the mid-1960s is that traditional Marxist organizations are sexist. In other words, those organizations that are dedicated to the kind of revolutionary change that is supposed to liberate women are in fact perpetuating that oppression. The original feminist criticism was simply that individual men in Marxist organizations were personally oppressive to women and insensitive to their concerns. Feminists at first saw the problem as one that could be solved by a change in interpersonal relationships between male and female members of Marxist organizations. Later, however, they moved to claiming that sexism was inherent in traditional Marxist strategies and methods of organizing for social change and was indeed inherent in the Marxist conception of politics.

1. WOMEN IN REVOLUTIONARY ORGANIZATIONS

Feminist historians are beginning to examine the origins of the women's liberation movement that emerged in the 1960s. The women who sparked this movement were primarily from two characteristic backgrounds: either they were middle-class "professional" women or they were women involved in the radical organizations then struggling against nuclear arms, for black civil rights or against the war in south-east Asia. Inspired by ideals of equality, justice or liberation, the women in radical organizations were outraged to discover that they were expected to be "housewives to the revolution": making coffee, doing typing, providing support and being sexually available. In reaction to this discovery, many women dropped out of the "mixed left" to form their own autonomous organizations. Fearing total defection by women, most socialist groups became more sensitive at least to the more blatant forms of male domination. "Women's issues" began to be addressed and childcare was often provided at meetings and events. In spite of these reforms, however, feminists continue to criticize the positions given to women in revolutionary socialist organizations.

The basic complaint is the difficulty encountered by women in achieving full participation or being accepted as independent leaders in "mixed left" organizations. This difficulty is due only partly to men's habits of dominance and women's habits of submission. Some feminists argue that it is also due to the conceptions of democracy and of revolutionary leadership current in traditional Marxist organizations. Because revolutionary organizations are born and continue to survive in an extremely oppressive society, it is inevitable that some of the values of that society will emerge even within groups committed to opposing those values. Obviously, it would be utopian to expect that revolutionary organizations would be immune to racism, to careerism, to competition, to disproportionate respect for "intellectuals" and, of course, to male dominance. What feminists criticize is not so much that these problems crop up; rather they criticize the fact that many traditional Marxists are not committed to developing systematic ways of combating these forms of oppression within their own organizations. Instead, Marxists tend to trust to the goodwill of their members as individuals. Many feminists, however, believe that male dominance (and other forms of oppression) are embedded in the organizational structure of traditional Marxist groups and in the traditional conception of what it is to be a revolutionary leader. The model of revolutionary organization to which these feminists object is often referred to as "Leninism."

Many revolutionary socialist groups, at least in Britain and in the United States, typically have described themselves as Marxist-Leninist. Lenin is viewed as the practical organizer who, with history on his side, was able at least to begin to put into practice the political theory formulated by Marx and Engels. (Left groups differ ferociously, of course, over how far the revolution begun by Lenin was betrayed by Stalin.) Lenin's conception of revolutionary organization was developed within the extremely repressive conditions of czarist Russia and his view bears the marks of its birth.[66] Central to Lenin's conception of revolutionary organization is the idea of the "vanguard party," the organization destined to lead the revolution. Lenin believed that the members of the vanguard party must be politically experienced, highly trained and disciplined. He thought that the members of such a party, in virtue of their intensive study of political texts and their equally intensive sharing and discussion of their own political experience would be able to obtain an overview of the current political situation that was unavailable to most members of the working class, whose experience would be limited to local struggles and specific forms of oppression. The theoretical task of the vanguard party, therefore, was to distil the collective wisdom of the working class from the various political experiences of its members and to develop a unified and effective strategy for toppling the entire capitalist system. The practical task of the vanguard party was to join with the most "advanced elements" of the working class and to attempt to escalate struggles against specific grievances into a successful attack on the whole political and economic system of capitalism. To carry out this historic task, Lenin believed that the vanguard party must be a tightly knit organization, subject to rigid discipline and with a high degree of centralization. Democracy within the organization was to be preserved by the principles of democratic centralism. The system of democratic centralism requires that each branch of the party should elect delegates to the party congress, the supreme authority of the party. The delegates at this congress would decide on the main problems facing the party and finally would elect a central committee to govern the party until the next congress met. Between congresses, members were to be bound by the authority of the central committee, although in principle the committee was subject to recall at an emergency conference if enough branches expressed no confidence in it. Democratic centralism was claimed to reconcile discipline and efficiency with basic democracy, and its principles are still accepted by contemporary Marxist-Leninist organizations. Unlike Lenin's illegal and therefore secret Bolshevik party, however, contemporary Marxist-Leninist organizations usually function openly in the advanced capitalist nations. This openness in itself fosters more democracy within the organization than was possible in pre-revolutionary Russia or in the crisis conditions immediately following the revolution. Some contemporary Marxist-Leninist organizations even allow opposing factions to exist within the organization—which Lenin banned in 1921.

Ever since its inception, the Leninist model of revolutionary organization has come under constant attack; from Mensheviks in 1903, from the British New Left in the 1950s, from the American New Left in the 1960s, and from anarchists, anarcho-syndicalists and council communists all along. One common criticism is that democratic centralism is inherently undemocratic. The centralization of information creates a leadership elite which is then able to use its power in an arbitrary and coercive way. The leaders' control of the information and communication networks in the organization is said to make it practically impossible for those who disagree with the leadership to organize effective opposition, even though this possibility exists in principle. Once leaders are entrenched within the so-called vanguard party, critics argue, they develop a vested interest in maintaining their own control, an interest which is often incompatible with furthering revolution. Critics charge that such leaders, because of their reluctance to take risks, invariably try to inhibit rather than to encourage revolutionary action and are even prepared to compromise with the capitalist class. In order to further their own ends, which they define as revolutionary, the leaders "sell out" particular struggles. According to some critics, the very notion of a vanguard party is incompatible with a revolution whose direction is determined by the people themselves.

Contemporary feminists are often sympathetic to these traditional criticisms of Leninism, but their characteristic objections to this model of revolutionary organization focus particularly on its consequences for women. One of their criticisms is that the Leninist process for arriving at decisions stifles women's participation. On the surface, the process of voting on political decisions and delegate selection is sex- (as well as race- and class-) neutral. In practice, however, this process discriminates against all those who are less articulate, less self-confident, less familiar with Marxist theory and less assertive. Women, because of their historical experience, tend to be all those things—as do many minority and working-class members. A speaker with an air of confidence and authority is received by her or his listeners with respect, but both women and men give greater credence to men than to women. Men feel more free to interrupt women than other men and women are trained to listen. If women are to have an equal voice in any organization, these sorts of problems must be confronted publicly and ways devised to deal with them. Feminists complain that this is not done in Marxist-Leninist organizations and so these organizations tend to replicate the power imbalances of the larger society. Leadership tends to be assumed by educated white males, whose position then increases both their knowledge and their self-confidence and so makes them seem even better-qualified to be leaders. People lacking those qualities when they join the organization have little hope of acquiring them within it and so remain in the position of followers. Prospects are not quite as bleak for manual workers, blacks, and other minority men because traditional Marxists perceive manual workers, who are often minority group males, as constituting a particularly important segment of the working class. Minority men may therefore be treated with some deference in a Marxist-Leninist organization. The class position of most women, however, is thought to be of less strategic importance and so women, particularly white women, are often considered as having less valuable experience to offer. Feminists charge that the women who do achieve prominence in Marxist-Leninist organizations are often the wives or lovers of male leaders and their opinions tend to be indistinguishable from those of their mentors.

The Leninist model of revolutionary organization is also criticized by feminists as being unconcerned with feeling or emotion. Discussion of the "objective" political situation and the need to perform a multitude of practical tasks leave little time for considering the feelings of the members of the organization. Some Marxists, indeed, tend to dismiss concern with feeling and emotion as a self-indulgent luxury of the privileged classes. Their narrow interpretations of "practice" and of "material conditions" lead them to dismiss feelings as "subjective" or "personal." By contrast, women's training as nurturers has taught them to be acutely aware of the feelings of others and, to a lesser extent, of themselves. Most women find it difficult to work in a group if some of the members have hostile or otherwise negative feelings and in the past this difficulty has led women to avoid confrontations in an effort not to provoke hostility. Feminists are not content to behave in traditionally devious, manipulative or subservient ways, but neither are they willing to leave the ensuing feelings unresolved. Consequently, they criticize Marxist-Leninist groups for providing no means of pursuing such a resolution. They argue that the Marxist-Leninist conception of organizational efficiency is a narrow and ultimately self-defeating conception. Its disregard for feelings and its insistence on conformity in pursuit of short-term goals make genuine democracy impossible. Leninist values increase tensions, insecurities and hostilities within the organization, make schisms and defections more likely and diminish the chances for long-term revolutionary commitment by the members.

Because a Leninist organization is so highly centralized, its leaders bear a heavy burden of responsibility. They are forced to become "professionals" or at least to devote to the organizations much of the time not spent at their paid employment. Sheila Rowbotham provides the following caricature of the Leninist conception of the revolutionary leader:

> This individual militant appears as a lonely character without ties, bereft of domestic emotions, who is hard, erect, self-contained, controlled, without the time or ability to express loving passion, who cannot pause to nurture, and for whom friendship is a diversion.[67]

Rowbotham points out that, on this model, few women will become revolutionary leaders: not only is the feminine character structure quite different from this but most women have family responsibilities which simply will not allow them to commit so much time to political activity. A handful of women indeed have been charismatic revolutionary leaders: they include Mother Jones, Rosa Luxembourg, Clara Zetkin, Allexandra Kollontai and Emma Goldman. All were childless at the time of their political activity, however, or else gave their children to others to raise. They also found it especially difficult to maintain long-term intimate relationships.

Even if the traditional model of revolutionary leadership were one that women could adopt, Rowbotham's characterization suggests that she does not view it as a desirable model. Radical feminists, in particular, have subjected the Leninist model of revolutionary leadership to a thorough critique which will be explored in Chapter 9. They believe that it overemphasizes the importance of individual action and minimizes the importance of collective action. It romanticizes the strength of certain individuals, usually men, and fails to acknowledge the support these leaders received, usually from women. Confronted by such heroes, portrayed larger than life and free from conflict, ambivalence or self-doubt, most women feel inadequate. Berenice Fisher argues that it is important to provide a more realistic picture of women heroes, a picture that does not

> deny or ignore the internal and external contradictions involved in [political] struggle or mask how uneven any heroic commitment may be. When such conflicts and unevenness are denied, heroic images stand *between* women, obscuring our common situation and common struggle.[68]

Fisher also suggests that,

> Just as we may have a special stake in restructuring the notion of work, to account (among other things) for the demands of childbearing, so we

may have a similar stake in restructuring the notion of political action, to make room for the part-time (part of her day, her month, her life) hero.[69]

Fisher concludes:

> Crucial to the development of more realistic images of women-as-heroes is the problem of collective action and the deep rifts that exist among us as women. Although there is obviously no simple solution to this problem . . . , the questions posed by heroism are suggestive. A clear-eyed look at feminist heroes reveals the central role that networks or collectivities have played in making heroism possible. Women political activists have not acted alone. The more we explore this central fact of our political history, the more we are forced to question the strongly individualistic bias of the concept "hero", in all its various uses. Feminists may need to go far beyond the democratic theory of heroism to articulate a more genuinely collective theory of heroic action.[70]

In the late 1960s, the eruption of the women's liberation movement was marked by the formation of innumerable feminist groups whose membership was closed to men. Some of these groups are called autonomous women's organizations because they are organizationally independent of any groups that include men. This means, of course, that they are organizationally independent of Marxist-Leninist vanguard parties. Women formed autonomous organizations because they found that, for all the reasons just described, they had been systematically dominated in Marxist-Leninist organizations. Marxist-Leninist organizations, however, have been extremely hostile to autonomous women's organizations, denying that they constitute a legitimate part of a revolutionary socialist movement. Because they see the interests of women as ultimately coinciding with the interest of the working class as a whole, they believe that a long-term strategy for revolution can be developed only by a relatively traditional vanguard party. They do admit the legitimacy of separate women's (or black or youth) groups that have organizational links with the party. Traditional Marxists fear that autonomous women's organizations will fall prey to what Marxists regard as bourgeois ideology, that is, to an analysis identifying men as a group or class with substantial material interests opposed to the interests of women. They fear that this analysis will divide the working class and make socialist revolution impossible. Contrary to the traditional Marxist view, many contemporary feminists claim that the working class is already divided by male dominance, and that only independent or autonomous women's organizations can ensure that women's interests are not neglected in a so-called socialist revolution. The plausibility of each side in this argument rests in large part on the adequacy of their alternative political analyses of women's situation. I have argued already that men have certain material interests that are opposed to women's interests; in my view, consequently, women need separate organizations to defend those interests and to ensure that the male-dominant structure of the larger society is not replicated in the vanguard party and ultimately in the post-revolutionary socialist society. In the next two chapters, I shall discuss different conceptions of autonomous women's organizations, their structure and their relationship to "mixed" organizations.

2. REVOLUTIONARY STRATEGY

The Leninist revolutionary organization is designed to carry out a specific revolutionary strategy: to lead the struggles of the industrial working class. Marxist-Leninists focus on the industrial working class because they believe that only this class can be the agent of revolutionary change. Other classes or social groups are oppressed or even exploited under capitalism; but only industrial workers have the strategic location that enables them to bring to a halt the capitalist system of production. The efforts of the vanguard party, therefore, should be directed primarily toward these workers, supporting their struggles and attempting to develop their consciousness of themselves as a class whose long-term interests are totally incompatible with the interests of the capitalist class.

On the surface, this time-honored strategy does not sound oppressive to women. It is expressed, after all, in language that is sex-neutral. Nevertheless, feminists have begun to argue that, beneath the surface, this strategy is sexist. It is sexist because it discounts the revolutionary potential of women. For traditional Marxists, the paradigm worker wears a blue collar and operates a machine at the "point of production." Marxists assume, perhaps unconsciously, that this worker is male. Marxists recognize that there are many women machine operators in advanced capitalist countries, but they see that such workers are employed primarily in small shops, in marginal industries or in industries such as the clothing industry, whose shutting down would not paralyze society.[71] Most women workers in the traditional heavy industries of the advanced capitalist nations, however, are "pink collar" workers, performing clerical functions which Marxists have viewed as nonessential to industrial production. Consequently women, even women wage workers, have been seen as peripheral rather than central to the revolutionary struggle. Their strategic location under capitalism, both within the paid labor force and outside it, is thought to allow them to function primarily in a supportive capacity to "real" revolutionaries. Women do not constitute the vanguard. Lydia Sargent describes the traditional Marxist strategy:

> Workers at the point of production (read white working class males) will make the revolution led by revolutionary cadre of politicos (read middle class white males steeped in marxist economic theory). Women (mostly white) would keep the home fires burning during it, functioning as revolutionary nurturers/secretaries: typing, filing, phoning, feeding, healing, supporting, loving, and occasionally even participating on the front lines as quasi-revolutionary cheerleaders.[72]

This strategy has a well-established record of failure. With the possible exception of the Bolshevik revolution, it is not clear that it has resulted in a single socialist revolution. Many contemporary critics attack it as "economistic," focusing too narrowly on one aspect of the total capitalist system. These critics point out that capitalism affects every aspect of daily life, that the working class creates itself not only at the workplace but also in the neighborhood and in recreational activities, and that capitalist values are strengthened and legitimated in every social institution: in homes, schools, and hospitals and through entertainment. In order to undermine the legitimacy of the capitalist system, critics emphasize the importance of "cultural" as well as industrial struggles. They argue that socialists should take up not only issues of wages and working conditions, but also such issues as education, the environment or health. They believe it is easy to show how the capitalist system inevitably creates not only alienation and poverty but also a polluted environment, unhealthy citizens and an inadequate and repressive educational system.

Many feminists, again, share these criticisms. What they would add is that "economism" is sexist. It rests on a conception of productive labor that is not only narrow but also sex-biased. Even apart from the controversial question of whether procreation is a form of production, technical developments in industry, coupled with the export of much manufacturing industry to the so-called Third World, means that the classic "point of production" workers constitute a steadily decreasing proportion of the workforce in advanced capitalist nations. Replacing them is a rapidly growing number of clerical, sales and service workers employed not only in trade and industry, but also in the mushrooming state bureaucracies. Many of these workers are women. Since 1947, in fact, the labor force participation of men has declined steadily while that of women has increased.[73] In the advanced capitalist countries, women now predominate in those categories of labor that are both fastest growing and lowest paid.[74] The largest of these categories is clerical work, which now occupies 20 percent of the paid labor force in the United States, and whose workers are 80 percent female.[75] Their work is now vital because the so-called paper revolution has made previously auxiliary clerical functions essential to the running even of industrial organizations. Thus women now predominate in a job category that is central rather than peripheral to an industrial economy.[76] Feminists argue that only sexist bias could allow traditional Marxists to ignore the revolutionary potential of women wage workers under advanced capitalism. Even Marxists may not be impervious to the bourgeois ideological perception of women's place as in the home.

If women had more of a voice in revolutionary organizations, they might point out this potential. But the sexism of traditional Marxist organizations and the sexism of traditional Marxist strategy reinforce each other. Women have only a limited voice in revolutionary organizations, in part because they are viewed as being only peripheral members of the working class. Conversely, one reason that women wage workers tend to have a less-developed sense of themselves as members of the working class is that socialist organizing efforts have not focused on women workers.

A deeper feminist criticism of the traditional Marxist strategy for revolution is that such strategy is directed only toward a certain limited goal, namely, the goal of democratizing production, in the conventional sense. Feminists complain that traditional Marxism provides no strategy for democratizing procreation, nor even a conception of what that might mean. This criticism will be developed later in this chapter.

3. "WOMEN'S ISSUES"

Since the early 1970s, it has become more common for traditional Marxist organizations to take up certain so-called women's issues. These are issues that are seen to involve some sex-specific oppression of women, as opposed to issues that are thought to affect the working class in a gender-neutral way. As we shall see in Chapter 10, some feminists criticize the whole conception of women's issues because such a conception assumes that the domination of women is limited to certain areas of social life. Radical and socialist feminists argue that this assumption is false: the pervasiveness of male dominance means that women and men are affected differently by all historical developments. For these feminists, therefore, every issue is a women's issue, just as, for traditional Marxists, every issue is a class issue. Radical and socialist feminists claim that the identification of certain issues as "women's issues" in fact serves to limit awareness of the extent of women's oppression. Moreover, by defining certain issues as being of concern primarily to women, it reinforces conventional views about women's place and recreates a sexual division of labor even within revolutionary organizations that are supposed to overcome male dominance.

Many traditional Marxists are unaware of this criticism and often are proud of their commitment to so-called women's issues. In taking up these issues, Marxists are influenced partly by the general critique of "economism" and by their recognition of the importance of issues that are more broadly "social." From this perspective, the traditional Marxist interest in women's issues is analogous to the Marxist concern for health, environment, education or other so-called social issues. Feminist criticism, however, has given Marxists an additional incentive to prove that they are indeed concerned about women. By participating in women's struggles, traditional Marxists hope to interest women in socialism and possibly to recruit them into the vanguard party.

Although some feminists view this Marxist move as a step in the right direction, many remain sceptical that it indicates a genuine commitment to feminism. They point out that it is typically women Marxists who work on the "women's issues," while the male leaders occupy themselves elsewhere. Feminists agree that women Marxists should take leadership positions, especially on issues where the question of women's oppression is raised explicitly, but they would like to see Marxist men supporting women's leadership, not only by appearing in demonstrations but by making picket signs, doing typing and providing childcare. Until this happens, feminist critics argue that the Marxist commitment to women's liberation is little more than tokenism.

A deeper criticism concerns the particular "women's issues" with which Marxist organizations choose to involve themselves. According to some feminists, these issues are never the ones that directly challenge male privilege. The most usual "women's" campaigns for Marxists to support are the campaign for the right to abortion (although a few so-called left dissenters refuse to associate themselves with this) and the campaign against the forced sterilization of women. General Marxist support for these issues is followed by rather lukewarm support for lesbian and gay rights (again denied by a few Engelsian fundamentalists), and by rather more enthusiastic Marxist support of campaigns for childcare. Occasionally, Marxists support campaigns against rape by participating in marches to "take back the night." It is very unusual for traditional Marxists to participate in campaigns for affirmative action, against occupational segregation, wife-beating, incest, pornography, or sexual harassment, or in favor of enforcing fathers' child-support payments. Marxists do not typically take up the question of housework or childcare in the home as public political issues, although, like everyone else, they certainly struggle over them in private.[77] They tend to dismiss feminists' frequent interest in alternative living arrangements as a utopian distraction from the real struggle.

Feminist critics point out that the issues supported by Marxists are typically those that are in the self-interest of men as well as women. If women have the right to abortion, husbands will not have unwanted children to support and unmarried men will not face pressure to marry their pregnant lovers or at least to support the children they have fathered. As Barbara Ehrenreich says, the flip side of the claim that abortion is a woman's right is that it is no longer a man's responsibility.[78] Campaigns against involuntary sterilization, which is imposed primarily on women of color, in no way undercut the power of working-class men, and campaigns for lesbian rights are obviously campaigns for gay male rights as well. The provision of childcare would ease the burden on fathers as well as on mothers: once the mother were free to obtain a paid job, she could contribute to the family income if she were married, and would require lower child-support payments if she were not married.

Marxists can often provide a rationale for their reluctance to support certain feminist campaigns. "Reclaim the night" marches, for instance, may be racist or classist if the march is held in predominantly minority or white working-class areas. Marxists may view affirmative action as a bourgeois reform benefiting token middle-class women. And they may fear that restrictions on pornography would simply increase the power of the state to control freedom of expression— a power that would ultimately be used against the political expression of socialists. Usually, however, it is possible to support the feminist purpose of these campaigns while answering Marxist objections. "Reclaim the night" marches can be routed carefully, and affirmative action can be extended from "professional" to skilled and unskilled jobs. It may be possible to formulate restrictions on pornography in such a way that they cannot be used against leftist publications. Feminists sometimes suspect that Marxist reasons for failing to support such issues are actually rationalizations for their reluctance to confront male dominance.

On other issues, this feminist suspicion hardens into certainty. Many feminists believe that male Marxists simply do not want to struggle against the domestic abuse of women. Traditional Marxist organizations are unconcerned with the fact that divorced fathers usually fail to make their full child-support payments so that, with no man in the house, mothers and children sink into poverty. Similarly, traditional Marxist organizations tend to ignore occupational segregation, prostitution, incest and the sexual harassment of women. And the male members of these organizations are often unwilling to transform their own "personal" lives in such a way that they will have less control over decisions, more domestic chores to perform, and less time to spend on political activity, as they conceive political activity.

Male Marxists reject this criticism. They acknowledge that violence, poverty, discrimination and harassment are part of women's oppression, and they say that they oppose this oppression. Nevertheless, they do not choose to make these problems the focus of their political activity; to do so might offend the male members of the working class whom they view as the most important constituency of their revolutionary organization. On the traditional Marxist view, the sex-specific oppression of women is merely a by-product of capitalism and on this view, the most effective strategy for ending that oppression is to focus on overthrowing capitalism, an achievement which requires the united efforts of the working class. Once socialism is achieved, the sex-specific oppression of women can be dealt with. In the meantime, male Marxists claim, they are not sexists as individuals: they do not beat the women in their lives, they fulfill their child-support obligations, they refrain from rape and sexual harassment and, so far as possible, they share the domestic work in their homes.

This answer evades the basic disagreement between traditional Marxists and their feminist critics. For these feminists, the main question is not how far Marxists are sexist as individuals but whether the material basis of male dominance will be eliminated with the advent of socialism, as traditional

Marxists conceive socialism. Feminists see that, in contemporary society, men of all classes have systematic economic and political power over women. This power varies according to the traditionally defined class relations of the men and women involved, but it is always substantial. It is evident both outside and inside the home, manifested both by women's low status as wage workers and also by women's lack of control over their procreative capacity and over the ways in which they may express their sexuality.

Traditional Marxists acknowledge the existence of male dominance, but their recognition is not central to their theory or their practice. Traditional Marxists do not take seriously the systematic nature of women's oppression nor search conscientiously for the material basis of male dominance. Marxism's answers are inadequate because it does. not ask the right questions. Marxist practice gives low priority to struggles against male dominance and even excludes the home from the sphere of politics. Engels writes that any demand for equality which goes beyond the abolition of classes is absurd. This may be true, but it presupposes that we have an adequate concept of class: if our concept of class is gender-blind, the effect of Engels' claim is to delegitimize demands for an end to women's sex-specific oppression. On the traditional Marxist view, such oppression *cannot really exist,* once classes in the conventional sense have been abolished! Feminists do not see contemporary Marxism as being energetically committed to challenging male dominance, either in its theory or in its practice; consequently, they see no reason to believe that the traditional Marxist commitment to feminism will be any stronger in the future. They are sceptical that socialism, at least as it has been envisioned by traditional Marxists, will ever liberate women.

4. THE POLITICS OF PERSONAL LIFE

The women's liberation movement was born in the late 1960s at a time of social upheaval in the capitalist world. In Europe and North America, people, especially young people, were rebelling against the capitalist values of competition, hierarchy and commodity consumption. In the late 1960s, almost every aspect of capitalist society was called into question: its inequality, its racism, its imperialist foreign policy, its alienation, its "consumerism", its educational system and its sexual mores. The nuclear family was one of the institutions which came under heavy attack from what was then called "the counter culture." Some of the criticisms to which it was. subjected were specifically feminist; some were not. The nuclear family was said to fulfill certain economic functions which made it a cornerstone of the capitalist economic system; those functions have been listed earlier in this chapter. In addition, the nuclear family was said to transmit capitalist ideology, instilling the values of competition, discipline, and possessiveness. Feminists argued that it was oppressive to women; gay liberationists argued that it discriminated against homosexuals; many people complained that it was emotionally and sexually repressive to the marriage partners and some saw it as oppressive to children.

Seeking an alternative to the nuclear family, many people experimented with what in the United States were called "alternative life styles". Sometimes these alternatives were limited to so-called "open marriage" or "swinging"; sometimes they took the form of single-sex couples or households; sometimes they were rural or urban "communes". All these alternatives shared a common rejection of the norm of heterosexual monogamy and many of them were also inspired by ideals of sexual equality and non-possessiveness in personal relationships. The more politically conscious communes developed elaborate systems for sharing expenses and sometimes incomes, for sharing domestic chores and childrearing, and even for sharing sexual partners.

Traditional Marxists stood apart from these experiments. They shared some of the prevailing criticisms of the nuclear family but they saw it as an integral part of the capitalist system. They believed it was impossible for the majority of working people to establish alternatives to the nuclear family in the absence of a fundamental transformation of the mode of production. They were afraid that the attacks on the family would alienate working-class people for whom the family still offered economic and emotional support. They charged that the "alternative life styles" were a form of middle-class self-indulgence and that the so-called politics of personal life was simply a distraction from "real" political struggle. Many refused to question Engels' assumption that sexuality was "naturally" expressed in heterosexual couples and viewed "open" and homosexual relationships as symptoms of bourgeois decadence.

Many alternative households were short-lived. Sometimes they succumbed to direct attacks from the state, attacks which took such form as zoning restrictions (which made illegal the occupation of single household units by more than a limited number of unrelated adults) or conditions on the receipt of public assistance (which made such aid unavailable to individuals in alternative households). In addition to external attacks, alternative households also suffered from internal problems. They were often emotionally overwhelming for their inhabitants, who had been brought up to believe in "privacy," individualism, heterosexuality, sexual exclusiveness and the idea that children should be seen but not heard. Indeed, alternative households often disintegrated in anger and bitterness. People who remained often found that the frequent changes in the population of large households did not satisfy their needs for emotional stability and they tended to fall once more into primary couple relationships. Although some communal or collective households remain, most radical women currently live alone (with or without children) or in couples, although their partner now is often a woman or an unmarried man, rather than a husband. Except for some radical feminists, of whom more will be said in the next chapter, people again tend to think of politics as something pursued outside rather than inside the home.

The current retreat from the politics of the personal may bear out traditional Marxist scepticism about the possibility of radical changes in domestic life while the capitalist system remains intact. It may even seem to support the romantic Marxist notion of the working-class family as an egalitarian "haven from a heartless world." However, I think this retreat is better understood in terms of the power of an internalized ideology over people's feelings and emotions and in terms of the substantial economic privilege that men hold over women. It is true indeed that, although the family functions in the interests of capital in some ways, it also provides a means by which the working class pools its resources in order to survive and even to struggle against capital.[79] On the other hand, the eagerness of middle-class women to try out alternative living arrangements suggests that, at least from the point of view of those women, the nuclear family was unsatisfactory. Moreover, the fact that most working-class women continue to live with a male partner may be due less to the emotional support they receive from him than to the fact that, for most women, poverty is the only alternative to marriage.

Engels was keenly aware at least of bourgeois women's "domestic slavery" in the family. As we have seen, he thought that equality could exist between husbands and wives only when each was economically independent of the other. Contemporary Marxists have not developed Engels' insights. On the contrary, they have tended to ignore them and to view the working-class family as a unit with a common interest in survival and, ultimately, in overthrowing capitalism. They are right that family members in every class share certain interests. But, for feminists, it is important to remember that family members in all classes also have interests that conflict with one another. Under capitalism, the family, including the working-class family, is an economic unit. But it is a unit that is hierarchically ordered—the wife subordinate to the husband and the children to the parents. The reality of the sexual hierarchy is partially concealed, often even from the family members themselves, by an ideology of romantic love, natural complementarity and Mothers' Day. But the reality emerges in studies revealing who makes major family decisions, who physically abuses whom, who does the housework, who has more leisure time and who receives more sexual satisfaction.

Middle-class women have certainly been the most vocal in pointing out women's oppression within the family—just as they have been the most active in trying to escape it. But this does not mean that their observations are entirely invalidated by class bias. Historically, the middle class has always been a source of radical ideas, from liberalism to feminism to Marxism itself. Marx, Engels, Lenin, Trotsky and Mao all came from relatively privileged backgrounds, but traditional Marxists do not charge that their views are class-biased. Sex-specific oppression has been particularly noticeable to middle-class women because they have not been subject to the additional forms of class and racial oppression that afflict working-class women and women of color and so perhaps they have been initially less sceptical of the liberal ideals of equality and freedom. Middle-class women have had more leisure and more resources for developing a critique of women's oppression in the family and perhaps more options for struggling against it. But all this does not mean that oppression in the family is a problem only for middle-class women. It is arguable that the nuclear family is even more oppressive to working-class than to middle-class women, simply because working-class women have even fewer options for survival outside it.

For traditional Marxists, a woman who struggles with her husband is diverting energy away from the class struggle. She should recognize that family life can never be ideal under capitalism and should stand with him, shoulder to shoulder, against the enemy outside the door. From the point of view of feminism, however, the woman's enemy is within the door as well as outside it. He is present in the incestuous father and in the abusive husband—perhaps even in the political activist who requires her to support his work through domestic and sexual service. From the perspective of a woman, the nuclear family is not a haven in a heartless world; it is one of her workplaces, perhaps her only one, and the one in which she suffers some of her most direct oppression. A woman who struggles with her husband may not be confronting capitalism directly, but she is in a direct confrontation with male dominance. And when a woman leaves her husband to live alone or with another woman, she is not necessarily abandoning a struggling comrade or even seeking an individual solution. She may be attempting to establish a liberated zone.

Traditional Marxists cannot see this because they are blinkered by their narrow interpretations of class and of work, of politics and of struggle. Even they should see, however, that a woman who has a job and who also has a husband and children is unlikely to have much time or energy left over for sustained revolutionary activity. On those grounds alone, Marxists who are genuinely committed to women's liberation should support women's efforts to find alternatives to the nuclear family rather than encourage them to wait until "after the revolution." For if women are unable to play a leading part in the revolutionary struggle, they will be unable to direct the course of the revolution so that it meets the needs that are specific to women as a result of women's special historical circumstances.

These needs are sometimes difficult for working-class women to articulate, even though there is no doubt that such women are dissatisfied with their lives in the family: "I don't know what's the matter with me that I don't appreciate what I've got. I feel guilty all the time, and I worry about it a lot."[80]

In spite of the limited opportunities available to them, many working-class women welcome a paid job as an opportunity to get out of the house: "The days go faster and they're more exciting when you work."[81] On the other hand,

> Working is hard for me. When I work, I feel like I want to be doing a real good job, and I want to be absolutely responsible. Then, if the little one gets a cold, I feel like I should be home with her. That causes complications because whatever you do isn't right. You're either at work feeling like you should be home with your sick child, or you're at home feeling like you should be at work.[82]

> It's like my mind battles with itself all the time—like, "Stay home" and "Go to work."[83]

Working-class women express similar ambivalence about their relations with their husbands:

> I don't want you to think I'm complaining now. He's a good man, a lot better than most. Any woman who's got a man who hardly ever gets violent and who doesn't drink much hasn't got a lot to complain about.[84]

On the other hand, "It sounds silly, I know, but here I am in a house with three kids and my husband, and lots of times I feel like I might just as well be living alone."[85] Another woman says,

> I sometimes get worried because I think maybe I want too much. He's a good husband; he works hard; he takes care of me and the kids. He could go out and find another woman who would be very happy to have a man like that, and who wouldn't be all the time complaining to him because he doesn't feel things and get close.[86]

Working-class women's dissatisfaction with their domestic lives does not mean that they are ready to abandon their families. The jobs available to them may get them out of the house but they are hardly fulfilling, economic survival is difficult outside the family and, in spite of the sexual hierarchy within it, the family is still the major source of emotional commitment under capitalism. But the woman who says, for so many others, "It feels like somebody's always wanting something from me,"[87] knows clearly that she needs a new way of organizing her domestic life in which she will receive as well as provide emotional support and in which her time and energy are not exhausted by housework and childrearing. Many women share this speaker's feelings: "I get mad sometimes and wish I could change places with him. It would be such a relief to worry only about one thing. It feels like I drag around such a heavy load."[88]

Traditional Marxism promises that things will be better under socialism, but it offers little immediate help. The problem is not so much that Marxism is committed irrevocably to the nuclear family as that it has never seriously investigated alternatives to it. It has tended to brush aside women's concern with sexuality, childrearing and emotional life, endlessly postponing their consideration to a later date. This tendency may be a result of the residual biologism of Marxist categories. Marxists have not considered in any systematic way the political implications of birth and infancy and are still too often content to talk about "the sexual act" as though there was a single privileged, natural or even biologically determined mode of sexual expression.[89] Such biologism is not built into the conceptual foundations of Marxism and in fact is inconsistent with those foundations, but the male theoreticians of Marxism have felt little urgency about correcting the biological determinist prejudices of Marx and Engels. In fact, often they have shared those prejudices.

Lenin is notorious for his scolding of Clara Zetkin because she failed to discourage the women of the German Social Democratic (communist) Party from discussing sexual issues.

The record of your sins, Clara, is even worse. I have been told that at the evenings arranged for reading and discussion with working women, sex and marriage problems come first. They are said to be the main objects of interest in your political instruction and educational work. I could not believe my ears when I heard that. The first state of proletarian dictatorship is battling with the counter-revolutionaries of the whole world. The situation in Germany itself calls for the greatest unity of all proletarian revolutionary forces, so that they can repel the counter-revolution which is pushing on. But active Communist women are busy discussing sex problems and the forms of marriage—"past, present and future". They consider it their most important task to enlighten working women on these questions.[90]

Contemporary Marxists often have attitudes similar to Lenin's. Note the condescension and the blame of the victim expressed in this sentence:

The culture of class society has inculcated in women the notion that they can fulfill themselves within the narrow limits of sex; they still do not understand that the development of their true capabilities can come only from work.[91]

In the Marxist tradition, productive activity has become equated with the sort of work that men do under capitalism, and this sort of work is then viewed as the only source of human dignity. In fact, however, women's concern with the sexual, emotional and procreative aspects of human life speaks to needs that are equally deep and to human capacities that are equally capable of development. Within capitalist society, the sexual division of labor has given men such a limited access to this side of human life that they are hardly aware of how their potentialities for full sexual, emotional and procreative expression have been stunted and distorted. By contrast, the contemporary assignment to women of the primary responsibility for childbearing and childrearing, for sexual gratification and for emotional nurturance has placed them in a privileged position for perceiving the oppression endemic to the present mode of organizing these types of production. In the same way, women's historical experience has placed them in a privileged position for envisioning ways of childrearing that go beyond state nurseries, modes of sexual expression that go beyond heterosexual intercourse and forms of emotional connection that go beyond either romantic love or impersonal comradeship. Radical women are developing a vision of liberation that goes far beyond workers' control over the means of production, as traditionally defined. They pursue the abolition of sex-class as well as of class in the Marxist sense, and they see that classes must be abolished not only in the so-called public sphere but also in the private. Women will never be liberated by a politics that accepts the bourgeois view of family life as a private or personal matter and that regards the restructuring of intimate, sexual and parent-child relationships as something beyond the scope of politics. Nor will women ever be satisfied by a vision of socialism which assumes that true human fulfillment is to be found only through activity in the so-called public realm, outside the sphere of intimate relations.

Notes

1. Karl Marx, *The Poverty of Philosophy* (New York: International Publishers, 1963), p. 147.
2. Karl Marx, *Capital: A Critique of Political Economy.* Vol. 1: *The Process of Production* (New York: International Publishers, 1967), pp. 183-84.
3. Max Weber, *The Protestant Ethic and the Spirit of Capitalism,* trans. by T. Parsons (London, 1930).
4. Marx, *Capital,* vol. 1, p. 177.
5. Karl Marx, *Grundrisse: Foundations of the Critique of Political Economy,* trans. with a foreword by Martin Nicolas (New York: Vintage Books, 1973), p. 488.
6. Karl Marx, *Capital: A Critique of Political Economy,* Vol. 3: *The Process of Capitalist Production as a Whole* (New York: International Publishers, 1967), p. 820.
7. Ibid., p. 820.
8. Karl Marx, *Early Writings,* trans. and ed. by T.B. Bottomore (New York: McGraw-Hill, 1963), p. 125.
9. Marx, *Grundrisse,* p. 611.
10. Thomas Robert Malthus, *An Essay on the Principle of Population, as it Affects the Future Improvement of Society with Remarks on the Speculations of Mr. Godwin, M. Condorcet, and Other Writers,* ed. by Anthony Flew (Harmondsworth: Penguin Books, 1970), p. 203. Originally published 1798. Bob Young brought these views of Malthus to my attention.
11. Ibid., pp. 205-206.
12. Ibid., p. 203.
13. Karl Marx and Frederick Engels, *The German Ideology,* ed. by C. J. Arthur (New York: International Publishers, 1970), p. 61.
14. For discussions of the Marxist understanding of the public/private distinction, see the following: Charles E. Ellison, "Marx and the Modern City: Public Life and the Problem of Personality," paper read to the Mid-west Political Science Association, Cincinnati, Ohio, April 15-18, 1981; Linda J. Nicholson, " 'The Personal is Political': An Analysis in Retrospect," *Social Theory and Practice* 7, no. 1 (Spring 1981):85-98; and Nancy L. Schwartz, "Distinction Between Public and Private Life: Marx on the *Zoon Politikon,*" *Political Theory* 7 (May 1979):245-66; Richard Sennett, *The Fall of Public Man* (New York: Alfred A. Knopf, 1977).
15. Marx, *Grundrisse,* p. 488.
16. Karl Marx, *The Eighteenth Brumaire of Louis Bonaparte,* in Karl Marx and Frederick Engels, *Selected Works* (New York: International Publishers, 1968), p. 97.
17. Frederick Engels, "Socialism: Utopian and Scientific," in Marx and Engels, *Selected Works,* p. 432. Italics in original.

18. Marx says that, under capitalism, "labour always appears as repulsive, always as *external forced labour;* and not-labour, by contrast, as 'freedom and happiness'." Marx, *Grundrisse,* p. 611.

19. Engels writes: "And always this [ideal of justice, *eternal* justice] is but the ideologised, glorified expression of the existing economic relations, now from their conservative, and now from their revolutionary angle. The justice of the Greeks and Romans held slavery to be just; the justice of the bourgeois of 1789 demanded the abolition of feudalism on the ground that it was unjust . . . The conception of eternal justice, therefore, varies not only with time and place, but also with the persons concerned, and belongs among those things of which Mulberger correctly says, 'everyone understands something different'." Karl Marx and Frederick Engels, *Selected Works,* Vol. 1 (Moscow: Foreign Languages Publishing House, 1962), p. 624. This passage is quoted by W. L. McBride, "The Concept of Justice in Marx, Engels and Others," *Ethics* 85, no. 3 (April 1975):204-18. My present discussion owes much to this article.

20. *The Letters of Karl Marx,* trans. and intro. by Saul K. Padover (Englewood Cliffs, N.J.: Prentice-Hall, 1979), p. 275.

21. A number of major contributions to the debate on Marxism and justice have been collected in *Marx, Justice and History,* ed. by Marshall Cohen, Thomas Nagel, and Thomas Scanlon (Princeton: Princeton University Press, 1980). Cf. also *Marx: Morality. Canadian Journal of Philosophy,* Suppl. vol. 7, 1981. Also *Marx and Justice: The Radical Critique of Liberalism* (Totowa, N.J.: Littlefield Adams, 1982).

22. I. M. Young, "Toward a Critical Theory of Justice," *Social Theory and Practice* 7, no. 3 (Fall 1981):284.

23. John Rawls, *A Theory of Justice* (Cambridge: Harvard University Press, 1971), p. 3.

24. Marx, *Early Writings,* p. 153.

25. Ibid., p. 155.

26. Frederick Engels, *Herr Eugen Duhring's Revolution in Sciences,* trans. by E. Burns (New York: International Publishers, 1939), pp. 117-18. Quoted in McBride, "The Concept of Justice in Marx."

27. Marx, *Capital,* vol. I, p. 176.

28. Marx, *Early Writings,* p. 123.

29. Ibid., p. 125.

30. Ibid., p. 127.

31. Ibid., p. 127.

32. "Marriage Contracts for Support and Services," *N.Y.U. Law Review* (December 1974):1166. Cited by Muriel Nazzari, "The Significance of Present-Day Changes in the Institution of Marriage," *Review of Political Economics* 12, no. 2 (Summer 1980):63-75.

33. This is shown in detail by Nazzari.

34. A number of contributions to this debate have been conveniently collected by Bonnie Fox, ed., in *Hidden in the Household: Women's Domestic Labour Under Capitalism* (Toronto: The Women's Press, 1980). One influential contribution to the debate that is not included is John Harrison, "Political Economy of Housework," *Bulletin of the Conference of Socialist Economists,* Spring 1970. Another useful collection of papers on the topic of housework and one that represents a wider range of perspectives than Fox's is Ellen Malos, *The Politics of Housework* (London: Allison & Busby Ltd., 1980).

35. Marx, Appendix to *Capital,* vol. I (New York: Vintage Books, 1977), p. 1042. Cited by Nazzari, "Institution of Marriage."

36. Frederick Engels, *The Origin of the Family, Private Property and the State* (hereafter *Origin*) (New York: International Publishers, 1972), p. 137.

37. Marx and Engels write: "The bourgeois sees in his wife a mere instrument of production." Karl Marx and Frederick Engels, "Manifesto of the Communist Party," in Marx and Engels, *Selected Works,* p. 50.

38. Engels, *Origin,* p. 139.

39. Ibid., p. 134.

40. Ibid., p. 138.

41. Ibid., pp. 144-45.

42. Ibid., p. 135.
43. V. I. Lenin, *On the Emancipation of Women* (New York: International Publishers, 1934), p. 64.
44. Engels, *Origin,* p. 137.
45. Ibid., pp. 113-14.
46. Ibid., p. 135.
47. Marx, *Early Writings,* p. 156n.
48. Engels writes that, within the bourgeoisie, "the marriage is conditioned by the class position of the parties and is to that extent always a marriage of convenience . . . this marriage of convenience turns often enough into the crassest prostitution—sometimes of both partners, but far more commonly of the woman, who only differs from the ordinary courtesan in that she does not let out her body on piecework as a wageworker, but sells it once and for all into slavery. And of all marriages of convenience Fourier's words hold true: 'As in grammar two negatives make an affirmative, so in matrimonial morality two prostitutions pass for a virtue.' " Engels, *Origin,* pp. 134-35.
49. Ibid., p. 137 and Marx and Engels, "Manifesto," p. 50.
50. Juliet Mitchell, *Psychoanalysis and Feminism* (New York: Vintage Books, 1975).
51. Of course, this analysis was not developed by Marx and Engels, who seem to have shared the belief that only heterosexuality is natural. Marx describes "the relation of man to woman [as] the *most natural* relation of human being to human being." Marx, *Early Writings,* p. 154. Engels describes male homosexuality as an "abominable practice" (*Origin,* p. 128). Engels also seems to have held a romantic belief that women were "naturally chaste" or sexually exclusive (*Origin,* p. 117). Most contemporary Marxists, however, with some exceptions, mainly among the Maoists, assume that these remarks of Marx and Engels were mere expressions of Victorian prejudice and that the true spirit of Marxism is expressed by Engels's statement that we cannot imagine the form that a liberated sexuality would take (Engels, *Origin,* p. 145).
52. Engels, *Origin,* pp. 137-38.
53. Marx, *Capital,* vol. 1, pp. 489-90.
54. Ibid., pp. 394-95.
55. Engels, *Origin,* p. 137.
56. Ibid., p. 139.
57. Ibid.
58. Ibid., p. 144.
59. Ibid.
60. Ibid., p. 139.
61. Ibid., p. 128.
62. Engels writes: "The more the traditional sexual relations lost the naive primitive character of forest life, . . . the more oppressive and humiliating must the women have felt them to be, and the greater their longing for the right of chastity, of temporary or permanent marriage with one man only, as a way of release. This advance could not in any case have originated with the men if only because it has never occurred to them, even to this day, to renounce the pleasures of actual group marriage" (*Origin,* p. 117). On the other hand, Engels does castigate those "moralizing philistines" who judge the sexual norms of earlier societies by the standard of their own (*Origin,* pp. 96ff).
63. Ibid., p. 145.
64. Contemporary Marxists have also involved themselves in a number of other issues which are less obviously "class" issues; these issues include racism, destruction of the environment, nuclear power and war. The Marxist motivation for involvement in these issues is parallel to the motivation for their involvement in gender issues. In other words, they seek to demonstrate that all these social problems are generated originally by the capitalist mode of production and that, in order to solve these problems, it is necessary to transform that mode of production.
65. This is obviously a very controversial claim and to evaluate it adequately requires acquaintance with a vast literature. A clear overview of many of the main issues from a feminist perspective is Maxine Molyneux, "Women in Socialist Societies: Problems of Theory and Practice," in Kate Young, Carol Wolkowitz and Roslyn McCullagh, eds., *Of

Marriage and the Market: Women's Subordination in International Perspective (London: CSE Books, 1981), pp. 167-202.

66. Lenin's classic exposition of his conception of revolutionary organization occurs in V. I. Lenin, *What Is To Be Done? Burning Questions of Our Movement* (New York: International Publishers, 1961).

67. Sheila Rowbotham, "The Women's Movement and Organizing for Socialism," *Radical America* 13, no. 5 (September–October 1979):12. Rowbotham's article was later expanded and published with two others as a book: Sheila Rowbotham, Lynne Segal, and Hilary Wainwright, *Beyond the Fragments: Feminism and the Making of Socialism* (London: Merlin Press, 1979). The book struck a chord among many women on the left and was the focus of a large conference in Britain in the summer of 1980.

68. Berenice Fisher, "Who Needs Woman Heroes?" *Heresies* 3, no. 1 (Issue 9): 12-13.

69. Ibid:13.

70. Ibid.

71. In so-called third world countries which are being "developed" by the establishment of foreign-owned industry, the workers in many of the most profitable forms of factory production are predominantly female. The potential of these women for disruption of the capitalist system may be greater than that of women industrial workers in the advanced capitalist nations. Cf. Dian Elson and Ruth Pearson, "The Subordination of Women and the Internationalisation of Factory Production," in Young, Wolkowitz and McCullagh, eds., *Of Marriage and the Market,* pp. 144-166.

72. Lydia Sargent, *Women and Revolution: A Discussion of the Unhappy Marriage of Marxism and Feminism* (Boston: Southend Press, 1981), p. xiii.

73. Harry Braverman, *Labor and Monopoly Capital: The Degradation of Work in the Twentieth Century* (New York: Monthly Review Press, 1974). See especially chapter 17, "The Structure of the Working Class and Its Reserve Armies."

74. Ibid., p. 391.

75. Karen Nussbaum, "Women Clerical Workers," *Socialist Review* 49, pp. 151-59.

76. Evelyn Nakano, Glenn and Roslyn L. Feldberg, "Clerical Work: The Female Occupation," in Jo Freeman, ed., *Women: A Feminist Perspective,* 2nd ed. (Palo Alto, Calif.: Mayfield, 1979), p. 324.

77. Cuba is unique in writing into its marriage agreement the condition that both marriage partners are equally responsible for housework. Nevertheless, informal reports suggest that little effort is made to enforce this law.

78. Barbara Ehrenreich, "The Long View," *Moving On* (December 1977):19.

79. This is argued by Jane Humphries, "The Working Class Family, Women's Liberation and Class Struggle: The Case of Nineteeenth Century British History," *The Review of Radical Political Economics* 9, no. 3 (Fall 1977):25-41. It is also shown by Carol B. Stack, *All Our Kin: Strategies for Survival in a Black Community* (New York: Harper Colophon, 1975).

80. Lillian B. Rubin, *Worlds of Pain: Life in the Working-Class Family* (New York: Basic Books, 1976), p. 115.

81. Ibid., p. 172.

82. Ibid., p. 172.

83. Ibid., p. 171.

84. Ibid., p. 104.

85. Ibid., p. 114.

86. Ibid., p. 120.

87. Ibid., p. 151.

88. Ibid., p. 106.

89. Marx and Engels, *The German Ideology,* p. 51.

90. Lenin, *The Emancipation of Women,* p. 101.

91. Isabel Largnia and John Dumoulin, "Towards a Science of Women's Liberation," originally circulated under the title "For a Scientific Feminism."

9
The Politics of Radical Feminism

The Political Values of Radical Feminism

A distinguishing feature of the radical feminist conception of human nature is its attention to human reproduction. Reflection on modes of organizing procreation generates radical feminist insights on the basic structure of society, prompts radical feminist ideas for changing that structure and even suggests new social values for radical feminism.

Because human beings reproduce sexually, and because babies are extremely immature at birth, radical feminism points out that one of the fundamental tasks of every society must be to organize sexual activity and the rearing of children. Almost universally, societies organize these activities by allocating them according to sex. Men impregnate women, of course, but women are then assigned to perform most of the work required to rear infants and young children. Radical feminists claim that the sexual division of labor established originally in procreation is extended into every area of life. Even when pregnancy is not desired, women are expected to provide sexual gratification to men and they are expected to tend men's daily physical and emotional needs, just as they tend the needs of their children. Even those radical feminists who regard the distinction between the sexes as being ultimately a social construct claim that, in contemporary society, as in all other known societies, an individual's sex is the single, most influential factor in determining her social position, her life experiences, her physical and psychological constitution, her interests and her values. The distinction between the sexes, a distinction defined originally by reference to procreative function, is used to structure every aspect of human nature and human social life.

According to radical feminists, the bifurcation between male and female experience means that every society in fact has two cultures—the visible, national, or male culture and the invisible, universal, female culture. "There is always a women's culture within every culture."[1]

Males define and control all the institutions of all "national" cultures—including every purportedly socialist nation that has ever existed.

Because the male culture is dominant and in control in every nation, the "national" culture becomes synonymous with, and in fact is, the male culture. The female culture exists "invisibly", in subjection to the male-defined "national" culture.

What appears as one national culture, due to male propaganda, is in reality the male culture setting itself up as *the* national culture through the subordination of the female. The male army, the male government, the male religion, the male-run economy, the male-defined institution of the family, along with the male culture in the "narrower" sense—i.e., the male arts, sciences, philosophy, and technology—are defined as *the* national culture when in fact they represent nothing but the male view and interests.[2]

In fact, however, a female culture exists. It is based on "the cooking, cleaning and child 'raising' chores of the society" (page 338).

Radical feminists believe that the dominant male culture or patriarchy promulgates a certain picture of social reality, a picture that is clearly colored by male values. In this picture, male culture is portrayed as the only culture of a given society. Different male cultures may emphasize different values but, in general, "Men are seen as 'day', positive, forceful, aggressive, dominant, objective, strong, intellective, etc." (page 352). By contrast, "the concepts, habits, skills, art, and instruments of women in any period have been different from men's and have been ridiculed and/or suppressed by them" (page 336). Women's culture is denied and women are defined, in opposition to men, "as weak, 'night', passive, emotional, intuitive, mysterious, unresponsible, quarrelsome, childish, dependent, evil, submissive, etc." (page 352). Although these characteristics are considered undesirable for men, the patriarchy considers that at least some of them are appropriate for women. Passivity, vanity, subservience and self-sacrifice are not masculine virtues, but the male culture accepts and even values these qualities in women.

Feminists have usually accepted this male picture except for its evaluation of women. They have expressed dissatisfaction not with the picture itself, but rather with the world that it portrays. They have pointed out that this is a world of male dominance. Women may indeed be weak, emotional, vain, passive and subservient, but that is only because the male culture has made them that way. In fact, feminists typically claim, these characteristics are no more appropriate for women than they are for men; women and men should be judged by the same standards. Typically, then, feminists argue that women are capable of participating in male culture and of living up to male values. Liberal feminists claim that women are capable of autonomy and rationality; traditional Marxists claim that women are capable of transcending narrow family preoccupations and of participating fully in public life. The usual feminist response to male culture, therefore, has been to accept the accuracy of its picture of the world and to seek to change the social reality that this picture portrays.

Radical feminists respond quite differently to the dominant male picture. They too wish to change social reality, but they claim that even the existing reality is distorted by the way men present it, which is to glorify whatever has been defined as masculine and to disparage whatever has been defined as feminine. Thus, the male picture conceals the destructive values that underlie the male culture and obscures the positive contributions of the female culture.

Radical feminism acknowledges that there is considerable superficial variety in different male cultures. For instance, some male cultures value entrepreneurial talent, while others may value contemplation and withdrawal from practical life. Underlying the superficial differences, however, radical feminists believe that male cultures share a number of common but often unacknowledged values. These values include respect for formalism and abstraction, contempt for the routine tasks of bodily maintenance, disdain for infant care and, by association, for infants, a colonial attitude toward women's bodies, particularly women's sexuality, womanhatred and, according to Mary Daly, necrophilia or "love for those victimized into a state of living death."[3]

Even less accurate than its portrait of itself is the patriarchy's portrait of women. Radical feminists acknowledge that this portrait does capture certain aspects of women's culture:

> Because of the child raising role and the emphasis on personal relationships, women have a more personal, subjective view of things. Because of our subjection, women have a more fatalistic, passive view of the world. We are more in touch with our emotions and often find it necessary to use emotions in manipulating men. Through the imposition of a servant status on women, the female culture has elaborated a whole servile ethic of "self-sacrifice".[4]

Other aspects of female culture, however, fail to appear in the patriarchal picture. If they do appear, they seem to emerge by accident rather than by intention and they are not valued and respected as they deserve. According to radical feminists, the patriarchy fails to appreciate that women's culture values life rather than death. Women's culture is grounded on the values that inform women's work as mothers, nurturers and healers. These values include emotional expressiveness, gentleness, sensitivity to the feelings of others, closeness to nature, flexibility rather than rigidity, a distrust of abstract principles, the acceptance of all bodily functions and an acknowledgement of their capacity to bring pleasure.

According to radical feminists, liberal and Marxist feminists have internalized the values of the male culture. They want women to live according to male standards. Radical feminists, by contrast, challenge the values of the male culture. They do not want women to be like men. Instead, they want to develop new values, based on women's traditional culture.

> We are proud of the female culture of emotion, intuition, love, personal relationships, etc., as the most essential human characteristics. It is our male colonizers—it is the male culture—who have defined essential humanity out of their identity and who are "culturally deprived."
>
> We are also proud as females of our heritage of known and unknown resisters to male colonial domination and values.
>
> We are proud of the female principle and will not deny it to gain our freedom.[5]

The only aspects of female culture to be rejected are "all those that keep us subservient, such as passivity, self-sacrifice, etc."[6]

At first glance, radical feminism might appear to be advocating a straight-forward inversion of male values. After all, it condemns male culture for many of the same attributes on which that culture typically has prided itself. These attributes include military prowess, sexual aggression, analytical thinking, emotional "cool," adherence to principle and transcendence of everyday life. Moreover, radical feminism values many of those qualities that the male culture traditionally has despised. These qualities include an ability to nurture, a willingness to express emotion, a distrust of abstraction, a readiness to "take things personally," spontaneity, flexibility and an enjoyment of the routine details of everyday life. It is too simple, however, to interpret radical feminism as simply reordering patriarchal priorities. For one thing, radical feminists tend not to be concerned to order values hierarchically;[7] for another, radical feminists seem to share certain values with the patriarchy. Both patriarchy and radical feminism, for instance, value power and strength, and neither admires passivity or subservience. It is perhaps closer to the truth to say that radical feminism rejects some of the values of the patriarchy outright but that it accepts others with reservations. The reservations depend on a feminist reinterpretation of traditionally accepted values. Joyce Trebilcot calls these reinterpretations "feminist reconceivings."

A feminist reconceiving may involve a shift in the descriptive meaning of a concept, in its evaluative meaning or in both. An example is the concept of strength. Trebilcot states that strength is valued both by feminists and by the male culture but argues that each culture makes different judgments about what counts as strength, particularly strength in women. Under patriarchy, Trebilcot believes that a woman is not viewed as strong unless she is unattached and unattractive to men, often because of age; if an actual or even a possible man is around to protect her, then the term "strong" is reserved for him. By contrast, the feminist view of a strong woman allows a young or conventionally beautiful woman to be strong and allows her strength to be expressed in struggles with men: "The feminist strong woman is likely to be noisy, even loud; she is inclined to protest, to complain, to call attention to her difficulty."[8] Feminists also believe that strength is more likely to be indicated by flexibility than by rigidity.

The radical feminist concept of integrity, discussed briefly in Chapter 5, is another example of feminist reconceiving. So are the radical feminist reflections on power, to be discussed later in this chapter. A more surprising example, perhaps, is the radical feminist attention to wildness. Patriarchy views wildness as bad because it is rebellious and destructive. To radical feminists, however, wildness in women is a quality to be cherished. Susan Griffin associates women's wildness with the wildness of nature and of non-domestic animals. All these forms of wildness are victims of male taming and conquest.[9] For Mary Daly, women's wildness expresses their resistance to male domination.

> The call to wild-ize our Selves, to free and unfreeze our Selves is a wild and fantastic calling to transfer our energy and our Selves and to Sister Selves. . . .
>   Our call of the wild is a call to dis-possess our Selves of the shrouds, the winding sheets of words. . . . to dis-possess our selves of pseudo-bonding.[10]

Honor is another value which feminists are reconceiving. Adrienne Rich defines male honor as

> having something to do with killing: *I could not love thee, Dear, so much/ Lov'd I not Honour more* ("To Lucasta, on Going to the Wars"). Male

honor as something needing to be avenged: hence, the duel. . . .
  Men have been expected to tell the truth about facts, not about feelings.
They have not been expected to talk about feelings at all.[11]

Under patriarchy,

Women's honor, something altogether else: virginity, chastity, fidelity to
a husband. Honesty in women has not been considered important. We
have been depicted as generically whimsical, deceitful, subtle, vacillating.
And we have been rewarded for lying.[12]

Rich wants to redefine honor as an ideal that applies primarily not to relations
between men and men or even to relations between men and women, but to
relations between women.

It isn't that to have an honorable relationship with you, I have to understand
everything, or tell you everything at once, or that I can know, beforehand,
everything I need to tell you.
  It means that most of the time I am eager, longing for the possibility
of telling you. That these possibilities may seem frightening, but not
destructive to me. That I feel strong enough to hear your tentative and
groping words. That we both know we are trying, all the time, to extend
the possibilities of truth between us.
  The possibility of life between us.[13]

  A final example of feminist reconceiving is the value of nurturance. Nurturance
is viewed with approval by the patriarchy as well as by the feminist community,
but by patriarchy it is seen "as second-rate. Nurturing is a good thing for
women to do, but not good enough for men."[14] Under patriarchy, however,
nurturance is associated with self-sacrifice—which is why it is relegated to
women. By contrast, radical feminists emphasize that it is important for women
to nurture themselves as well as others. Sally Gearhart even defines a lesbian
as "a woman who seeks her own self-nurturance"[15]—in defiance of the patriarchal
mandate to sacrifice herself to men.
  What radical feminists seek, then, are new values around which to organize
society. They are looking for a way of expressing their vision of wholeness,
which will transcend the patriarchal dualisms of self and world, nature and
spirit, reason and emotion.[16] In part, radical feminist values are inspired by
women's spiritual or mystical experiences of connectedness with non-human
nature or with other women. In part, although their values are not identical
with the values of the female culture under patriarchy, they have their roots
in that traditional culture.
  Sara Ketchum distinguishes between female culture, which is the subdominate
or subordinate culture of women under patriarchy, and womanculture, which
is a counterdominant or resisting culture consciously created by feminists. In
creating the womanculture, feminists will draw on the best aspects of the female
culture but will reject "the values and concepts [that] tend to favor dominant
members of the dominant culture."[17] Many of the values of the womanculture
turn out to be values that have been traditionally relegated to the "private"
domain of spirituality or of "personal relations," and they are expressed in
concepts that sound foreign to political theory. For many radical feminists,
however, it is precisely the absence of those values that is their main reason
for rejecting "male" politics. In a review of Mary Daly's *Gyn/Ecology,* Susan
Leigh Star writes:

> In creating her web of language around the ideas of spinning, sparking and spooking, Mary uses words that have had profound meaning for me in my life, but which I have often felt embarrassed to talk about in a "political" environment: hope, innocence, courage, gentleness, compassion, *sacredness. Gyn/Ecology* frees up some of the coopted language and silences associated with these ideals, gives them new strength.[18]

Politics is concerned with the management or government of social groups. Political theory prescribes the acceptable or legitimate modes of government and criticizes modes of social organization that fail to meet its standards. Typically, political theory focuses on the structure of relations between the governors and the governed and ignores their experiential quality. It discusses liberty, equality and justice or citizenship, collectivity and freedom. These relations are conceived as "impersonal" ones. They hold between people who may or may not be acquainted with each other, who may love or hate each other, or have no emotional bond at all. By contrast with traditional political theorists, radical feminists emphasize the experiential quality of human relations—what are sometimes called "relationships." They are concerned about feelings and emotion and they advocate openness and trust, caring and affection, respect and non-manipulation.[19] These values presuppose people relating to each other as unique individuals rather than as interchangeable fellow citizens or comrades. The radical feminist value of sisterhood, for instance, is not at all symmetrical with the patriarchal value of brotherhood or male comradeship.

> Sisterhood, like female friendship, has at its core the affirmation of freedom. Thus sisterhood differs radically from male comradeship/brotherhood, which functions to perpetuate the State of War.
> Since sisterhood is deeply like female friendship, rather than being its opposite (as in the case of male semantic counterparts) it is radically Self-affirming. In this respect it is totally different from male comradeship/brotherhood, in which individuals seek to lose their identity.[20]

Radical feminists recognize, of course, that a superior experiential quality in relationships does not come about simply because it is wanted. Such a quality has structural preconditions. The basic precondition is the absence of institutionalized relations of power and domination. It is difficult to resist manipulation when that is one's only means of control; it is stupid to be open and trusting toward one who exploits you; and it is impossible to nurture adequately when one is not being nurtured oneself. Radical feminists recognize that there are many institutionalized relations of domination other than legal privilege or class prerogative. Naturally, radical feminists are particularly aware of gender domination and they perceive a gender hierarchy in every institution of daily life. To instantiate their values and to make possible the kinds of relationships they advocate, radical feminists believe that it is necessary to abolish gender as well as all other forms of hierarchy. As we shall see, much of the radical feminist critique of women's oppression focuses on gender domination in intimate relations and many of their proposals for social change concern the reorganization of the so-called private rather than the so-called public or political sphere.

To say this is misleading, however, for radical feminism does not recognize the legitimacy of a distinction between the private sphere of personal relations and a public sphere of impersonal politics. Although their values derive from women's experience in intimate relations, radical feminists believe that these values are appropriate to regulate all of society. One group describes its vision as "a nurturant society of love and trust."[21] This radical feminist approach constitutes a sharp break with the western tradition in political theory. Machiavelli argued forcefully that it was irresponsible and morally wrong to apply in politics the same moral standards that are appropriate in intimate relations. He thought that betrayal, deceit and violence were necessary and therefore justified in pursuit of public policy. Liberalism and Marxism are less forthright, but they preserve Machiavelli's distinction between a public and a private sphere with different standards of conduct appropriate in each. The liberal tradition distinguishes between public and private morality,[22] and the Marxist tradition insists that people should be judged by their "politics" rather than by their "private" reputations.[23] Capitalist propaganda attributes exclusively to Marxism-Leninism the view that the end justifies the means, but liberal states, too, expect their officials to perform acts that would be unthinkable for a private citizen. Only the anarchist tradition has required that political life should be judged by "personal" standards of caring, spontaneity and playfulness, "strength, vitality and joy."[24] I shall argue later that there are strong similarities between contemporary radical feminism and some traditional forms of anarchism.

Radical feminism popularized the slogan "the personal is political." In Chapter 5, we saw that one meaning of this slogan is that sexual politics, the systematic male domination of women and women's resistance to this domination, occurs in the so-called private as much as in the so-called public sphere. For radical feminists, the slogan has an additional meaning: that women's experience in personal life can provide the inspiration and the basis for a new vision of politics. Paradoxically, this is a vision of the withering away of politics as we know them because, in the radical feminist vision, all institutionalized relations of domination have disappeared.

Male Control of Women's Bodies: The Radical Feminist Analysis of Women's Oppression

On the radical feminist view, contemporary society is a patriarchy. It is organized in such a way as to negate the values of radical feminism. Radical feminist values are practiced only occasionally, in relations between women and in relations between women and children. Relations between men, however, exemplify values precisely opposed to those of radical feminism, as do the relations between men and women. The radical feminist analysis of women's oppression exposes the destructive quality of women's relations with men and shows how that destructiveness is rooted in the systematic coercive power that men have over women.

Radical feminists conceive patriarchy as a total system of domination. Through imperialism, racism and class society, groups of men seek to dominate each other. Most of all, however, they seek to dominate women who suffer characteristic forms of oppression in every patriarchal society. To legitimate its domination, the dominant male culture invents ideologies that define subordinate groups as inferior for one reason or another: as lazy, shiftless, stupid, greedy, emotional, sly, childish, barbaric or uncultured. Under patriarchy, many of these attributes are applied to women as well as to subordinate groups not defined primarily by sex. In addition, however, patriarchal ideology defines women in a way specific to their sex, as beings whose special function is to gratify male sexual desires and to bear and raise children. This ideology limits what women may do under patriarchy and delegitimizes whatever they in fact do that goes beyond the limits of the patriarchal definition.

The radical feminist analysis of women's oppression seeks to uncover the specific relations of domination that are concealed or legitimized by patriarchal ideology. While this ideology defines women as natural mothers or as sexual objects, the reality, according to radical feminism, is that women under patriarchy are forced mothers and sexual slaves.

1. FORCED MOTHERHOOD

The conventional wisdom of centuries has linked and sometimes identified women with motherhood. The earliest artistic representations of women stress their fertility and even in. the 20th century the identity between women and mothers often goes unquestioned. For instance, when Helene Deutsch, the noted Freudian analyst, wrote a two-volume work on *The Psychology of Women* in the mid-1940s, the first volume was called *Girlhood,* the second, *Motherhood.*

Not only have women always given birth to children; in every culture, they have been assigned the primary responsibility for the routine care of young children. For this reason, human motherhood has been seen not only as a biological relationship, but also as a special kind of social relationship that invariably exists between mothers and their offspring. "Mothering," for example, means the characteristic relation of nurturance that mothers are thought to establish with their children, and frequently "mothering" is extended to any relationship in which one individual nurtures and cares for another.

Patriarchal ideology has explained and justified the connection between women and children in a variety of ways. Sometimes women have been thought to possess a maternal instinct or some innate capacity for nurturance that is supposed to make them especially well suited for childrearing. Often women have even been thought to resemble children. For the ancients, women, slaves and children were considered to be similarly deficient in rationality, and even in modern times women and children are thought to lack the ability to look after themselves. Consequently, women and children are accorded special protection: certain language is not supposed to be used before them and in wars and shipwrecks they are supposed to be the first to be evacuated. The conventional psychological stereotypes of women and children are similar and disparaging; both are conventionally characterized as willful, emotional, weak and dependent. Even the prevailing standard of physical beauty for women portrays them as resembling children with wide eyes, a small nose, and an almost hairless body.

A successful ideology is never straightforwardly false; it does not describe the world as totally other than it is. Instead, a successful ideology is a seductive blend of truth and misrepresentation that distorts and obscures the facts rather than denying them completely. According to radical feminism, the patriarchal ideology of motherhood does exactly this. It identifies more or less correctly many of the special qualities that women develop as mothers, but it obscures the fact that these qualities are developed in a situation of domination.

Radical feminists assert that women are forced to be mothers. Patriarchy has many means of compulsion. Contemporary patriarchy deprives young women of adequate contraceptive information, and the contraceptives it does make available are inconvenient, unreliable, expensive and dangerous. Patriarchy limits abortions and often seeks to deny them entirely, but at the same time it subjects women to intense and unremitting pressure to engage in sexual relations. Usually the pressure is to engage in intercourse, a form of sexual interaction which does not give maximum sexual gratification to most women but which is the only form of sexual expression that results in pregnancy. Often women are simply raped: in the contemporary United States, a rape is said to occur every five minutes.

Patriarchal ideology and economics are additional forces compelling women to be mothers. According to patriarchal ideology, motherhood is the only way in which a woman can discover true fulfillment and genuine respect. Women who are unable to bear children are pitied; those who do not want to do so are described as "immature," "unfeminine," "unnatural" or "selfish." The poor conditions and low pay of most jobs available to women impel them into marriage, and having children is invariably the price a woman must pay in return for support from a man. Even when women engage in paid labor, radical feminists assert that they are often expected to perform for other adults the same kinds of nurturing tasks that mothers typically perform for their children.

Patriarchy not only forces women to become mothers; on the radical feminist view, it also determines the conditions of their motherhood. The male title "head of the household" is not merely honorific, even in contemporary industrial society. Individual men dominate within their homes: they are recognized as the ultimate source of discipline for children, and they evaluate their wives' childrearing performance by reference to their own criteria of how children should behave. Even if the individual father is absent, the system of patriarchy dictates the values to which women's childrearing should conform. According to radical feminism, these are the values of hierarchy and competition, abstract rationality and control, buying, fighting and winning. These patriarchal values are most clearly evident in capitalist society but radical feminists perceive them as modified only slightly under socialism. Given the predominance of these values, children must be reared to accept them. They must learn to submit to "superiors" and to dominate "inferiors"; they must learn to control their emotions and to take their places in existing institutions. Radical feminists view the apparent differences between patriarchal societies as merely superficial:

> The mode of childrearing in patriarchy is to control and dominate the child's will. In capitalism the child's will is directed towards serving the interests of corporations; in socialism it is directed towards serving the state. In patriarchy to nurture oneself is actually a revolutionary act.
>
> Therefore, although women are told that they are the nurturers of the world, women in patriarchy do not have the power to nurture—if by nurturance we mean supporting the unique will of the child to grow into its full potential as a self-regulating individual. Capitalism and socialism, the institutions of patriarchy—which control the mother and child—both conflict with nurturance.[25]

Mothers under capitalist patriarchy are expected to absorb the impact of two opposing sets of values. In opposition to a society that values individualism, mothers are expected to embrace their servitude voluntarily, to sacrifice their own interests completely to those of others and even to deny that they could have interests that conflict with those of their children. In addition, mothers are expected to create a nest of emotional warmth and security that will give life to beings who must leave that nest to survive in a death-dealing culture. Mothers under patriarchy continuously confront a dilemma: should they rear their children according to the life-giving values of trust and nurturance that their own experience as mothers allows them to realize, however incompletely? Should they encourage their children's desire "to live openly, creatively, trustfully and safely with others?"[26] Or should they foster instead the dominant patriarchal values that will enable their children to be accepted and to survive in male culture?

Under patriarchy, mothers are trapped between contradictory values. Inevitably, the experiential quality of their relationships is conflictual and ambivalent. Adrienne Rich has described some of those experiences. She speaks of the "tragic, unnecessary rivalry" she felt toward her own mother, and of her relationship with the father of her children: "I experienced my depressions, bursts of anger, sense of entrapment, as burdens my husband was forced to bear because he loved me; I felt grateful to be loved in spite of bringing him those burdens."[27] She speaks of the ambivalence that feminist mothers feel in rearing their sons:

> What do we fear? That our sons will accuse us of making them into misfits and outsiders? That they will suffer as we have suffered from patriarchal reprisals? Do we fear they will somehow lose their male status and privilege, even as we are seeking to abolish that inequality? Must a woman see her child as "the enemy" in order to teach him that he need not imitate a "macho" style of maleness? How does even a mother genuinely love a son who has contempt for women—or is this that bondage, misnamed love, that so often exists between women and men?[28]

Rich also speaks of the ambivalence that daughters have for their mothers:

> "Matrophobia" as the poet Lynn Sukenick has termed it is the fear not of one's mother or of motherhood, but of *becoming one's mother.* Thousands of daughters see their mothers as having taught a compromise and self-hatred they are struggling to win free of, the one through whom the restrictions and degradations of a female existence were perforce transmitted. Easier by far to hate and reject a mother outright than to see beyond her to the forces acting upon her. But where a mother is hated to the point of matrophobia there may also be a deep underlying pull towards her, a dread that if one relaxes one's guard one will identify with her completely. An adolescent daughter may live at war with her mother yet borrow her clothes, her perfume.[29]

The structure of mothering under patriarchy has consequences that stretch far beyond the individual family. It creates the masculine and feminine character types that, in the view of some radical feminists, are the main supports of patriarchy. Shulamith Firestone provides a revised Freudian account of how the emergence of femininity in girls and masculinity in boys is a response not to the difference in their parents' anatomy but rather to the difference in power between their mothers and their fathers in the context of a male-dominant culture.[30] According to Firestone, both girls and boys are attracted initially to their mothers because their mothers are their first caretakers. Soon, however, both sexes come to envy and admire their fathers' opportunities for what Firestone calls "travel and adventure." Both girls and boys try to win favor with their fathers but, whereas boys can do this by imitating masculine characteristics, girls can win male approval only by the feminine wiles of flirtation and seduction.

Firestone's politicized version of Freud is only one of several radical feminist accounts that demonstrate how the patriarchal institution of motherhood reproduces the fathers and mothers of the future. Adrienne Rich writes:

> Even if contraception were perfected to infallibility, so that no woman need ever again bear an unwanted child; even if laws and customs change—as long as women and women only are the nurturers of children, our sons will grow up looking only to women for compassion, resenting strength in women as "control", clinging to women when we try to move into a new mode of relationship. As long as society itself is patriarchal— which means antimaternal—there can never be enough mothering for sons who have to grow up under the rule of the Fathers, in a public "male" world separate from the private "female" world of the affections.[31]

Dorothy Dinnerstein argues a similar thesis.

> The deepest root of our acquiesence to the maiming and mutual imprisonment of men and women lies in a monolithic fact of human childhood: Under the arrangements that now prevail, a woman is the parental person who is every infant's first love, first witness, and first boss, the person who presides over the infant's first encounters with the natural surround and who exists for the infant as the first representative of the flesh. . . .
> It is in the relation with [the mother] that the child experiences the earliest version of what will be a lifelong internal conflict: the conflict between our rootedness in the body's acute, narrow joys and vicissitudes and our commitment to larger-scale human concerns.[32]

Dinnerstein's argument is complex but it consists at least partly in the assertion that cultural misogyny is rooted in infants' primitive rage toward their mothers, since mothers are the ones who, under traditional childrearing arrangements, must introduce children to their "irreparable" grief.

> the loss of this infant illusion of omnipotence—the discovery that circumstance is incompletely controllable, and that there exist centers of subjectivity, of desire and will, opposed to or indifferent to one's own— is an original and basic human grief.[33]

Dinnerstein believes that the motherrearing of children also explains the apparently universal identification of women with non-human nature: because "the early mother's boundaries are so indistinct," we fail "to distinguish clearly between her and nature, we assign to each properties that belong to the other."[34]

Motherhood is central to many radical feminist analyses of women's situation. On the one hand, motherhood is seen as the source of women's special values and characteristics, the basis of female culture.

> feminist culture is based on what is best and strongest in women, and as we begin to define ourselves as women, the qualities coming to the fore are the same ones a mother projects in the best kind of nurturing relationship to a child: empathy, intuitiveness, adaptability, awareness of growth as a process rather than as goal-ended, inventiveness, protective feeling toward others, and a capacity to respond emotionally as well as rationally.[35]

On the other hand, motherhood, as it is institutionalized under patriarchy, is one of the bases of women's oppression. The point is not simply that rearing children is hard and demanding work: the patriarchal sentimentalization of motherhood is challenged by authors as diverse as Betty Friedan and V. I. Lenin. Nor is the point even that the patriarchal definition of women as mothers excludes women from the public world outside the home, although that is certainly part of it. What radical feminists point out, and what no other feminists have stated so clearly, is that motherhood under patriarchy is forced labor. Men determine whether children are born, under what conditions they are reared and what counts as successful childrearing. Women have responsibility only for the daily details of a process whose totality is male-controlled. The structure of the patriarchal institution of motherhood corrupts and debases the quality of relationships between fathers, mothers, and children. Moreover, the patriarchal institution of motherhood is perhaps the fundamental process in reproducing male dominance. Male dominance is grounded in men's control of procreation, in the dominance of fathers over mothers. It is indeed rule by the fathers, and it is aptly called patriarchy.

2. SEXUAL SLAVERY

Women under patriarchy are not only mothers; according to radical feminism, women under patriarchy are also sexual slaves. These two aspects of women's condition are not independent of each other; most obviously, forced motherhood begins with sexual coercion. Patriarchal ideology, however, typically opposes women as sexual beings to women as mothers. The cult of the Virgin Mary is perhaps the most extreme example of this feature of patriarchal ideology, but the same phenomenon is also evident in the exaggerated respect given to mothers, as contrasted with the contempt and disgust shown toward women's sexuality. Of course, the patriarchal separation between motherhood and sexuality is largely an ideological illusion for, as we shall see, most mothers are still forced to exploit their sexuality, either for their husbands or in their paid work.

With the partial exception of mothers, the male culture defines women as sexual objects for male pleasure. For much of her life, every woman is evaluated continuously in those terms. Within the patriarchal culture of advanced capitalist nations even women's paid work is sexualized, and "sex appeal" is often an explicitly acknowledged qualification for "women's jobs." Not only do men evaluate women in terms of their sexual desirability; they also assume that women themselves are concerned primarily with being sexually desirable to men. When a man wears baggy clothing or refuses to shave or to curl or straighten his hair, he is assumed to be doing it for his own comfort. When a woman does the same thing, she is interpreted as "lazy" or as "punishing" men.[36] In the context of patriarchal culture, she is indeed defying men. If she is young, whatever she does is interpreted in sexual terms; she cannot avoid either reinforcing or challenging the patriarchal stereotype of women as sexual objects. Only when she is older and when male standards define her as no longer desirable does sexual interest in her fade. She then sinks into invisibility.[37]

Having defined women as sexual objects, men seek possession of those objects. They use ideological, economic, legal and even physical coercion to gain sexual possession of women. Superficially, women's sexual experiences differ widely from each other: some women are prostitutes, some are virgins; some women are raped, while others are protected with obsessive care. Beneath the superficial variety, however, radical feminists assert the underlying fact that men control women's sexuality for their own purposes. Radical feminists believe that women, whether they recognize it or not, are the sexual slaves of men.

Consequently, women's sexual relation with men is typically that of rape.

The form of rape most commonly recognized is straightforward physical coercion. Rape may not have existed in every society, but it is a defining feature of patriarchy. Women are always raped in war and are considered by the winning side to be part of its legitimate booty.[38] In the United States, the F.B.I. lists forcible rape as one of the three most violent crimes (the other two are murder and aggravated assault); it is the most frequently committed violent crime and, according to statistics, it is committed with increasing frequency. F.B.I. statistics reveal that reported rapes doubled from 27,620 in 1967 to 56,730 in 1976.[39] Only one rape in ten is reported to the police, but feminist publicity may be encouraging a higher rate of reporting. For this reason, it is difficult to know how much of the statistical increase in rape is due to increased frequency of reporting. If present trends continue, however, it is estimated that one woman out of three in the United States will be forcibly raped in her lifetime.

Overtly, patriarchal ideology condemns rape; covertly, it legitimizes rape by viewing it as normal. Under patriarchy, not only are women defined as sexual objects but men are regarded as having a "drive" toward heterosexual intercourse that is almost overwhelming and kept in check only by fear of the law and by respect of women's "honor." Sometimes these constraints are inadequate. Law enforcement may be uncertain, as in time of war, at night, or in secluded places, or there may be an excuse to disregard a women's "honor." In courts of law, accused rapists often use the defense that the victim "asked for it." As defined by the patriarchy, "asking for it" may include speaking to a man, dating him, allowing him into one's home, wearing "provocative" clothing or even going out alone at night. Because patriarchal culture defines women as sexually passive or receptive, it is thought reasonable to interpret a woman's uninterested behavior as expressive of sexual interest. Sometimes even outright refusal is interpreted as assent.[40] A woman is invariably considered to have assented to rape if she has previously engaged in sexual relations with anyone other than her husband. When a rape case comes to court, the investigations into the accuser's sexual history often make it seem as though the woman rather than the man is on trial. Although patriarchal ideology officially condemns rape, its asymmetrical definitions of male and female sexuality provide an implicit legitimation of rape.

According to patriarchal ideology, rape is wrong because it violates a woman's "honor." Her honor is defined either as her virginity or as her sexual fidelity to her husband. If a woman is unmarried, her "power to withhold or grant sexual access is an important bargaining weapon" in her search for a husband.[41] Rape laws are justified by partriarchy as being necessary in part to defend a woman's power to bargain her virginity. Under patriarchy, however, a woman's virginity is intrinsically valuable not to the woman herself, but only to her future husband.

> The consent standard in our society does more than protect a significant item of social currency for women; it fosters, and is in turn bolstered by, a masculine pride in the exclusive possession of a sexual object. The consent of a woman to sexual intercourse awards the man a privilege of bodily access, a personal prize whose value is enhanced by sole ownership . . . An additional reason for the man's condemnation of rape may be found in the threat to his status from a decrease in the "value" of his sexual "possession" which would result from forcible violation.[42]

Radical feminists point to this kind of statement to demonstrate that rape law is designed in fact to protect the interests of men rather than of women. "The man responds to this undercutting of his status as possessor of the girl with hostility toward the rapist; no other restitution device is available. The law of rape provides an orderly outlet for his vengeance."[43] That rape laws exist to protect the rights of men over women's bodies rather than the rights of women over their own bodies is shown even more clearly, if possible, by the fact that almost nowhere can a man be convicted of raping his own wife. Under patriarchy, her body is assumed to belong to him.

Needless to say, the radical feminist condemnation of rape is based on quite different grounds from the patriarchal condemnation. Radical feminists see rape as a political act which is oppressive on many levels. Susan Griffin quotes a group of French feminists whose statement against rape, delivered at the International Tribunal on Crimes Against Women, included the following words:

Legally, rape is recognized as a crime with physical aspects only; namely the penetration of the vagina by the penis against the will of the victim. In effect, however, the real crime is the annihilation by the man of the woman as a human being.[44]

Griffin herself writes:

Rape is an act of aggression in which the victim is denied her self-determination. It is an act of violence, which, if not actually followed by beatings or murder, nevertheless always carries with it the threat of death. And finally, rape is a form of mass terrorism, for the victims of rape are chosen indiscriminately, but the propagandists for male supremacy broadcast that it is women who cause rape by being unchaste or in the wrong place at the wrong time—in essence by behaving as though they were free.[45]

Continually, radical feminists emphasize that:

Rape is a punishment without crime or guilt—at least not subjective guilt. It is punishment, rather, for the *objective* crime of femaleness. That is why it is indiscriminate. It is primarily a lesson for the whole class of women—a strange lesson, in that it does not teach a form of behavior which will save women from it. *Rape teaches instead the objective, innate, and unchanging subordination of women relative to men.*[46]

It may be objected that men as well as women are raped, particularly in total institutions such as military forces, boarding schools and prisons. The recognition of this may seem to weaken the radical feminist claim that rape is the archetypal act "by which *all men* keep *all women* in a state of fear."[47] Radical feminists acknowledge that the rape of men occurs, but they claim that the special humiliation of rape for men lies precisely in the fact that a raped man is treated as a woman. He is subordinated, humiliated, and even called by the names that refer to women. It is not impossible for a woman to rape another woman but, one feminist has argued that it is impossible for a woman to rape a man.[48] According to Louanna Aptheker, the reason why a woman cannot rape a man is that a sexual assault on a man by a woman has a different social meaning from a sexual assault by a man on a woman or on another man. A female victim of male rape is considered to have lost her honor and to have been degraded, and something similar is considered to have happened to the male victim of male rape. But the male victim of a female "rapist" is either overtly envied by other men, if the rape is not painful, or else he is viewed as the victim of a perverted torturer. The divergent standards of masculine and feminine sexual "normality" under patriarchy result in very different interpretations being assigned to physically similar acts, depending on whether they are performed by males or by females. Whatever one thinks of this argument, the situations in which it could even arise are extremely atypical. The fact remains that, in contemporary society, it is extremely rare for there to be an event that even remotely resembles the rape of a man by a woman. Rape is typically an act performed by men and its social meaning is to degrade and "feminize" the victim.

> Rape, then, is an effective political device. It is not an arbitrary act of violence by one individual on another; it is a political act of *oppression* (never rebellion) exercised by members of a powerful class on members of the powerless class. Rape is supported by a consensus in the male class. It is preached by male-controlled and all-pervasive media with only a minimum of disguise and restraint. It is communicated to the male population as an act of freedom and strength and a male right never to be denied.[49]

To radical feminists, the rape carried out under the overt threat of physical force is only the tip of the iceberg. Another form of rape is prostitution. In *Female Sexual Slavery*, Kathleen Barry has documented the existence of a worldwide "traffic in women." Women are forced into prostitution through a variety of means, from deceptive promises of jobs or marriage, through the "invisible enslavement" of love and loyalty for a pimp, to physical kidnapping and imprisonment. Barry maintains that:

> *Female sexual slavery is present in ALL situations where women or girls cannot change the immediate conditions of their existence; where regardless of how they got into those conditions they cannot get out; and where they are subject to sexual violence and exploitation.*[50]

It is possible to enslave women only because patriarchal society has institutionalized the patriarchal definition of women as valuable primarily for their sexuality. Like rape, conventionally defined, prostitution is defined as a normal response to female sexual seductiveness and male sexual "drive." Even where prostitution is illegal, male law enforcement officials look away and the women themselves see no alternatives open to them. Barry writes:

> because it is invisible to social perception and because of the clandestine nature of its practices, it is presently impossible to statistically measure the incidence of female sexual slavery. But considering the arrested sexual development that is understood to be normal in the male population and considering the numbers of men who are pimps, procurers, members of syndicate and free-lance slavery gangs, operators of brothels and massage parlors, connected with sexual exploitation entertainment, pornography purveyors, wife beaters, child molesters, incest perpetrators, johns (tricks) and rapists, one cannot help but be momentarily stunned by the enormous male population participating in female sexual slavery. The huge number of men engaged in these practices should be cause for a declaration of a national and international emergency, a crisis in sexual violence. But

what should be cause for alarm is instead accepted as normal social intercourse.[51]

Patriarchal ideology refuses to acknowledge that prostitutes are coerced by men. Instead, it identifies prostitutes as seducers and exploiters of men, as masochists or as nymphomaniacs. Prostitutes are viewed as "fallen" or dishonorable women—by contrast with those women who preserve their honor for their husbands. Thus patriarchy draws a sharp line between prostitutes and "respectable" women, the latter being wives and especially mothers.

In response to the stigmas of patriarchal ideology, liberal feminism has sought to rehabilitate the reputation of prostitutes by asserting that prostitution is a legitimate job option for women, provided that no coercion is involved. The liberal conception of coercion, however, is much narrower than radical feminist or even than the·Marxist conceptions. Marxists see that people can be coerced by economic necessity, but radical feminists point out the total coerciveness of a social system in which the primary criterion for evaluating women, other than their fertility, is their sexual attractiveness to men. For this reason, radical feminists assert that even marriage, under patriarchy, is a form of prostitution or sexual slavery. As Karen Lindsey puts it, "We have long held that all women sell themselves: that the only available roles of a woman— wife, secretary, girlfriend—all demand the selling of herself to one or more men."[52]

Women are coerced into marriage by the same forces that impel them into prostitution—with the exception that, at least in the advanced capitalist nations, there is less physical kidnapping of wives. Women marry not only because they are deceived by the patriarchal ideology that defines "love and marriage" as women's highest fulfilment, but because they have few other options open to them. Occupational segregation forces women into the lowest-paid job categories and often requires of them the same kinds of service and nurturing functions that are expected of wives. "Free marriage" under patriarchy is therefore as illusory as the "free contract" between employer and employee under capitalism.

Once married, the wife has even less freedom than the typical wage worker. An early radical feminist examination of the legal institution of marriage found it structurally similar to the institution of American slavery. Sheila Cronan notes:

> Whereas the legal responsibilities of the wife include providing all necessary domestic services—that is, maintaining the home (cleaning, cooking, washing, purchasing food and other necessities, etc.), providing for her husband's personal needs and taking care of the children—the husband in return is obligated only to provide her with basic maintenance—that is, bed and board.[53]

Cronan claims that the husband has the right to decide where the couple will live and that he can charge his wife with desertion if she refuses to move— even if such a move requires her to change her citizenship. Although the legal requirement that the wife must reside with her husband may have changed in some places since "The Feminists" did their research for Cronan's article, the fact remains that most wives are forced to live with their husbands, simply because the husband is the major breadwinner. In these circumstances, a legal requirement of residency is unnecessary. In addition, the marriage laws of most advanced capitalist countries require wives to engage in sexual relations with their husbands and rarely admit even the legal possibility of rape within marriage. The inequality in the husband/wife relation allows radical feminists to argue that sexual relations occurring within marriage are in fact a form of rape.

From the radical feminist perspective, indeed, most heterosexual relations are indistinguishable from rape. The reality of the coercion involved is concealed, however, often even from the participants themselves, by the patriarchal mystification of romantic love. In consequence, Firestone says, "love, perhaps even more than childbearing, is the pivot of women's oppression today."[54]

Not only do women need a husband for economic support but they are taught to develop an emotional need for a man's commitment. In trying to achieve such a commitment, "one of (their) most potent weapons is sex."[55] The emotions which accompany this transaction are called "love" by the patriarchy. They are in fact, for women, a clinging possessiveness and, for men, an unrealistic idealization of the woman concerned—in order to elevate her to the man's social level. Firestone writes: "when we talk about romantic love we mean love corrupted by its power context—the sex class system—into a diseased form of love that then in turn reinforces this sex class system."[56] Firestone shows how this corruption occurs through the concentration of almost all emotional needs into erotic heterosexual relationships, through the "sex privatization" of women which blinds women to the depersonalized nature of men's attraction to them as sexual objects, and through the promulgation of a "beauty ideal" which controls and stereotypes women.

The rape of women is often concealed by the patriarchal mystique of romance. Sometimes, however, the patriarchy romanticizes unmistakable rape. Kate Millett was one of the first to point out that the degradation and humiliation of women is considered erotic by the patriarchy. In the first chapter of her best-selling *Sexual Politics,* Millett analyzes descriptions of heterosexual encounters as they occur in three respected 20th-century male novelists, D.H. Lawrence, Henry Miller, and Norman Mailer.[57] In all these encounters, Millett shows how the man uses his sexuality as a way of controlling and degrading women. She examines in detail the attitudes toward women that are implicit in these authors' descriptions of heterosexual activity and concludes that, for each author, heterosexual activity is a way of subjugating women. For Lawrence and Miller, the penis is a kind of deity, while for Mailer it is a gun or an avenger. Sex is identified with excretion or with violence and so women are viewed as "sexual comfort stations" or as legitimate victims.

Millett's exposure of the sadistic and womanhating values inherent in contemporary literary conceptions of heterosexual activity has been followed by increasing radical feminist protest against pornography. Feminists have always been aware that "pornography is sexist propaganda, no more and no less" because of its portrayal of women as glamorous sex objects for male pleasure.[58] Radical feminists now point out that contemporary pornography not only portrays women as sexual beings, it also seeks to eroticize the pain, humiliation, torture, dismemberment and even murder of women. For this reason, Kathleen Barry defines pornography as "the ideology of cultural sadism."[59] Robin Morgan sees pornography as providing a rationale for the rape of women, which is the core of male culture.

> Pornography is the theory, and rape the practice. And what a practice. The violation of an individual woman is *the* metaphor for man's forcing himself on whole nations (rape as the crux of war), on nonhuman creatures (rape as the lust behind hunting and related carnage), and on the planet

itself (reflected even in our language—carving up "virgin territory", with strip-mining often referred to as "rape of the land").[60]

Women under patriarchy are raped or romanticized—often both simultaneously. Partly for this reason, radical feminists argue that, under patriarchy, heterosexuality itself is oppressive to women. They claim more than the obvious point that patriarchy institutionalizes heterosexuality as a cultural norm, sometimes called heterosexism, a norm that deprives lesbian women of their right to sexual self-determination and defines them as sick, abnormal, and even criminal. Nor is the radical feminist point simply that heterosexism forces women to turn away from primary relations with other women, often preventing them from even considering the lesbian alternative. Although radical feminists make both these points, they argue in addition that heterosexuality is oppressive even to non-lesbian women—although the coercive power of patriarchy makes it impossible to tell for certain whether any woman is indeed non-lesbian.

Apart from the pressure it puts on women to suppress the lesbian side of their sexuality, patriarchal norms of heterosexuality define masculine and feminine sexuality in such a way that the woman is an object for the man. Adrienne Rich writes: "all objectification is a prelude to and condition of slavery."[61] The social inequality between women and men is reflected inevitably in heterosexual relations, even if the man decides not to utilize his male privileges and so makes the most conscientious efforts to participate in an egalitarian relationship with a woman. One radical feminist puts it this way: "every fuck is a rape even if it feels nice because every man has power and privilege over women, whether he uses it blatantly or subtly."[62] Another radical feminist writes:

> We do not doubt that there are straight relationships that derive their meaning and content from the people involved and not from the norm alone. But even in those relationships the male partner always has the option of falling back on "masculine" behavior in the sense of his conditioning, thereby forcing his partner to fall back on "feminine" acceptance in the sense of her conditioning. He has that option because the oppression of women by men has the status of a universal axiom: no one is surprised by "axiomatic" behavior, but this is precisely how everyone confirms it. That is why the important thing is not that there are men who do not exercise the option they have. The important thing is that the option exists whether or not it is exercised.[63]

3. MALE CONTROL OF WOMEN'S BODIES

According to radical feminism, the oppression of women is rooted in male control of women's fertility and women's sexuality. The accepted shorthand way of referring to this situation is as the male control of women's bodies.

From a non-patriarchal perspective, it is obvious that women's bodies are not only capable of but actually perform far more than sexual and procreative functions. It is on these functions, however, that radical feminism usually focuses, at least the radical feminism of the advanced capitalist nations. Women, indeed, suffer systematic exploitation by men in non-sexual and non-procreative ways: in African peasant societies, women do much of the heavy farming work;[64] in the new industries of the so-called Third World, women are the new industrial proletariat.[65] But it has been unusual for radical feminists in the United States to attempt to develop a feminist economic analysis, where "economics" is construed in the conventional sense of explaining the prevailing system of producing and distributing food, shelter, clothing, etc.[66] Even radical feminist discussions of women's work outside the home usually emphasize the sexualization of that work or its similarity to mothering.

Several explanations are possible for the radical feminist emphasis on sexuality and mothering. One might be a belief that the patriarchal definition of women as mothers and sex objects in fact reflects the reality of women's situation under patriarchy. Radical feminism flourishes mainly in the advanced capitalist nations; it may be that women's work is defined more in terms of sexuality and procreation under western capitalism than it is in other parts of the world where women are also primary food producers. Another reason for the radical feminist emphasis on sexuality and procreation might be a belief that male dominance in all its manifestations is grounded ultimately on men's control over women's sexual and procreative capacities. This belief would fit well with the tendency of many radical feminists to believe that biological differences are the cause of male dominance. Certainly it is true that patriarchal culture has virtually excluded procreation and sexuality from the domain of politics and in that way excluded them from systematic critical scrutiny. The radical feminist emphasis on fertility and sexuality may be a necessary counterbalance to patriarchal political theories.

The first radical feminists, writing at the end of the 1960s, modeled their writings on existing political theory, particularly, though not exclusively, on Marxist theory. The influence of traditional ways of theorizing can be seen in the work of Ti-Grace Atkinson, who wrote a conventionally outrageous article challenging "the institution of sexual intercourse," but whose definition of "institution" appealed to the work of the established, liberal, Harvard philosopher John Rawls.[67] Similarly, Shulamith Firestone imitated the language of Marxist theory in her attempts to identify the "material base of male dominance."[68] The radical feminist writers who emerged in the 1970s gradually abandoned the "linear" "male" style of traditional male political theory. Radical feminist writing has always been lively and colloquial, scattered with vivid and immediately jolting examples of women's oppression. In the 1970s, radical feminist authors continued their use of striking examples, but they tried less frequently to incorporate these into an explicit and comprehensive system. Instead, the most influential radical feminist writing became increasingly poetic, broadening its appeal but becoming more difficult to translate into traditional political terms. Susan Griffin, whose own feminist writing began with an analysis of rape that, in form at least, was fairly traditional but who moved rapidly into poetry, reports:

> In a recent conversation with Kathy Barry, a feminist scholar, thinker, writer, friend, she told me that she no longer likes to use the word *theory* for our thought since that word implies a special kind of separation between thought, feeling and experience which has sprung from patriarchy.[69]

What constitutes a theory, of course, is open to a number of interpretations. These interpretations depend in part on one's epistemology or theory of knowledge, in part on the phenomena that need a theoretical explanation. For instance, one might expect a theory of film criticism to take a different form from a theory of geological formation. When social phenomena have to be explained, it is common to think of a theory as postulating certain underlying mechanisms that will provide a causal explanation of observed patterns of regularities in those phenomena. If one thinks of a theory in this way, it is evident that an adequate theoretical account of any social phenomena presupposes an adequate description of those phenomena: if the phenomena in question are misdescribed, if existing regularities are unrecognized or if regularities are asserted that are unimportant or even nonexistent, then the theoretical inquiry will be misdirected. For this reason, although it is possible to distinguish between theories and descriptions in terms of the levels of reality to which they refer, it is impossible to make a sharp separation between theory and description. Descriptions of reality are theory laden, at least in the sense that they are compatible or incompatible with certain theoretical accounts; similarly, although theories are supposed to explain rather than contradict observations or descriptions, they may imply that certain observations have been misinterpreted or that the supposed data should be redescribed.

When some radical feminists deny that they are building theories, their denial can be interpreted in several ways. On the one hand, they may mean to reject prevailing epistemological views about the ways in which systematic accounts of reality are created and validated. This interpretation will be discussed in Chapter 11. On the other hand, they may mean that they are doing something that is often thought of as preliminary to theory, namely, that they are engaged in description. Radical feminists claim that even existing descriptions of reality are male-biased and that patriarchal language itself distorts reality. In particular, patriarchal language conceals the way in which women are systematically oppressed and exploited. Consequently, radical feminists see their first task as being simply to redescribe reality and, in so doing, to reconstruct patriarchal language. Radical feminists in the United States often call this process "naming." Mary Daly writes, "women have had the power of naming stolen from us."[70] She believes that women must reclaim the right to name, that the "liberation of language is rooted in the liberation of ourselves."[71]

> The truth behind the manifestations of the charism of "tongues" is the need to break out of the iron mask of language forms that are strangling us. Women's new hearing and naming is cosmic upheaval, in contrast to this charism which is a controllable and cooptable ripple of protest. Feminist naming is a deliberate confrontation with language structures of our heritage. It transcends the split between nonrational sounds of "tongues" and the merely rational semantic games of linguistic analysis, for it is a break out of the deafening noise of sexist language that has kept us from hearing our own word.[72]

What radical feminism offers, then, is a fundamental challenge to conventional ways of describing reality. In this, it differs from liberal feminism, whose critical thrust consists in its making new value judgments about facts that are generally recognized. For instance, liberal feminism might argue that the lack of maternity leave or sex-segregated sports programs are unjust. The radical feminist analysis, however, challenges not only conventional value judgments about existing reality, but also conventional descriptions of that reality. It suggests that what has been called consent must be renamed coercion, that supposedly free women are in fact enslaved. The goal of radical feminist analysis is a "change in consciousness,"[73] a change that might be described as a paradigm shift. Radical feminist analysis aims to redescribe reality, to make us see old facts in new ways and to perceive regularities where we saw none before. The radical feminist use of poetry and metaphor is designed to facilitate this shift of paradigm.

The radical feminist paradigm is still emerging. As Griffin says, "The atrocities continue, and we have not yet even named them all."[74] Radical feminists differ somewhat in how they name reality. Mary Daly speaks of men as necrophiliacs and as "nothing-lovers."[75] Andrea Dworkin writes:

> Men love death. In everything they make, they hollow out a central place for death, let its rancid smell contaminate every dimension of whatever still survives. Men especially love murder. In art they celebrate it, and in life they commit it. They embrace murder as if life without it would be devoid of passion, meaning and action, as if murder were solace, stilling their sobs as they mourn the emptiness and alienation of their lives.
> Male history, romance, and adventure are stories of murder, literal or mythic. Men of the right justify murder as the instrument of establishing or maintaining order, and men of the left justify murder as the instrument of effecting insurrection, after which they justify it in the same terms as men on the right. In male culture, slow murder is the heart of eros, fast murder is the heart of action, and systematized murder is the heart of history.[76]

Adrienne Rich disagrees. She insists that "slavery and death are in fact two different states" and believes that it is more accurate to understand patriarchy in terms of slavery.[77] Kathleen Barry uses the concept of "sex-colonization," showing it is a "cross-cultural network" or system

> which includes wife-battery; incest; marital rape; the Muslim code of "honor" regarding female chastity; marriage through seclusion, arrangement, and bride-price; genital mutilation; and enforced prostitution, of which pornography is the ideology. She includes in this system . . . taboos on and punishment for lesbian behavior, including the vogue for pseudolesbian pornography . . . and the wipeout of actual lesbian history and expression.[78]

At the end of this chapter and in Chapter 11, I shall discuss some of the ways in which radical feminist thinking both resembles and differs from traditional conceptions of theory. Whether or not it is theoretical in the traditional sense, however, radical feminist writing is clearly not neutral with respect to traditional political theory. It is developing an account of social reality which forms a sharp contrast with the account presented by male theory and language. Central to this account is the concept of male dominance expressed universally through male control of women's sexual and procreative capacities. Artemis March writes:

> "feminist materialists" (Griffin, 1971; Dworkin, 1974, 1977; Brownmiller, 1975; Morgan, 1978; Firestone, 1971) believe that the primary object of patriarchal control is women's bodies/sexuality. They view the exploitation of women as direct, and as physically violent and coercive. Their work points to the patriarchal inseparability of violence and sexuality and most of these writers find that behavior to be motivated by fear/awe/envy/ hatred of women. These writers (and I include myself) are more likely to turn to religious and medical institutions and sources as the primary agencies solidifying, enforcing and reproducing male control and misogyny.[79]

Similarly, Catherine A. MacKinnon, writing in a more formal, academic mode than many of the most influential radical feminists, sums up in this way the contemporary feminist analysis of women's oppression:

> Sexuality is to feminism what work is to Marxism: that which is most one's own, yet most taken away . . .
> The molding, direction, and expression of sexuality organizes society into two sexes—women and men—which division underlies the totality of social relations . . . As the organized expropriation of the work of some for the benefit of others defines a class—workers—the organized expropriation of the sexuality of some for the use of others defines the sex, woman. Heterosexuality is its structure, gender and family its congealed forms, sex roles its qualities generalized to social persona, reproduction a consequence, and control its issue.[80]

Radical feminists may vary in their naming, but they share a general agreement about the basic structure of social reality. It is a total system of male domination whose institutions form an almost impenetrable grid. This grid is a male construction that enables men to control women's bodies and that traps women as forced mothers and as sexual slaves.

Living the Revolution:
Radical Feminist Proposals for Social Change

"The way a question is asked limits and disposes the ways in which any answer to it is given." The way a problem is stated limits and disposes the ways in which its solution is conceived. The way that radical feminism formulates its analysis of women's oppression suggests a certain politics of women's liberation and rules out certain other political approaches.

Most urgently, the analysis of radical feminism points to the need for women to escape from the cages of forced motherhood and sexual slavery. The immediate goal of radical feminist politics must be for women to regain control over their own bodies. In the long run, radical feminism seeks to build a womanculture, a new society informed by the radical feminist values of wholeness, trust and nurturance, of sensuality, joy and wildness.

In order to create such a society, radical feminists need to prepare themselves. They need a womanspace, a space free from male intrusion. In this space, women can nurture each other and themselves. They can begin to practice their own values and become clearer about them by doing so. They can develop the skills and the strengths forbidden to women under patriarchy. They can begin to lay the foundations on which the womanculture will be built.

Feminism has always required a degree of separatism. Patriarchy, after all, has separated women from the rest of humanity, forcing them to inhabit a subordinate culture and providing images of women that tend to be "negative and derogatory. . . . Since most members of a given society think in terms of the concepts and assumptions of the dominant culture, this situation will foster a sense of inferiority in members of the oppressed group."[81] To overcome this sense of inferiority and to develop their own solidarity as an oppressed group, feminists have always found it necessary to band together against their oppression. The groups they have formed have not always excluded men entirely, although men have always been a minority in them. Nor have such groups always provided a context in which women can live much of their lives. Most often, feminist groups have been interest group organizations, organized along traditional political lines to further the interests of women as such. In the 1960s, women also separated from men for the purpose of "consciousness raising," to discuss their own experience and to reinterpret that experience in the light of an explicit recognition of male dominance. The contemporary radical feminist concept of womanspace or separatism is an extension of the kinds of separatism that have always been practiced by feminists, and by other oppressed groups. Instead of just separating themselves for brief periods, however, many radical feminists try to separate as much as possible of their lives from men, particularly the most intimate parts of their lives.

1. LESBIANISM

Given the radical feminist analysis of women's oppression, separatism in intimate relationships makes good sense. Unlike other feminists, radical feminists do not define women's oppression primarily in relation to the world outside the home. For radical feminists, women's oppression does not consist primarily in the lack of equal job opportunities or in exclusion from full participation in the public world. Instead, radical feminists see women as oppressed primarily in so-called intimate relations: in sexual and procreative relations, in the home, in the sphere of life that the male culture defines as personal rather than as political.

On the radical feminist analysis, marriage is one of the primary institutions oppressing women since it sanctions the most widespread forms of forced motherhood and sexual slavery. The first condition for escaping from forced motherhood and sexual slavery is escape from the patriarchal institution of marriage. Consequently, radical feminists urge women either not to marry or to leave their husbands. A few women who define themselves as radical feminists reject this tendency. Pat Mainardi complains that some of the arguments used against marriage are contradictory:

> The line used by the Feminists: that married women had a class privilege over other women, that single women were more oppressed, that therefore married women must give up their class privilege of marriage and leave their husbands, was actually contradictory to their other line that married women were more oppressed.[82]

Mainardi's voice is part of a tiny minority, however, and is quite out of harmony with the dominant radical feminist view that marriage is a way in which women are seduced into betraying their own deepest needs and into supporting the system of male dominance.

> I realized that when I was married I had been bought off. I had accepted being subservient, sexually available, and keeper of his home in return for some degree of economic security and social acceptance. I had become a fat hen who gave up her freedom for regular corn.[83]

Even more firmly entrenched than the institution of marriage is the institution of heterosexuality.

> Heterosexuality keeps women separated from each other. Heterosexuality ties each woman to a man. Heterosexuality exhausts women because they

struggle with their man—to get him to stop oppressing them—leaving them with little energy for anything else.[84]

The normative status of heterosexuality forces women to limit themselves sexually and emotionally to relationships with members of the caste that oppresses them, while denying them the possibility of establishing meaningful relationships with other women. Viewed in this light the straight norm is not really a sexual norm at all, but a powerful instrument in the perpetuation of the power relationship between the sexes.[85]

Because heterosexuality buttresses patriarchy, genuine feminists must be lesbians. Charlotte Bunch writes:

Being a Lesbian means ending identification with, allegiance to, dependence on, and support of heterosexuality. It means ending your personal stake in the male world so that you join women, individually and collectively, in the struggle to end your oppression. Lesbianism is the key to liberation and only women who cut their ties to male privilege can be trusted to remain serious in the struggle against male dominance.[86]

Ti-Grace Atkinson argues similarly:

(Can you imagine a Frenchman serving in the French army from 9 to 5, then trotting "home" to Germany for supper and overnight? That's called game-playing, or collaboration, not political commitment.)
It is this commitment, by choice, full-time of one woman to others of her class that is called lesbianism. It is this full commitment, against any and all personal considerations if necessary, that constitutes the political significance of lesbianism.
There are women in the Movement who engage in sexual relations with other women, but who are married to men; these women are not lesbians in the political sense. These women claim the right to private lives; they are collaborators.
There are other women who have never had sexual relations with other women, but who have made and live a total commitment to this Movement; these women are lesbians in the political sense.[87]

The definition of "lesbian" that Atkinson uses here is unusual because it does not define lesbianism primarily in terms of sexual interest. Elsewhere Atkinson argues that, while the primary emotional and political bonds of feminists should be with other women, it is better to refrain from sexual relations since those are too disruptive of the smooth functioning of feminist organizations.[88] Within radical feminism, there has been a tendency to define a lesbian "not by where she puts her hands but by where she puts her energy." Adrienne Rich talks about the "lesbian continuum," by which she means

a range—through each woman's life and throughout history—of woman-identified experience; not simply the fact that a woman has had or consciously desired genital sexual experience with another woman. If we expand it to embrace many more forms of primary intensity between and among women, including the sharing of a rich inner life, the bonding against male tyranny, the giving and receiving of practical and political support; if we can also hear in it such as associations as *marriage resistance* and the "haggard" behavior identified by Mary Daly . . . we begin to grasp breadths of female history and psychology which have lain out of reach as a consequence of limited, mostly clinical, definitions of "lesbianism".[89]

Some radical feminists, however, have rejected the tendency to broaden the term *lesbian* on grounds that this would understate the sexual component of women's relationships with each other and make *lesbian* mean little more than *feminist*. A purely "political" definition of lesbianism obscures the fact, deeply threatening to male dominant society, that women are often interested in each other in a sexual way. For many radical feminists, precisely the fact that lesbianism is sexual makes it political. Even lesbians who did not consciously choose lesbianism or who have not developed a sophisticated feminist consciousness defy the patriarchy directly, simply by being lesbian. Merely by virtue of their sexuality, they challenge the patriarchal definition of women.

> Lesbianism is a threat to the ideological, political, personal, and economic basis of male supremacy. The Lesbian threatens the ideology of male supremacy by destroying the lie about female inferiority, weakness, passivity, and by denying women's "innate" need for men.[90]

This is as true of lesbians of color as it is of white lesbians.[91]

Because lesbianism has deeply subversive political implications within a society where women are defined as sexual objects for men, radical feminism encourages women to become lesbians. A few self-defined radical feminist women have resisted this push, claiming that it denies women the freedom to determine their own form of sexual expression.[92] To most radical feminists, however, this claim reasserts the liberal view that sexuality is a matter of personal choice or private morality, of no concern to anyone other than the individuals directly involved. Radical feminists reject this liberal conception of a private moral realm because it constitutes a denial that the personal is political.

> As the question of homosexuality has become public, reformists define it as a private question of who you sleep with in order to sidetrack our understanding of the politics of sex. For the Lesbian-Feminist, it is not private; it is a political matter of oppression, domination, and power.[93]

> In a world devoid of male power and, therefore, sex roles, who you lived with, loved, slept with and were committed to would be irrelevant. All of us would be equal and have equal determination over the society and how it met our needs. Until this happens, how we use our sexuality and our bodies is just as relevant to our liberation as how we use our minds and our time.[94]

Under patriarchy, radical feminists see lesbianism as inherently revolutionary. Women who refuse to come out as lesbian are "fat hens" who "primarily wanted the farmer to treat them a little better."[95] They are bought off with heterosexual privilege: "legitimacy (you are a real woman if you are with a man—a sexual definition again), prestige, money, social acceptance, and in some token cases political acceptance."[96] Those who are genuinely committed to the defeat of the patriarchy must come out as lesbians:

> A lesbian is the rage of all women condensed to the point of explosion.[97]

> We live in a male supremacist shitpile. At its most basic level this shitpile is upheld by fucking, marriage and breeding. Straight women serve this system by serving their men. Lesbians reject it by saying we won't fuck,

we won't marry, we won't breed and we'll damn well do as we please.[98]

To be a Lesbian is to love oneself, woman, in a culture that denigrates and despises women. The Lesbian rejects male sexual/political domination; she defies his world, his social organization, his ideology, and his definition of her as inferior. Lesbianism puts women first while the society declares the male supreme. Lesbianism threatens male supremacy at its core. When politically conscious and organized, it is central to destroying our sexist, racist, capitalist, imperialist system.[99]

In the early 1970s, the politics of intimate relations assumed great importance within the radical feminist community. Once heterosexuality had been left behind, new ways for women to live together would have to be developed. Rita Mae Brown wrote:

> We must move out of our old living patterns and into new ones. Those of us who believe in this concept must begin to build collectives where women are committed to other women on all levels—emotional, physical, economic and political. Monogamy can be cast aside, no one will "belong" to another. Instead of being shut off from each other in overpriced cubicles we can be together, sharing the shitwork as well as the highs. Together we can go through the pain and liberation of curing the diseases we have all contracted in the world of male dominance, imperialism and death. Women-identified collectives are nothing less than the next step towards a Women's Revolution.[100]

Lesbian collectives, however, experienced many of the same difficulties that were encountered by "mixed" collectives of the same period. One lesbian remembers with pain: "About a year ago I joined a lesbian collective that lived together one painful week and broke up, largely because several of us had not dealt with our class privilege."[101] Like heterosexual women, most lesbians are presently living alone or in couples, although they do not necessarily view this state of affairs as permanent. Yet radical feminists are now prepared to acknowledge that emotional changes come slowly and cannot be forced. The restructuring of intimate relations must occur in response to felt needs rather than for the sake of abstract political principles or what has come to be called, tongue in cheek, "political correctness." Political correctness is seen as a typically male concept and Rita Mae Brown now advises women not to act only "on principle."[102]

In spite of their suspicion of abstract political correctness, radical feminists have not abandoned their central principle that the personal is political. One indication of the importance of this principle is the volume and intensity of the recent debate over the propriety of sado-masochistic forms of sexual expression within the lesbian community. For liberal feminism, the form in which one expresses one's sexuality is a private matter, so long as the participants are all consenting adults. Traditional Marxism has also excluded sexuality from the sphere of politics, with the exception of some recent reflections on how the oppression of homosexuals supports the capitalist family.[103] For radical feminism, however, lesbian sadomasochism is a matter of intense political concern.

The radical feminist controversy over sadomasochism is not a controversy over whether sadomasochistic practices should be tolerated or even outlawed. No radical feminist would call on the patriarchal state in order to ban any voluntary lesbian practice. The debate is rather over the question whether sadomasochism can be accepted as a legitimate part of the womanculture. Some radical feminists attack sadomasochism as a coercive form of sexuality that is typically patriarchal; those who practice it are accused of violating the central values of feminism:

> For women to degrade and hurt each other is to conform to and to confirm male myths that women are first and foremost sexual objects with all else peripheral, that we are so sex starved and orgasm focused that we will do whatever it takes to make us come—a myth that has steeped our psyches all too often in self loathing.
>
> Lesbian-feminist s&m clearly models itself after straight and gay male cultures, cultures in which there is little room for women to discover and define sexuality beyond male constructs. We will, as women identified feminists, survive and flourish only to the extent that we can create positive, loving and life affirming relationships with each other, relationships that are the very pulse of our women's culture.[104]

In reply, those who advocate sadomasochism argue that sadomasochism is concerned with fantasy rather than with reality, that the appearance of violence may be illusory. They point out that both participants agree to engage in a sadomasochistic encounter and that, contrary to appearances, the masochist is actually in control because she can halt the encounter at any time. Sadomasochists are engaging in radical sexual exploration but, by condemning sadomasochism, "The women's movement has become a moralistic force and it can contribute to the self-loathing and misery experienced by sexual minorities."[105]

Even so, reply the critics, sadomasochism eroticizes violence and thus perpetuates the values of the male culture.

> If we are unlikely to choose to give and take abuse, to humiliate and be humiliated, to exploit and be exploited in ordinary encounters, then to affirm this behavior in our sexual relationships is possible only when we separate our sexuality from the rest of our lives and objectify it. The separation between our sexual lives and everything else that we do is patriarchal through and through. So is objectified sexuality.
>
> Sadomasochistic sexuality presupposes and advocates fragmented modes of being and doing. These modes are so fragmented that different, indeed contradictory, rules are employed to govern the different fragments. This kind of fragmentation stands in polar opposition to feminist visions. Feminism is about reintegration into an holistic mode of being and doing. We must reaffirm our commitment to the integrity of our bodies and our selves, a commitment which the vindication of sadomasochistic sexuality renders hopelessly compromised.[106]

While the radical feminist discussion of sadomasochism cannot be recapitulated here in full, the discussion does illustrate the centrality of sexuality in the radical feminist conception of human nature and gender politics.

2. BUILDING A WOMANCULTURE

Although lesbianism is one step on the way to "a Women's Revolution," radical feminists are well aware that there are many other steps along the way. Lesbianism provides the basis for restructuring intimate relations so that they can instantiate radical feminist values. To restructure other relations of daily life, it is necessary to create other institutions that will fulfill women's daily needs. These new institutions must be built by women only. Men's presence would bring the inevitable intrusion of male values; men's absence is necessary for women to heal their male-inflicted wounds, to strengthen their bonds with other women and to develop a distinctively female perspective on the world.

Radical feminist women are in the process of creating a wide variety of alternative institutions. A few of these are total communities, usually rural communities, where women seek to build new lives, as independently as possible of the patriarchy. Other radical feminist institutions focus on fulfilling particular needs, and the list is practically endless. It includes women's health centers which provide services ranging from abortion to feminist therapy, which stress disease prevention, and which teach women how to treat themselves through such techniques as herbal medicines and cervical self-examination. It includes women's educational projects that range from automobile maintenance to reading the tarot, from menstrual extraction to acupressure massage, from karate to feminist political theory. It includes the revival of a specifically women's spirituality, based on wicca or witchcraft, the ancient goddess religion driven underground by Judaeo-Christianity. It includes women's businesses, ranging from printing and publishing, through bookshops and restaurants, to carpentry and furniture removal. It includes services to women in crisis, such as telephone crisis lines, anti-rape squads and the provision of shelters to battered women. It includes the creation of a new world view, seen from women's perspective and expressed through journalism, radio, music, film, dance, poetry, painting, photography, sculpture and literature.

In spite of the variety of these radical feminist enterprises, they are all directed toward certain common purposes. Simultaneously, they are supposed to benefit those who build the new institutions, those who are their clients and feminism itself. In the radical feminist view, these purposes ultimately are inseparable from each other.

The most immediate aim of radical feminist enterprises is to fulfill women's needs since, in the radical feminist view, women's needs are not being met adequately by the patriarchy. Either women's needs are being ignored entirely or they are being exploited for male profit. For instance, until feminists opened shelters for battered women, there was simply nowhere for such women to go. Women's need to prevent pregnancy is not ignored by the patriarchy in the same way (perhaps because men have an interest in preventing pregnancy too), but the need is answered by the male medical profession with expensive and life-threatening contraceptives. Similarly, women's anger and despair are met with tranquilizers and incarceration. Radical feminist enterprises offer goods and services to women that are less expensive than those offered by patriarchy and that, in many cases, are simply not available through patriarchal institutions. They offer food that is nutritious in a non-sexist environment, sensitive and client-centered medical care, and spiritual experiences that foster women's values. In opposition to the patriarchal ideology that demeans women, their values and their experiences, radical feminist culture offers new political and aesthetic ideas and the vision of a woman-centered world.

For radical feminists, only the creation of a womanculture can fulfill women's true needs. Feminist enterprises demonstrate to women how far the patriarchy has perverted and manipulated their needs, training women to find satisfaction in fashionable clothes and male compliments rather than in genuine achievements and the pleasures of women's company. Feminist enterprises can help women to discover their real needs and to begin to fulfill their potentialities, so long repressed by patriarchy. Not only clients, however, benefit from radical feminist enterprises. Such enterprises provide equal or even greater benefits to those who participate actively in building them.

Where radical feminist enterprises provide economic support for those who construct them, one benefit is immediately obvious. Such enterprises allow some women to survive economically within institutions that are not male-dominated. Women can do work whose value they believe in without being subjected to the daily insults and humiliations that come from working with men. This prospect is so attractive that many radical feminists devote their main energies to feminist enterprises, even when the enterprise is unable to pay or pays them very little. Within those enterprises, women experience the rewards of working with other women to realize a shared vision and the pleasure of developing new skills and capacities in areas hitherto reserved for men.

Unlike a male business, a radical feminist enterprise is not established for the sole benefit of its entrepreneurs; on the other hand, it is not simply a social service. The benefits received by the creators of a radical feminist enterprise are not viewed simply as by-products, incidental to the main purpose of the project. On the contrary, a radical feminist enterprise is typically organized in such a way as to maximize benefits to the workers as well as to the clients, to break down male assumptions about work and to instantiate radical feminist values. For radical feminists, the process by which a product is created is just as important as the product itself. Indeed, the product is inseparable from the process of its creation: the process is the product.

Radical feminists are very sensitive to hierarchy, to its destructive effects on people's character and on their relationships. Radical feminism associates hierarchy and domination with male culture and seeks to minimize or abolish these within the womanculture. Accordingly, it seeks to avoid traditional forms of the division of labor in which a small number of people supervise the rest and each worker performs, in a routine and monotonous manner, a small part of the work required to accomplish the overall project. This division of labor places some people in a position of authority over others and removes responsibility from the rest. Moreover, it deprives individuals of the opportunity to learn new skills and so perpetuates and reinforces the relative advantages and disadvantages with which each individual entered the enterprise. By contrast with traditional male enterprises, radical feminists try to equalize relations between project workers, to challenge patriarchal estimates of the value of different kinds of work and to rotate tasks so that each worker develops new capabilities. Jennifer Woodul summarizes her conception of how a radical feminist business should operate:

> The nature of business will be changed by feminist operation of it. There should be structures for worker input, working toward meaningful worker control. Salaries should be set within a narrow range, with consideration of each woman's particular needs as well as her role in the company. Structures should be clear to all and determined on concrete bases. Decision-making methods should be set out, with the understanding that decision-making must presume responsibility. There must be a consciousness of accountability to the women's community. There must be a commitment to channel money back into the community or the movement. Finally, there must be a commitment to radical change—to the goals of economic and political power for women.[107]

Coletta Reid provides further elaboration of the principles that should govern the internal organization of a radical feminist business:

Insofar as possible, the internal organization of women's businesses should be consistent with the goals of the future socialist economy they're working toward. All the workers need to be all the owners. Going to rich women or other corporations for investment/ownership is no solution . . .

All the people who work should have some say over what they do and participate in determining the direction of the business, the organization of the work, etc. . . . The most efficient production methods seem to be centralization of decisions, rigid hierarchies, extreme specialization and constant supervision; but these are not necessarily the conditions that we want to perpetuate in the future. . . .

Workers should be paid equally or nearly equally according to need. Special needs include children, health problems, etc. . . . The idea of equal pay is tied to the realization that all work that is necessary to the success of an enterprise is equally valuable. . . .

There should be no divisions between white-collar/blue-collar or working class/middle class jobs. . . . Everybody has a head and two hands and should learn how to use both. . . .

We all can and should share the maintenance tasks of our businesses, such as cleaning, but we cannot all equally share skilled jobs because none of us would get enough experience at any one thing to do it really well. . . .

Women should also try to develop businesses that are not closely related to the female role . . . Women need to learn to farm, to mine, to sell, to build buildings, be machinists, etc.

Every effort should be made not to farm out work to other businesses which are exploitative. . . .

A similar effort should be made to give as much work as possible to other women's businesses—even if they're more expensive and slower, which they probably will be. . . .

The business should be providing women with a good or a service that is important both to their needs and to their developing consciousness.[108]

Radical feminist living communities are based on similar values:

THE SPIRAL WOMIN'S LAND COOPERATIVE is an expanding group of Lesbians co-founding/creating a rural Lesbian community in southeastern Kentucky. We are committed to understanding cooperative process and consensus decision making. And to the decision to build and maintain ourselves and our community cooperatively . . .

We are working actively to create a strong womoon owned, built, governed and shared land space.[109]

Not all radical feminist enterprises are living communities or businesses, even in the extended sense of "business" that radical feminists use. Even in their health clinics, crisis centers and battered women shelters, however, radical feminists try to minimize hierarchy, particularly the hierarchy that exists in the male culture between the (typically male) "professional" workers and their (typically female) clients. One way in which radical feminists do this is by trying to break down the actual distinction between worker and client. For instance,

In "Jane", an early underground Chicago-based abortion clinic, for example, women developed models of abortion care which included sharing all processes and procedures, discussion of feelings and the trading of mutual experiences among the women abortion-workers and the women seeking abortions.[110]

The Detroit Women's Clinic stated: "We do not examine women. We show women how to examine themselves . . . We neither sell nor give away self help . . . we share it."[111] A member of the Coalition on Battered Women which formed in Austin, Texas, described the vision of the founders in these words:

At the time, there seemed to be general agreement on issues such as the value of a feminist perspective in the shelter, the inclusion of lesbians as visible members of the collective, and the need for workers and residents in the shelter to share in decision-making and leadership.[112]

It is clear that radical feminist enterprises, even service projects, are not designed primarily to help women cope or even to "make it" within patriarchal society; instead, they are designed to bring about social change. This intention is stated most clearly by Laurie MacKenzie and Sue Kirk. "The most concise working definition of Radical Feminist Counseling employed by our component is as follows":

Problems women come with for counseling, however personal, are rooted in the social and political condition of our existence as people and as women; therefore, counseling takes the dual form of both personal and socio-political analysis of the problems, with an attempt to synthesize the two and arrive at, or work for, tenable creative solutions at both levels.

Accordingly, the core of Radical Feminist counseling practice is education. Our unique form of counseling, whether one-to-one or in groups, is fundamentally an active learning process, an opportunity for women to learn the truth about themselves and the world in an atmosphere of dignity, honesty, trust, and support.

The immediate aims of our various counseling processes . . . are: to foster self-determination and independence; to open up the great diversity of choices that can be struggled for in companionship with, and support of, other women; and to encourage the development of a collective feminist consciousness (without laying political trips) so that women need no longer be isolated and alienated from themselves and one another. Thus, Radical Feminist Counseling is a process of personal integration, growth, and change as well as of social and political transformation.[113]

By now it is obvious that radical feminist enterprises are quite different from liberal and Marxist projects, even those that they resemble superficially. Liberal feminists, for instance, both found women's businesses and establish service programs for women, but their goals are, respectively, to make profits for women or to help women cope with the system. Radical feminists explicitly eschew both of these goals. Marxists are less likely either to run businesses or to offer services, but occasionally may open a bookshop or provide some service such as legal aid; in these cases, their main goals are political education and agitation, with the possible side benefit of earning a little money for their group. Apart from not being directed specifically toward women's needs, traditional Marxist projects differ from radical feminist enterprises in that they focus more exclusively on the end result to be achieved and place less emphasis on the process by which it is achieved.

A number of writers have pointed out that the radical feminist conception of a womanculture, emphasizing social change through the building of alternative institutions, is strikingly similar to traditional social anarchism. As Lynne Farrow puts it, "Feminism practises what Anarchism preaches."[114] The trouble with this epigram is that "anarchism" preaches many things. Etymologically, the word "anarchy" comes from the Greek and means literally "without government." What anarchists all have in common, therefore, is a denial of the legitimacy of state institutions, and much anarchist writing has been directed toward working out in detail just how various state institutions, far from curing a variety of social ills, in fact constitute their ultimate cause. For instance, law is said to create crime and property to create (or even, as Proudhon said, to be) theft.[115] From its original root, however, the meaning of "anarchism" (like the meanings of "socialism" and especially of "feminism") extends outward to cover a broad spectrum of ideas and practices. These range from individualistic anarchism, which preaches a return to what an unsympathetic outsider might characterize as a Hobbesian state of nature, to various varieties of social anarchism. Social or socialist or communist anarchism is what radical feminism most resembles. Social anarchists share a Marxist critique of capitalism, but they reject the Marxist belief that the way to establish a new society is through an extension of state power and a dictatorship of the proletariat. Far from withering away, anarchists believe that the violence inherent in state coercion will only breed more violence. One of their most basic beliefs is that means are inseparable from ends.

> There can be no separation of the revolutionary process from the revolutionary goal.[116]

> We have nothing but our freedom. We have nothing to give you but your own freedom. We have no law but the single principle of mutual aid between individuals. We have no government but the single principle of free association. You cannot buy the Revolution. You cannot make the Revolution. You can only be the Revolution. It is in your spirit or it is nowhere.[117]

Like radical feminists, anarchists value feeling, intuition, and spontaneity. An anarchist slogan proclaims: "All power to the imagination!" Social anarchism also values cooperation and mutual aid, the latter being the title of a classic anarchist work by Peter Kropotkin.[118] Lizzie Borden has pointed out that many radical feminist institutions recall Proudhon's ideas of rebuilding society by creating a federation of communes and cooperatives organized on principles of mutual aid and on the exchange of skills and services.[119] Like radical feminism, social anarchism focuses not on large abstractions but on the immediate transformation of daily life:

> It is plain that the goal of revolution today must be the liberation of daily life. Any revolution that fails to achieve this goal is counter-revolution. Above all, it is *we* who have to be liberated, *our* daily lives, with all their moments, hours and days, and not universals like "History" and "Society."[120]

Like radical feminists, social anarchists realize that the transformation of daily life both presupposes and results in the transformation of the self. The hierarchy and power relations of traditional institutions produce people who are mutilated remnants of what they could have been. Traditional social anarchism does not analyze how gender has distorted human nature but, like radical feminism, it does emphasize a vision of human wholeness, balance and integrity. Like radical feminism, social anarchists believe that this vision can be realized only through the restructuring of the institutions of daily life.

> The self must always be *identifiable* in the revolution, not overwhelmed by it. The self must always be *perceivable* in the revolutionary process, not submerged by it. There is no word that is more sinister in the "revolutionary" vocabulary than "masses." Revolutionary liberation must be a self-liberation that reaches social dimensions, not "mass liberation" or "class liberation" behind which lurks the rule of an elite, a hierarchy and a state. If a revolution fails to produce a new society by the self-activity and self-mobilization of revolutionaries, if it does not involve the forging of a self in the revolutionary process, the revolution will once again circumvent those whose lives are to be lived every day and leave daily life unaffected. . . .
>
> If for this reason alone, the revolutionary movement is profoundly concerned with lifestyle. It must try to *live* the revolution in all its totality, not only participate in it. It must be deeply concerned with the way the revolutionist lives, his [sic] relations with the surrounding environment and his degree of self-emancipation. In seeking to change society, the revolutionist cannot avoid changes in himself that demand the reconquest of his own being.[121]

By building alternative institutions, radical feminists pursue what an anarchist would call the "hollowing out" of the patriarchal system. By withdrawing from patriarchal institutions, they weaken and delegitimate them. Peggy Kornegger perceives this withdrawal as hidden subversion. She writes: "As women, we are particularly well-suited for participation in this process. Underground for ages, we have learned to be covert, subtle, sly, silent, tenacious, acutely sensitive, and expert at communication skills."[122] To radical feminists, however, the creation of feminist institutions constitutes a direct rather than an indirect challenge to the patriarchal system. They see the creators of these institutions as "living in the open", courageously allowing themselves to become visible to the patriarchy.

Radical feminist institutions differ from liberal feminist enterprises in being firmly anti-capitalist. Radical feminists hope to create a gradually developing network of communities and enterprises that will enable increasing numbers of women to become economically independent of patriarchy. Thus, their long-term vision is for a kind of socialism, but not the socialism of Marx and Engels.

> feminism presupposes a socialist economy of some kind. Communism was not invented by Marx, as we know. It has been an integral part of matriarchal society, and, in one form or another, it is a continual guiding principle as feminists decide what things we want to keep in our world.[123]

> We are all socialists. We refuse to give up this pre-Marxist term which has been used as a synonym by many anarchist thinkers. Another synonym for anarchism is libertarian socialism, as opposed to Statist and author-itarian varieties. Anarchism . . . is the affirmation of human freedom

and dignity expressed in a negative, cautionary term signifying that no person should rule or dominate another person by force or threat of force. Anarchism indicates what people should not do to one another. Socialism, on the other hand, means all the groovy things people can do and build together, once they are able to combine efforts and resources on the basis of common interest, rationality and creativity.[124]

Unlike traditional Marxists, who believe in the need for a powerful state, at least in the period immediately following the revolution, radical feminists, like social anarchists, seek ways of organizing social life that avoid all uses of coercive power. The masthead on the early radical feminist journal *It Ain't Me Babe* carried the slogan "End all hierarchies!" Mary Daly writes: "The development of sisterhood is a unique threat, for it is directed against the basic social and psychic and model of hierarchy and domination."[125] The radical feminist search for non-coercive models of social life is reflected in feminist science fiction and in feminist discussions of power.[126] Over and over, radical feminists condemn conceptions of power that define it in Hobbesian terms of conquest and domination over others, rather than in terms of the social development of human capacities. "*This* revolution has got to go for broke: *power to no one, and to every one: to each the power over his/her own life, and to no others.*"[127]

One way in which anarchists have attempted to get rid of conventional power relations is by organizing society through small, intimate groups rather than through large, impersonal bureaucracies or parties. The anarchist Murray Bookchin writes:

They would try to foster a deep sense of community, a rounded human relationship that would transform the very subjectivity of the people involved. Groups would be small, in order to achieve the full participation of everyone involved. Personal relationships would be intimate, not merely issue-oriented. People would get to *know* each other, to *confront* each other; they would *explore* each other with a view toward achieving the most complete, unalienated relationships. . . .

From this intimacy there would grow, hopefully, a supportive system of kinship, mutual aid, sympathy and solidarity in daily life . . . This "extended family"—based on explored affinities and collective activities— would replace relationships mediated by "organizers", "chairmen", an "executive committee", *Robert's Rules of Order,* elites, and political manipulators.[128]

Bookchin's vision is startlingly close to the radical feminist "reconceiving" of a cooperative model of power relations, beginning with "personal" relations.

Although women cannot help but be influenced by the competitive power model, women try in the groups we establish to create different forms. Women, in groups, seek to build the trust necessary to support each other, to cooperate, and to work together to reach both individual and group goals. In personal interactions, at both informal and formal group levels, women grope toward a cooperative, societal kind of power relationship. There is at least as much attention to *process* as to final goals, to devising ways to work through conflicts at the small group level. If such groups become models for power interactions in the larger society, the personal can be transformed into the political.[129]

3. CONFRONTING PATRIARCHY

The creation of female culture is as pervasive a process as we can imagine, for it is participation in a VISION which is continually unfolding anew in everything from our talks with friends, to meat boycotts, to taking over storefronts for child care centers, to making love with a sister. It is revelatory, undefinable, except as a process of change. Women's culture is all of us exorcising, naming, creating toward the vision of harmony with ourselves, each other, and our sister earth. In the last ten years our having come faster and closer than ever before in the history of the patriarchy to overturning its power . . . is cause for exhilarant hope—wild, contagious, unconquerable, crazy HOPE! . . . The winning of life over death, despair and meaninglessness is everywhere I look now—like taliswomen of the faith in WOMANVISION.[130]

In spite of the beauty of this vision, patriarchal culture impedes its realization. Radical feminism sees patriarchy as a total system, a male culture characterized by violence, domination and death. The male culture manifests itself in every aspect of life except those defended by women; as Mary Daly says, "Patriarchy appears to be 'everywhere'."[131] Because it is so pervasive and familiar, patriarchy appears as the natural order of things. To shatter the appearance of naturalness, radical feminists sometimes engage in direct attacks on the more blatant manifestations of patriarchy, which they take as symbols of the entire system. The symbols vary, depending on the male culture in question; to rip the *chador* or veil, for instance, is a symbolic attack only on the male culture of Islam. In contemporary capitalist society, recent targets of attack have included beauty contests (symbols of the sexual objectification of women), bridal fairs (symbols of women's enslavement to men), pornography (a symbol of violence against women), the Pentagon (a symbol of male militarism and imperialism) and nuclear power stations (symbols of male greed, destructiveness and the rape of the environment).

Radical feminist attacks on the symbols of patriarchy typically are carried out in a dramatic manner that emphasizes the symbolic nature of these attacks. They are the activist equivalents of the poetic forms of verbal expression chosen increasingly by radical feminist authors. Like radical feminist poetry, radical feminist attacks on patriarchy aim to jolt our perceptual field, to bring it into a new focus, to interpret it in terms of a new paradigm. With this aim, radical feminists perform guerilla theater; they throw red meat onto the stage at beauty contests;[132] they hex or cast spells on anything from Wall Street stockbrokers, to inflationary prices in supermarkets, to the Pentagon itself; they organize public confrontations with accused rapists or spray-paint "rapist" on their property;[133] they destroy pornography in bookshops and record shops;[134] they have even set fire to pornographic bookshops.[135]

Washington, D.C., WITCH—after an action hexing the United Fruit Company's oppressive policy on the Third World *and* on secretaries in its offices at home . . . claimed that WITCH was "a total concept of revolutionary female identity" and was the striking arm of the Women's Liberation Movement, aiming mainly at financial and corporate America, at those institutions that have the power to control and define human life.[136]

The radical feminist attacks on male culture, like their alternative institutions, most clearly resemble the methods of social anarchism. It is true that radical feminist actions are nonviolent to human beings whereas anarchists in the past have sometimes resorted to violence. In its symbolic character, however, the radical feminist apocryphal bra-burning is "propaganda by the deed," just like the symbolic anarchist assassinations of heads of state. Moreover, the radical feminist small group is very similar to the *grupo de afinidad* (affinity group) which was the basis of the Iberian Anarchist Federation in pre-Franco Spain. Murray Bookchin describes affinity groups in these words:

> The affinity group could easily be regarded as a new type of extended family, in which kinship ties are replaced by deeply empathetic human relationships—relationships nourished by common revolutionary ideas and practice. Long before the word 'tribe' gained popularity in the American counterculture, the Spanish anarchists called their congresses *asambleas de las tribus*—assemblies of the tribes. Each affinity group is deliberately kept small to allow for the greatest degree of intimacy between those who compose it. Autonomous, communal and directly democratic, the group combines revolutionary theory with revolutionary lifestyle in its everyday behavior. It creates free space in which revolutionaries can remake themselves individually, and also as social beings.
>
> Affinity groups are intended to function as catalysts within the popular movement, not as 'vanguards'; they provide initiative and consciousness, not a 'general staff' and a source of 'command.' The groups proliferate on a molecular level and they have their own 'Brownian movement.' Whether they link together or separate is determined by living situations, not by bureaucratic fiat from a distant center.[137]

The direct attacks that radical feminists make on patriarchy are carried out typically by small groups of women. Even their names are chosen for dramatic impact. They include WITCH (acronym of many sources including Women's International Terrorist Conspiracy from Hell), BITCH, and SCUM (Society for Cutting Up Men). "A certain common style—insouciance, theatricality, humor and activism, unite the [WITCH] Covens—which are otherwise totally autonomous, and unhierarchical to the point of anarchy."[138]

The pornographic bookshops in Leeds, England, were burned by a group called Angry Women, and feminist vandalism in California was carried out by the Preying Mantis Women's Brigade. In May 1981, U.S. Senate committee hearings on abortion were disrupted by the Women's Liberation Zap Action Brigade. The Women's Pentagon Action of November 1980, in which feminists attacked the Pentagon in a variety of symbolic ways, was unusually large for a radical feminist action, but it was not organized in a centralized and hierarchical manner. Instead, its mode of organization

> reaffirmed the need for small scale initiative and autonomy. To keep from taking energy from individuals and local groups, we refrained from constructing much of an over-all co-ordinating framework opting instead for information sharing bulletins, an emergency phone tree and a date for our next general meeting April 25–26 in NYC. To quote one of our many sages, the WPA went forward with an unusually small amount of baggage. In times like these, it's best to travel light.[139]

Some radical feminist groups are entirely structureless in their internal organization.

There is no "joining" WITCH. If you are a woman and dare to look within yourself, you are a Witch. You can make your own rules. You are free and beautiful. . . .

You are a Witch by saying aloud, "I am a Witch" three times, and *thinking about that*. You are a Witch by being female, untamed, angry, joyous, and immortal.[140]

Other radical feminists are critical of what Joreen called "The Tyranny of Structurelessness."[141] Joreen pointed out that if a group had no formal or explicit structure for decision making and leadership, then it would have an informal structure and some individuals would become *de facto* leaders. In order to ensure genuine internal democracy, some radical feminist groups invented very careful organizational structures. A good example is THE FEM-INISTS: A Political Organization to Annihilate Sex Roles:

THE FEMINISTS is an organization without officers which divides work according to the principle of participation by lot. Our goal is a just society all of whose members are equal. Therefore, we aim to develop knowledge and skills in all members and prevent any one member or small group from hoarding information or abilities.

Traditionally official posts such as the chair of the meeting and the secretary are determined by lot and change with each meeting. The treasurer is chosen by lot to function for one month.

Assignments may be menial or beyond the experience of a member. To assign a member work she is not experienced in may involve an initial loss of efficiency but fosters equality and allows all members to acquire the skills necessary for revolutionary work. When a member draws a task beyond her own experience she may call on the knowledge of other members, but her own input and development are of primary importance. The group has the responsibility to support a member's efforts, as long as the group believes the member to be working in good faith. A member has the duty to submit her work for the group—such as articles and speeches—to the group for correction and approval.

In order to make efficient use of all opportunities for writing and speaking, in order to develop members without experience in these areas, members who are experienced in them are urged to withdraw their names from a lot assigning those tasks. Also those members, experienced or inexperienced, who have once drawn a lot to write or speak must withdraw their names until all members have had a turn.

The system of the lot encourages growth by maximizing the sharing of tasks, but the responsibility for contributions rests ultimately with the individual. One's growth develops in proportion to one's contributions.[142]

Sometimes, radical feminists are not in a strong enough position to engage in open confrontation with patriarchy. In this case, they are encouraged to fight back in covert ways.

We in offices have our own ways of spittin' in Massuh's soup. We manage to break typewriters, steal supplies, forget to relay messages, use the day's mail to cover our heads on rainy days. These reactions to being dehu-manized should be recognized for what they are, sabotage.[143]

Radical feminist attacks on what they call patriarchy are clearly very different from liberal feminist and traditional Marxist struggles against male dominance.

Unlike liberal feminists, radical feminists do not direct their efforts toward legal reform:

> We simply cannot look to the government to rid us of pornography; legally there are no "final solutions." The feminist movement against pornography must remain an anti-defamation movement involved in education, consciousness-raising, and the development of private strategies against the industry.[144]

The Preying Mantises, who destroy pornography, state: "We do not want official censorship."[145] Although the Preying Mantises describe their actions as civil disobedience, they act in secret, unlike liberals who engage in civil disobedience. and they do not acknowledge the legitimacy of the state by accepting the legal penalty for their actions. Radical feminist resistance to patriarchy is also unlike the political struggles in which Marxists engage. Radical feminists deliberately eschew "mass actions" and disciplined, centralized, vanguard parties.

> The spirit of the women is just too large to be guided and manipulated by a 'movement.' Small groups, acting on their own and deciding upon their own actions, are the logical expression of revolutionary women.[146]

> Feminism is a many-headed monster which cannot be destroyed by singular decapitation. We spread and grow in ways that are incomprehensible to a hierarchical mentality.[147]

Radical feminist propaganda by the deed is not conceived as a direct, frontal onslaught on patriarchy, an assault which, if escalated sufficiently, would bring the patriarchy down. Instead, radical feminist actions are conceived as a type of consciousness raising—making visible the destructive power of patriarchy, a destructiveness that is invisible because it is so familiar as to appear natural and because it is disguised by the ideology of romance, fun, and national security. Radical feminist actions are supposed to disrupt the spectacle and to show it for what it is. Often their actions combine art with politics in a way that enlarges our conception of both.[148] How patriarchy will finally come to an end is a question radical feminists discuss only rarely. Often male supremacy seems so powerful that its end can be imagined only in the pages of science fiction. However, there seems to be a general belief that patriarchy will be undermined rather than overthrown. Perhaps it will even self-destruct, leaving the way open for women to build a new society founded on radical feminist values.

Problems with Radical Feminist Politics

Radical feminism has shattered the illusions of male culture. It has demonstrated the degradation and drudgery that underlie the dominant male ideology of motherhood, romance and equality. Through analysis, metaphor and poetry, through music, literature and art, radical feminism has revealed the pain beneath the lives of countless women whose view of themselves and their world will never again be the same.

Without the change in consciousness effected by radical feminism, no social revolution will truly liberate women. But does radical feminism itself show us the way to women's liberation? My own view is that radical feminist ideas and practice are a necessary part of the revolutionary transformation of society but that, in themselves, they are insufficient to bring it about.

1. PRACTICE WITHOUT THEORY

Radical feminism is not like traditional political theory. It has different political values; it asks and seeks to answer different questions; it focuses on different areas; and it has developed a very different mode of expression. The first radical feminist writings most closely resembled those of traditional political theory: although lively and polemical, their authors seemed to be trying to produce political analyses of women's situation that were formally identical with traditional analyses. As the radical feminist movement mushroomed, however, its forms of expression became increasingly imaginative and "non-linear." Radical feminists created new music, new poetry, new drama, and new science fiction. Even the prose writing of radical feminism became more impassioned, metaphorical and epigrammatic. Every available linguistic resource was employed to jolt the audience out of its accustomed ways of perceiving the world and to reveal "a counter-reality, a mutually guaranteed support of female experience undistorted by male interpretation."[149]

Radical feminism indeed has revealed different reality. It has shown us a world in which men control women's bodies and force women into motherhood or sexual slavery. Radical feminism has also described how much of this occurs; it has demonstrated an interlocking system of male-dominant institutions that trap women and leave them with few routes of escape; it has also explored the psychic mutilation of women imprisoned in these institutions. What radical feminism has not yet done is provide an account of the underlying causes of the patriarchal system. Why have men built these institutions and why do they maintain them?

To answer these questions would require a comprehensive theory of human nature and human society. Only such a theory can explain why men seek to enslave women, why men are what Daly calls necrophiliacs, why men, as Dworkin puts it, are lovers of murder and death. These are crucial questions, but radical feminism has not developed a theory capable of answering them. For most radical feminists, it is enough to show what men are like: to show that heroes rape, that bosses rape, that husbands rape, that fathers rape. To reveal these secret atrocities is indeed an achievement, but it is only the first part of ending them.

Early radical feminists, such as Firestone or the New York Radical Feminists, made some attempt, however unsatisfactory, to answer the question of what keeps patriarchy going. But the popularity of those early writers has now been eclipsed by more poetic and impassioned authors such as Daly, Rich and Griffin. These writers demonstrate vividly *how* men enslave women, but they do not provide a theoretical explanation of *why* men do so. As we have seen, indeed, some radical feminists explicitly reject the need for theory in the traditional sense. Griffin, for instance, writes:

> We rejected the theory that capitalism had raped us. If they said patriarchy was just a form of capitalism, we said that capitalism was a form of patriarchy. But our departure from these old ways took place on a far deeper level than this dialogue. There were other leftist theories from which we departed, but our most serious difference was that theory has

ceased to impress us as much as it had. Experience had become more important.[150]

A few pages later, Griffin suggests that radical feminists have not abandoned theory so much as tried to "reconceive it." Theory in the traditional sense, abstract and unemotional, is inadequate to express women's suffering. Theory must be guided by feeling.

> We did not move from theory; we moved quite simply, as I wrote before, to the sorest wounds, and in this sense, we were no longer "thinking" in the way that Western man thinks, in the realm where thought is divided from feeling, and objectivity is imagined to exist. We were discovering a different sense of clarity, one achieved through feeling, in which thought followed a direction determined by pain, and trauma, and compassion and outrage.[151]

The anarcha-feminist Lynne Farrow distrusts political theory on somewhat different grounds.

> Feminists have always possessed an exuberant disregard for the "why?" questions, the theoretical mainstay of our menfolk. Kate Millett's *Sexual Politics* for one was severely attacked by reviewers for spending all those pages *not* formulating a theory on why sexism existed. Our disinterest in theoretical speculation has been construed as a peculiar deficiency. Of course. Similarly our distrust for logic and that which has been unscrupulously passed off as the Known in the situation. We can't "argue rationally" we are told and it probably is true that we avoid this kind of verbal jigging. But the fact is we haven't any real stake in the game. KNOWLEDGE and ARGUMENT as it relates to women is so conspicuously alien to our interests that female irreverence for the intellectual arts is rarely concealed. In fact, women seem to regard male faith in these processes as a form of superstition because there appears no apparent connection between these arts and the maintenance of life, the principal female concern.[152]

Farrow thinks that political theory is used as a substitute for political action.

> Feminism as situationism means that elaborate social analysis and first causes à la Marx would be superfluous because changes will be rooted in situations from which the problems stem: instead change will be idiosyncratic to the people, the time and the place . . . Discussing "male chauvinism" is as fruitless as discussing "capitalism" in that, safely reduced to an explanation, we have efficiently distanced ourselves from a problem and the necessity to immediately interact with it or respond to other people. *Such theoretical over-articulation gives one the illusion of responding to a critical situation without ever really coming to grips with one's own participation in it.*[153]

"Theoreticism" is certainly a familiar phenomenon among so-called revolutionaries—especially among academics. It involves the elaboration of an abstract and jargonized mode of discourse that separates theoreticians from those about whom the theory is constructed, and makes these theoreticians the authoritative source of knowledge.[154] Obviously, women's liberation will never result from theory and analysis alone. Outrage is necessary to motivate people to political action. On the other hand, outrage is not necessarily the best guide to the action that should be taken. Griffin and Farrow seem to suggest that feminists should focus directly on the immediate problems.

focusing on the source of the problem is not necessarily the problem . . . the energies of feminism will be problem-centered rather than people (or struggle) centered . . . Feminism has tried to find ad hoc solutions appropriate to needs at the time, i.e., centered around the family or community of friends.[155]

Farrow ignores the possibility that women might exhaust their energies in tackling symptoms rather than underlying causes. Griffin suggests the creation of rape-protection centers. She acknowledges that "we do not yet have the end of rape. All we have is the feat of naming rape a crime against us."[156] This is indeed a feat; rape-protection centers have succoured women and healed them. But it is also necessary to discover how to end rape completely, so that it no longer needs to be named and so that women no longer require succour and healing. Theory alone will not liberate women. But women's liberation seems equally unlikely to result from simple activism, not grounded in a systematic understanding of women's situation.

Activism is never pure activity. Even if people are responding to very immediate problems, their response rests on certain assumptions and has certain implications. This is true whether or not the assumptions and implications are recognized explicitly. If the assumptions and implications are not reflected on consciously and systematically, that is to say, if they are not part of a theory, then they are likely to be problematic.

Radical feminist action is not entirely impulsive, of course. As we have seen, it is grounded on a systematic analysis of women's subordination. This analysis is theoretical insofar as it specifies a few concepts, such as rape and slavery, in such a way as to bring a variety of apparently disparate phenomena, such as marriage, prostitution, Indian *suttee,* Chinese foot-binding, African genital mutilation, European witchburning, and American gynecology, within a unified conceptual framework.[157] Thus, the radical feminist analysis goes beneath the conventional appearance of women's equality and even privilege to reveal an underlying pattern of subordination and degradation. Reality, however, has more than one level; to speak less metaphorically, it can be conceptualized in many different ways. The radical feminist analysis is theoretical in that it offers a reconceptualization of women's situation that makes it more intelligible in some ways—that helps us to understand, for instance, why so many women take anti-depressant or tranquilizing drugs. But the radical feminist analysis still leaves important questions unanswered. In particular, it does not explain the material reasons for men's subjugation of women. The existing radical feminist analysis needs to be supplemented by an account that embraces yet a deeper level of reality. Another way of putting this point is to say that the radical feminist analysis provides a redescription of women's reality, a redescription that is not theory-neutral but that is also not theoretically complete or adequate because it does not provide a causal explanation of the reality that it describes. It is static rather than dynamic; it presents a still rather than a motion picture.

As long as radical feminists do not attempt to identify the underlying causes of patriarchy, as long as they do not try to explain why men are rapists, slavers and murderers, women are likely to jump to one of two conclusions. The first is that rape, slavery and murder are so obviously enjoyable in themselves or offer such obvious benefits to their perpetrators that anyone would engage in these practices if the opportunity arose. It follows from this view that women would be just as likely as men to rape, enslave and murder if only they had the chance. This conclusion is not one that many feminists are likely to adopt. Consequently, for lack of a better answer, many radical feminists assume that there is simply something wrong, biologically, with men that impels them to act in such cruel and wanton ways. Radical feminists often tend toward this view not because they are convinced of any specific biological determinist theory about the difference between the sexes; rather they drift into it because, given the prevailing dominance of biological reductionist forms of explanation, they see no other way to explain all the forms of male violence against women.

Biological determinism, as we saw in Chapter 5, is conceptually incoherent. It is also politically undesirable because it drastically narrows the options available for political action. Since feminists reject a fatalistic acceptance of the status quo, and since they are not in a position to practice biological engineering or systematic patricide, separatism becomes their only remaining option. As we have seen, it is the option that, in one form or another, radical feminists typically take. Separatist political strategies are also encouraged by the radical feminist reliance on feeling and by the radical feminist emphasis on healing or nurturing oneself. For many women, withdrawal from men is far more attractive than the grinding struggle to resist male dominance in its daily manifestations.

The reluctance of contemporary radical feminists to search for theoretical explanations of male dominance thus leads naturally to a political practice of separatism. In the rest of this chapter, I shall consider various aspects of separatism as a strategy for social transformation.

2. WOMEN'S CONTROL OF THEIR BODIES

A different source of at least one kind of separatist politics is the radical feminist emphasis on women's control of their bodies. This slogan is capable of many interpretations, but the radical feminist analysis of women's oppression as consisting in forced motherhood and sexual slavery encourages radical feminists to interpret women's control of their bodies in sexual and in procreative terms. Women are seen as controlling their bodies when they determine their own mode of sexual expression and when their decisions about whether or not to bear children are based on their own desires and needs. In other words, women are seen as controlling their bodies when they are free from forced motherhood and sexual slavery.

Given this understanding of the slogan, the only way in which women can take control of their bodies under patriarchy seems to be through lesbianism; that is, through separatism in intimate relations. Because of the social inequality between women and men, radical feminists argue that it is impossible for women to take control of their bodies as long as they remain in intimate relationships with men. Radical feminists consistently refer to heterosexual relations as rape, prostitution, "servicing men's needs" or "licking up to men." Of course radical feminists recognize that even lesbians do not have complete control over their bodies under patriarchy; for instance, radical feminists are aware that lesbians, like all women under patriarchy, are still vulnerable to rape. But radical feminists believe that lesbianism, or separatism in intimate relations, is not only a necessary condition for women's taking back control of their own bodies but, in most circumstances, goes a long way toward achieving that goal.

Given this conception of women's control over their bodies, and given this strategy for achieving such control, it seems almost possible for women to win back control of their bodies through individual action. Of course, collective action against rape is still required but, once a woman becomes a lesbian, she no longer needs contraception or abortion. "Political" campaigns to win a safe contraception or free abortion become irrelevant to her; they may even seem to be a way in which non-lesbian women seek to escape the consequences of engaging in sexual relations with men. One angry lesbian wrote:

> Abortion is a reform measure. Its analysis is good when it says that women should seize control of their own bodies, but it patently ignores the contradiction that women will not have control of their own bodies if they keep on voluntarily giving them to men. Abortion, then, does not threaten male supremacy. It assumes that women are going to keep on fucking and breeding and makes it easier for some women to lick up to men.[158]

This author is correct in pointing out that abortion alone does not give women full control over their bodies and that the abolition of compulsory heterosexuality is at least equally important. But other aspects of women's control over their bodies are overlooked by those who believe that this goal can be largely achieved by the individual decision to become a lesbian.

Exclusive lesbianism would indeed free women from forced motherhood and sexual slavery. By offering an alternative to these almost universal conditions, lesbianism presents a fundamental challenge to patriarchy. What is rarely recognized explicitly by radical feminists, however, is that lesbianism is not an alternative that is open to all women. Apart from existing heterosexual conditioning and affections, the radical feminists' own claims that many women are forced, either physically or economically, to become mothers and/or sexual slaves implies that many married women and many prostitutes who might prefer to be exclusively lesbian are unable to take that option. Exclusive lesbianism is a choice available primarily to young women without children and to women who have the marketable skills that allow them to survive in the patriarchy without direct dependence on marital or sexual relations with men. Consequently, lesbianism is an alternative that is far more available to white and to middle-class women, although of course there do exist many working-class lesbians and lesbians of color. The point is that there are economic preconditions for women to achieve the degree of control over their bodies that lesbianism offers. The choice of separatism, even in intimate relations, is not just a simple issue of political principle, unconnected with issues of class, race and occupational discrimination.

In seeing lesbianism as the way in which women can take immediate control over their bodies, radical feminism ignores another aspect of the issue. It fails to confront the facts that, for women to have full control over their own sexuality and fertility, they should be able to choose to have sexual relations with men as well as to refuse them and to choose to bear children as well as to refuse to bear them. Radical feminists consider the latter as a more legitimate issue than the former. As we have seen, radical feminists perceive the imbalance of power between men and women under patriarchy to be so great that they cannot conceive of circumstances in which a woman could be said to have made a free choice to engage in sexual relations with men. By contrast, radical feminists look much more favorably on motherhood; after all, many radical feminists believe that motherhood is the source of women's special power and the inspiration for feminist values. In spite of their respect for motherhood, however, radical feminists do not emphasize that to become a mother is just as legitimate a choice for women as the refusal to do so. Of course, radical feminists are operating in a patriarchal society whose ideology and institutions all push women into motherhood. In this context, it is vital for feminists to emphasize a woman's right to say: No! On the other hand, a full understanding of what it would mean for women to control their own fertility must also include an acknowledgment of those social forces that prevent women from exercising their right to become mothers. Radical feminist struggles on behalf of the custody rights of lesbian mothers do indeed begin to acknowledge those forces. But radical feminists rarely mention the forced sterilization of poor women, especially women of color; they do not discuss the fact that poverty makes many women unable to afford the number of children they would like; and they do not point out how the lack of childcare facilities makes it impossible for many women both to engage in paid labor and to bear children. Their recognition that patriarchy forces many women into motherhood and into sexual slavery inspires radical feminists to assert a woman's right to control her body by refusing motherhood and by refusing heterosexuality. In focusing almost exclusively on these important claims, however, radical feminists often neglect to mention other features of contemporary society that restrict in an opposite but equal way women's right to control their own bodies.

The radical feminist conception of women's control of their own bodies is too narrow in still another respect. This is in its construal of women's bodies primarily in sexual and procreative terms. Once again, radical feminist emphasis on the political significance of male control of women's sexuality and fertility is important in the context of a political tradition that has relegated those aspects of human life to the private sphere and defined them as non-political. But the almost exclusive radical feminist focus on sexuality and on procreation ignores the fact that, under patriarchy, men control women's bodies in many other ways. Women are exposed not only to rape; they are also exposed to pollution and to industrial hazards. Women are imprisoned not only in the home; they are imprisoned as well in sweat shops, fields and factories.

Radical feminists do not deny this when it is pointed out to them, just as traditional Marxists do not deny that women are subjected to sexual harassment and rape. But radical feminist theory and practice have tended to ignore the non-sexual and non-procreative aspects of women's lives. It is true that some radical feminists have begun to concern themselves with issues of militarism and nuclear power, but they are only beginning to develop a distinctively feminist analysis of these issues. Most radical feminists continue to conceive of women's control of their bodies primarily in terms of the right to refuse motherhood and sexual slavery. Consequently, they continue to believe that lesbianism will give them a large measure of control over their own bodies.

To some degree they are right. In a patriarchal context, there is no doubt that lesbianism is a political choice. Lesbians do have more control than most women over their sexuality and their fertility. But not only is exclusive lesbianism an unavailable option for many women; even for lesbians themselves, it offers only a limited degree of control over their own bodies. For one thing, many women feel that lesbianism is the only choice that they can make, given the nature of patriarchal society, but the absence of alternatives hardly makes it a "choice" at all. A lesbian also pays a certain price for the "choice" she makes; she is better able than most women to refuse motherhood but, unless she is a mother already, it then becomes very difficult for her to bear children, the possibility of parthenogenesis notwithstanding. Finally, it is obvious that no lesbian can insulate herself completely from the impact of patriarchal society. Most lesbians have to work for male bosses in economic situations that are male-defined; lesbians, like other women, are exposed to economic discrimination and industrial hazards; even the relatively few lesbians who support themselves in the womanculture are exposed to pollution, radiation, street violence and the threat of war. There is no individual solution to these problems. But for lesbians and other women to have full control over their bodies, they would have to be free from these dangers, not only from forced motherhood and sexual slavery.

The radical feminist conception of women's control over their own bodies is both revolutionary and reactive. It is revolutionary insofar as it asserts that women's bodies can no longer be viewed as territory to be colonized by male culture. In its emphasis on women's control of their sexuality and their fertility, however, radical feminism comes close to accepting the patriarchal definition of women as primarily procreative and sexual beings. Of course, radical feminism's point is precisely to deny that definition. But when it construes women's control over their bodies to mean control over their sexual and reproductive organs, radical feminism seems to forget that women's bodies have other parts as well. It seems to view women as vaginas and wombs on legs. Sexual activity and childbearing indeed involve women's bodies in very intimate ways, but those ways are no more intimate than the ways in which women's bodies are involved in tending dangerous machines, eating contaminated food or breathing polluted air.

The very formulation of the slogan "Women's control over their own bodies" seems to reify or objectify women's bodies in a way that radical feminists view as typically patriarchal. It suggests that women's bodies are objects, separate from women themselves, which men have colonized so far but which women will now liberate. In this way, the slogan suggests a dualistic conception of human nature, even though dualism is a patriarchal concept that radical feminists typically reject. Interpreted in the usual way, the slogan also suggests that sexual interaction and childbearing are physical processes that a woman passively undergoes rather than activities that she actively performs. Instead of control over their bodies, a more appropriate goal for radical feminism would be women's control over their lives.

Control over their own lives, of course, is what radical feminists really want. Those who reject individual solutions know that this control cannot be achieved through lesbianism alone, and that is why they try to build an alternative womanculture. In the next section, I shall discuss whether women can gain control over their lives through this more thoroughgoing form of separatism.

3. SEPARATISM

There is no doubt that women's liberation requires some kinds of separatism. Feminists have always known that women require separate political organizations in order to formulate their own demands and to ensure that those demands are taken seriously. Radical feminists provide additional and valid reasons why women need times and places in which to gather apart from men. Separatism is necessary for women to develop new ways of relating to each other without male disruption; it is necessary for women to learn new skills, to hear other women, to share experiences and to develop their own distinctive perspective on the world. Separatism is necessary for women to create a womanculture that will challenge the values of patriarchy and prefigure an alternative future. But although some forms of separatism must always be available for women under patriarchy, separatism alone cannot transform society. Lynne Farrow writes: "feminism begins at home and it generally doesn't go a whole lot further than the community."[159] In her view, feminists should avoid grandiose plans for social transformation and should concentrate instead on solving immediate problems. The hope of those creating women's businesses and communities is that feminist enterprises will expand laterally to form an economic network that is increasingly adequate to meet women's needs and that will undermine the patriarchal economy. Carol Anne Douglas expresses doubt that such a non-violent strategy will work: "But won't forcing men to accept women's right to freedom take a certain amount of coercion? Won't it take coercion to stop rape and woman-beating? Won't it take coercion to take our share of the means of production and its fruits?"[160] Douglas raises difficult questions. Can force be stopped without force? Can non-violence really work? There are some historical examples where it has worked, where so many people refused to support the dominant system that the dominant group has been unable to impose its will.[161] It is not inconceivable that the male culture would collapse if enough people withdrew from it and joined the alternative womanculture. Unfortunately, there are overwhelming reasons why a separatist women's movement will never grow large enough to constitute a serious threat to patriarchy.

One problem, which has been experienced already by many radical feminist enterprises, is that the economics of capitalism make it almost impossible for alternative businesses to survive. For instance, because women's publishing houses are so small, their overheads are much higher than those of the established houses. Consequently, their books are often more expensive—even though they are trying to reach a female readership whose average earnings are little more than half those of men. The same problem affects the women's music industry, perhaps the most successful branch of the womanculture. Feminist music still has a relatively small audience and it is not a wealthy one. But it is relatively more expensive to produce a small than a large run of records and feminist performers still have to live. For feminist enterprises to survive, women working in the womanculture usually suffer what Polly Laurelchild calls "reverse exploitation" but what is in fact little different from conventional exploitation, except that the exploited women choose to accept their situation for feminist political reasons.[162]

Many feminist enterprises have not survived, and those which have survived have been forced to revise their business practices. A recent article on women's music announced the abandonment of collective structure by most of the remaining producers of feminist music.[163] This collective process is too slow and, by capitalist standards, inefficient. Kay Gardner, a well-known feminist musician states:

> You cannot have high political ideals and run a business. Let's put it this way: most of the political ideals are anti-capitalist, whether they are Marxist or whatever you want to name them. It's very hard to have a high anti-capitalist ideal and be running a business in a capitalist manner.[164]

Many radical feminist enterprises are being forced economically to revert to the politics of liberal feminism. Trotskyists often assert that you cannot have socialism in one country. It is equally impossible to have radical feminism in one commune, one business or even a network of businesses. A few such enterprises may survive, making compromises and gaining a partial independence. Nevertheless, they will always remain marginal to the patriarchal capitalist economy and never be able to constitute a real challenge to it.

Because of the economic difficulties facing feminist business enterprises, women's culture is forced to limit itself mainly to what Marxists would call superstructural forms, such as art and spirituality. As we have seen already, radical feminists view these forms of cultural expression as important political activities. Performance art dramatizes specific aspects of women's oppression; women's music celebrates women's love, humor, and courage; women's literature renames reality; the Goddess symbolizes "the newfound beauty, strength, and power of women."[165] The creation of an alternative culture is a vital part of any revolutionary movement, and the creation of a woman's culture is a vital part of feminist revolution. Women's culture changes women's consciousness and provides necessary havens of refuge from the psychological and sometimes physical assaults of patriarchal culture. By itself, however, a separate women's culture can never effect the changes in the material base of society that are required to bring down patriarchy. To believe that it can do so is a form of idealism. Patriarchy will not fall to words, spells or songs.

Apart from material limitations, there are also political limitations on the strength of the separatist movement. Early radical feminist authors claimed frequently that the domination of women was the deepest division in society. They saw it as historically the first form of oppression and as having given rise to later divisions of class (in the Marxist sense) and of race.[166] With the loss of interest in systematic political theories, this claim has not often been made explicit in the last few years. Nevertheless, many radical feminist authors, such as Griffin and Daly, have continued to speak about women in universal terms which suggest that all women share certain fundamental common experiences, regardless of differences of class or race.

Other feminists have attacked this assumption as classist and racist. They point out that it is an assumption that denies the special oppression of working-class women and women of color. In response to this criticism, radical feminists have recently made extra efforts to combat the special forms of oppression suffered by certain groups of women. These include not only working-class women and women of color, but other groups such as Jewish women and differently abled (or disabled) women. Almost a decade ago, Charlotte Bunch wrote: "Race, class and national oppressions come from men, serve ruling class white men's interests, and have no place in a woman-identified revolution."[167] Radical feminists now are trying not only to eliminate oppressive forms of behavior as individuals; they are making efforts to eradicate classism, racism, anti-Semitism and able-bodyism from the institutions of the womanculture. In their conferences and their publications, they are attempting to ensure that the voices of all groups of women are heard, and they try to make feminist events accessible even to those who are physically challenged.

These efforts to encourage more women to participate in the womanculture can only enrich and strengthen it. Nevertheless, the very concept of a womanculture suggests that, in spite of their different experiences under patriarchy, all women have a fundamental interest in joining together with other women. Similarly, the radical feminist characterization of contemporary society as patriarchy reveals a continuing assumption that the most significant division in our society is gender, just as the Marxist characterization of contemporary society as capitalism reveals a continuing assumption that its most significant division is class in the conventional sense. The politics of total separatism presuppose that women's interests are in permanent opposition to those of men.

There is some truth in these assumptions. In spite of their differences, women seem to share certain aspects of oppression across the boundaries of class or race. For instance, "the black lesbian has had to survive also the psychic mutilation of heterosexual superiority."[168] Women of all class and ethnic backgrounds have suffered, although in different ways, from forced motherhood and sexual slavery. Given these common forms of oppression, all women do have some interests in common. What the politics of total separatism ignore, however, is that some groups of women also have interests in common with some groups of men. Working-class women have interests in common with working-class men; Jewish women have interests in common with Jewish men; differently abled women have interests in common with differently abled men; and women of color have interests in common with men of color. One black lesbian collective writes:

> Although we are feminists and lesbians, we feel solidarity with progressive Black men and do not advocate the fractionalization that white women who are separatists demand. Our situation as Black people necessitates that we have solidarity around the fact of race, which white women of course do not need to have with white men, unless it is their negative solidarity as racial oppressors. We struggle together with Black men against racism, while we also struggle with Black men about sexism.[169]

A limited separatism is healthy and necessary. But a politics of total separatism is necessarily classist and racist, no matter how far classism and racism are eradicated inside the womanculture. In part it is classist and racist because access to the womanculture is more difficult for poor women and women of color, just as it is more difficult for such women to be exclusively lesbian. On the most fundamental level, however, total separatism is classist and racist because it denies the importance of class and racial divisions. It assumes that these can be overcome without the full participation of the groups who suffer from them.

By definition, female separatism excludes the male half of the population. It also excludes women with any emotional attachment to or shared political interest with men. Since these are not only all non-lesbian women but also all working-class lesbians and lesbians of color, it excludes most of the population. For these reasons, a women's movement that calls for maximal as opposed to limited separatism and that views separatism as the major strategy for revolutionary change is doomed to remain a small minority. Consequently, it can never be effective in bringing about far-reaching social transformation. One American woman of color states clearly the limitations of separatist politics.

> Black people alone cannot make a revolution in this country. Native American people alone cannot make a revolution in this country. Asians alone cannot make a revolution in this country. Chicanos alone cannot make a revolution in this country. White people alone cannot make revolution in this country. Women alone cannot make revolution in this country. Gay people alone cannot make revolution in this country. And anyone who tries it will not be successful.[170]

Notes

1. Judith Moschkovich, "—But I Know You, American Woman," in Cherrie Moraga and Gloria Anzaldua, eds., *This Bridge Called My Back: Writings by Radical Women of Color* (Watertown, Mass.: Persephone Press), p. 82.

2. Barbara Burris in agreement with Kathy Barry, Terry Moore, Joann DeLor, Joann Parreut, Cate Stadelman, "The Fourth World Manifesto," in Anne Koedt, Ellen Levine, and Anita Rapone, eds., *Radical Feminism* (New York: Quadrangle Books, 1973), p. 342. The following references are all to this volume and will show only page numbers.

3. Mary Daly, *Gyn/Ecology: The Metaethics of Radical Feminism* (Boston: Beacon Press), p. 59.

4. Burris et al., "The Fourth World Manifesto," p. 340.

5. Ibid., p. 355.

6. Ibid., p. 355.

7. Joyce Trebilcot, "Conceiving Women: Notes on the Logic of Feminism," *Sinister Wisdom*, Fall 1979, pp. 43-50.

8. Ibid., p. 46.

9. Susan Griffin, *Woman and Nature: The Roaring Inside Her* (New York: Harper & Row, 1978). See especially the chapter entitled "HIS POWER (He Tames What Is Wild)."

10. Daly, *Gyn/Ecology, pp. 343 and 345.*

11. Adrienne Rich, Women and Honor: Some Notes on Lying (Pittsburgh, Pa: Motheroot Publications), p. 1.

12. Ibid., p. 1.

13. Ibid., p. 9.

14. Trebilcot, "Conceiving Women", p. 46.

15. Sally Miller Gearhart, "The Spiritual Dimension: Death and Resurrection of a Hallelujah Dyke," in Ginny Vida, ed., *Our Right to Love* (Englewood Cliffs, N.J.: Prentice-Hall, 1978), p. 187.

16. Carol P. Christ, *Diving Deep and Surfacing: Women Writers·on Spiritual Quest* (Boston: Beacon Press, 1980), p. 13. Thanks to Penny Smith for giving me this book.

17. Sara Ann Ketchum, "Female Culture, Womanculture, and Conceptual Change: Toward a Philosophy of Women's Studies," *Social Theory and Practice* 6, no. 2 (Summer, 1980):153.

18. Susan Leigh Star, "To Dwell Among Ourselves," *Sinister Wisdom* 8 (Winter 1979):95.

19. Barbara Love and Elizabeth Shanklin, "The Answer is Matriarchy," in Vida, ed., *Our Right to Love,* pp. 183-86.

20. Daly, *Gyn/Ecology,* pp. 369-70.

21. *The Matriarchist,* vol. 2, is. 1, p. 4. *The Matriarchist* is published by The Foundation of Matriarchy, P.O. Box 271, Pratt Station, Brooklyn, N.Y., 11205.

22. For recent liberal discussions of this issue, see Stuart Hampshire, ed., *Public and Private Morality* (Cambridge: Cambridge University Press, 1978).

23. Charles E. Ellison, "Marx and the Modern City: Public Life and the Problem of Personality," paper read to the Annual Meeting of the Mid-west Political Science Association, Cincinnati, Ohio, April 15-18, 1981, p. 30 of typescript.

24. Murray Bookchin, *Post-Scarcity Anarchism* (San Francisco: Ramparts Press, 1971), p. 77.

25. Love and Shanklin, "The Answer is Matriarchy," pp. 184-85.

26. Ibid., p. 184.

27. Adrienne Rich, *Of Woman Born: Motherhood as Experience and Institution* (New York: W.W. Norton, 1976), p. 27.

28. Ibid., p. 205.

29. Ibid., p. 235.

30. Shulamith Firestone, *The Dialectic of Sex* (New York: Bantam Books, 1971), Chap. 3: "Freudianism: The Misguided Feminism."

31. Rich, *Of Woman Born,* pp. 211-12.

32. Dorothy Dinnerstein, *The Mermaid and the Minotaur: Sexual Arrangements and Human Malaise* (New York: Harper Colophon, 1977), pp. 28-29.

33. Ibid., p. 60.

34. Ibid., p. 108.

35. Jane Alpert, "MotherRight: A New Feminist Theory," *Ms.,* August 1973, p. 92.

36. Sara Ann Ketchum and Christine Pierce, "Sex Objects, Sexual Partners, and Separatism" (unpublished ms.), p. 5. A later version of this paper was published as "Separatism and Sexual Relationships," but it omitted this point made in the earlier paper.

37. Doris Lessing's *The Summer Before the Dark* (New York: Alfred A. Knopf, 1973) provides a vivid account of this process.

38. Susan Brownmiller, *Against Our Will: Men, Women and Rape* (New York: Bantam Books, 1976), chap. 3: "War."

39. Susan Griffin, *Rape: The Power of Consciousness* (San Francisco: Harper & Row, 1979), p. 88.

40. In the United Kingdom, three men were acquitted of raping a woman despite her screams and struggles, because they accepted the assurance of her husband that, in spite of her behavior, in fact she consented to sexual intercourse with them. *D.P.P.* v. *Morgan* (1975) 2 W.L.R. 913.

41. "Forcible and Statutory Rape: An Exploration of the Operation and Objectives of the Consent Standard," *Yale Law Journal* 62, no. 1 (December 1952):70. Cited by Jill Bley, "The History of Rape," *The Women Helping Women Manual* (Cincinnati, OH, 1978).

42. Ibid., pp. 72-73.

43. Ibid., p. 73.

44. Griffin, *Rape,* p. 39.

45. Ibid., p. 21.

46. Barbara Mehrhof and Pamela Kearon, "Rape: An Act of Terror," *Notes from the Third Year: Women's Liberation* (New York: 1971), p. 80.

47. Brownmiller, *Against Our Will,* p. 5.

48. Louanna Aptheker, "Can a Woman Rape a Man?" (unpublished).

49. Mehrhof and Kearon, "Rape: An Act of Terror," pp. 80-81.

50. Kathleen Barry, *Female Sexual Slavery* (Englewoods Cliffs, N.J.: Prentice-Hall, 1979), p. 33 (italics in original).

51. Ibid., p. 220.

52. Karen Lindsey, "Prostitution and the Law," *The Second Wave* 1, no. 4 (1972): p. 6.

53. Sheila Cronan, "Marriage," in Koedt, Levine and Rapone, eds., *Radical Feminism,* p. 217.

54. Firestone, *The Dialectic of Sex,* p. 126.

55. Ibid., p. 140.

56. Ibid., p. 146.

57. Kate Millett, *Sexual Politics* (New York: Avon Books, 1971).

58. Robin Morgan, "Theory and Practice: Pornography and Rape," in Laura Lederer, ed., *Take Back the Night: Women on Pornography* (New York: William Morrow, 1980), p. 139.

59. Barry, *Female Sexual Slavery,* chap. 9.

60. Morgan, "Theory and Practice," pp. 139-40.

61. Adrienne Rich, "Afterword" to Lederer, ed., *Take Back the Night,* p. 320.

62. Sharon Deevey, "Such a Nice Girl," in Nancy Myron and Charlotte Bunch, eds., *Lesbianism and the Women's Movement* (Baltimore: Diana Press, 1975), p. 24.

63. The Purple September Staff, "The Normative Status of Heterosexuality," in Myron and Bunch, eds., *Lesbianism and the Women's Movement,* p. 83.

64. Juliet Mitchell, *Women's Estate* (New York: Random House, 1971), p. 104, cites Rene Dumont, *L'Afrique Noire est Mal Partie,* 1962, p. 210.

65. Barbara Ehrenreich and Annette Fuentes, "Life on the Global Assembly Line," *Ms.*, January 1981.

66. Atypical is Kathy Parker and Lisa Leghorn's "Towards a Feminist Economics: A Global View," *The Second Wave* (Summer/Fall 1979):23-30. This article was the forerunner of their book, *Woman's Worth: Sexual Economics and the World of Women* (Boston and London: Routledge & Kegan Paul, 1981). This pioneering and exciting book offers a new way of conceptualizing the economic realm that illuminates the international reach of the sexual division of labor, that makes visible much of women's hitherto invisible economic activity, and that demonstrates how this activity is organized for men's benefit.

67. Ti-Grace Atkinson, "The Institution of Sexual Intercourse," in *Women's Liberation: Notes from the Second Year* (New York, 1970), p. 42.

68. Firestone, *The Dialectic of Sex*, chap. 1.

69. Griffin, *Rape: The Power of Consciousness*, p. 26 fn (italics in original).

70. Mary Daly, *Beyond God the Father: Toward a Philosophy of Women's Liberation* (Boston: Beacon Press, 1973), p. 8.

71. Ibid., p. 8.

72. Ibid., p. 167.

73. Griffin, *Rape: The Power of Consciousness*, p. 30.

74. Ibid.

75. Daly, *Gyn/Ecology*, pp. 59 and 424.

76. Andrea Dworkin, "Why So-Called Radical Men Love and Need Pornography," in Lederer, ed., *Take Back the Night*, pp. 148-49.

77. Adrienne Rich, "Afterword" to Lederer, ed., *Take Back the Night*, p. 318 fn.

78. Ibid., pp. 316-17.

79. Artemis March, "A Paradigm for Feminist Theory," paper delivered at the Second Sex Conference, NYC, September 1979.

80. Catherine A. MacKinnon, "Feminism, Marxism, Method and the State," *Signs: Journal of Women in Culture and Society* 7, no. 3 (Spring 1982):515-16.

81. Sara Ann Ketchum and Christine Pierce, "Separatism and Sexual Relationships," in Sharon Bishop and Marjorie Weinzweig, *Philosophy and Women* (Belmont, CA: Wadsworth, 1979), p. 164. This article is a very clear and illuminating discussion of a highly emotional issue, and the argument of the rest of this paragraph is based on Ketchum and Pierce's discussion. In another excellent article, Marilyn Frye argues that separatism is a way of taking power and escaping male parasitism ("Some Reflections on Separatism and Power," *Sinister Wisdom* 6 [Fall, 1978]). Also published as a pamphlet by Tea Rose Press, PO Box 591, East Lansing, Michigan, 48823.

82. Patricia Mainardi, "The Marriage Question," in Redstockings, *Feminist Revolution* (New York: Random House, 1977(?)), p. 121.

83. Coletta Reid, "Coming Out in the Women's Movement," in Myron and Bunch, eds., *Lesbianism and the Women's Movement*, p. 96.

84. Rita Mae Brown, "The Shape of Things to Come," in Myron and Bunch, eds., *Lesbianism and the Women's Movement*, p. 71.

85. The Purple September Staff, "The Normative Status of Heterosexuality," p. 83.

86. Charlotte Bunch, "Lesbians in Revolt," in Myron and Bunch, eds., *Lesbianism and the Women's Movement*, p. 36.

87. Ti-Grace Atkinson, "Lesbianism and Feminism," in Phyllis Birkby, Bertha Harris, Jill Johnston, Esther Newton, Jane O'Wyatt, eds., *Amazon Expedition: a lesbianfeminist anthology* (Washington, N.J.: Times Change Press, 1973), p. 12.

88. Ti-Grace Atkinson, *Amazon Odyssey* (New York: Links, 1974), pp. 13–23,83–88.

89. Adrienne Rich, "Compulsory Heterosexuality and Lesbian Existence," *Signs: Journal of Women in Culture and Society* 5, no. 4 (Summer 1980):648-49.

90. Bunch, "Lesbians in Revolt," p. 33.

91. Cheryl Clarke, "Lesbianism: An Act of Resistance," in Moraga and Anzaldua, eds., *This Bridge Called My Back*, pp. 128-37.

92. I am thinking of the Redstockings group who published the anthology *Feminist Revolution*, and also the journal *Meeting Ground*.

93. Charlotte Bunch, "Lesbians in Revolt," pp. 31-32.

94. Coletta Reid, "Coming Out in the Women's Movement," p. 103.

95. Ibid., p. 97.

96. Rita Mae Brown, "The Shape of Things to Come," p. 71.

97. Radicalesbians, "Woman-Identified Woman" in *Liberation Now: Writings from the Women's Liberation Movement* (New York: Dell Publishers, 1971), p. 287.

98. Barbara Solomon, "Taking the Bullshit by the Horns," in Myron and Bunch, eds., *Lesbianism and the Women's Movement*, p. 41.

99. Bunch, "Lesbians in Revolt," p. 29.

100. Rita Mae Brown, "Living with Other Women," in *Women: A Journal of Liberation* 2, no. 2, p. 34.

101. Sharon Deevey, "Such a Nice Girl," p. 25.

102. Rita Mae Brown, *Plain Brown Rapper* (Oakland, Calif: Diana Press, 1976), p. 213.

103. A typical example is Donald Milligan, *The Politics of Homosexuality* (London: Pluto Press, 1973).

104. Letter to the editors by Andrena Zawinski, *Off Our Backs* 9, no. 2 (February 1981):28.

105. Pat Califia, "Feminism and Sadomasochism," *Heresies* 3, no. 4 (Is. 12):30. It was Pat Califia's book of lesbian sexuality, *Sapphistry*, which brought this issue out of the closet and to the attention of the broader women's community.

106. Bat-Ami Bar On, "Feminism and Sadomasochism: Self-Critical Notes," in Robin Ruth Linden, Darlene R. Pagano, Diana E. W. Russell, and Susan Leigh Star, eds., *Against Sadomasochism: A Radical Feminist Analysis* (East Palo Alto, CA: Frog in the Well Press, 1982), p. 80. For more on this topic, see the various reports on Barnard College's ninth Scholar and the Feminist Conference: Towards a Politics of Sexuality, in *Off Our Backs* 12, no. 6 (June 1982).

107. Jennifer Woodul, "What's This about Feminist Businesses?" *Off Our Backs* 6, no. 4 (June 1976). Reprinted in Alison M. Jaggar and Paula M. Struhl, eds., *Feminist Frameworks: Alternative Theoretical Accounts of the Relations Between Women and Men* (New York: McGraw-Hill, 1978), pp. 197-98.

108. Coletta Reid, "Taking Care of Business," *Quest: A Feminist Quarterly* 1, no. 2 (Fall 1974):18-21.

109. Advertisement in *Matrices: A Lesbian-Feminist Research Newsletter* 4, no. 3 (June 1981):10.

110. Ann Withorn, "Helping Ourselves: The Limits and Potential of Self Help," *Radical America* 14, no. 3 (May–June 1980):32.

111. Quoted in ibid.

112. Lois Ahrens, "Battered Women's Refuges: Feminist Cooperatives Vs. Social Service Institutions," in *Radical America* 14, no. 3 (May-June 1980):42.

113. Laurie MacKenzie and Sue Kirk, "What is Radical Feminist Counseling?" duplicated by the Center for Women's Studies and Services, 908 'F' St., San Diego, CA., 92101.

114. Lynne Farrow, "Feminism as Anarchism," Black Bear Pamphlet 2, c/o 76 Peckham Rd., London SE5, p. 1. This article first appeared in 1974 in *Aurora*, a New York feminist magazine.

115. Pierre-Joseph Proudhon, *What is Property? First Memoir—An Inquiry into the Principle of Right and of Government*, trans. by Benjamin R. Tucker (Princeton, Mass.: B.R. Tucker, 1876), p. 11. Proudhon (1809–1865) was a French socialist whose ideas formed the basis for the anarcho-syndicalist movement which flourished at the turn of the century.

116. Bookchin, *Post-Scarcity Anarchism*, p. 45.

117. Ursula LeGuin, *The Dispossessed*, quoted by Lizzie Borden, "Women and Anarchy," *Heresies* 1, no. 2 (May 1977):73.

118. Peter Kropotkin, *Mutual Aid: A Factor of Evolution*, London, 1902. In contrast to prevailing interpretations of Darwinian theory, which stressed individual competition as the sole motive force of biological evolution and social progress, Kropotkin (1842–1921)

argued that cooperation or mutual aid was also an important factor in biological and social evolution.

119. Borden, "Women and Anarchy," p. 72.

120. Bookchin, *Post-Scarcity Anarchism,* p. 44.

121. Ibid., pp. 44-45.

122. Peggy Kornegger, "Anarchism: The Feminist Connection," *The Second Wave: a magazine of the new feminism* 4, no. 1 (Spring 1975):31.

123. Woodul, "What's This about Feminist Businesses?" p. 197. Barbara Love and Elizabeth Shanklin, authors of "The Answer is Matriarchy," write: "matriarchy implies a worldwide socialist economic base, but a liberation of reproduction from subordination to the socialist state" (p. 186).

124. Chicago Anarcho-Feminists, "Anarcho-Feminist Manifesto," *Siren: A Journal of Anarcho-Feminism* 1, no. 1 (1971). Reprinted as Black Bear Pamphlet 1, c/o 76 Peckham Rd., London SE5.

125. Daly, *Beyond God the Father,* p. 133.

126. Examples of feminist science fiction include the following: C.P. Gilman, *Herland: A Lost Feminist Utopian Novel* (New York: Pantheon, 1979); Dorothy Bryant, *The Kin of Ata are Waiting for You* (Berkeley, CA and New York: Moon Books and Random House, 1976); Marge Piercy, *Woman on the Edge of Time* (New York: Fawcett, 1976); Sally Miller Gearhart, *The Wanderground: Stories of the Hill Women* (Watertown, Mass: Persephone Press, 1979); and many of the novels of Ursula LeGuin, perhaps especially *The Left Hand of Darkness.*

127. Women's Majority Union (Seattle, Washington), "*Lilith's Manifesto—1969*" in Robin Morgan, ed., *Sisterhood is Powerful: An Anthology of Writings from the Women's Liberation Movement* (New York: Vintage Books, 1970), p. 529 (italics in original).

128. Bookchin, *Post-Scarcity Anarchism,* pp. 232-33.

129. Joan Rothchild, "Taking Our Future Seriously," *Quest: A Feminist Quarterly* 2, no. 3 (winter 1976):26. Thanks to Marilyn Myerson for drawing this article to my attention.

130. Laurel, "Toward a Woman Vision," *Amazon Quarterly* vol. 1, is. 2, p. 40. Quoted by Kornegger, "Anarchism: The Feminist Connection," p. 36.

131. Daly, *Gyn/Ecology,* p. 1.

132. Loie Hayes, "Preying Mantis Urges Vandalism," *Off Our Backs* 11, no. 6 (June 1981):12.

133. *Time,* April 23, 1973. Quoted by Griffin, *Rape: The Power of Consciousness,* p. 78.

134. Hayes, "Preying Mantis."

135. Loie Hayes, "Feminist Arsonists in England," *Off Our Backs* 11, no.6 (June 1981):13.

136. WITCH leaflet reprinted in Morgan, ed., *Sisterhood is Powerful,* p. 538.

137. Bookchin, *Post Scarcity Anarchism,* pp. 221-2.

138. WITCH leaflet, p. 538. On p. 539 can be found other meanings of the acronym WITCH.

139. Loie Hayes, "Women's Pentagon Action: Herstory and Future," *Off Our Backs* 11, no. 4 (April 1981):9.

140. WITCH leaflet, p. 540.

141. Joreen, "The Tyranny of Structurelessness," reprinted in Koedt, Levine, and Rapone, *Radical Feminism,* pp. 285-99.

142. "The Feminists: A Political Organization to Annihilate Sex Roles," Atkinson, ed., *Women's Liberation:* in *Notes from the Second Year,* New York, 1970. p. 115. This article was reprinted in Koedt, Levine, and Rapone, *Radical Feminism.*

143. Madeline Belkin, "Drowning in the Steno Pool," in *Liberation Now! Writings from the Women's Liberation Movement* (New York: Dell, 1971), p. 77.

144. Wendy Kaminer, "Pornography and the First Amendment: Prior Restraints and Private Action," in Lederer, ed., *Take Back the Night,* p. 247.

145. Hayes, "Preying Mantis Urges Vandalism."

146. Red Rosia and Black Maria, "Blood of the Flower," Black Bear Pamphlet, 1.

147. Kornegger, "Anarchism: The Feminist Connection," p. 33.

148. Among the best examples of this sort of combination is so-called performance art which developed in Los Angeles during the 1970s. A brief account of this art form, together with pictures of some of the most striking examples, is given by Suzanne Lacy, "Organizing: The Art of Protest," *Ms,* October 1982, pp. 64-67.

149. Mehrhof and Kearon, "Rape: An Act of Terror," p. 233.

150. Griffin, *Rape: The Power of Consciousness,* p. 31.

151. Ibid.

152. Farrow, "Feminism as Anarchism," p. 11.

153. Ibid., p. 7.

154. Annette Kuhn and Ann Marie Wolpe, "Feminism and Materialism," in Kuhn and Ann Marie Wolpe, eds., *Feminism and Materialism: Women and Modes of Production* (London, Henley, and Boston: Routledge & Kegan Paul, 1978), p. 6.

155. Farrow, "Feminism as Anarchism," pp. 6, 7, and 8.

156. Griffin, *Rape: The Power of Consciousness,* p. 31.

157. Most of the items on this list come from Mary Daly's *Gyn/Ecology.* As we have seen earlier, however, radical feminists are not in complete agreement about the precise definition of their central concepts, and so not all would accept the appearance of all these items on a single list.

158. Solomon, "Taking the Bullshit by the Horns," p. 44.

159. Farrow, "Feminism as Anarchism," p. 10.

160. Carol Anne Douglas, "Review of *Reinventing Anarchy,*" *Off Our Backs* 11, no. 4 (April 1981):21.

161. For some of these examples, see *Disregarded History: Case Studies of European Nonviolent Defense,* pamphlet available from the Fellowship of Reconcilation, Youth Action, Box 271, Nyack, NY, 10960.

162. Laurelchild's expression was quoted by Maida Tilchen, "Women's Music: Politics for Sale?" *Gay Community New Music Supplement,* June 1981. Thanks for Teresa Boykin for bringing this article to my attention.

163. Ibid., p. 2.

164. Ibid., p. 2.

165. Carol P. Christ, "Why Women Need the Goddess: Phenomenological, Psychological and Political Reflections," in Charlene Spretnak, ed., *The Politics of Women's Spirituality: Essays on the Rise of Spiritual Power Within the Feminist Movement* (New York: Anchor Books, 1982):84.

166. Early radical feminists who made this claim include Shulamith Firestone in *The Dialectic of Sex;* "The Feminists: A Political Organization to Annihilate Sex Roles," in *Radical Feminism,* p. 370; and Charlotte Bunch, "Lesbians in Revolt," p. 32.

167. Bunch, "Lesbians in Revolt," p. 33.

168. Clarke, "Lesbianism: An Act of Resistance," p. 130.

169. Combahee River Collective, "A Black Feminist Statement," in Zillah R. Eisenstein, ed., *Capitalist Patriarchy and the Case for Socialist Feminism* (New York: Monthly Review Press, 1978), pp. 365-66.

170. Pat Parker, "Revolution: It's Not Neat or Pretty or Quick," in *This Bridge Called My Back,* p. 241.

10
The Politics of Socialist Feminism

The Political Values of Socialist Feminism

Socialist feminism views human nature as defined in part by biological characteristics of the human species. These characteristics, however, are subject to change because a unique feature of the human species is that it continuously transforms itself through its conscious and cooperative productive activity. Through this activity, human beings continuously re-create their physiological and psychological constitution. Thus, human nature is a historically changing phenomenon. Stated in its most abstract form, the socialist feminist conception of human nature is identical with that of traditional Marxism. We have seen already, however, that socialist feminists and traditional Marxists draw very different implications from this conception, partly because they have divergent conceptions of human productive activity, partly because they have different categorical frameworks for analyzing that activity.

The socialist feminist conception of productive activity acknowledges the historically determined and changing character of the production of people, including the production of sexuality, as well as the historically determined character of the production of other goods and services. In its analyses of contemporary society, socialist feminism goes beyond conventional definitions of "the economy" to consider activity that does not involve the exchange of money. Within its concept of productive activity, therefore, it includes the procreative and sexual work that is done by women in the home. In analyzing all forms of productive activity, socialist feminism supplements the analytic tool of class with the additional conceptual tool of gender. It perceives that human productive activity is organized invariably around a sexual division of labor and that the specific historical form taken by the sexual division of labor has always been basic in determining the historically prevailing constitution of human nature. Socialist feminism's distinctive contribution to our understanding of human nature is its recognition that the differences between women and men are not pre-social givens, but rather are socially constructed and therefore socially alterable.

Implicit in the socialist feminist conception of human nature, as in all conceptions of human nature, are certain social values. Chief among these is the value of productive activity or work. Since socialist feminism shares the basic Marxist conception of human nature, it is inevitable that it should share the Marxist belief that human fulfilment is to be found in free productive activity. But because socialist feminism has a broader view than traditional Marxism of what counts as distinctively human productive activity, its conception of freedom is very different from that of traditional Marxism. In many ways, indeed, the socialist feminist vision of the good society is quite similar to that of some radical feminists, even though the theoretical basis of their social and political values is quite different.

Socialist feminism is a very recent political tendency and it is still under-developed, both practically and theoretically. For this reason, one cannot turn to an existing body of systematic theory explaining the philosophical foundations of the position. Instead, one must attempt to extrapolate a systematic theory from the existing fragments and from the tentative beginnings of practice. To expound socialist feminist theory, to a far greater degree than for better-developed theories, is also to participate in constructing that theory. The following exposition of the political values of socialist feminism is an attempt to reinterpret traditional Marxist theory so that it is compatible with socialist feminist practice.

Within the Marxist tradition, work is valued both for its direct products, which fulfil specific and historically determined human needs, and also for the possibility it offers of developing the potentialities of the workers. Because socialist feminism acknowledges sexuality and procreation as historically changing forms of productive activity, socialist feminist theory must regard these as important avenues for possible human development. Of course, socialist feminism does not have to envision precisely what the full flowering of human procreative and sexual capacities would be like, any more than Marxism can envision clearly the full flowering of other kinds of human productive capacities. Nevertheless, it does need to identify the material preconditions for such a flowering. Marx's distinction between "the realm of freedom" and the "realm of necessity" seems well adapted for this task.

In Chapter 8, we saw that the boundaries of the realm of necessity were determined by two interrelated conditions: a certain level of development of the forces of production and a certain organization of the social relations of production. When the level of development of the productive forces is low or when exploitation or forced labor exists, the realm of necessity is relatively large and most of the lives of most people are spent in that realm. When the level of development of the productive forces is high and when exploitation is reduced or eliminated, then the realm of necessity is relatively small and everyone can spend a good portion of their lives in the realm of freedom. The relation between the technical and social boundaries of the realm of necessity is, of course, a dialectical relation. On the one hand, certain forms of technological development have shaped the social relations of production; that is, they have set limits to the ways in which people can organize themselves if they are to utilize those types of technology. On the other hand, exploitative class relations have allowed the development only of certain kinds of productive techniques, techniques designed primarily to maximize productivity regardless of their damaging effects on the workers. When we look at the historical development of modes of sexual and procreative activity, it is easy to see how that activity has been subject to constraints that are simultaneously social and technological.

The sexual and procreative labor of most societies has been performed primarily by women. Obviously, men have played a role in conceiving children but they have not had to give birth to them and their role in childrearing usually has been quite limited. Men's work has been defined primarily as belonging to the public sphere of "politics," "culture," government and war. It is women's work which has been defined as belonging to the private sphere and it is mostly women who have performed what society has defined as necessary sexual and procreative labor.

Much, though never all, of women's energy has been consumed in sexual and procreative labor—and most of this labor has always been forced rather than free. Both technological and social conditions have limited women's sexual and procreative activity to the realm of necessity. First, low levels of development in the productive forces have often resulted in high infant mortality and the consequent need for a high birthrate. Moreover, primitive contraceptive techniques may sometimes have resulted in the birth of more babies than women desired. These factors, however, were inseparable from the prevailing system of social relations. For instance, the rate of infant mortality was (and often still is) linked to the class, race and sex of the infants. Moreover, the desired rate of birth has depended largely on social factors: a high birthrate has been desired primarily when the dominant class has needed labor power that it could exploit. In primitive hunting and gathering societies, with little opportunity to create a surplus and so little exploitation, a low birthrate was desired and was generally achieved, although it was accompanied sometimes by infanticide. A high birthrate became desirable only when the development of agriculture made possible the accumulation of surplus wealth and again when the Industrial Revolution offered new opportunities for the exploitation of labor. At these times, women were forced to produce more children, partly by suppressing knowledge and availability of the contraceptive and abortion techniques that were in existence already. For these reasons, the procreative labor in which women have engaged historically is viewed more accurately as resulting from "social" rather than from "natural" necessity, insofar as these two categories can be given any distinct meaning. Women's sexual labor is even more clearly a result of "social" rather than of "natural" necessity: in male-dominant societies, women have always been compelled to engage in more and different kinds of sexual activity than were required simply in order to conceive children.

If sexual and procreative activity is constrained both by technological and by social conditions, then sexual and procreative freedom requires developments in both technology and social organization. A basic technological requirement for free sexual and procreative activity is the availability of means for controlling fertility, for avoiding babies when procreation is not desired and for producing babies when they are desired. Procreative freedom also presupposes the material resources for raising children to adulthood in a certain fashion.

Social as well as technological preconditions exist for the free development of human sexual and procreative potentialities. Most simply, those who engage in any kind of sexual or procreative activity must do so freely rather than out of coercion. A certain level of sexual and procreative activity will always be needed in any society, just as there will always be the need for a certain level of other kinds of productive activity. At this stage, socialist feminists do not specify exactly how this socially necessary work should be assigned, any more than traditional Marxists specify exactly how other kinds of socially necessary work should be assigned. Nor do socialist feminists anticipate in any detail just what freely creative rather than coerced sexual and procreative activity would be like. But socialist feminists do point out that free sexual and procreative activity requires the abolition of exploitation. Given their understanding of political economy, this means not only the abolition of capitalism but also the abolition of male dominance. Without the elimination of both these forms of exploitation, the full development of human sexual and procreative potentialities is impossible.

Although the socialist feminist conception of freedom is rooted in the traditional Marxist conception, its actual vision of the realm of freedom differs almost as much from the traditional Marxist view as it does from the liberal view. For liberal feminism, freedom lies primarily in the private realm outside the scope of state regulation, although paradoxically, as we have seen, liberal feminism looks to the state to guarantee that freedom. Traditional Marxism, by contrast, holds a more classical view of freedom as existing only in the public realm, where citizens engage in conscious political action to change the course of history. Both these views of freedom are challenged by the socialist feminist conception of human nature and of human productive activity. Socialist feminism conceives sexuality and procreation as human activities which are no more biologically determined than any other and so are equally capable of social development. Thus, on the one hand, socialist feminism denies the liberal belief that sexuality and procreation are matters purely of individual or "personal" concern; on the other hand, socialist feminism denies the traditional Marxist assumption that sexuality and procreation are not possible arenas of human development and will vary relatively little from one society to the next. For these reasons, the socialist feminist conception of freedom is defined neither by the traditional Marxist nor by the liberal versions of the public/private distinction. Indeed, the socialist feminist conception of freedom is incompatible with the maintenance of any traditional version of the public/private distinction. For socialist feminism, freedom consists in transcending the realm of necessity in every area of human life, including sexuality and procreation. Freedom is a social achievement and cannot be achieved by isolated individuals in the absence of a general reordering of society.

In its rejection of the public/private distinction, the socialist feminist vision of the good society is closest to the vision of radical feminism. All earlier political theories have devalued, in one way or another, the daily work of bodily maintenance, particularly the care of children, and have seen human freedom and fulfilment as consisting in the transcendence of this work. Only radical feminism and socialist feminism have seen how human nature and human society are shaped by prevailing modes of organizing sexuality and procreation and have speculated on how human history may be reshaped by conscious political activity directed toward transforming traditional modes of organizing those activities. Of course, radical feminists differ widely between themselves on the sorts of changes in procreation they think are desirable or even possible. They are also bolder in envisioning new modes of procreation than are socialist feminists, whose adherence to historical materialism makes them sceptical that those forms can be determined in much detail in advance.

Another convergence between the political values of radical and of socialist feminism is their shared concern for ecology. Respect for non-human nature has always been an important value of radical feminism. In the penultimate chapter of *The Dialectic of Sex*, Firestone linked feminism and ecology, and later radical feminists have grounded feminist ecological concern in women's spiritual experience of communion with non-human nature. Socialist feminists share the radical feminist concern for the environment, but their Marxist conception of human nature allows them the possibility of providing a materialist, as opposed to a spiritual, grounding for that concern. On the Marxist view, human and non-human nature cannot be conceived separately from each other: human beings depend on non-human nature for their sustenance and they also shape and transform that nature by their labor. This conception of the dialectical unity between human and non-human nature constitutes the theoretical basis for socialist feminist ecological concerns, a basis which is not incompatible with the radical feminist intuition of a spiritual unity between human and non-human nature. Of course, this way of conceptualizing the relation between human and non-human nature could also provide the basis for traditional Marxist ecological concerns, but Marxists in the past have tended to stress the domination rather than the balance of nature. As we shall see in the next chapter, some socialist feminists believe that the traditional dominating attitude towards nature is the psychological result of a certain mode of organizing procreation.

In the rest of this chapter, we shall see how the basic values of socialist feminism generate a distinctive analysis of women's oppression in contemporary society and a set of distinctive political proposals for overcoming that oppression.

Alienation: The Socialist Feminist Analysis of Women's Oppression

In analyzing the oppression of the working class under capitalism, Marxists in the latter part of the 20th century have often made use of the concept of alienation. As we have seen, Marxists disagree about the propriety of this concept, since it is mentioned primarily in Marx's earlier and less "scientific" writings. Bertell Ollman has suggested, however, that even though the later Marx rarely uses the word "alienation," still Marx's mature critique of capitalism rests on his earlier perceptions of the structure and quality of capitalist social relations, perceptions that he expressed in terms of alienation. Socialist feminists, too, mention alienation only occasionally as they analyze women's oppression in contemporary society. Even so, I suggest that the concept of alienation can provide a theoretical framework for systematizing the socialist feminist critique of women's contemporary oppression. In utilizing this concept, of course, socialist feminists cannot rely on its religious interpretation, which describes the separation of the individual from God, nor on its psychological interpretation, which focuses on an individual's feelings of being an outsider, lonely or unwanted. Instead, the socialist feminist conception of alienation must be an extension of the traditional Marxist conception, which describes the structure of relations that define the typical human condition in capitalist society.

The traditional Marxist conception of alienation was developed primarily to explain the condition of wage workers but it does not exclude capitalists, who are thought to suffer their own special form of alienation. On the traditional Marxist view, alienation is a condition specific to humans under capitalism, although certain features of it may exist in other modes of production. Consequently, those who do not participate directly in the social relations that characterize the capitalist mode of production are not alienated. For instance, peasants are not alienated, although they certainly are exploited, nor are servants. Women are alienated insofar as they participate in capitalist relations of production either as wage laborers or, more rarely, as capitalists. According to the traditional Marxist interpretation of alienation, however, women are not alienated insofar as they are excluded from capitalist relations of production: thus, not all women are alienated, and those who are do not suffer special gender-specific forms of alienation. These are the main features of the traditional Marxist conception of alienation that socialist feminism wants to revise. It wants to show that, in contemporary society, women are alienated in all aspects of their lives. Moreover, this alienation takes special, gender-specific forms.

The Marxist conception of alienation has been outlined already in Chapter 8. As I said there, the central feature of alienation is that things or people which in fact are related dialectically to each other come to seem alien, separated from or opposed to each other. The situation of the wage laborer under capitalism constitutes the paradigm case of alienation. For Marx, labor is the essential human activity which links human individuals to the non-human world and to each other and which makes possible the development of their own capacities. Under capitalism, however, labor is organized in such a way as to disguise these links, making it appear that individuals must always be separate or alienated from the non-human world, from their own products, from the process of their work and from their co-workers and that labor must always prevent them from fulfilling their own potentialities. What accomplishes this apparent separation is that, under capitalism, individuals are deprived of control over their own labor power; they are forced to work according to the dictates of the capitalist class. Consequently, workers' products are taken from them and used against them, their fellow workers are made into competitors and the work process becomes an exhausting interruption of their "real" lives, an interruption which forces them to overdevelop a few primitive skills while preventing them from developing more complex and "global" capacities. In this way, alienation fragments not only the human community; it also fragments the human individual.

A few socialist feminist authors, building on radical feminist insights, have argued that women's experience in contemporary society is a perfect example of alienation. Socialist feminist explorations reveal the ways in which women are alienated as sexual beings, as mothers and as wives. One socialist feminist author writes that femininity itself is alienation.

The (hetero)sexual alienation of women was probably the first form of women's special alienation to be given explicit recognition. In 1971, Linda Phelps wrote an article entitled "Death in the Spectacle: Female Sexual Alienation," and Sandra Bartky has since written two papers using the concept of alienation to explore the relation between the contemporary forms of female sexuality and other features of women's lives. References to women's sexual alienation are also made by a number of other authors.[1] All these authors stress the coercive aspects of heterosexuality in contemporary society. Women are viewed relentlessly as sexual objects, whether or not they welcome sexual interest, and they are subject continually to sexual assaults and harassment. In addition, economic survival requires most women to present themselves in a way that is sexually pleasing to men: male superiors penalize women who seem to be "punishing" or defying men through their appearance; much of women's paid work is sexualized; and, in the end, the best chance of economic security for most women remains the sale of their sexuality in marriage. For economic reasons, therefore, women are compelled to spend large amounts of time and money on make-up, hair, diets, figure salons and alluring clothes. They are expected to titillate male sexuality in situations that are not overtly sexual and, in overtly sexual situations, they are expected to fascinate, to arouse and to satisfy men. In short, men rather than women control the expression of women's sexuality: women's sexuality is developed for men's enjoyment rather than for women's. In this respect, women's sexual situation resembles that of wage workers who are alienated from the process and product of their labor.

The way in which males control female sexuality also alienates women from themselves. In contemporary society, women are not regarded as whole persons with a multitude of desires, interests and capacities. Instead, they are seen as sexual objects, evaluated primarily in terms of their physical attributes and secondarily in terms of their skill (charm) in displaying these attributes. Pictorial and linguistic "dismemberment," in which parts of a woman's anatomy are portrayed or referred to in isolation from the whole women contribute to the idea that a woman is nothing more than the sum of her bodily parts.[2] The sexual fetishization or reification of parts of their bodies is an extreme way of fragmenting women. It forces a split not only between their bodies and other aspects of their persons but also between different parts of their bodies.

It is difficult for women to resist the definition of themselves that is purveyed by the dominant male culture. Women come to accept the male identification of their selves with their bodies, sometimes just with the fetishized parts of their bodies. Simultaneously, however, women separate themselves from their bodies; their bodies are treated as recalcitrant nature which has to be overcome by a multitude of aids to "beauty." Sandra Bartky has described how the organization of contemporary heterosexuality encourages the development of feminine narcissism. Through narcissism,

> objectifier and objectified can be one and the same person: a woman can become a sex object for herself, taking toward her own person the attitude of a man. She will then take erotic satisfaction in her physical self, reveling in her body as a beautiful object to be gazed at and decorated.[3]

As a result, not only are women's minds separated from their bodies and their bodily parts separated from each other, but fragmentation occurs even within women's minds. "The sexual objectification of women produces a duality in feminine consciousness. The gaze of the Other is internalized so that I myself become at once seer and seen, appraiser and the thing appraised."[4]

Given this fragmented consciousness, it is impossible for women to develop even their full sexual potential, let alone their non-sexual potentialities. The problem of women's sexual alienation is not just that women are not free to express their sexual preferences; more fundamentally, it is that women cannot discover what are their sexual preferences. As a result, many women never reach orgasm in heterosexual encounters and many more achieve it only rarely. Those who do receive gratification from heterosexual encounters often do it by fantasizing themselves in the place of the man; they are aroused by what is being done to them rather than directly making love to the man.[5]

> In these fantasy episodes, the female does not always play the masochistic role. The female who is focusing on sexual imagery can take the part either of the male, the female, or an onlooker, but in any case eroticism is still dealing in female powerlessness.[6]

Feminine narcissism is thus an extreme example of the alienation of women from themselves and from their own potentialities.

The final aspect of women's sexual alienation is that the masculine definition of women as sexual objects for male enjoyment alienates women from each other by making them compete for the sexual attention of men. Women appraise each other's sexual attributes and compare them with their own. This is not to deny that women often provide each other with substantial help and support. Lesbian feminists have pointed out, however, that where female support conflicts with male demands, loyalty to the man invariably comes first. The sexual competition between women often makes them unable to perceive their underlying shared interests, just as wage workers are often unable to perceive the interests they share with their co-workers.

Women's sexual alienation is not the only form of specifically feminine alienation in contemporary society. Women are also alienated as mothers. Just as women do not control how and how often they express their sexuality, neither do they control the conditions of their motherhood. In past times, women have often been forced to bear more children than they wished, in order to satisfy the demand for labor power. By contrast, in advanced capitalist society, where children have become an economic burden rather than an economic benefit, women are often unable to bear the number of children they wish: either they cannot afford to support children alone, their husbands resist more children or they suffer involuntary sterilization. The involuntary sterilization of poor women has become a widespread practice in the United States, affecting disproportionate numbers of black, hispanic, and Native American girls and women.[7] In either case, whether women are forced into motherhood or prevented from becoming mothers, it is not they who decide how many children they bear.

Just as women do not determine the "product" of their procreative capacities, neither do they determine the process in which those capacities are used. The cultural regard for slimness makes many people regard pregnancy as grotesque and so pregnant women, especially those who are unwillingly pregnant, may feel alienated from their bodies. Several authors, moreover, have described contemporary childbirth as "alienated labor." Within the Judaeo-Christian tradition, the pain of childbirth is interpreted as punishment for Eve's sin, and for this reason alone "childbearing is seen as working against the woman, as an experience in which the woman is at odds with her body, not as an opportunity to be in unison with one's body."[8] In contemporary society, modern obstetrics and the discovery of anaesthesia in some ways have reduced the danger and pain of childbirth, but their price has been a progressive loss of control by mothers over the birth process. In the contemporary United States, it has become commonplace for women to be anaesthetized or even tied down when they give birth. Adrienne Rich described her own experience of giving birth in the 1950s.

> We were, above all, in the hands of male medical technology. The hierarchal atmosphere of the hospital, the definition of childbirth as a medical emergency, the fragmentation of body from mind, were the environment in which we gave birth, with or without analgesia . . . The experience of lying half-awake in a barred crib, in a labor room with other women moaning in a drugged condition, where "no one comes" except to do a pelvic examination or give an injection, is a classic experience of alienated childbirth. The loneliness, the sense of abandonment, of being imprisoned, powerless, and depersonalized is the chief collective memory of women who have given birth in American hospitals.[9]

In the years since Rich became a mother, birth has become even more of a high technology event resulting in even further loss of control by the birthing woman.[10] Perhaps the most blatant example is Caesarian sections which, between 1970 and 1980 rose from 5.5 percent to 18 percent of total U.S. births.[11] Giving birth by Caesarian section alienates women even further from their procreative capacities. Birthing women are viewed less as individuals than as the "raw material" from which the "product" is extracted. In these circumstances, the physician rather than the mother comes to be seen as having produced the baby. "In the common view, she has been delivered rather than given birth."[12]

There is, of course, no "natural" or biologically determined way either of giving birth to children or of rearing them. Childrearing, even more obviously than childbearing, is always done in accordance with prevailing norms of what constitutes acceptable behavior in children and desired characteristics in adults. In male-dominant society, as radical feminists have pointed out, women have never completely controlled the process of childrearing, but have always had to raise their children according to patriarchal standards. In the 20th century, however, there have been qualitative changes in childrearing. These changes make the concept of alienation especially applicable to mothers who are rearing children in contemporary capitalist society. The changes are, first, the application of "science" to childrearing and, second, the isolation of mothers.

The development of the "science" of child development has reduced mothers' control over childrearing almost as much as the development of modern obstetrics has reduced mothers' control over the birth process. In pre-industrial society,

> The mother-child relationship had been shaped by the round of daily tasks; it was always in part an apprenticeship relationship. "Child raising" meant teaching children the skills and discipline required to keep the home industries running. It was not something that one *did,* so much as it was something that happened, or had to happen, if the family's work was to be done.[13]

By the 20th century, however, most goods and services were no longer produced in the home. Child labor was eliminated except for the poorest families and fewer women worked outside the home. In consequence, childrearing came to be defined as the central task of women's lives. Now that the mode of childrearing no longer seemed to be determined by immediate economic necessity, childrearing became a "question," just as the options for women that were opened up by the industrial revolution had earlier raised "the woman question." Just as men were ready with answers to "the woman question," so they rushed to answer the question of how children should be reared. The 20th century was dubbed "the century of the child,"[14] and self-styled experts began to propound "scientific" methods of childrearing.

If childrearing is a science, it is one that changes with extraordinary rapidity. At the beginning of the century, the rigid suppression of children's spontaneity and the imposition of "regular habits" resembled the rigid control of workers' "time and motion" which was advocated by the principles of so-called scientific management, introduced into the industry at the end of the 19th century by Frederick Winslow Taylor.[15] By the middle of the century, the expert's advice had changed to the extreme "permissiveness" of the 1950s. Current standards of childrearing require that children receive large quantities of adult attention and "stimulation." Here is one great-grandmother's perception of how standards of childrearing have changed during the 20th century:

> Well, babies, they're a bit tough to figure. When mine were wee, we figured all they needed was feeding and a bit of loving now and again.

I left mine to sleep most of the first year. But my daughter, her babies were born in the 1940s and she was all modern and they were on a schedule so she fed them when the book said, and she took them for a walk when the book said, and bathed them and talked and played with them, all when the book said. She spent more time with them than I did but it seemed odd to me. And now my granddaughter has a wee one and she thinks it needs all sorts of attention. She says babies need talking to and music and she has her sit on the table with her and that baby's never alone except at night. And the baby seems to thrive on it but her mother's never alone and gets no peace. [Generation 1 b. 1893][16]

Mothers are often baffled by the variety of the experts' advice.

Having children is a really difficult thing to do. I never realized it until I had kids but it's all so confusing. You never know if what you're doing is right. Everybody tells you to do something different and it all happens so fast anyway. [Generation II, b. 1924]

I used to think having a baby was just natural. I mean women have done it for thousands of years, right? But now, every time I go to do something, I have to think about it. Is this the right thing or not? It makes me very anxious. [Generation III, b. 1947][17]

In spite of their variety, the methods of scientific childrearing all share two assumptions. The first is that the child is a product which has to be produced according to exact specifications. The second is that mothers are ignorant of how to rear children and have to be instructed by experts. These "experts", of course, are mostly male.

The child-raising science which developed was a masculinist science, framed at an increasing distance from women and children themselves. It was a science which drew more and more on the judgments and studies of the experts, less and less on the experience of mothers—until it comes to see the mothers not only as the major agents of child development but also as the major *obstacles* to it.[18]

Although mothers are not paid for rearing their own children, the increasing subjection of the domestic childrearing process to scientific control suggests that mothers' experience is parallel in this respect to the experience of wage laborers and provides one reason for characterizing mothers' work as alienated.

The second major change in mothers' situation in the 20th century is that they have been isolated from other women in a way that is new. Industrial capitalism took men out of the home and contemporary urban life has progressively decreased the size of households so that ordinarily they contain only one or two adults. Of course, this varies according to class; poor and very rich families are less likely to conform to the official nuclear norm.[19] Most middle-class and the more secure working-class households, however, no longer contain the grandmothers, aunts, boarders, and maids who used to inhabit them. The erstwhile nannies, for instance, have moved into higher-paying and otherwise more attractive jobs. As a result, most 20th-century mothers face alone the enormously demanding work of childrearing.

In 1918, the editor of *The Ladies' Home Journal* rejoiced in the knowledge that, if present trends continued, the postwar generation of American children would be the first generation to be raised by its mothers; they would be healthy in mind and body and, as a result, they would lift the sagging fortunes of the race.[20]

The isolation of contemporary mothers means that, at least when their children are infants, they must face single handed a tremendous amount of work.

Dr. Lovshin . . . says that mothers develop the Tired Mother Syndrome because they are tired. They work a sixteen-hour day, seven days a week. Automation and unions have led to a continuously shortened day for men but the work day of housewives with children had remained constant. The literature bears him out. Oh, it is undoubtedly true that women have today many timesaving devices their mothers did not have. This advantage is offset, however, by the fact that fewer members of the family help with housework and the task of child care, as it is organized in our society, is continuous. Now the woman puts the wash in a machine and spends her time reading to the children, breaking up their fights, taking them to the playground, or otherwise looking after them. . . .

What hits a new mother the hardest is not so much the increased workload as the lack of sleep. However unhappy she may have been in her childless state, however desperate, she could escape by sleep. She could be refreshed by sleep. And if she wasn't a nurse or airline stewardess she generally slept fairly regular hours in a seven- to nine-hour stretch. But almost all babies returning from the hospital are on something like a four-hour food schedule, and they usually demand some attention in between feedings. Now children differ, some cry more, some cry less, some cry almost all the time. If you have never, in some period of your life, been awakened and required to function at one in the morning, and again at three, then maybe at seven, or some such schedule, you can't imagine the agony of it.

All of a woman's muscles ache and they respond with further pain when touched. She is generally cold and unable to get warm. Her reflexes are off. She startles easily, ducks moving shadows, and bumps into stationary objects. Her reading rate takes a precipitious drop. She stutters and stammers, groping for words to express her thoughts, sounding barely coherent—somewhat drunk. She can't bring her mind to focus. She is in a fog. In response to all the aforementioned symptoms she is always close to tears.[21]

The foregoing description of the new mother's condition recalls vividly Marx's description of the alienated wage laborer's conditions, whose work "mortifies his body and ruins his mind."[22] As their children get older, mother's work becomes easier in some ways, but the sheer physical work and the real responsibility of single-handed childrearing continue to impose tremendous stress on mothers. This stress is increased by the mystique of "scientific" childrearing which makes the mother feel that a single word or action, let alone any of her habitual failings, may damage the child for life. As a result, it is very difficult for mothers to assert their own needs, especially since, as women, they are trained to be passive. The mother's needs become subordinate either to the child's rigid schedule or, when permissive childrearing is in vogue, to the whim of the child:

I used to let them turn over all the furniture and build houses in the living room that would stay up for days, so there was no place for me even to sit and read. I couldn't bear to make them do what they didn't want to do, even take medicine when they were sick. I couldn't bear for them to be unhappy, or fight, or be angry at me. I couldn't separate them from myself somehow. I was always understanding, patient. I felt guilty leaving them even for an afternoon. I worried over every page of their homework; I was always concentrating on being a good mother.[23]

The unmet needs of mothers are driven underground and emerge in depression, alcoholism, child abuse and suicide.

The unique circumstances of contemporary motherhood result in intensely ambivalent feelings on the part of both mothers and children. These feelings arise because of their socially imposed mutual dependence, a dependence that is quite different from a healthy interdependence. The utter dependence of the child upon her arouses feelings of love and protectiveness but also of resentment in the mother. Here is one (university-educated, financially secure, British) mother's description of what she felt when her second child was a few months old.

Isolation, a sense of never being able to keep up with the constant mess and chaos, an inability to respond adequately (according to my high ideals) to the children. Guilt at my inability to be calm and coping, maintaining an orderly house in the face of an apparently ordered world. A profound sense of bewilderment and guilt, that I wasn't what I could describe as "happy" looking after the children and being a housewife. Loving the children, and after the first two hours of the day, longing for the moment when they both slept in the afternoon so that I could be alone.[24]

A similar ambivalence is expressed by a Canadian mother: "I look at them sometimes and I wonder. I love them more than life itself and I wish they'd go away forever." (Generation III, b. 1939)[25]

The dependence that the mother develops on the child often is not obvious until the child leaves home. At this point, the mothers who have been most devoted to their children suffer most intensely from the "empty nest" syndrome. They often become extremely depressed because they feel unloved, unwanted and as if there were no meaning left in their lives.[26] The ambivalent feelings that they directed toward their children in childhood now intensify. They may be intensely proud of their children but feel resentment because the children are now independent. One depressed empty nest mother said "My children have taken and drained me."[27]

The ambivalent feelings that mothers exerience toward their children, like mothers' feelings of helplessness, are created by contradictions that are inherent in their situation. Just as mothers' feelings of inadequacy result from their losing their status as childrearing experts simultaneously with being assigned sole responsibility for their children, so mothers' feelings of ambivalence about their children result from the contrast between the enormity of the sacrifices mothers make to produce children and the small value that contemporary society places on their products.

I watch him go off to work for the Company just like his dad. Eighteen years I've raised that lad. I cared for him; I taught him. I don't feel very good about doing all that just so he can go work for the Company and kill himself like his dad is. [Generation II, b. 1931]

I complain about my son having to work but it's true for her, too. I want for her to be happy and I'm glad she's married, but I see her doing just what I had to do all my life, keeping house, raising kids, caring for her husband—and I wonder if that's really what I raised her for. [Generation II, b. 1931][28]

The feelings that contemporary mothers develop for their children have only a limited parallel in the way that wage workers feel toward their product. It is true that wage workers, like mothers, may feel drained by their jobs while they are performing them, only to suffer feelings of emptiness and meaninglessness after retirement. But wage workers rarely have the same emotional investment in their jobs that mothers have in theirs. Even so, the existence of these intensely ambivalent feelings does seem to mark a sense in which contemporary mothers are alienated from their children. The extreme mutual dependence of mother and child encourages the mother to define the child primarily with reference to her own needs for meaning, love and social recognition. She sees the child as her product, as something that should improve her life and that often instead stands against her, as something of supreme value, that is held cheap by society. The social relations of contemporary motherhood make it impossible for her to see the child as a whole person, part of a larger community to which both mother and child belong.

If the conditions of contemporary motherhood alienate mothers from their children, they equally alienate children from their mothers. Some aspects of this form of alienation may have existed prior to the emergence of contemporary industrial society. Dorothy Dinnerstein, for instance, believes that children have always had feelings of hostility toward their mothers (and, by extension, to all women) because mothers have always been the ones to bear the brunt of shattering the infant's illusions of omnipotence.[29] Freudian authors claim that daughters have always viewed their mothers as rivals for the affection of the powerful father, and that sons have always come to dominate and despise their mothers. Feminist reinterpreters of Freud agree, although they argue that these phenomena are inevitable only in a situation of male dominance. If Freudian claims are correct and if male dominance has been universal, children have never been able to see their mothers as whole persons. Nevertheless, in many societies mothers and daughters have worked together at the same women's tasks. In the 20th century, it seems likely that children's alienation from their mothers has increased. For one thing, the modern invention of adolescence creates a youth subculture from which parents, by definition, are excluded. In addition, the separation of home from workplace and women's increasing entry into wage labor means that all sons and most daughters must move out of the home into a world beyond their mothers' experience. Finally, the increasing pace of technological and social change creates a generation gap that is particularly difficult for mothers to bridge since they are often ignorant of the world outside the home.

The conditions of contemporary motherhood also result in alienation between mothers and the fathers of their children since, rather than being parental co-workers with mothers, fathers often function as agents imposing the standards of the larger society. Moreover, mothers' situation alienates them from other mothers, and not just because their places of work are separated. It is also a result of the fact that childrearing "science," with its rigid timetables of child development and its batteries of "objective" developmental tests, makes it almost impossible to avoid comparisons between children. These comparisons, coupled with the conception of children as "products," often make mothers feel intensely competitive with other mothers and in that way alienated from them.

Women's alienation from their sexuality and from their motherhood are among the most obvious forms of women's alienation in contemporary society, but women's alienation takes other forms too. Sandra Bartky identifies women's alienation from cultural production: women are allowed limited participation in this production and often see it result in images of women that are truncated, demeaning and directly opposed to women's own interests.[30] In addition, women are alienated from science and scholarship which, as I have argued in earlier chapters and as I shall continue to argue in Chapter 11, present a male-biased model of human nature and social reality. Women's participation in male-dominated political activity might also be described as alienated, and so might the maintenance services that women provide for men and children in the home. Even within wage labor, the sexualization of women's work and the sexual harassment of women create a gender-specific form of women's alienation. These various forms of women's alienation are interrelated. For instance, as Sandra Bartky has argued, the form taken by women's sexual alienation results in an alienation from their intellectual capacities that may be even more damaging than the alienation of their sexuality.

Ann Foreman sums up the socialist feminist analysis of women's oppression by declaring that femininity itself is alienation.[31] Her claim might be elaborated as follows: in contemporary society, women are alienated from all aspects of their own labor, from other women and from children. Above all, their definition as feminine alienates them from men and from themselves. Male-dominant culture, as all feminists have observed, defines masculinity and femininity as contrasting forms. In contemporary society, men are defined as active, women as passive; men are intellectual, women are intuitive; men are inexpressive, women emotional; men are strong, women weak; men are dominant, women submissive, etc.; ad nauseam. To the extent that men and women conform to these definitions, they are bound to be alienated from each other, holding incompatible values and views of the world. To the extent that men dominate women, the sexes are bound to be alienated from each other for they have incompatible interests: men in maintaining their dominance and women in resisting it. And to the extent women and men conform to gendered definitions of their humanity, they are bound to be alienated from themselves. The concepts of femininity and masculinity force both men and women to overdevelop certain of their capacities at the expense of others. For instance, men become excessively competitive with and detached from others; women become excessively nurturant and altruistic. Whether one believes with liberal feminism that men more than women have been allowed to develop their more human capacities or whether one believes with radical feminism that women are more fully human than men, the fact remains that both sexes have been prevented from the full and free development of their productive capacities. Both sexes are fragmented distortions of human possibility. Both sexes are alienated from their humanity.

The socialist feminist contribution to the analysis of women's oppression does not consist in the discovery of new facts that were previously invisible to other feminists. All feminists acknowledge the sexual objectification of women; the fatigue, boredom and occasional desperation of mothers; the conflicting demands made on women; and their lack of self-determination in all areas of life. The special contribution of socialist feminism is to begin the construction of a new theoretical framework that will show the quality and systematic interrelations of the now-familiar facts of women's contemporary oppression. This new theoretical framework is based on but must go beyond the framework provided by the Marxist theory of alienation. Within this framework, the facts of women's oppression may be reinterpreted and given a new meaning. For instance, use of the theoretical framework of alienation identifies women's contemporary oppression as a phenomenon peculiar to the capitalist form of male dominance. The apparent universality of women's subordination is revealed as taking a form that is historically specific. The framework of alienation, moreover, links women's oppression in the home with women's and men's experience in wage labor. The experience of all who live in capitalist society is shown to have basic similarities. Recognition of these similarities may generate some motivation on the part of male Marxists to take seriously women's specific forms of oppression, just as in the 1960s the repeated comparisons between sexism and racism motivated male liberals to take seriously discrimination against women. Whether or not reliance on the concept of alienation has this effect, it promises to provide a coherent conceptual framework for understanding many features of women's contemporary oppression. Properly understood, moreover, it may provide a guide for determining how that oppression may be eliminated.

The Socialist Feminist Proposals for Social Change

To analyze the contemporary oppression of women in terms of the concept of alienation is to link that oppression inevitably with capitalism. It is to deny that "patriarchy" is an unchanging trans-historical and cross-cultural universal and to assert instead that the subordination of women takes different forms in different historical periods. The alienation of contemporary women is a historically specific product of the capitalist mode of production. It results from such historically specific features of capitalism as the fetishism of commodities, the rise of positive science, and especially the separation of home from workplace, accompanied by the characteristic split between emotion and reason, the personal and the political.

This is not to say, of course, that women's oppression stems from capitalism alone, nor that the abolition of capitalism would eliminate that oppression. The abolition of capitalism would end the specifically capitalist form of women's oppression, but there is no reason to suppose that it could not be succeeded by a new form of "patriarchy" or male dominance and perhaps by new modes of alienation. The socialist feminist analysis of women's oppression shows that women's liberation requires totally new modes of organizing all forms of production and the final abolition of "femininity." Traditional Marxism has taken the abolition of class as its explicit goal, but it has not committed itself to the abolition of gender. Socialist feminism makes an explicit commitment to the abolition of both class and gender.

It is one thing to say that class and gender must be abolished, of course, and quite another to say how that abolition should be achieved. Socialist feminists, like everyone else, offer no guaranteed route to the overthrow of male dominance and capitalism. One thing that they do have, however, is a conception of the material base of society that includes the mode of producing sexuality and children as well as the mode of producing what are ordinarily called goods and services. For this reason, several of their proposals for social change, like many of the proposals of radical feminism, are directed toward the transformation of sexuality and procreation.

1. REPRODUCTIVE FREEDOM

Reproductive freedom for women is a central concern for socialist feminism. Basically, it means control over whether and in what circumstances women bear and rear children. Sometimes this idea is expressed as "reproductive rights" but, for reasons that I shall explain shortly, I think the terminology of rights is misplaced.

In developing their conception of reproductive freedom, socialist feminists do not begin from a vision of some ideal society. Instead, they begin by identifying existing constraints on women's reproductive freedom. In identifying these constraints, they draw from the insights of other groups of feminists. From liberal feminism, they draw a recognition of some of the factors that force women into unwanted motherhood, including the legal and the economic unavailability of contraception and abortion, as well as the lack of opportunities for women to fulfill themselves through avenues other than motherhood. From traditional Marxism, socialist feminists draw a recognition of the factors in contemporary society that deprive many poor women of the opportunity to be mothers. These factors include the involuntary sterilization of poor, black, Hispanic, and native American women in the United States, and the lack of economic support for children who are born to such women. Finally, socialist feminists draw from radical feminists the recognition that women are often forced into motherhood by compulsory heterosexuality, that compulsory heterosexuality also deprives many lesbian mothers of custody of their children, and that no woman under patriarchy is really free to raise her child as she wishes.

As long as any of these constraints exist, socialist feminists argue that women lack reproductive freedom.

> *Genuine control over one's own reproductive life* must mean, among other things, the universal availability of good, safe, cheap birth control; and adequate counseling for *all* women and men about *all* currently existing methods. It must mean adequate abortion services and an end to involuntary sterilization. It must mean the availability to *all* people of good public childcare centers and schools; decent housing, adequate welfare, and wages high enough to support a family; and of quality medical, pre- and post-natal and maternal care. It must also mean freedom of sexual choice, which implies an end to the cultural norms that define women in terms of having children and living with a man; an affirmation of people's right to raise children outside of conventional families; and, in the long run, a transformation of childcare arrangements so that they are shared among women and men. Finally, all these aspects of reproductive freedom must be available to *all* people—women, minorities, the disabled and handicapped, medicaid and welfare recipients, teenagers, everyone. Women have never had reproductive freedom in this sense.[32]

The socialist feminist conception of reproductive freedom starts from the material conditions of contemporary society, it is not designed to offer a model of reproductive freedom in some ideal society. This is obvious from the fact that the statement above assumes the continuation of the wage system—although in fact it is less obvious that some elements in the above definition are compatible with the continuation of the wage system. Nor does this typical socialist feminist statement of reproductive freedom call, for instance, for the development of the means to make possible parthenogenesis or the fertilization of one ovum by another so that two women could be the biological parents of a child, nor for the option of extra-uterine gestation, so-called test-tube babies. Because of its historical materialist methodology, socialist feminism eschews any final or abstract definition of reproductive freedom and instead is content to allow the notion of reproductive freedom to be defined relative to the material possibilities of a given society. For instance, in a technologically advanced society the unavailability of amniocentesis or of test-tube conception may be seen as constraints on women's reproductive freedom in a way that their absence cannot be construed to limit the reproductive freedom of women in a less technologically advanced society. The socialist feminist call for reproductive freedom must be interpreted in a historical and materialist way. It functions less as a clearly envisioned end goal than as a heuristic device. As such, it urges us to identify specific restrictions on women's freedom to choose or to refuse motherhood, to understand the material basis of these restrictions, and to seek the real possibility of eliminating them.

Although it starts from existing material conditions, the socialist feminist conception of reproductive freedom does not accept those conditions as unchangeable. For instance, this conception of reproductive freedom is clearly much broader than the liberal "right to choose" contraception and abortion. What it actually calls for is a transformation of the social conditions in which "choices" are made. Construed thus broadly, it becomes obvious that reproductive freedom is incompatible either with the compulsory heterosexuality and mandatory motherhood that have characterized all male-dominated societies or with the economic inequality that necessarily characterizes capitalism. Because it cannot be achieved within the existing social order, reproductive freedom is in fact a revolutionary demand.

Socialist feminists are careful to emphasize that reproductive freedom must be available to all women, but they rarely discuss what reproductive freedom would be for men. As Rosalind Petchesky points out, two reasons exist for the socialist feminist assumption that women rather than men should control reproduction. One is the biological fact, unalterable until the present time, that babies are gestated and born from the bodies of women; the other is the social fact that, in contemporary society as in other known societies, the sexual division of labor assigns women most of the work and responsibility for infant and child welfare.[33]

When reproductive freedom for women is justified solely by reference to the facts of female biology, rather than including a reference to women's social situation, it tends to emerge in a demand for "reproductive rights." Petchesky criticizes this formula because she believe that

> it can be turned back on us to reinforce the view of all reproductive activity as the special, biologically destined province of women. Here it has to be acknowledged that this danger grows out of the concept of "rights" in general, a concept inherently static and abstracted from social conditions. Rights are by definition claims that are staked within a given order of things and relationships. They are demands for access for oneself, or for "no admittance" to others, but they do not challenge the social structure itself, the social relations of production and reproduction. The

claim for "abortion rights" seeks access to a necessary service, but by itself it fails to address the existing social relations and sexual divisions around which responsibility for pregnancy and children is assigned. And in real-life struggles, this limitation exacts a price, for it lets men and society neatly off the hook.[34]

"Reproductive rights" may come to be viewed as ends in themselves, as something belonging permanently to women in virtue of their unalterable biological constitution. A more consistently socialist feminist approach would focus less on biological "givens" and more on the social relations of procreation. Ultimately, socialist feminists are not interested in a mode of society that assigns rights to some individuals in order to protect them from others; they are interested in transforming the mode of procreation.

Apart from the fact that children are born from the bodies of women rather than men, the other ground for asserting that reproductive freedom should belong to women rather than to men is that present day relations of procreation assign most procreative work and responsibility to women. In previous societies, this work and responsibility was usually shared by a group of women but, as we saw in the preceding section, the special conditions of modern capitalism have confined most contemporary mothers in an isolation that is historically unique. It is in part this unique isolation that makes it plausible to interpret reproductive freedom as a "right" of individual women. Part of the socialist feminist conception of reproductive freedom, however, is to challenge the traditional sexual division of labor in procreation so that childcare comes to be shared between women and men. If this goal were achieved, and if the community as a whole came to assume responsibility for the welfare of children (and mothers), then the birth or non-birth of a child would affect that community in a much more direct and immediate way than it does at present. In this case, it would seem reasonable to allow the community as a whole to participate in decisions over whether children were born and how they should be reared. In these changed social circumstances, it would no longer be even plausible to interpret reproductive freedom as a "right" of individual women. Instead, reproductive freedom would be seen clearly to be a social achievement and something to be shared by the entire community, men as well as women.[35]

Under the rubric of reproductive freedom, socialist feminists propose to transform existing arrangements for organizing sexuality and procreation. They believe that their proposals will have far-reaching social consequences. The most obvious, of course, is that women's release from compulsory motherhood will allow them to develop their capacities in many other areas. On a deeper level, many socialist feminist theorists believe that the equal involvement of men in infant and childcare is the key to eliminating the gendered structure of the unconscious mind. Dorothy Dinnerstein, as we have seen, argues that the mother-rearing of children instills an ineradicable (though often unacknowledged) misogyny in both men and women, a misogyny that "conspires to keep history mad."[36] Nancy Chodorow traces the way in which women's responsibility for early childcare results in the imposition of a different character structure on girls and boys. Boys grow up to be achievement-oriented and emotionally closed to others; girls grow up to be emotionally vulnerable, open to and even dependent on the approval of others. In the end, boys and girls become men and women who repeat the traditional sexual division of labor in childrearing and so perpetuate psychological and social inequality between women and men.[37] Both for Dinnerstein and for Chodorow, men's full participation in infant and child care is essential to eradicating the deep roots of gender in the unconscious mind.

Not all socialist feminists accept the psychoanalytic theories of Dinnerstein and Chodorow. Some socialist feminists argue that they repeat the errors of Freud in being ahistorical, in falsely universalizing childhood experience, and in ignoring differences of period and of class. Critics who are non-Freudians deny that people's character structures are fixed in childhood with such finality and argue that in fact people may continue to change in fundamental ways throughout their lives. Other critics argue that the problem is not so much that mothers rear children as that they do so in a context of male dominance and compulsory heterosexuality. A male-dominated society is always likely to be misogynistic, no matter who rears the children. It may be that women rear children because they have low status, rather than that they have low status because they rear children. After all, childcare is a demanding though socially necessary task which provides no material as opposed to emotional return until the child is old enough to work, and often not even then. For this reason, childcare is a task which is likely to be relegated to the less powerful members of the society, while the more powerful devote their energy to increasing their power. Historically, this has certainly held true, and even today much childcare is left to relatively powerless teenage, minority or elderly women.

Rather than focusing on relatively long-term attempts to alter the psychic structure of our daughters (and our sons) by involving men immediately in childrearing, some socialist feminists argue that it is more important to alter the external social structures that channel women into motherhood and childrearing.[38] The most important single factor contributing to this channeling is probably the sex-segregated job market, which keeps women in low-paid and low-status jobs. In these circumstances, childrearing appears to many women to be the only kind of fulfilling work available to them. In order to take this option, however, a woman is forced economically to find a man who will help support her and her children. Because of men's economic privilege in the market, it is usually impossible for women to support the family while men stay at home with the children. Their economic situation thus tends to push women into childrearing, regardless of whether they have unconscious drives toward mothering.

The socialist feminist conception of reproductive freedom seeks to enlarge women's options so that they are not forced to choose between childlessness and the alienation of contemporary motherhood. It calls for economic security for women, for paid maternity leaves and for the provision of publicly funded and community-controlled childcare. If these were established, women would have the real option of choosing motherhood without being forced to abandon or drastically limit their participation in other kinds of work or to become economically dependent on a man. These changes, particularly the assumption of public responsibility for childcare, would make visible the way in which childrearing is real work and would constitute an enormous step toward eliminating the public/private distinction.

If women were fully active participants in worthwhile work outside the home, enjoying the economic security and self-respect that such participation would bring, it is doubtful that, from the child's point of view, a male presence would be required for successful childrearing. Without the occurrence of these structural changes, several authors have expressed concern that male presence in childrearing could simply deprive women of control over even this aspect of their work.[39] If these structural changes were to occur, however, women would be in a stronger position to demand that men should share the responsibility for childrearing. In these circumstances, men might even want to do so. In these changed circumstances, too, childcare would be less exhausting and alienated and this is one way in which increased reproductive freedom for women could also result in increased reproductive freedom for men.

Included within the socialist feminist conception of reproductive freedom is a recognition of the necessity for sexual freedom. The statement of reproductive freedom quoted earlier, for example, includes a call for "freedom of sexual choice." The announcement that reproductive freedom includes sexual freedom is not just an arbitrary definition nor is it an opportunistic attempt to cram as many good causes as possible under one slogan. Instead, it is an explicit recognition that there exist not only biological but also social connections between sexuality and procreation. Limitations on women's procreative freedom have been used to control their sexual freedom; for instance, men in early societies used a ban on birth control to force monogamy on women.[40] Conversely, limitations on women's sexual freedom have been used to control their procreative freedom; most obviously, forced heterosexuality has also forced women into motherhood. These are not the only connections between sexuality and procreation. As we shall see, there are a number of other reasons why sexual freedom for women is not possible without procreative freedom and procreative freedom is not possible without sexual freedom. Consequently, an adequate conception of reproductive freedom must include an ideal of sexual freedom.

Although there are in fact many connections between sexuality and procreation in women's lives, sexual and procreative freedom are possible only if the expressions of women's sexuality are viewed as activities which need not result in procreation. Feminists have not always recognized this: in the 19th century, many American feminists saw non-procreative sex as "a means for men to escape their responsibility to women. They saw contraception as a tool of prostitutes and as a potential tool of men in turning women into prostitutes."[41] In the 20th century attitudes changed, partly because women were in fact achieving a degree of economic independence from men, partly because the pressures to bear large numbers of children were reduced. Increasingly, sexuality itself became a "question" and sexual pleasure began to be acknowledged as a legitimate aspiration of women. In the first part of the 20th century, however, it was men who defined sexual liberation, even for women, and the male definitions were blatantly self-serving. Female sexuality was characterized by Freud as inherently passive, masochistic and narcissistic—a perfect rationale for the sexual objectification of women and for sexual aggression toward them. Heterosexual intercourse was taken as the paradigm of sexual activity, and women were blamed for frigidity if they did not experience orgasm during intercourse.

With the rise of the contemporary women's liberation movement in the 1960s, feminists began a thoroughgoing critique of the prevailing conception of sexual liberation. They pointed out the coerciveness of heterosexual relations; they identified the alienation in the sexual objectification of women; they exploded the "myth of the vaginal orgasm";[42] they demystified the ideology of romantic love; they criticized the emphasis on an exclusively genital conception of sexuality, which ignored the possibilities for a more diffuse sexuality; they showed how dominance and submission were reinforced by being eroticized; above all, they identified the heterosexual norm as a means by which women were divided from each other. Women began to explore and define their own sexual needs, many of them in the context of lesbian relationships. Linda Gordon writes:

> The lesbian liberation movement has made possibly the most important contribution to a future sexual liberation. It is not that feminism produced more lesbians. There have always been many lesbians, despite high levels of repression; and most lesbians experience their sexual preference as innate and nonvoluntary. What the women's liberation movement did create was a homosexual liberation movement that politically challenged male supremacy in one of its most deeply institutionalized aspects—the tyranny of heterosexuality. The political power of lesbianism is a power that can be shared by all women who choose to recognize and use it: the power of an alternative, a possibility that makes male sexual tyranny escapable, rejectable—possibly even doomed.[43]

The abolition of compulsory heterosexuality would have an enormous impact on the system of male dominance. One effect might be to disrupt the way in which gender is imposed on the infant psyche, as described by Freud. Gayle Rubin has pointed out that the Freudian account of child development presupposes a norm of heterosexuality as well as a context of male dominance. Without this norm, girls would not have to give up their early attachment to their mothers. "If the pre-Oedipal lesbian were not confronted by the heterosexuality of the mother, she might draw different conclusions about the relative status of her genitals."[44] The abandonment of compulsory heterosexuality would reshape the sexuality both of girls and of boys and, if psychoanalysis is correct, would have tremendous consequences for the structure of the unconscious and for people's sense of their own gender identity. This speculation suggests a further way in which procreative freedom presupposes sexual freedom.

Another connection between sexual and procreative freedom lies in women's tendency to become pregnant in order to compensate for unsatisfactory heterosexual relationships.[45] Sometimes, too, women become pregnant in an attempt to try to consolidate a heterosexual relationship.

> Women get pregnant "accidentally on purpose" as a way of punishing themselves. But they may also be protecting themselves and punishing men. Nothing illustrates better than reproduction that unless women can be free, men will never be. Pregnancy is woman's burden and her revenge.[46]

Thus, the connections between women's sexual and procreative activity are quite complicated, and sexual and procreative freedom for women are inseparable from each other. This is why the socialist feminist conception of reproductive freedom includes both aspects.

Comprehensive as it is, the socialist feminist conception of reproductive freedom is not a self-contained ideal which can be achieved or even understood simply with reference to sexuality and procreation. For instance, as we saw earlier, one of the preconditions of reproductive freedom for women is economic independence from men, without which reproductive freedom would degenerate into sexual and procreative exploitation. Thus, reproductive freedom requires the abolition of male dominance in the "public world." Linda Gordon points out that reproductive freedom also requires the abolition of hereditary class society:

> The prohibition on birth control was, as we have seen, related to the defense of class privilege. Today the powers and privileges that can be

passed on to succeeding generations through the family are more varied: property, education, confidence, social and political connections. But the essential nature of class divisions is unchanged and depends on the generational passing down of status. Thus in class society children are never individuals and cannot escape the expectations, high or low, attached to their fathers' position. These expectations also distort the reproductive desires and childrearing practices of parents, making it more difficult for them to view their children as individuals.[47]

Once again, we see that full reproductive freedom is incompatible with the maintenance of capitalism and male dominance.

Socialist feminists are discovering that "in thought and practice, neat distinctions we once made between sex and class, family and society, reproduction and production, even between women and men seem not to fit the social reality with which we are coping."[48] Socialist feminist explorations of reproductive freedom illustrate this well by showing that reproductive freedom for women requires a transformation of what has been called traditionally the mode of production. Equally, however, a feminist transformation of the mode of production cannot be achieved without reproductive freedom for women or a transformation of the mode of procreation. Since one cannot precede the other and since both are dialectically related, both must occur together. Procreation and "production" in the narrow sense are simply two aspects of an integrated capitalist and male-dominant mode of producing and reproducing every aspect of life.

2. WOMEN AND WAGES

Women have more than one workplace. A woman's place may be in the home when young children need care or when meals need to be prepared, but at other times, as one socialist feminist author put it, "a woman's place is at the typewriter."[49] Women are a steadily increasing proportion of the paid labor force in the United States, with mothers of young children constituting the fastest growing category.[50] Most women in the U.S. will engage in paid labor at some time in their lives. Whether or not it was once true to say that women were oppressed primarily in virtue of their exclusion from public production, it is true no longer.

Within the wage labor force, however, the sexual division of labor is almost as striking as the sexual division of labor between home and outside work. Token women can now be found in almost every category of paid labor, including coal mining, but women cluster predominantly in a relatively few occupations. The largest of these is clerical work: in 1977, more than one-third of all wage-earning women in the United States were clerical workers.[51] Clerical workers now constitute 20 percent of the paid labor force in the US and they are 80 percent female.[52] Women who are not clerical workers tend to work in retail sales or in service occupations such as social work, teaching, or nursing.

The categories of labor where women congregate are both the fastest growing and the lowest paid.[53] On average, a woman wage worker earns 59¢ for every dollar earned by a man. Low pay, however, is only one characteristic of women's paid work in contemporary society. Women's paid labor also tends to require from its workers those qualities that contemporary society describes as feminine: submissiveness, toleration of tedium, the ability to communicate and empathize with people, nurturance and sexual attractiveness to men.

The availability of a large "reserve army" of labor, prepared to work for relatively low wages and with relatively few fringe benefits, is obviously advantageous to capital. The existence of such a reserve pool of labor accommodates fluctuations in the demand for labor, exerts a downward pressure on all wages and, through the threat of strikebreaking, increases capitalist control over labor. This functionalist argument has often been used by Marxists to explain the sex-segregation of the wage labor force and it does have considerable explanatory value. What it fails to explain is why women constitute this reserve pool and why "women's work" acquires its specifically "feminine" character.

The nursing profession provides an excellent example of how work is defined not only by the categories of class and of the mental/manual distinction but also by the category of gender. Eva Gamarnikow explains that nursing in Britain was established during the 19th century as an occupation for women, and she shows how the assumption that nurses would be female influenced the definition of the work.[54] Nurses were defined as assistants and subordinates of the (male) physician; nursing was seen as less important than medicine, in spite of the fact that patients can be cured by nursing alone but rarely by medical treatment alone; nursing was seen as emotional rather than instrumental and so nurses were defined by their moral qualities (patience, humility, self-abnegation, neatness, cleanliness, punctuality, cheerfulness, kindness, tenderness and honesty) rather than by their professional skills. Around the turn of the century, explicit links were made between nursing and mothering and between nursing and women's domestic work. The good nurse was considered to have the same qualities as a good wife and mother.

The structure of contemporary health care is still defined by gender. A sharp distinction is still made between medicine and nursing, and medicine is still overwhelmingly a male profession while nursing is a female one. More than 92 percent of the physicians in the United States are male, while over 96 percent of the nurses are female. Tim Diamond has shown how traditional sex stereotypes still influence the respective definitions of medicine and nursing: medicine is concerned with curing specific maladies, it transforms sickness, often by "aggressive" means, and it charges for specific units of medical intervention; nursing, by contrast, is concerned with care rather than cure, it provides a service to the whole patient and it does not charge per unit for its services.

> The mode of human service for the nurse becomes indistinguishable from that of the wife, the mother or the nun. In the case of health services, the woman's world is, once again the emotive, the man's world, the instrumental: the nursing model is feminine, the medical model is masculine.[55]

The gendered structure of paid labor is equally obvious in education. In this field, women work mostly with very young children where education, nurturance, and physical care are inseparable, while men work mostly in higher education, dealing with adult students and abstract ideas. Contemporary conceptions of gender also influenced the redefinition of clerical work around the turn of the century. In 1870, men were 97.5 percent of the clerical labor force in the United States,[56] and a clerk was often viewed by his employer as "assistant manager, retainer, confidant, management trainee, and prospective son in law."[57] With the influx of women into clerical work, however, that work was redefined to fit the prevailing stereotype of femininity. The work became less skilled and more of a personal service. Good clerical workers were no longer required to

326 The Politics of Socialist Feminism

have business acumen; instead, they were supposed to have the feminine qualities of docility, passivity and manual dexterity. Personal secretaries were supposed to be a cross between wives and mothers.[58]

An obvious example of the gendered definition of wage labor is the prevalence of physical appearance and sexual attractiveness as formal or informal requirements for women's jobs. Jobs with these requirements include not only prostitution and entertainment but also many jobs such as being a waitress, stewardess or receptionist and other forms of service work. Sexual attractiveness is not related logically to the performance of any of these jobs except prostitution and possibly entertainment (given current ideas about what is entertaining), but that it is an unstated requirement for women's employment is shown by the way in which employment becomes progressively more difficult for a woman to find as she gets older and becomes, according to conventional definitions, less sexually desirable.[59]

Even the low pay that women wage workers typically receive may be viewed in fact as a gendered characteristic. Women's low wages used to be justified on the grounds that a man was working to support his family, while a woman was working merely for "pin money." Many feminist authors have pointed out that this is false: millions of women are the sole support of their households, and the wage of many other women is necessary to lift their family income above the poverty level. Although the traditional rationale for women's low pay is less often stated explicitly nowadays, continuing low wages for women actually provide it with some basis in fact. Veronica Beechey has argued that new forms of wage labor are being created specifically for women at ever-lower real wages, often at less than the cost of their own subsistence.[60] Women can afford to work at these jobs only because they are part of a family unit whose chief support is the male wage. If Beechey's supposition is correct, the contemporary form of women's wage labor reinforces male dominance in two ways: on the one hand, the definitions of women's work reinforce the ideological perception of women as "naturally" nurturant, subservient and sexy; on the other hand, women's low wages make it very difficult for women, especially for mothers, to survive alone and women are forced into dependence on men. The fact that most women have been forced to form family units then can be used to justify continuing their low pay.

The genderization of wage labor means that women wage workers suffer a special form of alienation. They are not alienated simply as genderless (male!) workers; they are also alienated in ways specific to their sex. In order to earn a living, they are forced to exploit not only their physical strength and skill or their intellectual capacities; they are also forced to exploit their sexuality and their emotions.

Socialist feminist proposals for social change must take into account the special alienation of women outside the home. In developing their conception of free productive activity, it is not enough to talk in general terms about transcending the realm of necessity or about worker control of production. It is also necessary to talk about eliminating sex segregation in production, so that male workers do not end up controlling mining, forestry and the steel industries while female workers end up controlling laundry and food services. Traditional Marxists have always asserted that free productive activity requires the restructuring of the labor process so that it abandons a detailed division of labor and overcomes the distinction between conception and execution, mental and manual labor. Socialist feminists add that work must be redefined so as to eliminate the distinction between "masculine" and "feminine" work as well.

To overcome this distinction would not mean necessarily that all work would assume the characteristics of masculine work under contemporary capitalism, that all work would be impersonal, unemotional and asexual. Free productive labor in fact might be more similar to contemporary feminine work in that workers would be able to express their emotions and their sexuality and would view others as unique individuals. Unlike the contemporary situation for women workers, however, these forms of emotional and sexual expression would be freely chosen rather than coerced and alienated.

Marxism's ultimate solution to worker alienation has always been to overthrow the capitalist mode of production. To alleviate intolerable working conditions in the short term and as a transitional step on the way to its ultimate goal, Marxism has supported the organization of workers into trades unions. Trades unions allow workers to bargain collectively with their employers and also to exert collective influence in electoral politics. In the United States and in most other capitalist countries, a much higher proportion of male than female workers is unionized. Even where women are union members, most union officials are men, and unions tend to bargain for the issues of wages and working conditions that are of most concern to men. The specific interests of women are not well represented by existing unions.

In the United States, clerical work is the largest category of wage work that remains unorganized into unions.[61] It is also, of course, the largest category of women's wage work. Trade union officials have not been eager to "organize" clerical workers, explaining that the workers themselves do not want to be organized. Women clerical workers are said to be committed primarily to their families rather than to their paid jobs and to be too "feminine" to be militant.[62] In the 1970s, socialist feminists rejected these explanations and have begun to organize women workers, especially women clerical workers. They organize them not as genderless workers, however, but rather as workers who are women.

Some socialist feminist organizing efforts have resulted in the formation of union locals. Others have resulted in the formation of organizations that are not unions but that address the concerns of women office and service workers. "Active groups include Nine-to-Five in Boston; Women Office Workers in New York; Women Employed in Chicago; and Union Wage and Women Organized for Employment in San Francisco."[63] Many of the local groups affiliate with a national organizational network, Working Women. "They are hybrid groups, neither pure women's rights nor pure labor rights, but an amalgam of both evidencing women's great need for organizations that will advance their cause as women at work."[64]

Working women's organizations concentrate not only on the issues that have preoccupied the male trade union movement; they also focus on issues that are of specific concern to women. These issues include dress codes and expectations by bosses that women will provide "personal services" such as running errands or making coffee. Sexual harassment, of course, is one of the most important issues of concern. Sexual harassment seems to have been a problem for women as long as they have been employed in wage work.[65]

> It is consistent, systematic, and pervasive, not a set of random isolated acts. The license to harass women workers, which many men feel they have, stems from notions that there is a "woman's place" which women in the labor force have left, thus leaving behind their personal integrity. . . .

Words, gestures, comments can be used as threats of violence and to express dominance. Harassment often depends on this underlying violence—violence is implied as the ultimate response. Harassment is "little rape", an invasion of a person, by suggestion, by intimidation, by confronting a woman with her helplessness. It is an interaction in which one person purposefully seeks to discomfort another person. This discomfort serves to remind women of their helplessness in the face of male violence. To offer such a model is to suggest that it is not simply an individual interaction but a social one; not an act of deviance but a societally condoned mode of behavior that functions to preserve male dominance in the world of work.[66]

Today it is used "to control women's access to certain jobs; to limit job success and mobility; and to compensate men for powerlessness in their own lives."[67] Lin Farley cites innumerable examples of women who have been forced out of jobs by sexual harassment.[68] A few organizations, such as the Alliance Against Sexual Coercion in Boston, devote themselves entirely to combating this form of women's oppression.

An increasing proportion of the women who work for wages also have children. Because childcare is still predominantly women's work, women wage workers often have to perform two jobs. The stress of coping with the demands of both their paid and their unpaid work has had damaging consequences on women's health.[69] Women's entry in large numbers into the wage labor market has shown how 20th-century wage labor is defined implicitly, if not explicitly, as "men's work" insofar as it is structured on the assumption that the wage laborer is a man with a woman at home to do his laundry, cook his meals, rear his children, and provide him with emotional and sexual consolation. Without "wives," women and especially mothers pay enormous costs for their survival in wage labor.

Women wage workers are beginning to refuse to pay those costs. They are demanding the restructuring of non-procreative work so that it is compatible with parenting. Through their organizations, they are beginning to seek out not only the traditional benefits of adequate pay and job security; they are also seeking the provision of day care, paid maternity leaves, the availability of leave to look after sick children, and work hours that correspond to the school day.

Women are concerned not only about the structure of their wage labor; they are also concerned about their wage. Women's work is becoming increasingly "deprofessionalized" and more "proletarianized." That is to say, women wage workers have decreasing control over the conditions of their work, their work is becoming less skilled and their real wages are diminishing. These trends can be seen in education, in nursing and especially in clerical work. As women workers become more proletarianized, they are beginning to develop a more "proletarian" consciousness. In the spring and summer of 1974, nurses in Britain took industrial action for the first time;[70] nurses in the United States are also organizing.[71] Clerical workers are beginning to strike, and teachers' strikes are increasingly frequent. What should be noted is that, even when women strike for pay and not for specifically "women's" demands, their actions still have a different meaning from the same actions taken by male workers. When women workers achieve a living wage, they are not just workers winning a concession from capital: they are also women winning economic independence from men.

Women's experience in wage labor brings out more connections between women's procreative and their non-procreative work. For instance, the assumptions that women are wives and mothers influences definitions of women's work and rationalizes women's low pay. Just as economic independence for women is a precondition of reproductive freedom, so reproductive freedom is a precondition for an end to sexual segregation in other kinds of productive activity and for women's full participation in these.

In the 1970s, some women who defined themselves as socialist feminists began to demand that women should receive wages for that aspect of procreative work that hitherto had received no pay—the work of rearing their own children. The wages for housework movement began in the early 1970s in Italy, where relatively few mothers were employed in wage labor,[72] and spread across Europe to Britain and Canada. It never achieved much of a foothold in the United States, although Wages for Housework groups did spring up in a few U.S. cities. Wages for housework were demanded as a way of recognizing the value of the work that all women perform and also as a way of ensuring women economic independence from men. In the mid-1970s, the demand was debated frequently by feminists, but in the 1980s the movement seems to be disappearing. This may be because the continuing entry of women into existing forms of wage labor gives relatively fewer women any interest in defining themselves as paid houseworkers. It seems unlikely that pay for housework would be sufficient to raise its status and it would not diminish the isolation of women in the home. Even if the idea has merit in some circumstances as a tactical step toward women's liberation, the provision of wages for housework is incompatible in the long run with the goals of socialist feminism. It would reinforce the sexual division of labor to which feminists object and would extend the capitalist form of exploitation which socialists want to overthrow.

It is indeed this demand for the abolition of the wage system that most sharply distinguishes socialist feminists from liberal and radical feminists. Most of the specific issues around which socialist feminists organize are supported by feminists who are not socialists, but socialist feminism explains these issues in terms of exploitation and alienation, thus showing how male dominance cannot be eliminated without the abolition of capitalism.

3. WOMEN AND ORGANIZATIONAL INDEPENDENCE

In 1865, Marx wrote:

> Trades Unions work well as centres of resistance against the encroachments of capital. They fail partially from an injudicious use of their power. They fail generally from limiting themselves to a guerilla war against the effects of the existing system, instead of simultaneously trying to change it, instead of using their organized force as a lever for the final emancipation of the working class, that is to say, the ultimate abolition of the wages system.[73]

Trade union consciousness is not revolutionary consciousness, as Marx well knew. The most that wage working women's organizations can hope to achieve is to modify contemporary wage labor so as to enable women to juggle two jobs. The goal of socialist feminism, however, is not for women to be able to juggle two jobs. It is to overthrow the whole social order of what some call "capitalist patriarchy" in which women suffer alienation in every aspect of their lives. The traditional Marxist strategy for revolution is to form a Leninist vanguard party. The socialist feminist strategy is to support some "mixed" socialist organizations, but also to form independent women's groups and ultimately an independent women's movement committed with equal dedication to the destruction of capitalism and the destruction of male dominance. The women's movement will join in coalitions with other revolutionary movements, but it will not give up its organizational independence.

Independent women's organizations are obviously a form of separatism: they do not accept male members, and they refuse permanent organizational links with "mixed" organizations. They are not separatist, however, in the radical feminist sense of requiring their members to have as little contact with men as possible outside the organization. Nor are they separatist in the sense that their ultimate goal is a "matriarchy," a "lesbian nation" or a society in which men and women are separated formally from each other. On the contrary, their goal is a society in which maleness and femaleness are socially irrelevant, in which men and women, as we know them, will no longer exist. Organizational independence for socialist feminists is thus a form of tactical separatism, a step on the way to an ultimate goal of complete integration between the sexes.

The need for independent women's organizations springs from the basic socialist feminist understanding of society as male-dominated. On this analysis, the interests of men are in some ways opposed to those of women, even though certain groups of men share a number of interests with certain groups of women. Men have an interest in maintaining their dominant position: in earning more than women, in having sexual power over women and in keeping the larger share of leisure time which results from their relative freedom from housework. Women have an immediate interest in getting rid of those male privileges and they need separate organizations to fight for this interest.

Some feminists deny the need for independent women's organizations. It is common for both liberals and Marxists to assert that the enemy that women face as women is not men but the system of sexism. Traditional Marxists believe that, if women came to see men as their enemy, then they would not perceive the interests that women share with men as members of the working class. To state that women's enemy is the system rather than men themselves, however, is to ignore the question of who perpetuates that system and in whose interest it operates. Both men and women in fact help to perpetuate the system of male dominance (just as workers as well as capitalists help to perpetuate the capitalist system), but women's objective interests as women also encourage them to resist that system in many ways. Men, too, may sometimes resist the system of male dominance, but, because that system provides them with privileges, they are much less likely to resist it. Radical feminists perceive that the system of male dominance is enforced primarily by men, and so they draw the unambiguous conclusion that it is men who are the enemy for women.

In an obvious sense, men are the enemy for women, just as colonizers are enemy for the colonized and capitalists are the enemy for workers. In saying that men are the enemy for women, however, it is important to remember two things. One is that the enmity between women and men is part of a specific system of social relations which defines what it is to be a man and a woman; consequently, change in that system could eliminate the enmity between female and male persons. The enmity is not necessarily permanent. The other point to remember is that there are many other divisions in society as well as the division between the sexes: differences of nationality, race, age, ability, religion and class. Because these other divisions cut across sex lines, there are respects in which women have shared interests with men and in which men are not the enemy. For instance, colonized women have interests in common with colonized men, differently abled women have interests in common with differently abled men, girls have interests in common with boys, etc. In the same way, the working class of a colonized nation will cooperate with that nation's upper class in resisting colonization and, in the context of a struggle for national liberation, will not regard it as the enemy.

Radical feminists view men as "the main enemy"[74] of women because they claim that the subordination of women by men was the first form of oppression and that it remains causally basic to all other forms. Traditional Marxists, by contrast, view capitalists as the main enemy because they believe that this contemporary form of class oppression is now the main support of all other forms of oppression. Many traditional Marxists borrow Maoist terminology and justify their claim that capitalists are the main enemy by asserting that class (traditionally construed) is the "principal contradiction" in society today. Their arguments for this view are theoretical and tend to the conclusion that revolutionary activity should always focus on class struggle as traditionally understood. Hartmann and Markusen have pointed out that these sorts of Marxist arguments in fact misinterpret the notion of "principal contradiction." As developed by Mao, the notion was strategically rather than theoretically determined; it was designed to identify the focus of revolutionary activity in specific periods rather than in all situations.[75] Socialist feminists avoid not only the language of "primary" or "principal" contradiction but in general are suspicious of attempts to assert that either class or gender is causally basic to the other. They see the various systems of oppression as connected inseparably with each other and believe that it is mistaken to try to identify a single group as being permanently "the main enemy."

> We claim that in the current situation it is entirely in keeping with Marxist and Maoist tradition to see capitalist patriarchy at the root of the principal contradiction, to label the enemy as such, and to build a strategy that insists on the duality (and with racism and ageism, the multiple aspects) of the principal contradiction. We see the insistence on "class first" as an antifeminist practice, not a proworking class practice.[76]

Traditional Marxists argue that it is divisive to speak of men as the enemy, that it diverts the working class from its primary struggle against capitalism. They fear that if women join independent women's organizations rather than the "vanguard party," they will lose their revolutionary perspective, will mistake symptoms for causes and will focus on reforms for women rather than on the transformation of the system as a whole. These fears reveal distrust of women's revolutionary commitment and a belief that women cannot maintain their socialist vision without men to hold it continually before their eyes. They seem to overlook the fact that women, just as much as men, are members of the working class.

The organizations advocated by socialist feminists, however, are socialist as well as feminist. They are not dedicated simply to winning reforms for women or to integrating women into the capitalist system. Nor, on the other hand, are they dedicated simply to overthrowing the capitalist system and replacing it with a dictatorship of the male proletariat. They are concerned with the ways in which even working-class men perpetuate male dominance: through their resistance to affirmative action, through rape, through woman beating, through sexual harassment, through refusal to take an equal share of household responsibility—and through sexism in their revolutionary organizations. In order to combat male dominance, women must form their own independent organizations.

To say that socialist feminist women should form their own independent organizations is not to preclude them from also joining "mixed left" groups, nor to deny that women's organizations should work with the mixed left. But independent women's organizations are necessary to ensure that women's voices are heard, both individually and collectively.

> Working class women and men must be allied in their struggle against the ruling class, but this alliance must be among equals: women should not be subordinate to men in a "revolutionary" movement. Equality of women and men requires a direct struggle against patriarchy and an autonomous power base for working class women. It is not enough for the Party to organize women: women must become "subjects" of history, able to act in their own behalf.[77]

Ann Foreman agrees.

> In short, the organized presence of women could prevent the traditional exclusion of women in both its crude and more sophisticated forms. And by asserting the right of women to define their own identity within political structures, the self-organization of women strikes at the heart of the feminine attitude of alterity on which this exclusion rests. Ultimately, then, autonomy provides a political and not simply an organisational link between the feminist and the working class struggle.[78]

Only the organizational independence of women can ensure that women's concerns are addressed and that women escape from their traditional role of "wives to the revolution."

4. BEGINNING AT START: STRATEGIES FOR SOCIAL TRANSFORMATION

Socialist feminist strategies for ending oppression seek to combine the traditional Marxist emphasis on changing the material conditions of life with the 20th-century emphasis on the importance of changing ideas and feelings. The special socialist feminist conception of human nature provides the basis for a distinctively socialist feminist approach to each of these aspects of human life.

All those who struggle against oppression must try to discover the underlying causes of that oppression and to separate these causes from the more superficial symptoms. Within the Marxist tradition, the distinction between the symptoms of a certain form of oppression and its underlying causes is formulated in terms of "base" and "superstructure." The "material base" of a certain form of oppression is taken to be those social relations which fundamentally sustain that form of oppression and which therefore must be transformed in order to eliminate that form of oppression. In investigating the fundamental causes of women's oppression, socialist feminists have developed a conception of material base as that set of social relations which structures the production and reproduction of the necessities of daily life, the production of people, including the production of sexuality, as well as the production of goods and services. On the socialist feminist view, these relations are simultaneously capitalist and male-dominant, and both aspects must be changed to liberate women.

The inclusiveness of the socialist feminist conception of the material base of women's oppression has implications for the socialist feminist conception of revolutionary strategy. Most obviously, the enlarged conception of the material base means that many more forms of political activity than previously thought can now be described as challenges to the basic system of social relations. For example, even when working women's organizations do not bring directly into question the capitalist mode of production, they do begin to challenge the gendered definition of women's work. Similarly, campaigns for various aspects of reproductive freedom, such as campaigns for free abortion, against rape and sexual harassment, and for free and community-controlled childcare all challenge existing male-dominant and capitalist relations of procreation and sexuality.

In addition to making direct challenges to the prevailing male dominant and capitalist mode of production, it is necessary also to challenge the system of ideas that justify and reinforce this mode of production. In the 20th century, even those political theorists who aspire to a materialist method have placed considerable emphasis on the importance of "consciousness" in explaining historical change—or the absence of change. These theorists have not denied the materialist insight that consciousness is determined in some ultimate sense by the material conditions of daily life, but they recognize that systems of ideas may establish considerable autonomy from the existing historical circumstances and may also have considerable causal influence on those circumstances. This recognition has been made by influential tendencies within the Marxist tradition whose theorists, as we have seen, have elaborated the notions of ideology, false consciousness and hegemony and have made a number of attempts to graft some form of Freudian psychology onto Marxist political economy. The same recognition has also been made by radical feminism, which has contributed the technique of consciousness raising to political practice and has emphasized "cultural" critique and re-creation. Socialist feminism is firmly in this 20th-century tradition and so claims that an effective revolutionary strategy must include techniques for demystifying the prevailing male-dominant and capitalist ideology and for developing alternative forms of consciousness, that is alternative ways of perceiving reality and alternative attitudes toward it.

A vital part of organizing for social change is the creation of a sense of political unity among oppressed groups. A class is identified not only by its "objective" position relative to the means of production, but also by its "subjective" sense of itself as having a common identity and common interests. Unless it is a class "for itself" as well as a class "in itself," the group will not move to political action. For instance, although the peasants in 19th-century France shared a common relation to production, Marx argued that their isolation from and poor communication with each other prevented them from developing a sense of community and shared political purpose.[79] Contemporary women are in a position that in some ways resembles that of 19th-century French peasants though in other ways it differs from theirs. By and large, as we have seen, women do share a common relation to production: unlike men, they are all responsible for housework, for childrearing, for emotional nurturance and for sexual gratification; in addition, they are clustered in a few gender-defined paid occupations. Insofar as they work together in the paid labor force, the conditions do exist for women to develop a shared political identity and, as we have seen, that is beginning to happen with the growth of working women's organizations. Insofar as they are isolated from each other in the family, it is much harder for women to develop a shared identity as workers in the home. In the late 1960s, the explosion of consciousness-raising groups showed the

334 The Politics of Socialist Feminism

need that women felt to overcome their isolation, and many kinds of support groups still continue. In this context, socialist feminists agree with radical feminists that the creation of a women's culture is essential to facilitating women's sense of themselves as a group with common interests and to encourage their political organization.

During the 1970s, women's culture mushroomed in the advanced capitalist nations. There are now feminist novels, feminist science fiction, feminist dance troupes, feminist films, feminist theater groups, feminist music and feminist visual art. Moreover, women's past cultural productions are being retrieved and women's traditional crafts are being revived. In addition, there are cultural events, restaurants, etc. for women only, "womanspaces" in which women can be together physically and which foster a sense of community between women. The values expressed in the women's culture are quite diverse, even though they are all feminist in one way or another. At one extreme, they fantasize a world without men; at the other extreme, they show women "making it" in a man's world. Some feminist artists, such as Judy Chicago in her "The Dinner Party," show that women can be rulers, doctors, warriors, etc., just as well as men; others try to present alternative models of female achievement. The values presented depend in part on the intended audience and sometimes are modified to suit that audience. For instance, Marilyn French's best-selling novel *The Women's Room* ends with the central character walking alone on the beach, despairing of women's liberation or even of a degree of personal happiness, at least for feminist women. By contrast, the TV version of the book, perhaps in an attempt to make feminism palatable to an audience with less feminist sophistication than the readers of the book were presumed to possess, ended with the same character, smartly dressed, delivering a rousing feminist speech to a college audience and being wildly applauded.

As one aspect of feminist political activity, women's culture emphasizes the process as well as the product of artistic creation. Where possible, it uses collective rather than individual forms of creation and tries to minimize the gaps between creators, performers and technicians. It may also try to narrow the gap between artist and audience. The dance troupe Wallflower Order raises explicitly on the stage the question of process.

> Wallflower examines the problems of working collectively in one of their pieces. Lack of money, feeling fed up with seeming endless criticism and self-criticism, feeling closed in by the group, wanting to reach out to other people and not being certain how. These are real problems faced by all of us who have attempted to work collectively. And it is wonderful to see these problems portrayed on stage in a way that allows us to both examine our difficulties and to laugh at ourselves.[80]

Judy Chicago's "The Dinner Party" is accompanied on its travels by a film, "Right Out of History," which documents the four-year creation of the piece by a group of more than 400 people. Often the process of creating feminist art is imperfect; for instance, the process of creating "The Dinner Party" was clearly hierarchical and perhaps exploitative. Nevertheless, the very recognition by feminists of the importance of process raises important political questions about the relation between artistic and other kinds of production.

Socialist feminists view cultural work as a necessary part of political organization for social change. They do not accept uncritically all aspects of women's culture, but seek to encourage those aspects which explore new ways in which the artist and the community can relate to each other, which link women's oppression with that of other oppressed groups, and which emphasize the possibility of women's collective political action against their oppression. For socialist feminists, the creation of a women's culture is an important way in which women can develop political self-consciousness. Of course, such development is possible only because women do in fact already share objective political interests.

One of the interests shared by women is the availability of quality goods and services such as food, clothing, housing, medical care and education. Of course, everyone has an interest in these, but women have a special interest because it is they who, according to the prevailing division of labor, are responsible for making these goods and services directly available to their families. Women buy and cook food, buy or make clothing, furnish homes, take their children to the doctor and worry about schooling. Weinbaum and Bridges characterize this work as consumption work. They point out that it is time-consuming, exhausting and alienating.[81] Women who find this work intolerable have two options. One is to demand that the work be shared by men. This option challenges the sexual division of labor but has the disadvantages that men may not be available, that men's economic privilege puts them in a strong position to refuse and, finally, that this option does not make the goods and services any more available: it just gives somebody else the responsibility for procuring them. Women's other option is to organize politically against the unavailability of goods and services, and this option has often been chosen by working-class women. Women have taken the lead in forming tenants' unions, in boycotting expensive or racist stores or products, in protesting cutbacks in services such as welfare or childcare and in taking militant action against the high price of, for example, public utilities. Socialist feminists believe that all these "community based" political activities are necessary parts of the struggle for a socialist and feminist transformation of society.

In order to achieve a thoroughgoing socialist and feminist transformation of social relations, socialist feminists believe that a wide range of political activity is necessary. It includes community struggles, the organization of women against their alienation in wage labor, the creation of a distinctive socialist feminist culture and attempts to restructure sexual and childrearing relations. All these struggles must be linked together to ensure that the social transformation is total and that all aspects of women's alienation are overcome.

One obvious problem with the strategy as presented so far is that it offers no political priorities: it suggests that everything must be done at once. Socialist feminists refuse to assign permanent priority to any one type of political activity over the others; they believe that a socialist and feminist revolution cannot happen without struggle on all these fronts. Yet they do suggest some general criteria that socialist feminists might use in deciding where to direct their political energy. Charlotte Bunch offers five criteria that are similar to those proposed by other socialist feminist writers.

Material reforms should aid as many women as possible and should particularly seek to redistribute income and status so that the class, race and heterosexual privileges that divide women are eliminated . . .

Reform activities that help women find a sense of themselves apart from their oppressed functions and which are not based on the false sense of race, class, or heterosexual superiority are important. . . .

Women need to win. We need to struggle for reforms that are attainable. . . . Victories and programs, especially when linked to specific organizations, give us a clearer sense of what we can win and illustrate the plans, imagination, and changes that women will bring as they gain power . . .

Since winning one reform is not our final goal, we should ask if working on that issue will teach us new and important things about ourselves and society. Particularly when a reform fails, political education is important to motivate women to continue, rather than to become cynical about change. . . .

As women, we want to improve the conditions of our daily lives. In order to do this, we must have power over the institutions—the family, schools, factories, laws, and so on—that determine those conditions . . . above all, we should demand that those most affected by each institution have the power to determine its nature and direction. Initially, these challenges and reforms help to undermine the power of patriarchy, capitalism and white supremacy. Ultimately, these actions must lead to the people's control of all institutions so that we can determine how our society will function.[82]

With respect to her final criterion, Bunch suggests that one way of building power is by creating alternative institutions "such as health clinics that give us more control over our bodies or women's media that control our communications with the public." Bunch adds, "Alternative institutions should not be havens of retreat, but challenges that weaken male power over our lives."[83] In this sentence, Bunch sums up the difference between the socialist feminist conception of alternative institutions and the radical feminist conception of a womanculture. Radical feminists intend that their alternative institutions should enable women to withdraw as far as possible from the dominant culture by facilitating women's independence from that culture. They have high hopes for creating a womanspace that provides a total contrast to patriarchal space and is a refuge from it. Socialist feminists, by contrast, argue that women's independence from the dominant male, white and capitalist culture is an impossible fantasy: they build alternative institutions as a way of partially satisfying existing needs and also as a way of experimenting with new forms of working together. The difference here between radical and socialist feminists is not clear-cut: both radical and socialist feminists might work on the same alternative project, such as a health center. But socialist feminists expect that social relations within the project will be distorted by the pressures of the larger society outside, and they do not anticipate that their project will become part of a permanent women's counterculture.

One institution to which some socialist feminists are seeking immediate alternatives is the stereotypical 20th-century nuclear family, with its familiar sexual division of labor, according to which the wife is assigned responsibility for childrearing and housework while the husband has responsibility for economic support of the family. Socialist feminists, like many other feminists, see this family structure as a corner-stone of women's oppression: it enforces women's dependence on men, it enforces heterosexuality and it imposes the prevailing masculine and feminine character structures on the next generation. In addition, the traditional nuclear family is a bulwark of the capitalist system insofar as it makes possible the use of women as a reserve army of labor, sustains a high level of demand for consumer goods, and inculcates in children the values of dominance and submission, of alienated labor and consumption and of competition. Many points in the socialist feminist critique of the family are identical with points made by traditional Marxists, but socialist feminists differ from traditional Marxists in their belief that immediate changes in living arrangements can be a significant part of a broader strategy for social transformation. Unlike traditional Marxists, socialist feminists do not believe that consciously designed changes in family structure must wait until "after the revolution." They believe that immediate changes are necessary in order to enable women to participate fully in the revolutionary process and to ensure that process is feminist as well as socialist.

Many commentators have pointed out that in fact the classic nuclear family is disappearing rapidly in advanced capitalist countries at the end of the 20th century. Increasing numbers of women, regardless of their politics, are living in alternatives to that family, either because they bring a second wage into the home or because they are bringing up children as single parents. What distinguishes socialist feminist alternatives is that they are self-conscious attempts to incorporate socialist feminist values in their daily living arrangements. These values include equality, cooperation, sharing, political commitment, freedom from sexual stereotyping and freedom from personal possessiveness.

Many socialist feminists live in family structures that are not obviously different from those of most other women: they are the structures of marriage or cohabitation with a man or of single motherhood. Within these relatively traditional structures, it is impossible to practice all the socialist feminist values. For instance, a single mother cannot model the range of alternatives possible for women and a heterosexual couple cannot demonstrate the validity of alternatives to heterosexuality. Even within these relatively traditional structures, however, many traditional values can be challenged: fathers and mothers can refuse the traditional sexual division of labor, reversing the traditional roles or sharing equally the responsibility for breadwinning and childcare; single mothers can hardly fail to present a model of an independent woman. It is in larger households, however, that the dominant values of possessiveness, privatism, emotional dependence and consumerism can be challenged more thoroughly. Larger socialist feminist households may be all women or may include men. Ann Ferguson lists seven goals for such socialist and feminist "revolutionary family-communities":

1. To alter childrearing inequalities between men and women, to provide the structural base for men and women to be *equal nurturers* to children and to each other as well as *equally autonomous* . . .
2. To challenge the sexual division of labor . . .
3. To break down the possessive privacy of the two primary sets of relationships in the American patriarchal family: the couple and the parent-child relationship . . .
4. To equalize power as far as possible between parents and children and, in general, between adults and children . . .
5. To eliminate the base for heterosexism in a society which, along with patriarchy and capitalism, contributes to women's oppression. This means openly allowing gay persons, including gay mothers and fathers, openly into the revolutionary family-community . . .
6. To break down elitist attitudes about the superiority of mental and professional work to manual work.
7. To deal with racism and classism.
8. To introduce economic sharing in the family-community which allows its members to develop a sense of commitment to each other.[84]

Ferguson realizes that no single revolutionary family-community can achieve all these goals easily, if at all. In addition to the "internalized" psychological problems of emotional insecurity, jealousy, competitiveness or heterosexism, such communities are subject to external or social constraints: women will find it harder than men to obtain adequately paying jobs, and people's work or study plans may require them to leave the area. Revolutionary family-communities are certainly not envisioned as utopian refuges from male dominance, racism and capitalism. They are places where people can experiment with new ways of organizing childrearing and sexuality, prefiguring, though imperfectly, some of the new forms of social relations that will be part of a socialist feminist revolution. In the meantime, they will also provide people with the "material support needed to continue to challenge the combined domination systems of capitalist patriarchy."[85]

Delores Hayden recognizes that only a relatively few women are ready for the revolutionary family-communities outlined by Ferguson. For those who are not ready, Hayden proposes the less immediately radical alternative of HOMES: Homemakers Organized for a More Equal Society.[86] HOMES groups would own housing cooperatively. Their property would contain private dwelling units and some private, fenced, outdoor space, but it would also include public outdoor areas and the facilities to provide a number of services, such as childcare, laundry, food preparation, van transportation and home help for the elderly, the sick and employed parents whose children are sick. Existing suburban blocks could be converted for use by HOMES groups. In designing their living arrangements, Hayden states that HOMES should be guided by the following principles to

> (1) involve both men and women in the unpaid labor associated with housekeeping and child care on an equal basis; (2) involve both men and women in the paid-labor force on an equal basis; (3) eliminate residential segregation by class, race, and age; (4) eliminate all federal, state, and local programs and laws which offer implicit or explicit reinforcement of the unpaid role of the female homemaker; (5) minimize unpaid domestic labor and wasteful energy consumption; (6) maximize real choices for households concerning recreation and sociability.[87]

Alternative living arrangements are one way in which socialist feminists seek to translate into practice their insight that the personal is political. Another way is in their general concern for the process as well as the product of political activity. They are aware that organizational form is not politically neutral, and they have seen how the centralized and hierarchical forms of traditional political organization have perpetuated the subordination and passivity of women—and of other groups. Like radical feminists, socialist feminists are experimenting with new forms of organizational structure that can help people to overcome the partial and distorted development of their capacities that has been imposed by the capitalist and male-dominant division of labor. Without direct efforts to contradict these distorted developments of contemporary human nature, revolutionary organizations will only reinforce that which they are ostensibly struggling against. A hierarchical, undemocratic, sexist and racist organization can achieve only a hierarchical, undemocratic, sexist and racist "revolution."

Although they seek to avoid replicating within their own organizations the division of labor imposed by the dominant society, socialist feminists do not go to the opposite extreme of insisting that everybody should do every job. In a sensitive discussion of the problems involved in restructuring the labor process,

Nancy Hartsock points out that alienation does not result simply from specialization in one kind of work, but rather from the social relations within which, in contemporary society, specialized work is usually performed. Within these relations, work is coerced and execution is separated from conception. Hartsock believes that a socialist feminist restructuring of the labor process can avoid both coercion and the separation of execution from conception without requiring that everyone should do everything:

> By rotating all members through the various tasks of the group, and by insisting that every member of a collective do every activity that the group as a whole is engaged in, the collective, in practice, treats its members as interchangeable and equivalent parts. It reproduces the assembly line of the modern factory, but instead of running the work past the people, people are run past the work.[88]

Hartsock suggests that a better alternative is to allow individuals or groups to have responsibility for whole aspects of projects, involving both planning and executing the work to be done.

> Having responsibility for some parts of the work done by a group allows us not only to see our own accomplishments but also to expand ourselves by sharing in the accomplishments of others. We are not superwomen, able to do everything. Only by sharing in the different accomplishments of others can we participate in the activities of all women.[89]

In their recognition of the inseparability of means from ends, socialist feminists are closer to radical feminists than to any other group of feminists. Unlike radical feminists, however, socialist feminists do not see themselves as "living the revolution." This is true for two reasons. First, socialist feminists recognize the ways in which the larger society imposes limits on the possibilities of alternative ways for living and working.

> Our strategies for change and the internal organization of work must grow out of the tension between using our organizations as instruments for both taking and transforming power in a society structured by power understood only as domination and using our organizations to build models for a society based on power understood as energy and initiative . . . There are real pressures to reproduce the patterns of estranged labor in the interests of efficiency and taking power. At the same time, there are pressures to oppose estranged labor by insisting that each of us do every job.[90]

The other reason why socialist feminists do not see themselves as "living the revolution" is because they do not think that social transformation can occur through the gradual accretion of socialist and feminist reforms and through the gradual undermining of dominant by alternative institutions. Radical feminists depend on slow, evolutionary rather than sudden, revolutionary change both for moral and practical reasons. On the one hand, they eschew the use of force as a patriarchal tactic; on the other hand, even the potential constituency of radical feminism is so small that there seems little chance of its winning a violent confrontation with the patriarchy. Socialist feminists, by contrast, are sufficiently Marxist to be skeptical that the white male ruling class would give up its power without a violent struggle; however, they are confident that such a struggle could be won by the overwhelming majority of the population whom they see as their potential allies. Socialist feminists expect that there will be a distinctive revolutionary period, characterized by acute social turmoil, but they also expect that the outcome of this turmoil will be determined by the kind and quality of the pre-revolutionary activity that has preceded it. To this extent, they see themselves not so much as living the revolution as preparing for it and attempting in limited ways to prefigure it.

The socialist feminist contribution to revolutionary strategy is not simply to add women's issues to the list of concerns that a revolutionary movement must address. Socialist feminism does indeed broaden the traditional Marxist conception of revolutionary struggle to include, for instance, reproductive freedom. But ultimately socialist feminism denies the separation between so called class issues, race issues and women's issues. It argues that every issue is a women's issue, just as every issue has race and class implications. That is to say, socialist feminism argues that a feminist perspective can illuminate understanding not only of family life or of education but also of foreign policy, of imperialism and of political organization. To ask how a certain practice or institution affects women is different from asking how it affects the working class or the colonized nation as a whole. Because male dominance structures every area of life, a foreign policy based on explicit concern for women's interests would be quite different from a foreign policy that was based only on a concern for the working class conceived as a unified whole or for some ethnic minority within that class. On the socialist feminist view, it is necessary to approach all political issues with a consciousness that is explicitly feminist as well as explicitly anti-racist and explicitly socialist. This consciousness will change both the form and the content of revolutionary political practice.

Problems with Socialist Feminist Politics

Grounded on a conception of human potentiality as virtually limitless, socialist feminist politics are informed by the vision of a society where all the members are able to participate freely and fully in every area of life. Socialist feminism seeks a society where people can integrate their capacities for mental and manual labor, for rationality and for emotional connection, for work, for sexuality, for art and for play, until those categories no longer describe separate human activities. In particular, socialist feminism seeks a society in which "masculinity" and "femininity" no longer exist. The vision is inspiring, the analysis of women's contemporary oppression is incisive, and the political practice, which refuses to separate means from ends, is appealing. The problems with socialist feminist politics are less in what they prescribe than in what they fail to prescribe. The strength of socialist feminism is in raising questions for other political traditions; its weakness is sometimes in answering those questions.

One distinctive feature of socialist feminism is its emphasis on democracy. Following radical feminism, it has argued that women's voices are unheard not only in conventional liberal politics but also in Marxist organizations; in addition, it has argued that it is necessary to institute not only democratic control of the economy, as traditionally construed, but also democratic control of pro-creation. So far, however, socialist feminism has not shown clearly just how more genuine democratic practices can be instituted.

One problem with the socialist feminist call for the democratization of procreation is that it may conflict with what is sometimes called "women's right to their own bodies." In contemporary society, procreation is ostensibly a private matter: individuals or couples decide how many children they want, if any, and how they should be reared. In practice, men have more control than women over procreation, for reasons that we have explored, and the state also exerts considerable direct and indirect control over procreation through policies regarding the availability of contraception and abortion, childcare, compulsory schooling, etc. Socialist feminists justify their call for establishing explicit and democratic procedures for community control over procreation by appeal to the interests of women, of children and of the community as a whole. So far, however, socialist feminists have made little attempt to explain just what democratization of procreation would mean in practice. It is, of course, utopian to expect that detailed blueprints for a new society should be drawn up far in advance of the time when there exists the material possibility for constructing that society. On the other hand, failure to think through exactly what would be implied in democratizing procreation has allowed most socialist feminists to overlook the possibility of conflict between the needs of the community for babies and the wishes of the women who, as procreative technology now stands, would have to bear those babies. Rosalind Petchesky asks:

> even in a society where the collective responsibility for reproduction and child rearing is taken seriously at all levels of public and interpersonal life, would there not still be aspects of reproductive and sexual relations that remain a "personal affair"? In particular, would women not still retain a preemptive claim to reproductive autonomy, especially around questions of abortion and childbearing, based on the principle of "control over one's body"? Even in the context of new, revolutionary social relations of reproduction, it would never be legitimate to compel a person to have sex or to bear a child, to have an abortion or be sterilized, to express or to repress sexuality in some prescribed way, or to undergo surgical or chemical or other bodily intervention for reproductive or contraceptive purposes. A sense of being a person, with personal and bodily integrity, would remain essential to the definition of social participation and responsibility under any historical conditions I can imagine.[91]

Petchesky's discussion suggests a number of difficult questions for those who call for the democratization of procreation. A central question is what counts as social coercion. Is it coercion, for instance, if the community announces reluctance or refusal to care for more children? Is it coercion if the community offers rewards or incentives to women for bearing children? Would this be a form of prostitution or is it only fair to reward those who perform less desirable jobs? Could women even use their childbearing capacity to win special privileges for themselves? All these questions would confront those who attempted to put into practice the ideal of democracy in procreation. Petchesky herself doubts that they can ever be given an answer that is totally satisfactory.

In any society, there will remain a *level of individual desire that can never be totally reconciled with social need,* without destroying the individual personalities whose "self-realization," as Heller and Marcuse stress, is the ultimate object of social life. How would an individual woman's desire to have a child, or not to have a child, be harmonized in every case with a social policy that determines, on the basis of social need, the circumstances in which people should or should not have and raise children? Even if reproduction and pregnancy were technologically relegated to the laboratory, in the vision of Firestone, there would no doubt remain women who resisted the "technological revolution" as usurping a process that belonged to them individually, personally, to their bodies. The provision of adequate, universal child care services or male sharing in child rearing will eliminate neither the tension between the principles of individual control and collective responsibility over reproduction, nor the need to make reproductive choices that are hard.[92]

The socialist feminist conception of organizational democracy is no more complete than its conception of procreative democracy. Socialist feminists have provided an incisive critique of the ways in which centralized forms of political organization replicate sexual and other divisions in the larger society. As alternatives to centralism, they have experimented with networks of small and often short-lived groups organized to undertake specific projects. As we saw in the last chapter, however, the lack of formal organizational structure can lead to "the tyranny of structurelessness."[93] Sheila Rowbotham notes:

Our lack of structure can make it difficult for women outside particular social networks to join. It can lead to cliquishness and thus be undemocratic. The stress on personal experience makes it hard to communicate ideas which have been gained either from the women's movement in the past or from other forms of radical politics.[94]

One popular alternative to centralized forms of organization has been "participatory democracy" in which decisions are made by those who are present at meetings. Again, however, Rowbotham is aware of the weaknesses of this form of organization:

The problems about participatory democracy are evident. If you are not able to be present you can't participate. Whoever turns up next time can reverse the previous decision. If very few people turn up they are lumbered with the responsibility. It is a very open situation and anyone with a gift for either emotional blackmail or a conviction of the need to intervene can do so without being checked by any accepted procedure. Participatory democracy only works if everyone accepts a certain give and take, a respect for one another's experience, a desire and need to remain connected. If these are present it can work very well. If they are not it can be a traumatic process.[95]

Socialist feminists have prided themselves on developing a form of political practice which concerns itself with people's feelings and refuses to separate the personal from the political. Ann Foreman speaks for many women when she writes:

By failing to consider personal interaction a political question, the forms of organisation and discussion that the left groups adopted both internally and in the campaigns that they initiated prevented the full participation of women. The aggressive and often destructive approach of men to political debate reflects their traditional ability to distance themselves from their political practice. Historically, the political and personal lives of men have been structurally separate. Unlike women, their involvement in politics has not required them to question their very individuality. The left groups, in their lack of sensitivity to personal interaction, reproduced a traditionally male approach to politics and with it an effective exclusion of women from real political involvement.[96]

The socialist feminist refusal to separate the personal from the political makes for a more integrated politics but it also has its drawbacks. Entire meetings for instance, can be consumed by trying to resolve problems between individuals and total personal identification with one's politics makes it difficult to separate a political criticism from a personal attack.

Though setting ourselves more exacting practical and personal standards in politics than the contemporary left, we nonetheless have found that criticism and differences bear too closely upon us for comfort. The distancing which is present in male-dominated groups is alienating. Yet it allows for the release of differences. The agony of division can be turned outwards rather than imploding the soul. Sisterhood can become a coercive consensus which makes it emotionally difficult for individual women to say what they feel rather than a source of strength. Consciousness raising can put too great a pressure on women to change by an effort of will alone. Feminist politics can become preoccupied with living a liberated life rather than becoming a movement for the liberation of women.[97]

A final inadequacy in the socialist feminist discussion of democracy is its lack of interest in extending democracy to children. There has been considerable liberal interest in the question of children's rights,[98] and Shulamith Firestone, among radical feminists, published in 1970 her ringing call for the abolition of childhood.[99] Yet radical feminists generally have not heeded Firestone's call, nor have socialist feminists taken up the issue.[100] This omission by socialist feminists is especially significant in light of the socialist feminist conception of human nature which utilizes both the Marxian notion of human self-creation and the Freudian view that the main features of an individual's character structure are socially imposed at a very early age. Taken together, these views suggest that children must be fully active participants in making the decisions that affect them most directly and so participate in controlling their own lives. The work of Wilhelm Reich and others suggests that children who are subjected consistently to externally imposed authority are likely to develop the sort of authoritarian character structure that will fit them only for conformity in an authoritarian society.[101] Even if they reject the dominant ideology and espouse some apparently revolutionary alternative, they will hold the new view as a dogma; they will tend to hero worship certain powerful leaders and to condemn those who challenge authority. It is hard to see how adults with this sort of character structure could establish genuinely democratic forms of social life or even participate in such forms. Children are smaller and weaker than adults; they are less skilled and have less information. Like adults, however, they create their own nature through their own forms of daily praxis. Both the dignity of children now and a concern for the future society they will construct require that revolutionaries take seriously the notion of extending democracy to children. Of course, they should include children in those reflections. It may be that such reflections will lead to the conclusion that it is necessary to abolish the entire status of childhood. It may be that the call for children's rights reflects the limitations of a liberal perspective analogous to the limitations reflected in the call for women's or workers' rights. Just as socialist feminists are committed to abolishing workerhood and womanhood as social categories, so their political values and their conception of human nature may require them also to abolish childhood.

In sum, socialist feminists have demonstrated a number of inadequacies in contemporary conceptions of democracy, but they have not yet succeeded in creating alternatives that are entirely satisfactory. Of course, no alternative will ever be entirely satisfactory in a society split by divisions of class, race, sex and age. Full democracy requires that decisions regarding every area of life should be made by everyone affected by those decisions in a situation where each person is fully confident to participate freely in debate and is heard with equal respect. Democracy in this sense is presently impossible, but it is important that it be kept in mind as a heuristic ideal, inspiring the goals and strategies of socialist feminism.

Socialist feminist consideration of racism is even less complete than its consideration of democracy. Most socialist feminists pay lip service to the need for their struggle to be directed against racism, but so far only limited success has been achieved. The vast majority of socialist feminists are still white and "middle-class", although this may be slowly changing. Socialist feminists recognize that it is necessary to combat racism within their own organizations, and the non-centralized structure of their organizations is less likely to perpetuate racist divisions than a more centralized structure. Socialist feminists are also aware of racial dimensions in issues such as employment, rape, the family, abortion or international relations, but they remain uncertain how to conceptualize in a systematic way the connections between racism, sexism and capitalism. Ann Ferguson expresses very clearly this uncertainty.

> Many socialist feminists include racial oppression as a concept of equal importance in understanding the social conflicts basic to U.S. capitalism. However, I know of no one who presents a historical analysis which makes clear how *race* fits in as a basic social division between people rather than as an effect of capitalism and/or patriarchy. A worked out theory would have to develop an analysis of the special position of minorities in class and sex struggles, something I cannot do in this paper, in part because I don't know the best way to do it.[102]

In developing their understanding of the interconnections between racism, sexism and capitalism, socialist feminists cannot limit their view to a single society nor even to a single type of society, such as advanced capitalism. They need to explore how racism, sexism and capitalism operate internationally so that, for instance, an imperialist power may simultaneously reinforce racism and male dominance by drawing men into dangerous and exhausting forms of wage labor, often far from home, and by leaving women behind to rear children and practice subsistence agriculture. Without an international perspective, there is a danger that increased freedom for women in the advanced capitalist nations may be won at the expense of women elsewhere. For instance, women under advanced capitalism seem likely to win a degree of reproductive freedom, but only because the burden of reproducing the labor force needed by capitalism is falling on women in less developed nations. Most advanced capitalist nations now have a very low birthrate and they often fill their need for labor by temporary immigration from the less-developed nations. Nations such as France, Switzerland, and Germany import temporary workers from North Africa, Turkey or Italy in arrangements such as the German "Gastarbeiter" or "guest worker" system. The United States relies heavily on the labor of undocumented Mexican workers and currently seems likely to implement some sort of guestworker system, within which immigrant workers are issued temporary work permits for a limited time, after which they must return to their native land. This system allows the capitalist class of an advanced industrial nation to exploit the labor power of less-developed nations without having to pay for the full costs of producing that labor power. A system like this obviously intensifies divisions of race, class and sex. If socialist feminists are serious about eliminating these divisions in one society, they cannot allow them to be replicated on a world scale.

The last problem that I want to mention for socialist feminist politics requires shifting from a global perspective to a reflexive focus on socialist feminists' own daily lives. It is the problem of discovering viable ways of living in the long haul toward a socialist feminist revolution, ways of living with contradictions that are presently ineradicable. The socialist feminist insistence that the personal is political has raised the possibility of liberating women through a total transformation of social relations. While this is an exciting prospect, the insight that the personal is political can, in the meantime, be a heavy burden to socialist feminist women. When racism, capitalism and male dominance are seen to penetrate political organizations, the home and even the bedroom, socialist feminist women are left with no place of refuge from the struggle. They are always on the front lines. When even clothing is seen to have political significance, the choice of what to wear ironically can become even more difficult for the woman with a socialist feminist consciousness than for the woman who lacks that consciousness.[103]

The burden of daily life is particularly acute for socialist feminists who are heterosexual. Barbara Haber calls it a crisis.[104] She recognizes that millions of women in the U.S. and other advanced capitalist countries are suffering a crisis of personal, that is, of emotional and family life as a result of social and economic changes, particularly women's massive entry into wage labor, the drop in the birthrate and the decline of the traditional family. But Haber argues that those socialist feminists who are heterosexual are in a particularly difficult position. They seek sexual and emotional intimacy and many of them would like to be mothers. Like all contemporary women, they suffer from "social isolation, lack of gratifying work, absence of intimacy and sexual closeness, or the threat of violence."[105] Unlike most women, however, and unlike most feminists except for radical feminists, socialist feminists also have an acute awareness of the ways in which conventional solutions, marriage, a career, romantic love, even heterosexuality itself, are "unprogressive." Yet there seem to be few alternative ways for people to fulfill some deep needs. In these circumstances, Haber, a socialist feminist, writes: "As an ordinary heterosexual woman, with a limited span of life before me, I sometimes partake of the desire to turn back from the path that we as feminists have set out upon."[106]

Haber does not want to repress either her heterosexuality or to "come slinking back individually to grit my teeth and repress my hard-earned awareness of male supremacy and sexism."[107] She wants a way of living in the present that satisfies her need for emotional and sexual intimacy but that does not violate her socialist and feminist principles. Socialist feminist analysis teaches us that there are no "individual solutions," that separatism is utopian, that life under capitalism and male dominance will always be alienated. At the same time, people need a way of surviving within the contradictions of the system.

The contemporary women's liberation movement began with a deep critique of "personal" relations. Haber claims that this critique has been suspended in the last few years.

The fear that men may look like a bad compromise for most women leads us to turn away from looking at our own experiences with men and from using our own life dilemmas as the basis of political theory and practice. Our fears tempt us to lower the consciousness we once struggled to raise, in the hopes that we can find a rationale for making do with what is available. This, on the perfectly understandable ground that a limited marriage is better than loneliness, and raising children with an inadequate partner is better than raising them alone, or foregoing motherhood altogether.[108]

Haber calls for reviving the critique of personal life, for "another round of consciousness raising, (for entering) once again, into a relationship of collective confrontation and dialogue with men."[109]

Lesbian socialist feminists might not share Haber's urgent wish for confrontation and dialogue with men, but they too have emotional and sexual needs whose fulfilment is thwarted by racism, capitalism and male supremacy. All socialist feminists need communities that provide supportive criticism and critical support as they struggle with the contradictions of their daily lives. They need ways of balancing the insight that every aspect of life has a political dimension against the recognition that contemporary society allows only limited means for the satisfaction of individual need and that, in any case, the needs of us all have been shaped and distorted by an authoritarian, male supremacist and capitalist society.[110] As long as the basic structure of contemporary society remains unchanged, these contradictions are unresolvable. In the meantime, however, socialist feminists must discover how to live with these contradictions in such a way as to find not despair and defeat, but joy and strength in the struggle against them.

Notes

1. Linda Phelps, "Death in the Spectacle: Female Sexual Alienation," *Liberation,* May 1971; Sandra L. Bartky, "On Psychological Oppression," in Sharon Bishop and Marjorie Weinzweig, eds., *Philosophy and Women* (Belmont, CA: Wadsworth, 1979), pp. 33-41; also, "Narcissim, Femininity and Alienation," *Social Theory and Practice* 8, no. 2 (Summer 1982):127-43. See also Bettina Aptheker, "The Humanization of Woman: Toward a Materialist Theory of Woman's Alienation", unpublished manuscript; also Ann Foreman, *Femininity as Alienation: Women and the Family in Marxism and Psychoanalysis* (London: Pluto Press, 1977).

2. This point was made to me by Alan Soble in correspondence. He was drawing on the work of Jean Kilbourne.

3. Bartky, "Narcissism, Femininity and Alienation," pp. 131-32.

4. Ibid., p. 134.

5. Shulamith Firestone, *The Dialectic of Sex* (New York: William Morrow, 1970), p. 178.

6. Phelps, "Death in the Spectacle," p. 26.

7. Sarah Lawrence College Ad Hoc Women's Studies Committee Against Sterilization Abuse, *Workbook on Sterilization and Sterilization Abuse* (Bronxville, N.Y., 1978), p. 20.

8. Andy Ferguson, "Childbirth as Alienated Labor," *Breaking Ground* 1 (Spring 1980):25.

9. Adrienne Rich, *Of Woman Born: Motherhood as Experience and Institution* (New York: W.W. Norton, 1976), p. 176.

10. Shelley Day, "Is Obstetric Technology Depressing?" *Radical Science Journal* 12 (1982):17-45.

11. *Newsweek,* Oct. 6, 1980, p. 105.

12. Brigitte Jordan, *Birth in Four Cultures: A Crosscultural Investigation of Childbirth in Yucatan, Holland, Sweden and the United States* (Montreal: Eden Press, 1980), p. 50.

13. Barbara Ehrenreich and Deirdre English, *For Her Own Good: 150 Years of the Experts' Advice to Women* (New York: Anchor/Doubleday, 1979), p. 192.

14. Ibid., p. 184.

15. Sandra Bartky pointed this out to me. A good account of Taylorism as it was called is given by Harry Braverman, *Labor and Monopoly Capital: The Degradation of Work in the Twentieth Century* (New York: Monthly Review Press, 1974), chap. 4: "Scientific Management."

16. Meg Luxton, *More Than A Labour of Love: Three Generations of Women's Work in the Home* (Toronto: Women's Educational Press, 1980), p. 104.

17. Ibid., p. 91.

18. Ehrenreich and English, *For Her Own Good,* pp. 184-85 (italics in the original).

19. For an account of family structure in one poor subculture, see Carol B. Stack, *All Our Kin: Strategies for Survival in a Black Community* (New York: Harper Colophon, 1975).

20. R.S. Cowan, "Two Washes in the Morning and a Bridge Party at Night: the American Housewife between the Wars", *Women's Studies,* vol. 3 (1976):153.

21. Beverly Jones, "The Dynamics of Marriage and Motherhood" in Robin Morgan, ed., *Sisterhood Is Powerful: An Anthology of Writings from the Women's Liberation Movement* (New York: Vintage, 1970), pp. 55-57.

22. Karl Marx, *The Economic and Philosophic Manuscripts of 1844,* ed. and intro. by Dirk J. Struik (New York: International Publishers, 1964), p. 110.

23. Anonymous mother cited by Betty Friedan in *The Feminine Mystique* (New York: Dell, 1963), p. 276.

24. Michelene Wandor, "The Conditions of Illusion," in Sandra Allen, Lee Sanders, and Jan Wallis, eds., *Papers from the Women's Movement,* (Leeds: Feminist Books, 1974), p. 193.

25. Luxton, *More Than a Labour of Love,* p. 87.

26. Pauline Bart, "Mother Portnoy's Complaints," *Trans action* 8, nos. 1 and 2 (November-December 1970), pp. 69-74.

27. Ibid., p. 72.

28. Luxton, *More Than a Labour of Love,* pp. 88-89.

29. Dorothy Dinnerstein, *The Mermaid and the Minotaur: Sexual Arrangements and Human Malaise* (New York: Harper Colophon, 1977), p. 60.

30. Bartky, "Narcissism, Femininity and Alienation," p. 129.

31. Foreman, *Femininity as Alienation.*

32. CARASA (Committee for Abortion Rights and Against Sterilization Abuse), *Women Under Attack: Abortion, Sterilization Abuse, and Reproductive Freedom* (New York: CARASA, 1979), p. 11 (italics in original).

33. Rosalind Pollack Petchesky, "Reproductive Freedom: Beyond 'A Woman's Right to Choose,' " *Signs: Journal of Women in Culture and Society* 5, no. 4 (Summer 1980):662. This paper is reprinted in Catharine R. Stimpson and Ethel Spector Person, eds., *Women, Sex and Sexuality* (Chicago and London: University of Chicago Press, 1980), pp. 92-116.

34. Ibid., pp. 669-70.

35. For a more extended discussion of this claim, see my "Abortion and a Woman's Right to Decide," *Philosophical Forum* 5, nos. 1-2 (Winter 1975). Reprinted in Robert Baker and Frederick Elliston, eds., *Philosophy & Sex* (Buffalo, N.Y.: Prometheus Books, 1975), pp. 324-37.

36. Dinnerstein, *The Mermaid and the Minotaur.*

37. Nancy Chodorow, *Mothering: Psychoanalysis and the Sociology of Gender* (Berkeley and Los Angeles: University of California Press, 1978). Chodorow's views are summarized in Chapter 6.

38. One who has made this argument is Ann Ferguson, panel discussant of Nancy Chodorow's book, Radical Caucus/Society for Women in Philosophy Joint Session, Eastern

348   *The Politics of Socialist Feminism*

Division meetings of the American Philosophical Association, Boston, 29 December 1980.

39. Petchesky, "Reproductive Freedom," p. 682. Also Adrienne Rich, "Compulsory Heterosexuality and Lesbian Existence," *Signs: Journal of Women in Culture and Society* 5, no. 4 (Summer 1980):638.

40. Linda Gordon, "The Struggle for Reproductive Freedom: Three States of Feminism" in Zillah R. Eisenstein, ed., *Capitalist Patriarchy and the Case for Socialist Feminism,* (New York: Monthly Review Press, 1979), p. 109. A number of the following points are made by Gordon in her excellent essay.

41. Ibid., p. 113.

42. Anne Koedt, "The Myth of the Vaginal Orgasm," in Ann Koedt, Ellen Levine, and Anita Rapone, eds., *Radical Feminism,* (New York: Quadrangle Books, 1973), pp. 198-207. The article was first published in 1970 in *Notes from the Second Year.*

43. Gordon, "Struggle for Reproductive Freedom," p. 123.

44. Gayle Rubin, "The Traffic in Women: Notes on the 'Political Economy' of Sex," in Rayna R. Reiter, ed., *Toward an Anthropology of Women* (New York: Monthly Review Press, 1975), p. 187. Abridged version reprinted in Alison M. Jaggar and Paula R. Struhl, eds., *Feminist Frameworks: Alternative Theoretical Accounts of the Relations between Women and Men* (McGraw-Hill, 1978), p. 164.

45. Gordon, "Struggle for Reproductive Freedom," p. 127.

46. Ibid., p. 127.

47. Ibid., pp. 123-24.

48. Joan Kelly, "The Doubled Vision of Feminist Theory: A Postscript to the 'Women and Power' Conference," *Feminist Studies* 5, no. 1 (Spring 1979):220.

49. Margery Davies, "Woman's Place Is at the Typewriter: The Feminization of the Clerical Labor Force," in Eisenstein, ed., *Capitalist Patriarchy,* pp. 248-66.

50. The participation of women in the paid labor force has steadily increased since 1947, while that of men has steadily decreased. Harry Braverman, *Labor and Monopoly Capital: The Degradation of Work in the Twentieth Century* (New York: Monthly Review Press, 1974), chap. 17.

51. *Employment and Earnings,* January 1978, pp. 151-53. Cited by Evelyn Nakano Glenn and Roslyn L. Feldberg, "Clerical Work: The Female Occupation," in Jo Freeman, ed., *Women: A Feminist Perspective,* 2nd ed. (Palo Alto, CA: Mayfield Publishing Co., 1975), p. 317.

52. Karen Nussbaum, "Women Clerical Workers," *Socialist Review* 49, pp. 151-59.

53. Braverman, *Labor and Monopoly Capital,* p. 391. Cf. also Pat Armstrong and Hugh Armstrong, *The Double Ghetto: Canadian Women and Their Segregated Work* (Toronto: McClelland and Stewart, 1978), chap. 2.

54. Eva Gamarnikow, "Sexual Division of Labour: The Case of Nursing," in Annette Kuhn and AnnMarie Wolpe, eds., *Feminism and Materialism: Women and Modes of Production* (London: Routledge & Kegan Paul, 1978), pp. 96-123.

55. J. Timothy Diamond, "The Dialectical Relationship of Medicine and Nursing: A Proposal for Research" (unpublished), December 1978, p. 16.

56. Davies, "Woman's Place Is at the Typewriter," p. 249.

57. Braverman, *Labor and Monopoly Capital,* p. 294.

58. Davies, "Woman's Place Is at the Typewriter."

59. Lin Farley, *Sexual Shakedown: The Sexual Harassment of Women on the Job* (New York: Warner, 1978), pp. 131-37.

60. Veronica Beechey, "Women and Production: A Critical Analysis of Some Sociological Theories of Women's Work," in Kuhn and Wolpe, eds., *Feminism and Materialism,* pp. 155-97. Tim Diamond brought this article to my attention.

61. Glenn and Feldberg, "Clerical Work," p. 331.

62. Ibid., p. 331.

63. Ibid., p. 334.

64. Nussbaum, "Women Clerical Workers."

65. Mary Bularzik, "Sexual Harassment at the Workplace: Historical Notes," *Radical America,* July–August 1978, p. 2. Reprinted as a pamphlet by the New England Free Press, 60 Union Square, Somerville, Mass. 02143.

66. Ibid., p. 2.
67. Ibid., p. 2.
68. Farley, *Sexual Shakedown.*
69. Jeanne Mager Stellman, *Women's Work, Women's Health: Myths and Realities* (New York: Pantheon, 1977).
70. "This is Nursing: Introduction to a Struggle," in Wendy Edmond and Suzie Fleming, eds., *All Work and No Pay: Women, Housework, and the Wages Due* (Bristol: Power of Women Collective and Falling Wall Press, 1975), p. 61.
71. The Boston Nurses Group, "The False Promise: Professionalism in Nursing," *Science for the People,* May–June 1978 and July–August 1978. Reprinted as a pamphlet by the New England Free Press.
72. The most influential statement in English of the Italian wages for housework movement was Mariarosa Dalla Costa and Selma James, *The Power of Women and the Subversion of the Community,* 3rd ed. (Bristol: Falling Wall Press, 1975). A shorter statement is Giuliana Pompei, "Wages for Housework" in *WOMEN: A Journal of Liberation* 3, no. 3 (1972):60-62. A good short critique of the position is Carol Lopate's "Women and Pay for Housework," *Liberation,* June 1974, pp. 8-11. Both articles are reprinted in Jaggar and Struhl, eds., *Feminist Frameworks.* More arguments in favor of wages for housework can be found in Edmond and Fleming, eds., *All Work and No Pay.*
73. Karl Marx, "Wages, Price and Profit, in Karl Marx and Frederick Engels, *Selected Works* (New York: International Publishers, 1968), p. 229.
74. This is the title of an influential pamphlet by Christine Delphy: *The Main Enemy: A Materialist Analysis of Women's Oppression,* trans. by Lucy ap Roberts (London: Women's Research and Resources Centre Publications, 1977).
75. Heidi I. Hartmann and Ann R. Markusen, "Contemporary Marxist Theory and Practice: A Feminist Critique," *The Review of Political Economics* 12, no. 2 (Summer 1980):91.
76. Ibid.
77. Charlotte Perkins Gilman Chapter of the New American Movement, "A Socialist-Feminist Response to the Durham Organizing Collective's 'Towards a Marxist Theory on Women's Oppression and a Strategy for Liberation' " (mimeographed), circulated in the mid-1970s.
78. Foreman, *Femininity as Alienation,* p. 157.
79. Karl Marx, "The Eighteenth Brumaire of Louis Bonaparte," in Marx and Engels, *Selected Works,* pp. 171-72. I owe this reference to Ann Ferguson, "Women as a New Revolutionary Class in the United States," in Pat Walker, ed., *Between Labor and Capital* (Boston: South End Press, 1979), p. 285.
80. Part of the publicity for Wallflower Order, said to be from a review of the Wallflower's performance in Vancouver and an interview with them in *Kinesis,* 1980.
81. Batya Weinbaum and Amy Bridges, "The Other Side of the Paycheck: Monopoly Capital and the Structure of Consumption," *Monthly Review,* July–August 1976. Reprinted in Eisenstein, ed., *Capitalist Patriarchy and the Case for Socialist Feminism,* p. 198.
82. Charlotte Bunch, "The Reform Tool Kit," in *Building Feminist Theory: Essays from Quest* (New York: Longman, 1981), pp. 197-98. Similar lists are given by the Hyde Park Chapter, Chicago Women's Liberation Union, *Socialist Feminism: A Strategy for the Women's Movement,* a pamphlet published in 1972, pp. 9-15; and by Nancy Hartsock, "Political Change: Two Perspectives on Power," in *Building Feminist Theory,* p. 17.
83. Ibid., p. 198.
84. Ann Ferguson, "The Che-Lumumba School: Creating a Revolutionary Family-Community," *Quest: A Feminist Quarterly* 5, no. 3 (Feb/Mar. 1980):15-17.
85. Ibid., p. 1.
86. Dolores Hayden, "What Would a Non-Sexist City Be Like? Speculations on Housing, Urban Design, and Human Work," *Signs: A Journal of Women in Culture and Society, Special Issue: Women and the American City* 5, no. 3 (Supplement Spring 1980).
87. Ibid., p. 181.
88. Nancy Hartsock, "Staying Alive," in *Building Feminist Theory,* p. 120.
89. Ibid., p. 119.

90. Ibid., p. 121.

91. Petchesky, "Reproductive Freedom," p. 685.

92. Ibid.

93. Joreen, "The Tyranny of Structurelessness", reprinted in Koedt, Levine, and Rapone, eds., *Radical Feminism,* pp. 285-99.

94. Sheila Rowbotham, "The Women's Movement and Organizing for Socialism," in Sheila Rowbotham, Lynne Segal, and Hilary Wainwright, *Beyond the Fragments: Feminism and the Making of Socialism* (London: Merlin, 1979), p. 41.

95. Ibid., p. 76.

96. Foreman, *Femininity as Alienation,* p. 154.

97. Sheila Rowbotham, "The Women's Movement," p. 41.

98. Paul Adams, Leila Berg, Nan Berger, Michael Duane, A.S. Neill, Robert Ollendorf, *Children's Rights: Towards the Liberation of the Child* (New York: Praeger, 1971); Richard Farson, *Birthrights* (New York: Macmillan, 1974); Harvard Educational Review, *The Rights of Children,* (Cambridge: Harvard Educational Review, 1974); Laurence D. Houlgate, *The Child and the State: A Normative Theory of Juvenile Rights* (Baltimore: The Johns Hopkins University Press, 1980); Onora O'Neill and William Ruddick, eds., *Having Children* (New York: Oxford University Press, 1979); W. Aiken and Hugh LaFollette, *Whose Child? Children's Rights, Parental Authority and State Power* (Totowa, N.J.: Littlefield, Adams & Co., 1980).

99. Shulamith Firestone, *The Dialectic of Sex: The Case for Feminist Revolution* (New York: William Morrow, 1970), chap. 4: "Down with Childhood."

100. Two exceptions of which I am aware include: Lorenne M.G. Clark, "The Rights of Children vs. Parental Rights: Problems in the Foundations of a Coherent Approach to the Question of Children's Rights," paper read to the Conference on Children's Rights, Carleton University, Canada, October 12-14, 1979; J. Timothy Diamond and Judith A. DiIorio, "The Status of Children Under Advanced Capitalism: A Critical Perspective," paper circulated by the Red Feather Institute for Advanced Studies in Sociology, Red Feather, Colorado.

101. Wilhelm Reich, *The Mass Psychology of Fascism,* trans. by Vincent R. Carfagno (New York: Pocket Books, 1978).

102. Ann Ferguson, "Women as a New Revolutionary Class in the United States," p. 280. fn.

103. Acute self-consciousness over her dress is expressed, for example, by Carol Ascher, "Narcissism and Women's Clothing," *Socialist Review* 11, no. 3 (May-June 1981):75-86.

104. Barbara Haber, "Is Personal Life Still a Political Issue?" *Feminist Studies* 5, no. 3 (Fall 1979):417-30.

105. Ibid., p. 427.

106. Ibid., p. 424.

107. Ibid., p. 429.

108. Ibid., p. 424.

109. Ibid., p. 429.

110. A fascinating example of this sort of dilemma is discussed by Sandra Bartky in her paper "On Masochism," read to the midwest division of the Society for Women in Philosophy, Bloomington, Indiana, 23 October, 1982. Bartky describes the difficulties of personal transformation through a "decolonization of the imagination" and clearly identifies some of the questions that must be faced in the future by socialist feminist theory.

part four
Feminist Theories
of Political Knowledge

11
Feminist Politics and Epistemology: Justifying Feminist Theory

There are many ways of being a feminist. Contemporary feminists are united in their opposition to women's oppression, but they differ not only in their views of how to combat that oppression, but even in their conception of what constitutes women's oppression in contemporary society. Liberal feminists, as we have seen, believe that women are oppressed insofar as they suffer unjust discrimination; traditional Marxists believe that women are oppressed in their exclusion from public production; radical feminists see women's oppression as consisting primarily in the universal male control of women's sexual and procreative capacities; while socialist feminists characterize women's oppression in terms of a revised version of the Marxist theory of alienation. Each of these analyses of women's oppression reflects a distinctive feminist perspective on contemporary society and each of them is associated with a characteristic conception of human nature. While these distinctive feminist perspectives have been in some ways cross-fertile, they are ultimately incompatible with each other. In other words, one cannot view contemporary society simultaneously from more than one of these perspectives. The question then arises which perspective one should choose. What are the reasons for preferring one feminist theory to another? This chapter is concerned with answering that question.

On television commercials, the rational consumer is sometimes shown comparing one brand with another. In these comparisons, the consumer has a list of the qualities desired in the product and uses that list to determine which brand possesses most of these desiderata, be they fuel economy, clean lemon scent or gentle overnight action. In comparing different feminist theories to each other, the obvious procedure might seem to be to prepare a similar list of theoretical desiderata and then to check off which feminist theory possesses most of the desired qualities. In fact, however, this is not as simple as it sounds. While it is not difficult to reach agreement in general terms over the criteria of an adequate feminist theory, there is enormous controversy between feminists over what counts as satisfaction or fulfilment of these criteria of adequacy. One reason for this controversy is systematic disagreement over how the criteria should be interpreted and applied. In this chapter, I shall explain the epistemological and political reasons for this metatheoretical disagreement. Later, I shall try to defend one specific interpretation of the general criteria of theoretical adequacy and to show that, on this interpretation, socialist feminism is the most adequate of the feminist theories formulated to date.

Feminist theory is simultaneously political and scientific. This is true of all theory, but it is particularly evident in the case of feminist theory. Feminist scholars are distinguished from non-feminist scholars precisely by their common political interest in ending women's oppression, and they see their scholarly work as contributing to a comprehensive understanding of how women's liberation should be achieved. Feminist political theorists, whose work has been the special focus of this book, give more attention than other feminist theorists to examining explicitly normative arguments about the nature of the good society and to developing a vision of women's liberation. Like all political theorists, however, they must draw on scientific knowledge to give substance to their ideals, to discover the causes of women's past and present oppression and to identify workable strategies for ending that oppression. Each of the political theories that has been examined in this book is thus a complex network of conceptual, normative, empirical and methodological claims, and each of them, I have argued, centers around a distinctive conception of human nature. Because feminist theory has both a political and scientific aspect, the criteria for evaluating its adequacy must be both political and scientific.

Identifying the appropriate criteria for evaluating normative and scientfic theories is a primary preoccupation of moral philosophers and philosophers of science.[1] Unfortunately, however, these philosophers are able to reach agreement only when the theoretical desiderata are stated in the most general terms. Most moral philosophers, for instance, agree that an adequate moral or political theory must express values that are morally desirable, that it should provide a guide to conduct that is consistent, comprehensive and practicable, and that it should be in some sense impartial. Unfortunately, however, they differ on what counts as impartiality, on which ideals are practicable, on which conduct is morally significant or insignificant and, of course, on which values are the most desirable morally. Similarly, most philosophers of science agree that an adequate scientific theory should be self-consistent, that it should be well supported by the available evidence, that it should be comprehensive in accounting for all the data and that it should be illuminating or have explanatory power. However, they too disagree on what counts as evidence, on what are the data that need explanation and on which explanations are illuminating. Feminist theorists have no characteristic disagreement with non-feminist theorists about the general desiderata for an adequate political and/or scientific theory, but they do disagree with non-feminist theorists about how those general criteria should be interpreted and applied. In addition, as we shall see, they differ systematically not only from non-feminists but also among themselves over the interpretation and application of such theoretical desiderata as impartiality, objectivity, evidential confirmation, comprehensiveness or completeness and explanatory power.

Feminist disagreements over these metatheoretical issues are related conceptually to the rest of their political theory and in particular to their distinctive conceptions of human nature. This is because every conception of human nature involves a characteristic conception of human knowledge—its sources, its extent and the proper criteria for distinguishing truth from falsity. In other words, commitment to a theory of human nature carries with it commitment to a certain epistemology. Thus every political theory, like every other theory, involves at least an implicit commitment to a certain method for understanding social reality and to certain criteria of theoretical adequacy. In what follows, I shall explain the metatheoretical disagreements between various groups of feminists, linking these with the rest of their political theory and with their conceptions of human nature. I shall argue that the most politically appropriate and theoretically illuminating interpretations of theoretical desiderata are those associated with socialist feminism. Finally, I shall show, unsurprisingly, that socialist feminism best fulfils the criteria of theoretical adequacy thus interpreted, and so constitutes, despite its incompleteness, the best available theory of women's liberation.

Liberal Feminism and the Elimination of Bias

Liberal feminism rests on a conception of human nature that is radically individualistic. What this means, in part, is that human beings are conceived as isolated individuals who have no necessary connection with each other or even with non-human nature. Of course, liberals recognize that human individuals in fact engage in all kinds of interactions with each other and with non-human nature, but they do not see these interactions as essential to human beings. On the liberal view of humans as essentially separate rational agents, it would be logically possible for human individuals to exist in total isolation from each other and perhaps even from non-human nature.

Just as the individualistic conception of human nature sets the basic problems for the liberal political tradition, so it also generates the problems for the tradition in epistemology that is associated historically and conceptually with liberalism. This tradition begins in the 17th century with Descartes, and it emerges in the 20th century as the analytic tradition. Because it conceives humans as essentially separate individuals, this epistemological tradition views the attainment of knowledge as a project for each individual on her or his own. The task of epistemology, then, is to formulate rules to enable individuals to undertake this project with success. Within this broad epistemological tradition, several different tendencies have emerged. The rationalist tendency, typified by Descartes, views knowledge as achieved by inference from indubitable first premises; by contrast, the British empiricist tendency views knowledge as achieved by inference from basic individual sense experiences. In either case, however, the attainment of knowledge is conceived as essentially a solitary occupation that has no necessary social preconditions.

The empiricist strand in Cartesian epistemology culminated in the theory of knowledge known as positivism. According to positivism, the paradigm of knowledge is physical science and positivism has a distinctive view of what constitutes the scientific enterprise and the proper method of scientific discovery. One basic assumption of this view is that all knowledge is constructed by inference from immediate sensory experiences. Thus knowledge, that is science, is atomistic in structure and the task of epistemology and the philosophy of science is to formulate the rules for making valid inferences from the basic sense experiences on which knowledge is thought to be founded. The assumption that knowledge is atomistic in structure means that a good scientific explanation must be reductionistic; that is, it must show how the characteristics of a complex entity are built up from its simplest components.

The requirement of epistemological atomism obviously incorporates a metaphysical assumption that reality itself is atomistic in structure. If reality were not in fact atomistic, then an atomistic type of explanation would misrepresent the reality that it was supposed to describe. The assumption that the forms of explanation appropriate for physics are the only forms appropriate for any explanation leads positivist epistemology to prefer quantificational or mathematical types of explanation. Thus, positivism is favorable to the classical Newtonian model of physical reality as composed of indistinguishable atoms which are related to each other through mechanical causal interactions. The qualitative properties of physical reality are explained by the mathematical formulae which express the atomic laws of motion.

On the positivist view, the adequacy of a scientific theory is thought to be guaranteed by its objectivity or lack of bias. The positivist conception of objectivity has several aspects. First, objectively produced claims are capable, in principle at least, of being verified by anyone. It is assumed that similar circumstances would stimulate similar perceptions in anyone with normal faculties of sensation, and from this assumption positivists conclude that, as long as they follow the same rules of valid inference, everyone should emerge with the same scientific conclusions. The possibility of intersubjective verification is thus part of what is meant by "objectivity." A second aspect of the positivist conception of objectivity is that it excludes any evaluative element. Positivism requires that scientists should take empirical observations as their only data and should scrupulously control their own values, interests and emotions, since these are viewed as biasing or distorting the results of scientific enquiry. For positivism, objectivity is defined by the inquiry's independence from the "subjective" values, interests and emotions of those who engage in scientific enquiry or who deal with its results. Positivists view this second requirement of value neutrality as necessary for fulfilling the first requirement of intersubjective verifiability. Since people, including scientists, have widely differing values, interests and emotions, intersubjective agreement is thought to be impossible unless these values, interests and emotions are prevented from directing the scientific enterprise. On the positivist view, therefore, good scientists are detached observers and manipulators of nature who follow strict methodological rules, which enable them to separate themselves from the special values, interests and emotions generated by their class, race, sex or unique situation. Thus, the good scientist of positivism is the abstract individual of liberal political theory.

The narrow positivist paradigm excludes many aspects of human intellectual and cultural activity from the realm of knowledge; indeed, positivism's criteria for knowledge are so strict that many critics argue that they cannot be met even by the physical sciences. However that may be, positivists agree that value judgments cannot be part of genuine knowledge because value judgments cannot be justified empirically by the scientific method as they conceive that method. A consequence of this claim is that moral and political theories are not part of knowledge because value judgments are integral to such theories. The logical positivists of the mid-20th century accepted this consequence and declared the death of normative, that is, explicitly evaluative, moral and political philosophy, though not of the supposedly empirical political science.

In the latter part of the 20th century, the more extreme versions of positivism have been rejected, explicitly normative moral and political philosophy has undergone a revival and the liberal tradition has been revitalized.[2] Nevertheless, the conception of moral and political philosophy that dominates this revitalized tradition still retains some positivist or neo-positivist assumptions. One of the most important of these is the assumption that an adequate moral or political theory must be objective in the sense of being unbiased. In the case of normative theory, objectivity or lack of bias obviously cannot consist in independence from value judgments, since normative theories by definition express values. Instead, objectivity is defined to mean independence from the value judgments of any particular individual. Objective or unbiased value judgments are those that would be made by an individual who was impartial in the sense of giving no special weight to her own or to any other special interests. In other words, the good moral or political philosopher of the contemporary liberal tradition resembles the good scientist of positivism in being able to detach herself or himself from such "contingent" properties as race, class or sex.

The contemporary liberal tradition has experimented with a number of theoretical devices in its efforts to achieve the supposedly unbiased and objective standpoint of the abstract philosopher. Some versions of utilitarian theory, for instance, have postulated a perfectly rational spectator whose own interests are not involved and who is therefore considered to be sufficiently unbiased and impartial to assign appropriate weights to the human desires that are compared and balanced in the utilitarian calculus.[3] John Rawls has tried to guarantee objectivity in a somewhat similar way by stipulating that the imaginary individuals who formulate his principles of justice should be ignorant of their own particular interests and their place in the society to be regulated by those principles. By concealing their particular interests behind a "veil of ignorance", Rawls believes himself to have guaranteed the impartiality of his imaginary political theorists and to have established an "Archimedean point," outside the society, from which the justice of that society's basic institutions can be evaluated objectively.[4] Yet another version of this conception of objectivity can be found in Bruce Ackerman's elaboration of the "Neutral dialogue" as the proper method for arriving at conclusions in political philosophy.[5]

If the conception of objectivity that is held by the revitalized liberal/positivist tradition is used to evaluate the various contemporary feminist theories, one theory emerges as clearly superior. That one, of course, is liberal feminism. Unlike other versions of feminism, liberal feminism makes a sharp distinction between what it takes to be the normative and the empirical aspects of the theory. It does not rest on mystical notions of women's special relation to nature, nor does it rely on concepts such as alienation whose logical status, from the neo-positivist point of view, are quite unclear. In stating the non-empirical or normative aspects of its theory, moreover, liberal feminism relies on values that are claimed to be universal human values and which in consequence, liberal feminism assumes, cannot reflect only the special interests of a particular group. Most notably, liberal feminists insist that they seek no special privileges for women; they claim to demand only equal rights and equal opportunities for all. Their basic demand is that everyone should receive equal consideration with no discrimination on the basis of sex.

Given what they take to be the universal applicability of their values, liberal feminists assume that the validity of their theory will be evident to all who set aside their own special interests. In their view, after all, their version of feminism does not favor the interests of any one group or class over another. If men rationally think about why they should set aside their own special interests, they should be just as well able as women to see the soundness of liberal feminist arguments and there is no reason in principle why men should not be just as good feminists as women. In short, liberal feminists assume that their view reflects the impartial perspective of the rational, detached observer and consequently constitutes the most unbiased and objective feminist theory.

Other versions of feminism do not claim to be more objective than liberal feminism in the liberal/positivist sense of objectivity. Instead, they challenge precisely the conception of objectivity that liberals take as a primary condition of theoretical adequacy. In particular, they challenge the liberal assumption of a sharp fact/value distinction and they attack the claim that there is any such standpoint as that of the neutral observer.

Traditional Marxism and the Science of the Proletariat

The traditional Marxist conception of theoretical adequacy is in sharp contrast with the liberal conception. It is part of a theory of knowledge generated by a view of human nature that is quite different from liberal feminism's view.

Traditional Marxism conceives of human individuals as existing necessarily in dialectical interrelation with each other and with the non-human world. On this view, the essential activity of human beings is praxis and the development of knowledge is seen as just one aspect of praxis. In other words, knowledge is developed as part of human activity to satisfy human needs. Rather than viewing knowledge as the purely intellectual construct of a detached spectator, therefore, Marxism sees knowledge as emerging through practical human involvement in changing the world, an involvement which also changes human beings themselves. Moreover, since human productive activity always takes a definite historical form, all knowledge must be seen as growing out of a specific mode of production.

The Marxist conception of knowledge challenges two basic assumptions of liberal epistemology. First, since praxis is necessarily a social activity, it challenges the view that knowledge can be the achievement of a single isolated individual. Instead, Marxism views knowledge as socially constructed and the expansion of knowledge as a social project. Secondly, since knowledge is one aspect of human productive activity and since this activity is necessarily purposive, the basic categories of knowledge will always be shaped by human purposes and the values on which they are based. For this reason, Marxists conclude that even so-called empirical knowledge is never entirely value-free. The conceptual framework by which we make sense of ourselves and our world is shaped and limited by the interests and values of the society that we inhabit. Marxists express this by saying that all forms of knowledge are historically determined by the prevailing mode of production.[6]

At least since the inception of class society, however, societies have not been characterized by a single set of interests and values. Instead, societies have been composed of classes whose interests have been in opposition to each other and whose values have conflicted with each other. In such a situation, one cannot say that the prevailing world view or system of knowledge reflects the interests and values of society as a whole. Instead, one must specify which class's interests and values are reflected. Marxism's answer to this question is that the system of knowledge that is generally accepted within a society reflects the interests of the dominant class. In a much quoted passage, Marx and Engels write:

> The class which has the means of material production at its disposal has control at the same time over the means of mental production, so that thereby, generally speaking, the ideas of those who lack the means of mental production are subject to it. The ruling ideas are nothing more than the ideal expression of the dominant material relationships, the dominant material relationships grasped as ideas; hence of the relationships which make the one class the ruling one, therefore, the ideas of its dominance.[7]

In class societies, the prevailing world view supports the interests of the ruling class by obscuring or by justifying the reality of domination. In this sense, Marxism views all existing claims to knowledge as "ideological," that is, as distorted representations of reality. Only a classless society will produce an undistorted and genuinely scientific representation of reality.

Although class societies are governed by a ruling system of ideas, they also contain some ideas that are subversive to that system: slaves perceive reality differently from their masters. As long as the society is relatively stable, however, subversive ideas will not be generally accepted or even understood; they will receive widespread consideration only during a period of social upheaval. During times of relative stability, the dominant ideology is imposed in a number of ways. The most obvious of these ways involve the direct suppression of potentially subversive observations or theories. One effective means of doing this is by denying a voice to those classes from which such ideas are likely to emerge. Those classes are denied education and even literacy, and their ideas are labeled as superstition. By contrast, honors are heaped on those who invent theories that can be used to justify the status quo, and their ideas are popularized in the mass media. Those who do develop subversive theories are ridiculed and denied jobs or research facilities. If their ideas seem to be gaining popularity anyway, the ruling class resorts to outright censorship and persecution; for instance, subversive groups may be prohibited from access to the media or denied the right to assemble.

In addition to direct forms of thought control, the plausibility of the dominant ideology is enhanced by the very structure of class society. Daily life itself tends to generate historically specific forms of false consciousness. In capitalist society, for instance, individuals are forced to compete with each other to survive, and the apparent universality of competition seems to confirm the view that humans are "naturally" aggressive and selfish. Similarly, the provision of inferior educational resources and facilities for the subordinate classes appears to provide confirmation of the view that the members of these classes are more lazy and/or stupid than members of the dominant class, and so seems to justify their subordinate position. The structure of capitalist society also seems to confirm the validity of the prevailing socio-economic categories; for instance, it encourages the perception of capital as an independently existing object with its own properties, especially the property of generating capital, rather than as the expression of a certain system of social relations.[8] On some interpretations of Marxism, less prevalent now than in the 19th century, the physical sciences are thought to be less "ideological" and more "objective" than the human sciences. Contemporary Marxists, however, have argued that there is an irreducible ideological element in the fundamental categories of even the most formal sciences—perhaps even especially in those. Alfred Sohn-Rethel, for instance, has argued that the concept of pure reason itself was generated in classical Greece during the sixth century B.C. as a reflection of the relations of a monetary economy in which production began to be undertaken for exchange rather than for use, and in which intellectual was divided from manual labor.[9] Similarly, Sohn-Rethel sees the emergence of capitalism, which necessitates the unending movement of money, as generating the Galilean concept of inertial motion which is the fundamental category of Newtonian physics. On this view, the basic structure and categories of contemporary science reflect alienated relations of production, and what is generally accepted as the most "objective" science is in fact a form of alienated consciousness.

According to this interpretation of Marxist epistemology, all systems of knowledge bear the marks of their social origin within a particular mode of production. This is true even of knowledge about knowledge. In class society, not only is there an ultimately ideological element, according to Marxism, in the concepts and categories through which we constitute our reality; there is also an ideological bias in the standards for determining what is to be accepted as knowledge or science and what is to be rejected as myth or superstition. Marxists have claimed that an ideological bias is working especially strongly in the positivist notion of objectivity, which connotes the possibility of knowledge that is value-free and independent of the social context in which it originates. This conception of objectivity has its roots in the 16th or 17th centuries, a period in which, according to R.M. Young, "the rise of capitalism, the development of the Protestant ethic and the development of the foundations of modern science must be seen as a single movement."[10] In the philosophy of both Descartes and Galileo, a clear demarcation was made between mental and physical being. Only the latter was thought to be susceptible to mechanical explanation; the former was taken to be the realm of value and purpose. The domain of science was now defined as the physical world, and so it became plausible to regard science as value-free, objective in a new sense. What Marxist philosophers of science point out, however, is that this notion of objectivity was formulated for a particular purpose, the purpose of defining an area for free scientific enquiry, unhampered by the restrictive interference of Church and State. In the 19th century, Max Weber made a similar claim for the objectivity of social science as a value-free enquiry.[11] In both instances, the claim that science was value-free was made for the conscious political purpose of defending the scientists from the charge of subverting existing social values. As a political tactic, this claim served its purpose in the 17th and 19th centuries, but Marxist philosophers of science argue that the prevailing positivist notion of objectivity now serves a reactionary purpose, for it obscures the political assumptions that lurk within science and even within apparently common-sense observations of social events. Thus it obscures the reality of domination. As Sohn-Rethel puts it:

> The objectivity of science demands its neutrality with respect to social issues, and this acceptance of social neutrality is part of the training that every scientist undergoes. Scientific truths are held to be valid regardless of the time and conditions of their genesis and their application. In his [sic] professional life the scientist blinkers himself from all the rest of existence. But is this neutrality really intrinsic to science and conditional to its objectivity? Is it not perhaps a more profound blinkering to the

role played by the scientist and science in the interests of capital? In that case, the very objectivity of science would be an expression of its alienation, denying the scientist an awareness of the significance of separating intellectual from manual labor.[12]

The Marxist conception of existing claims to knowledge as ideological provides the conceptual basis for the enquiry known as the sociology of knowledge. Sociologists of knowledge study the way in which systems of thought are related to the social contexts from which they emerge. Investigations in the sociology of knowledge reveal that reality is perceived very differently by different groups and that these different perceptions depend not only on the social order that the groups inhabit but also on their position within that social order. Different social positions provide different vantage points from which some aspects of reality come into prominence and from which other aspects are obscured. For instance, if we look at capitalist society from the standpoint of the owners of capital, Marx writes ironically that society appears to be:

> a very Eden of the innate rights of man. There alone rule Freedom, Equality, Property and Bentham. Freedom, because both buyer and seller of a commodity, say of labour-power, are constrained only by their own free will. They contract as free agents and the agreement they come to is but the form in which they give legal expression to their common will. Equality, because each enters into relation with the other, as with a simple owner of commodities, and they exchange equivalent for equivalent. Property because each disposes only what is his own. And Bentham, because each looks only to himself. The only force that brings them together and puts them in relation with each other is the selfishness, the gain and the private interest of each. Each looks to himself only, and no one troubles himself about the rest, and just because they do so, do they all, in accordance with the pre-established harmony of things, or under the auspices of an all-shrewd providence, work together to their mutual advantage, for the common weal and in the interest of all.[13]

If we look at capitalist society from the point of view of the producers of commodities, however, Eden is transformed into hell. From this perspective, we can see that:

> within the capitalist system all methods for raising the social productiveness of labour are brought about at the cost of the individual laborers; all means for the development of production transform themselves into means of domination over, and exploitation of, the producers; they mutilate the labourer into a fragment of a man, degrade him to the level of an appendage to a machine, destroy every remnant of charm in his work and turn it into a hated toil; they estrange from him the intellectual potentialities of the labour-process in the same proportion as science is incorporated into it as an independent power; they distort the conditions under which he works, subject him during the labour-process to a despotism the more hateful for its meanness; they transform his lifetime into working-time, and drag his wife and child beneath the wheels of the Juggernaut of capital. . . . Accumulation of wealth at one pole is, therefore, at the same time accumulation of misery, agony of toil, slavery, ignorance, brutality, mental degradation, at the opposite pole, i.e., on the side of the class that produces its own product in the form of capitalism.[14]

Once we look at the real conditions in which knowledge is produced, Marxists believe that we will see that the ways in which we conceptualize the world are always shaped by our interactions with that world. Moreover, we will see that it is inevitable that all systems of thought should be constructed from some standpoint within the social world. There is no Archimedean point outside the world where we may stand to gain a perspective on reality that is neutral between the interests and values of existing social groups. Consequently, no knowledge can be objective in the liberal or positivist sense.

This recognition raises a problem for Marxist epistemology. If all existing knowledge is ideological in the sense that its categories reflect the interests and values of a certain social group, then what are the grounds for selecting between competing theories or systems of thought? Does Marxism condemn us to epistemological relativism, so that our world view is necessarily limited by our class origins and truth is relative to class? Or are there rational criteria capable of justifying the preference for one standpoint over another?

This question is the central controversy within Marxist epistemology and different interpreters of Marxism answer it in different ways.[15] The positivist interpretation of Marxism exempts "science" from the relativization of knowledge and suggests that "objective" truth may be found through empirical experimentation. It proposes a naive correspondence theory of truth, according to which the adequacy of a theory is tested by how closely its claims correspond to or mirror "the facts." Structuralist Marxism proposes a coherence theory of truth. It claims that the main criterion of theoretical adequacy is the comprehensiveness and lack of contradictions within a particular system of thought; bourgeois thought is inadequate largely because of its antinomies and contradictions. Practical or interventionist Marxism proposes a pragmatic criterion of truth. It suggests that the ultimate criterion of theoretical adequacy is its usefulness in making a revolution. Finally, the "totalistic" Marxism of Georg Lukács argues that we should prefer the standpoint of that class whose interests, at a particular historical juncture, most closely approximate to those of the totality of humankind.[16] On Lukács's view, classes whose interest lies in perpetuating the existing social order have an interest in perpetuating the myths that justify their own domination. By contrast, classes whose interest most closely approximates the interests of the social totality will have an interest in overthrowing the established order. Consequently, they are more likely to construct conceptual frameworks that will reveal accepted views as myths and provide a more reliable understanding of the world. Lukács's view offers a plausible explanation of the success of the scientific revolution of the 16th and 17th centuries. This revolution was the intellectual product of a rising bourgeois class whose interests lay in undermining the geocentric view of the universe that was used to justify the power of the Church and of the feudal aristocracy. Lukács also provides a plausible explanation of the birth of the social sciences in terms of a similar social situation which existed in 19th-century Germany. Of all existing interpretations of Marxist epistemology. Lukács's is the most convincing: its insights into the sociology of knowledge are illuminating and it recognizes the inevitability of social influences on all systems of thought at the same time as it acknowledges that the adequacy of theories must also be subject to the constraints of an "external" reality. Lukács provides a conception of "objective inquiry" that is a persuasive alternative to the liberal/positivist conception.

Marxist political economy analyzes contemporary society into two fundamentally opposed classes, the bourgeoisie and the proletariat. Lukácsian epistemology accepts this analysis and concludes that these two class positions provide the two major epistemological standpoints from which contemporary society may be viewed. As we have seen already, these two standpoints yield very different pictures of capitalist society: from the standpoint of the capitalist, contemporary society appears to be Eden while from that of the worker it appears to be hell. Of course, the workers' standpoint does not automatically provide them with a full, comprehensive and coherent alternative to the ruling ideology; they cannot help being influenced by the dominant world view. But the workers' position in society forces them to take as problematic what the capitalist class takes as given, for instance, "the quantification of object, their subordination to abstract mental categories."[17] According to Lukács, the standpoint of the proletariat is epistemologically preferable to that of the bourgeoisie, because it drives the working class to demystify the myths of bourgeois society and to develop a new world view that will reveal more clearly the real regularities of social life and the underlying causes of those realities, including the causes of its own domination.

On the traditional Marxist view, of course, Marxist theory itself constitutes the most comprehensive picture of the world from the standpoint of the proletariat. Precisely because it reflects the interests and values of the working class, which are thought to be those of the totality of humankind, Marxist theory provides the most-unbiased and objective available representation of social reality, as well as the most-useful method of investigating the non-human world. For this reason, Marxists sometimes describe their theory, perhaps with a slightly positivist ring, as the science of the proletariat. Proletarian science ultimately will defeat bourgeois science but the struggle will not be simply an intellectual one. The superiority of proletarian science will be demonstrated ultimately by the fact that it will enable the working class to abolish the class relations that have given rise to the forms of bourgeois consciousness.

> Those manifestations [of bourgeois consciousness] are by no means merely modes of thought, they are the forms in which contemporary bourgeois society is objectified. Their abolition, if it is to be a true abolition, cannot be simply the result of thought alone, it must also amount to their *practical* abolition as the *actual forms of social life.*[18]

Given the epistemological framework of traditional Marxism, there is room for only two basic kinds of feminism. Inevitably, the dominant kind must be liberal or bourgeois feminism, which expresses the aspirations of upper- and middle-class women and which is grounded on the assumptions of capitalist ideology. By contrast, Marxist, or revolutionary, feminism expresses the aspirations of working-class women and is grounded on the science of the proletariat. On the traditional Marxist view, what appear to be independent versions of feminism, such as lesbian feminism, radical feminism, anarchist feminism, or socialist feminism, are simply distorted forms of one of the two major types. All versions of feminism are seen either as expressing ideals that are basically capitalist or as expressing "progressive" alternatives to capitalism, ideals which are flawed, however, by an incomplete understanding of Marxist science. The apparently ungendered categories of traditonal Marxism, which do not allow women an independent class position, make it impossible for traditional Marxists to conceive that women might have their own epistemological standpoint. This inability to conceive that there might be a specifically feminist perspective on reality is expressed clearly by Barbara Winslow:

Ideas, political programs and to some extent organizations are neither male nor female . . . The political perspectives put forward by women's groups will be neither "male" nor "female." Rather they will reflect the dominant or competing forces within the society and they will be conservative, reformist, revolutionary, etc.[19]

To the traditional Marxist, of course, men and women as such do not represent "dominant or competing forces within the society," and a traditional Marxist class analysis provides the only possible standard for measuring who is conservative, reformist, revolutionary, etc.

If contemporary society affords only two basic epistemological standpoints, then Marxist epistemology naturally recommends that feminists adopt the standpoint of the proletariat. Given Marxist epistemological presuppositions, the political theory of liberal feminism is bound to be totally inadequate. By suggesting that women's liberation can be achieved primarily through legislative reform, liberal feminism obscures what Marxists take to be the fact that women's oppression is "built into the capitalist system."[20] Consequently, liberal feminism is unable to point the way to overthrowing the capitalist system which Marxists believe is the material base of women's contemporary subordination. Traditional Marxist feminism, by contrast, takes itself to be an epistemologically superior perspective because it reveals what Marxists claim to be the essential identity of interest between working-class women and working-class men. Marxist epistemology concludes that only the traditional Marxist conception of women's oppression provides the theory that will guide the simultaneous abolition of capitalism and women's oppression. As for the other varieties of feminism, traditional Marxist epistemology measures their adequacy by estimating how effectively they contribute to undermining the capitalist system and to strengthening the power of the working class as a whole.

Like liberal feminism, traditional Marxist feminism justifies itself on the basis of its own interpretation of the generally accepted criteria of theoretical adequacy. Just as traditional Marxism rejects the liberal interpretations of theoretical adequacy, however, so other versions of feminism reject the Marxist interpretations.

Radical Feminism and the Upward Spiral

Radical feminism is developing its own distinctive conception of what counts as reliable knowledge and how such knowledge may be achieved. Like a number of the foundational concepts of radical feminism, this conception of knowledge is nowhere expounded in a systematic or linear way. Instead, various authors mention various aspects of it in passing, often in the context of a critique of "patriarchal" conceptions of knowledge. From these scattered references, however, a number of common epistemological assumptions emerge. Not all radical feminists share all of these assumptions: in particular, some radical feminists accept mystical or spiritual experiences as a reliable source of knowledge, whereas others reject them. In spite of this and related disagreements, I think it is possible to identify the outlines of a fairly consistent radical feminist epistemology. This epistemology is in some ways strikingly similar to that of traditional Marxism, especially in its critique of the dominant conception of knowledge, a conception which radical feminists characterize as "patriarchal." In many ways, the radical feminist critique of patriarchal modes of knowing recalls traditional Marxist critiques of the liberal/positivist paradigm of knowledge. Like traditional Marxism, radical feminism seems to recognize a distinction between science and ideology and to assume that, in any society, the dominant group will impose its own distorted and mystifying version of reality. Radical feminist epistemology also generates an ontology that bears a remarkable resemblance to some aspects of traditional Marxist ontology. Unlike traditional Marxism, however, radical feminist epistemology is a self-conscious elaboration and justification of a specifically feminist view of reality.

Radical feminist epistemology starts from the belief that women know much of which men are ignorant and it takes one of its main tasks as being to explain why this should be so. Radical feminist epistemology explores the strategies women have developed for obtaining reliable knowledge and for correcting the distortions of patriarchal ideology. One of the best known of these strategies is the "consciousness-raising" process, a process that is often considered paradigmatic of the feminist method of inquiry. It was primarily through consciousness-raising groups that women involved in the contemporary women's liberation movement began to make visible, first to themselves, the hitherto invisible depths of their own oppression. Kate Lindemann lists the following major characteristics of consciousness-raising groups:

> First, the experience is more than communal, it is collective. In the context of collective reflection women found the power to name oppressive experiences and to disassociate themselves from both external and internalized models of oppression. Second, the group is dialogic and it is without a formal, appointed leader. Honest, mutual sharing without regard to status has been freeing and has generated keen insights for such groups. Third, the group emphasizes non-judgemental behavior. Members engage in non-judgemental listening to the naming of personal experience by other members. All experience, as long as it is owned by someone, is worthy subject matter. Fourth, in the consideration of someone's experience, members respond with supportive, collaborative experience, or with questions to aid clarification or critical reflection. They do not seek to tell, to "narrate answers" to another. Fifth, grounding in personal atmosphere characterized by honesty, vulnerability, and cooperation. Finally, the aim of such groups is praxis. Words are grounded in past action(s) and consideration of these words leads to proposed new actions. New actions lead to further reflection, etc.[21]

Nancy Hartsock writes that the consciousness-raising method of gaining knowledge is remarkably close, in many respects, to the Marxist method of analysis. Certainly it is obvious that the knowledge gained through consciousness raising is a collective product and that the process of gaining it is guided by the special interests and values of the women in the group. It is clear, too, that the aim of such knowledge is ultimately practical. In addition, through the practice of consciousness raising, as Hartsock writes,

> Women have learned that it was important to build their analyses from the ground up, beginning with their own experiences. They examined their lives not only as thinkers but, as Marx would have suggested, with all their senses.[22]

In spite of these similarities, there are also important differences between the epistemologies of radical feminism and of traditional Marxism. One of these differences is the contemporary lack of radical feminist interest in political theory, as theory has been understood within the Marxist tradition. This lack of interest in theory construction is most marked among contemporary American radical feminists. As we have seen, it was not evident among early American radical feminists, such as Firestone, nor is it shared by the French materialist feminists, such as Christine Delphy. Not only do American radical feminists begin with women's experience, however; often, as we saw in Chapter 9, they are also content to end with that experience. Radical feminists seek to construct a new picture of the world as it is seen through women's eyes, but currently they give low priority to providing a deep explanation of the social reality that they depict. Of course, the construction of an alternative description of reality is certainly an important part of theory-building, especially if it is true, as some philosophers claim, that all observations are "theory-laden." By pointing to previously unremarked social phenomena, such as violence against women or women's sexual and domestic slavery, by identifying connections among these phenomena and by showing how the institutions of patriarchy form an inter-locking grid within which women are trapped, radical feminism demonstrates the inadequacy of patriarchal descriptions of the world and simultaneously demonstrates, at least by implication, the inadequacy of patriarchal political theories which purport to explain why it is that way. In other words, radical feminism demonstrates that patriarchal political theory is not even asking the questions that are important for women and hence produces only incomplete and distorted versions of reality. Moreover, radical feminist redescriptions of reality constitute the basis for reformulating the questions of political theory. As we saw in Chapter 9, however, many radical feminists themselves do not seem to feel an urgent need to answer those questions, to identify the motor of patriarchy and the underlying causes of male dominance. They name but ultimately do not explain.

Perhaps the most striking difference between radical feminist epistemology and the epistemology of the western tradition, both Marxist and non-Marxist, is that a conspicuous strain of radical feminism accepts the reliability of certain human faculties which are considered highly unreliable within the western (though not necessarily within the eastern) epistemological tradition. Many radical feminists believe that these faculties are especially well developed in women, although they do not make it clear whether this higher development is due to some special aptitude genetically inherited by women, or is simply due to the fact that the male culture inhibits men from developing those faculties whereas the female culture encourages their development in women. However that may be, one of the faculties that radical feminism regards as a special source of knowledge for women is the faculty of intuition, through which women are thought to have direct, non-inferential access to the feelings and motives of others.[23] Women's intuition is both a cause and an effect of their special sensitivity to and empathy for others, capacities in which radical feminists take great pride.[24] Another faculty that radical feminists accept as a source of special knowledge for women is the spiritual power of experiencing a mystical sense of connection or identification with other people or with the universe as a whole.[25] This is well expressed by Susan Griffin, in a passage quoted already in Chapter 5:

> We know ourselves to be made from this earth. We know this earth is made from our bodies. For we see ourselves. And we are nature. We are nature seeing nature. We are nature with a concept of nature. Nature weeping. Nature speaking of nature to nature.[26]

Finally, some radical feminists believe that women have the capacity for developing what are now viewed as parapsychological powers, such as "mind-stretch" and "lonth."[27]

Women's special modes of knowing encourage a conception of the world that is totally opposed to what radical feminists characterize as the patriarchal world view. According to radical feminism, patriarchal thought is characterized by divisions, distinctions, oppositions, and dualisms. Patriarchy opposes mind to matter, self to other, reason to emotion, and enquirer to object of enquiry. In each of these oppositions, one side of the dualism is valued more than the other side. For this reason, radical feminists claim that hierarchy is built into the fundamental ontology of patriarchy. Robin Morgan writes: "The either/or dichotomy is inherently, classically patriarchal."[28] Griffin emphasizes the artificial, quantitative, and abstract nature of patriarchal measurements:

> The mile. The acre. The inch and the foot. The gallon and the ton. The upper and lower, left and right, side, front, back, under, ante, post. The large and the small. Number and name. Perimeter. Classification. Separation. Shape.[29]

By contrast with the dualistic and hierarchical ontology of patriarchy, radical feminism claims to be developing a world view that is non-dualistic and non-hierarchical. Instead, radical feminists conceive the world as an organic whole, in which "everything is connected to everything else."[30] The patriarchal oppositions between mind and body, thought and feeling, fact and value, public and private, and theory and practice are said to fragment and so to make unintelligible a reality which is an organic whole. Even linear conceptions of time obscure the reality that past, present and future exist simultaneously.

> When women live on the boundary, we are vividly aware of living in time present/future . . . The center of the new time is on the boundary of patriarchal time. What it is, in fact, is women's *own* time. It is our *life-time*. It *is* whenever we are living out of our own sense of reality, refusing to be possessed, conquered, and alienated by the linear, measured-out, quantitative time of the patriarchal system. Women, in becoming who we are, are living in a qualitative, organic time that escapes the measurements of the system. For example, women who sit in institutional committee meetings without surrendering to the purposes and goals set forth by the male-dominated structure, are literally working on our own time while perhaps appearing to be working 'on company time.' The center of our activities is organic, in such a way that events are more significant than clocks.[31]

Not only is everything connected with everything else, but everything is always in a process of change. Radical feminists see the world "as structures of relations in process, a reality constantly in evolution."[32] Carol Christ writes: "The circle, which also emerges as a key symbol in women's art, is a powerful image of the impulse toward wholeness in women's culture."[33]

The ontology and epistemology of radical feminism each imply the other, just as the atomistic liberal ontology and epistemology imply each other and just as the Marxist ontology of class both implies and is implied by the Marxist epistemological categories of class standpoint. Because radical feminist ontology conceives "everything as connected to everything else," Gerri Perreault points out that radical feminist epistemology is committed to the view that the observer is inseparable from the observed, the knower from the known.[34] If this is so, then it is both proper and inevitable for theory to be guided by practical interests and to be informed by feelings. Feminist thinking "entails a refusal of (the) false clarity"[35] of the conceptual frameworks of patriarchy: "We were discovering a different sense of clarity, one achieved through feeling, in which thought followed a direction determined by pain, and trauma, and compassion and outrage."[36]

Given this conception of how adequate theories are developed, radical feminists conclude that the liberal/positivist conception of objectivity is a myth. Knowledge does not grow in a linear way, through the accumulation of facts and the application of the hypothetico-deductive method, but rather resembles "an upward spiral, so that each time we reevaluate a position or place we've been before, we do so from a new perspective."[37] Mary Daly uses the same image of spiraling to describe the growth of knowledge. She recommends that feminists spin a new web of ideas and then compares the spider's web to "a spiral net."[38] A few pages later, Daly writes: "Genuine Spinning is spiraling, which takes us over, under, around the baffle gates of godfathers into the Background."[39]

Although radical feminists continually contrast their world view with that of "the patriarchy," in fact their view contrasts most clearly with the atomistic world view of classical Newtonian physics, liberal politics and positivist epistemology. We have seen already that radical feminist epistemology parallels Marxist epistemology in important ways, particularly in its conception of theory building as a practical and a social activity and in its rejection of the liberal standard of objectivity. The relational ontology of radical feminism also recalls the relational ontology of traditional Marxism, although radical feminists and Marxists of course disagree on which social relations are most deserving of critical examination: traditional Marxists focus on conventional class relations and radical feminists on gender relations. Radical feminist epistemology differs most markedly from Marxist epistemology in its reliance on mystical or spiritual experiences as a source of knowledge, but even this feature of radical feminist epistemology does not distinguish it sharply from all forms of "patriarchal" thought. For instance, Gerri Perreault has argued that the world view of contemporary radical feminism bears striking resemblances to the relational world view of modern, post-Newtonian physics, the world view expressed in Einstein's relativity theory and Planck's quantum theory.[40]

The post-Newtonian conception of physical reality requires a transformation in the positivist conception of science. In this transformed view, the scientist can no longer be seen as a detached observer whose values are irrelevant to his or her science but rather must be acknowledged as a "participator" whose science reflects his or her values. Subatomic elements are not independent of the observer but can only be understood as correlations between various processes of observation and measurement. As Fritjof Capra puts it, the properties of matter depend on the apparatus we use to investigate it: if we ask a particle question, we will get a particle answer; if we ask a wave question, we will get a wave answer. Capra concludes that we cannot speak of nature without at the same time speaking about ourselves.[41] Capra claims that the world view of modern physics resembles that of the Hindu, Buddhist and Taoist mystics, who perceive reality as an inseparable whole, always alive and always in motion, simultaneously spiritual and material. Perreault argues that this world view also resembles that of radical feminism, especially those radical feminists who are concerned with rehabilitating women's spiritual powers and reviving the

"Old Religion" of wicca or witchcraft. Witches perceive deep connections between humans and the universe, they perceive non-human nature as divine and the human body as holy.[42] At least according to Fritjof Capra, modern physics also generates communitarian and ecological values.[43] Thus, although wicca has its roots in the Stone Age[44] while modern physics is a 20th-century phenomenon, and although modern physics is primarily a male creation while the revival of wicca is overwhelmingly the work of women, the ontology and epistemology of each are remarkably similar in certain respects.

By the epistemological standards of liberal feminism, the political theory of radical feminism is totally inadequate. It makes no pretence of detached impartiality, and the more spiritually oriented versions of radical feminism rest on non-empirical claims about women's special closeness to each other and to non-human nature. Radical feminism also fails the epistemological tests of traditional Marxism, especially the tests imposed by the more positivistic interpretations, according to which radical feminism is mystical and non-scientific. Even on less positivistic interpretations of Marxist epistemology, such as that developed by Lukács, radical feminism is an inadequate political theory. Traditional Marxists claim that, by dividing social reality according to the categories of male and female, patriarchal and feminist, radical feminism obscures the fundamental social division between the capitalist and the working class. It distorts the science of the proletariat and it implicitly strengthens the capitalist system by turning working-class men and women against each other.

By its own epistemological standards, however, radical feminism is indisputably the most adequate feminist theory. It is created directly from the experience of women, and it reflects women's pain and anger. It does not arbitrarily limit its sources of information, but utilizes women's special ways of knowing. Its non-linear mode of exposition reflects the human learning process, and the highly charged language of its authors evokes an emotional response in its readers and helps to jolt their consciousness out of the conceptual framework of patriarchy and into a women-centered paradigm. It reveals men's domination of women and demystifies myths through which that domination is concealed. Radical feminism is the collective product of feminist "Spinsters."

> Spinsters spin and weave, mending and creating unity of consciousness. In doing so we spin through and beyond the realm of multiple split consciousness. In concealed workshops, Spinsters unsnarl, unknot, untie, unweave. We knit, knot, interlace, entwine, whirl, and twirl. Absorbed in Spinning, in the ludic cerebration which is both work and play, Spinsters span the dichotomies of false consciousness and break its mind-binding combinations.[45]

Like the other feminist theories that we have considered, radical feminism justifies itself through its own epistemological standards. Let us turn now to one more feminist theory of knowledge and examine one final interpretation of the generally accepted criteria for theoretical adequacy.

Socialist Feminism and the Standpoint of Women

The socialist feminist theory of human nature is structurally identical with that of traditional Marxism and so, consequently, is the structure of its epistemology. Like both traditional Marxists and radical feminists, socialist feminists view knowledge as a social and practical construct and they believe that conceptual frameworks are shaped and limited by their social origins. They believe that, in any historical period, the prevailing world view will reflect the interests and values of the dominant class. Consequently, they recognize that the establishment of a less mystified and more reliable world view will require not only scientific struggle and intellectual argument but also the overthrow of the prevailing system of social relations.

Where social feminist differs from traditional Marxist epistemology is in its assertion that the special social or class position of women gives them a special epistemological standpoint which makes possible a view of the world that is more reliable and less distorted than that available either to capitalist or to working-class men. Socialist feminists believe, therefore, that a primary condition for the adequacy of a feminist theory, indeed for the adequacy of any theory, is that it should represent the world from the standpoint of women. A number of theorists are working to develop this insight, although they do not all use the terminology of women's standpoint or even mean quite the same thing by it when they do. These theorists include Elizabeth Fee, Jane Flax, Sandra Harding, Nancy Hartsock, Evelyn Fox Keller and Dorothy Smith.[46]

Both liberal and Marxist epistemologists consider that, in order to arrive at an adequate representation of reality, it is important to begin from the proper standpoint. Within liberal epistemology, the proper standpoint is the standpoint of the neutral, disinterested observer, a so-called Archimedean standpoint somewhere outside the reality that is being observed. Marxist epistemology, by contrast, recognizes that there is no such standpoint: that all systems of conceptualization reflect certain social interests and values. In a society where the production of knowledge is controlled by a certain class, the knowledge produced will reflect the interests and values of that class. In other words, in class societies the prevailing knowledge and science interpret reality from the standpoint of the ruling class. Because the ruling class has an interest in concealing the way in which it dominates and exploits the rest of the population, the interpretation of reality that it presents will be distorted in characteristic ways. In particular, the suffering of the subordinate classes will be ignored, redescribed as enjoyment or justified as freely chosen, deserved or inevitable.

Because their class position insulates them from the suffering of the oppressed, many members of the ruling class are likely to be convinced by their own ideology; either they fail to perceive the suffering of the oppressed or they believe that it is freely chosen, deserved or inevitable. They experience the current organization of society as basically satisfactory and so they accept the interpretation of reality that justifies that system of organization. They encounter little in their daily lives that conflicts with that interpretation. Oppressed groups, by contrast, suffer directly from the system that oppresses them. Sometimes the ruling ideology succeeds in duping them into partial denial of their pain or into accepting it temporarily but the pervasiveness, intensity and relentlessness of their suffering constantly push oppressed groups toward a realization that something is wrong with the prevailing social order. Their pain provides them with a motivation for finding out what is wrong, for criticizing accepted interpretations of reality and for developing new and less distorted ways of understanding the world. These new systems of conceptualization will reflect the interests and values of the oppressed groups and so constitute a representation of reality from an alternative to the dominant standpoint.

The standpoint of the oppressed is not just different from that of the ruling class; it is also epistemologically advantageous. It provides the basis for a view of reality that is more impartial than that of the ruling class and also more comprehensive. It is more impartial because it comes closer to representing the interests of society as a whole; whereas the standpoint of the ruling class reflects the interests only of one section of the population, the standpoint of the oppressed represents the interests of the totality in that historical period. Moreover, whereas the condition of the oppressed groups is visible only dimly to the ruling class, the oppressed are able to see more clearly the ruled as well as the rulers and the relation between them. Thus, the standpoint of the oppressed includes and is able to explain the standpoint of the ruling class.

The political economy of socialist feminism establishes that, in contemporary society, women suffer a special form of exploitation and oppression. Socialist feminist epistemologists argue that this distinctive social or class position provides women with a distinctive epistemological standpoint. From this standpoint, it is possible to gain a less biased and more comprehensive view of reality than that provided either by established bourgeois science or by the male-dominated leftist alternatives to it. An adequate understanding of reality must be undertaken from the standpoint of women. As socialist feminists conceive it, however, the standpoint of women is not expressed directly in women's naive and unreflective world view. We have seen earlier that socialist feminists recognize that women's perceptions of reality are distorted both by male-dominant ideology and by the male-dominated structure of everyday life. The standpoint of women, therefore, is not something that can be discovered through a survey of women's existing beliefs and attitudes—although such a survey should identify certain common-alities that might be incorporated eventually into a systematic representation of the world from women's perspective. Instead, the standpoint of women is discovered through a collective process of political and scientific struggle. The distinctive social experience of women generates insights that are incompatible with men's interpretations of reality and these insights provide clues to how reality might be interpreted from the standpoint of women. The validity of these insights, however, must be tested in political struggle and developed into a systematic representation of reality that is not distorted in ways that promote the interests of men above those of women.

Considerable work still needs to be done in elaborating the concept of women's standpoint. A number of arguments used to establish it are still speculative and require further development and investigation. Even so, the concept of women's standpoint promises to provide an important criterion for evaluating the adequacy of feminist theory. It is supported by a variety of arguments: by psychological research, which demonstrates that women's per-ceptions of reality are in fact different from those of men; by psychoanalytic theory, which offers an explanation of those differences in terms of the different infant experiences of girls and boys; by investigations in the sociology of knowledge, which link the distinctive social experience of women with dis-tinctively feminine ways of perceiving the world; and by feminist critiques of existing knowledge, which reveal how prevailing systems of conceptualization are biased because they invalidate women's interests and promote the interests and values of the men who created them. Of course, the epistemological superiority of women's standpoint will be demonstrated conclusively only through a distinctively feminist reconstruction of reality in which women's interests are not subordinated to those of men. This reconstruction must be practical as well as theoretical.

Feminist critiques of existing knowledge have been undertaken in a variety of fields.[47] Already in this book we have seen how the categories of western political theory, from Aristotle to Marx, have systematically excluded consideration of women and women's work. Similarly, feminist historians have pointed out that established history is the history of men. Not only have women's lives and achievements been excluded, but the prevailing historical categories distort women's past. For instance, historians commonly view classical Athens, Renaissance Italy and 18th-century revolutionary France as periods of progressive social change—in spite of the fact that women lost significant status and power during these periods.[48] In the field of ethology, feminist researchers have shown that what animals do is entirely misrepresented by categories that rest on assumptions of individual competition and male dominance.[49] In psychology, the work of Carol Gilligan has demonstrated that the categories used to describe the moral development of children in fact fit the development only of boys; the moral development of girls follows quite a different course.[50] Gilligan's work even suggests that the basic categories of western moral philosophy, categories such as rationality, autonomy and justice, are drawn from and reflect the moral experience of men rather than that of women. A final example of the contemporary feminist critique of knowledge is the claim made by some feminist historians of science that the categories developed by the scientific revolution of the 16th and 17th centuries, together with the conception of scientific rationality that was established at the same time, are not only typically bourgeois but also typically masculine modes of conceptualization.[51] During this scientific revolution, the organic conception of nature as a mother who should be respected and cherished gave way to a conception of nature as an unruly female who needed to be tamed and finally to a mechanistic conception of a passive, inert and dead nature which could be exploited with impunity. At the same time, Copernican theory replaced the female (earth)-centered universe with a male (sun)-centered universe. Finally, the Baconian experimental method, which encouraged the "inquisition of nature" by scientists who conceived themselves as quite separate from the objects of their study, has been shown to draw its inspiration from the witch trials of the 15th, 16th and 17th centuries.

Of course, women have not yet been able to construct systematic alternatives to the prevailing masculine science and ideology. For one thing, they are still in the process of discovering ways in which their thought is constrained on both conscious and unconscious levels by assumptions that reinforce male dominance. Powerful interests discredit women's ideas and minimal social resources are allocated to developing a science that is profoundly subversive. As Elizabeth Fee says,

> At the moment, the production of feminist knowledge and theory is a cottage industry; it depends on the energy and ideas of a small number of women, working individually, in response to a collective social movement, but without any significant institutional or financial base.[52]

Despite these obstacles, some theorists believe that it is possible to discern at least the outlines of a distinctively feminine perspective on reality and to see how these are generated by the sexual division of labor.

Within contemporary capitalism, the society with which they are concerned primarily, socialist feminist theorists remind us that the sexual division of labor assigns to women work that is very different from that of men. Dorothy Smith argues that women's work is primarily in what she calls "the bodily mode"; it focuses on the transformation of the immediate and concrete world. Men's work, by contrast, is in what Smith calls "the abstracted conceptual mode" which is the ruling mode in industrial society. The rulers are able to operate in the conceptual mode, abstracting from the concrete realities of daily existence, only because they participate in a system of social organization which assigns bodily work to others—others who also "produce the invisibility of that work."[53]

> The place of women, then, . . . is where the work is done to facilitate man's occupation of the conceptual mode of action. Women keep house, bear and care for children, look after him when he is sick, and in general provide for the logistics of his bodily existence. But this marriage aspect of women's work is only one side of a more general relation. Women work in and around the professional managerial scene in analogous ways. They do those things which give concrete form to the conceptual activities. They do the clerical work, giving material form to the words or thoughts of the boss. They do the routine computer work, the interviewing for the survey, the nursing, the secretarial work. At almost every point women mediate for men the relation between the conceptual mode of action and the actual concrete forms on which it depends. Women's work is interposed between the abstracted modes and the local and particular actualities in which they are necessarily anchored. *Also, women's work conceals from men acting in the abstract mode just this anchorage*[54] (my italics).

Nancy Hartsock provides a similar account of women's work in contemporary capitalism. She too points out that women's domestic work mediates much of men's contact with natural substances; women cook the food that men eat and wash the toilet bowls that men use. This sexual division of labor hardly permits women to think in abstractions, such as the abstraction of human beings from the non-human world, and instead requires women to focus on the sensuous and ever-changing qualities of the material world. Women's child-rearing work further discourages abstraction and instrumentalism. Many studies have shown that children cannot thrive on bread alone; they must also receive love and affection. To rear children successfully, women must concentrate on the quality rather than the quantity of the relation, they must be sensitive to the changing needs of the child and they cannot remain emotionally detached from their work. Finally, Hartsock claims that the intimate involvement of women's bodies in pregnancy, childbirth, and lactation has epistemological consequences:

> The unity of mental and manual labor and the directly sensuous nature of women's work leads to a more profound unity of mental and manual labor, social and natural worlds, than is experienced by the male worker in capitalism. The unity grows from the fact that women's bodies, unlike men's, can be themselves instruments of production: in pregnancy, giving birth or lactation, arguments about a division of mental from manual labor are fundamentally foreign.[55]

Of course, women do not spend their whole lives as adults. Like men, their distinctively human labor in fact begins in infancy when they create their first conceptions of themselves, of other people and of the non-human world. According to the psychoanalytic tradition, this first labor is especially important because early infantile attitudes and conceptualizations often set the direction for adult life, becoming the unconscious and invisible foundation on which adult attitudes and conceptualizations are grounded. Psychoanalysts since Freud have claimed that girls typically tend to develop perceptions of reality that differ from those of boys because their infant experiences are different. We have seen already that a number of socialist feminist theorists have drawn on psychoanalytic theory to explain the social formation and relative fixity of the masculine and feminine character structures that are typical of contemporary society. Some socialist feminist theorists also draw on psychoanalytic theory in attempts to identify the psychological links between gendered systems of conceptualization and the earliest experiences of girls and boys.

Contemporary feminist psychoanalysis is designed primarily to understand how prevailing norms of gender are imposed on infants and come to structure the human mind. Although gender in fact structures much more of the social reality than the human mind, feminist psychoanalytic theory is often referred to briefly as "gender theory." The theory begins from the "object relations" post-Freudian theory of Margaret Mahler, D.W. Winnicott, and Harry Guntrip, which distinguishes the physical birth of an infant from its psychological birth.[56] In contrast to the relatively short-lived event of physical birth, psychological birth is a process that stretches over approximately three years and which results in the establishment of the child's personal identity. According to object relations theory,

> The most important tasks of the first three years of life are first, establishing a close relationship with the caretaker—usually the mother—(symbiosis) and then moving from that relation through the process of separation and individuation. Separation means establishing a firm sense of differentiation from the mother, of possessing one's own physical and mental boundaries. Individuation means establishing a range of characteristics, skills and personality traits which are uniquely one's own. Separation and individuation are the two "tracts" of development; they are not identical, but they can reinforce or impede each other.[57]

In a male-dominated society, the processes of separation and individuation are not the same for girls and for boys. Because children are born into a deeply gender-structured society, even the early processes of separation and individuation are gender-structured and result in the formation of individuals whose identity centers around their gender. The apparently universal division of labor by sex means that women, usually mothers, are the primary caretakers of most young children and consequently women are the individuals with whom children develop their earliest and most intense relationship. It follows that women, usually mothers, must also be the ones from whom children have to separate themselves and in relation to whom they must individuate themselves. Because girls will grow up to be women, like themselves, mothers often unconsciously treat daughters as an extension of themselves rather than as separate persons, and this makes it difficult for girls to achieve separation and individuation. Girls often remain for an extended period in an ambivalent relationship with their mother, unable to distinguish clearly between her needs and feelings and their own. In contrast with their perceptions of their daughters, their social context encourages mothers to perceive sons as clearly other than themselves. Boys are encouraged to separate themselves from their mothers much earlier than girls and they do so in a much more complete way. Because women are socially devalued, boys find it necessary not just to separate from their mothers as individuals but to reject all identification with the feminine. Boys' love for their mothers is threatening to their new masculine identities; consequently, they deny their emotional need for their mothers and develop an exaggerated contempt for women.

Psychoanalytic gender theory predicts that the differences in their early experiences of separation and individuation will result in girls and boys developing very different ways of understanding themselves, their relation to others and their relation to non-human nature. Girls will have relatively less-rigid ego boundaries: they will be more concerned to make connection with others rather than to separate from them, they will be more sensitive to the needs and feelings of others and they will be open to the persuasion and judgments of others. They will seek greater complexity and intimacy in rela-tionships, rather than preserving distance from others. By contrast, boys will have rigid ego boundaries and will be preoccupied with distinguishing themselves from others. They will repress their longings for fusion with the mother and they will seek to dominate their feelings, their own bodies, other people and non-human nature because all of these threaten to betray the boys' ultimate lack of separateness and their ultimate dependence on others.

If this psychoanalytic account is correct, there is a remarkable "fit" between women's infant and adult experiences. Both as infants and adults, women are encouraged to immerse themselves in relationships with other people, first with their mothers, then with their children. Moreover, given women's adult re-sponsibility for the daily maintenance of life, it is more difficult for them than it is for adult men to enter the "conceptual, abstracted mode of action" that Smith sees as the governing mode of industrial society. Socialist feminist theorists argue that a consideration of the distinctive differences between the experience and work of women and the experience and work of men, both as infants and as adults, sheds light on certain distinctive differences in the way that each sex tends to conceptualize reality. Specifically, they claim that such a consideration can be used to explain why some systems of conceptualization distort reality in ways that are typically masculine and how the standpoint of women offers the possibility of correcting these distortions.

Several socialist feminist theorists claim that the preoccupations of infant males are reflected in the fundamental categories of western science and philosophy. For instance, Sandra Harding uses feminist psychoanalysis to supplement Merchant's explanation of what is typically masculine about the scientific revolution of the 16th and 17th centuries. In the course of this revolution, as we have seen already, the organic conception of nature as a mother who should be respected and cherished was replaced by a conception of nature as a collection of inert atoms, connected by mechanistic causal relations whose movements, expressed in the abstract and quantitative terms of math-ematical formulae, are supposed to account for the qualities of nature as those are perceived by the senses. Harding identifies the unconscious masculine preoccupation with separation and control in these new metaphysical categories. Similarly, Harding suggests that the new positivist account of scientific rationality also reflects a characteristically masculine emphasis on abstraction, the repression of feelings, and the domination of nature.[58] Working on similar lines, Nancy Hartsock and Jane Flax have traced the unconscious masculine preoccupation with separation and domination in the fundamental categories of western philosophy, the same categories that define the basic problematic of western epistemology and political theory.[59] We have seen already that the insistence on making sharp distinctions between mind and body, reason and passion, knowledge and sense, culture and nature, permanence and change poses in-superable philosophical problems concerning the possibility of knowledge and the relations of mind to body, value to fact and of individuals to each other. Hartsock to some extent and Flax to a much greater extent draw on feminist psychoanalysis to explain why these perennial philosophical problems spring from unconscious attitudes to the world that are typically masculine. In these problems, Flax finds reflected the masculine repression of the infantile longing for union, the masculine fear of desire and dependence, and the masculine need to control both nature and the body. She suggests that "apparently insoluble dilemmas within philosophy are not the immanent structure of the human mind and/or nature but rather reflect distorted or frozen social relations."[60]

Although feminist psychoanalysis is currently popular among socialist feminists as an explanation of the psychological mechanism through which gendered conceptual frameworks emerge from the sexual division of labor in childrearing, socialist feminist epistemology does not stand or fall with feminist psychoanalysis. Socialist feminist epistemology claims that the social experience of women is so different from that of men that it shapes and limits their vision in substantially different ways—in other words, that women's position in society provides the basis for an autonomous epistemological standpoint. Socialist feminist epistemology is not committed, however, to any specific account of the psychological relation between the sexual division of labor and the gender structuring of knowledge; it is quite compatible with socialist feminism for the gender-structured adult experience of women and men to be more influential than their infant experience in shaping their world view. Whenever and however this shaping occurs, growing empirical evidence shows that women tend to conceive the world differently from men and have different attitudes towards it.[61] The discovery of the precise nature and causes of these differences is a task for feminist psychologists and sociologists of knowledge. The task for feminist scientists and political theorists is to build on women's experience and insights in order to develop a systematic account of the world, together with its potentialities for change, as it appears from the standpoint of women.

As we saw earlier, women are far from creating systematic alternatives to the prevailing male-dominant ways of conceptualizing reality. Even to imagine what such alternatives might be like is, as Elizabeth Fee says, "rather like asking a medieval peasant to imagine the theory of genetics or the production of a space capsule; our images are, at best, likely to be sketchy and insubstantial."[62] Socialist feminist theorists claim, however, that women's experience has generated at least the outline of a distinctive world view, even though this outline is, as Fee predicts, sketchy and insubstantial. Nancy Hartsock provides this outline:

> The female construction of self in relation to others, leads . . . toward opposition to dualisms of any sort, valuation of concrete, everyday life, sense of a variety of connectednesses and continuities both with other persons and with the natural world. If material life structures consciousness, women's relationally defined existence, bodily experience of boundary challenges, and activity of transforming both physical objects and human beings must be expected to result in a world view to which dichotomies are foreign.[63]

The standpoint of women generates an ontology of relations and of continual process.

The basic structure of the world, as Hartsock claims that it appears from the standpoint of women, bears a strong resemblance to the world as described by radical feminism. Indeed, my characterization of several of the theorists mentioned above as socialist rather than radical feminist is perhaps presumptuous and may not be in accord with their own definition of themselves. The writings of Sandra Harding, Nancy Hartsock and Dorothy Smith could all be described as radical feminist insofar as they all seem to suggest that the sexual division of labor has more causal primacy than other divisions and so generates a deeper and more permanent division in knowledge. An additional radical feminist element in Hartsock's work is her discussion of procreation, where she seems to suggest that the difference between women's and men's world views is partly rooted in certain of women's experiences that she calls "inherent in the female physiology." Specifically, she mentions "menstruation, coitus, pregnancy, child-birth and lactation."[64] The claim that certain distinctive differences between women and men's perceptions of reality are rooted in "inherent" biological differences rather than in a sexual division of labor is more typical of radical feminism than of socialist feminism, as I have characterized these positions. My criterion for identifying all these theorists as socialist feminist, however, is that all of them adhere in principle to a historical materialist approach for understanding social reality. Hartsock explicitly commits herself to this method, and so she is precluded from regarding even physiology as a pre-social given and must see it ultimately as socially constructed, although certainly less immediately susceptible to social alteration than some other aspects of human life. In general, the work of all those theorists whom I have characterized as socialist feminist is clearly a development of radical feminist insights and shows how great is the debt that socialist feminism owes to radical feminism.

In spite of this debt, the socialist feminist concept of the standpoint of women is rather different from the superficially similar concept that is assumed in the writing of many popular American radical feminists. In the next section, I shall focus on the contrasts between radical and socialist feminist epistemology and also on the contrasts between socialist feminist epistemology and the epistemology of liberalism and of traditional Marxism.

The Standpoint of Women as a
Condition for Theoretical Adequacy

So far in this chapter, I have shown how each of the major versions of contemporary feminism offers its own interpretation of the generally accepted criteria of theoretical adequacy. For instance, each version of feminism has its own conception of what constitutes bias, objectivity and comprehensiveness; there is even disagreement, although I have not discussed this, on what counts as inconsistency with liberal positivists sometimes accusing "dialectical" Marxists of self-contradiction. My own exposition of these various epistemological positions has not been neutral, of course; throughout my discussion, I have given indications of what I regard as the major advantages and disadvantages inherent in each position. In this section, I want to summarize my criticisms, to state exactly why liberal feminism, traditional Marxism and radical feminism do not offer appropriate criteria of theoretical adequacy and to explain why I regard the socialist feminist concept of the standpoint of women as providing an indispensable standard for measuring the adequacy of competing theories.

Liberal feminism, as we saw earlier, is committed to certain neo-positivist assumptions about theoretical adequacy. In particular, it is committed to a distinctive conception of objectivity. This conception is fundamentally similar for both so-called empirical and normative theories, even though liberal positivism, unlike the other epistemological traditions that we have considered, postulates a sharp break between so-called facts and values and assigns a different "logical status" to normative and to "scientific" theories. According to the liberal/positivist conception, a "scientific" enquiry is objective if it utilizes methodological controls to eliminate the influence of social interests, values, and emotions; political or moral philosophy is objective insofar as it introduces devices for eliminating the influence of special interests and values. Such devices include the postulation of "rational spectators," "veils of ignorance" and "neutral dialogues." In both "science" and philosophy, the aim of these methodological constraints is ultimately the same, to provide justification for the claim that the theories produced by these methods are not biased in favor of any particular social group. On the basis of this claim, theories produced by these methods are viewed as presenting conclusions that are universally applicable and as embodying universal or human values.

The liberal/positivist conception of objectivity rests on the belief that it is possible to identify the Archimedian standpoint of a disinterested and detached spectator. By contrast, I accept Marxist arguments that there is no epistemological standpoint "outside" social reality and that all knowledge is shaped by its social origins. In class society, the origins of knowledge are necessarily class origins; there is no standpoint outside all classes. Consequently, in class society, all knowledge is bound to represent the standpoint either of the rulers or the ruled. In this situation, claims that knowledge is objective in the sense of being uninfluenced by class interests are themselves ideological myths. Such claims operate in fact to obscure the ruling-class interests that are promoted by the dominant world view. In reality, the interests of the rulers and of the ruled conflict in a way that cannot be resolved within the prevailing system of social organization. For the ruled, it is imperative to focus on these conflicts and to discover the underlying reasons for them. It is equally imperative for the ruling class to minimize the class nature of these conflicts and to conceal their origins in the prevailing system of social organization. To do this, the ruling class develops interpretations of reality that mystify the existence and nature of class conflict. This mystification is itself concealed by the myth that knowledge, especially that part of knowledge regarded as science, is neutral between class interests. The myth hides the fact that established knowledge, in class societies, is a weapon in the hands of the ruling class. Because existing knowledge is grounded on ruling class interests, moreover, it is not a weapon that can simply be taken over by oppressed groups. If science is to be useful to the oppressed, it must be reconstructed on new foundations. The myth of scientific neutrality misleads the oppressed about the class bias of existing knowledge and encourages them to believe that it expresses universal truths. So technology is seen as having its own imperatives. Human beings are too. Oppressive aspects of the status quo are justified as inevitable. Knowledge is an effective weapon for the ruling class only as long as it remains a secret weapon. The liberal/positivist conception of objectivity provides established knowledge with its cover of neutrality. For this reason, it is an entirely inappropriate standard for measuring theoretical adequacy.

Marxist epistemology in many ways is a total contrast to liberal/positivist epistemology. It views the constitution of knowledge as a social achievement that necessarily reflects certain interests and values. Some interpretations of Marxism seem to exempt the physical sciences from this characterization and to assume that these are purely objective in the liberal/positivist sense. The positivist streak in Marxist epistemology finds some justification in the writings of Marx and Engels, especially in their rather physicalistic interpretations of such concepts as "production" and "material life," which were commented on in earlier chapters. A positivist bias may also be detected in what I earlier called the residual biologism of Marxist categories, that is, in the tendency to take biological facts as "given" and as setting fixed limits to social possibility.[65] Where positivist preconceptions have not been eradicated entirely from the

Marxist method, they certainly have had a deleterious effect on the Marxist analysis of women's situation. Nevertheless, as I argued earlier, a positivist epistemology is fundamentally incompatible with the historical materialist method whose establishment remains one of Marxism's most important contributions. It is far more conformable with the historical materialist method to recognize explicitly that knowledge always expresses a certain epistemological standpoint and to identify the most advantageous standpoint with that of the oppressed classes.

My differences with this Lukácsian interpretation of traditional Marxism lies not in our general account of knowledge but rather in our views about the adequacy of the political economy of traditional Marxism, according to which capitalism is divided into two conflicting classes, the proletariat and the bourgeoisie. Other groups, such as peasants, people of color and women, are seen as being oppressed in characteristic ways but the maintenance of their oppression is ultimately attributable to the requirements of the capitalist system. According to the political economy of traditional Marxism, the class position of peasants is a carry-over from the mode of production that preceded industrial capitalism; consequently, the class position of peasants does not provide them with a particularly advantageous standpoint for understanding the capitalist system. As groups, women and people of color are thought to occupy no distinctive class standpoint. Some of them are certainly in the proletariat, but others are peasants, lumpenproletariat or even part of the ruling class. Whatever may be said about the position of peasants and people of color, feminist analysis has shown conclusively that the class analysis of traditional Marxism obscures important features of women's situation. Although women are indeed part of all classes in the traditional Marxist sense of "class," there are also important commonalities in their experience, commonalities significant enough to justify claiming that women share a distinctive social location that can provide the basis for a distinctive epistemological standpoint.

Feminist analysis has shown that the situation of women cannot be explained adequately in terms of the class analysis of traditional Marxism. This analysis, which purports to represent the standpoint of the proletariat, in fact represents the standpoint only of the adult male proletariat—and perhaps only of the white proletariat. As I have argued earlier, the class analysis of traditional Marxism obscures important features of women's oppression in a way that is closely analogous to the way that bourgeois ideology obscures the systematic exploitation of the working class under capitalism. Feminist analysis shows that the apparently gender-blind categories of traditional Marxism must be revised, so that the proletariat can be seen to be comprised of women as well as men, of people of colors other than white and of children as well as adults. It must also be seen to labor in many places other than the factory. As traditionally understood, the concept of the standpoint of the proletariat legitimates the social analysis of traditional Marxism and conceals its male bias. As traditionally understood, therefore, this concept is entirely inappropriate as a criterion of theoretical adequacy.

Radical feminism recognizes explicitly that women's perceptions of reality often differ from those of men. Moreover, it claims that male interpretations of reality often are misinterpretations, that prevailing knowledge distorts reality in a typically ideological fashion. Radical feminists believe that only women can correct these masculine distortions and they offer a variety of reasons for this belief. Their reasons include assertions that women are able to draw on special and innately female modes of knowing, claims that women's lives have encouraged them to develop a special sensitivity to data that men fail to notice and observations that the circumstances of women's lives provide them with a perspective on reality that is different from and more dependable than that of men. In my view, radical feminist epistemology constitutes in some ways a remarkable advance on Marxist epistemology. In other ways, however, I think it is problematic.

One of the problems with at least some versions of radical feminist epistemology is its postulation of conventionally unrecognized modes of knowing. No evidence shows that women have innate faculties of perception that are unavailable in principle to men. On the other hand, it is very plausible that women's lives of subordination have encouraged them to develop a special sensitivity to behavioral cues and a remarkable creativity in interpreting those cues. Something like this is probably the explanation for the undoubted phenomenon of "women's intuition."

Radical feminists are also correct in calling attention to the role of feeling and emotion in the construction of knowledge. As we have seen already, all investigations are motivated by certain interests, and interests inevitably generate emotions and feelings. Susan Griffin is right to applaud an enquiry which recognized explicitly that, as we saw earlier, "thought followed a direction determined by pain, and trauma, and compassion and outrage." The existence of strong feelings helps to identify the questions that are important for investigation.

What feelings cannot do, or at least cannot do unassisted, is provide systematic answers to those questions. One reason for this is that, as we have seen already, feelings and emotions are not simply immediate, unsocialized responses to situations. They depend both on our perception of the situation, for instance, on whether we perceive the wolf whistle as an insult or as a compliment, and also on what we conceive as appropriate emotional responses to certain situations. Our conception of what emotional responses are appropriate is socially determined on more than one level. For instance, our socialization as women or as middle class may have made it difficult for us to express certain emotions, such as anger. Or our political views may have convinced us that it is inappropriate to feel compassion for members of certain groups. On the deepest level, as we saw in Chapters 3 and 5, even our identification of our feelings presupposes the existence of social norms about what constitute appropriate emotional responses to certain types of situations. Like so-called cognitive knowledge, therefore, feelings and emotions are social constructs, and this means that they are not self-authenticating. Like our perceptions, our feelings and emotions may be distorted in various ways by the prevailing ideology and even by the oppressive structure of daily life; these encourage us, for instance, to feel anger at ourselves, at those close to us or at some easily identifiable ethnic group rather than at the real causes of our suffering. Radical feminists correctly recognize that feelings and emotions are essentially involved in knowledge and that we should not pretend to be uninfluenced by them. Because feelings and emotions are socially constructed, however, radical feminists are wrong if they suppose, as some do, that the feelings and emotions of feminists should always be accepted as appropriate to the situation or even that those who experience them always identify them correctly. It is not just a case of stripping away patriarchal myths to get back to the basic "female experience undistorted by male interpretation."[66] All aspects of our experience, including our feelings and emotions, must be subjected to critical scrutiny and feminist political analysis.

Its somewhat uncritical attitude toward feelings may itself be just a symptom of the basic problem that I see with radical feminist epistemology, that it does not place enough emphasis on the distinction between description and explanation. This is not to say that radical feminists rest content with women's immediate and naive perceptions. Of course they realize that not all women are feminists and they recognize that women's perceptions in contemporary society are distorted by what radical feminists call patriarchal mystification. On the other hand, radical feminists recognize that women's experience, even distorted as it is, provides the basis for an alternative to the dominant interpretation of reality. Among the main contributions of radical feminism has been the way in which it has drawn on women's experience to expose the male bias in existing knowledge. Radical feminism has begun to create a "counter-reality", to show us the world not just as it appears to women who are confused by patriarchal ideology but as it appears to those who have a consciousness of their own oppression, who are aware that they inhabit a patriarchy. It has drawn on the experience of feminist women to show us, often through poetry and literature, that prevailing world views are male-biased and descriptively inadequate.

I have already argued that description and explanation cannot be distinguished sharply from each other. Some theorists claim that all descriptions are theory-laden, and it is certainly true that alternative descriptions of reality set different questions for theorists to answer and different limits of theoretical adequacy. While descriptions are an important part of a theory, however, they are not the whole of it. Theory is needed to explain the relationship between various descriptions or observations; typically, a theory shows that the world as we immediately perceive and describe it is merely the appearance of an underlying reality. Thus a theory may require that we revise even the descriptions of the world on which the theory itself is based. Contemporary American radical feminism does not explicitly recognize this. It has painted, vividly and movingly, a picture of women's oppression, but it has not created a working model of that oppression. Since its early days, American radical feminism has not acknowledged the need for a dynamic theory that goes beneath the appearance of women's oppression to identify the oppressive forces and their laws of motion. It has encouraged women to name their own experience, but it has not recognized explicitly that this experience must be analyzed, explained and theoretically transcended. Radical feminism has shown us that women have a distinctively valuable perspective on the world; it has not fully comprehended that an adequate expression of the standpoint of women must be a theoretical and scientific achievement as well as a political and artistic one.

The socialist feminist conception of the standpoint of women is radical feminist in its inspiration, but it rests on a more complex and self-conscious epistemology. In part, the differences between the two conceptions may be due simply to the rather different preoccupations of the two groups of feminist theorists: the most influential radical feminist theorists are typically concerned to redescribe reality as it appears to women; socialist feminist theorists are typically concerned to give a systematic explanation of that reality. To this extent, the work of radical and socialist feminists may be seen as complementing each other. I think, however, that the different methodological commitments of radical and socialist feminists also lead to substantive differences in their accounts of how knowledge may be reconstructed from the standpoint of women and especially to differences in their estimate of what is required as a precondition for such a reconstruction.

One of the main contributions of radical feminism has been its demonstration that the prevailing culture is suffused with the perceptions and values of male dominance. In response to this recognition, radical feminists have made it one of their political priorities to create an alternative women's culture. Sometimes this alternative culture takes practical forms, such as women's health centers and women's businesses. As we have seen earlier, however, these projects are constantly under financial pressure from the larger economic system and frequently fail to survive. Moreover, relatively few radical feminist women can participate in these projects. As a consequence, the more permanent and influential forms of women's culture are music, books or religious rituals that express women's values and perceptions and provide a radical challenge to the prevailing male-dominated interpretations of reality. In contemporary society, however, most women reject this challenge: they dismiss feminist ideas as distorted, crazy or perverse. Any theory that claims to express the standpoint of women must be able to explain why it is itself rejected by the vast majority of women. Radical feminist epistemology suggests an answer to this question in terms of the dominance of patriarchal culture. Socialist feminist epistemology, however, is explicitly historical materialist and so is able to explain why this culture is dominant and to link the anti-feminist consciousness of many women with the structure of their daily lives. At the same time, the socialist feminist account preserves the apparently contradictory claim that women occupy a distinctive epistemological standpoint that offers unique insight into certain aspects of reality.

According to the socialist feminist conception, a standpoint is a position in society from which certain features of reality come into prominence and from which others are obscured. Although a standpoint makes certain features of reality visible, however, it does not necessarily reveal them clearly nor in their essential interconnections with each other. The daily experience of oppressed groups provides them with an immediate awareness of their own suffering but they do not perceive immediately the underlying causes of this suffering nor even necessarily perceive it as oppression. Their understanding is obscured both by the prevailing ideology and by the very structure of their lives. The women who form the majority though not the leaders of the anti-abortion or so-called right-to-life movement provide a good example of the mixed consciousness of the oppressed. As Deirdre English analyzes their thinking, the women who oppose the legalization of abortion are quite conscious that the structure of the economy allows few women the opportunity for genuine economic independence. The women "right-to-lifers" are acutely aware that most women must depend on marriage to a man in order to achieve a standard of living that rises above bare subsistence and this awareness reflects their recognition of what may be the most fundamental aspect of women's oppression. English writes:

> The antifeminist woman is, like all other women, grappling with the weight of her oppression. She is responding to social circumstances—a worsening economy, a lack of aid and commitment from men—which feminists did not create and from which feminists also feel the conse- quences. The issues that she faces are the issues that face us too: her fears are nothing less than our fears.[67]

In English's view, anti-abortionists see the pro-choice movement supported by most feminists as posing a threat to women's economic security by depriving women of their most important lever for getting men to marry them. If abortion were freely available, women would no longer be able to refuse sex on the grounds that it might lead to an unwanted child, for the availability of abortion ensures that no child need be unwanted. As English points out, giving women the right to choose takes away their ability *not* to choose. What the anti-abortionists see is that

> men have reaped more than their share of benefits from women's liberation. Woman's meager economic independence, a result of her new-found presence in the job market, and her sexual liberation have allowed men to garner new freedoms.[68]

Men no longer feel any obligation to stay in their marriages, and most of them default, in whole or in part, on their child support payments.[69] "Under these circumstances, the fear has awakened that feminism will free men first—and might never get around to freeing women."[70] In spite of being women, anti-abortionist women obviously have not been able to develop a comprehensive vision of feminism as a total and liberating transformation of society that would be in the long-term interests of all women. Instead, they conceive of feminism only in terms of certain very limited demands that they perceive as contrary to the immediate interests of working-class and older women.

It is possible to debate specific details of English's analysis. Other theorists claim that the opposition of some women to the legalization of abortion is due to envy of what they perceive as the freedoms of the Cosmo girl and a fear that the legalization of abortion will further lower the status of full-time wives and mothers.[71] On either account, women "right-to-lifers" provide an interesting example to illustrate the socialist feminist conception of women's standpoint. This example shows clearly the way in which "false consciousness" is generated by the structure of women's everyday lives as well as by ideologies of male dominance. It also demonstrates how a reconceptualization of reality from the standpoint of women is not readily available and requires a protracted political and theoretical struggle.

In addition to the mystifications created by the dominant ideology and by the structure of our lives, Jane Flax claims that women face another obstacle as they seek to develop a systematic feminist alternative to the masculine modes of conceiving the world. This obstacle is the typically feminine set of attitudes and modes of perception that have been imposed on women in a male-dominated society. While this set of attitudes and modes of perception provides part of the basis for an alternative to the masculine view, it cannot be the only basis of such an alternative. Flax writes:

> Women's experience, which has been excluded from the realm of the known, of the rational, is not in itself an adequate ground for theory. As the other pole of the dualities, it must be incorporated and transcended. Women, in part because of their own history as daughters, have problems with differentiation and the development of a true self and reciprocal relations.[72]

In other words, while women's experience of subordination puts them in a uniquely advantageous position for reinterpreting reality, it also imposes on them certain psychological difficulties which must themselves be the focus of self-conscious struggle.

Simply to be a woman, then, is not sufficient to guarantee a clear understanding of the world as it appears from the standpoint of women. As we saw earlier, the standpoint of women is not discovered by surveying the beliefs and attitudes of women under conditions of male dominance, just as the standpoint of the proletariat is not discovered by surveying the beliefs and attitudes of workers under capitalism. The standpoint of women is that perspective which reveals women's true interests and this standpoint is reached only through scientific and political struggle. Those who construct the standpoint of women must begin from women's experience as women describe it, but they must go beyond that experience theoretically and ultimately may require that women's experience be redescribed. One's class position as a woman may encourage certain perceptions and present certain problems but it will not automatically provide the answers to those problems by generating a systematic feminist alternative to the prevailing masculinist ideology. Such an alternative can only be the product of a long process of political and scientific struggle in the pursuit of feminist goals. Only such a struggle will reveal the intricate and systematic reality of male dominance. In the process of this struggle, partial analyses will appear but their partiality will be demonstrated by their failure to lead to women's liberation. In the end, an adequate representation of the world from the standpoint of women requires the material overthrow of male domination. Donna Harraway writes:

> A socialist-feminist science will have to be developed in the process of constructing different lives in interaction with the world. Only material struggle can end the logic domination. . . . It is a matter for struggle. I do not know what life science would be like if the historical structure of our lives minimized domination. I do know that the history of biology convinces me that basic knowledge would reflect and reproduce the new world, just as it has participated in maintaining our old one.[73]

Even though we do not yet know how the world looks from the standpoint of women, I think that the socialist feminist concept of women's standpoint constitutes a valuable epistemological device for identifying certain necessary conditions of theoretical adequacy. It provides a politically appropriate and theoretically illuminating interpretation of such generally acknowledged conditions as impartiality, objectivity, comprehensiveness, verifiability and usefulness.

First, the concept of women's standpoint presupposes that all knowledge reflects the interests and values of specific social groups. Since this is so, objectivity cannot be interpreted to mean destitute of values, and impartiality cannot be interpreted to mean neutrality between conflicting interests. If these interpretations are ruled out, and given that we want to preserve the conditions of objectivity and impartiality, the question for epistemology becomes the following: if claims to knowledge are to be objective and impartial, whose interests should they reflect? Socialist feminists answer that they should reflect the interests of women. Women's subordinate status means that, unlike men, women do not have an interest in mystifying reality and so are likely to develop a clearer and more trustworthy understanding of the world. A representation of reality from the standpoint of women is more objective and unbiased than the prevailing representations that reflect the standpoint of men.

The concept of women's standpoint also provides an interpretation of what it is for a theory to be comprehensive. It asserts that women's social position offers them access to aspects or areas of reality that are not easily accessible to men. For instance, to use one of Hartsock's examples, it is only from the standpoint of women that household labor becomes visible as work rather than as a labor of love. The same might be said of socializing children, of empathizing with adults and even, often, of engaging in sexual relations. Thus the standpoint of women provides the basis for a more comprehensive representation of reality than the standpoint of men. Certain areas or aspects of the world are not excluded. The standpoint of women reveals more of the universe, human and non-human, than does the standpoint of men.

Every epistemological tradition requires that genuine claims to knowledge be verified in some way and several of them require that genuine knowledge be useful. The socialist feminist conception of women's standpoint specifies certain interpretations of verification and of usefulness. It asserts that knowledge is useful if it contributes to a practical reconstruction of the world in which women's interests are not subordinate to those of men. Whether or not knowledge is useful in this way is verified in the process of political and scientific struggle to build such a world, a world whose maintenance does not require illusions.

The concept of women's standpoint is not theory-neutral. Like every epistemology, it is conceptually linked to a certain ontology: its model of how knowledge is achieved necessarily presupposes certain general features of human nature and human social life. Whether or not one accepts socialist feminist epistemology thus depends in part on whether or not one accepts the general view of reality on which it rests. One thing that may be said in favor of the concept of women's standpoint, however, is that it is itself more comprehensive than the other interpretations of theoretical adequacy that have been examined already. It explains not only why prevailing representations of reality are systematically male-biased but even why the conditions of theoretical adequacy themselves have been interpreted in characteristically male-biased ways. Thus it provides the basis for a new historical materialist critique of epistemology. It also offers at least a method for discovering the material reasons for its own emergence in this particular historical period.[74]

The concept of women's standpoint is not entirely unproblematic and in the next section I shall discuss one important problem with it. Even so, I think that this concept shows us how to construct a standard for judging the adequacy not just of feminist theory but of all claims to knowledge. I shall conclude this book by showing how the concept of women's standpoint enables us to evaluate the feminist theories that are presently available.

Identifying the Standpoint of Women

Liberal political theory speaks of human rights; Marxist political theory speaks of class conflict. Feminist theorists have used the concept of women's standpoint as a way of criticizing the abstractness and overinclusiveness of such male-generated categories that conceal the special nature of women's oppression. As Sandra Bartky has pointed out, however, the concept of women's standpoint is itself overinclusive and abstract if it presupposes that all or most women share a common social location.[75] From what I have said so far, it may seem as though socialist feminism, whose political analysis stresses the differences in women's social experience, is developing an epistemology that obscures those differences. If socialist feminist epistemology is accepted, then knowledge must be reconstructed from the standpoint of women. But do all women really occupy the same standpoint? And if they do not, which women occupy the standpoint that is most advantageous?

Until recently, socialist feminist theorists have been preoccupied primarily with establishing that women indeed have a distinct epistemological standpoint.

386 Feminist Politics and Epistemology: Justifying Feminist Theory

Occasionally they have shown some awareness that women's different experiences generate perceptions of reality that differ significantly from each other as well as sharing certain common features. Dorothy Smith, for instance, remarks: "To begin from (women's) standpoint does not imply a common viewpoint among women. What we have in common is that organization of social relations which has accomplished our exclusion."[76] Only very recently, however, have socialist feminist theorists begun considering seriously the epistemological consequences of the differences as well as the commonalities in women's lives.

Sandra Harding points out that "We theory-makers are our own subject/objects but not a very historically representative part of 'women.' "[77] She suggests that contemporary feminist theory is likely to be biased itself by its predominantly white, middle-class origins. White middle-class women, for instance, are likely to experience their family life as a source of oppression and to make generalizations about "the family" that are quite incongruent with the experience of women in "cultures of resistance," for whom the family may be a source of individual and collective strength. Harding suggests, however, that the differences in women's experience need not be a source of division and weakness. If we learn how to use them, she claims, these differences can be a "scientific and political resource" for feminism. Her idea is not that feminist theory should reflect only the experience of a single group of women, presumably of the most oppressed; for instance, feminist theory does not have to be grounded only on the experience of physically challenged Jewish lesbians of color. Women's oppression is constantly changing in form and these forms cannot be ranked. Consequently, we cannot identify the standpoint of women with the standpoint of physically challenged women, or of lesbian women, or of women of color or of colonized or immigrant women. For each of these overlapping groups of women, some aspects of reality may be clearly visible and others may be blurred. A representation of reality from the standpoint of women must draw on the variety of all women's experience.

In order to do this, a way must be found in which all groups of women can participate in building theory. Historically, working-class women and women of color have been excluded from intellectual work. This exclusion must be challenged. Working-class women, women of color, and other historically silenced women must be enabled to participate as subjects as well as objects in feminist theorizing. At first it may be impossible for such women to work collectively with middle-class white/Anglo women. Maria Lugones writes: "We cannot talk to you in our language because you do not understand it. . . . The power of white/Anglo women vis-à-vis Hispanas and Black women is in inverse proportion to their working knowledge of each other."[78]

Because of their ignorance, white/Anglo women who try to do theory with women of color inevitably disrupt the dialogue. Before they can contribute to a collective dialogue, they need to "know the text," to have become familiar with an alternative way of viewing the world. To acquire such understanding is not easy:

> You need to learn to become unintrusive, unimportant, patient to the point of tears, while at the same time open to learning any possible lessons. You will also have to come to terms with the sense of alienation, of not belonging, of having your world thoroughly disrupted, having it criticized and scrutinized from the point of view of those who have been harmed by it, having important concepts central to it dismissed, being

viewed with mistrust, being seen as of no consequence except as an object of mistrust.[79]

As we saw earlier, the construction of a systematic theoretical alternative to prevailing ways of interpreting the world is an achievement linked inseparably with a transformation of power relations. Only when women are free from domination will they have access to the resources necessary to construct a systematic and fully comprehensive view of the world from the standpoint of women. In the meantime, within a class-divided and racist society, different groups of women inevitably have unequal opportunities to speak and to be heard. For this reason, the goal that women should begin to theorize together is itself a political goal and to succeed in collective theorizing would be itself a political achievement. Women who can theorize together can work together politically; indeed, in theorizing together they are already doing one kind of political work.

In beginning the scientific reconstruction of the world from their own standpoint, women must draw on the experiences of all women. As they do so, their representation of reality will become increasingly adequate—and its adequacy will be tested constantly by its usefulness in helping women to transform that reality. Since women cannot transform reality alone, they must also find ways to work politically with men without being dominated by them and men may even be able to contribute to women's theoretical work. To do so, however, men will have to learn women's "text," a process that will require at least as much humility and commitment as that needed by white/Anglo women to understand the experience of women of color. Even when men contribute to the construction of a systematic alternative to the dominant world view, it is still accurate to describe this alternative as a representation of reality from the standpoint of women. As we have seen, the socialist feminist conception of the standpoint of women does not refer to a perspective that is immediately available to all and only to women. Instead, it refers to a way of conceptualizing reality that reflects women's interests and values and draws on women's own interpretation of their own experience. Women's standpoint offers a perspective on reality that is accessible in principle to men as well as to women, although a materialist epistemology predicts that men will find it more difficult than women to comprehend this perspective and that widespread male acceptance of it will require political as well as theoretical struggle.

The concept of women's standpoint is complex and is still being developed. It does not offer a one-dimensional yardstick against which the adequacy of competing claims to knowledge can be measured mechanically. Even though it provides fairly specific interpretations of the generally accepted criteria of theoretical adequacy, there is still room for discretion and disagreement over how those interpretations should be applied—as there is over the applicability of any concept. Moreover, all feminist theory can find some justification for maintaining that it represents the standpoint of women. In spite of this unavoidable looseness, I think that the concept of women's standpoint is sufficiently specific to provide a way of evaluating the real strengths and weaknesses of the feminist theories presently available. In particular, I think that it provides a way of justifying the socialist feminist approach to theory and of indicating further directions for theoretical development.

Liberal feminist theory constitutes the first attempt to represent reality from the standpoint of women and the importance of this contribution cannot be overestimated. As we saw in earlier chapters, however, liberal feminism is still committed to the conceptual framework of traditional liberal theory, a framework that maintains rigid distinctions between mind and body, reason and emotion, fact and value, and public and private. Although apparently gender-neutral, these dichotomies justify a social system that perpetuates the subordination of women to men. For instance, they exclude from political consideration precisely that "private sphere" into which women historically have been relegated. Liberal feminism rests on an abstract conception of human nature that minimizes the importance of such "accidental" properties as class, sex, color and age. It focuses on a commitment to so-called human values that obscures the real conflict of interest between the oppressors and the oppressed and especially between women and men. Viewed from the standpoint of women, liberal feminism is not impartial, comprehensive nor conformable with the experience of many groups of women. It is therefore inadequate as a feminist theory.

Although traditional Marxism is in many ways a contrast with liberalism, it shares some of the same assumptions. Like liberalism, traditional Marxism assumes that certain activities, such as childbearing and -rearing, housework and sexual activity, are more "natural" and less "human" than the making of physical objects. Like liberalism, therefore, although in a different way, traditional Marxism excludes these activities from serious political consideration by excluding them from the realm of political economy. Like liberalism's categories, the categories of traditionl Marxism are apparently gender-neutral and, like those of liberalism, they divert attention away from men's domination of women. From the standpoint of women, therefore, traditional interpretations of Marxism are also inadequate as feminist theory. Rather than being impartial, they promote masculine interests; rather than being comprehensive, they systematically exclude important aspects of human life; and rather than being tested in experience, they disregard the experience of women.

Radical feminism is the first theory to recognize explicitly the need for a total reconceptualization of reality from the standpoint of women. It demonstrates the concealed masculine bias in the conceptual frameworks and dualisms that traditional political theory has used to justify the subordination of women. Its insight that the personal is political provides the basis for a political theory that is truly comprehensive rather than arbitrarily excluding "women's sphere". Radical feminism expresses the changes of attitude and consciousness that are needed to represent reality from the standpoint of women. In constructing this representation, however, many versions of American radical feminism are held back by assumptions unconsciously absorbed from the dominant culture: their theory shows tendencies toward biologism, idealism and toward the false universalization of women's experience. The effect of these tendencies is to minimize the effects of racism, classism and imperialism on women's lives, to encourage giving priority to "cultural" efforts to bring about social change and to eternalize the conflict of interest between women and men. As it currently exists in the United States, therefore, radical feminist theory tends to represent the standpoint only of certain relatively privileged women, rather than of all women. Nevertheless, if radical feminists were to recognize and explicitly renounce the assumptions that I have identified, as some are beginning to do, it is probable that radical feminist insights could be elaborated into a systematic reconceptualization of the world that truly represented the standpoint of women.

Such a development, in effect, is the theoretical project of socialist feminism. Since I have distinguished between radical and socialist feminism primarily in terms of their different methods, a change in the methodological assumptions of radical feminism may make this distinction no longer tenable. In the meantime,

I think that socialist feminism offers the best available representation of reality from the standpoint of women. Its ideals and categories are designed to overcome the narrowness and masculine bias of prevailing theory by drawing directly on women's experience of their lives and labor. As we have seen, the socialist feminist analysis is incomplete and leaves many questions unanswered. Even so, it offers us the vision of a new society based on a much more comprehensive and less biased conception of what constitutes fully human activity.

> What we desire and need is not only "to hunt in the morning, fish in the afternoon, rear cattle in the evening, criticise after dinner . . . without ever becoming hunter, fisher . . . , shepherd, or critic." We also desire and need sometimes to cook and clean, sometimes to make babies and raise children, and often, spontaneously, to play with our bodies, with ourselves, and with other women, men, and children, without even becoming "only a housewife", somebody's mother, "the head of the household", or perpetual children.[80]

Socialist feminism shows that to reconstruct reality from the standpoint of women requires a far more total transformation of our society and of ourselves than is dreamt of by a masculinist philosophy.

Notes

1. On my view of the integral connection between politics and science, values and facts, this division of academic labor misleads us about the necessarily scientific aspects of moral and political theory and about the normative components of science. For ease of exposition, however, I shall speak in this paragraph as though it were possible to make a sharp distinction between moral and political theory, on the one hand, and scientific theory, on the other.

2. Contemporary liberal theorists who are influential, systematic and in some ways innovative include John Rawls, *A Theory of Justice* (Cambridge: Harvard University Press, 1971); Robert Nozick, *Anarchy, State, and Utopia* (New York: Basic Books, 1974); and Ronald Dworkin, *Taking Rights Seriously* (Cambridge: Harvard University Press, 1978).

3. This idea goes back to David Hume, *Treatise of Human Nature*, L. A. Selby-Bigge, ed. (Oxford, 1888), esp. pp. 574-84; and to Adam Smith, *The Theory of Moral Sentiments*, in L. A. Selby-Bigge, *British Moralists*, vol. 1 (Oxford, 1897), pp. 257-77. Contemporary versions can be found in Roderick Firth, "Ethical Absolutism and the Ideal Observer," *Philosophy and Phenomenological Research* 12 (1952); and in F. C. Sharp, *Good and Ill Will* (Chicago: University of Chicago Press, 1950). See also C. D. Broad, "Some Reflections on Moral-Sense Theories in Ethics," *Proceedings of the Aristotelian Society* 45 (1944-45); and W. K. Kneale, "Objectivity in Morals," *Philosophy* 25 (1950).

4. Rawls, *A Theory of Justice*, esp. pp. 260-63 and 584.

5. Bruce A. Ackerman, *Social Justice in the Liberal State* (New Haven, Conn.: Yale University Press, 1980).

6. On some interpretations of Marxism, the physical or "hard" sciences are exempted from this characterization. They are seen as being "objectively" true, and their fundamental categories are not thought to be tied to the social context from which they emerged. While the writings of Marx and Engels provide some evidence to support this positivistic interpretation, I believe that such an interpretation runs counter to the overriding epistemological orientation of Marxism. In making this claim, I am influenced by the work of many authors, including R. M. Young, " 'Non-Scientific' Factors in the Darwinian Debate," *Actes du. XIIᵉ Congres International d'Histoire des Sciences Naturelles et de la Biologie*, vol. 8 (Paris, 1971), pp. 221-26; Sandra Harding, "Does Objectivity in Social

Science Require Value-Neutrality?" *Soundings* 60, no. 4, and "Four Contributions Values Can Make to the Objectivity of Social Science," in Peter Asquith and Ian Hacking, eds., *PSA 1978, vol. 1,* (East Lansing: Philosophy of Science Association, 1978); Alfred Sohn-Rethel, *Intellectual and Manual Labour: A Critique of Epistemology* (London: Macmillan & Co., 1978); Norman Diamond, "The Politics of Scientific Conceptualization in Les Levidow and Bob Young, eds., *Science, Technology and the Labour Process,* Marxist Studies, Volume 1 (London: CSE Books, 1981), pp. 32-45.

7. Karl Marx and Frederick Engels, *The German Ideology* (New York: International Publishers, 1970), p. 64.

8. Bertell Ollman, *Alienation: Marx's Conception of Man in Capitalist Society* (New York: Cambridge University Press, 1976), p. 196.

9. Sohn-Rethel, *Intellectual and Manual Labour.* An easier introduction to Sohn-Rethel's work can be found in his essay "Science as Alienated Consciousness," *Radical Science Journal* no. 2/3 (1975):65-101.

10. R. M. Young, "Who Cares About Objectivity? - And Why" (unpublished)

11. Alvin Gouldner, "Anti-Minotaur: The Myth of a Value Free Sociology," in M. Stein and A. Vidrich, eds., *Sociology on Trial,* (Englewood Cliffs, N.J.: Prentice-Hall, 1963).

12. Sohn-Rethel, "Science as Alienated Consciousness", p. 79.

13. Karl Marx, *Capital,* volume 1 (New York: International Publishers, 1967), p. 176. I owe this and the following example to Nancy Hartsock. As will become obvious shortly, I am much indebted to Hartsock's work in this area.

14. Ibid., p. 645.

15. The following summary of Marxist theories of truth draws on the article by Peter Binns, "The Marxist Theory of Truth," *Radical Philosophy,* Spring 1973, pp. 3-9.

16. G. Lukács, "Reification and the Consciousness of the Proletariat," in Lukács, *History and Class Consciousness: Studies in Marxist Dialectics,* trans. by Rodney Livingstone (Cambridge: MIT Press, 1971). The following brief exposition of Lukács's view draws on Sandra Harding's "Philosophy and History of Science as Patriarchal Oral History" (unpublished).

17. Lukács, *History and Class Consciousness,* p. 165.

18. Ibid., p. 177 (italics in original).

19. Barbara Winslow, "Women's Alienation and Revolutionary Politics (a review of Anne Foreman, *Femininity as Alienation) International Socialism* 4 (Spring 1979):11-12.

20. Ibid., p. 9.

21. S. K. Lindemann, "A Feminist Method of Inquiry" (unpublished), pp. 3-4 of typescript.

22. Nancy Hartsock, "Feminist Theory and the Development of Revolutionary Strategy," in Zillah R. Eisenstein, ed., *Capitalist Patriarchy and the Case for Socialist Feminism,* (New York: Monthly Review Press, 1979), p. 59.

23. I have heard radical feminists claim that if a woman's intuition is particularly well developed she may be a witch, one whom radical feminists view as an especially wise woman.

24. "We are proud of the female culture of emotion, intuition, love, personal relationships, etc., as the most essential human characteristics." Barbara Burris in agreement with Kathy Barry, Terry Moore, Joann DeLor, Joann Parent, Cate Stadelman, "The Fourth World Manifesto," in Anne Koedt, Ellen Levine, and Anita Rapone, eds., *Radical Feminism* (New York: Quadrangle, 1973), p. 355.

25. Carol P. Christ, *Diving Deep and Surfacing: Women Writers on Spiritual Quest* (Boston: Beacon Press, 1980), p. 13.

26. Susan Griffin, *Woman and Nature: The Roaring inside Her* (New York: Harper Colophon, 1980), p. 226.

27. The development of these and other powers is foreseen in Sally Miller Gearhart's popular novel *The Wanderground: Stories of the Hill Women* (Watertown, Mass.: Persephone Press, 1979).

28. Robin Morgan, *Going Too Far: The Personal Chronicle of a Feminist* (New York: Random House, 1977), p. 15. This quotation from Morgan is cited by Gerri Perreault

in her groundbreaking paper "Futuristic World Views: Modern Physics and Feminism. Implications for Teaching/Learning in Higher Education," a paper presented at the Second Annual Conference of The World Future Society—Educational Section, October 18, 1979. The paper was also read at the National Women's Studies Association Second National Conference, Indiana University, Bloomington, May 16-20, 1980. Much of the inspiration for this section comes from Perreault, and I am extremely grateful to her for allowing me to draw on her work.

29. Griffin, *Women and Nature,* p. 107.

30. Mary Daly, *Gyn-Ecology: The Metaethics of Radical Feminism* (Boston: Beacon Press, 1978), p. 11.

31. Mary Daly, *Beyond God the Father: Toward a Philosophy of Women's Liberation* (Boston: Beacon Press, 1973), pp. 42-43.

32. Nancy Hartsock, "Fundamental Feminism: Process and Perspective," *Quest: A Feminist Quarterly* 2, no. 2 (Fall 1975):73.

33. Christ, *Diving Deep and Surfacing,* p. 122.

34. Perreault, "Futuristic World Views," pp. 15-16.

35. Daly, *Beyond God the Father,* p. 43.

36. Susan Griffin, *Rape: The Power of Consciousness* (San Francisco: Harper & Row, 1979), p. 31.

37. Morgan, *Going Too Far,* p. 14.

38. Daly, *Gyn-Ecology,* p. 401.

39. Ibid., p. 405.

40. Perreault, "Futuristic World Views." In making this claim, Perreault draws heavily on the work of Fritjof Capra in *The Tao of Physics* (New York: Bantam, 1977). Capra presents modern physics as constructing a model of reality that is in fundamental opposition to the model embodied in Newtonian physics. The Newtonian world view is dualistic, postulating a complete break between spirit and matter. It conceives of spirit as self-moving, but matter is thought to consist of discrete, solid and inert atoms moved only by external forces. These atoms interact in a mechanistic way, and they are governed by exact and absolute causal laws, the formulation of which is the job of the physical sciences. Space is three-dimensional and time is one-dimensional, linear and separate from space. On this atomistic conception of the world, scientists are separate from the world they observe, and their theories do not affect its properties. The world view of modern physics, by contrast, is non-dualistic. At the subatomic level, mass is a form of energy (Einstein's famous formula, $e = mc^2$, expresses the relation between mass and energy), and mass and energy change unceasingly into each other. The elementary particles of modern physics are not solid and inert building blocks. At the subatomic level, matter has only "tendencies to exist," tendencies which are expressed as mathematical probabilities. The mathematical structures used to describe these probabilities are the same as the mathematical structures used to describe waves, and subatomic elements can be understood either as particles or as waves. Because particles are also waves, atomic matter is "fundamentally restless," in motion rather than inert. According to relativity theory, space and time are not independent of each other but exist in a four-dimensional continuum called space-time. Reality is not a collection of independent parts but a "complicated web of relations between the various parts of a unified whole" (*The Tao of Physics,* p. 23). Cf. also Robin Morgan, *The Anatomy of Freedom: Feminism, Physics, and Global Politics* (New York: Doubleday/Anchor, 1982). An extract from this book, "A Quantum Leap in Feminist Theory," was published in *Ms.,* December 1982, 101-106.

41. Fritjof Capra in a lecture entitled "Physics, Mysticism and Social Change" delivered at Xavier University, Cincinnati, on 23 March 1981.

42. Jade River, "Witchcraft: A Political View," talk given at conference on Women's Spirituality, Cincinnati, 22 March 1981. River draws heavily on Margot Adler, *Drawing Down the Moon* (Boston, Mass.: Beacon Press, 1979).

43. Capra, "Physics, Mysticism and Social Change."

44. Starhawk, *The Spiral Dance: A Rebirth of the Religion of the Great Goddess* (San Francisco: Harper & Row, 1979).

45. Daly, *Gyn-Ecology,* p. 386.

46. Elizabeth Fee, "Is Feminism a Threat to Scientific Objectivity?" *International Journal of Women's Studies* 4, pp. 378-92. Jane Flax, "Political Philosophy and the Patriarchal Unconscious: A Psychoanalytic Perspective on Epistemology and Metaphysics," forthcoming in M. Hintikka and S. Harding, eds., *Discovering Reality: Feminist Perspectives on Epistemology, Metaphysics, Methodology and the Philosophy of Science* (Dordrecht: Reidel, 1983). Sandra Harding, "The Norms of Social Inquiry and Masculine Experience," in P. D. Asquith and R. N. Giere, eds., *PSA 1980*, Vol. II (East Lansing, Mich.: Philosophy of Science Association); "The Discovery of the Sex/Gender System Calls for a Strong Program for Epistemology," in Hintikka and Harding, eds., *Discovering Reality;* "Is Gender a Variable in Conceptions of Rationality? A Survey of the Issues," *Dialectica* 36, nos. 2-3 (1982), to be reprinted in C. Gould, ed., *Beyond Domination: New Perspectives on Women and Philosophy* (Totowa, N.J.: Rowman & Allanheld, forthcoming); "Towards a Reflexive Feminist Theory" (unpublished). Nancy Hartsock, "Social Life and Social Science: The Significance of the Naturalist/Intentionalist Dispute," *PSA 1980* (in press); "The Feminist Standpoint: Developing the Ground for a Specifically Feminist Historical Materialism," in Hintikka and Harding, eds., *Discovering Reality.* Evelyn Fox Keller, "Gender and Science," *Psychoanalysis and Contemporary Thought,* reprinted in Hintikka and Harding, eds., *Discovering Reality;* "Feminism and Science" (unpublished, 1981). Dorothy Smith, "Women's Perspective as a Radical Critique of Sociology," *Sociological Inquiry* 44 (1974); "Some Implications of a Sociology for Women," in N. Glazer and H. Waehrer, eds., *Woman in a Manmade World: A Socioeconomic Handbook* (Chicago, Rand-McNally, 1977); "A Sociology for Women," in *The Prism of Sex: Essays in the Sociology of Knowledge* (Madison: University of Wisconsin Press, 1979).

47. An introduction to some of these critiques is provided by Dale Spender, ed., *Men's Studies Modified: The Impact of Feminism on the Academic Disciplines* (Oxford & New York: Pergamon Press, 1981). Many of the following examples have been brought to my attention by Sandra Harding, to whose work in this area I am much indebted. Harding has been particularly generous in helping me to clarify my views about the issues dealt with in this chapter.

48. Joan Kelly-Gadol, "Did Women Have a Renaissance?" in Renate Bridenthal and Claudia Koonz, eds., *Becoming Visible: Women in European History* (Boston, Mass.: Houghton Mifflin, 1977).

49. A variety of examples is cited by Elizabeth Fisher in the first two chapters of her *Woman's Creation: Sexual Evolution and the Shaping of Society* (New York: McGraw-Hill, 1979). More examples are given by Donna Haraway in her "Animal Sociology and a Natural Economy of the Body Politic," Parts I and II in *Signs: Journal of Women in Culture and Society,* Special Issue on Women, Science and Society 4, no. 1 (Autumn 1978). See also Haraway's "The Biological Enterprise: Sex, Mind, and Profit from Human Engineering to Sociobiology," in *Radical History Review* 20 (Spring/Summer 1979). See also Lila Leibowitz, " 'Universals' and Male Dominance Among Primates: A Critical Examination," and Ruth Bleier, "Social and Political Bias in Science: An Examination of Animal Studies and their Generalizations to Human Behavior and Evolution," both in Ruth Hubbard and Marian Lowe, eds., *Genes and Gender II* (Staten Island, N.Y.: Gordian Press, 1979).

50. Carol Gilligan, "In a Different Voice: Women's Conceptions of Self and of Morality," *Harvard Educational Review* 47, no. 4 (November 1977). See also Gilligan's "Woman's Place in Man's Life Cycle," *Harvard Educational Review* 49, no. 4 (November 1979). Also Gilligan, *In a Different Voice: Psychological Theory and Women's Development* (Cambridge: Harvard University Press, 1982).

51. Carolyn N. Merchant, *The Death of Nature: Women, Ecology, and the Scientific Revolution* (San Francisco: Harper & Row, 1980). Cf. Brian Easlea, *Witch-hunting, Magic and the New Philosophy: An Introduction to Debates of the Scientific Revolution, 1450-1750* (Brighton: Harvester Press, 1980), p. 152: "The *emboîtment* mechanical philosophy was clearly a sternly masculine one. It may not have been, after all, a statement of no moment when in 1664 Henry Oldenburg, the Royal Society's Secretary, asserted that its business was to raise 'a Masculine Philosophy.' "

52. Fee, "Is Feminism a Threat to Scientific Objectivity?" p. 388.

53. Smith, "A Sociology for Women," p. 166.

54. Ibid., p. 168.

55. Hartsock, "The Feminist Standpoint," p. 24 of typescript.

56. D. W. Winnicott, *The Maturational Processes and the Facilitating Environment* (New York: International Universities Press, 1965); Margaret Mahler, Fred Pine, and Anni Bergman, *The Psychological Birth of the Human Infant* (New York: Basic Books, 1975); H. Guntrip, *Personality Structure* and also his *Psychoanalytic Theory, Therapy and The Self* (New York: Basic Books, 1971). My exposition of psychoanalytic object-relations theory draws heavily on the work of Jane Flax, who has developed the feminist implications of this theory. See especially Jane Flax, "Political Philosophy and the Patriarchal Unconscious: A Psychoanalytic Perspective on Epistemology and Metaphysics," in Hinkikka and Harding, eds., *Discovering Reality.*

57. Flax, "Political Philosophy and the Patriarchal Unconscious," pp. 9-10 of typescript.

58. Harding, "Is Gender a Variable in Conceptions of Rationality?"

59. Flax, "Political Philosophy and the Patriarchal Unconscious"; Hartsock, "The Feminist Standpoint."

60. Flax, "Political Philosophy and the Patriarchal Unconscious," p. 6.

61. See the essays in Julia A. Sherman and Evelyn Torton Beck, eds., *The Prism of Sex: Essays in the Sociology of Knowledge* (Madison: University of Wisconsin Press, 1977); Marcia Millman and Rosabeth Moss Kanter, eds., *Another Voice: Feminist Perspectives on Social Life and Social Science* (New York: Anchor Books, 1975); Shirley Ardener, ed., *Perceiving Women* (New York: Halstead Press, 1975). A less academic account is Anne Wilson Schaef's *Women's Reality: An Emerging Female System in the White Male Society* (Minneapolis: Winston Press, 1981). This book is currently enjoying considerable popular success.

62. Fee, "Is Feminism a Threat to Scientific Objectivity?", p. 389.

63. Hartsock, "The Feminist Standpoint," p. 23.

64. Ibid., p. 17.

65. Tim Diamond pointed this out to me.

66. Barbara Mehrhof and Pamela Kearon, "Rape: An Act of Terror," in Anne Koedt, Ellen Levine, and Anita Rapone, eds., *Radical Feminism* (New York: Quadrangle, 1973), p. 233.

67. Deirdre English, "The War Against Choice: Inside the Antiabortion Movement," *Mother Jones* 6, no. 11 (February/March 1981):28.

68. Ibid.

69. *Divorce, Child Custody and Child Support,* Current Population Reports, Special Studies Ser. P-23, No. 84, U.S. Department of Commerce, Bureau of the Census, Superintendant of Documents, U.S. G.P.O., Washington, D.C. 20402. English reports that more than 50 percent of fathers default within the first year after divorce.

70. English, "The War Against Choice," p. 28.

71. Sandra Bartky suggested this in private correspondence.

72. Flax, "Political Philosophy and the Patriarchal Unconscious," p. 37.

73. Haraway, "The Biological Enterprise," pp. 232-33.

74. Sandra Harding suggests that the distinctive insights of contemporary feminism became possible only with the recent emergence of what she provisionally calls "wage-laboring mothers." Only these insights could generate the concept of the standpoint of women. Harding, "Towards a Reflexive Feminist Theory."

75. Sandra Bartky, private correspondence. Maria Lugones and E. V. Spelman make a similar criticism of prevailing interpretations of the concept of speaking in "the woman's voice," a concept closely related to the concept of women's standpoint. See Lugones and Spelman, "Have We Got a Theory for You! Feminist Theory, Cultural Imperialism and the Woman's Voice," paper read to the Tenth Anniversary Conference of the Eastern Division of the Society for Women in Philosophy, Northampton, Massachusetts, October 1982. Alan Soble is another critic of the concept of women's standpoint or the perspective of women because he claims that it reifies women. He argues that reification can be avoided only by taking into account the variety of "racial ethnic, political, geographical and religious factors" that distinguish women from each other. Once this is done, he

argues, we shall see that "there is no such thing as 'the perspective of women.' " Alan Soble, "Feminist Epistemology and Women Scientists," *Metaphilosophy* (1983) (in press), page 9 of typescript.

76. Smith, "A Sociology for Women," p. 163.

77. Harding, "Towards a Reflexive Feminist Theory," p. 17 of typescript.

78. Lugones and Spelman, "Have We Got a Theory for You!", pp. 7, 20 of typescript.

79. Ibid., p. 22.

80. Muriel Dimen, "Toward the Reconstruction of Sexuality", forthcoming in *Social Text*, pp. 22-23 of typescript. Available from 700 W. Badger Rd., Suite 101, Madison, WI 53713.

Index

Abstract individualism. *See* Individualism, abstract

Abortion: abolition of restrictions on, 180, 198 controlled by patriarchy, 257; economic access to, 186; opposition to legalization, 382, 383; as reform measure, 291; as a right, 238

Abuse: child, 201, 314; domestic, 186, 238; physical, 77, 226, 241, 332; wife, 94, 219, 222, 237. *See also* Harassment; Rape; Violence

Ackerman, Bruce, 357

Activism: radical feminist, 289; socialist feminist, 163

Activity, productive, 53–59, 75, 211, 212, 216; equation with men's work, 243; and Marxist epistemology, 358; as praxis, 208; procreation as, 303; under socialism, 225; socialist feminist conception of, 303, 304; and women's nature, 63

Adequacy, theoretical, 7, 9, 18, 19, 143, 353–89; and feminist political economy, 160–62; identifying criteria for, 31, 354; liberal criteria for, 31, 355–58; Marxist criteria for, 358–64; radical feminist criteria for, 364–69; socialist feminist criteria for, 150, 369–77, 385; standpoint of women as condition for, 369–77, 377–85

Adolescence, 315

Affinity group, 284

Affirmative action, 183, 190–93, 237

Age, abolition of distinctions based on, 67. *See also* Children

Aggression, 104, 107–8

Agnosticism, liberal, 38, 128, 174, 195. *See also* Autonomy, of empirical desires; Scepticism

Alienation, 57–59, 216; central to socialist feminist analysis, 307–17; concept as male-biased, 131; feminity as, 308, 316; as moral foundation in Marxist critique, 59; in motherhood, 310–15; as new theoretical framework, 316–17; from non-human nature, 217; from other human beings, 216; paradigm case of, 308; revision by socialist feminists, 131–32, 307–8; sexual, 309; and women in paid labor, 217

Alliance Against Sexual Coercion, 328

Alpert, Jane, 94–95

Althusserian Marxism, 98

Altruism, 18, 31, 45, 50 **n.**43

Anarcha-feminism, 11, 228

Anarchism: and alternative institutions, 280, 281; as critique of liberal feminism, 202–3; elements in four conceptions, 11; similarity to radical feminism, 203, 255, 280–82; and social organization, 282; vision of revolution, 280–81

Androcentrism, 22, 47, 79, 169, 186

Androgyny, 67–69, 132; as conception of human nature, 85–88; as inadequate ideal, 88, 97; as inappropriate political objective, 88; as liberal feminist ideal, 38–39; as radical feminist ideal, 87; as reconceived by Dworkin, 100

Angry Women, 284

Anthropology, political, 9, 72, 73, 81 **n.**49, 149

Antifeminist women, 382–83

Aptheker, Louanna, 262

Aristotle, 28, 36, 371

Astell, Mary, 27

Atkinson, Ti-Grace, 101, 267, 272

Authoritarian character structure, 71, 343

liberal feminist, 355–58; Marxist, 359–60, 362; and political philosophy, 9, 16; radical feminist, 364–69; socialist feminist, 369–77, 384–85
Equal distribution, 214
Equality, 5; concept as critique, 16; economic dimension of, 17; "formal," 47; ideology of, 286; liberal conception of, 17, 39, 42, 46, 193; in liberal feminist theory, 176, 178, 181, 182, 193–94; in Marxist theory, 230, 361; as new democratic ideal, 4; as philosophical question, 7, 15; in public life, 178; in socialist feminist theory, 154; as traditional concern of political philosophy, 6–7; for women, 7
Equal Rights Amendment (ERA), 47, 182
Equal opportunity, 37, 39, 61, 62, 170, 176, 181, 183, 196, 228, 357; as challenge to individual liberty, 195; as contradictory ideal, 62; impossibility of, in capitalism, 201; and meritocracy, 193–97
ERA. *See* Equal Rights Amendment
Essence, human, 32, 38, 52, 53, 57
Ethnicity, 77
Evolution, biological, 55
Experience, sensory, 356
Experience, women's: as basis of epistemology, 381; commonalities in, 12, 77–78; diversity and complexity of, 118; as inadequate theory base, 383; universalization of, 388; variations· in, 8, 66, 139, 386
Exploitation, 58, 71, 73; abolition of, 306; as relation of capitalist and worker, 215; of women's labor, 155, 157
Ezorsky, Gertrude, 196

False consciousness. *See* Consciousness, false
Family, 4, 27, 64–69, 70–74, 241, 386; as center of private realm, 70, 144, 146, 199; as consumers, 244; critiqued by middle-class women, 241; and emergence of feminism, 3; as historically variant, 128–29; ideology of, 153; liberal feminist critique of, 199, 200; Marxist view of, 223–24; and need for alternatives to, 239–40, 336–38; as oppressive, 239, 241; revolutionary goals for, 337–38; and sexual division of labor, 64, 68; transformation under socialism, 226; values of, 337
Farley, Lin, 328
Farrow, Lynne, 280, 288, 294
Fee, Elizabeth, 370, 372, 376
Feelings. *See* Emotion, and reason
Female Sexual Slavery (Barry), 263

Feminine psychology, 38, 140. *See also* Femininity; Freudian theory; Psychoanalysis
Femininity: abolition of, 317, 340; as alienation, 308, 316; and androgyny, 87–88; contemporary definition of, 316; in personality development, 92, 114, 140, 154, 374–76; as influenced by social relations, 130
Feminism: anarchist, 11, 228; black, 10–11; cultural, 84, 104; emergence of organized, 3–4; lesbian, 8, 11, 84, 310; materialist, 22, 87, 88, 98, 99, 366; origin of term, 5; and political philosophy, 3–23; and reconstruction of theories, 12–13; and women's liberation, 5–6. *See also* Liberal feminism; Liberation, women's; Marxism, traditional; Radical feminism; Socialist feminism
"Feminists, The," 86, 285
Ferguson, Ann, 128, 140–141, 156; on connection of racism, sexism, and capitalism, 344; on goals for socialist feminist households, 337–38
Firestone, Shulamith, 85, 267; on abolition of childhood, 154; as influenced by Marxism, 90; on masculinity and femininity, 258; reinterpretation of Freud, 92; revision of historical materialism, 90–91; on romantic love, 265; unpopularity of work, 93
Fisher, Berenice, 233–34
Flax, Jane, 126, 370, 375, 383
Folbre, Nancy, 140–41, 156
Foreman, Ann, 128; on femininity as alienation, 316; on need for independent women's organizations, 332; on the personal and political, 342–43
Freedom, 228, 361; labor as, 58; liberal conception of, 33–35, 39, 43, 62, 210–11; liberal feminist conception of, 306; Marxist conception of, 61–62, 209–13, 215, 304–6; necessity for sexual, 322; socialist feminist conception of, 154, 304, 306; as traditional concern of political philosophy, 6–7
Freedom, reproductive, 318–24; demand for, 201; historical and materialist view of, 319; as revolutionary demand, 319; socialist feminist concept of, 318, 320
Frankfurt School, 127
French feminists, 84, 98–100, 107, 120 **n.**34, 366
French, Marilyn, 334
Freudian theory: adaptation of (Rubin), 140; compatibility with historical materialism, 127; debiologizing of, 126–27; model of

human mind, 18; as reinterpreted by Firestone, 92; use of as problematic, 151
Freud/Marx synthesis, 166 **n.**70
Freud, Sigmund, 37, 126. *See also* Freudian theory; Psychoanalysis; Psychology
Friedan, Betty, 37, 178
Friere, Paulo, 154
Fulfilment, human, 19, 20, 41, 131, 174, 188, 190, 244. *See also* Self-fulfilment; Self-realization
Functionalism, Marxist, 71
Furies collective, 118

Gamarnikow, Eva, 325
Gardner, Kay, 294
Gay males, 69, 227, 238
Gearhart, Sally, 97, 253
Gender, 21, 22, 23 **n.**8, 47, 68; abolition of, 67–68, 254, 317; bias, 78–79; blindness, 74, 77–78; in capitalist relations, 158; conflict, 77; and dialectical relation with sex, 112; identity, 69; invisibility of, 85; and male privilege, 86; norms of, 126, 374; psychoanalytic theory of, 374–75; as system of male domination, 85; as unjust, 39
German Ideology, The (Marx), 53, 68, 69, 75, 129, 138
Gibson, Mary, 41
Gilligan, Carol, 50 **n.**38, 372
Girlhood (Deutsch), 256
Gintis, Herbert, 141
Goldberg, Steven, 94, 107
Goldman, Emma, 233
Good, the: human, 6, 194; and human needs, 17
Good society, the, 15, 16, 17, 21, 45, 173, 207, 305, 340; liberal conception of, 33, 43, 174–75; liberal feminist vision of, 38–39; Marxist conception of, 51
Goods, social, 30, 31, 195
Gordon, Linda, 5, 323
Gramsci, Antonio, 151
Griffin, Susan, 252, 267, 366, 367, 380; on rape, 262; and rejection of reason, 115; on rejection of theory, 287–88; on women and non-human nature, 95–96
Grupo de afinidad (affinity group), 284
Guerilla theater, 283
Guérillères, Les, 103
Guntrip, Harry, 374
Gyn/Ecology (Daly), 104, 253

Haber, Barbara, 345–46
Harding, Sandra, 50 **n.**43, 370, 376; on the democratic ideal, 196–97; on feminist theory, 386; on meritocracy, 196–97; on procreation, 156; on scientific rationality, 375
Harassment, sexual, 86, 179, 221, 308, 331, 333; as concern of women's labor organizations, 327–28; as discrimination, 182; as functional to capitalism, 223, 227; ignored by Marxist organizations, 237, 238
Harraway, Donna, 384
Hartmann, Heidi, 71, 122 **n.**79, 331
Hartsock, Nancy, 50 **n.**35, 163 **n.**4, 370, 375, 376–77; on consciousness-raising method, 365; on restructuring labor process, 339; on women's work and epistemology, 373
Hayden, Delores, 338
Health: care, gendered structure of, 325, 335, 336; as concern of feminist businesses, 276, 278, 382; criteria of, 20; as revolutionary socialist issue, 236; women in medicine, 188
Hegel, G.W.F., 36
Hegemony, 44, 151, 333, 359
Heroes, women, 233–34
Heterosexual activity, 265
Heterosexual couple, 226–27
Heterosexual privilege, 273
Heterosexuality, 69, 78, 86, 290, 345; as buttress for patriarchy, 271–72; as compulsory, 105, 308, 318, 322, 323; as "normal" sexual expression, 227; as normative, 132, 140–41, 272; as oppressive to women, 266
Hierarchy: by gender, 254; minimization in radical feminist enterprises, 277, 278; as natural order, 33
Hobbes, Thomas, 29, 30, 90, 151, 280
Homemakers Organized for a More Equal Society (HOMES), 338
Homology, conjectural nature of, 108
Homophobia, 227
Homosexuality, 69, 140, 180, 223. *See also* Gay males; Lesbianism
Honor, women's, 261
Household work, 70, 72, 74–75, 77, 101, 177; and capitalism, 217; in contrast with industrial work, 145; effect of monogamy on organization of, 220; as form of praxis, 219; liberal feminist objection to, 198–99; organization of, 217–18; as outside public realm, 145, 237; pay for, 329; as privatized, 220; as professionalized, 170, 184–85, 197; as public, 220
Households, alternative, 240
Housework. *See* Household work
Houston Women's conference, 201
Human beings, production of, 152–55. *See also* Procreation

Lesbian Peoples: Material for a Dictionary
(Wittig and Zeig), 100
Lesbianfeminism, 8, 11, 84, 310
Lesbianism, 69, 128, 223, 271–75, 290, 386;
and heterosexism, 266; political definition
of, 272–73; as revolutionary, 273; and
sexual freedom, 227–28; as threat to male
supremacy, 105, 273; as unavailable option, 291, 292
Lesbians of color, 273, 291, 296, 386
Liberal feminism: contradictions in, 28; and
elimination of bias, 355–58; as false consciousness, 66; goal of, 35; Marxist opposition to, 197; and political values,
173–75; and standpoint of women, 388;
theoretical problems of, 39–47, 378; and
women's nature, 35–39; and women's
rights, 36
Liberalism, contemporary, 357
Liberalism, traditional: emergence with cap-
italoism, 27; and human nature, 28–33
Liberation: black, 5; gay, 5, 239; human,
62, 131; lesbian, 323; third world, 5;
women's, 52, 64, 70, 223, 229, 242, 289,
329, 364 / existential and religious conceptions of, 10 / and feminism, as terms,
5–6 / four conceptions of, 10–13 / and
political philosophy, 6–7 / vision of, 354
Liberties, civil, 27, 34, 35, 40, 174. *See also*
Civil rights; Rights
Liberty, 170, 178, 180, 181, 193, 195, 230;
worth of, 177
Life style, alternative, 239–40
Lindemann, Kate, 365
Lindsey, Karen, 264
Lloyd Thomas, D. A., 195, 196
Locke, John, 28, 29, 30, 32
Love, romantic, 345; as ideology, 219, 241,
286, 322; and women's oppression, 265
Lowe, Marian, 126
Lugones Maria, 386
Lukács, Georg, 362, 379
Luxembourg, Rosa, 233
Luxton, Meg, 312

Machiavelli, 255
MacKenzie, Laurie, 279
MacKinnon, Catharine, 105, 270
Mahler, Margaret, 374
Mainardi, Pat, 271
Male privilege, 86, 193, 237–38
Malthus, Thomas, 210
Manual/mental distinction: critique of, 187,
189–90; use of, to control women, 187–88;
in health care systems, 188
March, Artemis, 105
Markusen, Ann, 331

Marriage, 135, 138, 139; bourgeois, 222;
contracts for, 198, 199; of convenience,
246 **n**.48; and economic motivation, 226;
economic structure of, 218; as form of
female sexual slavery, 264–65; as historically variant, 128–29; ideology of, 153,
199, 264; and lack of analysis in Marxism,
222; monogamous, 65; "open," 239; as
oppressive, 271; pairing, 73; relations of,
217, 218, 219
Marx, Karl, 51–59, 63–64, 68–69, 71–72,
197; on alienation, 216; on capitalist society, 361; on communism, 215; on equal
distribution, 214; on equality, 214; Freud
synthesis, 166 **n**.70; on justice, 213, 214;
on labor as process, 208; on realm of
freedom, 209; on realm of necessity, 209;
on value of work, 209
Marxism, Althusserian, 98
Marxism, totalistic (Lukács), 362–63
Marxism, traditional, 8, 11, 51–52, 78; adequacy of vision, 208, 229; analysis of
women's oppression, 215–24; and human
nature, 51–82; political problematic in,
229–44; political values of, 207–15; praxis
as central concept in, 55; proposals for
social change, 224–28; and standpoint of
women, 388; theoretical adequacy, 358–64
Masculinism, 162, 384, 388
Masculinity, 130; abolition of, 340; and
androgyny, 87–88; contemporary definition of, 316; in personality development,
92, 140, 374–76; radical feminist characterization of, 114
Masters, William H., 89
Material base. *See* Base, material
Materialism: feminist, 87, 88; historical, 56,
60, 62–63, 73, 90–91, 124, 125, 127, 207;
Marxist, 52, 213
Maternal instinct, 256
Matriarchy, 73, 103
Mead, Margaret, 107
Means, and ends: in anarchist thought, 280;
inseparability of, 280, 339; as instrumental reason, 30; non-violence as, 294; and
praxis, 54; questions of, as normative,
16; rational argument as inadequate, 183;
strategies and goals, 16–17
Medicine, women in, 188. *See also* Health
care
Men: and children, 321–22; and learning
women's "text," 387; normative attributes, 250; and parenting, 128, 315, 337;
as potential co-revolutionaries with
women, 387. *See also* all categories per-
taining to maleness

Mensheviks, 231
Menstruation, 110, 121 **n.**70, 126, 377
Mental/manual distinction. *See* Manual/ mental distinction
Meritocracy, 181, 193–97
Mill, John Stuart, 32, 35, 37; on equal opportunity, 178; on the good life, 174; on natural differences in sexes, 38; on opportunity for women, 36; on "sympathetic selfishness," 31
Millett, Kate, 86, 265
Minority women, 190, 201. *See also* Blacks; Women, of color
Misogyny, 105, 259, 320–21
Mitchell, Juliet, 71, 124, 126, 223
Monogamy, 65–66, 219
Moral neutrality, 195; and political institutions, 41
Morality: capacity for, 31; development in children, 372, 373; differences between men's and women's, 50 **n.**38, 372; in liberal theory, 29, 30; liberal values of, 33; and women's factory work, 68
Morgan, Robin, 265, 367
Mother Jones, 233
Motherhood (Deutsch), 256
Motherhood: and alienation, 310–15; as basis of women's oppression, 259; choices about, 292, 321; conditions of, 257; and dependence on children, 314; forced, 144, 256–60, 270, 271, 287, 292, 293; ideology of, 144, 153, 199, 256–57, 286; isolation of, 313; and lesbians, 292, 318; organization of, 140; psychological qualities of, 94–95; as reproducing male dominance, 260; radical feminist emphasis on, 94–95, 259, 267, 291; single, 337; social relations of, 315; structure of, under patriarchy, 258
Music, women's, 294, 295
Myths of Male Dominance (Leacock), 81 **n.**49

Naming, 88, 155–62, 268, 366
Narcissism, feminine, 309
National Abortion Rights league (NARAL), 203 **n.**7
National Organization for Women (NOW), 893, 188
Nature, and culture, 96, 110–11
Nature, human: as ahistorical, 32, 117; basis for theory of, 18–21; competing conceptions of, 18–21; control of, 59, 69; and epistemology, 355; as historical product, 56, 303; and liberal feminism, 27–44; male bias in liberal theory of, 46–47; Marxist conception, 52–59, 105–6; nor-

mative elements in theory of, 20; and political philosophy, 15–23; problems for liberal theory of, 39–47; problems for Marxist conception of, 69–79; and socialist feminism, 123–67; as socially alterable, 304; and traditional liberalism, 28–33; transformation of, 54, 130, 132; and women's nature (*see* Nature, women's); universal characteristics in, 19
Nature, non-human: transformed by labor, 53–54, 60; women as closer to, 46
Nature/nurture controversy, 62
Nature, women's: and human nature, 21–22; and liberal feminism, 35–39; and Marxism, 63–69; and radical feminism, 94–100; and socialist feminism, 126–32; theoretical assumptions about, 21
Nazism, 127
Necessity, realm of physical (Marx), 209, 304, 305
Necrophilia, 269
Needs, human, 42, 74, 111, 135, 243; as biologically based, 53–54, 60; changing through praxis, 54; for children, 135, 157; as determined by mode of production, 56; flexibility of, 112; identification of, 17; redefinition of, 58; scepticism regarding, 42; social perversion of, 44; universal, 59; variation in, 47, 62; women's, 63, 276
Networks, 184
Neutral dialogue (Ackerman), 357
Neutrality, 232, 385; in formulation of questions, 133, 143; gender, 78–79, 387; in language, 182, 235; moral, 195; of observation, 358; scientific, 360, 378; of the state, 35, 61; Charles Taylor on, 18–19; of theory, 269, 289; value, 41, 360
New Left, 11, 231
New York Radical Feminists, 87, 92, 287
Newtonian physics, 356, 368, 391 **n.**40
Non-violence, as strategy, 294
Normative dualism. *See* Dualism, normative
Normative heterosexuality, 132, 140–41, 272
NOW. *See* National Organization for Women
Nozick, Robert, 21, 29, 30, 34
Nursing, 325
Nurturance: as feminist reconceiving, 253; in organizations, 232–33; as productive activity, 141; as special women's power, 94; as women's responsibility, 46, 114, 148, 156, 157, 243, 256

Objectification, sexual, 137, 221, 223, 283, 293, 309, 316. *See also* Sex objects
Objectivity, 9, 356, 357, 359, 360, 362, 368, 377

Index

Ollman, Bertell, 307
On the Subjection of Women (Mill), 36
O'Neill, Onora, 195
Ontology: in Dworkin's view, 99; and Marxist critique, 59–60; and political philosophy, 19; in radical feminist theory, 367–68; of relations, 367, 368, 369, 376
Opportunity, equal. *See* Equal Opportunity
Oppression: of children, 154, 225, 226; of elderly, 225, 226; etymology and use of term, 5–6; internalized, psychology of, 149–51; of women (*see* Oppression, women's)
Oppression, women's, 8, 63, 69, 76–78, 353; diagnosis of, 133; within the family, 241; as fundamental form, 12; as historically changing, 317; liberal feminist analysis of, 175–81; link with capitalism, 317; Marxist analysis of, 215–24; material basis of, 67, 70, 88–92; obscured in Marxist analysis, 77, 379; prostitution as paradigm of, 221; racial, 241 (*see also* Racism); radical feminist analysis of, 101–2, 255–70; sex-specific forms of, 221; socialist feminist analysis of, 307–17; varying conceptions of, 353. *See also* Subordination, women's
Organization, social, 43–44, 274; and children, 155; determined by mode of production and family, 129, 147; goal of, 59; theories of as ideological, 62–63; of procreation, 128–32, 138–40, 142–43, 249, 320, 338; as related to biology, 76, 91, 109, 110; socialist feminist claims about, 127
Organizations: revolutionary, 230–34; women's independent, 329–32
Origins of the Family, Private Property, and the State (Engels), 52, 63, 73, 129

Paradigm: androcentric, 22; feminist theory as, 9, 10, 11, 12; liberal, as male-biased, 46–68; of rationality, 45; shift of, 268
Parenting, 140, 147, 315, 337. *See also* Childrearing; Motherhood; Nurturance
Patriarchy: as distorted world view, 366–67; radical feminist conception of, 102–3, 116–18, 255–56, 367; radical feminist confrontation with, 283–86; socialist feminist conception of, 122 **n**.79, 160. *See also* Dominance, male
Personal life, politics of, 239–44; "Personal is political," 7, 101, 143, 198, 255, 273, 274, 317, 338, 342, 345, 388
Perreault, Gerri, 119 **n**.28, 367, 368, 391 **n**.40

Petchesky, Rosalind, 147, 319, 341–42
Phelps, Linda, 308
Philosophy, moral, 356–57
Philosphy, political: domain and problematic of, 7, 9, 41, 62, 100, 106, 155, 255, 385–89; feminism as 3–23, 133; goals of, 15; and human nature, 15–23; and interpretation of concepts in, 15, 18; liberal view of, 35, 44; Marxist view of, 62–63; as normative enterprise, 15; and positivism, 356–57; radical feminist view of, 100; and scientific knowledge, 9, 17; socialist feminist view of, 134; strategy as integral part of, 16–17; use of term, 16
Physics, Newtonian, 356
Plato, 16, 83
Poetry, and radical feminism, 267
Political correctness, 274
Political economy. *See* Economy, political
Political theory: liberal, 33–35; Marxist, 59–63; radical feminist, 100–105; socialist feminist, 133–48. *See also* Philosophy, political; Theory
Politics, feminist: and epistemology, 353–93; and goals of liberal feminism, 35; and goals of radical feminism, 270; and goals of socialist feminism, 132; problems for liberal feminism, 185–203; problems for Marxism, 229–44; problems for radical feminism, 286–96; problems for socialist feminism, 340–46; value differences in, 170
Politics, sexual, 100–105
Pornography, 105, 159, 180, 199, 237, 265, 283, 286
Positivism, 355–57, 378
Poverty, 158, 177, 183, 240, 3189, 326
Praxis, 54–60, 134, 208; and Marxist epistemology, 358; and psychology, 127, 151
Preferential treatment, 190–93
Preying Mantis Women's Brigade, 284, 286
Privacy, as a value, 174, 198–99, 213
Private/public distinction. *See* Public/private distinction
Private realm, 33–35, 61, 70, 112–13, 124, 129, 144, 180, 213, 253, 273, 305, 388
Privilege: heterosexual, 273; male, 86, 88, 193, 237–38
Procreation, 74–79; as cross-cultural universal, 138; democracy in, 148, 342; democratization of, 236, 340–41; interrelationship with production, 75, 131, 141, 152, 157, 303; as labor, 131, 152–53; as material base of women's oppression, 91; as natural rather than historical, 107; organization of, 128–32, 138–40, 142–43, 249, 320, 338; radical feminist focus on,

Reconceiving, radical feminist, 252–53, 288, 289
Reductionism, 105, 290, 356
Reed, Evelyn, 133
Reich, Wilhelm, 71, 127
Reid, Coletta, 278
Reiter, Rayna R., 81 n.49. *See also* Rapp, Rayna
Relations: gendered, 158; interpersonal production of, 156; need for conceptual framework, 158; ontology of (*see* Ontology); power, 282; of procreation, 320; radical feminist emphasis on, 254
Relativism, epistemological, 362
Reproduction, 70; as basic to women's subordination, 105; conceptualization of, 156; control of, 136; of labor power, 71; and production, 157–58; in socialist feminist terminology, 156. *See also* Procreation
Resistance, 149–51
Revolution: as solution to women's oppression, 224–25; women's part in, 230–34, 242
Revolution, Industrial, 175
Revolution, Women's, 274, 275
Revolutionary leader. *See* Leader, revolutionary
Revolutionary organization. *See* Organizations, revolutionary
Revolutionary strategy, 235–36
Rich, Adrienne, 88, 118, 266, 269; on childbirth, 310; on feminist mothers, 258; on lesbian continuum, 272; on reconceiving honor, 252–53; on women as sole nurturers, 259
Right-to-life movement, 382
Rights: abortion, 238; children's, 38, 343; civil (*see* Civil liberties; Civil rights); equal, 38, 46; gay, 238; individual, 35, 180, 193; and marital status, 176; natural, 27, 31; political, 28, 35, 61, 385; reproductive, 7, 318, 319; sex as irrelevant to, 37; women's, 35, 36, 38
Role-models, 191
Roles. *See* Sex-roles
Romantic love, 92, 101, 104, 219, 241, 265, 322, 345. *See also* Ideology
Romanticism, sexual, 5
Rorty, Richard, 40
Rosaldo, M. Z., 117
Rousseau, Jean-Jacques, 29
Rowbotham, Sheila, 233, 342
Rubin, Gayle, 126, 130, 132, 138, 156, 323; on Freudian theory, 140; on kinship systems, 139; on a political economy of sex, 147–48; on sex-gender system, 139
Russell, Bertrand, 30

Sadomasochism, 274–75
Sargent, Lydia, on Marxist strategy, 235
Sartre, Jean Paul, 77, 127
Scepticism, 40–42, 60, 175, 189, 194, 240
Scheman, Naomi, 42–43
Science: atomistic, 356; controlled by ruling class, 57, 58, 359, 370–71; Marxism as, 52–53, 59; and neutrality, 21, 360, 378; as objective, 360, 377, 378; political, 15, 16; and political philosophy, 9, 17, 18–21; proletarian, 363, 369; socialist-feminist, 384. *See also* Knowledge
Scientific reconstruction, 387
SCUM, 284
Second Sex, The (de Beauvoir), 10
Second Sex Conference, 98
Self-actualization, 18
Self-fulfilment, 33, 34, 35, 39, 47, 184
Self-improvement, 184
Self-interest, 31, 33, 35
Self-realization, 19; labor as means of, 58–59; impeded by capitalism, 58
Sen, Amartya, K., 45
Separatism, 270–71; black, 11; as political strategy, 11, 103, 290–94; tactical, 330; total, as classist and racist, 296; as utopian, 345; viability of, 293–96
Services, women's, 184
Sex objects, 128, 179, 181, 223, 227, 256, 260, 265, 267, 308, 309
Sex-affective production, 141
Sex-blindness, 182
Sex, and gender dialectic, 112
Sex-role conditioning, 37, 43, 44, 125, 192
Sex-roles: and androgyny, 85–88; as consciously chosen, 86; as descriptor of women's oppression, 86, 87
Sexism: connection with racism and capitalism, 344; in Marxist organizations, 230; in revolutionary strategy, 235
Sexual Politics (Millett), 265
Sexuality: as excluded from production, 138–43; and historical transformation, 129; and mode of production, 75; and nature, 116; organization of, 101, 124, 227–28, 320, 338; as private, 180; radical feminist emphasis on, 267, 292; standards as oppressive, 178–79; women's, 101, 218–19, 309, 322
Sherfey, Mary Jane, 89
Sisterhood, 254, 282
Sisterhood Is Powerful (Sherfey), 89
Slavery: sexual, 105, 241, 260–66, 270, 271, 287; wage, 211
Smith, Adam, 39, 178
Smith, Dorothy, 370, 373–74, 376, 386